Dedication

This book is dedicated to me. I mean, I may as well. Neither Jon Stewart (first edition) nor Stephen Colbert (second edition) demonstrated anything close to the proper level of appreciation for having a textbook dedicated to him. In fact, if it weren't for the restraining orders, it would have been hard to even be sure they had noticed the dedications or the hundreds of other professionally sycophantic gestures I have made over the years. Besides, it's not like anyone else is ever going to dedicate a book to me. And who could have inspired and supported my work more than me? It's not like it's easy forcing yourself to roll out of bed at the crack of noon every Tuesday and Thursday and do all the other things it takes to work for ten, sometimes eleven grueling hours every month for two whole semesters a year, every year.

A NOVEL APPROACH TO POLITICS 3RD EDITION

Introducing Political Science through Books, Movies, and Popular Culture

DOUGLAS A. VAN BELLE

Victoria University of Wellington

SAGE | CQPRESS

Los Angeles | London | New Delhi
Singapore | Washington DC

Los Angeles | London | New Delhi
Singapore | Washington DC

FOR INFORMATION:

CQ Press

An Imprint of SAGE Publications, Inc.

2455 Teller Road

Thousand Oaks, California 91320

E-mail: order@sagepub.com

SAGE Publications Ltd.

1 Oliver's Yard

55 City Road

London EC1Y 1SP

United Kingdom

SAGE Publications India Pvt. Ltd.

B 1/I 1 Mohan Cooperative Industrial Area

Mathura Road, New Delhi 110 044

India

SAGE Publications Asia-Pacific Pte. Ltd.

3 Church Street

#10-04 Samsung Hub

Singapore 049483

Acquisitions Editor: Elise Frasier
Production Editor: Laura Stewart
Copy Editor: Judy Selhorst
Typesetter: C&M Digitals (P) Ltd.
Proofreader: Stefanie Storholt
Indexer: Judy Hunt
Cover Designer: Michael Dubowe
Marketing Manager: Jonathan Mason
Permissions Editor: Adele Hutchinson

Printed in the United States of America

Library of Congress Cataloging-in-Publication Data

Van Belle, Douglas A., 1965-

A novel approach to politics : introducing political science through
books, movies, and popular culture / Douglas A. Van Belle. — 3rd ed.

p. cm.
Includes bibliographical references and index.

ISBN 978-1-4522-1822-9 (pbk.)

1. Political science. 2. Popular culture—United States.
3. Politics and culture—United States. 4. Mass media—
Political aspects—United States. I. Title.

JA66.V28 2013
320—dc23   2012027066

This book is printed on acid-free paper.

Certified Chain of Custody
SUSTAINABLE FORESTRY INITIATIVE
Promoting Sustainable Forestry
www.sfiprogram.org
SFI-01268
SFI label applies to text stock

12 13 14 15 16 10 9 8 7 6 5 4 3 2 1

Brief Contents

CONTENTS

Detailed Contents

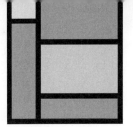

PREFACE

This is not your grandparents' textbook, and I mean that in a way that goes well beyond the simple fact that it's all shiny and new. I also mean it in a way that goes beyond the fact that I use novels, films, television, and pop culture to introduce students to the study of politics. The marketing people may be all giggly and twittery over the films and such, and people may like the idea so much that suggestions for novels and films to put in the book get flung at me like they were American Dodgeball Association of America regulation dodgeballs.* However, the real difference that sets *A Novel Approach* apart from the shuffling hordes of intro to politics textbooks out there can be found in the way it expresses humankind's pathological fear of zombies.

I am, of course, talking about zombies in terms of the metaphorical roles they play in the narratives of the genre. Even when given a comedic twist in films like *Shaun of the Dead*[1] zombies are always used to represent the slow but relentless threats to life that we all must face. The fear of aging is a significant subtext in *Night of the Living Dead.*[2] In *Shaun of the Dead,* it's the weight of social entanglements with friends, lovers, and family. In *Zombies from Mars,*[3] it's bureaucracy. And for an introduction to politics course, zombies represent the threat posed by a textbook that is so chock full of soul-crushing boredom that it will smother the mind and rot the flesh right off of students' faces. That part I mean quite literally. As a certified Zombitolgist I'm kind of an expert on these things.

Generally speaking, introduction to politics instructors who aren't undead themselves, hate using those kinds of soul-crushing textbooks. Enduring the overwhelming stench of a lecture hall full of half-living corpses is a bit unpleasant, but there isn't really that much of a gap between the personal hygiene skills of zombies and hung-over 18-year-old boys, so that's not the real worry. Professors dislike mind-numbing textbooks because they make it really, really difficult to teach. In theory, a textbook should provide a foundation of material and information that all students share and that the instructor can teach from. The problem with that theory is that it presumes that the students read and engage the material in the text, and even when you manage to force students to read the book, getting them to actually engage the material on their own is, unfortunately, rare. That was the real challenge that I wanted to tackle way back when I put together the first edition of this book. I wanted to create a book that professors could teach from, rather than teach at. When instructors step up to the lectern, they need to know that there are certain sparks of thought and knowledge hidden behind that sea of undead faces.

---

* While it is true that if you can dodge a wrench, you can dodge a ball, books are a bit tougher. They open up and flop around in the air and don't fly straight.

[1] Directed by Edgar Wright, distributed in the United States by Universal Pictures (2004).

[2] Directed by George A. Romero, distributed by the Walter Reade Organization (1968).

[3] Douglas A. Van Belle, "Zombies From Mars," *The Andromeda Spaceways Inflight Magazine* 40 (2009).

The use of fiction is one of two critical aspects of *A Novel Approach* that accomplishes this. In fact, fictional examples allow me to both increase the complexity and nuance of the political dynamics addressed and create a book that all students can and will read. Because of the way that fiction exaggerates the forces driving characters, the way it often explicitly explores the political and social dynamics of choice, action, and consequence, *A Novel Approach* can actually engage the often-complex dynamics that underlie political phenomena more completely and more thoroughly than most introduction to politics textbooks.

Fiction, however, is only one of the two keys. The second is the style, or lack thereof, that I bring to the text. The narrative tone is casual, sarcastic, and occasionally just a bit crass. The argumentative structure varies from topic to topic. I play with the chapter structure. I even mess with the overall structure of the book. I have fun with it whenever and however the opportunity arises. This may not appeal to everyone. In fact, if you're a British academic who uses the word "proper" with serious intent, this book may very well endanger your health. However, for the humans reading the book, my snarky style should be mostly harmless and, more important, it serves a purpose well beyond providing an admittedly modest bit of entertainment. I also want to inject some uncertainty into the text. I want the turn of every page, the start of every paragraph, the jump to every footnote to include just a little anticipation of the unexpected. I want students looking for the next non sequitur, the next nearly appropriate example, or the next bit of crude narrative commentary. That uncertainty, that anticipation of the unexpected, does more to keep the reader engaged than all the car chases and sex scenes in the history of cinema.

The result is a text that can be used just like a regular textbook. It has all of the necessary stuff. In fact, because this approach makes it easier to get across some relatively complex theoretical ideas, in many ways there is more of the important stuff in here than you would usually find in an intro textbook. An instructor can add a couple of lectures to reinforce the topics and add a few examples each week, and the semester will just fly merrily by. I have tested that approach with this material, and it works quite well. Very few of the cute and fuzzy little lab animals suffered serious harm.

A Novel Approach can also be thought of as a textbook that reduces or eliminates most of the substantial barriers to using fiction in the classroom. Not only will students quickly get used to using fiction, they can and will read it quickly. Two, or even three, chapters can be assigned per week, leaving half the semester or more for instructors to show or discuss any of the myriad of novels, films, and television programs of their choosing.

Another valuable result of this approach is a textbook that focuses on the "why" rather than the "what." *A Novel Approach* is a textbook that builds upward from the underlying theories and dynamics, a textbook that has several chapters that come before the starting point of most introduction to politics textbooks. This usually leads to students who can explain how the tragedy of the commons can be applied to Marx's conceptualization of the

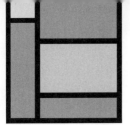

pool of labor. By the end of the text, students will be armed with Arrow's Theorem, the dynamics of power in anarchic environments, the role of ideologies in practical politics, Downs's spatial representation of the electorate, social contracts, the mediated construction of political reality, core and periphery in world systems theory, the differences between political structures and institutions . . . Students should have these, and a whole lot of other conceptual weapons, in their arsenal, ready for attacking the complexity of social and political statements being made in fiction and, by extension, the world around them.

Of course, now that I'm chugging along into the third edition, I've gotten bored with all that. First edition, just getting it together was a challenge. Second edition I pushed the editorial army about as far as I could push them with my references to "naughty" things like purple smoke and the "stuff" that your neighbor's dog leaves in steaming piles on your front lawn. So with the Third edition I had to come up with something new to amuse myself. My solution was to see just how far I could push it when it came to slipping self-aggrandizing self-references into the text. Come to find out that it is pretty easy to bribe a copy editor and convince her not to mention the "minor corrections" I made to the text after it was approved by the edition editor. By the time it gets back on the desk of anyone who would have (and probably should have) objected, it will be all printed up and too late. Mwa Ha Ha.

I strongly suggest that instructors examine Chapter 13 very carefully before writing their syllabus.

Introduction/Warning/ Parental Advisory

This Book Contains Politically Explicit Material

If you have ever dreamed of reading an introduction to politics textbook written by an overeducated jackass, this is your lucky day. Unless of course the dream was a nightmare. But then again, people pay good money to watch horror films, especially those really horrific ones with sparkly vampires, so even if it is a nightmare . . . Whatever. Either way, your esteemed professor, the one with impeccable taste in textbooks, picked this one and that means you're stuck with it. So I guess the real point I'm trying make here, in addition to the jackass thing, is that this book is written without any apologies, express or implied.

This is a dangerous book. Even after the valiant struggles of CQ Press's legions of brave editors—none of whom will ever be the same—this book far exceeds the acceptable levels of collateral damage for a textbook. Somewhere along the line, something in this book will upset you, at least a little. I make no attempt whatsoever to relate to youth culture. I don't bother to even try to engage the student experience or in any other way pretend that I'm anything other than an old and sometimes cranky overeducated jackass. I will poke fun at, sometimes to the point of tormenting, everyone and everything. Liberal, conservative, moderate, capitalist, socialist, ecofacist, pirate banker, or beloved cartoon character, I will upset you all.

I blame politics.

Because of the very nature of politics as a subject of study, I don't even have to try to upset you. Don't get me wrong, as part of teaching about politics I will occasionally try to annoy or provoke you. I will do whatever is necessary to force you to consider ideas that are contrary to what you believe or want to believe, if only so you can recognize some of your unnoticed beliefs, presumptions, and cognitive frameworks that provide the foundation for what you hold dear. This is a necessary part of learning to understand the dynamics of politics, and if I do not infuriate you at least once with a topic or pointed comment, or a snide little evisceration of something you value highly, then I have probably failed to get you to really think about politics. Sometimes you need to get a bit riled up before you are motivated to look beneath the surface of the politics you see around you. I will blame you, the student, if I fail to inflict some minor mental trauma—I am a professor, after all, and blaming the student is the first thing they taught us in training

camp—but given my ability to annoy just about everyone else in the world, I will be truly disappointed if I cannot manage to get you pissed off about something as controversial and as personal as politics.

Politics is personal. It limits, defines, or enables even the most intimate aspects of your life. You cannot escape politics, and you cannot help but have preexisting ideas about politics, and it is those preexisting ideas that I must disturb in order to expose the underlying dynamics of the subject. Take the nice, safe, and completely uncontroversial topic of teenage sex as an example. Politics intrudes into just about every aspect of this most frantically brief but intimate of topics. In 1996, a seventeen-year-old girl was arrested in Idaho because she was both unmarried and pregnant. It seems that in an effort to reduce teen pregnancies, officials in Gem County decided to enforce an old and disregarded law forbidding sex outside of marriage, and the county's police officers were told, literally, to arrest young women who appeared to be pregnant but were not wearing wedding rings. While this incident probably deserves an honorable mention in one of those "bizarre but true" lists, the truly scary part was that the girl in question was actually convicted. She was found guilty of the alleged crime of fornication, fined ten dollars, and sentenced to three years of probation.

Most would probably agree that getting pregnant at seventeen is unwise, but if unwise were criminal, authorities would be obligated to arrest the entire cast, crew, and audience of Two and a Half Men.[1] And regardless of how socially conservative or liberal you may be, you almost have to think that there has got to be a better way to curb teen pregnancy than arresting girls for getting knocked up. However, it is in that thought that you will find the key to understanding why and how any political example I might use or any political subject I might discuss will find a way to upset someone. If you look through the letters to the editor related to this incident, it is clear that many people would be offended by my suggestion that everyone must believe there had to be a better policy than giving unwed teenage mothers criminal records to help them through the difficulties of single parenthood. In response to the letters criticizing the arrest and conviction of the girl, many people wrote scathing letters that savaged the critics of the action and defended the policy as long overdue and a perfect way to change the thinking of the criminally promiscuous teens of the day.

If this political act of criminalizing pregnancy offends you, you might well suggest an alternative, such as education and contraception. Do realize, however, that what a social liberal and the vast majority of moderates might consider to be a far less offensive policy is going to be deeply offensive to a large minority others. For many religious and social conservatives, a group that probably makes up 25 to 30 percent of the U.S. population, any public policy supporting the use of birth control methods other than abstinence is morally reprehensible. When it comes to a public policy regarding teen pregnancy and teen sexuality—forgive me for assuming they kind of go together—all options, including the option of having no policy on the subject, is going to offend or upset someone.

Perhaps sexuality, as a political subject, does not bother you. How about fairness and justice? After all, even if you are not a feminist, it is hard to deny that arresting just the girl in a case of teenage pregnancy is grossly unfair. I do not claim to be a biologist, unless there's cash involved, but I am pretty sure there was an alleged father of the alleged child, and there is no mention of a guy getting prosecuted. That is unquestionably unfair.

Or is it?

It turns out that the prosecution of the girl and not the boy for fornication is not the biggest gender inequity in the politics and resulting laws that meddle in the sex lives of Idaho's alleged teenage population, and there was a very good reason the guy was not prosecuted. If convicted of fathering the child, the boy that I presume was involved would have faced a sentence of life in prison. Yes, life in prison. In the alleged state of Idaho, sexual intercourse with a woman under the age of eighteen is rape, period, full stop, end of sentence. There are no exceptions.* It does not matter how old the boy is or even if he is younger than the girl. The reverse, however, is not true. While there are Idaho statutes that a girl could be charged with violating for having sex with an underage boy, the punishments for women do not include anything close to a sentence of life in a maximum-security prison. And do remember that the fine people of Idaho are extremely serious about the "life" part of the life sentence. Clearly that is a disparity in the ways that boys and girls are treated in Idaho, and if gender equity or even just plain old fairness is important to you, that should upset you.

Have I raised any hackles yet?

The political meddling in your sex life goes well beyond this example. In Idaho, no matter how old the two parties are, any sex outside of marriage is defined as fornication and is punishable by a fine of up to three hundred dollars and six months in jail. If it is an extramarital affair, it is even worse, because adultery is punishable by a fine of up to one thousand dollars and three years in prison. I suspect these laws are the primary reason no soap operas are set in Boise.

---

*It is not clear how that exceptionless law for statutory rape fits with the fact that you can marry at the age of sixteen in Idaho, or even younger if both sets of parents approve.

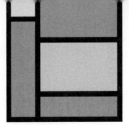

The intrusion of politics into your sex life is not limited to Idaho. In Indiana mustaches are illegal for those who have a "tendency to habitually kiss other humans." Note that the statute specifies humans. Hmmm? In Minnesota, it is illegal for any man to have sexual intercourse with a live fish. It is a little more complex in Utah, where sex with an animal is illegal, *unless* you are doing it for profit. Sex while standing in a walk-in meat freezer is specifically banned in New Castle, Wyoming, and in Washington, D.C., anything other than the missionary position is still illegal. The penalty for masturbation in Indonesia is decapitation. Virgins are forbidden to marry in Guam, but that is balanced out by the fact that in Washington State it is illegal to have sex with a virgin—no exceptions, even for a wedding night. I used to use that for a joke about why billionaire geek Bill Gates had to fly to Hawaii for his wedding, but that's starting to seem a bit lame, even for me.

While these may seem to be amusingly misguided and forgotten laws that are left over from an ancient age, on September 17, 1998, police arrested two men for violating Texas sodomy laws after entering the men's apartment and bursting into their bedroom in response to a prank burglary call. In 2003, the U.S. Supreme Court struck down the Texas sodomy laws in *Lawrence v. Texas,* making it extremely difficult for states to convict someone for breaking any of the myriad U.S. state laws forbidding particular sexual acts between consenting adults. However, most of these laws are still on the books, and there is nothing to stop a future set of Supreme Court justices from deciding differently on a future case. There is also nothing to stop a future arrest and trial and all the associated trauma and costs, even if the case is certain to be thrown out eventually by the Supreme Court.

You might argue that government has no place interfering in what consenting adults do in the privacy of their bedroom. However, that socially liberal position is clearly not universal. Chances are there is a fellow student in your course who would argue that government must act to preserve what he or she considers to be the moral fabric of society. Chances are that someone in your class considers the act of figuring out how to unhook a girl's bra to be a legally binding marriage proposal. This kind of socially conservative perspective is likely to include the belief that it is necessary to outlaw anything related to "immoral" sexual acts, which can include the distribution of condoms by school nurses, sex education, homosexuality, pornography, naughty bits on HBO, and anything lacy. These are all subjects tied to public policy issues involving politics in this most intimate aspect of young people's lives. All of these topics are controversial, and pretty much any position that might be taken on any of these subjects or issues related to them is guaranteed to upset someone.

In this text I do not shy away from issues because they might provoke; I cannot. I try to keep it casual and lighthearted. I also try to spread it around and torment just about everyone, especially if they are French or, to a lesser degree, Belgian. However, I make no apologies if a topic or a sarcastic comment hits a nerve or two—it should. Going back to

where I started, politics is deeply personal. To make it easier to engage these very personal topics openly, I use a bit of sarcasm and some admittedly questionable humor, but that does not alter the fact that many of the topics and examples, even the fictional ones, are sensitive and likely to upset someone. The movie *A Clockwork Orange*[2] will probably offend your sensibilities, but just because it might offend I cannot hesitate to suggest it as an example of the complex interplay between the rights of criminals versus the rights of victims versus the role government needs to play in protecting society.

HOW TO READ THIS BOOK

My unconventional style should not get in the way of the fact that this book is a serious effort to delve into the complex concepts and theories that underlie politics as a subject of study. Just because an example is from the *Phineas and Ferb*[3] or a beer commercial does not make the underlying point about politics any less relevant than if it were tied to an example I might pull from a discussion of comparative political institutions. It is just more fun. In fact, lightening things up with a bit of sarcasm and using fiction and pop culture to help give you a different perspective on the subject enables me to include more of the good stuff. It makes it easier to get past what you think you already know, or the things you did not realize were hiding something about politics, and delve into the underlying dynamics.

There are a lot of ways to write a textbook on politics, and as you read this book you should keep in mind that when I designed it, I wanted to create something that focused on the how and why of politics rather than just the what. I also made a conscious decision to repeatedly take advantage of opportunities for self-promotion. My editor tried to stop me, but I can be persistent and devious, and it turns out to be really easy to bribe the copy editors who go through the book just before it goes to layout. I had to agree that I would be subtle and not crass about it. In fact, it all ended up so subtly and tastefully done that you probably won't even notice how many times I tell you that you can buy my novel *Barking Death Squirrels* from most online book retailers. The subtlety of how I pimp my other books makes it easier for you to focus on my concerted effort to coax/cajole/coerce you into engaging the dynamics that underlie the politics that pervades every aspect of your lives. It will be even easier, and the headache from the subliminal messages will go away, once you buy a novel or two.

As a wizened and extremely brilliant professor, I am struck by something about the papyrus scrolls that I read as my introduction to politics text way back in college, and that is how many of the specifics in those old textbooks, how many of the details and facts I remember being tested on, are no longer relevant. There were entire chapters on Politburo politics. The odds are pretty good that most students reading this text have no idea what that could possibly refer to. That is the nature of the subject, and it is an important part of why new editions of textbooks are constantly being churned out. It also exposes the problem of focusing on the "what" of politics. For both the teacher and the student, it is horribly

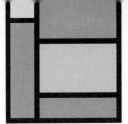

tempting to focus on the what. Different types of parliaments, different categories of executives, different legal foundations, the history of different ideologies, different systems for serving this function or that function—it is easy to write exams that test that sort of knowledge, and it is easy for students to study categories and lists of things. The problem is that the world changes, and the what of politics changes.

In contrast, the parts of those old textbooks that delved into the hows and whys of politics still seem to be relevant. As an obvious example, my discussion of why some democratic governments have two parties and why some have dozens is not that different from the one that I was taught. The specific examples from my old textbooks are no longer all that relevant, but the explanation is as strong as ever. The basic theory is more than a half century old, yet it has lost none of its value. Thus, throughout this text I focus on hows and whys. All of the examples I use—whether they are real-world examples or fictional— are chosen to get at the underlying logic of politics. As I explain in the first chapter, fictional examples are excellent for this purpose. For the student, my pursuit of this goal should provide a hint of how to engage this text. You know, help me out a bit, and look for the reason, cause, process, or dynamic I am trying to get you to understand.

Actually, I expect a great deal from you when you are reading this textbook. I expect you to explore the material. I expect you to think about the examples. I expect you to look for the dynamics of politics in fiction. I expect you to consider the arguments of people who disagree with you. I expect you to realize that an introduction to political science is just that, an introduction, a starting place, and it is neither definitive nor complete. The one thing I most sincerely hope to provoke with this text is your interest in knowing more about politics.

Beware the Kahutahuta!
Available soon!

ABOUT THE AUTHOR

A dozen things most people don't know about

DOUGLAS A. VAN BELLE

1. I once backed over a Peugeot with a loaded dump truck—all the way over. But it was okay—Officer Van Lierop gave the screaming realtor lady a ticket for parking in a marked construction zone.

2. Ten days later I backed into the front bumper of that same woman's brand-new insurance-money Peugeot. It was just a little bump, but it was enough to break off the little pin in the transmission that held the car in park, and that was enough to send it rolling down the hill. The car was going at least fifty when it suddenly realized it was going backward and did a full Starsky and Hutch around and into a very large tree. A passing botanist saved the tree. Officer Van Lierop gave the screaming realtor lady another ticket for parking in a marked construction zone.

3. Less than a week later, I was moving a flatbed trailer with two eight-foot-long sections of four-foot-diameter concrete pipe when I discovered that the physics of mass and momentum will kick the $#*& out of a 1972 Datsun pickup. I slammed on the brakes and managed to stop the roll backward down the hill before it turned into a train wreck, but the concrete pipes shifted and snapped the chain holding them in place. The first pipe hit the Peugeot (less than two hours off the lot) just behind the front door and spun it around so the second pipe hit the other side in almost exactly the same spot. The two back doors ended up touching each other in the middle of the backseat. Officer Van Lierop gave the screaming realtor lady yet another ticket for parking in a marked construction zone. The realtor lady walked home crying, and no one ever saw her again.

4. I used to call my Datsun pickup Hoser Truck. Hoser Truck was killed by a fat lady in a Ford Fairlane. She was going "at least fifty" when she hit it broadside. After rolling and tumbling nearly half a block down University Avenue, Hoser Truck came to rest, on its wheels (okay, three of its wheels) in the middle of a used-car lot. The car lot's fence was undamaged, and Hoser Truck had somehow ended up inside a ring of cars parked very close to one another. The cars in the lot were undamaged, and the police had to call the owner of the lot to unlock the gate so I could get out. The car lot was called "Buy a Wreck Cheap, Nothing over $500." I left the car there and rode the bus home.

5. If you're going to park a 1972 Datsun pickup near the edge of a small cliff, try to remember that the parking brake never really worked right. Otherwise it will cost you fifty bucks to have an old guy with a bulldozer pull it up off the beach for you.

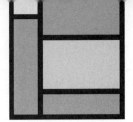

6. At the end of my second-worst date ever, I ended up in a hospital emergency room with my possibly broken wrist handcuffed to a gender-indeterminate biker (who smelled like Pine-Sol) while I tried to explain to a similarly gender-indeterminate police officer (who spit when she/he screamed) how the cute blonde girl had ended up with a broken nose.

7. Until my second-worst date ever, I thought that my Austin-Healey Sprite was the best date car in the world. It was kind of ugly and most motorcycles could put its motor to shame, and girls didn't really like it, but it was so small that just getting a girl in the passenger seat counted as foreplay. The problem was that when two of the pistons in that screaming little engine decided to leave the other two, they took the entire drivetrain out of the bottom of the car with them. That snapped the gearshift handle hard to the right, and there was nowhere for the hand sitting on the gearshift knob to go except up and into the face of the cute blonde girl in the passenger seat.

8. If you happened to be driving down I-5 just outside of Woodburn, Oregon, in September of 1987, and you saw a bunch of fraternity boys roasting marshmallows and hot dogs over the smoldering remains of a Winnebago, I was the one wearing a green sweatshirt.

9. Just in case you were wondering, a 1972 Datsun pickup won't fit inside one of those big ten-foot concrete sewer pipes. Not even if you get a running start.

10. Also, just in case you were wondering, a tow truck isn't powerful enough to extract a 1972 Datsun pickup that is jammed halfway into a ten-foot sewer pipe. A 1968 GMC pickup is. It has to get a running start, and you want to be smart enough to realize straightaway that the back bumpers of the trucks just ain't gonna handle it, but if you hook the chain to the frames, it'll work.

11. I once set the unofficial Kansas record by flying a motor home more than fifty yards through the air. On the third day of a grand, summerlong tour of the United States, I was driving down the freeway just outside WaKeeney, Kansas, when the aforementioned motor home was hit by what the people in the insurance business call a "lateral microburst." Humans call it a big gust of wind. It lifted the brand-new motor home from the right-hand lane, flipped it over, and deposited it on its side on the far side of the center median, blocking both oncoming lanes. No one was hurt, but I did suffer a deep muscle bruise when I was hit in the head by a thirteen-inch TV that I had just set up to play *The Lion King* for the kids. I had also just told my lovely wife, "Stop being neurotic, the stupid TV isn't going anywhere."

12. My lovely wife repeatedly and frequently reminds me that she is going to carve "Stop being neurotic, the stupid TV isn't going anywhere" into my tombstone.

Introducing the Ancient Debate
The Ideal versus the Real

Back in the "good old days,"* on televisions that resembled Laundromat dryers, geeky tykes rejoiced as Adam West, the only Batman with a beer belly, spouted the campiest of campy lines while employing the Batmobile, Batcomputer, Batcopter, Batladder, Batcanopener, and Shark-Repellent Bat Spray† to thwart the evildoers who plagued Gotham City. *Batman* was such a classy show that the words "POW!!!" and "BAAAAM!!!" flashed across the screen as the masked superhero tackled his enemies. These "special effects" were quite important. Not only did they distract viewers from the glaringly obvious fact that the show's producers were too cheap to hire stuntmen to fake fights properly, but also the Technicolor-graphics-instead-of-sound effects were pretty much the only part of the show that came anywhere close to capturing *Batman*'s comic-book origins. The television series may have been so campy it was a joke, but there was nothing campy or comedic about the comic-book version of Batman. Batman made his first appearance in 1939 in DC Comics' *Detective Comics,* and in spring 1940, DC published the first comic book featuring the caped crusader as a title character. The Batman in this first comic book—just as he was some 682 issues later—was dark, sullen, and almost villainous.

Nowhere is the dark and conflicted Batman better depicted than in *The Dark Knight* (2008)[1]—dare I call it the best offering from a franchise that includes not just the classic TV series and the comics but also graphic novels, traditional novels, cartoons, and feature films. Looking past the truly fantastic performance of the late Heath Ledger, and past the action-packed fights and chases, and past the wretched hint of a lisp that Christian Bale gives Batman, you can see the heart of a film beating

---

*Feel free to inform mom, dad, granny, aunty, etc., that I have scientifically tested the concept, and there have never been any "good old days." Of course, I accept no liability for the anguish that'll befall you when you tell them.

†The Shark-Repellent Bat Spray actually made the shark explode. Seriously, YouTube "Batman exploding shark."

with the eternal conflict between ideals and reality. Batman, the idealist, is willing to sacrifice absolutely everything he values for Gotham City's future—despite knowing that doing so will make *him* appear a villain to those for whom he has risked it all. Harvey Dent is such a committed idealist that the brutal reality of fighting a sociopath quite literally breaks him, and he turns into Two-Face, a man who loses all faith in reason, rationality, or ideals. The couture-clad Rachel Dawes abandons her romantic ideals to accept the reality that she will always come second to Bruce Wayne's idealistic crime-fighting alter ego. Each of these characters is driven by an idealized image of what ought to be, and each is, in one way or another, forced to struggle against the fact that the real world will never match his or her ideals.

The clash between the real and the ideal is a common theme in film and fiction, and it even became part of the comic-book franchise itself. The 2011 reboots, redesigns, and reimaginings of several classic DC comics, including Batman, ignited a geekstorm of controversy—some of the dedicated even called it a geekageddon. It was a classic clash between competing ideals and reality. The reboots were clearly driven by the realities of a publishing genre that had changed drastically over the previous seven decades. Batman and the other DC classics had stalled both creatively and in terms of sales and needed drastic changes if they were going to continue. That reality did not sit well with many long-time fans. Some idealized all the classical comic elements that put Batman out of sync with the modern, flashier, and more extravagant graphic novels that have risen to lead the genre. Others complained that the oversexualization inherent in the idealization of the female figures in the reboots was actually harmful to women who had to deal with the reality of femininity in a media-saturated world. Others argued that DC should have shut the characters down rather than pander to economic realities. A common theme in all the debates and discussions was the question of what should be, ideals, versus what reality would allow or enable.

In films and literature, this conflict is commonly embodied by two contrasting characters thrown together on the same side of a conflict. How often does the plot of a good story turn on the relentless enthusiasm of the young idealist who reignites the jaded realist's squashed idealism? How many movies feature a tough, salty older realist who rescues a younger, more naive idealist? In the original *Star Wars,*[2] which for some unfathomable reason is Episode 4, the young, energetic idealist Luke Skywalker is driven to rescue the princess because it is the noble thing to do.* Han Solo, the gritty smuggler and worldly realist in debt up to his eyeballs, deals with the universe as it is rather than dreams of how it could be. Han is not at all interested in rescuing the princess until Luke convinces him that she will reward him well. But in the end, after Han has received his reward, Luke's idealism touches something within Han, who returns to help save the day. In Brian De

---

*Well, Luke also appears to be enamored of her, which is kind of cute until we find out she's his sister.

Palma's *The Untouchables*[3] Kevin Costner plays Eliot Ness, the idealistic federal agent whose mission is to bring the notorious gangster Al Capone to justice. Ness believes that law enforcement officers should play by the rules and shouldn't break any laws in the process of bringing criminals to justice. In contrast, Sean Connery's character, a veteran police officer and a man of experience, teaches Ness that if he wants to get Al Capone he will have to play by a different set of rules, those created by the reality of the streets: "He pulls a knife, you pull a gun. He sends one of yours to the hospital, you send one of his to the morgue. That's the Chicago way. And that's how you get Capone."

In *Star Wars,* the idealist brings out the best in the realist. In *The Untouchables,* the realist gives the idealist the tools to succeed. Eliot Ness abandons at least some of his ideals as he tosses a criminal off a rooftop on his way to bringing down Capone. Regardless of the specifics of the particular fictional scenario, the struggle between the ideal and the real has always been an attractive, dramatic, and dynamic theme. Shakespeare's plays are filled with examples. In *Julius Caesar,*[4] the idealistic Brutus joins in the plot to assassinate his friend, Caesar, for the noble goal of preserving the republic, while other characters, such as Cassius, act to better their own personal positions. From *West Side Story*[5] to *Twilight,*[6] every rip-off of *Romeo and Juliet*[7] casts the idealism of the two young lovers in sharp contrast to the harsh reality of the rivalry between their families, gangs, vampire clans, nations, tribes, religions, or dodgeball teams.

I would be criminally negligent if I didn't at least mention a particularly horrific example of the clash between ideals and realities. In the case of *Indiana Jones and the Kingdom of the Crystal Skull,*[8] the audience's idealistic expectation of an awesome new Indy film is crushed by the gruesome confrontation with the steaming pile of celluloid that Steven Spielberg pulled out of the cat box and flung at the screen. And on behalf of the geeks who got all excited about the mention of Batman at the opening of this chapter, I think I can safely say that *Watchmen,*[9] *Green Lantern,*[10] and *The Green Hornet*[11] were all cat-box-worthy examples of the reality that Hollywood executives will do whatever they can to take advantage of the 120,000 idealistic brethren and sisteren who flock to Comic-Con every year.* Although, *The Avengers*[12] . . . awesomeness embodied.

We can all identify with the struggle between idealists and realists. Every one of us can probably even identify a little bit with both sides. This reflection of our own internal conflict is much of what makes the fictional contest so engaging. The struggle that torments all the characters in *The Dark Knight* reflects what we all face in trying to balance the drive to do what we think would be best (**idealism**) with what we must do or are able to do (**realism**). The hopeful Luke Skywalker within us looks at the world and envisions a better place, looks at our fellow human beings and sees creatures that are capable of so much more. The realistic Han Solo in us looks at how our fellow human beings actually behave

---

Watchmen was particularly egregious. About halfway through, I said, "The director is going to get desperate pretty soon and try to save it with boobs," and two scenes later, the busty girl was naked.

rather than focusing on their potential for doing good. This inner pragmatist argues that we must work with the unseemly, self-interested side of life in the here and now to make the best out of an inherently bad situation. And, of course, our inner Batman wants to wear a mask and a cape while driving a gnarly black car to the grocery store.

The clash between the real and the ideal also makes a most excellent theme for a textbook that uses fiction to explore the fundamentals of politics. In novels and films this clash is a common motive that drives the heroic characters and often the central dynamic in plots and story lines. You can even see the duality in the settings, contexts, and imagery, such as in the contrast between the cartoon realm and photographed New York in Disney's *Enchanted*.[13]

In politics, the tension between the real and the ideal is prominent both in theory and in practice. Virtually all who engage in politics must balance the dreams of what they would like to accomplish against real-world limitations. A legislator with an idea for a law may have to change the original concept to gain the support of other lawmakers. The threat of revolt often limits the power of dictators and constrains their actions. The harsh realities of economics, the constraints of history, and the dynamics of culture often force revolutionaries to stop far short of the social transformations they envisioned when they first stormed the radio station. A negotiator cannot go into peace talks without understanding that stopping the bloodshed may require distasteful compromises, such as leaving a dictator in power or offering amnesty to the perpetrators of atrocities.

For people like your beleaguered professor, who went to school far longer than anyone really ever should and who now gets to bask in the unmitigated joy of lecturing to constantly texting kids who are in the class only because they have to gather enough social science credits to finish the annoying distribution requirements for their business degrees,* the greatest articulation of the contrast between realism and idealism is found in the work of the ancient Greek philosopher Plato.† Plato's *Republic* is a centerpiece of political theory, and the characters of Thrasymachus and Socrates represent two sides engaged in a discussion about the purpose of politics. Thrasymachus is a **sophist**: one who teaches promising young men the practical skills, such as rhetoric and deceptive accounting practices of questionable legality, that they need to be personally successful in public life. Thrasymachus and his fellow sophists are realists. Success means attaining tangible wealth and power, and the sophists have little if any concern with ethics, furry pettable creatures, or the good of the society. In contrast, Socrates represents the idealist position. He believes that there is more to politics than mere skill at reaching goals or attaining

---

*Oh, by the way, one reviewer described my writing style as "eloquently snarky." Many dispute the "eloquent," but none dare argue that I am not the master of all that is snarky. Nobody's exactly sure what *snarky* means, but I embrace it.

†Plato is not that brightly colored and funny-smelling modeling clay that your pediatrician was constantly digging out of your ears. Plato was a philosopher, which appears to be a person who has found a way to make a living by admitting that he listens to imaginary people talking to each other. It's a good gig if you can get it.

rewards. Socrates believes that the true leader must have genuine knowledge about ethics and about how to govern in the best interest of the entire community.

In a famous section of the *Republic,* Socrates argues that a good shoemaker's interest lies not in making money but in making the best possible shoes; a ship's captain should be concerned not with profit but with the crew; an excellent doctor is concerned with the health of patients, not with the money they pay. Similarly, a skilled governor's interests should be in the happiness of the governed, not in the personal power or fortune of the leader. According to Socrates, the purpose of the state and the purpose of politics should be to ensure the happiness of the citizenry. Thrasymachus counters with the example of the shepherd. A good shepherd does indeed do everything possible to keep the sheep healthy, but he does so to turn them into nice, tasty lamb chops that people will pay good money for. And so it is with the politician and the state.[14] For the leader, the purpose of caring for the citizenry and the state is to keep them both healthy so they can continue to provide the benefits the leader seeks.

Clearly, Thrasymachus has a point. If we look at how the world operates, we must realize that there are people who view others only as sheep to be fattened up to turn a profit at the slaughterhouse. If idealists ignore the realities of this world, there is a good chance that some calculating tyrant or even just some self-interested politician will take advantage of them. However, Socrates also has a point. If all people were interested only in making the most out of the existing reality, then no one would take the risks to make the world a better place. People often do eschew profit, or personal benefit, or even what seems like the very nature of the world, to pursue noble goals. What kind of world would it be if nobody had ever questioned the practice of slavery, if no one had ever fought for women's suffrage, if no one had ever demanded religious freedom, if no one had ever dared to combine malted barley, hops, water, and yeast? What kind of horrible world would this be if no visionary had ever imagined an entire television network dedicated to around-the-clock coverage of obscure sport-like activities such as Aussie-rules football? How precarious the survival of Western civilization might be if that greatest of all Swedish visionaries, Mr. Torgo Espn, hadn't pursued that ideal despite the fact that only six people had cable TV at the time?

In many ways, politics is all about the ongoing struggle between the dreamer and the pragmatist, the pursuit of tomorrow's ideals within the context of today's reality. Keeping in mind the contrast between the ideal and the real also makes it easier to write a textbook that examines many complicated political concepts and theories. We can explore the simplified and idealized version of a concept while recognizing that reality demands compromises and imposes limitations on the application of that ideal. We can discuss competing ideals. We can also take just about any concept to its idealized extreme as a way of exposing its underlying dynamics, its limitations, and its possibilities. For example, we can envision an idealized version of democracy where the majority always rules and everybody

SOCRATES

Team: **Classical Greek United**

Position: **Short Mid Wicket**

Status: **Totally Dead**

Socrates (469–399 B.C.) was basically the controversial talk radio host of his day. Of course, there was no radio in ancient Greece, but he talked a lot, pissed a lot of people off, and, as far as we know, he didn't write anything down.

Most of what we know about Socrates comes to us from the writings of his contemporaries, including his student Plato. Plato's writings are a bit difficult and we have to be careful to separate the fictional Socrates that Plato uses as the main character in his dialogues from the historical Socrates. Plato's fictional Socrates is a mechanism for expressing Plato's philosophical ideas rather than a representation of the real Socrates. Also, Plato's fictional Socrates wins every argument, and we know that Socrates lost at least one very important argument—the argument at his trial over his own execution.

Socrates was a well-known critic of the faith that most Athenians placed in popular opinion, particularly as it related to the simple democratic government practiced in Athens. However, most scholars would argue that critical reasoning represents Socrates' true legacy to the study of politics. Some would even argue that it is the philosophical foundation of the Western culture that eventually evolved from Athenian Greek culture.

Socrates's method of critical reasoning centered on the dialectic. The term dialectic has taken on a number of meanings and nuances in the last few millennia, but for Socrates it was quite literally a dialogue or discussion in question and response format. As a method of teaching this is still quite common, and when an instructor forces a conversation in class by asking pointed questions and demanding a response, he or she is in fact using what is commonly referred to as the Socratic Method. Plato's Dialogues are modeled after Socrates's dialectic teaching methods and Plato used the dialectic as a systematic method of conceptual inquiry. Plato's student Aristotle was a critic of this method, though Aristotle did use the dialectic argumentative structure in his writings and many would argue that the Socratic dialectic is the foundation that underlies the Aristotelian methods of logic and inquiry. This connection has tremendous implications since it is the Aristotelian method that serves as what many would consider to be the cornerstone of the modern Western model of scientific inquiry.

votes on everything, but we must also acknowledge that reality demands limits on what majorities can impose on minorities. We don't have to look back at too many horrific but extremely popular trends, such as sparkly vampires who like to watch emo high school girls sleeping, to cringe at the thought of subjecting politics to the raw and untamed whims of the majority. Reality limits the number of issues that the entire population is informed enough to cast a vote on. At the very least, a functioning democracy must prevent a majority from undermining the future of democratic competition. If a system is to remain a democracy, the majority cannot vote to limit speech or persecute peaceful political critics and opponents.

Considering politics as a balance between ideals and reality* also serves as a good transition to a discussion of some of the challenges to learning the fundamentals of politics. While I note and explore many of these challenges as I examine different subjects throughout this book, from the very start, you, the reader, must realize that one of the very real problems inherent in introducing you to the study of politics is, quite frankly, you.†

THE DOLLHOUSE

In Joss Whedon's *Dollhouse*,[15] the dolls are the perfect secret agents, hunks of very pretty but empty meat who are turned into exactly what is needed for their missions through downloads of the perfect sets of memories, experiences, and personality traits for those missions. Unfortunately for the agents, for all that downloaded stuff to work properly, everything that is already in their heads has to be erased. The dynamic of the storytelling in the series revolves around the imperfections of mind wipes, how what the dolls begin to remember and how what persists in their heads complicates what is added. Unfortunately, this pop-culture reference was cancelled before most students even got their hands on the last edition of this textbook, and chances are that only the geekiest of Whedonites know anything about it, but it is still an awesome example of the point that what's already in your head can be a real problem when it comes to adding something new.

Contrary to what you might have divined from the fountain of truth that is talk radio, no matter how criminally liberal and vegetarian your professor might be, he or she cannot brainwash you.‡ In some ways, that's too bad, because one of the most difficult obstacles to teaching you about politics is all the other stuff you already have in your head. It would be a heck of a lot easier to teach you about politics if your instructor could just go in and erase a few things. The simple fact is that people make sense of new ideas and make judgments about their political preferences by referring to what they already know. Thus, none of us approaches the study of politics with a blank slate. We all have our own preferences and biases. Even if you don't realize it, you have been immersed in politics your entire life. In fact, politics is the very definition of your never-opened SAT/ACT preparation guide's word of the day, *ubiquitous.* Politics is absolutely everywhere.

The essence of politics is the attempt by some to influence the actions and/or choices of others. Think about all the efforts that we make to persuade, cajole, manipulate, convince, and even deceive each other at school, work, home, and the Laundromat. Complicating matters further, even though you are constantly aware of and affected by the political behavior around you, your day-to-day involvement in politics actually hinders your

---

*The reality I talk about should not be confused with "reality shows," which of course are not reality shows, but shows that people appear on in order to trade their dignity for fifteen minutes of fame.

†Please note that this represents a legally binding assignment of responsibility for your D– on the first exam.

‡It's mostly a technical problem. With university budgets the way they are, no one will pay for the really good brainwashing equipment, and it's just not a good idea to use the cheap knockoffs.

instructor's heroic efforts to teach you about politics. The fundamental underlying causes of political behavior are often muddied by the specifics of situations, histories, contexts, cultures, and personal biases. We respond to these muddy pictures by organizing and simplifying our understanding of politics, by using our own **conceptual frameworks,** which we draw from the personal experiences, preferences, and expectations that we all use to make sense of the world.

For example, when media mogul Rupert Murdoch introduced his overtly partisan Fox News network into a U.S. political environment that was previously dominated by centrist, mass-market news networks, he was both hailed as the savior of truth and vilified as the defiler of journalistic integrity.* However, neither of these perspectives accurately reflects the relatively simple underlying political and economic dynamics that bred Fox News. In reality, the cost of running a cable news network had fallen far enough to make it economically viable for Murdoch to cater to a strongly partisan minority of the overall U.S. audience. The political and social conservatives occupying the so-called red states were not only the largest, wealthiest, and most easily identifiable partisan audience in the United States but also the most dissatisfied with the centrist news outlets that dominated the television and print news markets. As a result, political and social conservatives were the most obvious first subset of the overall audience to target with news that catered to their political beliefs and biases. However, even in courses focused on studying the business and economic dynamics of the news industry, it is remarkable how few students can look past what they "know" about politics and journalism to see Fox News for the very simple, very rational, very profit-oriented economic product that it is. Fox News is there to make money; all other motives are incidental. Perhaps the best evidence of this economic dynamic was MSNBC's response to Fox, which was to try to capture the more liberal segment of the U.S. media market by airing shows hosted by Chris Matthews, Keith Olbermann, Rachel Maddow, and that guy who talks like a Muppet.

Conceptual frameworks plague all efforts to engage political subjects in the classroom, and we can see this in something as simple as a discussion of a political debate or a speech. A Democrat and a Republican watching the same presidential debate will notice different details about the questions asked and how the candidates respond. Because each individual uses a unique conceptual framework to organize details into a coherent, simple conclusion, two different people watching the same event are quite likely to come to drastically different understandings of what happened. Furthermore, neither the Democrat nor the Republican will agree with the conclusions about the same event drawn by a radical environmentalist, a white supremacist, your mother, or the motivational speaker who lives in a van down by the river.* Our backgrounds and personalities shape our

---

*It is probably fair to say that choosing "Fair and Balanced" as a motto for a partisan news network was delusional, deeply cynical, or the expression of an underappreciated sense of humor.

*A moment of silence please, for the late Chris Farley.

RELEVANT BUT STILL LAME EXCUSE FOR PIMPING STUFF I WROTE

Believe it or not, I actually used the whole idea of cognitive frameworks as the basis for a short story I wrote a few years back. "Detritus of a Second-Hand Mind" is about a scientist's very personal struggle to escape the bounds of what she knows so she can gain the insight she needs to find another way to attack a vexing puzzle. She bounces around through everything from fundamental societal roles to the imperative to reproduce. She eventually finds what she needs, but in the oddest place, well outside the bounds of what she thought the puzzle was.

Douglas A. Van Belle, "Detritus of a Second-Hand Mind," in *The Tangled Bank: Love Wonder and Evolution,* edited by Chris Lynch (Albuquerque: Tangled Bank Press, 2010).

understandings of politics, sometimes to the point of determining what we can or cannot believe. As a result, every real-world example offered in this book and every political dynamic discussed here will mean something different to every reader.

This is partly why I use fiction to teach about politics. Usually it is easier to separate your personal viewpoint from the characters, plots, and settings of books and films than it is to find objectivity in your assessments of real events. Even when this separation is not entirely possible, fiction makes it easier for you to recognize how your conceptual frameworks color your appreciation of the work. This means that fiction can provide examples that we can all understand similarly, even if we do, ultimately, reach different conclusions. However, as professors always do, I am going to ask you to do most of the work.[†] As we move through subjects, I will often ask you to recognize, explore, and challenge your own perspectives and opinions and to be open to at least understanding other perspectives that you may not have considered before or that you oppose. It should come as no surprise that many aspects of politics are subjective, prompting normative questions about ideals, about what should be or how things should work. You may consider some of the answers to be disturbing, inhumane, or horrific. In fact, even though most would agree that making anyone live in your mother's idea of a perfect world would violate the Geneva Conventions, there will be a few people, such as your aforementioned mother, who would disagree. It is important that even as you recoil in horror and disgust, you still try to understand such bizarre, unpleasant, or even torturous perspectives as your mother's idea of whom you should date. First, because she is your mother, and second, because those borderline-insane people with those bizarre preferences are part of the real world, and it is highly likely that reality is going to demand that you find some way to compromise with them.

[†]Again, legally binding.

For those of you who actually agree with your mothers' opinions on your current or future spouses, life partners, or love-monkeys, I suggest consulting a mental health professional as soon as possible. For the rest of you, I suggest that you prepare to be offended (if you aren't already offended). To break through all that you already know and to drag you kicking and screaming into something resembling an understanding of the underlying dynamics that drive politics, I must often challenge or disparage some deeply held and cherished beliefs. This is difficult for all involved, and, as noted in the introduction,* if you do not become annoyed or downright angry at some point along the way, you are missing part of the introduction to politics. Politics is an intensely personal subject.

FICTION AS A TOOL FOR EXPLORING POLITICS

I have chosen fiction as a means to introduce you to politics for several good reasons. First, fiction provides a much better variety of examples and analogies than does invertebrate zoology, but a very close second reason is that fiction, whether it is presented on film, in a novel, or even in a Nickelodeon cartoon marathon, can be used to address the difficulties inherent in the complex and individual nature of politics. As already noted, fiction provides a window into an environment where our conceptual frameworks more easily give way to the author's creativity. By viewing events through the eyes of fictional characters, we find it easier to set aside our own personal preferences, ideologies, and experiences while at the same time appreciating the adventures that the characters encounter. Thus, we can all share the characters' experiences and perspectives on a conflict, a struggle, or some other aspect of politics, and we can share that experience in a reasonably similar manner. Fiction, therefore, gives us an opportunity to at least partially transcend the individual, personal nature of politics.

Second, by living through the characters in novels, we can get a taste for political situations that we, as individuals, might never be able to experience in the real world, or would never want to. For example, George Orwell's novel *Nineteen Eighty-Four* shows us how government can be used to control every aspect of people's personal lives.[16] The narrative provides numerous extreme and obvious examples of how this might work, such as the government's placement of cameras in private homes and the use of children to spy on their parents. Most of us have never experienced such oppressive government, but through the eyes of the protagonist we can see how it works, and we get a feel for what it might be like to live in such horrible conditions. For those of us who would rather not have the government torture us by stuffing our heads into cages full of rats, there is the additional bonus that we can get a taste of such an experience without having to actually live it.

---

*The introduction is that part at the beginning of the book that you didn't bother to read because you didn't think it counted as a proper chapter or because it wasn't assigned.

A third aspect of fiction that makes it valuable for learning about politics is that it is fiction—the characters and institutions are not subject to practical limitations. Authors and directors often exaggerate aspects of human interaction that might remain hidden in real life. They do this for dramatic purposes, but these exaggerated social dynamics are often perfect illustrations of the very ideas, influences, techniques, and principles that I want you to recognize as part of the underlying dynamic of politics. Many of the books and films mentioned in this text are set in speculative contexts in which the authors extend particular aspects of politics, government, or society out to their logical extremes. For example, to show the dangers of powerful governments, *Nineteen Eighty-Four* presents us with a government that is so extremely powerful and invasive as to be almost unimaginable. Fictional politicians, such as the chancellor in the *Star Wars* prequels, can be portrayed as far more calculating than any human being could possibly be. These exaggerated contexts and personalities serve to highlight the forces that limit the characters' choices or motivate their actions. It is much easier to recognize these forces in a speculative fictional context than in real life, which is comparatively complex, murky, and very extremely beige.

The characters and plotlines of fiction can also help us to develop insights into human motivation that lectures and textbooks could never hope to match. This is crucial for the study of politics because, unlike courses you may have taken in biology, mathematics, anatomy,* or some other straightforward subject that lends itself to multiple-choice exams, understanding politics requires an intuitive sense for how people interact. Thus, a fourth reason for using fiction as a window into politics is that it is an engaging and interesting way to help you develop an intuitive feel for the subject. Once you truly understand politics, you can read a newspaper story or watch a television news account and come away with a much richer understanding of what is going on because you have learned to read between the lines. Knowing the underlying dynamics, you can sense the reasons for actions that might not be mentioned in the report.

You have to get used to uncovering the subtle aspects of politics in society, and developing that skill takes a fair bit of work. You must think critically. You must learn to be just as aware of the unspoken dimensions of how people, governments, and organizations behave as you are of what they say about themselves or what others say about them. It is the subtle details in William Golding's novel *Lord of the Flies*—such as the shipwrecked boys' experiences of anarchy (a society without any hierarchy)—that prompt us to develop an intuitive feel for how that environment influences and drives the collective pursuit of security.[17] In the real world, where you will almost certainly never have to deal with true anarchy, the fictional story may offer the only way for you to develop a feel for what the experience would be like. An instructor can explain anarchy and lecture about it until he/she/it is blue/red/mauve in the face, but until you investigate the issues and encounter the

---

*I mean actual college anatomy courses, not playing doctor behind the bleachers.

politics in a fictional yet realistic context, you will find it difficult if not impossible to imagine the implications of the situation.

Last, the use of fiction can support and in some cases instigate an active approach to learning. In this text, I introduce a concept or dynamic of politics and then mention some of the examples available from novels, films, and television shows.[†] Some of what I reference actually counts as literature, but more often than not you will see that I prefer to wallow in pulp fiction, films, television commercials, or even children's cartoons to illustrate my points. In doing so I avoid having to read too much of anything that English professors might like, but I also am trying to entice you with popular fiction so that you personally engage the subject and resolve to explore politics on your own, thereby learning even more than you would otherwise. I believe that if you actively explore the subject, you can discover more about politics than a professor can ever teach. The more you work at discovering insights and examples in the books and films you enjoy, the more you are likely to learn about the study of politics.

UTOPIAS IN FICTION AND POLITICS

Utopias are a seriously big deal in both fiction and politics.[*] Eden, Shangri-La, Lake Wobegon, Grandma's house, an attic apartment above Willy Wonka's factory, Euro Disney . . . images of a perfect world abound. Imagining an ideal world seems to be common throughout history and across societies, as is the desire to attain such a world. Religions, myths, philosophies, ideologies, dogmas, and folklore all frequently involve some aspect of utopian thought. The invocation of the ideal consistently arises whenever people move from the tangible reality around them into the realm of hopes, dreams, beliefs, faith, or the chemical alteration of brain function. Utopias may conform to the ideal of the warrior or the pacifist, the prudish or the stereotypical denizens of fraternity row, but they always seem to depart conceptually from empirical reality.

Contrasting images of the ideal with reality makes a perfect theme for a textbook using fiction to explore politics, and utopian literature is the ideal place to start, if only because the pursuit of utopia is such a common theme of both fiction and politics. Novels, films, cartoons—even the amusingly dysfunctional families of television sitcoms—often make use of idealized or utopian settings to explore certain aspects of society. Utopias are

---

[†]But obviously not all—I do not admit to watching that much TV.

[*]One reviewer of the previous edition of this textbook complained that I tried too hard to use youthful colloquialisms in a vain attempt to engage students. Nothing could be further from the truth. First, I never put in anywhere near enough effort for it to be considered "trying" to do anything. Second, if I had been trying to do something, my actual goal would have been to embarrass my children by acting like a dorky old man. With this edition, in order to avoid any misperception that I might be trying to act cool or hip, I rewrote the entire textbook in Klingon. This led to a restraining order from my copy editor's psychiatrist, and my legal counsel has insisted that I issue the following disclaimer: "I am not cool, I have never been cool, and I could scarcely manage to relate to college students when I actually was a college student. I am a hopeless geek who is pathologically obsessed with the study of politics, and any abuse of the English language that might appear in any way to be youthful is actually a manifestation of a congenital grammar deficiency."

particularly useful for our purposes here because in the fiction that depicts them, some ideal is almost always pushed to such an extreme that it starts to break down. This was the third reason I mentioned for why fiction is a valuable teaching tool, and if I had thought ahead a little better I would have made it the final one in that section and used it as a segue into this section, but I didn't and the editing budget is limited. Deal with it.

However, there is more to utopia than just ideals pushed to extremes. Utopian visions are actually part of the reality of politics, because the people in the world who are politically active are often people who are trying to make the real world more like whatever it is they imagine a perfect world to be. The similarities in the use of ideal societies in the two realms of fiction and politics are so extensive that at times it can be difficult to draw a clear line dividing literature from political theory. Indeed, Thomas More's *Utopia*—which is where the modern term originated—is just as likely to be assigned reading in college literature courses as it is in courses in politics or philosophy.[18]

Utopia Ain't What You're Thinking

A first step in understanding how utopias are used in literature, political theorizing, and even practical politics is to drop the assumption that perfection implies a good or pleasant result. Because utopias are inherently subjective and human societies are diverse, it is unreasonable to expect that everyone would consider any one context to be ideal. Although a utopia is a perfect world, that does not necessarily mean it is perfectly wonderful. Believe it or not, scantily clad people frolicking on sunny beaches with free beer served by singing llamas is not everyone's idea of utopia. How about the utopia of a neo-Nazi, or the ideal world of one of those television preachers with plastic-looking hair, or of a militant vegetarian, or your Aunt Daisy? How many of those perfect worlds would you find appealing or even tolerable? In fact, a utopia may be perfectly miserable, if only because one person's perfect world is quite likely to be another's nightmare.

The subjective nature of a perfect world is often made quite clear in fiction that addresses the concept of utopia directly. In Ursula Le Guin's *The Lathe of Heaven,* the main character is a mental patient who can change reality through his dreams.[19] Once his psychologist realizes that this man is not insane but actually is changing the world, the doctor begins using hypnosis to direct the changes, and the story evolves toward a focus on how the psychologist's effort to create a utopia pushes these two characters into conflict. The struggle between the doctor and the patient repeatedly demonstrates just how different their perfect worlds are and just how miserable each of them becomes as the world moves closer to the other's utopia.

Instead of expecting some joyously decadent spring break on steroids, we might better understand a utopia as an extreme version of an ideal, principle, or presumption about the nature of the world. The film *Logan's Run* is set in a world where the ideals of youth and beauty are taken to their logical extreme—the populace remains young and beautiful

Dances with Squirrels, the action-packed sequel to Douglas A. Van Belle's soon-to-be-classic novel *Barking Death Squirrels,* provides the universe's best example of the subjective nature of utopias. When Edgar discovers that he is the only man trapped on a spaceship full of women, he finds that his traveling companions are not nearly as happy as he is with the utopian scenario that he had been dreaming about since puberty.

"Far from arguing over who would be the first to win my intimate attentions, the women made it immediately

clear that the only reason they might want to get close to the lone man trapped in their midst was so they could gouge my eyes out. I figured that if I was lucky, they would pounce on me and savagely rip my eyes out with a rusty scrap of jagged metal, but given my experience with women, I was pretty sure that they were going to take their time and savour the experience. They were cold, tired, frightened and hungry, and they blamed everything male for their predicament. They seemed to have good reason for blaming men, but that didn't make it any less horrific for the unfortunate bearer of a Y chromosome when he wandered in from stage left to audition for the role of lynching victim number one."

Douglas A. Van Belle, *Dances with Squirrels* (Wellington, New Zealand: Random Static, 2013).

because the government kills everyone on his or her thirtieth birthday.[20] Even though Aldous Huxley wrote *Brave New World* in the 1930s, the novel might be described as a 1960s-style free-love hippie commune pushed to the point of perfection.[21] The diabolically intrusive government in Orwell's *Nineteen Eighty-Four,* which is sometimes referred to as a *dystopia,* might be instead thought of as a utopia in which government's control of society is perfected and pushed to an extreme. Featuring shipwrecked children devolving into brutal savagery, Golding's *Lord of the Flies* depicts the closest thing to perfect anarchy that might exist in the real world. The list of examples ranges from the obscure libertarian/anarchic utopia of L. Neil Smith's *The Probability Broach,* in which the idea of limited government sees the full light of day, to Captain Kirk and crew's exploration of some utopian planet on practically every third episode of the classic *Star Trek.*[22] The "perfect" societies of *Star Trek,* besides teaching you never to wear a red shirt on any planet that looks like a bunch of sand and Styrofoam rocks tossed together on a soundstage,* all take some idea and carry it through to its logical extreme.

---

*As any *Star Trek* groupie will tell you, it is the actor in the red shirt who is destined to die when the away team visits Planet Doom.

Although it is clearly impossible to get everyone to agree on one notion of perfection, and even if pretty much any image of perfect bliss is totally impractical, the idea of a utopia is still a valuable tool for political theory, political ideology, and even political action. Whenever one takes an idea (or social concept, or vision of the world) to its conceptual extreme, otherwise unforeseen aspects of the idea—particularly its flaws—are exposed. This effect is demonstrated in its simplest form when an author uses a utopia to provoke reflection on our presumptions about society or to warn us against adopting seductively simple solutions to any of the myriad complex problems that challenge the real world. Theorists invoke utopian visions both to critique flaws in political ideologies and political processes and to envision practical paths to a better, though imperfect, future. Even political actors conjure utopias, whether by drawing mental pictures of where their policy ideas will lead or by establishing landmarks to guide their strategies for tackling the endless daily decisions they must make. Martin Luther had his Ninety-Five Theses for a better church; Martin Luther King Jr. (no relation) had a dream about equality. Gandhi had both a unique fashion sense and a hope for peacefully attaining the freedom of India. All of them spoke of utopias and used utopian concepts to pursue political goals in the real world.

Utopias as Social Statement

The simplest and most obvious use of utopias occurs when an author of fiction makes a social statement by pushing an ideal, ideology, or political demand to its logical extreme in order to make it serve as a warning to society. For example, one can argue that Orwell wrote *Nineteen Eighty-Four* at the very beginning of the Cold War to demonstrate, among other things, what would happen if ardent anticommunists were actually to get what they were demanding. Zealously seeking to protect the capitalist way of life from what they perceived as a predatory communist political ideology, the anticommunists of the post–World War II era aggressively sought to identify and remove from positions of power or influence those who did not hold "proper" beliefs. Not only is mandating correct beliefs antithetical to the liberal ideology that underlies modern capitalist democracy, but also the tactics used and the powers demanded by the leaders of this effort threatened the very freedoms and ideals they said they wished to protect.

To see how Orwell's novel could be intended as a warning to those who might support the communist witch hunt, compare the tactics and actions of Senator Joseph McCarthy and the House Un-American Activities Committee as portrayed in the film *The Front* with those of the government in *Nineteen Eighty-Four.*[23] In the *The Front,* Woody Allen plays an average guy whose blacklisted screenwriter friends arrange to use his name on their scripts so that they can continue to work. Although it has a light edge, the film bluntly depicts the United States at the height of the anticommunist frenzy, when a McCarthyite Congress spearheaded the persecution of "traitors" with "communist leanings" in the

PLATO

Team: **Classical Greek United**

Position: **First Slip**

Status: **Long Dead**

There are those who claim that all of Western political theory is really only a response to **Plato** (427–347 B.C.). There are also those who claim the pyramids were built by aliens. Who are we to judge?

The reality is that the pyramids were built by humans. They were time-traveling clones of an art student who was supposed to be creating one of those junk and garbage sculptures that spring up around campus from time to time, but still, the reality is that the original art student is mostly human. The other reality was that Plato was also an elitist snob and his antidemocratic ideas, beliefs, and arguments would be distinctly out of step with the liberal ideology that permeates modern Western political theory. While Plato envisions an ideal society in the *Republic*, that society is not in any sense democratic. Plato did not believe that the majority should have its way, and he especially did not believe that any decision should be accepted as correct simply because the masses favored it. After all, he had witnessed the democratic majority in Athens condemn his friend and mentor Socrates to death for corrupting the youth of Athens. Plato's disregard, if not contempt, for the average person derived from his understanding of the very ability of people to perceive the world around them.

Plato believed that one could not rely on his or her senses to discover what was real. He believed that what we see, touch, and taste are just imperfect representations of another actual reality. Unlike the universe about which we are aware, the hidden "real world" is unchanging and perfect; it is a world of "forms." We may think we *know* what beauty is, but that is just our *opinion* of beauty. All we can have are opinions, because we do not know the true form of beauty. However, Plato would have us believe that there is such a thing as perfect beauty, which is real and unchanging. Similarly, he also believed that there was such a thing as perfect justice, or correct living, although this perfect form would correspond not with what a society commonly understood as just, but rather with a real, unchanging equity.

Plato believed that it was only philosophers, like him, who could obtain the ability to see the true forms and they are the only ones who are in a position to share it with the general public. Basically, it was a lot like our pretentious self-cloning art student saying that only artists understand why building a replica of Stonehenge out of old computers is art and not a pile of garbage in the middle of the Quad.

Key to Plato's theory is the belief that it is important for every person to do what he or she does well. Plato believed that people who are good at making shoes, for example, should stick to making shoes; that athletes should only concern themselves with athletics; and that those who can see the true forms (the philosophers) should be the ones to rule. Because of the importance of this governing class, much of the *Republic* is devoted to constructing a state that allows for the proper training of the elite ruling class of philosophers and to specifying the type of training that philosopher-kings should receive.

entertainment industry. From the presumption of guilt by association or innuendo to the exercise of government coercion to compel individuals to testify against friends and colleagues in order to save themselves, the similarities between the real and fictional settings are all too obvious.

Nineteen Eighty-Four can be argued to represent the extension of something like McCarthyism to the point at which the government regulates every aspect of life, from personal relationships to thoughts and language. In essence, one of many possible interpretations of Orwell's novel is that the anticommunist extremists, if successful, would impose the very dictatorship they claimed to be fighting against. The novelist's dire warning eerily resonates with the real Senator McCarthy's later actions. The imprisonment and torture of people for thought crimes depicted in *Nineteen Eighty-Four* found its perfect real-world parallel in the ability of the American anticommunists to ruin careers and lives in the name of defending freedom. When workers can be fired and generally shunned by employers for simply being named as communist sympathizers, you have to admit that sounds a lot like something a communist dictator would do to those accused of being sympathetic to capitalist pigdogs.* Regardless of the specifics, even the most pleasant fictional utopia comes at a very high price to someone.

Just as novelists and filmmakers utilize utopias to analyze social or political phenomena, political theorists use them to evaluate aspects or dynamics of politics and political or social structures. **Karl Marx,** for example, applied utopian thought in his harsh and influential critique of capitalism.[24] I explore Marx's theories more fully when I discuss the economic dimensions of politics in Chapter 4, but his work is notable here because of the way he extends capitalist ideals to their logical extreme for the purpose of exposing the social and political consequences of unfettered competition. Just as Orwell, the novelist, aimed to sound an alarm about the ramifications of giving the passionate communist hunters everything they wanted, Marx, the political theorist, envisioned a "perfect" capitalism to expose an aspect of its theoretical underpinnings that could be self-destructive if left unrestrained.

Utopias in Practical Use

More commonly, a political ideologue offers a utopian vision not only to conceptualize a better world but also to suggest a means to achieve it. Again, Marx provides an example.* Having identified what he believed to be the fundamental flaw in capitalism, he proposed an alternative model—socialism—wherein society controls the economics of production.

---

*I'm not sure exactly what pigdogs are—whether you should barbecue them or pet them—but all the communists in the movies talk about them a lot.

*Marx went both ways. He was both a theorist and an ideologist.

He projected socialism out to a communist utopia, a perfect socialist world, which he then used to prescribe specific instructions about how to get there from the starting point of a predominantly capitalist world. The fact that this road map to utopia included the revolutionary overthrow of capitalism and destruction of the governmental structures supporting that economic system is undoubtedly why Marx's theories continue to provoke a visceral response from capitalists and fearful political elites. Nevertheless, Marx's projection of a utopia as an orienting point for a political strategy is quite common for theorists, ideologues, and activists.

The evocation of utopias in theory, ideology, and practical politics probably reached its pinnacle in the wake of World War I. Sometimes referred to as the **idealist period,** at least in the study of international politics, the two decades between the world wars were marked by efforts to envision and attain a perfectly peaceful world. The attempt to pursue a utopian vision of global peace through world democracy, a concept first proposed by U.S. president Woodrow Wilson, was the most prominent example of this utopian thinking. The unbelievable carnage of World War I, which I describe in unpleasant if not gory detail in Chapter 12, instigated a desperate search for alternatives to violence as a means of settling disputes in international politics. The liberal democratic political structures and institutions that operated in the countries that had managed to win the war appeared to allow for the reasoned resolution of political, economic, and social conflicts. Consequently, these institutions provided a seemingly natural basis for a worldwide system of peaceful politics, and the **League of Nations** was built on this ideal.

Comprising an international court of justice, a legislative body, and lots of bureaucracy, the League of Nations appeared to be a substantial step toward a global democracy. However, like most paths toward perfection, it ran into the even more substantial imperfections of the real world. While the idea of a global government was tremendously appealing to the war-ravaged nations of Europe, that same vision of a path to world peace was frightening to the powerful and isolationist United States. The domestically oriented U.S. Congress would neither submit to the democratic structure of the League of Nations nor risk entanglement in the European politics that had repeatedly led to devastating wars. A similar resistance can still be seen, nine decades later, in the public and political attitudes of the United States toward the United Nations and toward an international criminal court. The U.S. rejection of the League of Nations during the interwar period weakened the institution and made it easier for the fascist governments of Japan, Germany, Italy, and Spain to refuse to participate or respect its role in world politics.

Whether it is depicted as utopian thinking in an imperfect world or as the gap between idealists and realists, the contrast between the real and the ideal is a constant throughout the practice, theory, and study of politics. It is also, incidentally, part of writing a textbook on politics. Ideally, I would have written a conclusion for this section that really drives the point home and also offers a bridge to the next section. The reality, I am sorry to report, falls far short of the ideal.

IDEOLOGIES

Karl Marx has already been identified as a notable political theorist, but as I've told you, his ideas can wait until we start talking about economics—please try to pay attention.* For present purposes, however, Marx's work offers a good way to talk about the contrast between a **political theory** and a **political ideology.** In essence, the difference between these two bodies of thought centers on their basic dynamics: political theory is aimed at developing knowledge, whereas political ideology is about organizing and directing goal-oriented action. The distinction is roughly the same as that between doing research on former baseball players, as many popular authors do, and actually plowing under your cornfield in the hope that they will magically show up for a visit, as Ray Kinsella does in *Field of Dreams.*[25] Marx explicitly wrote toward both ends. It is not difficult to interpret the meaning of *The Communist Manifesto,* which Marx wrote with Friedrich Engels in 1848.[26] Its blistering, sharply written conclusion—urging, "Workers of the world, unite!"—is unquestionably the capstone of an argument that is intended to translate ideals into action, to guide political struggle and change. This exhortation also stands in stark contrast to the theoretical and philosophical writings in which Marx makes use of utopias, idealized worlds, and other perfect but impractical concepts. The motivations of the two kinds of writing are clearly different, but, because both invoke perfect worlds, political ideology and political theory are easily confused.

Distinguishing Ideologies from Theories

A crude way of distinguishing between theories and ideologies—though one with which Plato would undoubtedly have agreed—is to consider the intended audience. While political theories are written for elites who think intently about the details of the nature of the political world, ideologies are written for the masses. Ideologies are used to convey simple messages, much like the brief moral at the end of each of Aesop's fables. To use yet another grossly oversimplified analogy, political theories are to political ideologies what great works of literature are to their TV movie adaptations. Charles Dickens's *A Christmas Carol* is a complex narrative with layer upon layer of imagery, nuance, and subtle references to religion, faith, society, and politics.[27] Scholars debate all manner of detail within its pages. In contrast, *Mr. Magoo's Christmas Carol* is an animated cartoon made for mass consumption, and, aside from the philosophical debate of whether or not there really is such a thing as "razzleberry dressing," the cartoon version intends to do little more than to teach kids to share and be nice.[28]

Political theories are usually very complex and logically robust, containing an epistemology (which is a theory of the nature of knowledge), and are written for a select audience.

---

*This also seems an opportune moment to mention that recent studies link marijuana use to memory loss. Of course, to communicate this information to the students in greatest need of it, I would have to mention it every third page or so, and I'm way too lazy to do that, so this whole footnote is something of a wasted effort.

They are, in some ways, timeless—not because they have been around for a long time and you are likely to find several dog-eared, highlighted copies at used bookstores, but because they raise questions and provide answers for problems that have persisted throughout the centuries.

An ideology, on the other hand, is created to convince large numbers of people to buy into a belief system. While political theorists often use utopian images to develop their central points or to critique the ideas of others, with an ideology, the image itself is the point. An ideology paints dramatic pictures of the utopia its proponents hope to achieve. It generally does this in a very cartoonish kind of way, in terms simple enough to be convincing. An ideology also often offers almost how-to instructions for assembling that utopia. Interestingly, it is not uncommon for the tenets of an ideology to be logically inconsistent: the proponents of an ideology may dedicate themselves to war and power struggles as a means of attaining peace, or advocate imprisoning those who disagree with them as a means of preserving freedom and liberty. Having made believers out of an audience, the purveyors of an ideology then provide a conceptual framework to make sense of a complex world. Inherent within that conceptual framework is a logic that consistently shapes judgments about specific policy questions. Because ideologies must appeal to large numbers of people in specific countries at specific times, they are also usually malleable enough that they can be changed to suit the relevant conditions. This explains why there are often many different versions of similar ideologies.[29]

We think of an ideology as something someone else follows, but we all adhere to or accept one or more belief systems ourselves. Whether our personal ideologies have been acquired through culture, religion, family, language, or conscious choice, we all view the world through lenses tinted by sets of beliefs that we share with others. It is important when studying politics to realize that we have these beliefs and to understand how our ideological lenses alter our vision, even if we cannot or do not wish to remove them. This reflection allows us not only to question why we hold a particular ideology but also to more fully understand others' perspectives and to appreciate how our own beliefs control our perceptions of the complex world of political preferences.

Classifying Ideologies

There are several ways to discuss ideologies. Because they are temporal—they are born, they evolve, they die, and they spawn variants—it is possible simply to give a history of prominent or influential ideologies. I could organize them into family trees and discuss their intellectual roots and how they evolved. I could even create a scheme for categorizing them, like the taxonomy of species that connects fossils and living animals. Because ideologies are meant to be implemented, the proponents of ideologies are constantly looking for new followers to join their ranks. As such, ideologies are like television commercials for ideal worlds: just as a commercial is supposed to make you want to get up off the sofa and

go buy something, an ideology is supposed to stir you to action. Therefore, I've decided to present to you with commercials for a few prominent ideologies. At first, I was just joking around while outlining this chapter and thought commercials for ideologies would be amusing. But then I realized that the concept works. Fake commercials are a perfect way to convey the idea that an ideology sells people the simplified image of an ideal as a way to enable groups or leaders to engage the realities of politics.

One more common thread characterizes ideologies. With the possible exception of classic conservatism, they all presume that human beings can make rational decisions and that people can mold their destinies. Although you may view this statement with something approaching the excitement of studying how paint dries,* the discovery of this genuinely fascinating fact was crucial to making modern political ideologies possible. Think about how many modern political ideologies could not have been imagined when people believed that kings ruled because God chose them. Think of how many ideologies remain inconceivable even now in countries where governments claim that they are ruling in response to a very polite request from the magic goat. This common thread also explains why the first great ideology bursts on the scene in 1776, when **Adam Smith** (1723–1790) published *The Wealth of Nations,* arguing that individual rational choices are the ideal way to foster efficient economic activity.[30]

Classic Liberalism: The Mother of All Ideologies

Although **classic liberalism** is rooted in the theories of freedom that were articulated by Thomas Hobbes and John Locke and were explicitly made part of the American insurrection against their divinely appointed British monarch, Adam Smith added economic freedom as a key variable. He believed a nation could achieve economic success by keeping the government out of the economy and allowing the "invisible hand" of the market to work unfettered. While this economic aspect of the ideology is extremely important, classic liberalism also emphasizes the belief that people should be generally free from governmental constraints. As Thomas Jefferson wrote, "The government that governs best, governs least." Most political scientists argue that freedom of speech and freedom of religion owe their existence to adherents of classic liberalism. A classic liberal's utopia would be a country in which the government provides for maximum human freedom by staying out of the way. It is worth noting the contrast of classic liberalism with the way many Americans currently misuse the term *liberal.*

The ideology closest to classic liberalism in existence today is probably libertarianism. Libertarians believe that the government should provide military protection, a police force, and basic infrastructure (such as roads and bridges), but do little more. It is an interesting

---

*Those of you considering taking advantage of the entertainment value of watching paint dry, don't bother. It dries from the edges first and gradually gets lighter in color and tone.

question whether classic liberals should be considered realists or idealists. Libertarians believe that government institutions are necessary to control the selfish nature of human beings—as is the case with the U.S. Constitution—so in that way they seem to be realists. However, some critics would argue that their faith in unregulated economic markets is just as idealistic as unbridled faith in human potential.

> **Classic Liberalism, the Commercial:** Row after row of identical bureaucrats wearing identical suits push tons of papers on their identical desks, which stretch off into the infinity of an impossibly vast office. Some of these identical men are seen stapling a cease-and-desist order on a half-built tree house as they march children off in handcuffs. More government clones are shown out in a rainstorm, posting signs saying "Wetlands" at the edge of every puddle. A lemonade stand is suddenly crushed as a dump truck buries it under a mountain of papers printed with big red letters that spell out "GOVERNMENT REGULATIONS." A teenager in a fast-food restaurant uniform excitedly opens his first paycheck just as one of the government clones pops up to snatch it away and then grabs all the others from the slots by the time clock. The Twisted Sister song "We're Not Gonna Take It" stops blaring as the voice-over proclaims: "There are rights that no one can take away. You know what is best for you. You work hard and you're entitled to life, liberty, and the pursuit of happiness. You deserve the opportunity to make the most of yourself without the government standing in your way or taking away your rewards with high taxes. Become a classic liberal and learn how to stand up for your rights."

Classic Conservatism

Generally associated with the eighteenth-century British parliamentarian Edmund Burke, **classic conservatism** developed as a reaction not to classic liberalism but to the excesses resulting from the French Revolution. It is often said that conservatives do not like change. However, even though this generalization originates with classic conservatives, it is not really accurate. What Burke objected to was the belief that unrestrained individual human reason could take the place of long-standing, traditional institutions. He believed that no group of people could possibly know all of the reasons why institutions such as the church and the aristocracy existed or why traditions evolved. These institutions served purposes that had been carefully honed by centuries of experience. They evolved through success and failure and had an incalculable wealth of built-in knowledge. Thus, these social institutions and traditions became shorthand for a volume of experience and information that was so vast that it would be impossible for any individual or group to understand it fully. Unlike the extreme views and aggressive rhetoric of many people or groups now associated with the term *conservative*, classic conservatism is a rational, considered belief that existing processes and norms have evolved into highly efficient and effective institutions. Classic conservatives believe that people should be very wary of

changing things until they understand all the ramifications of the proposed changes, because almost any change is certain to unleash unintended consequences, such as the havoc that followed the French Revolution. The perfect world envisioned by classic conservatives tends to be a negative one; it is a picture of the anarchy that might result from the careless elimination of treasured institutions.

> **Classic Conservatism, the Commercial:** Simon & Garfunkel's "59th Street Bridge Song (Feelin' Groovy)" plays in the background of a small-town setting out of a Norman Rockwell painting, where beautiful children are sitting on their grandparents' laps and selling lemonade in front of their white-picket-fenced houses. The music screeches to a halt and is replaced by the Talking Heads' "Burning Down the House," while on the screen an unruly crowd pushes down a pillar, causing the town hall to come tumbling to the ground. Footage of hippies from the 1960s, carrying "Down with Marriage" signs, are followed by additional shots of the poster children of every unusual counterculture group in existence, culminating in a scene of a crowd of them burning Bibles. The images conclude with a pan out to a vast desert, where ruins are visible in the background. The voice-over announces: "They want to change the world. Do they really know what they are doing? What happens when they are done? What is to become of you and the way of life that you hold so dear? It's worked well for your great-grandparents, your grandparents, your parents, and you. But they want to change everything. Become a classic conservative and stand up for the good things that have lasted for generations."

Communism

For Karl Marx,* the central problem with capitalism was the class division between the proletariat and the bourgeoisie. The bourgeoisie was made up of the capitalists who controlled the entire machinery of the state and who benefited from the inequities created by the capitalistic system, while the proletariat was the working class, workers who were paid only a fraction of the worth of the goods they produced and the services they provided. The members of the proletariat did not make enough to purchase the goods they supplied, and this resulted in constant overproduction and recurrent economic depressions. Marx saw the benefits of capitalism, including industrialization and the modernization of feudal society, but he believed that eventually the workers in advanced industrial nations would realize that they were being exploited and would revolt by casting off the rule of the capitalists and instituting **communism,** a classless society in which justice and fairness would prevail. In Marx's utopia, there would be no need for government as we know it because there would be enough material goods for all.

---

*Again, I'll get to a serious discussion of Karl later. This is just a tidbit. Put down the water pipe for a minute and pay attention.

Marx's ideology has often been adapted to meet circumstances completely unlike the context he was describing. Most notably, Vladimir Ilich Lenin applied communist principles to the conditions of czarist Russia in the early twentieth century. At the time, Russia was still a semifeudal agrarian land, which was about as far as you could get from the industrial capitalist society that Marx confronted with his analysis of capitalism. In crafting what has become known as Marxist-Leninism, Lenin shifted the focus from the exploitation of the proletariat within capitalist societies to the exploitation and colonization of countries—**imperialism**—by advanced capitalist countries. Lenin also changed Marx's revolutionary vision to depend on, instead of a spontaneous revolution by the proletariat, a central communist party that can organize the revolution.

> **Communism, the Commercial:** The scene starts with a black-and-white image of an ornate carriage in which laughing people in tuxedos and lavish gowns sip champagne and nibble caviar. Their laughter fades as the carriage slows and stops, and the driver climbs down from his perch to inspect the bedraggled men and women who have been pulling the carriage. Stopping in front of one woman who has collapsed on an injured leg, he unhitches her from her harness and throws her into a nearby trash bin before grabbing a random passerby off the sidewalk and hitching him to the cart in her place. Suddenly, a man runs toward the team of harnessed humans. "This is their world," he yells, pointing to the people in the carriage as uniformed police try to stop him. "It should be YOURS!" One of the harnessed draftees shimmers, changes from black-and-white to color, and says, "Ours." His harness falls away and he begins shaking the person next to him as the police close in. "It is ours!" he shouts gleefully, as a few others around him begin shimmering and gaining color. The police appear to panic as the color spreads to exhausted-looking factory workers, construction workers, teachers, coal miners, and salesclerks. The camera pans as color spreads across the formerly gray background, where flowers begin to sprout in empty flower boxes. Then, as it focuses in on a single flower, a voice-over intones: "Workers of the world, unite! Join your fellow workers in throwing off the yoke of your capitalist oppressors. Create a world where those who do the work make the rules and reap the rewards for their labor."

Democratic Socialism

While there were socialists who preceded Karl Marx, it is certainly true that those who followed him were influenced by his view of communism. Like Marx, the democratic socialists who emerged in the early twentieth century believed that people are inherently social beings and that classic liberalism places too great a stress on individualism. Like communists, the democratic socialists envisioned a society characterized by social, political, and economic equality. Their primary difference with Marx centered on the means of implementing this utopia. Whereas Marx believed in the violent overthrow of capitalist societies,

the social democrats favored operating political parties in democratic countries to achieve their ends.

There actually is a difference between democratic socialists and social democrats. Although it may appear to be as confusing a point as the ludicrous debate between the Judean People's Front and the People's Front of Judea in the Monty Python film *Life of Brian*,[31] the distinctions are significant. Democratic socialists believe that a socialist state can be achieved through democratic means, while social democrats aim merely to modify the harshness of capitalism through the infusion of some elements of socialism. A key advocate of **democratic socialism** was Eduard Bernstein (1850–1932), who was active in the German Social Democratic Party. Bernstein believed that Marx's critique of capitalism was accurate, but he advocated a more gradual or evolutionary approach to reaching utopia.[32]

> **Democratic Socialism, the Commercial:** Over an image of Bill Gates posing in front of his mansion, the words "One Vote" are stamped across the screen. Next, over an image of Donald Trump standing in the marble-and-gold lobby of the Trump Tower; again, "One Vote" is stamped across the screen. Rupert Murdoch on his yacht—"One Vote." Alex Rodriguez in front of his three Ferraris—"One Vote." An image of an elderly coal miner—"One Vote." The camera slowly zooms out, and as the frame widens to include the images of various downtrodden people, the words "One Vote" are stamped over each image, faster and faster, until the screen becomes a blur. Voice-over: "We are equal in the voting booth; why not in life? Social democrats ask you to use your vote wisely." As the camera zooms back in to focus on the coal miner, REM's "Shiny Happy People" blares from a distance, and the still picture of the miner's face comes to life. Voice-over, gently: "Shouldn't everyone have a home before anyone gets two?" The camera again zooms out as the miner walks into the front yard of a modest house and is hugged by a small child. "Everyone deserves the basic necessities."

Reform Liberalism

Motivated by the inequities of capitalism and the booms and busts of the economic cycles that occurred in the late nineteenth and early twentieth centuries, several theorists—chief among them Thomas Hill Green (1832–1882)—began to think that classic liberalism needed to be modified. These advocates of **reform liberalism** began to argue that government has a role to play in regulating the economy and removing the major inequities inherent in the capitalist system. Government could both remove the obstacles that hinder people from pursuing their individual goals and guarantee opportunities for those who might not otherwise be able to take advantage of this type of freedom by providing education, job training, health care, a safety net, and so forth. While classic liberals would agree with the first goal, which is known as *negative liberty,* they would not agree with government's involvement in securing equal opportunity, known as *positive liberty.* Classic liberals

believe that any governmental interference ultimately has a deleterious effect on the economy, whereas the utopia envisioned by the reform liberals includes a government that ensures that no one is left behind.* Adopting the ideal world of the classic liberals, reform liberalism hopes to spread it to all in society. This is closer to what many in the United States consider to be a liberal perspective.

> **Reform Liberalism, the Commercial:** The camera zooms in on a stadium track where runners wait for the start of a race—but in this race it is clear that there is more than one starting line. Poised at the first starting line are contestants dressed in expensive tracksuits and running shoes. Behind them, at the second starting line, are people dressed in working clothes, including construction workers in heavy boots, postal employees carrying bags of mail, and a farmer pulling futilely on the rope lead of a cow that seems interested in wandering off in a different direction. Far behind them, at the last starting line, are others in tattered clothes and with bare feet; these entrants include children, people with disabilities, and elderly people. Jackson Browne's "Running on Empty" plays in the background as the camera pans across the faces of those on the last starting line, and the voice-over pronounces softly: "One of these people could be the fastest sprinter in the world, but we will never know if we never give them all a reasonable chance. Reward success, but give everyone a chance to succeed. We're the reform liberals."

Fascism

Fascism, an ideology that was developed in the twentieth century, argues for the supremacy and purity of one group of people in a society. Fascists believe in strong military rule headed by the charismatic dictator of a ruling party that exercises total control over all aspects of social and cultural life and molds it to suit the history and traditions of the superior group. In countries where fascism has taken control, such as Italy, Spain, and Atlantis, the fascist party has usually risen to power during a severe economic depression, or when the island was sinking. The leader promises to take control of the economy and works with businesses to plan recovery. Public spectacles are staged to reinforce traditions and to motivate the people to support the ruling party. Historically, fascist governments have grown out of democracies in crisis. However, once in power fascists tend to dislike democracy because it allows for the dilution of custom and tradition and because it undermines the dictator's ability to express the will of the people. Nationalism plays a strong role in fascism, as does a belief in constant vigilance against enemies at home and abroad. The fascist utopia promises that people of the correct lineage can return to the supposed greatness of their roots undistracted by enemies who would change or corrupt their way of

---

*This slogan is not to be confused with "No Child Left Behind," which appears to be a policy designed to suck the life out of actual learning by turning all students into mindless droids who find joy in taking standardized tests.

life. Of course, the Nazis in Germany and the Italian and Spanish fascists all had the opportunity to try out their utopias.

> **Fascism, the Commercial:** On the screen, row after row of soldiers are marching. Patriotic tunes are playing in the background. Watching the parade are very Aryan-looking children waving flags and saluting. Voice-over: "Sick of all the political wrangling, the dirty deals, and the inability to cure our economic ills? We can have it all again and return to greatness. If you believe that REAL Americans should rule America, that someone who actually knows what REAL Americans want and need should make decisions that work—if you believe that the trains should run on time, even if that means running over some good-for-nothing un-American foreigners, then fascism's for you!"

Other Ideologies

Each of the ideologies described above has been rethought, remolded, and resold in different places at different times. It is not possible to characterize all ideologies in the space of one section of one chapter in an introduction to politics textbook. That's why there are hefty textbooks and entire university courses dedicated to exploring ideologies. Bear in mind also that virtually any vision of a utopia can be transformed into an ideology through a simplified description of how and why people should take part in the pursuit of that utopia. Imagine the commercials for nationalists, who hold that their own country is the best and that the rest of the world should emulate their way of doing things; for feminists (who can be divided further into several distinct ideologies), who look forward to a world in which women are not dominated by patriarchy; for environmentalists, who envision a time when the Earth and all its creatures are treated with respect and care; for technocrats, who eagerly anticipate a world in which people base decisions only on fact and not on belief; or for rugbyists, who dream of a world in which everyone is devoted to rugby or a rugby-like sport of their choosing.

Obviously, I made that last one up. Rugbyism isn't an ideology. It's a religion—all worship the black jersey. The point is that virtually any belief system that includes a utopian vision of a perfect world can become an ideology if believers try to use that utopia to shape or drive political action. The disembodied voice may not be telling you to build a baseball field in the middle of a cornfield; it's probably telling you to send lots of money to the author of this textbook. Regardless, remember that the call to action is a key part of an ideology. As you read the chapters that follow, I will be reminding you to try to recognize your preconceived notions and how they may be shaping your insights as we further explore the real, the ideal, and the political. Before I get to that dreaded rest of the book, however, I want to bludgeon you with one more thing. I want to ask a question that isn't quite as absurd as it might first appear.

WHAT IS POLITICS?

Writing a concurring opinion in a 1964 case involving pornography, U.S. Supreme Court justice Potter Stewart admitted his difficulty in defining specifically what types of adult films constitute pornography. Despite his trouble, he concluded, "I know it when I see it."[33] Students in introductory political science classes face the same dilemma. No, you do not have to define pornography,* but like the justices watching dirty movies in the basement of the Supreme Court, you are unlikely to be able to offer a clear definition of the similarly indistinct concept called *politics.* Still, more often than not, you will know politics when you see it. After thinking about it for a while, you can probably give examples of politics or political behavior, so the inability to define politics is not a sign of ignorance. Rather, the difficulty seems to arise because *politics* is a word that is so clouded with personal opinions and potentially conflicting examples that it defies a precise and complete description. You should also feel reassured by the simple fact that political scientists themselves disagree about how to define the term. In general, political scientists find it rather difficult to agree on anything,† but we all have to admit that to disagree about the very definition of the subject they study is truly bizarre.

What is politics? Well, you probably know it when you see it. Think about how you might have used the word in the past. Perhaps you were discussing office politics, and you were griping, whining, or laughing about something that someone did in an attempt to better his or her position within the company. You might remember a time when Pat, for example, spent weeks braving the boss's paint-peeling halitosis, flirting and laughing at all the bad jokes while pretending that your oblong, mentally defective boss was not the most offensive human on the planet. Pat, you may have thought, was "playing politics"—behaving in a calculating manner, trying to influence others to get something in return or attain a goal.

Politics does not end there. Those of you with a more critical eye for these sorts of things may have realized that "Pat" could be either a guy's name or a girl's name and that I did not identify the boss as a he or a she. You may be thinking that I have really gone to a lot of trouble to make this example gender-neutral and, hence, sexual-orientation-neutral. That took some work, and if I put even a tiny bit of effort into something, then there must be a very good reason for it. While I am not admitting anything, all the neutering in this example might well be a political effort to avoid the kind of typecasting that prolongs gender stereotypes. Or perhaps I may simply realize that it would be politically unwise to upset professors who might otherwise assign this textbook to their students.

Behave politically? Who, me?

---

*In fact, perversely enough, most of you can't even watch it legally. You can star in porn at age eighteen but in most U.S. states you can't watch it until age twenty-one, so please, for legal reasons, pretend that you have no idea what it is.

†An unfortunate exception is the unnatural tolerance all political scientists have for corduroy sport coats worn with pastel polyester pants.

Another way to get to the meaning of the word *politics* might be to engage in word association. Think of the first synonyms that come to your mind when you hear the word *Stewie Griffin on steroids.* Wait, sorry, I was thinking about something else—besides, that's four words. Try the word *political.* How many of your synonyms are positive? Do they include terms like *greedy, disingenuous, manipulative, sleazy,* and *selfish*? Do you think of someone who applies the ingenuity of Wile E. Coyote to construct elaborate plans for pursuing his or her own self-interest at the expense of others? Describing someone as political is not usually a compliment. Most people use the word in a derogatory sense. After all, the public seems to consider politicians to be somewhat less evolved than used-car dealers.

It is easy to see how Pat's fawning attitude toward the boss fits in with the derogatory connotation of politics, and there are undoubtedly plenty of other examples that you might associate with the word *politics.* But what exactly is Pat doing that is political? Pat is using a technique—in this case the art of flattery and perhaps even a bit of manipulative sexual flirtation—to try to get something from someone else. Pat is laughing at the boss's inane jokes in hopes of getting a better schedule, a raise, a promotion, a better work assignment, a new desk chair, or perhaps Pat wants the coveted cubicle that is farthest from the desk of the amateur taxidermist who showers only on Thursdays. Clearly, behavior can be classified as political when it is aimed at getting something from others. We call Pat's behavior political in the same way that we would classify as political the behavior of a candidate who shakes hands with constituents or a member of Congress who tries to make a deal with a colleague in order to get a bill passed into law. In each of these cases, someone is trying to get something from others, such as constituents' votes or colleagues' support for a bill. Whether the behavior is that of an individual, a group, or a government, this description seems to fit our popular understanding of the term *politics.*

Unfortunately, defining politics isn't as simple as including all efforts to manipulate people in pursuit of benefits. Would we call this kind of flirting and fakery political if it involved two Pats who had just met each other at the monorail stop on Aisle 374 of a Mega-Walmart? One Pat may indeed be trying to get something from the other, but if Pat is just after a date with the other Pat, would we call that political?

Of course, coming up with a definition is even more complicated than that. The word *political* is an adjective, describing the everyday acts of persuasion or calculation that we all engage in, but here we are concerned with defining what politics is. I'm going to take a bit of a risk here and say that the difference between behaving politically and politics is largely a matter of the context of the action.

There is one very clear difference between Pat's actions, in either the office or the Walmart, and those of a candidate or legislator: Pat's behavior is unlikely to affect more than a small number of people. Normally, when we use the word *politics,* we are referring to matters that directly or indirectly or potentially have impacts on a great number of

people. Thus, I can state that **politics** consists of individual or combined actions of individuals, governments, and/or groups aimed at getting what they want accomplished when those actions have public consequences.

Notice that this definition does not distinguish between what we might label "good" or "bad" behavior. I sort of did that on purpose.* People, countries, and organizations can have lofty moral purposes or they can have very low, nasty goals when they are engaged in politics. Both Darth Vader and Princess Leia are involved in politics. Both Adolf Hitler and Winston Churchill were politicians. In fact, most of those striving for what you might consider good purposes are successful precisely because they are knowledgeable about politics. Politics can be engaged in by individuals or by groups of people. It can be aimed at achieving societal goals or personal ambitions. Politics can be the product of private individuals or government officials.

On its face, characterizing politics as *goal-oriented actions with public consequences* is not too different from one classic definition of politics offered by Harold Lasswell: "who gets what, when, and how."[34] One major difference is that the definition I use places more stress on action—which means that the content of politics is never stagnant. New needs or desires arise. People are constantly coming up with new ideas about how to get what they want. Political entities are constantly changing. Advances in technology translate into new political strategies. The specifics about politics are always in flux. While this constant evolution of the specifics makes politics an interesting topic to study, it also means that the already difficult problem of definition is made all the more challenging because we are trying to hit a moving target.

Consider tweeting. It used to be something that birds did, but now it has something to do with Angry Birds and adolescent girls and cell phones or something. Regardless, a medium of communication that was apparently designed so Ashton Kutcher could announce when he's off to take a dump is not the sort of thing that one would normally think of as political, but Twitter and its social networking cousins played critical political roles in the Arab Spring of 2011. Activists used them to coordinate actions, disseminate information, and evade government efforts to restrict news coverage of protests and government responses. Governments went so far as to shut down the Internet completely, disrupting the international trade and other business that relied on it, to try to stop the political use of Twitter, but ultimately they failed and several governments fell.

That, however, shouldn't have been much of a surprise. Nobody thought of a fax machine as a political tool until 1989, when supporters of the political protesters occupying Tiananmen Square sidestepped the Chinese government's ban on domestic press coverage by faxing copies of newspaper articles from other countries into China. This action let key parts of the Chinese public know what was going on in Beijing even though the

---

*Fortunately, you can't prove otherwise.

government-run news agencies tried not to report on the events. By breaking the Chinese government's monopoly on information, the supporters of the political protesters made the protest a public event, and they drastically altered the context in which Chinese officials were making significant political choices. From that day on, the fax machine became a political tool as well as an office tool, and all governments have to take this now totally antiquated information-transmission method—and newer ones such as e-mail and blogs and the Ashton Kutcher bodily function announcement service known as Twitter—into account before they act. No matter how much the content of politics changes, it is always very much about action. It is about the things that people do or choose not to do. And please remember that choosing not to do something is an action.

This brings me to a very important point about politics. Many people are used to discussing politics as if they are the objects of those undefined others engaged in it—as in "They are raising my taxes," "They are starting a war," "They are letting too many immigrants into the country," "They made Newt Gingrich crazy and fat," or "They put the president's speech on all the good channels." But the very same people complaining about the political actions "they" are taking are also acting politically: even when actively avoiding political action, they are engaged in politics. Choosing not to participate leaves it to others to make decisions, and, just as surrender is a military option, inaction is a political option. If you have ever not voted in an election you were eligible to vote in, you have taken a political action. In many cases, people choose not to participate in politics because they are happy enough with conditions as they exist and have more interesting ways to occupy their time, but there can also be insidious reasons, such as fear, or a surrender to a feeling of futility. Whatever the reason, not voting is a political action. Even under a brutal dictatorship, people's decisions not to protest or not to rebel, while perfectly rational, are still political choices.

Inaction may be something that is taught as a proper response to authority, it may be driven by religious faith, or it may be the result of ignorance. Inaction can also be a very carefully thought-out, rational choice. In the case of revolt, you can think of inaction as the rational result of a calculation involving the potential gains versus the very high risks encountered in revolting against a government. With their use of injury, torture, and death, dictators are seldom very nice to participants in failed rebellions. Not all of the planets in *Star Wars* join in the rebellion against Darth Vader and the Emperor. This might be the wise or prudent decision—after all, most of us would like to stay alive and in one piece—but it is still a political choice.

The definition of politics used here also differs from another classic definition, offered by David Easton, that holds that politics is the "authoritative allocation of values for society."[35] According to this definition, politics is about how governments determine who is entitled to have whatever lots of people want. However, I do not want to limit you to the idea that government will be involved in all that is political. In fact, a number of important decisions with public consequences take place outside the control of governments.

One of the most fascinating things about studying political science is that the substance of politics is constantly changing. New political strategies are constantly being developed, new political actors arrive on the stage, and new political entities emerge. For example, faced with increasing globalization, whereby multinational corporations have exerted expanding power that cannot be checked by traditional governments, environmental and other interest groups have searched for new strategies to advance their particular objectives. Some have reached back to the 1980s for a strategy that many had utilized to fight apartheid in South Africa: they have begun trying to influence corporate decisions from the inside. By purchasing stocks in corporations or acquiring proxy votes from willing corporate stockholders, groups such as the U.S. Public Interest Research Group, Greenpeace, and the World Wildlife Fund have introduced proposals designed to heighten corporate responsibility. At one time, corporations scorned the activities of these groups, but the trend toward **socially responsible investing** (SRI) has had an increasing impact on these businesses. Even McDonald's, long the target of animal rights and environmental groups, has rethought its stance and now issues a report on its social responsibility. Its menu is still defined by what was killed to make the meal, so it would be hard to argue that the animal rights activists have won that one, but the organization's corporate behavior has been modified. Despite the fact that no direct governmental activity has taken place, the organized actions of such advocacy groups are clearly political.[36]

A society's religions, its customs and traditions, its resources, and its economy can all be part of its politics. People can even take actions with public consequences in their own homes. For years, feminists have argued that "the personal is political." Private and personal actions, those that are not traditionally thought of as occurring in the public sphere, can have serious political consequences if, for example, they keep others from participating freely in the political process or from sharing proportionally in a country's resources. Thus, spouses who discourage their partners from participating in public debates or elections are acting politically. They are making decisions with political consequences. Companies that frown on their employees participating in politics are acting politically. Furthermore, companies make decisions with public consequences all the time—when they close plant locations, hire workers, move their headquarters, or lop off the top of a mountain to get at the good stuff inside.

In *The Simpsons,* Mr. Burns's actions often have clear political implications.[37] When you think about all the radiation that has leaked out of the nuclear power plant owned by Homer's boss, and the impact of these leaks on the citizens and environment of Springfield, the political consequences are quite obvious. Michael Moore's documentary *Roger & Me* provides another good example, as Moore demonstrates the very public ramifications that the choices of the American automobile industry had on Detroit and the surrounding towns.[38] Those who are outside government commonly make decisions with political implications.

Politics is just one of many terms used in this book that have disputed, complex, or unclear definitions. *Power, legitimacy, authority, sovereignty, security,* and a host of other essential political science concepts present similar challenges to the effort to explore the fundamentals of politics. To deal with this barrage of ambiguity, I cheat. I also cheat when I play Grand Theft Auto with my kids, but that's just self-defense. When faced with disputed terms or concepts I will give you simplified—sometimes extremely simplified—definitions that capture the basic elements, and I will trust that you can later flesh out the ideas if necessary. I will try to remember to alert you to these deliberate oversimplifications because I want you to be aware that there are nuances and complexities involved in particular topics of discussion that you might encounter in other courses or other contexts, but I will simplify, sometimes horrifically. Hopefully, as you progress through the four years of political science that you will all be majoring in after the subliminal messages in this text take effect, you will be able to build on the simplified definitions offered here. However, for now, I do not want you to lose sight of the hows and whys of politics because you are bogged down in debates over definitions. The use of simplified definitions for some complex terms is meant to keep a focus on the dynamics.

WHAT IS POLITICAL SCIENCE?

If politics is about goal-oriented actions or choices that have public consequences, what, then, is **political science**? Strange as it may seem, political scientists do not agree on a definition of this term either. In fact, the disagreement can often become heated, and the scholarly debate often escalates to a point at which, even though food is seldom thrown, you would still have to call it an argument. For political scientists, the stakes can be substantial. How the discipline defines the *science* part of political science can influence which approaches to research will be published in journals and scholarly books. That, in turn, can have a tremendous effect on who can get jobs, promotions, and grants for research projects. Because of the stakes, the battle over the definition can be, well, political. For students, some aspects of how we define the science part of political science can be interesting and useful for understanding how researchers study political phenomena.

When you hear the word *science,* chances are you do not think of politics. You probably think of people in white coats conducting experiments—the typical *Dexter's Laboratory* full of chemicals, beakers, and electric gadgets. However, more than two thousand years ago, Aristotle spoke of a "political science."[39] Could he possibly have meant science as we now think of the term? The answer is plainly no. When Aristotle used the term, he was referring to a body of knowledge regarding how to organize a state in order to obtain happiness. Perhaps it is unfortunate that he used the word *science* at all. When we mention science we are usually thinking of the **scientific method,** a specific set of rules and processes for pursuing knowledge through observation, hypothesis building, experimentation, and replication.

ARISTOTLE

Team: **Classical Greek United**
Position: **Square Leg**
Status: **Quite Dead**

Although he was Plato's student, **Aristotle** (384–322 B.C.) was more of a realist, and—unlike our students—was highly critical of his mentor. Aristotle neither believed that one should strive for a perfect world nor did he assume that there is a perfect world of forms hidden in the shadows. Instead, he thought that we could learn far more by observing the world and drawing conclusions from what we see. He believed that we should study how things actually work and how people actually behave. As for states, he observed their functions and categorized them according to the type of rule exercised within each one. Thus, compared to Plato, Aristotle was pragmatic. Aristotle believed that people should do the best they can within the limits of the world, as it exists around them.

Also, according to Aristotle, everything works toward a specific end, or *telos*. The *telos* for an apple seed is the eventual apple tree. The *telos* for a baby gorilla is a full-grown gorilla. The *telos* for human beings is happiness, and, therefore, people should create governing institutions with this human end in mind. Furthermore, Aristotle believed that it is natural for people to form associations because human beings are inherently social—that is, "man is a political animal." The *polis,* or state, is but an extension of these individual associations and is, consequently, something natural. This is a key point. To argue that the state is natural means to argue that people form states because human beings are innately inclined to do so. In fact, Aristotle would argue, people move toward their *telos* through participation in the state.

Aristotle proceeded to demonstrate how some types of government are better than others at helping people achieve the goal of happiness. He also pointed out that it is possible to take a bad form of government and improve it. Therefore, we must be concerned not only with the ideal world, but also with making improvements to the flawed world that we know. Aristotle was clearly more of a realist than Plato, but Aristotle is still considered to be an idealist because he believed that there is a goal toward which people should strive—happiness. The primary aim of government, in his theory, is to create happiness for the people; thus happiness is still the ideal.

This is a way of finding factual information about what *is,* while Aristotle was clearly being normative when he used the term. He was offering opinions about what constituted the good life, and he sought to create a city-state capable of delivering that good life. Today, when we think of science, we try to separate it from discussion of what should be and try to concentrate on objectively gathered facts, sterilized as much as possible of opinions.

Much of the disagreement about the definition of political science stems from these fundamental differences. Some believe that political science should be a science in the same way that biology, chemistry, and physics are sciences—they believe that political scientists should employ a strictly defined scientific method. Of course, there are many practical difficulties with this approach. Think about why it would be difficult to study politics in the same way that one could study a subject such as botany.*

---

*There is a bad pun about shopping that could be made here. Please note that I refrained.

Consider something straightforward—let us say, the effect of high-intensity halogen lights on the growth of plants that can *legally* be cultivated hydroponically in your grandmother's basement. You can take two healthy *and perfectly legal* plants into the basement and put one under a lamp and the other in a closet without a lamp. You can then compare the growth of the two plants and draw conclusions about the effects that your independent variable, in this case the provision of light, has on your subjects, the plants. This scientific study of plant cultivation can be repeated again and again, and again, and again, until you are caught by the DEA. As you repeat this experiment, you can make changes to the environment or other factors that you think might influence the growth of these plants.*

In contrast, political scientists and other social scientists usually cannot isolate individuals, organizations, or groups in the laboratory. It is almost impossible to isolate them enough to allow for the careful manipulation of the political factors that might influence them. Instead, political scientists have come up with numerous ways of approximating the ideal of laboratory conditions, primarily through the use of statistics. Even so, some critics have argued that the use of statistics pushes researchers to examine whatever can easily be counted, cataloged, or quantified (money, votes, weapons) while other important concepts that cannot be counted (beliefs, expectations, hopes) are discounted or ignored entirely. For example, a researcher would have a much easier time studying *how* legislators vote than *why* they vote the way they do, although answering the latter question may be more important to improving our understanding of the political behavior of legislators. Nevertheless, despite the fact that statistical methods cannot perfectly replicate laboratory conditions, this approach to the study of politics has significantly increased our understanding and base of knowledge.

Other theorists believe that political scientists need not, and perhaps should not, try to force the study of politics into the mold of other sciences. They argue that it is not possible to be objective about politics in the way one can be objective about biology, or chemistry, or the hydroponic cultivation of commercially lucrative *but totally legal* plants. Political scientists making this argument have also significantly increased our understanding of politics by offering insights into the influence of rhetoric, decision process, and culture on the behavior of individuals and governments.

As suggested earlier, Aristotle may have done future generations a disservice by using the term *science* at all. After all, he also referred to politics as "the master art."[40] Perhaps politics should be viewed as an art or, even more appropriately, as a craft?[41] Regardless, the best way for the student to approach the science part of political science may be to

---

*An additional benefit of this experiment is that when your flagrant disregard of my suggestion that you cultivate a legal plant leads to a handcuffed, shirtless, kicking and screaming, involuntary guest appearance on an episode of *Cops,* instead of shouting something stupid, you can yell, "It was science, man!"

Even the political scientists who agree that researchers should act all scientific argue constantly about what the science part of it all means. I love that. Partly because I just like arguing but also because it totally gave me an excuse to go on a dinosaur dig and call it work. And it gives me another excuse to make a self-indulgent reference.

Douglas A. Van Belle, "Dinosaurs and the Democratic Peace: Paleontological Lessons for Avoiding the Extinction of Theory in Political Science," *International Studies Perspectives* 7 (2006): 287–306.

use a framework offered by social scientist Earl Babbie in his popular text on social science research methods.[42] Babbie argues that we all know two realities: **experiential reality** and **agreement reality.** This is a valuable concept for understanding the role of the news media in politics, and I use it a lot in Chapter 11, but it is also a good way to come to grips with the science part of political science. Experiential reality is composed of the things we directly experience—which, in fact, make up only a very small portion of what we know to be real even though we have never directly seen, touched, heard, smelled, or tasted a lot of those real things.

Agreement reality can be derived from interaction with parents, friends, authority figures, religious doctrines, celebrities, the media, and teachers. However, as Babbie argues, we can also think of science as a set of rules and processes that we use to generate agreement reality. Every single scientist does not go out to replicate every single experiment conducted in his or her area of expertise. Instead, scientists agree on common methods to be used in research. As long as they are convinced that other scientists have properly followed those methods, they accept their results as true, as part of reality. Thus, the science of political science is the effort to develop a greater understanding of politics by conducting research openly and transparently, utilizing methods that will convince other political scientists to accept the results as accurate and correct. The difficulty is that the personal, individual nature of politics extends to the study of politics. Just as there are a variety of reasonable perspectives on politics, there are a variety of reasonable and effective methods for pursuing an understanding of politics.

The intensity of the debate over the term *political science* centers on which set of research methodologies is best, and it probably has to be admitted that the different perspectives in that debate are often driven by the self-interests of scholars. An academic scholar invests a great deal of effort—often several years of intense work—in learning one of these sets of research methods. The rules, processes, and procedures are often quite involved, and a scholar would be in serious professional jeopardy if his or her preferred methodology were to lose the debate. For students, it is enough to know

that all of these definitions of the science part of political science require that researchers always be honest about their methods, transparent about the steps they have taken, open with their findings, and, ideally, receptive to criticism. In other words, in order to create agreement reality regarding politics, all researchers must carefully document their research, fully explain their findings, disclose any of their known biases, and acknowledge any known weaknesses in their research. They should do this not because they fear criticism, but because they wish to contribute to the development of knowledge and therefore welcome constructive criticism. It is through the accurate reporting of research and subsequent criticism that our knowledge of politics, or any discipline for that matter, increases.

Of course, even this is disputed. Some argue that this kind of structuring of inquiry so severely limits the questions that can be asked that we essentially define away much of what we need to study and debate.

I encourage students to be open to any methodology that, when used properly, increases our understanding about politics. The amazingly profound academic research conducted by the author of this text is obviously the most stupendous available, but in some very, very small ways I have learned a little bit of minor stuff from research conducted by others, and those others have employed a tremendous variety of methodologies.

Also, as I note later, it is true that the lines between political science, economics, history, philosophy, literature, geography, and even the natural sciences are not as clear as your university's course catalog makes them appear. They all play a part in the study of politics. I believe that is one reason political science is such an interesting and rewarding subject to study. Finding such an argument in this book should not be too surprising—after all, I wrote this text with the assumption that some of the best ways you can learn about politics include reading literature, watching TV, and viewing movies.

KEY TERMS

agreement reality / 36
classic conservatism / 22
classic liberalism / 21
communism / 23
conceptual frameworks / 8
democratic socialism / 25
experiential reality / 36
fascism / 26
idealism / 3
idealist period / 18
imperialism / 24
League of Nations / 18

Karl Marx / 17
political ideology / 19
political science / 33
political theory / 19
politics / 30
realism / 3
reform liberalism / 25
scientific method / 33
Adam Smith / 21
socially responsible investing / 32
sophist / 4

CHAPTER SUMMARY

People's preconceptions affect the ways they think about politics, which can make it very difficult for them to study politics systematically and to remain open to new concepts, different approaches, and alternative perspectives. Thus, it is important to find some mechanism that enables students of politics to take a step back from their biases, their own desires, their preference for realism or idealism, and so forth. The use of fictional examples can make it easier for us to set aside our predispositions, can help us to travel to places we typically could not visit, and allows us to share experiences that would ordinarily elude us. Fiction writers, political actors, political theorists, and ideologues commonly invoke images of utopia as a tool to communicate their views about politics. This can be an effective device because, by pushing an idealized vision to its conceptual extreme, a utopia can clearly project specific details of a better world—and it may, in fact, expose the dangers of that world.

Many people from many different professions have contributed to our understanding of politics. Political theorists often use utopias to explore what is possible and what is impossible within the realm of politics. Some of these theorists are realists, and others are idealists. Political theories differ from ideologies in a number of ways. Those who promote an ideology advocate specific programs that are meant to achieve their utopia.

The difficulty people have when attempting to define the term *politics,* the changing nature of the subject matter, and disagreements about how to conduct research all further confound the study of politics. Students should learn two very important lessons from this first chapter. First, the study of politics is fascinating. Second, reading only the chapter summary will not adequately prepare you for lecture or for an exam.

STUDY QUESTIONS AND EXERCISES

1. Why is fiction a good tool for the study of politics?

2. Why do political theorists and political actors use utopian themes? How can these themes help us to identify flaws in "perfect worlds"?

3. What are the differences between political theories and political ideologies?

4. As a potential consumer viewing the commercials for different political ideologies, what questions would you want answered before you would buy each product?

5. What is it that makes politics a difficult concept to define?

6. How is the study of politics different from the study of natural sciences (for example, biology and chemistry)?

7. Think of your own example to illustrate how a novel that you've read or a television show, movie, or film that you've seen demonstrates the difference between idealism and realism.

8. Send all of your money to the author of this text.

WEBSITES TO EXPLORE

www.political-theory.org. The Foundations of Political Theory is an organized section of the American Political Science Association that aims to promote the links between political theory and the discipline of political science.

http://plato.stanford.edu/contents.html. The Stanford Encyclopedia of Philosophy lists encyclopedic entries on relevant authors, concepts, and terms.

www.gutenberg.org. Project Gutenberg provides free electronic versions of many classic works, including several of the older texts mentioned in this chapter.

www.library.vanderbilt.edu/romans/polsci/polthought.html. Vanderbilt University Library's Political Thought Page offers a great collection of Web resources for students exploring an array of theories and ideologies.

www.etalkinghead.com. eTalkinghead, an online magazine, features in its Political Blog Directory a listing of political blogs covering an array of ideologies. Exploring these blogs is a great way to discover your own Field of Dreams.

www.cagle.com/politicalcartoons. Daryl Cagle's Professional Cartoonists Index is an up-to-date collection of editorial cartoons, which can be powerful tools for promoting ideologies and critiquing other ideologies.

www.theonion.com. The Onion provides a weekly satirical look at the major news of the day.

www.lib.umich.edu/govdocs/polisci.html. The University of Michigan Library Documents Center's Political Science Resources on the Web is a great collection for students engaged in political science.

Why Government?

Security, Anarchy, and Some Basic Group Dynamics

Sometimes you just have to go old school. For Max Rockatansky, hotshot motorcycle cop, it starts out as just another postapocalyptic summer day, the perfect kind of day for the beach, some ice cream, and the soothing sounds of rampaging motorcycle gangs. But then the brutal murder of Max's wife and son drives him over the edge, and he goes so medieval on their asses that everyone starts calling him *Mad Max.*[1] Realizing that the crumbling remnants of civilization can provide no justice for the murdering and raping rampage of Toecutter and his crew, Max takes the last of the V-8 interceptors from the motor pool, races into the outback, and starts dishing out some justice—old-school justice. It's kind of ugly, extremely violent, and deeply disturbing. In what has become a legendary film finale, Max handcuffs a man's ankle to the frame of a wrecked and burning car. Nodding at the leaking gas that's trickling toward the fire, Max tosses the man a hacksaw and tells him that it will take him ten minutes to cut through the chain, but only five to cut through his ankle. Yeah, I know, the guy who wrote *Saw*[2] totally stole that.

One of the best things about writing a new edition of this textbook is that it gives me the chance to update my examples to keep on top of the trends, or at least to stay within shouting distance, as I drag my sorry old desk-chair-shaped ass around in the futile pursuit of said trends. This is especially important for a book that uses pop culture to introduce politics. I decided to go old school here instead. *Mad Max* dates from 1979, so it's vintage old school . . . your-parents-were-barely-teenagers kind of old school.

Part of my reason for going totally old school on you is the sheer artistry of the symphony of violence that George Miller tosses up from down under. *Mad Max* presented such a graphic depiction of the horrors of brutal postapocalyptic anarchy that the Australian release was rated M-18, the

same adults-only rating that is given to porn. And that rating was probably the right call. There is a lot of violence in *Mad Max,* but the movie is not gratuitously violent. It is disturbingly violent. There is a kind of honesty to the brutality that makes it feel real and that curls your toes and makes you recoil in a way that a disemboweling chainsaw serial killer in a slasher film could never, ever match. Even if you saw the sanitized American version, in which the distributors somehow thought that dubbing over Mel Gibson's thick Australian accent would make the raping and killing less disturbing, it's hard not to cringe at the realization of just how "nasty, brutish, and short" life would be in the constant "war of every man against every man" of an ungoverned world,[3] and that is why I decided to go old school. *Mad Max* provides the best, most visceral and gut-churning example of the most horrific aspect of anarchy, and that kind of emotional understanding of anarchy provides the key to answering one of the most important questions in political science: Why do we have government?

Some of you may think it unnecessary, if not absurd, to try to explain why we have government. The joy we all experience when blessed with the chance to interact with government is so blissful* that the need for government all but explains itself. Whether it is the hot summer days we spend dancing through the intricate mazes of queues and taking of numbers involved in renewing our driver's licenses; or the paper shuffling, strutting, and other display rituals of the deodorant-challenged bureaucrats who hand out lawn-watering permits;† or the thrill of counting down the number of shopping days left before taxes are due; or a chance encounter with Officer Bubba, who doggedly pursues the ideal of swift and efficient customer service by filling out half the speeding ticket before you ever rolled through his radar trap—our every interaction with officialdom reminds us of the lasting legacy of hope and joy that is government. Seriously, why wouldn't we all love government?

Even people with an interest in politics are likely to describe their personal interactions with government as frustrating, infuriating, evil, satanic, bulimic,‡ or worse. We chafe at the restrictions government creates, we are annoyed by the taxes it imposes on us, we fume over its inefficiencies, we curse its wastefulness, we scream at the impediments it throws in our way, and we rage at its failures.§ Seldom does anyone praise government; yet, there it is. Except for passing moments of breakdown or revolutionary changes, government is always there. Whether in a communal tribe subsisting in an isolated jungle or in a virtual democracy emerging from a hypercaffeinated suburban cybercafe, nearly every human being who has ever set foot on this planet has lived in a governed society. Given the near-universal contempt for government, we must

---

*My copy editor cut out "orgasmic" here and suggested "nice" as a synonym . . . go figure.

†In Melbourne, Australia, the persistent drought has grown so bad that you actually need a permit to water your lawn, and such permits are very, very hard to get.

‡It's never too early to start studying for the GREs. Have fun looking it up!

§It's fascinating that we all do this while enjoying the benefits of government. Still, it's so much more cathartic to complain.

wonder why people repeatedly create, sustain, and submit to it. Whims of fate, freaks of nature, and simple accidents can cause anything to happen once or even twice, but rational explanations are needed for any phenomena that persist or occur frequently. There must be a reason we all live in governed societies, and it is the business of this chapter to offer you a convincing argument.

I could almost just point to *Mad Max* and its sequel and call that an answer. The violence in *Mad Max 2,*[4] which you might know as *The Road Warrior,* is tame in comparison to that in *Mad Max. The Road Warrior* merited only an MA-15 rating in Australia, roughly the equivalent of an R rating in the United States, instead of an adults-only, as-naughty-as-porn advisory. *The Road Warrior* is violent, but it is far less violent than *Mad Max,* partly because of a subtle but important difference in context. The story in *Mad Max* catches the world at the moment that civilization collapses. Max goes over the edge at the point when the world descends into anarchy. In that moment, all constraints on human action have been removed, and that moment of the complete absence of any hint of government is the most brutal moment—and that last bit is the key. The complete absence of government will last but a moment. Anarchy almost never persists for more than a fleeting instant, because the immediate, perhaps instinctual, human reaction to the horror of anarchy is to try to reestablish some semblance of a governed society. We can see this in *The Road Warrior.* This sequel to *Mad Max* is the story of a small, self-governed settlement trying to hold out against a well-organized—dare we say governed?—gang of marauders. Individuals existing within either of those governed contexts experience a degree of safety compared to those individuals caught outside them. As a result, people desperate for the slightest hint of security will flock to either group. People join Lord Humungus even though being a part of his gang of marauders is pretty horrific.

When confronted with anarchy, people will adhere to even the most unpleasant of governed environments. We can see this rush to government in several other classic examples of anarchy. In *Lord of the Flies,* the first thing the shipwrecked schoolboys do is create rules for debate and collective decision making. That effort fails, but government still arises, coalescing around the choir, of all things, and that governed group preys on those caught outside it. In David Brin's novel *The Postman,* government coalesces around the symbolism of an old, stolen U.S. Postal Service uniform.[5] In *Lucifer's Hammer,* it's a former senator and his effort to save a functioning nuclear power plant from an army of cannibals.[6] In all of these examples we see that the governed society, even a horribly governed society, offers security, and that is almost enough to explain why we have government. Security is a big part of it, but there is far more to government than joining the cannibal army so you're one of the people eating from the pot instead of going into it. Personal, physical security of the tribe is just one of the many types of security we seek from government.

As a way of getting to all that other stuff government provides, I'm going to start with a ridiculously simple and far less violent story of life in the state of nature and offer you the *Sesame Street* version of how the first government was formed.

A MODEL FOR THE EMERGENCE OF COOPERATION: BOBSVILLE

One Thursday morning[*] 9,342 years ago, Bob the intrepid caveman wandered down to a swampy area near a stream. He hoped to breakfast on the wild rice plants growing there, as he had done once every few weeks over his many years. However, on this particular morning, he tripped over his purebred hunting weasel, dropped the rice, and scattered his handful of grain across the muddy ground. After making heartfelt use of whatever foul language he had at his disposal, Bob quit trying to pick up the rice, shrugged off the minor disaster, and went to look somewhere else for his meal.[†]

A week or so later, in his always-difficult, never-ending search for food, Bob decided to look in the swampy place again. While there, he noticed that the rice grains he had dropped were sprouting. A few weeks later, he saw that the sprouts had grown into rice plants. Then, checking back regularly, Bob watched that one handful of grain grow into plants capable of producing dozens of handfuls. Somewhere in the creaky and seldom-used depths of Bob's mind, it all came together—he could do this on purpose! Instead of eating whatever rice he found, he could spread the grain around on the damp ground and grow all the food he could ever eat.

Bob, in his primitive way, had discovered agriculture. He quickly began scattering rice across the mud as he dreamed of the day when he would never have to worry about hunger again. Bob eventually realized, however, that his fantasy faced a very serious obstacle: he was not the only brute who enjoyed eating rice. Others saw the plants and knew what they were. The sudden concentration of this food source attracted dozens of cavemen down from the hills to forage. All of Bob's effort and all the rice grains he had planted instead of eating were now feeding the marauders. In the end, outnumbered by the influx of hungry barbarians, Bob received little, if any, return for his effort and sacrifice.

Presumably, Bob was not the first cave dweller to discover that he could grow food intentionally, and he was certainly not the first to encounter difficulty in reaping the rewards of his labor. Over and over again, all around the world, this discovery was made, and, it seems likely, the same hard lesson was learned again and again as this agricultural experiment failed. Growing food is relatively easy. Keeping the food you have grown is another thing entirely.

Somewhere along the way, one of the frustrated agricultural entrepreneurs had an inspiration. For the sake of my little story, let's assume it was Bob. Bob was the first who realized that several farmers working in close proximity could join together to protect the grain they grew. Even just a few cooperating farmers could defend the crops from the occasional barbarian wandering down from the hills. Coordinating their strength, several farmers could ward off all but the most organized efforts to steal their food.

---

[*]Things like this always happen on Thursdays.

[†]This is also when humans first decided to try domesticating dogs rather than weasels, but that is an entirely different story.

Inspired, Bob searched for allies who could see the value of growing food, perhaps even looking for them among the horde of cavemen who had wandered down to take his first crop. After promising not to attack each other, they also agreed that they would coordinate their efforts to defend the rice they grew. Add a few huts for shelter, and Bob had created the first sedentary village and, with it, the first vestiges of government.

COLLECTIVE ACTION

The story of Bob's foray into agriculture captures the essence of government— **collective action,** which is coordinated group activity designed to achieve a common goal that individuals acting on their own could not otherwise attain. Bob and his fellow farmers organized themselves to pursue a collective benefit, but what exactly was the specific goal that drew them together? Although raising food might be the first thing that pops to mind, farming was not the collective benefit this very first government was pursuing. Individually, each caveman or cavelady* could raise plenty of food for him- or herself, but he or she could not protect the crops from all the other thieving cave dwellers. Just like the people who flock to Lord Humungus and the protection his marauders provide against the horrors of the postapocalyptic outback in *The Road Warrior,* Bob's farmers needed the collective effort of the group first and foremost for **security**.

My admittedly cartoonish story of Bob's transformation from wandering caveman to enterprising farmer demonstrates some of the fundamental reasons we have government. Undoubtedly, historians and anthropologists who specialize in primitive governmental and social structures would offer valid criticisms of my "state of nature" story. Its biggest, but by no means only, flaw is the omission of the almost-certain role of family structures in the creation of Bobsville. The similarities between the organizational and power structures of extended families and the structures of primitive governments throughout history provide ample evidence of a connection between family and early government. In fact, many of these family-derived governmental structures persist to this day in the form of hereditary dictatorships such as that in North Korea and in the relationship between states or provinces and federal or national governmental structures. The United States, Canada, and Australia all have governmental structures that resemble the independent but connected relationships of an extended family. However, even a family-derived governmental structure would first have to confront the same problem that motivated Bob—having to protect itself from others. Thus, the story demonstrates that one essential element of government—if not its primary element—is collective action. In this case collective action is focused on the

---

Cavelady is obviously a gratuitously politically correct reference to a person who might be crassly referred to as a cavewoman. Unfortunately, this is necessary. To meet FCC requirements I am required to include enough inappropriately politically correct referents to offset the emotional trauma inflicted by my cavalier disregard for all those things everybody says I am disregarding. I actually tried to be a bit more over the top with this one, to earn extra credit, but I was surprised to discover that *Cave Queen, Duchess of the Stone Age,* and *Mistress of the Monkeymen* are all porn films.

attainment of security. Eventually, Bob and his friends will realize that the same organizational structure they created for protecting their crops could also be used to pursue other collective efforts.

Collective action is the essence of government because there are certain things, such as attaining security, that individuals simply cannot accomplish on their own. Consider the many things that a modern government does, such as building roads, protecting the environment, maintaining libraries, and constructing elaborate hoaxes about men landing on the moon. How many of those things would be difficult, if not impossible, for even the wealthiest or most powerful individual to do alone?

For now, however, let's stick with Bob and focus on the collective pursuit of security.

SECURITY

What do I mean by the word *security*? Though we all have a sense of the concept, the term can be problematic, particularly for the study of politics. Security can involve anything from China pointing ballistic missiles at Taiwan to the security blanket Snoopy is always trying to steal from Linus. Security can mean the ability to walk from the classroom door to your car without fear of bodily harm, the assurance that you will have a paycheck arriving next week, or the knowledge that you can always drop by your parents' kitchen and walk away with a full stomach. Even if I limit the term to how it has been defined and used in the study of politics, it is still difficult to nail down a definition. Some scholars have even argued that the effort to define security is futile. Moreover, when I attempt to define the term precisely and accurately, I wind up juggling so many nuances and variations that even the clearest result tends to be impossibly complicated.

Rather than wrestling with the complexities, I offer a definition that cuts straight to the heart of the concept, much as I did with the term *politics* in Chapter 1. Bob and his farmer friends attain security when they develop the ability to protect their crops. Thus, security is the ability to protect, preserve, or maintain control of something of value. Although this definition lacks the richness of some others, it nevertheless captures the basic idea.

The good part of defining security so simply is that you don't even have to hope that the brilliant author of this textbook knows what he is talking about. If you look at the way the term *security* is defined or applied in the research and commentary on politics, you can see that various definitions of security are differentiated by the specification of what is to be protected. For example, political scientist Brian L. Job lists four securities that are critical to understanding the political dynamics of developing nations.[7] The first is the protection of borders and governmental structures from outside threats. You probably think that kind of security is national security, but Job and most other political scientists refer to that as **state security.** Job's basic argument is that in the developing world, state security is not the most important consideration. Instead, these countries' foreign policies are dominated by **regime security,** which is defined by the leaders' ability to protect their hold on power. The pursuit of regime security is often complicated by issues related

to what political scientists define as **national security**: the protection of the interests or survival of tribal, ethnic, or other groups that exist within and across state borders.[*] These ethnic groups often clash within countries, and they are often spread across the borders between countries, making the pursuit of national security a particularly vexing international issue in the developing world. Lost in the politics of state, regime, and national security is a fourth category, **individual security,** which, just to keep you off guard, is exactly what it sounds like.

Notice that in this discussion of different securities, the key to understanding the politics of security is determining who is trying to protect what.

To truly grasp the concept of security and to understand why the collective pursuit of security is such a central element for government, you are going to need the grossly over-simplified definitions of a few other closely related terms.

POWER

While *security* is a contested term, the debate over its meaning is nothing compared to the disagreements surrounding the concept of **power**. The manifestation of power can be as obvious as a tank rolling in to break up the protests in China's Tiananmen Square or as subtle as a shopping-bag burdened student who stopped that tank by simply refusing to get out of its way. Power can be exercised through the brute physical force of a police officer's patrol stick or through the glorious leader's deft evocation of patriotism to provoke a desired response from a sycophantic crowd. It is this wide range of applicability that makes the term so difficult to define with accuracy.

Again, I resort to a simple definition to capture the fundamentals of the concept of power. At its core, power is the ability to get something done. While this definition is so elementary that it borders on the tautological, it cuts right to the heart of the notion of power. We tend to regard any successful effort to accomplish a goal as an exercise of power. The tank had the power to disperse the protesters because it posed a threat to their lives. The student had the power to stop the tank by stepping in front of it because he could force the driver to choose between halting or accepting responsibility for running over an unarmed, nonthreatening person. Brute force is power that surges toward a goal by means of a direct application of energy. The manipulation of language and imagery is power because it can channel the actions of a crowd. Whether direct or indirect—doing something yourself or getting others to do it for you—power is the ability to disturb the momentum of events. It is the ability to *influence.*

Power is widely believed to be the key variable in politics. Clearly, if politics is about acting to achieve a particular goal, then the ability to get the task done is of the utmost

---

[*]I know the world would be a better place if political scientists just defined national security as everyone else does, but if our definition of terms were less confusing, there would be less need to teach this stuff to suffering university students and, thus, fewer jobs for political scientists, so don't expect change to happen anytime soon.

importance. Power is so pervasive a concept that you likely take its role in your own life for granted, but think about all those people in your life who can get you to do certain things and how they go about getting you to do them. How do your parents get you to do what they want? What about your boss? Your professors? Why, exactly, are you reading this book?

When you think of power, you might picture a tangible implement of the use of force, such as a police officer's club. It's less likely that you will think of the officer's blue uniform and conspicuous patrol car and the way the mayor uses symbolism to alter people's behavior. However, the subtle uses of power can be by far the most important. Think of the relationship between boss and employee—Michael Scott and Jim Halpert in The Office,[8] Mr. Spacely and George Jetson in The Jetsons,[9] Mr. Slate and Fred Flintstone in The Flintstones,[10] Mr. Krabs and SpongeBob in SpongeBob SquarePants.[11] Michael is always demanding or manipulating the people in the office, particularly Jim. Poor George is constantly taking abuse from Mr. Spacely. Mr. Slate is always firing, or threatening to fire, Fred. SpongeBob doesn't get it, but if he did, he would realize that Mr. Krabs exerts power to get him to use his skills as the ultimate "fry cook to the gods." Why do Jim, George, Fred, and SpongeBob put up with it? Well, why does the supermarket clerk willingly clean up the baby's "accident" in Aisle 10? Why do millions of people comply with the wishes of their unarmed and physically unimpressive bosses? Is it because their kneecaps are in jeopardy? No, their acquiescence is probably due to the slightly subtler economic influence that all bosses have over their employees. At the extreme, bosses can fire their employees and deny them future paychecks, but they are more likely to exercise their power toward less drastic ends. After all, bosses also assign workloads, schedule vacations, distribute raises and promotions, and determine who gets the window office. In large corporations, the few sentences that a boss types into a performance review can facilitate or derail a worker's career. The diffuse power that the boss wields is probably why, in our androgynous workplace example way back in Chapter 1, Pat was laughing at the boss's jokes—it was all about power.

Easier yet, just watch Game of Thrones and marvel at how much violence and nudity the producers manage to throw on the screen.[12] And then, when you calm down, look at the huge variety of ways the characters make things happen and fight to get their way. From the brute force of a sword or army to deception, to imposition of vows and use of traditions, to family bonds, to logical arguments, to wealth, to creepy incestuous sexual stuff.

Stretching the employment analogy far beyond the bounds of prudence or caution, I will now split an infinitive to boldly suggest that power is to politics what money is to capitalism. The capitalist needs to accumulate money and then spend it carefully in the pursuit of profit and efficiency. The politician needs to amass power and then apply it carefully to gain the support of others, to win leadership positions, and to be effective in politics. In fact, we often use the term **political capital** to indicate the reserve of power on which some official can call to achieve political goals. While it is not a tangible resource like a stock option or a savings

account,* political capital can be stored or built up. Very often, individuals earn political capital by doing favors for others in the hope that they will deliver their support at a future date. A person might volunteer to help someone else campaign for office or contribute money to a political action committee. Someone in office might vote for another representative's bill or give a job to a colleague's nephew, or pay for the dry cleaning of an intern's nice blue dress. For years, political parties in many big cities provided jobs, food, and entertainment and performed other favors for their constituents in order to ensure their support on election day.

Do note that there is a critical difference between power and **authority.** The easiest way to make the distinction is to think of authority as a subcategory of power—a type of power. A person has authority when the social structure or context leads others to accept that person's commands, direction, or other forms of control over their actions. We often talk about authority in terms of enforced legal systems for allocating aspects of social control to certain individuals, such as police patrolling the roads. However, authority can arise even where no formal coercion is involved in creating the leader-and-follower relationship. In *Castle,* mystery writer Rick Castle often leads the investigative team's actions even though his official role is limited to observing.[13] In *Kitchen Nightmares,* the owners of skanky restaurants almost always follow Gordon Ramsay's instructions, commands, tirades, and invective-laden rants even though Ramsay has no official, legal position at all in the organizational chart of the business.[14] And James Cameron should really listen to an actual writer before he makes another *Avatar,* even though he doesn't have to. In all of these cases, something, such as specialized knowledge, experience, or insight, gives (or should give) people the opportunity to influence the actions of others, sometimes in profound and significant ways.

One of the key points about authority lies in the way it highlights the relationship between power and context. The particular kind of power that is appropriate in a given situation is intimately related to the specific political and social context. Different social environments affect how power is used. For example, a president exercises a type of power that is different from that exercised by a dictator. A country with a nuclear arsenal exerts a different type of power than does one that is rich in petroleum reserves. However, there is one context, one structure of human interaction, that is fundamentally different from all others: anarchy. In order to comprehend how power works and why security is a fundamental reason for government, we must first return to anarchy and develop an understanding of the dynamics of an anarchic environment.

ANARCHY

Unlike the concepts of security and power, the definition of anarchy is not something that political scientists argue about. However, in this case, it is the common usage of the term—equating anarchy with rioting werewolves run amok—that is likely to create

---

*Technically, stock options and bank accounts aren't tangible either, since they aren't physical things that can be touched.

Why Government?

confusion. I reinforced that misunderstanding of anarchy with the *Mad Max* example, but instead of apologizing I'm going to pretend that is exactly what I meant to do. It is a well-known fact-like belief that if you force students to intentionally rethink something, that process enriches their understanding of the nuances in a way that simply teaching them could never manage. Thus, making sure everyone was thinking of anarchy in terms of chaos and violence and now making you shift to think of it differently is a way to make you so totally smarter.*

When political scientists speak of **anarchy,** they are referring not to chaos but to an absence of any kind of overarching authority or hierarchy. In an anarchic situation, such as precooperation Bobsville, there is no means for policing behavior or enforcing agreements. This absence can lead to chaos and violence, and homoerotic biker gangs roaming the outback, but there is no reason that it necessarily has to. In fact, many **anarchists** are ideologues who long for a lack of **hierarchy** not because they desire chaos, but because they believe that human beings are capable of peacefully intermingling and ordering society without broad, formalized governmental structures.

Conversations in the classroom provide a good nonpolitical example of the difference between anarchy and hierarchy. Before the instructor arrives, there is no hierarchical structure in the room—no overarching authority—because none of the students has any control over the others. As a result, the conversation is reasonably anarchic. Any person can talk to any other person. The ability and desire to talk are the only things that really matter. Furthermore, as the relentless babbler next to you repeatedly demonstrates, it is not even necessary to find someone who agrees to listen before you start yapping. However, when the instructor arrives and starts class, the conversation

---

*That's my story and I'm sticking to it.

becomes structured and hierarchical. There are rules for who can speak. The instructor directs the exchange, deciding who will speak and when, thus controlling both the content and the tone of the discussion.

Anarchy and Power

The classroom conversation example also demonstrates the connection between power and anarchy, suggesting why both are crucial concepts for the study of politics. Anarchy is important because of its relationship to power. Before the instructor arrives, your ability, or power, to speak is all that is necessary to allow you to do so. We could even think of the volume at which you can speak as the amount of power you have in this situation. The louder you can bellow, the more effective you will be at getting words from your mouth to someone else's ears. In a hierarchical situation, however, the power of the individual is constrained. When the instructor is in the room and directing the conversation, the volume of your bellow is not the only factor relevant to your effort to get your words to someone else's ears. You must also consider the structure of the conversation. Your power to make yourself heard is tempered by the rewards and punishments that the authority in the room can direct toward you in response to your bellowing. By shutting out, quieting, waterboarding, muzzling, or exiling the loudest voices, the classroom structure makes it possible for the soft-spoken to be heard. The structure and hierarchy of interaction both enable and constrain participation in the classroom conversation.

We spend so much of our lives in structured, hierarchical situations that we can actually find it difficult to appreciate and comprehend anarchy, and this makes fictional examples particularly valuable. *Lord of the Flies,* for instance, is probably the classic story about anarchy.[15] The characters are boys who are stranded on a tropical island with no adults, no authority, and no rules. Their descent into barbarity contributes a human face to the definition of anarchy and illustrates the ways in which people—even children—form groups and attempt to create governments. Postapocalyptic stories and films also offer us a visceral brush with the true meaning of anarchy. I've already mentioned the *The Road Warrior,*[*] in which Mel Gibson wins the all-time award for fewest lines spoken by a leading actor as his character becomes the reluctant savior of a small band of people trying to survive in a land without laws. Fans of classic westerns will recognize the theme from countless films in which a lone cowboy rides in to enforce order in a Wild West town.

The frequent brutality that is characteristic of postapocalyptic stories demonstrates the connections among power, security, and anarchy. In an anarchic environment, power is the ultimate resource, because there is no overarching authority—no structure—no government to prevent the strongest individuals from using their power to get whatever they want. The only way those with less power can stop the bullies from acting as they wish is by mustering enough

---

[*]For those of you who missed it, it must be noted that *The Road Warrior* is actually a sequel. Most of the world knows it as *Mad Max 2,* which should be a hint that there probably was a *Mad Max 1.* Please, try to pay attention.

power to overcome the bullies' inherent advantage. In contrast, in a hierarchical situation, weaker individuals can rely on the coercive power of the authority structure to restrain more powerful individuals and protect the weak from the strong. The only hope for survival of the band of desperate people in *The Road Warrior* is to find enough power to defend themselves against the roving bandits. It is important to emphasize here that the white clothes they wear are totally symbolic of the good guys, but in the real world no amount of bleach would keep them clean while living around an oil well and refinery in the middle of the desert. It is also important to note that hierarchy need not result from formalized structures of government, though governments do provide hierarchy. In an anarchic situation, something as simple as an acknowledgment of status and power within a roving band of thugs may constitute enough of an authority structure to create something similar to a governed environment. If the scenario of *The Road Warrior* seems far-fetched, think about how warlords in places such as Somalia and Afghanistan are able to exercise power and draw bands of followers despite the lack of a con-stitution drawn up by a bunch of dead white guys.*

An Impetus for Government

Anarchy remains one of those ideal concepts that, if it ever really exists, is found only rarely and fleetingly in the real world, yet it is crucial for understanding government. Although it may come as something of a surprise, anarchy can even be thought of as the *source* of government. Why? Because anarchy sucks.

In an anarchic environment, the vast majority of people struggle to survive, and those who do survive live in a context of constant fear and constant threat. Every moment of every day, they live in fear of and seek to protect themselves from those who are more powerful. People need protection from bullies, and the bullies themselves need protection too. After all, even the nastiest of bullies has to sleep sometime. The collective pursuit of security—which is why Bob wants to form a village in the first place—provides an escape from this pervasive atmosphere of threat. In a governed society, people essentially hire government to protect them and the things they value from those who are more powerful.

We can make a reasonable sociopsychological argument that humans naturally tend to flee from anarchy toward hierarchical structures even when those structures are far from ideal. If you watch the way strangers herded into a cafeteria seem to congregate in small groups, there does seem to be some aspect of human nature involved. Think about what happens when you meet and introduce yourself to people. The whole pro-cess of becoming acquainted is, in many ways, a method of establishing hierarchy based on information elicited by such polite questions as "What do you do?" "Where do you live?" "How big are those pants?" An extreme example can be found in Japan,

---

*This is a tricky point, since most of the dead white guys who wrote constitutions weren't dead when they wrote them. Afghanistan is doubly tricky, since at least some of the white guys who wrote the country's newest constitution probably aren't even completely dead yet. This is, however, offset by the degree to which the current Afghan constitution is completely ignored by pretty much everyone with a gun.

where a round of introductions can make you feel like a Vegas table dealer as you swap business cards as fast as you can pull them out of your pocket. That exchange becomes a quick and direct means of establishing everyone's place in a social status hierarchy before the conversation can begin. Once the hierarchy is determined, the person at the top is often then expected to initiate and shepherd the discussion. Japan is one of the more formally hierarchical societies in the world, but all human societies are hierarchical to some extent.

Part of the explanation could simply be fear and the role it plays in survival and evolution. If *Mad Max* hasn't convinced you that Thomas Hobbes had good reasons for describing life in his anarchic state of nature as "solitary, poor, nasty, brutish, and short," try thinking of it in terms of accidentally walking past a couple of punks hanging out just inside the shadows of an alleyway. Think of how you feel in the moment you notice they are there. Think of that spike of fear in your gut when you realize that there's nothing to stop them from mugging you, or worse, right there.[*] There is no one else around, they are steps away, and they could drag you into that alley before you could speed dial 911 on your iPhone. That fleeting instant during which the protection of a governed society has abandoned you is what every moment is like in anarchy, and that surge of fear is constant in an ungoverned environment. Fear is an evolved human reaction that helps people to survive by helping them recognize danger, and the fact that people fear anarchy should provide a strong clue to why it is hard to find anarchy in the real world. A hierarchical structure, with its rules and the means to enforce them, can keep society under control, and, most important, hierarchy protects us from those of our neighbors who feel free to sport their highly fashionable swastika tattoos.

Still, we're stuck on that personal security aspect of government. This is important. Hopefully I have made that obvious by now, but even if we only talk of escaping anarchy, the collective pursuit of security is still just part of the equation. A governed environment is also appealing because anarchy is perhaps the most inefficient form of human organization, as can be seen in the story of Bobsville. Farming is, in essence, investing. Bob invests his time, his effort, and his food—the very thing that keeps him alive—in the belief that he will have a whole bunch to eat later. It is not rational to make an investment such as this, or any other, without security. The person making the sacrifice today must have some reasonable expectation that he or she will be able to reap the benefits in the future. Without that kind of assurance, without some reasonable expectation of being able to keep the fruits of his or her labor, a person would be crazy to invest all that effort and wealth. Would you put money into a savings account if there weren't rules, laws, and structures keeping random meerkats who wander into the bank from making withdrawals from your account? Hierarchical structures provide that economic security. Not all do equally good jobs, but

---

[*]My beloved copy editor insisted that "spike of fear" was better than any descriptive phrase using the word *sphincter.* I remain unconvinced.

THOMAS HOBBES

Team: **British Imperial Lions**

Position: **Deep Extra Cover**

Status: **Not Living**

If you're a dictator, king, or uptight schoolmarm with your hair pulled into a bun that's so tight you can't blink, **Thomas Hobbes** (1588–1679) is going to be your favorite political theorist. Influenced by the scientific revolution that occurred during his lifetime, Hobbes rejected all information that was not acquired empirically as he sought to craft a scientific theory of politics and government. In his most famous work, *Leviathan,* Hobbes sought to explain why government was necessary.[a] To accomplish this task, he asks us to engage in a thought experiment: what would life be like in this "state of nature"?

Imagine a time when there were no laws, no government, and no justice system at all, when individuals enjoyed perfect liberty to do whatever they pleased. Hobbes considered human beings to be essentially egotistical and self-interested rational pleasure seekers, but for some reason—a reason that will be difficult for university students to fathom—that belief did not lead him to predict that a world of complete freedom would lead to something like a constant spring break at Daytona Beach. Instead, he describes life in the state of nature as "solitary, poor, nasty, brutish, and short." It was a life of constant war and violence. It was *Lord of the Flies* in Technicolor.

Hobbes believed that people form governments because they want to escape this state of nature and they are willing to trade some of their liberty to achieve tranquility. According to Hobbes, government begins when people join together to form a "social contract" with each other. Under the terms of the contract, people agree to trade their liberty for protection from the harshness of the state of nature. Their individual freedom is turned over to a sovereign—a person or a group of people with supreme authority—who is responsible for securing and maintaining the peace. Once the people consent to join into this social contract, they must follow the will of the sovereign, and the dude in charge has the power to do whatever is necessary to ensure domestic tranquility. People have surrendered all of their rights, including their right to disagree. There is no such thing as freedom of speech or freedom of religion, and people should expect nothing except what is granted by the sovereign. Unlike Aristotle, Hobbes did not believe that government and the state were natural. Instead they were human creations that originated because they served a useful purpose.

Thus, not only does Hobbes provide the reason for the origin of the state, but he also tells us about the obligations of the individual and the sovereign. The sovereign's responsibility is to provide for the safety of the populace. Consequently, Hobbes contrasts the state of nature with the positive utopia of a life of security. However, that original, negative utopia always lurks in the background as a justification for the sovereign's rule.

[a]Thomas Hobbes, *Leviathan* (New York: Penguin, 1985).

virtually all are better than anarchy. I'll develop this point further when we discuss the relationship between government and the economy, but for now I'm going to cross my fingers and hope you can begin to see why a stable government is essential for a sound economy.

THE CONTEXT OF HIERARCHY

Since anarchy, defined as the complete absence of hierarchy, is on the extreme end of a continuum, any movement away from anarchy is a movement toward hierarchy, toward

some societal structure that elevates someone or some group to a position of authority over others. In fact, a single bully who dominates everyone else in an anarchic situation has created one type of hierarchy. When Bob and his hygienically challenged primal farmers cooperate in defense of their crops, they form a different type of hierarchy. When societies form governments they create institutionalized hierarchies, and different societies shape their own distinct governmental institutions to meet their specific needs, backgrounds, and values. The particular types of institutions chosen determine the context for how decisions are made and how people relate to one another in each society. As I hope you will become increasingly aware, this context has a tremendous effect on what options people have and how they act. Some theorists would even argue that context is the most important consideration in the study of politics.

To understand how hierarchy and context come together to shape human interaction, let's return to the classroom. Sitting atop a strong hierarchical structure, the instructor is a capricious dictator. The students get to be the worthy peasants who toil away at the evil dictator's erratic whim. The instructor has this dictatorial power because the university structure gives him or her the authority to assign the grades that will ultimately affect the students' prospects for graduation and, perhaps, their future careers. The tremendous value that students place on the grades that must be earned within this university structure gives the instructor immense power over them. The fact that students actually attend classes, listen to instructors, read texts, and study for tests—things they almost certainly would not otherwise do—is evidence of how effective the university structure is at empowering the instructor. If your instructor were just another poorly dressed person with mismatched patches on the elbows of his corduroy sport coat, and if he or she were lecturing from the backseat of a city bus, would you read what he or she recommended? Would you write papers at his or her command? Would you even stay on the bus?

The context of hierarchy is as crucial as its structure. When a student who also happens to be a police officer stops his or her instructor for speeding, the relationship is suddenly reversed. In the space of an hour, a professor may go from explaining a poor grade on an exam to handing over a driver's license and registration. The only difference is the context of interaction. The hierarchical structure of the university gives that professor power in the classroom, while the hierarchical structure of the local system of law enforcement gives that student power in the speed trap.

If people fear anarchy and seek hierarchy, if they institutionalize their collective effort to attain security, the next logical questions are: How are these structures created? How do people get from anarchy to hierarchy—to the government that we all like to complain about?

ALLIANCES

An **alliance** occurs when individuals or groups agree to combine resources and abilities for a purpose that benefits the members of the alliance individually. In some contexts, the term

coalition may be applied to such an arrangement. Alliances among countries are a key element of international politics, influencing prospects for war, peace, and complex diplomatic negotiations—we are all familiar, for example, with how the Allies joined together to defeat the Axis powers in World War II. For present purposes, the basics of alliance formation can illuminate how governmental structures emerge. The alliance is probably the simplest and the most obvious strategy for those pursuing security in an anarchic environment. Bob's primitive farmers protected their crops by joining together to gain power sufficient to ward off the neighboring marauders.

To illustrate the dynamics of alliances within anarchy, I can use a scenario very similar to that of *Lord of the Flies.* Among a group of seven children shipwrecked on an island, only one knows how to go out in the water and catch fish. We'll call this wimpy kid Gilligan—and if you don't understand why, then you have some serious reruns to watch. Since fish are particularly desirable when the only other thing you have to eat is coconuts, all of the kids want the fish. To catch the fish, Gilligan wades out until he is waist-deep in the ocean and then stands there for half the day until he eventually snags one of the slippery little entrées. In a fair and just world, Gilligan has just secured a nutritious dinner, but in an anarchic environment with no overarching authority, what happens when this scrawny kid emerges from the water with that tasty-looking fish?

Most likely, the biggest kid on the beach, whom we'll call the Skipper, walks up to Gilligan and snatches the fish. Can Gilligan do anything about it? No. The Skipper probably outweighs him by a hundred pounds, and there is no hierarchy, no police officer on the corner for the weak little fisherman to turn to for protection. If the Skipper can withstand some whining, crying, and tugging at his pant legs, there really is no way Gilligan can keep the bully from taking his fish. What is he to do? If he still wants to eat fish, Gilligan must go out and catch another one. So he wades out and catches another fish. However, when he brings it back in, the second-biggest bully on the beach, Mary Ann,[*] struts up and takes the fish. Gilligan is probably going to have to provide a fish for everyone bigger than he is before he gets to feed himself. What's more, long before he can feed all the others, the Skipper is hungry again. Poor Gilligan! He could spend his entire lifetime fishing and never get to eat any fish. On this anarchic island, any kid who is bigger and wants what Gilligan has can simply take it from him.

This situation is problematic, not only for hungry Gilligan but also for all seven of the castaways. Once Gilligan realizes that he is not going to get to eat any of the fish, why should he bother to catch any? Why would he work for no reward? The whole society would benefit if he were to stay out there catching as many fish as he could for as many of the kids as he could, but even if the bullies were to use their power to force him to do so, eventually Gilligan would become so weakened by malnutrition that he could not continue. Alliances offer a way out of such self-defeating situations by providing security within anarchy. Gilligan can make a deal

---

[*] Gilligan is seriously a wimp.

with the Skipper, offering to catch two fish—one for the bully and one for himself. In return, he asks the Skipper to protect him from all the others who might want his fish. In other words, the Skipper and Gilligan form an alliance. Gilligan gives up part of the yield of his labor in return for protection. He is buying security, in the form of the ability to eat his own fish, by sharing his resources with the bully who can protect him. Unlike the circumstances of the formation of Bobsville, Gilligan and the Skipper are not joining together to promote their common good; each is pursuing his individual interests.*

If this were the end of my fish story, we would have a plot similar to that of Bob and the first village full of grunting, hairy farmers. However, there is a dynamic here that is different from the collective action leading to the formation of Bobsville. There is a further complexity in this story of alliance formation that can help us to understand power, politics, and the way that government structures form in response to anarchy. To continue with the story: the second-biggest bully, Mary Ann, wants the fish just as much as the Skipper does, and Mary Ann is just as capable of forming an alliance as anybody else. If she teams up with the third-biggest bully, Mrs. Lovey Howell,† together they have more power than the Skipper. In fact, with a little bit of forceful persuasion, Mary Ann and Mrs. Howell can convince Gilligan that the biggest bully alone cannot protect him from their new alliance and that he will find life to be a lot less bruising if he joins their new alliance and agrees to catch three fish a day. The Skipper is not about to let that happen, however, so he recruits some additional thugs of his own, probably Ginger and the Professor, and forms another new alliance that is strong enough to overpower the rival team and force Gilligan back into the Skipper's camp. The Mary Ann–Mrs. Lovey Howell alliance is likely to reply in kind, adding sufficient power to overcome the alliance of the biggest bully. Of course, there is nothing (except the fact that there are only seven stranded castaways) to prevent the Skipper from then trying to amass even more power to force Gilligan back into his camp.

Aside from regurgitating some very unpleasant memories of the reality TV craze that I desperately hope will have finally died by the time you read this book,‡ this example of alliance formation as a response to anarchy demonstrates how groups ultimately lead to governments.[16] The alliance that is ultimately successful will form a group. In our fish story, the group forms around the competition for control of a resource—in this case, a skinny angler. However, there need not be a fight over Gilligan or any other person for a group to coalesce. Alternatively, the competition could involve a struggle to control farmland, grazing land, a bay full of fish, a grove of trees, water, or any other resource. The key is that the group needs to exist and persist in order to provide the collective benefit of security.

---

*This is actually an arguable point. Both in Bobsville and in this island scenario, everyone who participates in the group is better off, and, even though one dynamic is cooperative and one is coercive, the end result is the same.

†Mrs. Lovey Howell is actually pretty tough, in an old, rich lady kind of way.

‡Curse you, *Survivor* and your progeny!

Things really start to get complex, and nuances really start to matter, when we look at how such a group functions in everyday life. A momentary lapse in the group's ability to protect its valuables is all it takes for a rival to take advantage and for the group's members to lose everything. The need for security is constant. There are always more cavemen who may wander by. Thus, Bob's group of farmers must persist as a group, even after the initial bands of raiding cavemen have been driven away from the crops. This permanent group eventually becomes the government of Bobsville. Consequently, **government** results from the group's need to institutionalize—that is, to make permanent—its power. It accomplishes this by creating governmental institutions to provide the security that people continually need. Thus, to repeat the trend of providing overly simplistic definitions, I define government as a set of agreements, laws, or other political structures designed to provide permanent hierarchy.

Grasping the connection between groups and government can be difficult, because you must first drop your current expectations, which are based on what government is and does now. You must think about how, somewhere in the very distant past, the whole idea of government came to be. From this perspective, you can begin to see that it is from this essential first function that the governments we know evolved. With just a little modification, that collective effort that was put into rushing out and chasing the cavemen away from the field can be used to pursue other collective goals, and that, finally, is the answer to the question of why we have government.

Government is the primary mechanism through which people pursue collective actions. The collective pursuit of security is almost certainly the most fundamental of collective actions we ask government to coordinate for us, but it is by no means the only one. We ask government to build and maintain shared infrastructure, such as roads, bridges, subways, aqueducts, power grids, spaceports, and transdimensional wormhole transit stations. We ask government to regulate our activities and set standards so that we all drive on the proper side of the road (something they are still working on in China) and we can all be sure that the pint we buy at the pub is actually a full pint of beer.* We ask the government to perform services such as sewage disposal and educating all you young ruffians. We ask government to provide a context in which we can reap at least some of the reward for invested effort. We ask the government to manage shared or communal resources such as fish, clean air, and music that does more than go "Thumpa Thumpa Thumpa." We also ask government to accomplish things that no one, no matter how wealthy, could do alone, such as build the Panama Canal or mine asteroids. Wait, scratch the asteroids one. Anyway, all of these things are collective actions. Government isn't the only way to pursue a collective action—revolution against government is, after all, a collective action—but for most things that people need to pursue collectively, government (a really, really big group) provides the most efficient means for people to act. Consequently, in order to understand governmental dynamics, you need to understand group dynamics.

---

*By the way, all you Americans with your silly little pints, and miles, and Fahrenheit, it pays to go metric. A half liter of beer is bigger than a pint.

JOHN LOCKE

Team: British Imperial Lions

Position: Silly Mid Off

Status: M.I.A.—presumed "lost"

John Locke (1632–1704) was a Brit with a scary hairdo who also, in his *Second Treatise of Government,* begins with a state of nature.[a] However, unlike Hobbes's vision, Locke's state of nature is not a bad place. In his conception, all have natural rights to "life, liberty, and property." People are social, and since they deal with each other according to the rules of natural law, any social difference among them arises from how hard they work. However, the state of nature can suddenly turn into a state of war when a few people acting like playground bullies seek to violate natural laws and cause havoc for everyone.

Since Locke believed that the state of nature is not as nasty as Hobbes envisioned it, Locke argued that when people come together in a state of nature, they first form a "civil society," which then creates a government. Thus, the civil society is superior to the government, and the government that is created is a limited one. People surrender only as much of their rights as is absolutely necessary for the government to carry out its primary function, which, according to Locke, is "the preservation of property." Hence Locke's utopia is one in which the government exists as a subcontractor to the civil society, and this subcontractor continues to work as long as it performs its responsibility to protect the natural rights of the populace. All are free to enjoy their rights (including life and liberty), property, and the fruits of their labor.

Perhaps what is most important in Locke's theory is what is left implicit. If the government does not live up to its responsibility, can it be fired? Do the people have the right to cast off a government that fails to protect the rights and privileges of its citizenry or abuses its power? One answer can be found in the Declaration of Independence, which, building on Lockean theory, proclaims, "That whenever any form of government becomes destructive of these ends, it is the Right of the People to alter or to abolish it, and to institute new Government." While many think that Locke died, it is rumored that he was "Lost" on a tropical island and is now living with a bunch of other survivors of a plane crash.

[a]John Locke, *The Second Treatise of Government,* edited by J. W. Gough (Oxford, UK: Blackwell, 1966).

GROUPS AND GROUP IDENTITIES

Groups are fascinating beasts. They can suppress individuals and enforce conformity and, at the same time, elevate some people and drive others to rebel. They can aggregate the rational choices of individuals into collective irrationality. They can transform irrational fears and hatreds into a power that can be wielded to tremendous effect and lead to outcomes that appear rational in retrospect. However, before delving into group action and interaction, we need to explore the more basic notion of what makes a group—that is, what constitutes **group identity.** The degree to which members identify with a group, and, conversely, identify who is not part of that group, can affect its strength, its cohesiveness, and even its survival.

Group Identities

Think of some of the formal and informal groups that tolerate your presence: high school friends, college friends, a chess club, a church, that cluster of moody misfits in the back corner of the classroom, coworkers, the Jamaican curling team, siblings, a fraternity, an

ethnic organization, an honor society, or a high school alumni organization that doesn't really think it has to let you come to the reunion because some fool printed your name on a diploma. Chances are you identify more closely with the people in some of these groups than you do with those in others. This closeness can affect the strength of the bond you feel with a particular group, and that can affect what your group can accomplish, and that in turn is a big part of whether or not that group continues to survive. Group identity is not fixed. It can vary in response to events within the group or to the experiences of the group as a whole. How a group defines its identity gives it purpose and shapes its interactions with other groups. Identity and identity alone may even be the basis for justifying and maintaining the existence of the group.

Group identification first becomes important when the members ask, "Who can be a member of the group?" Groups constantly struggle over this crucial question. Leaders can manipulate the qualifications for membership in order to achieve their own political ends, because after they have decided what goals the group will pursue, leaders must call on members to do the actual work. The strength of the members' identification with the group directly affects the amount of effort and resources they are willing to contribute to the group's activities. Can you guess who can be a member of the Salish Tribal Council and, of those members, who is likely to feel a strong identification with this group?

Understanding groups is so critical to understanding government that those who study politics often equate current nations with groups, and they therefore study nations by applying to them concepts derived from theories of group dynamics. Thus, a good way to start delving into the subject of group identity and its role in group dynamics is to focus on the United States as a nation and ask the question, Who is an American?

The answer may at first seem obvious. With a quick glance around the classroom, relying on accents, appearances, and whatever you happen to know about the people around you, you can probably classify most of your classmates as either Americans or not Americans. While many cases are clear—such as the guy with the southern accent or the international exchange student with lutefisk breath—chances are that you will have trouble categorizing at least a few. The difficulty arises because Americans are missing a lot of the communal signifiers that many nations can rely on to identify citizens—Americans have no universally spoken language, no shared religion, and no common ethnic heritage. In the absence of an obvious marker such as language, people tend to fall back on more legalistic notions of citizenship. Thousands of pages of regulations and laws have been created in attempts to define American citizenship, but in some extreme cases, even these are insufficient. Furthermore, many of the people who do fit into the category of "U.S. citizen" may not match up with some of your expectations.

Take, for instance, someone born in Belgium who has always lived in Europe but has an American parent. While he meets the technical requirements for U.S. citizenship, he may not fit with your ideas of what it means to be an American. He may not even think of himself as an American. If a Japanese woman gives birth while waiting to change planes in a Chicago airport,

JACQUES ROUSSEAU

Team: Swiss National Bank

Position: Deep Gully

Status: Post-PreMortem

Jean-Jacques Rousseau (1712–1778) wasn't French. While that may seem an odd point to make, I got yelled at for calling him French in the first edition. Yes, he spoke French, wrote in French, and lived most of his life in Paris, which all seems pretty French to me, but he was born in Geneva, Switzerland, and lived there until he was ten and the cops chased his father out of the country. So he was the nearly French son of a petty criminal who lived in Paris, which I think is kind of like being a Canadian draft dodger living in North Dakota, but what do I know?

In the first edition I mistakenly called him French when I was trying to make a point about the normative nature of political theory. The answers an individual gives to questions about what is right or wrong, what is better or worse, what should or should not be, are all profoundly influenced by the culture of the society in which the person thinks and writes. Just as you would not mistake Canadian beer for Mexican beer, you must recognize that English and nearly French political cultures are quite different, resulting in a profound divergence in the political theories produced by their philosophers. Thus, even though Rousseau was not French, he was also not British, and you can see some aspects of that in the way Rousseau's political theory does not stress individualism to the degree that the works of his British predecessors and contemporaries do.

Rousseau did not believe that civilized society is an improvement on the state of nature. In *On the Social Contract,* Rousseau writes—in his characteristic dramatic style—"Man is born free, and everywhere he is in chains."[a] Rousseau believed that life in the state of nature is not all that bad, because the people may be primitive and simpleminded, but they retain their liberty. Rousseau believed that all of society, not just political society, is corrupt. It makes people focus on their individual desires, robs them of their compassion, and promotes inequality. Unlike Hobbes and Locke, who saw civilization as the answer, Rousseau thought it was the problem.

Rousseau believed that people need to reject societal inequality by placing the common good of all above their own personal interests. When the populace is prepared to make this commitment, it can form a new social contract that is unlike any of those previously discussed. Rousseau is not seeking democracy—at least not liberal democracy, wherein the voice of the majority is considered primary. Rousseau's new contract is formed by the "total alienation of each associate, together with all of his rights, to the entire community."[b] In exchange for the surrender of individual rights, each person gets to join in the solidarity of what Rousseau calls "the general will," which is the voice of the majority speaking for the common good. In essence, this is an experience in which participation is not just a means for reaching decisions but a process that is itself enlightening as well. All who participate grow through their participation in the general will. Since the general will is composed of equals with concern for everyone, and since it discounts private wills and personal stakes for the good of all, it can never be wrong.

Furthermore, the general will is the sovereign. Anyone who does not follow its rules will be "forced to be free."[c] The general will represents Rousseau's perfect world. It is a government that rules for everyone at nobody's expense. All who participate are enlightened by their participation, as the evils of society are cast aside.

[a]Jean-Jacques Rousseau, *On the Social Contract,* translated by Donald A. Cress (Indianapolis: Hackett, 1987), 17.

[b]Ibid., 24.

[c]Ibid., 26.

that baby is a U.S. citizen even if the entirety of her residence in the United States extends no further than a few hours at O'Hare. Both of these kids fit the technical definition of U.S. citizen, but would you put either of them in the group we call Americans? What if, instead, the little girl is born over international waters while flying toward the United States and her birth is recorded upon landing in the country, or, alternatively, what if the plane is merely in U.S. airspace, passing through on the way from Canada to Mexico, when the baby is born?

There are technical and legal answers to all of these questions, but the point is that human groups tend to be amorphous. There is usually a core of people who are clearly members, but groups are inevitably fuzzy at the edges, and they tend to overlap and blend into each other until it becomes nearly impossible to figure out precisely where one group ends and another begins. This lack of clear definition becomes especially problematic when we start talking about group dynamics, because it leads to questions such as these: Who must contribute to the collective effort of the group? Who is subject to the group's rules? Who has the right to the benefits the group provides?

Conflict between Groups

The difficulty in clearly identifying group membership has an effect on one of the first aspects of political group dynamics. Although we may not be able to define precisely and completely who *is* part of a given group, we can—often quite easily—define who is *not* part of the group. We may not always be sure who is an American, but we can easily spot a group made up of those who are clearly not Americans.* In other words, you can define the core membership of another group and use that definition to distinguish it from the membership of your group. You may not be able to identify clearly every member of your group, but you can absolutely define those who are not part of your group by instigating a conflict with them. That group becomes **the other**—the enemy—and you can be certain that one of "them" is not one of "us." This process is a matter of defining your group by what it is not rather than by what it is. And it explains the efficacy of President George W. Bush's remarks after the September 11, 2001, al-Qaeda attacks, when he announced to the nations of the world, "You're either with us or you are with the terrorists."

In this and several other ways, conflict is probably the central element in political group dynamics. A sociologist named Lewis Coser, who examined group conflict in terms of the social or political functions it serves, noted that intergroup conflict has a profound effect on a group's identity.[17] Specifically, Coser argued that the degree to which people consider themselves part of a group increases when that group is engaged in conflict with another group. Additionally, intergroup conflict tends to generate an increase in the willingness of group members to accept and actively support the leadership of the group. We can see how both of these dynamics connect to the collective pursuit of security, which, as you really should know by now, is central to the whole government thing.

---

*That'll teach you not to stand up for the national anthem! Whooo! U-S-A! U-S-A! We love Stephen Colbert!

Generally speaking, most scholars who study politics prefer to assume that people make rational choices based on self-interest, but the way groups respond to threats seems to be better explained as a sociopsychological process, an instinctual reaction. As you will see in Chapter 4, when we explore some of the concepts central to government's role in the economy, the rational choices of individuals tend to place immediate personal costs and benefits above the longer-term benefits of the group, and, in reference to that, the group response to threats presents a substantial challenge to the presumption of individualistic rational choice. Think of war as an intergroup conflict and then consider the extremes of patriotism people express during war and the willingness of individuals to sacrifice their lives to contribute to their groups' goals.

Although these extreme responses to threats to a group or to intergroup conflict appear to be individually irrational, they make a whole lot of sense in terms of human beings as social animals. You could even argue that there is a kind of Darwinian evolutionary benefit in this kind of reaction to intergroup conflict. We know that human beings are social animals. Humans have always lived in groups, and it is ingrained in us that being part of a group is a basic aspect of human nature. Why? Human beings are weak and fragile. We have no nasty claws or big deadly teeth, and we are slower than most predators. As a result, individual human beings in the wilderness are extremely vulnerable. However, just as Bob and his fellow agricultural pioneers discovered, if you get a half dozen humans together and coordinate their efforts, the group can become quite formidable. Working as a group, humans wandering the African savanna with pointy sticks were more than a match for any lions, and tigers, and bears (oh, my!) they encountered.[*] Language and intelligence allow for the coordinated execution of extremely complex strategies that amplify the power of individuals far beyond the sum of their strengths.

This leads to a Darwinian argument for the evolution of what appears to be an irrational instinct to contribute to the group in times of conflict. The fact that you need to be part of a group in order to survive in a hostile, anarchic environment means that if you as an individual are better at deferring to authority and committing your efforts to combating threats to your group's security, then your group is more likely to be able to ward off threats. Assuming that warding off threats makes your group more likely to survive, then you, as an individual who is dependent on that group for your own survival, are also more likely to survive. Traits that increase your likelihood of survival in this way should also make you more likely to bear and raise children. These survivors will then pass on the instincts that enhance the group's response to external threats.

Once this group defense strategy gets embedded as an instinct, or basic aspect of human nature, it may occasionally motivate action that is hard to explain in terms of rational benefits for the individual—such as the self-sacrifice of a young soldier.

---

[*]The ability to defeat lions, tigers, and bears in this setting is even more impressive when you consider that neither tigers nor bears live in Africa.

However, in the vast majority of cases, particularly in those similar to the specific context in which the trait evolved, such action will provide sufficient indirect benefits to the group's survival to justify its individual costs. Regardless of whether it is rational or instinctual, group identity and the influence it can have on individual actions are powerful factors in politics.

Group response to external threat is more than just a theoretical concept. Researchers have done a great deal of work on the topic, and there is clear evidence that groups tend to coalesce when confronted with external threats. This defensive identification is an important part of the dynamics of real-world politics. Scholars have found that regardless of the nature of a country, its type of government, or its historical, social, political, or religious heritage, the measures of group identification—such as nationalism and patriotism—tend to rise when a nation finds itself in an international conflict. In fact, the rise is often quite dramatic.

People tend to have an immediate, strong reaction to any threat to their nation. This phenomenon is very clearly demonstrated in the United States by what political scientists refer to as the "rally 'round the flag" effect. Whenever Americans perceive a threat to the nation, public opinion polls show a sudden upsurge in the president's approval ratings as well as in other measures of patriotism. Over the course of his occupation of the White House, George W. Bush averaged the lowest approval ratings of any U.S. president ever, but right after the September 11, 2001, attacks on the World Trade Center his approval rating surpassed 90 percent. Or, to cite a rather less "scientific" example, it is not surprising that flag sales shot through the roof in the wake of September 11, as Americans expressed their increased group identification in response to a clear and unmistakable threat.

Leadership Interests

In addition to defining who is or is not part of the group, the power of group identity can affect the purpose of the group, if not justify its existence. A perfect example can be seen in *Lord of the Flies,* with Jack and the choir. If you think of all of the kinds of school groups you might want to have with you if you should get stuck on a deserted island, it would be hard to think of one that might seem less useful than a choir. You might even be better off with the chess team, because at least its members have the proven ability to think logically and solve problems. The choir members in Golding's novel, however, have a very strong group identity, which makes them and their leader powerful.

The identity of the group is crucial to the power and the position of its leader. Jack leads the choir from the very beginning of the island adventure, and he struggles to find a new purpose for the choir. He tries to make them warriors, keepers of the fire, and then hunters. Why does he work so hard to change the group's identity? If you think about it, Jack must have once invested a great deal of effort in becoming the leader of the choir. And *investing* is exactly the right word in this context, because Jack devoted his efforts and his resources

to obtain leadership, which he believed would give him future or continuing benefits. Being the leader of the choir, or the hunters, or the clog-dancing flower pickers, gives Jack power. By controlling the efforts of a group, he controls a resource that can be used to accomplish goals beyond what an individual could manage, and through that control Jack can bring benefits to himself. On the island, Jack is the only one who has troops at the ready, and that gives him power. He is desperate to maintain this power, and he can do so only by keeping his group together. He may not even consciously realize it, but his actions clearly demonstrate that he wants and needs the group to continue. As a result, even though the choir's original purpose has disappeared, the group persists. In fact, much of the story is about the transformation of Jack's group from a choir into a band of hunters.

Groups usually form for specific purposes, but they also provide benefits to their members, and because of that they tend to survive even after they have accomplished the goals for which they were created. They adjust to meet new demands or changes in context. They take on added roles or expand upon what they have accomplished. Have you ever heard of the National Foundation for Infantile Paralysis? You have; you probably just don't realize it. The NFIP was founded by a group of North American housewives who organized a fund-raising campaign to pay for treatments for the victims of polio and to finance research dedicated to curing the disease. A lot of people put a lot of effort into getting this group together, and it was tremendously effective, collecting huge amounts of money and becoming enormously influential. Then, all of the sudden, some guy (Dr. Jonas Salk) invents a vaccine, and in a matter of a few years, polio dwindles from the most dreaded of diseases to a rare condition, threatening only those people who, for some reason, have not been vaccinated.

What happens to the NFIP? The group has accomplished its goal, so it folds up shop, right? Wrong. A group that controls the flow of huge amounts of money and has a vast membership is invariably led by someone who has a great deal of power and who receives substantial benefits from that power. Leaders of such groups have made tremendous investments, often spending decades building their organizations, designing structures to accomplish goals, crafting bylaws, and establishing headquarters. Whole armies of people depend on such organizations for their jobs, including the officers, the secretaries, and, most important, the leaders. The leaders of a group like the NFIP fly across the nation and around the world, talking to important people and enjoying the kind of access to government officials that most people can only dream of.[*] Is there any reason to expect that the leaders who benefit from such a group will suddenly just stop and give it all up? Of course not. The leaders of the NFIP responded to the eradication of polio exactly as Jack does with his suddenly useless choir.

---

[*]Okay, given the limited nature of commercial air travel at the time, the leaders of the NFIP probably didn't fly much, but it's a pretty sure bet they did ride on trains.

It doesn't matter that the choir is a bunch of skinny little wimps in robes. They are the warriors. No need for warriors? Fine, the choir will be the hunters. There is no longer a need for the NFIP? Fine, the leaders take the group and its structures and redefine them to focus on fighting birth defects. Thus, the group persists beyond the achievement of the original goal of its collective effort. In reality, there are probably several reasons the group persists, but one of the most important is that the leaders of the group have invested their time and effort to obtain benefits from the group's existence. Even if they gain only prestige, that is a thing of value. Today, the organization is known as the March of Dimes.

Even if we presume that the NFIP had a completely altruistic leader who selflessly wanted only to help other people (probably a reasonable presumption in this example, even for cynics), once polio was cured, the leader must have found it impossibly tempting to take advantage of the group's resources to help others. Having accomplished one good deed, why not pursue another?

Once formed, groups persist, as the NFIP did. Leadership interests, which always seem to be a part of politics, are often the best explanation for why groups act as they do. For example, the dynamics of group identity and intergroup conflict, as discussed by Coser, tend to support leaders' efforts to hold their respective groups together. If the individual members' attachment to a group is strong, it is easier for the leader to convince them to stay in the group and to contribute to its efforts—the group wants to stick together. Furthermore, because the group members respond to conflict with other groups by supporting the leader's directives, groups in conflict become not only more cohesive but also more willing to follow the demands of the leader.

What I have accomplished here is a totally slick transition into the next chapter, which is mostly about leaders and leadership. It probably would have been a better transition if I didn't go and point it out, but the whole smooth transition thing is tough to do, and I was pretty chuffed about managing to pull it off.

Anyway, while governments perform many functions, at root they are essentially groups formed for the pursuit of collective security and other collective goods. The process of government formation may be a little more complex than our tale of Bob and his cavemen farmers, but the basics are the same. This is why group dynamics can tell us a great deal about governments and politics. Since leaders usually make decisions on behalf of the group, direct its actions, apply its resources, and choose its goals, much of what a group does is determined by the interests of its leaders. Similarly, what a government does most often reflects the interests of its leaders. Thus, we must appreciate how leaders perceive their own personal interests if we are to understand why governments persist, how precisely leaders govern, and what they do to maintain control of society.

The end result is a "realist" view of the origins and nature of governments, but idealists need to try to hang in there. Even if I am totally correct in my view of how and why governments began, idealism survives. As you would have noticed if you were paying attention, I made a big

deal out of the fact that collective security is just the first collective good pursued with government. Once government is established, it can and often is used to pursue idealistic ends. Unfortunately, as you will see in the next chapter, idealism faces a substantial challenge in the face of leadership interests.

KEY TERMS

alliances / 54

anarchists / 49

anarchy / 49

authority / 48

collective action / 44

government / 57

group identity / 58

hierarchy / 49

individual security / 46

national security / 46

the other / 61

political capital / 47

power / 46

regime security / 45

security / 44

state security / 45

CHAPTER SUMMARY

Although government seems to be everywhere, we seldom think about why governments began and why they continue to exist. Logic suggests that, initially, government emerged from collective action aimed at providing security. We can learn more about the continued existence of government by understanding human beings' aversion to anarchy and their tendency toward hierarchy. Additionally, the concept of power and the dynamics of group behavior explain why governments persist. Students should learn two very important lessons from this chapter. First, the phenomena discussed here suggest that governments satisfy fundamental human desires. Second, as annoying as your state's Department of Motor Vehicles can be, it is unlikely that it or any other form of government is going anywhere soon.

STUDY QUESTIONS AND EXERCISES

1. What might some of the theorists I've highlighted in Chapters 1 and 2 think about our story of Bob the caveman? Which of the theorists would agree that government might have begun in as described in the story? Which would likely disagree? Why?

2. The news is consistently filled with stories involving conflict among groups. What current examples can you find in the news? How do your examples fit with this chapter's discussion of group identification, "the other," and threats to the group?

3. What are the four securities that are critical to understanding the political dynamics of developing nations? Why don't they have normal names?

4. Why is collective action the essence of government?

5. What is power, and what are the various forms that it can take? What fictional examples can you think of that demonstrate the different forms of power? What are some real-world examples?

6. How do hierarchy and context come together to shape human interaction?

WEBSITES TO EXPLORE

www.gwu.edu/~nsarchiv. The National Security Archive at George Washington University is filled with articles and documents that demonstrate the U.S. concern for security.

www.anarchism.net. This site defines and discusses the many forms of anarchism.

www.cato.org. The Cato Institute is an organization concerned with limited government, individual liberty, free markets, and national security.

www.archaeological.org. *Archaeology,* a publication of the Archaeological Institute of America, explores all aspects of human origins, including the origins of government.

www.dailyshow.com. *The Daily Show with Jon Stewart* maintains a site that accompanies the television show's satirical look at the news.

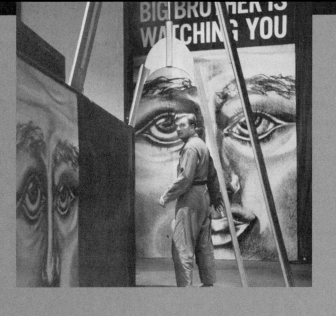

Governing Society
We Know Who You Are

She sees everything. She knows everything, and Jerry quickly learns that when the mysterious voice on the phone tells him to duck, he'd better duck. In fact, even as the cars start a-chasin' and bullets start a-flyin', Jerry realizes that he has no choice but to let her control his every action. "She" turns out to be "Eagle Eye," a computer. The only thing she can actually do is watch through a billion electronic eyes and share the information she observes, but that is enough power to enable her to manipulate and just about control each person's every action. She can kill. She can enslave. She could overthrow the government. She could rule the world.

Eagle Eye[1] is not the first film that has played on the coercive power of information manipulation. With the list including films such as *The Net, The Lawnmower Man,* and *1984* and books such as *Rainbows End, Cryptonomicon,* and *Snow Crash,*[2] there is a long history and a wide variety of fiction that plays on this theme. It shouldn't be surprising. Controlling information is one of the key tools that leaders employ to control those they govern, and some go so far as to claim that information *is* power. In fact, information control is a big part of how hated dictators can hold on to power with a combination of strategies to monitor their people and to repress the expression of opinion.

It all comes back to the weakness of individuals and the dynamics of collective action. In the discussion of governing society, it was selfish leadership interests that were the prime driver, and it again seems that the realists have carried the day. However, the idealists among you should not despair, because there is a long history of bending selfish motivations to serve idealistic collective ends. In the study of how societies are governed, a key difference between realists and idealists is how they view human nature. Idealists tend to believe that humans are essentially good, social beings who care for others.* From this

---

*I suspect that the typical idealist has never been involved in a mugging in any way. You would think that participating as either the perpetrator or the victim of a mugging would put a real damper on the belief that people are basically cooperative and good-natured. Thus, the biggest threat to an idealistic world would seem to be street crime.

perspective, idealists argue that we should judge governments and their leaders by how much they maximize these positive human qualities and how effectively they provide for their populations. Realists are more skeptical. Believing that human beings care only about maximizing their own self-interests, realists expect no more from their leaders. As discussed in Chapter 2, leaders usually make decisions on behalf of the group, direct its actions, apply its resources, and choose its goals. From a realist perspective, this means that much of what groups and governments do will serve the leaders' interests.

Since my goal in this chapter is to introduce you to how governments actually control the behavior of individuals rather than how governments ought to behave toward individuals, I rely heavily on realist approaches. Furthermore, the realist worldview provides a valuable conceptual tool to help cut through the bewildering complexity of politics. A surprisingly valuable rule of thumb is that whenever you are trying to understand a confusing aspect of politics, you should simply ask, "Who benefits?" and "How do they benefit?" The answers to these two questions will usually provide a solid first step toward unraveling the political puzzle. When examining politics, often the best line to remember is *Jerry Maguire*'s "Show me the money!"[3] Or, to paraphrase, "Show me the power."

The questions of who benefits and how are particularly helpful for looking at the strategies governments and leaders use to maintain control over their populations. I can argue that, regardless of the type of governments they head, all leaders try to maximize their self-interest. These two questions therefore allow us to make a little more sense of the excessive actions of totalitarian governments, such as the one portrayed in Orwell's *Nineteen Eighty-Four*. If I ask who benefits, you can begin to see how leadership interests determine how governments behave even in these extreme forms. When considered from the perspective of who benefits, heavy-handed, repressive tactics actually start to make sense. To get at the dynamics of how it all works, I draw heavily on the scenarios of fictional examples and on the real-world actions of totalitarian governments, but these extreme versions are just exaggerations of what leaders in all governments do. Examining the behavior of a ruthless leader who rules with an iron fist even helps explain the actions of democratically elected leaders. The chief executive who proposes a budget, members of Congress who work on committees, judges who interpret laws, and that annoying school board member who would dress up as a banana to get some coverage from the local newspaper—we can best understand them all by asking who benefits and how.

LEADERSHIP BENEFITS

From a realist perspective, people want to become leaders because holding the leadership position or being part of the elite group that controls the leadership position provides tremendous individual benefits. There is ample historical support for the argument that the leadership position enables those in charge to pursue a diverse set of personal benefits. Leaders may be power-hungry, such as Stalin in the Soviet Union, Mao in the People's Republic of China, and

Qaddafi in Libya, or they may be interested in extreme personal wealth, such as Ferdinand and Imelda Marcos in the Philippines, Mobutu in what was Zaire (now it is one of the many Congos), or the Saudi royal family. Leaders may thus be after different kinds of benefits, but they all pursue personal gains of some kind. Those of you still clinging to idealism will have to admit that even Winston Churchill, Abraham Lincoln, and Mahatma Gandhi benefited from their notoriety and/or prestige as leaders of their respective nations. They also were able to accomplish their goals through the political process. Admittedly those goals were largely altruistic, but they were their personal goals all the same. The concept of leadership benefits is such a powerful explanatory tool that some scholars even argue that personal benefits are the *only* reason people pursue leadership positions.

Given the potential for massive benefits, you can understand why someone might be willing to risk his or her life to take over a government. This potential for personal gains also explains why a leader might go to great lengths to hold on to the leadership position. The greater the benefits to be gained from leadership, the more willing people are to invest their own resources and take risks to attain it. You could even argue that battles for leadership are even more intense in poorer countries because, aside from leadership, these nations offer few, if any, alternate means to attain success. In a wealthy country, many motivated risk takers will go into business, sports, entertainment, academia, or the arts. Some will write best-selling textbooks or choose other avenues to pursue massive amounts of wealth or other measures of success, but in an impoverished and underdeveloped country, the only real option is politics. The poorer the country, the more constrained the opportunities, and, as a result, the proportion of talented and energetic people willing to take the extreme risks involved in pursing a leadership position increases.

Given these incentives for challengers, how can leaders stay in power? No matter how incompetent leaders may be at providing for the needs of their societies, it is not easy to oust them. In fact, some of the leaders who do the most damage to their countries manage to cling to power for years, sometimes decades. How? It is not enough to say that they use force. Although some leaders have massive armies and legions of secret police, in even the most brutal dictatorships the people outnumber the police by at least a hundred to one. How can so few maintain control over so many? How do leaders keep their subjects from revolting against them? Why don't the people lash out instead of knuckling under?

THE PANOPTICON

We saw part of the answer in the example of *Eagle Eye.* One of the fundamental mechanisms that leaders and governments use to control large populations is the **panopticon.** Though brutally dictatorial leaders throughout history (including your parents) have utilized it, the theoretical concept of the panopticon as a social mechanism for controlling populations comes from the political philosopher Michel Foucault's analysis of an eighteenth-century prison design that was crafted by the British theorist Jeremy Bentham. Bentham's panoptic prison features

cells built around a central tower. Those cells are arranged so that the guards in the tower can see the entire interior of every cell. However, the key to the design is that the guard tower is completely enclosed by mirrored windows. This is important because it means that the prisoners never know when they are being watched. The prisoners know that they are not being watched all of the time, but the severe and public punishments the guards mete out keep the prisoners constantly aware that they *could* be watched at any time. Thus, for the prisoners, the value to be gained from any type of misbehavior has to be weighed against the chance that one of the guards is watching at that very moment. If the punishments for misbehavior are severe enough, it will almost never be worth the risk of being seen misbehaving. Consequently, the prisoners will always behave as if the guards are watching them, even though they know they are not always watched. The only way the prisoners can be certain to avoid severe punishments is to police their own actions, constantly behaving as the rules dictate. In other words, most of the time, the prisoners serve as their own guards.

In a book titled *Discipline and Punish,* Foucault built upon the logic of that prison design by arguing that the panopticon's function of enabling a small number of guards to effectively control hundreds of prisoners is similar to the way in which governments and leaders maintain control over the societies they rule.[4] Indeed, this panoptic means of controlling behavior is a pervasive aspect of just about every government. An example you are almost certainly familiar with is the enforcement of traffic laws. Individual drivers are not constantly watched. In fact, very seldom do the police monitor any one person's driving. The vast majority of the time you drive mom's old minivan there are no police around. However, there always *could* be a cop around any bend in the road, and you never know when you are going to be watched. Does that white car behind you have a ski rack, or are those police lights on the top? You just never know. And because the cost of a ticket for even a minor infraction is usually outrageous, most of the time you will stay within shouting distance of the traffic laws. You police your own behavior. You watch your own speedometer.

It is impossible to overstate how deeply the fear that the government might be watching you influences your behavior. Most of us have had the experience of driving down the road and catching a glimpse of a state trooper in the rearview mirror. Even though the cop may be just driving along behind you minding his own business, your heart begins to race, you check your speed every two seconds, your palms get a little sweaty, you get a lump in your throat, and you start frantically reviewing everything you have done in the past few minutes to figure out how you accidentally drove yourself into a ticket. It's even worse when a state trooper pulls up behind you with his lights on. The instant you see that flash of blue, your mind's eye watches a whole semester's worth of beer and pizza money flying out the window.* Already halfway to the cardiac care unit, you pull over and the trooper goes whipping by you on his way to some other emergency. You've escaped with nothing worse than a need for a fresh set of tighty whities.

---

*This presumption of spending intent is pure speculation and does not constitute financial advice.

MICHEL FOUCAULT

Team: **Poiters Corps de Observé**

Position: **Deep Extra Cover**

Status: **Not Very Alive**

No matter what you think of modern French philosophy and the whole thing about people dressing all in black, gathering in the darkest corner of the nearest Starbucks and sharing the angst-ridden contemplation of critical nuances of this, that, or the other, you still gotta love a guy who started his career by writing about insanity.[a] **Michel Foucault** (1926–1984) is a love-him-or-hate-him kind of political philosopher and the haters have probably had a significant influence on how and where his work has had an impact on the study of politics. In the United States Foucault's work is most often associated with critical theory or poststructuralism and the related challenges to the conceptual and philosophical foundations of scientific approach to the study of politics. Many academics perceive this approach as a threat to the very nature of their research, and since that research is also the source of said academics' livelihood, that tends to provoke a bit of hostility. These hostile reactions have probably limited the interest in and the exploration of the many insights Foucault offered into power and the dynamics of society.

In addition to his discussion of the panopticon and how its dynamics related to political and social control,[b] Foucault's work was central to bringing discussions of the structure of knowledge, particularly as it related to language and representation of concepts, into the study of politics.[c] It's probably safe to say that the poststructuralist and postmodern research traditions, which became significant in the discipline during the 1980s, follow directly from Foucault's work, and research traditions that examine how knowledge, or identity or meaning are constructed through discourse and politics, such as the constructivist perspective on international politics, owe a significant intellectual debt to Foucault.

[a]Michel Foucault, *The History of Madness in the Classical Age* (Paris: Gallimard, 1961).

[b]Michel Foucault, Discipline and Punish: *The Birth of the Prison* (Paris: Gallimard, 1975).

[c]Michel Foucault, *The Order of Things* (New York: Penguin Books, 1970).

The fear that made you ruin your really sexy Captain America underwear is what causes you to police your own actions. The state troopers don't have to watch you all the time. They only have to be around often enough to remind you that they are out there watching. It also helps if the punishments are in some way public. You only have to see a few people pulled over here and there, you only have to hear one or two horror stories about a ticket so expensive that a kid had to sell his car to pay it, and you will fear being pulled over enough to keep watching what you do. You need only an occasional reminder of such things to keep those potential punishments constantly in your mind when you drive. You may never get a ticket, but seeing someone else get one reinforces that fear and slows your mad rush to the pizza place.

It is through this kind of **self-policing** that a few hundred police officers can control thousands upon thousands of drivers every day. Leaders put this same concept to work to prevent revolt and to control whole countries full of people who despise them.

Nineteen Eighty-Four presents several extreme examples of how the fear of being seen shapes people's behavior. The most prominent example is found in the affair between Winston and Julia. This unlikely couple has to go to some extreme lengths to avoid the prying eyes of a government that does not approve of personal connections such as love, or even lust. Just finding a way to communicate with one another to make the first personal contact is a struggle dominated by fear of the Thought Police and the punishments they might bestow. Julia contrives a fall and manages to pass Winston that first little love note, but he knows that he does not dare read it in the bathroom stall. There he is certain to be watched. He has to contrive a way to blend the reading of the note into his normal work routine, so that even if he happens to be watched when he does read it, his action will not be viewed as suspicious. Once he manages to read the note, his fear of the Thought Police makes him afraid to even glance at Julia. As a result, it takes him more than a week to find some way to respond. Winston and Julia then pursue their affair by meeting anonymously in crowds, going to great lengths to pretend they do not know each other, and taking different routes to their rendezvous in a pigeon-infested attic or a clearing in the woods.

The effects of the panoptic mechanism and the resultant self-policing of behavior are everywhere in the story. At times they are so pervasive that they seem almost unreal. The conduct of Orwell's characters, however, is merely an exaggeration of the way we all behave. It is the way our parents taught us to "behave" in the first place.* Is there any better example of the panoptic mechanism than Santa Claus? He knows when you are sleeping. He knows when you're awake. He knows when you've been bad or good. He's making a list and he's checking it twice. And if he knows that you have been bad, what does he do? He takes away Christmas! Is there any possible threat that a child would consider worse than losing Christmas? This truly is a punishment that outweighs the crime. All you have to do is be naughty, and that fat, musty-smelling guy at the shopping mall can take Christmas away.[†]

The panoptic mechanisms of the real world are usually less heavy-handed and brutal than what we see in *Nineteen Eighty-Four,* but they are a basic part of our adaptation to living in a complex social environment. Whether it is human nature to do so or some common social adaptation, the governing and social structures in every human society use panoptic structures to help maintain order and control. Leaders use these structures to prevent public behavior that might go against their interests. For the study of politics, it is probably important to note that from a leader's perspective, the worst kinds of behaviors are those that threaten that leader's ability to maintain control over society. Furthermore, because these are the behaviors that leaders are most intent on stopping, they are the ones on which panoptic mechanisms are most often focused.

---

*I would like to point out that my parents should have been more specific when telling me to behave. Technically speaking, behaving badly is just as much behaving as is pretending to be a sweet little angel.

†And parents wonder why kids cry when they are forced to sit on Santa's lap.

If leaders are most concerned about behaviors that threaten their control, why would the government in *Nineteen Eighty-Four* even care about the affair between Winston and Julia? More pointedly, why, at the end of the book, do the Thought Police stop the torture only when the threat of having his head stuck into a cage stuffed with rats drives Winston to betray Julia by telling them to "do it to her"? Why does the hyperparanoid government in Orwell's novel even care about the personal relationships of its citizens?

COLLECTIVE ACTION, REVOLUTION, AND THE USE OF FORCE

To understand why a leader might find the intimate personal relationships of societal members threatening, we have to return to the subject of collective action. As I pointed out in Chapter 2, government is, in essence, an institutionalized mechanism for collective action. One suggested motivation for the initial creation of government is the collective pursuit of security in an anarchic environment. However, once a government is formed, it serves as a framework that society can use to pursue a variety of other collective goals.

As it turns out, in the story about Bob and his fellow cavemen-turned-farmers, I skipped over any discussion of how they formed a group. I later offered one way to conceptualize the dynamics of group formation by introducing the skinny geek Gilligan and describing the alliances and counteralliances that formed around his ability to catch fish. In that story, however, I also glossed over several important details about the context and other factors shaping the choices individuals were making when deciding to join or not join particular groups. More specifically, I could talk of people choosing to accept or not accept the social contract of government to pursue the collective goal of security. So, what happens when people do not want to be a part of the governed society? What happens when they wish to cancel the social contract? I address some of these details here because they are important for understanding the most fundamental of threats to a government: revolution.

A **revolution** is a collective action, a mass uprising focused on the goal of tearing down and replacing the current government.* In fact, scholars who study collective action and the behaviors associated with it often use revolutions as cases for analysis. Because revolutions are such extreme forms of collective action, these scholars believe that many of the dynamics of choice and action that are general to all collective actions are magnified by the extreme nature of revolutions and easier to observe in a revolutionary context. While the initial formation of government may have occurred in anarchy, revolutions happen in hierarchical environments. Those at the top of the existing social hierarchy are driven by self-interest to actively oppose any collective effort to overthrow the system. Along with the panoptic self-policing mechanism, leaders use the techniques of atomization, peer policing, and preference falsification to prevent revolutionary groups from forming.

---

*Many argue that *revolt* would be a more appropriate term for the collective action to replace a government. Some limit the use of the term *revolution* to the collective effort to replace the political and economic or social structures of a state.

SURPRISINGLY RELEVANT GRATUITOUS SELF-REFERENCE

1996 was a magnificent year. It was unusually long, had a summer right in the middle, and had plenty of Tuesdays. It was also the year that *International Studies Quarterly* published a mind-shattering rational choice model of revolutionary collective action. The mind-shattering part was due to some very poorly constructed subliminal messages, but it was also an astoundingly tolerable article. The article maps out the rational choice of each potential participant in a revolution in terms of the information the individual has on costs, benefits, and the uncertainty surrounding the likelihood that the revolution will succeed. This graphic representation of the aggregate distribution of when it becomes rational for someone to join the revolution shows how information, particularly information regarding the certainty of how many revolutionaries it will take to win and how leaders can manipulate that for their own personal gain, is a critical aid for understanding both the mechanisms that dictators use to maintain power and the mechanisms that allow revolutions to appear seemingly out of nowhere.

Douglas A. Van Belle, "Leadership and Collective Action: The Case of Revolution," *International Studies Quarterly* 40 (March 1996): 107–32.

Atomization

In essence, **atomization** means exactly what you might guess. Since atoms are the smallest form of coherent matter, it follows that if you were to atomize something, you would break it down into its smallest components. Then, to keep it atomized, you would separate the parts and stop them from congealing into something larger. Leaders prevent the formation of revolutionary groups in a similar way. When people are isolated, they are kept from joining together in groups that could threaten a leader's hold on power. In the extreme case, a leader would want to prevent anyone from forming any kind of personal bond, such as the affair between Winston and Julia. You would have to be a pretty paranoid tyrant to go that far, but if you were out there on the edge of sanity, you might well be worried that such a close personal bond could someday be used as a means to overcome atomization, share discontent about government, and form a revolutionary group. Keeping people separate is atomization, and the two most important mechanisms for accomplishing this goal are peer policing and preference falsification.

Peer Policing

Peer policing means, literally, having people police each other. While peer policing can sometimes occur spontaneously, for it to work as a mechanism for preventing revolt leaders must usually put a few structural elements in place. First, they need to encourage citizens to engage in peer policing against potential revolutionaries. This might be most easily accomplished by making it a crime to *not* report someone's efforts to form a revolutionary group. While this deterrent alone might be effective, the government can make it even more effective—and, in fact, make it almost impossible to form a revolutionary group—by getting people to believe that government agents will test their willingness to turn in others to the authorities.

Borrowing the setting from *Nineteen Eighty-Four,* imagine that some bald guys with poorly faked Eastern European accents come up to you and say something like, "We know you are guilty and we are going to have to punish you." You have just become a pawn of the secret police. This shouldn't seem all that far-fetched. Even in the context of real-world totalitarian dictatorships, the secret police are always bald, creepy-looking guys with bad accents and an unnatural predilection for leather overcoats. They also do not actually need any evidence or any real justification to make such a claim. You are guilty as soon as they decide to say you are guilty. Working with this presumption of guilt, these leather-overcoated protectors of the government can offer to be magnanimous. They can give you the chance to redeem yourself by proving your loyalty. Perhaps you can do them the favor of testing the loyalty of your coworkers. Perhaps you can share some criticisms of the government with the person in your office you most suspect of having revolutionary inclinations, so the government can test that unsuspecting dupe's loyalty.

Everyone is aware that this is a common practice by the secret police. So, if a coworker comes up to you and complains about the government's policy for distributing a critical resource, such as ice cream, you are faced with three unpalatable choices:

1. You can turn your colleague in to the Ministry of Ice Cream Enthusiasm, knowing that even though he is a nice guy and not really a revolutionary, he is likely to be punished severely. Despite his innocence, you will have fulfilled your duty to turn him in, and you should escape punishment.

2. You can say nothing and decide not to turn him in, which is dangerous because he could be someone sent to test your loyalty. If that is the case, failing to turn him in is a crime for which you could be severely punished.

3. You can agree with him. This opens up the possibility of your getting together with him to revolt against the tyranny of MICE. This would give you a chance to attain an end that you both appear to desire. However, you will be at tremendous risk of severe punishment if he happens to have been sent to test your loyalty.

Regardless of how you feel about MICE, the only way you can be reasonably certain to avoid punishment is to report your coworker.

As a result, the leader has created a society in which people are constantly watching each other, constantly policing each other for revolutionary inclinations, and constantly ready to turn each other in. What does this accomplish? It separates people from one another. It atomizes them. How can you form a revolutionary group when every person you approach about joining the group is going to be afraid of not turning you in? If the punishment for failing to turn in your coworker for complaining about ice cream was going to be harsh, just wait until you see what you get for not turning in a revolutionary.

As far as government leaders are concerned, the worst crime a human or humanoid can commit is attempting to revolt against the political structure that gives the leaders their exalted position in the hierarchy.

You can see peer policing all over *Nineteen Eighty-Four*. Near the beginning of the story, Winston's comment about doublespeak sends his coworker into a tizzy. Visibly agitated and sweating nervously, the coworker vigorously defends the government's butchering of the language. He is afraid that Winston may be testing him or that the Thought Police may be listening and will somehow consider him guilty by association. Then there are Winston's neighbors. The father gets hauled off to the bowels of the government's police machinery after being turned in for thought crimes by his own children. When even within a coherent family unit one must fear being turned in for merely thinking the wrong thing, you have peer policing at its most extreme.

The use of peer policing helps to explain the behavior of the character V in *V for Vendetta*, a film about one man's crusade to take down a fascist government.[5] Only by staying out of sight, away from the prying eyes of the government and ordinary people, can V stage his revolt. He masks his identity because he must worry not only about the government punishing him for his terrorist activities but also that his fellow citizens may turn him in.

When just a few government agents are doing the actual policing, keeping people atomized can be a crucial element for maintaining control. As long as collective revolutionary activity remains impossible, there are plenty of police officers to keep order and handle individual "crimes" here and there. What the government is really afraid of, however, is that these individual actions might occur simultaneously. Mass action, coordinated or not, will quickly overwhelm the government's policing and enforcement mechanisms.

Think about what happens in a riot. With a few notable exceptions, the individual crimes committed during a riot are minor. There may be vandalism, breaking and entering, theft, simple assaults here and there, but seldom are very many offenses committed that are beyond the bounds of the typical junior high school day. Normally, the police would have little or no trouble handling such petty crimes. However, when all these minor crimes happen at once and there are far more offenders than officers, the police have no way to maintain order. Similarly, governments and their leaders can handle individual, isolated revolutionary actions, but they cannot stop large numbers of revolutionary activities that happen at the same time. To prevent revolt, governments have to prevent mass action, particularly coordinated mass action. Potential revolutionaries must be kept separate. A million revolutionaries marching on the capital one by one is nothing, but if those same revolutionaries should manage to arrive together, even the largest and most powerful government could be overrun. As the dictators of Tunisia, Libya, Egypt, and Syria discovered in 2012 and the dictators in the former Soviet satellite countries of East Germany, Czechoslovakia, and Romania discovered in 1989, revolutionaries acting in concert do not even have to be armed to overcome a government's police and military. They must simply act en masse.

Lest you think that atomization and peer policing are limited to totalitarian regimes, look around you. Examples are everywhere. Peer policing in particular is often encouraged in the United States and other democracies. A simple example comes from the Seattle area, where the combination of steep hills, lots of wet places called lakes, rivers, and harbors, and tremendous population growth has created horrible traffic problems. Like many other major cities, Seattle has created carpool lanes to try to alleviate some of the congestion, and right next to the signs detailing the carpool lane restrictions are other signs displaying a phone number for drivers to call to report those violating the lane restrictions. When you dial that number on your cell phone, an operator at the Washington State Patrol answers and asks for the license plate number of the vehicle illegally using the carpool lane. If three or more callers report the same license plate, the police send a ticket to the registered owner of the car. This is peer policing at its most effective. Because cell phones have long outnumbered car stereos on Seattle's freeways, you will probably never see anybody running solo in a Seattle commuter lane. So many people will call that number the instant they see someone illegally using the lane that the scofflaw is all but guaranteed a $200 ticket in the mail.

Another example—though of the spontaneous kind rather than the government-orchestrated variety—is from a small town in southern Louisiana. In a town with more churches than stop signs, an old gas station was converted to an adult video store, and this "remodeling" did not go over very well with the locals. Parishioners from several of the town's churches decided to camp out across the street and record the license plate number of every car in the store's parking lot. They then published the license plate numbers along with descriptions of the cars in the local newspaper under the headline, "Is This Your Neighbor's Car?" Within a month, the store closed down and a bunch of parishioners got high-speed Internet access.

Peer policing can be an extremely effective tool, particularly when governments encourage and direct it. The same strategy used to punish the road hogs and close down the naughty video store can be used to shut down crack houses and drive prostitutes out of a neighborhood. In reality, however, this voluntary form of policing will work only for a limited number of issues. It is particularly effective at getting rid of behaviors that many people already dislike, and when used in the right context, voluntary policing clearly works. However, to convince peers to police each other on other matters—such as revolutionary activities—governments must usually rely on the coercive methods discussed earlier.

Preference Falsification

Taken to an extreme in *Nineteen Eighty-Four,* in which the government feels that it can't even tolerate trust among family members or between lovers, peer policing is one mechanism that government uses to atomize the populace and consequently to prevent revolt. Another such tool is **preference falsification.** Also seen in an exaggerated form in Orwell's novel, preference falsification means exactly what it sounds like: it is hiding the way you truly feel while publicly expressing what those in power want to see and hear from you.

An obvious example of preference falsification occurs in *Nineteen Eighty-Four* when the citizens gather together in front of television sets to scream their hatred for the enemy during the "two minutes of hate." Does Winston really hate the enemy? No, but in public he expresses rage as expected. Julia is so enthusiastic during the two minutes of hate—screaming, spitting, and throwing her shoes—that Winston is convinced she must be with the Thought Police. Only later does he find out how different her true preferences are from those she expresses in public.

Governments employ methods to generate preference falsification as a key part of the atomization and peer policing process that keeps people separate and keeps potential revolutionary groups from forming. If people do not express their dissatisfaction with the current government or their desire for a new government, how can potential revolutionaries ever know that there are others who share their view? Aside from having a stuffy British name like Winston, this is Winston's greatest problem at the beginning of the novel. He wonders if he is the only one who feels the way he does because everyone else appears to support the government. As long as other people's true feelings about the government are hidden, it will be difficult for an individual like Winston to overcome the fear that atomization and peer policing cause. So long as atomization, peer policing, and preference falsification keep people apart, a potential revolutionary will be unable to form the group that is needed to overthrow the government.

Governments encourage preference falsification not only by making it illegal or dangerous to express dissatisfaction with the government but also by encouraging people to echo the leaders' preferences. Think of the massive progovernment demonstrations that take place in authoritarian regimes such as North Korea. You know the marches I'm talking about—the ones in which the people are spontaneously marching in tightly choreographed groups, carrying signs with Godzilla-sized pictures of the dear leader's face. Dictators can make these demonstrations materialize in a number of ways. They can send government officials to offices and factories to proclaim loudly, "Congratulations, today is a special holiday. You are all going to get to march in the plaza and you will carry these signs and chant these slogans." Do any of the marchers really hold the preferences they express at these demonstrations? A few of them do, but the majority probably do not. Nevertheless, regardless of their personal feelings, do you think any of these factory workers would dare to decline the government's invitation to march?

This tactic is not limited to totalitarian dictatorships such as the one in Orwell's fictional scenario. It can occur whenever the structure or context of interaction makes it clear that there will be unpleasant consequences for those who fail to endorse the leader's views. No matter how lame the boss's jokes, every employee forces a chuckle. Everyone who wants to keep his or her job nods and treats the boss's moronic idea as if it contained the wisdom of Solomon. Anyone who has ever seriously dated anyone at all knows that we often falsify our preferences under pressure: "No, those pants make you look so totally thin." "Sure, I'd love to see a movie with gratuitous nudity and mindless violence." "I *love* it that you watch twelve hours of football every Sunday." "Sure, I'd love to talk about feelings." Governments simply exaggerate this

common aspect of human interaction, and they take advantage of it to prevent people from engaging in collective action. Governments use preference falsification to reinforce their efforts at atomization and peer policing. Preference falsification adds to your uncertainty whether that person expressing dissatisfaction with the government is just testing you to see if you will follow the law and turn him in.

Leaders use all of the interrelated mechanisms discussed so far—fear, punishments, and even direct violence—to forcefully maintain control and prevent revolt. Still, we have to remember that *Nineteen Eighty-Four* is a work of fiction, and what makes fiction valuable is the way it exaggerates processes and dynamics such as these. While all governments use these mechanisms of force, real methods are often far less overt than those depicted in Orwell's extreme vision. In fact, there are some fundamental and very practical limits on the effectiveness of forceful control.

Limits on Forceful Control

The level of force leaders must use to maintain control of the government is related to the society's level of dissatisfaction. When the level of dissatisfaction is low, less force is needed to keep people from revolting against government, but when societal discontent outweighs the fear that government can instill in the populace, people will stop falsifying their preferences and start trying to overcome the government's mechanisms for atomization. If people are satisfied and happy, they are inclined to not fix what ain't broken. If people can't feed their families, it's going to be hard to keep them from doing whatever it takes to change things.

Think of the playground bully. When pushed too far, the other kids will stand up to a bully. If you've ever seen *A Christmas Story,* you'll recall how cute little Ralphie ultimately deals with the crazy bully who always pounds on his brother and his friends.[6] Ralphie usually deals with this intimidation through preference falsification—that is, by trying to say whatever the bully wants to hear so that he can pass unscarred. But one day, pushed by a series of events that have left him downtrodden and dispirited,* Ralphie instead flips out and pounds the bully until he bleeds.[†]

When people are pushed over the edge and into despair, they may also be pushed to revolt. Dissent, protests, inflammatory speeches by opposition leaders, marches, or perhaps even riots will occur. Consequently, when dissatisfaction rises to the point that it sparks open opposition, the government must increase the level of force to retain control. Punishments are made more severe and more frequent to increase self-policing enough to quell the unrest. Leaders take measures not only to increase peer policing but also to make

---

*Despite all his efforts, Ralphie will not get the BB gun he wants for Christmas.

†The bully bleeds, not Ralphie. I had a note to remind me to clear up that pronoun-verb confusion in the second edition, but I must have forgot or something, and now that I'm sneaking snarky footnotes into the third edition, it's a little too late to change things that might actually get noticed. We can always hope for the fourth edition.

peer policing more salient. As authoritarian leaders around the world have demonstrated repeatedly, this strategy works. Over the long run, however, there is a very serious problem with using large amounts of force, and this limitation can restore some of the idealists' faith in humanity.

Using force to maintain control usually does nothing to resolve the underlying causes of discontent. The people are usually dissatisfied for a reason. In fact, in a dictatorial environment it probably takes a pretty serious problem to get people past the fear of punishment that would normally keep them from expressing their true preferences. Left unaddressed, the underlying problem is likely to grow worse rather than better. There are times of transitory distress, such as a crop failure, when just buying six months will ease the problem, but in most cases if people are rioting because there are not enough jobs or because they can't afford to feed themselves, the application of more force will not fix the economy or provide cheaper food. When force is used but the underlying problem remains unsolved or ignored, the problem will likely grow worse over time, and the dissatisfaction will increase.

Unsolved and unsolvable problems can start a spiral of repression and dissent that is ultimately self-destructive for the government. If government leaders use force to quash unrest but don't fix the problem, what happens when the increasing dissatisfaction from the worsening problem exceeds the restraining effect of the higher level of force? The leaders must then exert even more force, but because the underlying problem still remains unaddressed, the festering dissatisfaction continues to grow until yet more force is needed. Once this vicious spiral starts, leaders may quickly find that they are stuck on a path with no escape, because the underlying problem has grown too large for them to fix with available resources. The leaders then have no real choice but to continue raising the level of force to maintain control, but this process cannot go on forever. The realist argument that human beings look to maximize their self-interest applies not only to leaders but to the public as well, and when the people come to believe that imprisonment, torture, or death is no worse than their miserable lives, the leaders have reached the point at which increasing force will have no effect. Starving people with starving children begin to believe that it is rationally worth the risk to revolt, even if the chance for success is slim. When you have pushed people to the point of desperation, force is simply not enough.

LEGITIMACY AND GOVERNMENT CONTROL

Fortunately for leaders who face these potential limits on the use of force, there is another way to maintain control. Instead of relying on threats and punishments, leaders can maintain control by pursuing **legitimacy,** which can be defined as the voluntary acceptance of their government. In other words, legitimacy exists when people have the sense that obeying the government's rules is rationally, economically, or morally the right thing to do. Like the definitions I have offered earlier, this one is overly simplified. It will work in the situations described

in this text, but it is by no means complete, absolute, or universally agreed upon, and students should be prepared to adjust and adapt to the nuances and complexities involved in less simplified contexts.

A complex array of social, psychological, political, and cultural processes and phenomena—including educational and socialization mechanisms and culturally defined responses to authority—can affect/effect a government's legitimacy.[*] There are many ways for a government to achieve legitimacy: by simply remaining in power for a long time; by receiving the blessing of a past leader whose rule was considered legitimate; by kicking the bejeebas out of the backsides of all the greatest warriors in the land; or by convincing the populace that God, Buddha, or the magic goat of Burbank has divinely selected the Glorious Leader to rule. However, from a realist's perspective, the primary focus should be on the rational, cost-benefit perspective of government legitimacy.

Perhaps the most effective way that a leader can gain legitimacy is by persuading the citizenry that it is in their best interest to accept his or her leadership voluntarily. Generally speaking, a leader can accomplish this goal by providing the things that people need or want. While this might mean anything from instilling religion in government to protecting ethnic culture or restoring national pride through military conquest, leaders most often accomplish legitimacy by providing the basic resources and opportunities that people need or expect. If the government is successful in providing such resources and opportunities, the level of discontent will be reduced, and the leaders will need to exert much less force to maintain control.

Got to Give the People What They Want: Elections and Public Goods

Popular elections provide the best example of how a government can use legitimacy as the primary means to avoid revolt. While I later devote an entire chapter to democracy—both the ideal and the dynamics of governments that try to achieve it—for present purposes, it is worth stealing some of the thunder from that chapter to note briefly the important connection between elections and legitimacy. Simply put, popularly elected leaders are legitimate leaders, at least when they first take office. They win their leadership positions and gain power by attaining the voluntary acceptance of a majority of those who vote, or from a majority of the representatives elected by a population. What is a vote but an expression that you choose to be ruled by a certain candidate?

Ironically, this means that electoral democracies deal with the threat of revolt by embracing it. Instead of trying to quash revolutionaries, they create political structures that tame and institutionalize the process of revolt. Instead of letting discontent build up until it erupts into massive bloody uprisings, a democracy holds periodic elections. These serve as planned, scheduled, and regular uprisings. Every few years, citizens have the opportunity to

---

[*]The grammatically obsessed language geeks in the class should note that the verb form of either *affect* or *effect* works here. These factors affect, or influence, the nature of legitimacy, but they can also effect legitimacy—cause it to be created.

throw out their leaders and replace those who have failed to provide for the needs or wants of the populace. The vote is a nonviolent way of meaningfully expressing satisfaction or dissatisfaction with the leadership.

The democratic electoral structure affects* the behavior of the leader and of those who hope to challenge for the leadership position. If you are in power, you want to stay in power or at least keep your party in power, so reelection is constantly in the back of your mind. You must continually work to convince a majority of voters to express their voluntary acceptance of you as the leader by casting their votes for you in the next election. To accomplish this goal, you must remain responsive to the populace and work to satisfy the needs and wants of the society by anticipating, addressing, and resolving the causes of dissatisfaction.

While popular elections serve as an excellent example of a mechanism that forces the leaders' personal interests to converge with those of the people they govern, there are other ways for leaders to pursue legitimacy. Most governments around the world try to find some balance between the use of force and the pursuit of legitimacy to maintain control. To some degree, the limitations on the use of force to control a society drive almost every leader to seek some degree of legitimacy. Even the vilest dictators have usually tried to strike this balance. Mussolini's Fascists were not above using force and violence, but they also tried to win voluntary acceptance of their rule by making the trains run on time* and doing many of the other simple things that earlier Italian governments had been unable to manage. Even Hitler did not rely on fear alone. His government undertook huge public works projects to revive Germany's economy and to provide jobs for the people. Leaders vary in the degree to which they try to satisfy the needs and wants of large portions of their populations. Surprisingly enough, the Libyan dictator Muammar al-Qaddafi provides one of the best nearly contemporary examples of a barely dead nondemocratic leader who pursued the voluntary acceptance of his rule.

When Qaddafi seized power from the Libyan royal family in 1969, the quality of life in Libya was miserably low: educational opportunities were almost nonexistent, doctors were scarce, jobs were hard to find, food was in short supply, life expectancies were low, and much of the population had little or nothing to call a home. Qaddafi embarked on one of history's most ambitious efforts to address the needs and desires of a society, spending the first decade of his rule focused on trying to better the life of the ordinary Libyan.† He took the country's oil money and used it to build schools, hospitals, and apartment buildings. He sent students to Europe to train as doctors and engineers. Irrigation projects

---

*Grammar-obsessed geeks will note that the verb form of *effect* doesn't really work here.

*I have been informed that Italy has now managed to find a way to get the trains to run on time without resorting to fascism, although, owing to the effect of strikes by rail workers, I have never actually seen an Italian train move. And yes, *effect* is used correctly there.

†Please note that I am talking about the Libyans living in Libya. Wealthy Libyans who had done well under Italian colonial rule and were economic and social elites in the kingdom that Qaddafi overthrew pretty much got screwed, which is, of course, a technical term for being driven into exile and having the land and assets they left behind seized.

increased farm output. Undoubtedly, he siphoned a great deal of money off for himself and his immediate supporters—his mansion was so big that Ronald Reagan had to send *several* U.S. warplanes to bomb it—but the resources Qaddafi devoted to meeting the needs and wants of the people of Libya were remarkable for a dictator exercising almost absolute power. The difference in the lives of the people became apparent in just a few years. By the end of the 1970s, the average Libyan's quality of life had improved so much and Qaddafi's leadership was considered so legitimate that the CIA is said to have told President Reagan that destabilization of Qaddafi was impossible.

Qaddafi pursued security in office by seeking legitimacy, by striving to attain the voluntary acceptance of his rule. Make no mistake—he was a brutal dictator, renowned for using murder and terror to enforce his rule. However, he did not rely solely, or even primarily, on the forceful mechanisms that are the mainstay of most authoritarian rulers. Perhaps just as notable is the fact that when force was the only mechanism Qaddafi had available for maintaining control, he couldn't.

Balancing Force and Legitimacy

How do leaders calculate the correct mix of force and legitimacy? In simple terms, the lower the level of dissatisfaction, the less force is necessary. But there are other considerations. For one, the pursuit of legitimacy tends to be a poor short-term strategy but a better long-term strategy. Provided there are resources available to pursue and maintain legitimacy, legitimacy can be a much more stable and efficient mechanism than force for maintaining control. First, because a leader who has legitimacy does not have to be constantly concerned about revolt and does not have to invest heavily in the tools of force, those resources can be directed toward improving the economy and doing other things that both support legitimacy and increase the resources available to government. However, it can take years, even decades, to turn an economy around or otherwise meet people's needs and expectations. That is usually far too long to satisfy the armed mob gathering at your palace door.

On the other hand, force is very effective in the short term. When people are marching in the streets, forceful actions such as arrests, torture, threats, and fear can have an immediate impact. When the leader is facing a riot, when revolution seems imminent, there is no time to wait for a new irrigation project to increase the food supply, and the leader would be long gone before new schools could be built.

Ideally, we would hope that a leader facing imminent revolt would use the short-term impact of force only to buy security while working to make the investments needed to attain long-term legitimacy. However, in the real world, leaders tend to be motivated only by immediate and visible threats to their hold on power. Once the immediate danger is removed through force, leaders tend to lose the motivation to pursue legitimacy. Taking away the threat of revolt also takes away the impetus to satisfy the needs of the people.

For an authoritarian leader to pursue the public interest seems to require either a moral commitment to the public welfare—a rare quality in an authoritarian leader—or the tremendous foresight necessary to realize the long-term value of pursuing legitimacy—yet another rarity.

Another aspect of pursuing legitimacy that is relevant for calculating the balance between force and legitimacy is that it is far cheaper in the short term to use force. It doesn't take that much wealth to pay off a small group of army officers and a small police force to maintain control by force compared to what it takes to invest in meeting the needs of the entire society. Furthermore, if the country does not have the wealth to invest in schools, economic infrastructure, and other services that can win the people's support, the leader cannot even make the effort. Qaddafi was able to pursue legitimacy because he had the resources available to make it work. He had oil money, the property he had seized from the wealthy, and a very small population to satisfy. Under other conditions, his strategy would not have worked. The leader of an impoverished country with no natural resources to exploit often simply cannot afford to pursue legitimacy. Consequently, some analysts have suggested that a country may need a minimum level of wealth in order to be a democracy. How can a government achieve legitimacy if no leader could ever accumulate the resources necessary to meet the public's wants and needs?

Legitimacy and Conflict within Groups

The concept of legitimacy brings us back to some of the basic theories on conflict and group dynamics introduced in Chapter 2.* As you'll recall from that discussion, conflict between groups can play an important role in group identification and in building support for leadership. Conflict also plays an important role—perhaps a more important role— *within* groups. To understand fully how this process works, you need to consider a bit of the early sociological research on social conflict.

The horrors of World War I—which I discuss in unpleasant detail in Chapter 12, where I go on and on and on about international politics and war—motivated the scholars of the interwar years to focus on understanding the nature of conflict. The "war to end all wars" was so hideously destructive that the aforementioned now dead scholars threw themselves into the study of international relations with the express goal of ensuring that such atrocities never occurred again. Every aspect of their research was dominated by the idea that conflict is an evil to be defeated or a disease to be cured. And, because they believed that no redeeming value is to be found in conflict, reducing it or minimizing it was not enough. These scholars believed that it had to be eradicated. However, as Georg Simmel and, later, Lewis Coser pointed out, there were problems with this drastic approach.[7] While horribly

---

*What would it take to convince you that I actually planned all along to return to group dynamics as a way of tying these two chapters and their concepts together?

bloody conflagrations* such as World War I should certainly be prevented, the complete elimination of conflict might be equally dangerous, because conflict serves constructive functions within human societies.

We can see some of these functions in intergroup conflicts, or conflicts between two or more groups. When a group's members are engaged in conflict with members of another group, their self-identification with their own group increases, along with support for the leadership. Both of these factors can benefit the leader and even the group as a whole by making the group more cohesive and enhancing the group's stability. Leaders can, and often do, use the effects of conflict between groups in self-serving ways, but for this discussion of legitimacy and government, the point is that managing an external conflict is one way that a leader or a government builds legitimacy. Most important, the work of Simmel and Coser redirected the study of conflict toward discovering how conflict *within* a group can also prove beneficial.

A Safety Valve

The first benefit of intragroup conflict (conflict within the group) is that it can serve as a **safety valve.** What do I mean by a safety valve? Most of you have probably never seen a pressure cooker, but if you or a family member has ever canned homegrown fruits and vegetables, or if you have lived at very high altitude, you may have encountered one. A pressure cooker is simply a cooking pot with a clamped lid that prevents steam from escaping. This mechanism creates a buildup of pressure—the same principle that powers a steam engine—and it also allows you to control the temperature at which the water boils—higher pressure creates a higher boiling point. Thus, you need a pressure cooker up in the mountains where the air pressure is much lower than at sea level, because without that clamped-on lid and the extra pressure the boiling water never gets hot enough to cook the noodles for your macaroni and cheese. In fact, if you go far enough up into the mountains—Mount Everest kind of up—the boiling point of water drops so low that you can actually stick your hand into boiling water without damaging the water or your hand.

Now, if you happen to be seven years old* and your mom is canning peaches in the kitchen, you just may wonder why the pot on the stove is whistling away. Because you are seven, you do not realize that when the pressure reaches a certain point, the safety valve pops open and lets out some of the steam, whistling and spitting a little bit. Instead, you are an industrious little boy who looks at this sputtering pot and thinks, "That is just not right." Then you go get a little wrench from the garage, put on some oven mitts, and start working on the safety valve, cranking it down tighter and tighter until it stops whistling and stops sputtering. Success! You've fixed it! Then you go outside and do whatever it is that seven-year-olds do outside around the end of summer.

---

*For a total of seventy-four cool-word points, not that I'm keeping score.

*I will not go into who actually did this because I think the guilty party's mother may have finally forgotten about it. At the very least, she has quit mentioning it at the start of every Thanksgiving dinner.

If you happen to be within earshot when that pressure cooker explodes, not only will you learn a lot of new words and phrases that no one ever used to be allowed to say on TV, but you will also learn that without a properly functioning safety valve, the pressure cooker can build up pressure to the point that it will blow the lid, quite literally, through the ceiling. That lid will blow straight up through the vent hood over the stove, the cupboard above that, the sheetrock, the insulation, the roof, and everything. As that lid bounces on the patio in the backyard, not only will your father start teaching you all those words and phrases, some of which can even today be found only on cable, but you will also learn that cooked peaches can become awesome projectiles. While canned peaches might ordinarily be soft, mushy things, when blown out of a pressure cooker with sufficient force, they can actually penetrate a wall with such gusto that there is no way you will ever get them out. Your dad will have to rip out and replace the entire kitchen, because after just a couple of warm days, the peaches you blasted into the walls really start to stink.

The point of this little story is the safety valve. Groups of people can often behave in the same way as a pressure cooker, and conflict within the group can function like the safety valve. Completely stopping group members from engaging in conflict creates a buildup of pressure. When people who are irritated cannot say or do anything about the source of tension, their frustration and anger builds until, eventually—as with Ralphie in *A Christmas Story*—just about anything will set them off. Conflicts, even small, controlled conflicts, allow people to vent their frustrations and dissatisfactions and thus serve the safety-valve function. Instead of a big blowup, the result is a series of minor, more manageable conflicts.

Spike Lee's *Do the Right Thing* provides a great example of what can happen when there is no working social version of that safety valve.[8] Throughout the film, racial tension mounts along with the temperature in a Brooklyn neighborhood. There is seemingly no relief from either the heat or the tension, which all comes to a head in a pizza joint with a white proprietor. Spike Lee makes the pressure of the situation tangible. Ultimately, it comes as little surprise that a riot breaks out after a racial epithet is used and the proprietor's friend and employee throws a garbage can through the window. The pressure built up with no controlled release. The explosion was inevitable.

Crosscutting Cleavages

This idea of a safety valve also relates to a second benefit described by Coser in regard to conflicts within a group: **crosscutting cleavages.**[*] If no conflict is allowed within a group, the things that do not work well in the group—those little things that cause irritation and frustration—will build up pressure. When conflict eventually does break loose within the group, it will tend to erupt intensely around a single issue. No matter

---

[*]If you chuckled at the mention of cleavage, either grow up or change your name to Beavis.

what the immediate cause may be, when a group has only one dividing line of internal conflict—a single cleavage—that division tends to split the group apart, threatening the cohesion or the very existence of the group. This threat to the group is significant, because everyone falls on one side or the other of that one issue.

On the other hand, if some conflict is tolerated or even fostered within a group, when cleavages appear they are not going to be as intense. Why? For one, the safety-valve principle allows these smaller conflicts to release some of the social tension and resolve some of the issues challenging the group's cohesion. Also, when a variety of different conflicts arise with a group, the divisions over them do not always coincide— the cleavages are crosscutting. In other words, if there are enough small points of debate or conflict, people who disagree on one issue are likely to agree on at least one other. The more internal cleavages that are allowed to surface, the more likely it is that any two people will be able to find some disputed issue on which they can agree despite their disagreements on other issues.

These crosscutting cleavages have several beneficial effects. First, they help to keep the society from dividing sharply over a single issue. Where no single divide exists and there are many things that many people agree on, it is easier for a leader to keep the group itself from splitting apart. Furthermore, the disagreements that do erupt will be less intense, because people will be less likely to act with extreme hostility toward people they disagree with on one issue if they agree with them on other issues. These crosscutting cleavages also provide a foundation for developing compromises. Facing multiple issues, a person or group can trade support on one issue for someone else's acquiescence on another. The more issues there are in play, the more opportunities there are for trade-offs, and the lower intensity of those conflicts also helps because it is easier to make concessions over smaller, less divisive issues.

Moreover, frequent small conflicts within a group can actually become a unifying force, as they tend to facilitate the resolution of underlying causes of disagreement. One of the reasons the safety-valve principle works in a social context is that small conflicts over small issues often leave those small issues at least partially resolved. This incremental resolution of small issues can keep them from growing into large ones, which leads to a consequence of group conflict that was addressed explicitly by neither Coser nor Simmel but is nonetheless important to the study of politics. Intragroup conflict can enhance the legitimacy of the group. Conflict within a group can actually reinforce the group's structure and its leadership.

Conflict as a Source of Legitimacy

While legitimacy derives from many sources, conflict is one important factor in people's voluntary identification with a group. Conflict between groups strengthens group identity by helping to define who is *not* part of the group. It causes people to turn to the

group for security and makes them more willing to accept direction from the leader voluntarily. But even conflict within a group can enhance the legitimacy of the group and its structures. Successfully resolving a conflict within the structures of the group enhances both the members' confidence in the group and their willingness to accept its structures voluntarily. This experience enhances the legitimacy of the group and its leaders. The more often this process occurs, the more it enhances the legitimacy of the group and its leaders.

Think about this phenomenon in terms of high-profile court cases, especially those in which the verdict makes you just shake your head and wonder what planet the judge or the jury were really on. Think of the bizarre criminal cases in which juries have failed to convict a rich or powerful person who is obviously guilty. Such cases erode confidence in the judicial system. They suggest that something is not right, that something has to be fixed, and they reduce your willingness to voluntarily accept the courts as a means of performing certain social functions. One ridiculous verdict may not cause you to believe that we need to scrap the entire judicial system, but it certainly does not help. Alternatively, court cases that come out the way you think they should tend to enhance your belief that the courts are doing their job. These cases increase the judicial system's legitimacy and reconfirm that the courts are an acceptable means to resolve conflict. The more legitimate a government structure, the less force will be needed to convince you to accept it and the rules or laws associated with it.

A skilled national leader understands and even exploits these potential benefits by manipulating and controlling conflict within the country. This concept can be extended so far that such a leader might actually promote or even create conflict so that the government can resolve it and thus establish or increase its legitimacy. Think about how countless leaders have effectively manipulated ethnic tensions, religious differences, and fear of crime first to promote conflict and then to find and implement a "solution" that enhances their legitimacy. Think about how effectively the government in *Nineteen Eighty-Four* magnifies the threat posed by Emmanuel Goldstein and the Brotherhood.

Another extreme example can be found in *The Prince,* in which Machiavelli relates the story of a duke who conquered a territory and then tried to establish his legitimate rule. Finding the place in disarray and plagued by theft, disputes, and violence, he hired the cruelest governor he could find to establish order and discipline—which that person brutally, maliciously, and promptly did. By this means, the duke had created a new conflict in the territory. The people now hated their governor. So the duke blamed the violent excess on the governor, had him killed, and used his body parts to decorate the public square. Thus, creating a conflict so that he could resolve it helped the duke win the support of the people. He manipulated group dynamics to achieve legitimacy. How's that for ending the chapter with a bang?

KEY TERMS

atomization / 75

crosscutting cleavages / 87

legitimacy / 81

panopticon / 70

peer policing / 75

preference falsification / 78

revolution / 74

safety valve / 86

self-policing / 72

CHAPTER SUMMARY

To understand the reasons governments do what they do, it is critical to appreciate the role of leadership interests. This perspective also provides a foundation for exploring how leaders and governments maintain control of those they govern. Whenever we seek to understand the complexities of politics, it always pays to begin by asking, "Who benefits?" and "How?" These questions apply regardless of the type of government under scrutiny. You may have no problem accepting this point when considering other countries, but it is equally appropriate to ask these questions of your own country. Even those who believe that governments seek to promote the social welfare must come to terms with this reality. It is also essential to appreciate the role that group conflict can play for groups (including governments) and their leaders. Students should learn two very important lessons from this chapter. First, people want to become leaders because holding the leadership position or being part of the elite group that controls the leadership position provides tremendous individual benefits. Second, while you should plan plenty of family time with children, it is a good idea to keep your progeny away from pressure cookers.

STUDY QUESTIONS AND EXERCISES

1. What is the principle behind the panopticon, and how do leaders use this means to control behavior?

2. What are atomization, peer policing, and preference falsification? How do leaders use these techniques to prevent revolutionary groups from forming?

3. What are the long-term risks to a leader who relies too much on force?

4. How can conflict within a group serve a beneficial function for the group and its leader?

5. In this chapter, I argue that to understand a confusing aspect of politics, one should ask, "Who benefits?" and "How do they benefit?" Apply this method while reading an article about politics in the newspaper or watching a report about politics on television. Does asking these questions help? Why or why not?

http://library.queensu.ca/ojs/index.php/surveillance-and-society/index. *Surveillance & Society* is an online journal dedicated to surveillance studies.

www.scrappleface.com. ScrappleFace is a site that pokes fun at the news.

www.ucl.ac.uk/Bentham-Project. University College London's Bentham Project offers information about Jeremy Bentham and the Bentham Project, including the Panopticon.

www.bbc.co.uk/history/historic_figures/orwell_george.shtml. The BBC's George Orwell page offers information about George Orwell and other links.

www.michel-foucault.com. This site is one of many dedicated to Foucault and his writings.

Government's Role in the Economy

The Offer You Can't Refuse

While idealists are likely to agree with the long-running credit card commercial and argue that there are some things that money just can't buy, realists are apt to respond that a trip to Vegas or a quick search of eBay will conclusively demonstrate that the list of things money can't buy must **be a very short one.** Realists tend to agree with the stereotypical Mafia don who appears in practically every gangster movie ever made to declare, "Every man has his price."

Idealists, however, prefer to believe the television commercial. They would like to emphasize the things you cannot buy, pointing to religious figures such as Mother Teresa and others who have eschewed wealth to follow a higher path. A lot of popular fiction adopts this idealist perspective, portraying money either as the source of evil or as a distraction from the things of true importance. Money convinces good cops to go bad, drives the runaway to commit desperate acts, and is at least part of every villain's passion. Idealism in fiction tells us that nobler motivations, such as the pursuit of justice or the bravery to withstand life-threatening pyrotechnics to perform a daring rescue, are the hallmarks of heroism. Heroes, it would seem, are never driven by greed. Remember the first *Star Wars* movie—the one actually called *Star Wars*? Han Solo doesn't truly become a hero until he drops his desire for the bounty money and joins the cause of the rebels. In the *National Treasure*[1] movies, Ben Gates is so heroically motivated by the quest that he gives the museums of the world almost all of the treasure he has risked his life to find. In *Zoolander*[2] the Evil Mugatu is driven by greed, trying to assassinate the Malaysian prime minister to keep his sweatshops working. In contrast, Derek Zoolander and Hansel are driven primarily by stupidity and ignorance, which may not be exactly heroic but is also not motivated

by money. In *Iron Man,*[3] Tony Stark ends up fighting the greed of his own corporation. In *Casino Royale*[4] and *Quantum of Solace*[5] the villains are all about chasing wealth while our flawed but still heroic James Bond is all about honor, revenge, and Photoshopped leggy women. Greed is never heroic. Of course, the realist counterargument points out that in real life, the lead actor usually demands about $22.6 million plus a percentage of the box office to portray a "selfless" hero, but still, we are talking fiction here.

Money may not actually make the world go 'round—the physics professor I occasionally eat lunch with insists that it is the residual angular momentum from the formation of the solar system that spins us through day and night. That one professor's "scientific" fantasy aside, it should be clear that the vast majority of people believe that money is a central part of life, and, consequently, it is an important political concern. I might even go so far as to say that economics, albeit in a rudimentary form, is the reason humans created government in the first place. In my story of the formation of the first government, caveman Bob pursues collective security so that he can become a farmer. Farming is, in essence, the most primitive form of investment. Bob gives up something of value—the grain he scatters on the muddy ground and his labor—with the expectation that he will obtain greater benefit in the future. When the barbarians come out of the hills to steal his first crop, however, Bob discovers that even this elementary economic investment is unworkable in a state of anarchy.

Bob needs a way to protect his investment. He needs the collective security of the village so that he can farm and reap the rewards of his effort. In a word, Bob needs government. Similarly, Gilligan, the geeky kid on the island, needs a bully's protection to employ his labor effectively. Government is intimately tied to economics, if only because people must have collective security to engage in even the most rudimentary of economic enterprises. The connection between economics and government is obvious in its simplicity, but it is actually a rich, dynamic relationship filled with subtlety and, sometimes, mystery. It's not exactly blockbuster film material, but it is far more interesting than most intro to macroeconomics textbooks. And it is profoundly political. We live in an age in which most people hold the government responsible for maintaining and improving the economy, yet the validity of that expectation is cast into doubt by the complexities of economic systems. This is compounded by many people's lack of understanding of the actual role of government in economics.

Suppose you have landed a job at the local North Korean chain restaurant, Glorious Leader's Bountiful Carcass Pucks of Eternal Wonderfulness. If you take a careful look at the pitiful paycheck you get for the countless hours spent standing in front of a lava-hot slab of iron flipping said carcass pucks with a Chinese-army-surplus spatula, you will realize that the government's role in economics goes far beyond providing the collective security needed for investment. Despite the official poster hanging in the back room, the one with the bright red numbers indicating the supposed minimum wage, the

government works very hard to guarantee that you never actually see that amount of money. In the United States there are federal taxes, state taxes, and various local taxes. But who is that FICA guy, and why does he get some of the money?[*]

The government is tied to the economy in other ways as well. For example, before you were allowed to start your career flipping carcass pucks, the state government probably forced you to get a certificate or read a pamphlet from some kind of hand-washing school. There is probably at least one government health inspector who comes by, from time to time, to pick up the unmarked envelope from the manager and to make sure that all employees are genuflecting toward the health code poster, wearing their funky hairnets, and washing their hands *after*[†] using the restroom and all that. Clearly the government is concerned with more than just providing the security needed for investment. It will also get involved when the assistant manager inevitably spills his strong "coffee" into the deep fryer, setting off a massive alcohol explosion. Not only will the government make sure that the corporate office pays your hospital bills, but it will also give the assistant manager disability checks while he trains at home to become a certified televangelist.

Sometimes the government's involvement in the economy is very clear. At other times it occurs in ways that are taken for granted or not easily noticed—often because it is hidden under a blizzard of infuriating little details. In *A Tree Grows in Brooklyn,* a film based on Betty Smith's novel of the same name,[6] the contemporary role of government is conspicuous by its absence. The book is filled with all kinds of literary stuff, and the film has a bunch of social commentary that high school teachers like to inflict on students, but poverty is at the heart of the story, and the harshness of that poverty is amplified a thousandfold by the absence of social or governmental intervention. Where are the food stamps to keep the family fed? Why must the next-door neighbor, the mother of a sick girl, worry about the cost of burials? Where are Johnny's unemployment checks? How can Francie be pulled out of school to work at her young age? Why must Katie give birth in her apartment? Where are the lawyers to recoup the grandmother's money when she gets swindled? Today, in most, if not all, developed countries, it would be shocking if no governmental mechanisms were in place for intervening in or mitigating all of these problems of living in poverty, but you may seldom think of these mechanisms as part of the government's role in the economy.

To get at some of the most basic yet often unnoticed elements of government involvement in the economy, I introduce in this chapter two prominent approaches to engaging government in the process of producing wealth: **socialism** and **capitalism.** As in other parts of this book, my effort to get at the basics leaves out much of the nuance and complexity of the ideas. I try to note some of the more significant simplifications, but let

---

[*]Just in case you really must know, FICA is short for Federal Insurance Contributions Act. The FICA deduction on your paycheck is the payroll tax that the government says it collects to pay for Social Security and Medicare. I can neither confirm nor deny the rumor that it is used to fund global conspiracies involving stealth helicopters and Canadian commandos wearing bear suits.

[†]If you are really supposed to wash your hands *after* using the restroom, why isn't the sink outside the restroom?

me reiterate that it is important to remember that I am cutting these theories down to the bare bones. The real world is far more complex, and it is likely that as you progress in your college career, or rise to command one of the Starfleet battle cruisers that drive the evil alien squids from the cosmos, you will encounter far more sophisticated applications of these arguments and theories. Before I get to these two economic systems, however, I'm going to force you to first consider some of the individual-level interactions that are kind of sort of a little bit nearly important.

THE TRAGEDY OF THE COMMONS

When Bob brings his group of future farmers together to engage in the collective pursuit of security, that first glimmer of governed society enables the earliest, most primitive manifestation of economy: agriculture. The transition to farming and village life also creates challenges that none of the grunting brutes could ever have imagined. Interestingly, these challenges originate from the very cooperation that makes government possible. Working together for the collective goal of security requires the development of community resources to be shared by several, or sometimes all, of the people in the village. For example, there may be a common well for water, a public garbage dump, a rugby pitch, or a communal meadow for grazing sheep. The exploitation of these shared resources creates a problem that is commonly known in academic circles as **the tragedy of the commons,** in which the rational choices of individuals collide with the needs or interests of the larger community. This is tragedy in a fatalistic kind of way,* a situation in which the horrible becomes inevitable. In a fatalistic tragedy, the protagonists cannot avoid the disastrous outcome even when they are aware that it lurks in their future. In this sense, the story of Sid and Nancy was also tragic: how predictable and unavoidable is the gruesome death of a punk-rock legend's junkie girlfriend? In contrast to either the classic Greek or the punk version of tragedy, the tragedy of the commons can be avoided, but not by individuals. In fact, according to the dynamics of the tragedy of the commons, people who realize that they are destroying a common resource through overexploitation will actually be driven to make the problem worse by exploiting the commons even more intensely.

The story of the tragedy of the commons can be told in many different ways. In fact, it is so important that I am going to tell you the story three times. Since I have been working the whole caveman-turned-farmer Bob thing the way a pop radio station plays a number one single until it induces nausea, I am going to keep at it. Thus, I begin with a brief story about farmers sharing grazing land.

Grazing Sheep and the Temptation to Cheat

After losing several limbs in a poorly considered effort to domesticate polar bears, Bob's descendants try raising sheep instead. Not only does this significantly reduce the

---

*This inevitable doom was the whole point of the Oedipus sleeping-with-your-mother-and-killing-your-father thing.

problem of herders getting eaten,* but also the project itself is far more successful. A nice round number of farmers—say, ten—come to share a large field for wintering their flocks. Through trial and error, they discover that if they limit themselves to the mathematically convenient one hundred sheep, they can use the field throughout the winter while maintaining just enough grass to support one hundred sheep through the next year's winter. If they put more than one hundred out there for the winter, the sheep will overgraze the field, eating not only the blades of grass but also the precious roots. It goes without saying that overgrazing ruins the pastoral view of the emerald-green field and devastates a prehistoric village's property values, but it also reduces the field's capacity to support sheep. So, if you put one hundred and ten sheep out there one winter, come next year, the field will grow only enough grass to support maybe eighty sheep through the winter months.

In this field, the villagers have a shared resource that is very fragile. If the sheep farmers overexploit it now, they will destroy its future value and its future ability to support livestock production. The obvious solution is for them to agree to share the field equally. Each of the ten farmers keeps only his or her ten best sheep through the winter and slaughters the rest. This would preserve the productivity of the field forever. Unfortunately, this idealistic solution faces a *big* obstacle. Each farmer faces an overwhelming temptation to increase the size of his or her flock by keeping an extra sheep alive through the winter. That extra sheep will give the farmer 10 percent more food, wool, and wealth the following fall. After all, what would be the harm of just one more little, tiny, cute sheep out on that field? There are sixty million sheep in New Zealand and it is not that big a country, so what could be the harm in putting just one more on a field?

It would also be pretty easy to get away with putting that one extra sheep out on the field. As it turns out, sheep have actually evolved so that they are hard to count—they blend together into a big fuzzy mass that mills about.† Since it is unlikely that anyone will notice, it is only a matter of time before one of the farmers does choose to add an extra sheep to the winter flock. Whether the cause is greed or desperation, somewhere along the line one farmer's personal wants or needs will outweigh his or her commitment to the interests of the community.

It is important to realize that the fact that the resource is shared plays a big role in making the situation tragic. If only one farmer owns and uses the field, the costs and benefits of overexploitation are balanced. The lone farmer obtains the full benefit of the extra sheep, but in subsequent years, the lone farmer also bears the full cost of the damage this extra sheep causes to the field. The individual farmer pays all the costs in reduced grazing

---

*Although, as we all learned in Jonathan King's 2006 hard-hitting documentary tour de force *Black Sheep,* raising sheep does not completely eliminate the problem of getting eaten by your livestock.

†For the wild ancestors of sheep, this increased the chance of survival by making it hard for predators to separate individuals from the flock. On the communal field, however, it makes it extremely difficult to figure out exactly how many of the cute little buggers are out there.

Government's Role In the Economy

capacity next winter for overexploitation of the field this winter. In contrast, when several people use the field, only the individual who cheats gets the benefit, while all of the shepherds share the costs associated with the damaged field. Even though the group of ten shepherds, as a whole, would be far better off if no one cheated, an individual sheep wrangler benefits from cheating by getting all the gain while suffering only a tenth of the cost. In other words, the benefits and the costs of that extra sheep are skewed in a way that motivates people to overexploit the resource. As the group sharing the resource increases beyond a handful of people, the disparity in benefits versus costs becomes more and more extreme, and it becomes more difficult to spot cheaters. As a result, at some point, cheating becomes inevitable.

At this point, it will be very tempting, particularly for you idealists out there, to try to play the **enlightened self-interest** card. Even invertebrates like SpongeBob SquarePants and Patrick Star can see that it is in everyone's best interest to preserve the commons for everyone. Surely, the farmers will be motivated by this enlightened self-interest to resist the short-term temptation to cheat to ensure that they and their descendants will benefit from the long-term continued value of the field. Unfortunately, this argument overlooks the fact that people's calculations are not based solely on their own behavior. When sharing a common resource, individuals have choices that are intertwined with the choices and actions of others who use the resource. Enlightened self-interest cannot prevent the tragedy of the commons because even when a person realizes that it is in everyone's best interest to preserve the shared resource, as soon as that person considers it likely that others will cheat, he or she is driven to overexploit the commons anyway. The logic behind this unenlightened behavior* becomes clear in my second tragic example, the stag hunt.

The Stag Hunt and Social Choice

The **stag hunt** is an old and commonly used parable that nicely demonstrates how the interdependence of actions and choices affects collective efforts to attain a goal, such as the preservation of the commons. Yes, I could have come up with my own story, but I decided to use this one, which illustrates the point so well, and reduce my workload enough to spend an afternoon sailing instead of writing. Call it my own personal form of enlightened self-interest.

For the benefit of the cinematically challenged reader who has not seen the black-and-white version of *Robin Hood,* a stag is a big deer with enough antlers to hold the hats of an entire baseball team.[7] Considered to be not only tasty but also a bit smarter than your average herbivore, the stag presented a substantial challenge to the spears and rocks that hungry human hunters relied on before the invention of bazookas. Hunting a stag required a collective effort—the hunters would surround the animal and slowly close in by drawing the circle tighter and tighter until they were close enough to attack effectively.

---

*I'm not sure if unenlightened behavior is dark or heavy.

It is the individual hunters' choices that are illustrative. Let us say that Bob's father, Bah, is one of the hunters. Holding his spear at the ready, Bah carefully keeps his place in the shrinking circle that surrounds the stag. Because Bah and his family have not eaten for a few days, the wife and kids are understandably a bit cranky, and Bah desperately needs to bring home something to eat. As the hunters close in on the stag, Bah notices that their slowly constricting circle has also been driving rabbits toward its center, and one of the floppy-eared rodents has trapped itself in a dead-end crevice between two large boulders. Bah has a choice. If he and all the other hunters stay in the circle, they have a 75 percent chance of killing the stag, which will feed everyone for two days—good odds, but by no means certain. Meanwhile, that rabbit is right there, with no way out. Bah can get it for certain—a 100 percent chance—but it will feed only his family, and it will feed them for only one day.

Assuming that Bah can do some quick calculations, he may figure out that a 75 percent chance of eating for two days is a better overall expectation of personal benefit (1.5 total meals of tasty stag) than the certainty of eating for one day (one total meal of rabbit, which happens to be a rodent, and rodents are icky). Furthermore, if you assume that Bah is not generally a jerk and that he cares about the other hunters, there is more reason to expect that he will pass up the rabbit. If Bah breaks from the circle, the stag will escape through the gap he leaves, and everyone will lose two days' worth of food. Thus, you expect the morally and socially upstanding Bah to walk past the rabbit.

It's not that simple, however. The stag hunt is a collective effort, therefore Bah must also consider the others hunters' choices and how those decisions will affect the outcome of the hunt. Every single hunter in the circle must pass up any and all of the rabbits he finds for the group to collectively get the stag. Thus, Bah must also consider the possibility that someone else will be tempted to break from the circle and take a rabbit. If Bah has any reason to doubt the commitment of any of the other hunters, then he must conclude that the stag will be lost. If it takes twenty hunters to kill the stag, how many of them will stumble across a rabbit? What are the odds that every single one will pass up the temptation of a rabbit? "Larry has always been a selfish and flatulent snarker, so he'll take the rabbit," thinks Bah. "If not Larry, then Moe or Shemp will do it."* As soon as Bah knows, or even just believes, that someone else will take the rabbit, then he has no choice but to conclude that the chance of successfully getting the stag is zero.

Thus, if Bah expects that someone else in the circle will take a rabbit, his personal calculation changes to one meal if he takes the rabbit and zero meals if he stays in the circle. Once he believes that there is no chance the group will succeed in the stag hunt, then Bah's *only rational choice* is to defect and take the rabbit. He realizes the impact of his choice, but he will choose to take the rabbit anyway out of fear that someone else will

---

*It goes without saying that Curly never would defect.

betray the group and leave him with nothing. Ironically, Bah causes the very failure that he fears. The social choice dynamic illustrated by the stag hunt is what drives even the enlightened to overexploit the commons. This dynamic is exacerbated by the economic realities of the situation, and my third example of the tragedy of the commons both illustrates this point and connects the ideas to current, real-world examples.

From Farming to Fishing

We seldom see shepherds sharing a field anymore, but fish stocks represent a good modern-day example of the tragedy of the commons. Let's return to Bob and his village, but fast-forward a few millennia. When that village grows into a town, complete with a Glorious Leader's Bountiful Carcass Pucks of Eternal Wonderfulness franchise and a Walmart, Bob's distant descendant Roberta, who is the assistant chief fry cook at the aforementioned Glorious Leader's Bountiful Carcass Pucks of Eternal Wonderfulness, is going to get yelled at for not wearing her hairnet. At some point, while this grill maestro is still contemplating the exact word to best express the physiology of where she would like to suggest that her boss can put that hairnet, it dawns on her that nets can also serve other purposes. Sooner or later she notices the bay into which the town's little stream empties, and it then occurs to her that she could use a bigger version of the hairnet to catch fish. After convincing an investment banker that people will pay some serious money for fish, she weaves a few nets, buys her cousin's bass boat, and hits the jackpot. As it turns out, the bay is full of slimy, flopping gold, which she hauls in and sells to a whole town full of people tired of eating nothing but rice, lamb chops, and those sorry excuses for hamburgers she's been flipping. People crowd around to buy every fish she can bring in to the dock. They even bid against each other for the best ones. In just a few weeks, her loan is repaid and our former fry cook is flipping money into her bank account.

As you might expect, other fry cooks notice Roberta's success and rush to copy her. Soon, bankers are lending money, factories are weaving nets, and shipyards are building boats—fishing is, like, so totally the rage. However, as everyone sails out to exploit the bay full of fish (a shared resource), the tragedy of the commons rears its ugly head. As long as the bay is not overfished, the fish that are not caught have a chance to go to their senior proms, accidentally reproduce in the backs of old minivans, and continue to supply the town. But if the fishers exploit the bay beyond the level at which the fish can reproduce fast enough to sustain the supply, this potentially limitless commons will be damaged or destroyed. The fish will become scarce or even disappear.

In the case of the sheep and the field shared by a few farmers, critical readers may be able to point out some relatively simple solutions to avert the tragedy of the commons. This real-world example, however, is far less tractable. The effects of fixed costs and the basic macroeconomics of supply and demand push the situation from difficult to tragic. As more masters of the sea bring fish to the docks, the supply of fish offered for sale increases. But

there is a limit to the amount of fish that the people of a small town will demand at the high price they were paying when only one boat was dragging a net around. Therefore, for the additional fish that are now coming in to the docks to be sold, the price charged per fish must come down. This law of supply and demand is the most basic idea of macroeconomics: as supply goes up, the price goes down, and vice versa.

In addition to problems caused by the falling price per fish, the members of the new generation of fish extraction engineers also have fixed costs—in this example, they have bank loans for boats and nets that must be paid off. In real life, fixed costs might also include the expenses of sustaining a basic living (rent, food, clothing) as well as the costs in fuel, maintenance, and supplies needed to actually go out and fish. As the price of fish drops because of the increase in supply, the fish extraction engineers are driven to catch and sell more fish to meet their fixed costs. While Roberta used to make ends meet by selling a hundred fish at ten cents each, now she must sell two hundred fish at five cents each to pay those same bills. Consequently, she is driven to catch more fish just to break even. Perversely, this need to cover fixed costs further drives supply in the market up and drives the price down, which, in turn, further increases the number of fish that have to be sold to meet those fixed costs. Once again, the market supply increases, the price drops, and so on.

It seems that the economics involved always drive the fishing fleet to increase the exploitation of the bay. When the price of fish is high, greed drives individuals to catch more fish. When the price is low, the need to meet fixed costs drives individuals to catch more fish. However, the limited nature of the common resource makes this dynamic even more pronounced. As the bay is overexploited, fish become scarce, and it gets harder and harder to catch the squirmy little buggers. Scarcity reduces supply, which drives prices up, and the renewed potential for making money motivates individual fishers to catch more of the ever-decreasing supply of fish.

This example also demonstrates that appeals to enlightened self-interest and awareness of the tragedy of the commons are not enough to save a shared resource. Everyone knows how to preserve the fish in the bay—reduce the level of exploitation. But again, it's not that simple. Like the successful stag hunt, the preservation of the commons works only if *absolutely everyone* cooperates. Everyone will cooperate only if they all agree that preservation is the right thing to do *and* if they all believe that absolutely everyone else will cooperate as well. An individual's decision not to fish will have little or no effect on the fish supply if others do not also restrict their fishing; if the fish do not go into your net, they will go into someone else's. As long as someone else is willing to go out and scour the bay, the commons will be ruined regardless of individual efforts to try to preserve it. The only rational choice, therefore, is to make as much money as you can, while you still can, and try to stash some in the bank for the day when the supply of fish runs out.

Escaping the Tragedy of the Commons

There are various solutions for the tragedy of the commons as laid out in these simplified examples, but if we consider them carefully, we see that they all involve collective actions. All the solutions require getting everyone to act in a certain way, such as limiting their fishing. Attaining universal compliance requires that someone regulate, monitor, and police those exploiting the commons. In the beginning,* I argued that government is all about collective action. It is about forming a group to pursue goals that cannot be attained spontaneously and would be impossible for any one individual to realize. The most fundamental of these goals is the collective pursuit of security, but once you go to the trouble of creating a group to establish a governed environment, it makes sense to use that same mechanism to pursue other collective goals that might arise.

One such goal is the preservation of a common resource. And since it makes sense for individuals to protect the commons only if they believe that all others will do so as well, you use government, through policing and the enforcement of laws, to make it rational for everyone to participate in the collective activity. This not only raises the potential cost of defecting from the collective effort but also assures everyone that no one else will defect, thereby lowering the motivation to cheat. Government regulation is what makes it possible to escape the tragedy of the commons. Those who graze sheep, hunt stags, or trawl for fish will be far less likely to make the choice that harms others—overexploiting the shared resource—if they must add the fear of punishment to their cost-benefit calculus.

The need to regulate the use of the commons represents a basic and continuing economic role for government. Society uses government to control some of the **means of production**—the mechanisms for transforming labor into wealth—and to escape the tragedy of the commons. Implicit in all our simplified examples of that problem, and also in the possible solutions you might imagine, are the dynamics of capitalism and socialism, which, at a basic level, can be thought of as two different answers to the question of who should control the means of production: individuals or society.

KARL MARX—STUDENT OF CAPITALISM?

Any reasonable exploration of the government's role in the economy must engage the concepts of capitalism and socialism. As a result, the discussion must examine the theories and ideas of **Karl Marx** (1818–1883).[8] Marx focused on economics as the primary element of politics, and nearly every political scientist identifies him as one of the Alpha Quadrant's most influential humanoid political theorists. Unfortunately, bringing him into the discussion always presents a challenge. Even though few, if any, of today's students know the Cold War as anything more than a historical term, mentioning the name of Karl Marx can still

---

*The beginning of this book, not the universe.

KARL MARX

Team: **Raging Proletariat**

Position: **Long On**

Status: **Infectious Nosferatu**

Karl Marx (1818–eternity) is not the monster under the bed. However, he may very well be a vampire. Even though he supposedly died in 1883, mobs with torches, credit cards, and wooden stakes are still running around the countryside chasing after him and the people he's bitten with his evil theories. Seems a bit extreme to me, but I don't read those vampire books that teenage girls really like, so what do I really know about vampires?

In addition to the very scary beard, there were plenty of reasons Marx raised the hackles of his contemporaries. The most important of those reasons, however, was probably embodied in the idea of *praxis,* which can be roughly thought of as a commitment not just to pursuing knowledge but to putting that knowledge into committed action. Thus, Marx wasn't just a theorist who criticized capitalism and argued that the contradictions inherent in its dynamics would cause a revolt against it and the governments that were dependent on it, he was a radical who was trying to change the world by putting those theories into action. In fact, it would be fair to say that he was hell-bent on changing the world.

Marx was active in socialist meetings. He published articles and essays critical of the very existence of governments. He edited several publications and managed to get pretty much all of the papers and journals he worked for banned or shut down because of what he printed. He set up the Communist Correspondence Committee to help link socialist leaders across Europe, and then he followed that up with the Communist League. The league's stated purpose was to overthrow pretty much everything capitalistic and create a society without private property. That was not real popular with the people who had stuff and liked having stuff. Marx was so unpopular with people who liked their stuff that he was chased out of Prussia, France, Belgium, and then France again. Seriously, what do you have to do to get chased out of Belgium?

provoke a response befitting a guy wielding a bloody chainsaw and wearing a mask sewn from human skin. Even before Marx became the namesake and poster child for the Soviet bloc dictatorships of the Cold War, his criticisms of the capitalist mode of production and his belief that meaningful theory must be combined with political action provoked a visceral reaction from economic, social, and governmental elites in the industrially developed world. Today, although the reaction to Marx may not be as passionate as it once was, his reception remains less than friendly.

For historical, economic, and cultural reasons, the negative reaction to Marx has been particularly intense in the United States and Canada, where most students learn to equate him with the mutant that scares the monster under the bed. He is the lurking threat to the capitalist society that they treasure, and it is difficult for them to engage his ideas and theories in a constructive manner. In reality, however, Karl Marx probably does not warrant such antipathy. A century of intense international politics, along with numerous domestic political struggles over economics and government, has created a mythology around Marx. He is deified by one side, demonized by the other, and distorted by both.

As a starting point, it is important for students to disassociate Marx's ideas from what the former Soviet Union, East Germany, China, North Korea, Rush Limbaugh, Newt Gingrich, and Sean Hannity label or have labeled Marxism. It is pretty safe to say that if Marx could see the oppression, brutality, and misery inflicted by so-called Marxist governments, or the way Glenn Beck uses the term *socialist,* he would roll over in his grave. In fact, it is all but certain that anyone using the word *socialism* or *socialist* on TV in the United States has absolutely no understanding of what the word actually means. Marx's version of socialism differed greatly from the anti-imperialist, party-driven, dictatorial variants that Vladimir Ilich Lenin (1870–1924), Joseph Stalin (1879–1953), Mao Zedong (1893–1976), Dick Cheney (1941–2009),* and others have used to justify placing strangleholds on their countries. Even when he was alive, Marx was quick to announce, "I am not a Marxist." Instead, among the many labels that could reasonably be applied to Marx, an important one is **humanist**—an idealist who is interested in and motivated by concern for the broader human condition and the quality of people's lives—although, ironically, that latter concern did not extend to his own family's hunger and misery. To understand how that altruistic attitude could fit with someone who criticized capitalism and advocated revolution to eliminate it, we must consider the social, historical, and economic context in which Marx was writing.

The Adolescence of Capitalism

Within his lifetime, Marx witnessed a critical historical period in the transformation of the global economy from the vestiges of what you might call a peasant or feudal system to the triumphant early forms of industrial capitalism.† There are some very distinct and important differences between these economic systems. One in particular is the relationship between those who perform labor and those who control the mechanisms for transforming labor into wealth. In the feudal system, most agricultural production occurred within some sort of peasant/landowner context. The landlord controlled and owned the land—and, in some cases, owned the peasants—and the peasants were little more than subsistence farmers. It is interesting that when most of us imagine living back in feudal times, we are likely to picture ourselves as lords, ladies, dukes, or duchesses, but the sober reality is that the vast majority of us would have been serfs. Picture

---

*Contrary to popular belief, Dick Cheney is not the reincarnation of Margaret Thatcher. He's actually a Cylon who was redownloaded and upgraded to an MS Vista 1.1 Beta operating system in 2009. It is also worth noting that Bill Gates attributes the failure of MS Vista to Dick's need for an operating system that supports a great deal of ancient and outdated legacy code.

†Although I put a lot of faith in gross oversimplifications, this one is more than a bit tricky. First, I should probably use the proper technical terms and discuss *modes of production,* which are the social and economic structures that transform labor into wealth. Second, I should probably be more specific about what kind of capitalist system I am talking about. I use early *industrial capitalism* as the example, but, depending on what country you use as a model, it could easily be argued that there were several transitional capitalist systems between feudalism and industrial capitalism, such as *mercantilism.* Finally, I should probably be clear that I am not discussing a specific historical example—rather, I'm generalizing to get the concept across. The working class in France reacted most forcefully to the capitalist changes and was really the first to act as a unified political force, but England provides a better example of the dynamic of give-and-take driving the evolution of a mixed capitalist and socialist system.

yourself not as a knight in King Arthur's court,[‡] but as a peasant living in filth and squalor, digging beets out of the mud with a stick, and using the mud to soothe the pain caused by festering open lesions.

Anyway, under **feudalism,** these peasants raised a diverse mixture of crops and live-stock on small plots within the landlord's estate. In turn, they were obligated to give a substantial percentage of their production to the landlord, who then converted it to wealth by selling or exchanging that modest surplus with others. It was an exploitative relationship that often bordered on slavery. However, one key aspect of this relationship was that the landlord and the peasant needed one another. Each brought something to the economic relationship that was valuable to the other, and each would find the other hard to replace.

The landowners were elites who seldom had any experience with the difficult and dirty essentials of farming. Lords were brought up to be knights, politicians, and scholars. They learned swordplay, Latin, philosophy, peasantry exploitation dynamics, and religion. By the standards of the time, they were highly educated, but as far as actually working the land, getting crops to grow in the dirt, or taking care of sheep out in the field, they were clueless. Farming was dirty, cold, and wet. It was peasant work that was beneath the dignity of the lords. As a result, the lords needed the peasants, who had the knowledge and the skills to work the land.

The result of this mutual dependence was something of a contract between the land-lords and the peasants. Sometimes it was codified in law, but more often it was just a matter of tradition. Still, it was always understood that both peasants and lords needed each other and that both had responsibilities. Let me be clear—this was in no way a fair or equal relationship. The peasants were ruthlessly exploited by the landowners, who got as much as they could out of them and gave back as little as possible, but there was always a bottom line. Much as a farmer would take good care of a horse to ensure that it could pull the plow next week, the landlords wanted their peasants to survive long enough to be exploited next year.

After a long period of transition, the industrial capitalism that emerged was different. Capitalists used factories as the means of production, as the means to transform labor into wealth. Though far more complex in reality, the concept of industrial capitalism can be understood in terms of the factory assembly line.[*] On an assembly line, complicated tasks that used to take a great deal of skill are broken down into a series of small steps, steps so simple that any chimp you might grab off the street could perform each of them.

Adam Smith, in his *Wealth of Nations,* used the example of the manufacture of sewing pins to highlight the benefits of the division of labor, which is a key aspect of the dynamic of industrial capitalism.[9] When an individual blacksmith made pins, he had to take the

---

[‡]By the way, King Arthur, if he actually existed, lived a millennium earlier, circa 600 A.D.

[*]While it is helpful to think about early capitalism in this context, remember that the assembly line had not yet been invented when Marx was writing.

Government's Role In the Economy

metal, pull it out into long wires, cut each pin to length, sharpen one end, pound the head onto the other, and then count, package, and even sell the pins. In the course of making even this simple product, the blacksmith had to switch from task to task repeatedly, and the starting, stopping, setting things up, and starting again took up a great deal of time. Furthermore, pins were only one of thousands of items that a successful blacksmith had to have the skills and tools to make. In contrast, by focusing on a single product and breaking the process up into many little tasks performed by different people—as you would on an assembly line—the factory system made production far more efficient. Because each specific task took very little skill, the workers could be paid less. Since the waste of time and effort caused by switching between different steps in the process was eliminated, more pins could be produced with less work. Additional money was saved because tools for other blacksmith tasks were not needed, and six people making pins could produce pins ten times faster and twenty times cheaper than a single blacksmith could.

Marx later used the same example of pin manufacturing, recognizing the efficiencies of the division of labor, but also pointing out that by removing the need for skilled and knowledgeable laborers, this factory or industrial style of capitalism significantly altered the social and political relationships surrounding the transformation of labor into wealth. In particular, it drastically shifted the relationship between those who owned the means of production and those who labored. The blacksmith had to acquire a tremendous array of skills and knowledge to create hundreds of products. This experience and expertise had value. The limited number of blacksmiths could charge good money for the products of those skills. However, a factory owner who focused on a single product and set up the machines properly could grab anything genetically close to a human off the street and teach it to perform a single, simple task—say, cutting the wire: snip, snip, snip—all day long. These laborers were not highly skilled artisans; they were simply replicable cogs in the productive machinery. And since each one could easily be replaced, why would the factory owner care for or be willing to provide for a person who broke his leg? Replacing him was a matter of grabbing a new primate off the street and giving him a few minutes of training. In other words, the mutual dependence that underpinned the implicit feudal contract between the landowner and the peasant did not carry over to the factories. The fact that any factory worker was easily replaceable with anyone else was a critical change in the owner-worker relationship, and that was one of the key things that Marx saw as a cause of many of the detrimental effects of capitalism. When combined with the competitive foundations of capitalism, the effect of this change on those who labored was devastating.

Competition as the Driving Force in Capitalism

The driving force in capitalism is the competition between capitalists. This is also the source of the system's greatest value: its efficiency. The capitalist who can make more with less can undersell the competition, capture market share, make more money, and, most important,

THINKER IN BOXES

ADAM SMITH

Team: **Capitalist Pigdogs**

Position: **Forward Short Leg**

Status: **Invisible**

Adam Smith (1723–1790) was not an angel sent down from capitalists in heaven. He was Scottish. He earned a lifelong pension in just a couple of years by tutoring some duke or lord, so he might actually have been some kind of deity befitting a capitalist pantheon, but he wasn't an angel. He was Scottish.

It's Adam Smith's invisible hand, which does sound kind of godlike and supernatural, now that I think about it, that marks him as one of the great theorists so beloved by the disciples of capitalism. Smith argued that the rational self-interest of people interacting in a free marketplace is the key to prosperity. The basic idea is that a self-regulating free market naturally shifts toward an equilibrium of maximum efficiency. As long as the market is unfettered, the dynamics of supply and demand will cause prices of goods and services to fluctuate, rising with undersupply and falling with oversupply. Rational individuals will then respond to those changes . . . rationally. As price goes up, more people will work to supply the product or service, and as price goes down, some will shift to other products or services that offer higher returns. A similar, but inverted, logic applies to purchasers, and the combination is what Smith called the invisible hand of the market. The free market is self-regulating and self-optimizing.

Sound familiar?

Smith applied a similar logic to wages, saying that those occupations that are hard to learn, or that require difficult-to-obtain expertise, or are just crappy and gross will earn higher wages than the easy jobs that everyone wants. In this, he is credited with creating the idea of human capital. Smith also argued that the division of labor is a key to economic efficiency, and it is notable that Smith's example of sewing pins was considered to be such a good example and argument for the efficiency of the division of labor as a fundamental part of capitalism that Karl Marx addressed it directly in his analysis and criticism of capitalism.

In short, if you examine just about any of the ideas found in modern macroeconomics, you'll find that they pretty much all build on Smith's arguments.

survive. Inefficient factories lose money, and inefficient capitalists go bankrupt. Constant competition and the continual entry of new competitors into the system drive an endless quest for greater and greater efficiency. This is probably the biggest benefit and the best aspect of capitalism. However, there is a dark side, too.[*] Constant competition between capitalists, if left unrestrained, pushes capitalists to continually demand more for every dollar that they pay workers. This is certainly the case with pure capitalism, or **laissez-faire capitalism,** an economic system characterized by very little, if any, government involvement in the economy. Marx argued that this drive has dire consequences that make the collapse of capitalism inevitable.

Take, for example, the production of cloth from yarn. During the early decades of industrial capitalism, the textile manufacturing industry made some of the most substantial gains in productive efficiency and endured some of the fiercest competition. All factories could

---

[*]Insert your own Darth Vader joke here. NOW!

produce roughly the same products, leaving customers to choose among their goods on the basis of price. And the prices the factories had to charge their customers can be broken down into four basic elements:

Profit

Materials

Overhead

Wages

I list profit first because, as the aspiring business majors in my classes argue, it is the most important. It is what motivates investors to risk their existing wealth to create the means of production. It is the reason this publisher asked me to write this book. However, another reason I put it first is to make the point that profit is not optional. It is not something you could do away with if only people were not so greedy. An entrepreneur must anticipate a minimum level of profit for it to be rational for him or her to put money at risk to build the factory and engage in production. An investor must expect to make enough profit to exceed the benefit to be gained from an alternate use of the money, such as earning interest in a bank. The potential profit must be enough to cover the risk of bankruptcy and the loss of the investment. The riskier the capitalist enterprise, the greater the potential payoff has to be. The greater the chance that your dorm-room emu farm will go bankrupt, the greater the expected profit must be in order to convince you to risk your money, at least when you're sober.

The costs of raw materials and overhead are also fundamental components of the final price of the product. Overhead includes everything necessary to build and maintain the factory, and the price of each yard of cloth sold has to contribute a small amount of money to pay for the building, the machines, repairs and maintenance, heat, and all the other expenses of keeping the factory running. Finally, the price of each yard of cloth must cover the wages for the labor necessary to produce it.

Competition among capitalists affects all four of these elements: profit, materials, overhead, and wages. In essence, if one capitalist can find a way to reduce any one of them, the savings will enable him or her to sell the product for less than the competition. Given roughly equal products, rational consumers will choose to buy the cheaper product. The factory that can sell for less will remain profitable. The others will find it difficult if not impossible to sell at a higher price, and, without sales, they will not make any money. In extreme cases, the more efficient producer can drive other factories out of business. In this kind of competitive environment, the financial survival of the factory owner is at stake every minute of every day. So, how do capitalists respond to cost cutting by their competitors? By matching or exceeding the reduction in costs. This strategy is not a matter of choice; it is the law of survival in the capitalist jungle.

The competitive dynamic drives all the components of price down as far as they will go. Thus, in an effort to minimize the costs of raw materials, factories will buy in bulk, seek cheaper overseas suppliers, and sign long-term supply contracts. To keep overhead costs down, they will be tempted to put off or limit plant maintenance, to ignore costly safety measures or environmental protections, and to do everything possible to maximize the production from every machine and every foot of factory space. In the early days of capitalism factory owners began to run machines around the clock rather than leaving them idle for part of the day, and they squeezed more and more machines into the factory space in order to get the highest possible return on the money invested in maintaining that space. Heating was cut to the bare minimum necessary to keep the machines functioning, and extra expenditures for the comfort or safety of the workers were eliminated.

Marx noted the benefits of an economic system driven by specialization and competition. He clearly understood the tremendous gains in efficiency and productivity that industrial capitalism offered over a feudal or artisan-based system of production, but he argued that the ruthless competition to cut costs and reduce prices was so severe that it would inevitably destroy the very political, economic, and social system that made all that efficiency and productivity possible. In efforts to cut overhead, textile factory owners often packed weaving machines so close together that no adult could fit between them to maintain them or fix the inevitable jams, and so they hired young children to perform these tasks. Not only did the hours in the factories put a serious crimp in these kids' ability to indulge in juvenile pranks, pickup softball games, and the other joys of youth, it was also dangerous work. A lot of kids lost a lot of fingers unjamming weaving machinery. Adult workers were also put in danger by the absence of nets, railings, and all the other safety measures that might have raised the factories' overhead. As it turned out, it was often cheaper to grab a new worker off the street than it was to invest in safety precautions that might keep the existing laborers alive. There were clearly some negative consequences to ruthlessly squeezing overhead. According to Marx, however, the real problem with capitalism would begin when the factory owners started squeezing wages.

Remember that the average worker in our simplified caricature of a capitalist factory does not have any special or unique skill to offer the factory owner; anyone can perform each simple task. The worker's labor is a commodity, and just as they search for the cheapest sources of raw materials, factory owners will seek the cheapest sources of labor. In fact, because some of the basic tenets of capitalism were spreading into agricultural production, and farmland was rapidly being consolidated into large plots that could be more efficiently farmed for single crops, peasants were being driven off the estates in massive numbers. Consequently, at the time that Marx was writing there was a substantial surplus of labor, which enabled factory owners to push wages below what individuals needed to survive. Furthermore, the relentless drive to reduce costs led to innovations such as the use of machines that required fewer workers to operate them. This change reduced wages as part of the cost, and it also left more people unemployed and searching for work.

If you are tempted to confuse these conditions with tough economic conditions you might experience today in the developed Western world, think again. They are probably a far distance beyond what you consider harsh. The hard economic conditions of earlier periods of capitalism are much closer to those found in the sweatshops of the Third World, or in the setting of *A Tree Grows in Brooklyn,* in which the family eats stale bread, winces when a guest puts too much cream in his coffee, and collects rags to sell for a few extra pennies. Marx's contemporary Charles Dickens offers an even more accurate picture: the lives of the poor characters presented in *Great Expectations, Oliver Twist,* and his other novels truly reflect the bleak urban landscape faced by workers under early capitalism.[10] In these grim conditions, people are desperate to find whatever employment they can.

When workers gather at the gates of the factory to plead for work, the efficiency-driven owner is able to pay minimal salaries. The starving workers literally bid their wages downward. Single people can work for less than those who have families to support, so if there are enough single people looking for work, wages will fall below the minimum a family needs to survive. Remember that at this time there were no ridiculously wealthy rock stars driving their Bentleys to mega charity concerts to buy food for the starving. In the early years of capitalism, and in any current system of pure capitalism, your survival was in your own hands. It was your responsibility. We are not talking about your inability to buy the latest Shihad CD or newest iPod, we're talking about the inability to afford crumbs to eat or to have a place to live.

Ironically, if you want to see capitalism in its rawest form, you might want to visit China. China today is radically different from China under Mao Zedong; labor is cheap, jobs are scarce, and people are desperate to make a living. There is a large gulf between the haves and the have-nots, and the government has slowly removed any safety net from underneath its people. Everywhere there is growth, construction, sales, commercialization, horrible pollution, and poverty. Present-day China is capitalism run amok, and the Chinese people must do whatever they can to survive.

In Marx's day, people were willing to put up with incredibly inhumane conditions to continue to work. Declaring personal bankruptcy was not yet an option. If you could not pay your bills, you were sent to the poorhouse or to debtors' prison. Who can forget the famous exchange from Dickens's *A Christmas Carol* when a not-yet-repentant Scrooge is approached in his place of business by some men collecting money at Christmastime for the "hundreds of thousands" in need:

> "Are there no prisons?" asked Scrooge.
>> "Plenty of prisons," said the gentleman, laying down the pen again.
>> "And the Union workhouses?" demanded Scrooge. "Are they still in operation?"
>> "They are. Still," returned the gentleman, "I wish I could say they were not."
>> "The treadmill and the Poor Law are in full vigor, then?" said Scrooge.
>> "Both very busy, sir."

"Oh! I was afraid, from what you said at first, that something had occurred to stop them in their useful course," said Scrooge. "I am very glad to hear it."

"Under the impression that they scarcely furnish Christian cheer of mind or body to the multitude," returned the gentleman, "a few of us are endeavoring to raise a fund to buy the Poor some meat and drink, and means of warmth. We choose this time, because it is a time, of all others, when Want is keenly felt, and Abundance rejoices. What shall I put you down for?"

"Nothing!" Scrooge replied.

"You wish to be anonymous?"

"I wish to be left alone," said Scrooge. "Since you ask me what I wish, gentlemen, that is my answer. I don't make merry myself at Christmas, and I can't afford to make idle people merry. I help to support the establishments I have mentioned—they cost enough: and those who are badly off must go there."

"Many can't go there; and many would rather die."

"If they would rather die," said Scrooge, "they had better do it, and decrease the surplus population."[11]

Bob Cratchit, Scrooge's clerk, did not put up with his boss's cruelty because he was meek. He did so because he feared unemployment and the resulting pain and hunger. He feared for his large family. He feared the starvation that would accompany the condition of unemployment.

Hunger can drive desperate men to work for less than it takes to survive. When you are starving to death, the other aspects of survival, such as clothing, housing, and so forth, come in a distant second to just getting something to eat. Getting some income, even if it is only enough for a single day's food, is better than getting none. If you have enough people who are that desperate, wages fall below what anyone can survive on. How long can people survive without housing or clothing? If you cannot even feed and clothe yourself, how do you feed a family or take care of your aging parents? Worse yet, you cannot go find yourself a second job because you are already working twelve-hour shifts, six and a half days a week, and still not making enough to survive at even the most basic level.

The Pool of Labor as a Common Resource

These are not fictional horrors. As the Dickens novels make clear, Scrooge's coldhearted vision represents what was actually happening in Europe when Marx was writing about capitalism: people were, quite literally, being worked to death. And this massive overexploitation of workers was what Marx saw as the fatal flaw of capitalism.*

---

*If you are a bit too perceptive for your own good, this is also the point at which you might be fooled into thinking I actually planned out the presentation of the material in this chapter. If you didn't know better, you might suggest that the chapter's sections fit together because this fatal flaw of capitalism is also a tragedy of the commons.

If you think of the pool of laborers as a commons—a shared resource that capitalists exploit for economic gain—you can also see that all the dynamics of the tragedy of the commons apply. This, in fact, is the critical link that connects economics with politics. Just as the shepherds need to protect the productivity of the field and the fishermen need to protect the fecundity[†] of the bay full of fish, the capitalists need to guard the productivity and the continued existence of the pool of workers. Without workers, the factories will sit idle and no profits will be made. However, despite this need, capitalists are driven by the dynamics of capitalist competition to overexploit the workers. This is just like the dynamic inherent in any shared resource, and a purely capitalist economic system provides no way for individual capitalists to end the overexploitation.

This is a fatal flaw in capitalism. In the same way that it does no good for the individual fisherman to unilaterally limit his own fishing in an effort to preserve the bay full of fish, an individual factory owner simply does not have the option of raising wages. Most capitalists are not overexploiting their workers because they are evil, or nasty, or even ruthless, but because the competition to gain customers by undercutting other producers drives all factory owners to match the price cuts made by the most ruthless, nastiest, and heartless scrooges. Anyone who chooses to pay his or her workers more than the stingiest of competitors will have to charge more for his or her product, which will quickly lead to bankruptcy. Thus, even the most enlightened and humane of capitalists could not choose to raise wages in this social Darwinist system in which any factory owner who fails to match a competitor's cost cuts is quickly driven out of business and eaten by polar bears.

While Marx pointed to a number of problems with the early vestiges of industrial capitalism, this tragedy of the commons—the overexploitation of the workers in the pool of labor—is a fatal flaw in the very concept of pure capitalism as an economic system. This creates two very big problems for capitalism and the political systems that support it. First, Marx argued that the constant push to lower workers' wages, which was aided by the advent of laborsaving machines, would eventually leave the workers unable to buy the goods they produced. If the workers could not afford to buy products, the result would be a serious reduction in demand for the factories' output. How could a capitalist system survive when there was insufficient demand for its products? Second, and more important, Marx pointed out that, unlike unmutated sheep or fish, people have the capability of acting with intent. Workers, he insisted, would eventually become so desperate that they would see no alternative to destroying the system. They would find some way to overcome the barriers to revolt—the atomization, peer policing, and preference falsification that had so far kept them isolated and powerless.

[†]Cool word, huh?

Marx argued that when this inevitable revolution happened, it would tear apart the whole capitalist economic system—not to mention a few factory owners—and replace it with a socialist system that would give workers control over the means of production. And Marx believed that this revolution would be a good thing, because the workers would then build a socialist political and economic system that would eventually lead to a communist utopia.

I Thought You Said There'd Be a Revolution?

Marx was incredibly insightful in his analysis of how capitalism and its related political dynamics work. In fact, there may not be a better discussion of the basic operation of the capitalist mode of production and how it drives everyone to become more efficient. But when it came to predicting the future, Marx was not quite as successful.* Let's just say you would have been better off making 1-900 calls to that late-night TV infomercial psychic who sometimes forgets to keep up her Jamaican accent than betting on the Marxist revolution. There was no cataclysmic revolution. The workers of the world did not unite, and they did not create a communist utopia or even the socialist economic system that was supposed to lead the way. Indeed, many of the more prominent Marxist theorists since Marx have expended considerable effort explaining why the inevitable collapse of the capitalist system did not arrive on schedule. For example, Lenin's best-known work, *Imperialism,* is essentially an explanation of how the expansion of the capitalist system delayed the revolt by exploiting the wealth of colonized foreign lands.[12]

Perhaps a better way to explain the revolution that never happened is to work with this tragedy-of-the-commons theme that I kind of stumbled upon for this chapter but will totally insist that I planned all along. If you think about the pool of labor as a common resource that is shared by capitalists, and if you ask how you can prevent destroying that resource through overexploitation, perhaps the solution is the same as the solution suggested earlier for the other examples of a tragedy of the commons—collective action. By forming a collective action group, or using the structures of an existing group such as the government, you can police the actions of all who use the commons to prevent its destruction through overexploitation and keep it productive year after year. You can limit or otherwise regulate the number of sheep and save the field, limit the number of fish caught and keep fishing in that bay forever. Perhaps you can limit and police the way the pool of labor is exploited by all capitalists and preserve it for the long term.

Through fits and starts, by accident and necessity more than by intent, this is essentially what has happened. Repeatedly, as dissatisfaction and unrest among workers threatened to grow into revolt, capitalists turned to the governments, upon which they exercised substantial, if not overwhelming, influence. Force was used and there were fights, arrests, and even massacres, but, as you all now know and are prepared to discuss on the essay exam, there are

---

*Most academics, including political scientists, are pretty good at explaining the past and the present. We're not so great at predicting the future.

limitations on the use of force, and governments gradually adopted policies that would give the workers some of what they demanded, which included the limitations on the exploitation of labor that were needed to prevent the collapse of the capitalist system.

SOCIALISM

Marx categorized political economic systems according to who controlled the means of production—the things necessary to transform labor into wealth—such as land and its natural products, factories, materials, and tools, as well as infrastructure. Since many people are quite fond of eating and the other simple pleasures of survival, control of this bit of economic life is critical. Under the feudal system, artisans such as smiths, coopers, shoemakers, fletchers, cat jugglers, and tailors controlled the means of production relevant to those crafts, but land was the primary means of production, and the church, along with a hereditary elite of royalty and landowners, controlled the land. In a capitalist system, individuals control the farms, factories, Glorious Leader's Bountiful Carcass Pucks of Eternal Wonderfulness franchises, and so on, and it is through the self-interested decisions of those individuals that the overexploitation of labor as a tragedy of the commons arises. I have yet to discuss, or even really describe, socialism, however.

Though students should bear in mind that this is an extremely simplified depiction of a very complex theory, socialism can be roughly defined as an economic system in which society controls the means of production. Instead of competition for profits, equality in the distribution of society's wealth is the driving factor in the decisions related to production. While many who are concerned about the effects of poverty and disparities of wealth may find this idea appealing, recognize that socialism is just as flawed as capitalism. I have spent a great deal of time discussing Marx's critique of capitalism and his discussion of its fatal flaw. I have done so because it is predominantly capitalism that most of us understand, and it is this system that students usually take for granted or defend with zealous vehemence.* However, socialism is also flawed. Pure socialism, just like pure capitalism, cannot work in practice. In fact, it has never even been tried on a large scale.

The idea of society controlling the means of production can be summarized by the statement, "From each according to his ability, to each according to his need." You produce what you can produce and society will make sure that everybody will get what he or she needs to survive. This system fixes the flaw in capitalism by making sure that people do not go hungry, but it creates a new problem: How do you get people off their butts to do something? In essence, socialism is very good at distributing goods, but very inefficient at producing those goods. Everybody gets whatever housing and food are available. The problem is getting the housing and food made. It is probably fair to say that Marx was a bit

---

*Another cool word, had to use it.

NEVER FLY STANDBY

"A Girl Named Rabies" is set in the far future, where they have kind of a socialist economy, and that's as good an excuse as any for talking it up. It is included in an anthology of New Zealand science fiction. The guy in the story ends up spending six hundred years on standby, waiting for a flight, and when he wakes up he has a really bad day, so I guess the basic moral of the story is never fly standby. That's probably a good moral for this textbook as well. Textbooks don't usually have morals, so that will be something cool

and new and different. Anyway, when Winston wakes to find the future waiting for him, the young woman at the airline customer service counter is named Rabies Biteme, and she is just as helpful as her name implies. Still, more by accident than by design, she becomes Winston's guide to this futuristic world that is so heavily regulated that they have quotas for petty street crime. A key question that is implied in this journey is the nature of an economy and people's place within it when all production is automated and there is no real need for human labor.

Douglas A. Van Belle, "A Girl Named Rabies," in *A Foreign Country: New Zealand Speculative Fiction,* edited by Anna Caro and Juliet Buchanan (Wellington, New Zealand: Random Static, 2010).

of a workaholic, and in his descriptions of socialism and the communist utopia he probably overestimated people's industriousness.[*]

You can probably think of a whole lot of jobs—such as being the night janitor at a sewage treatment plant for a nuclear power station—that get filled only because they pay a trainload of cash. Why do garbage collectors get paid more than teachers? Which job would you rather do? Would anyone regularly pick up trash just because it needed to be done? If you are getting exactly what you need regardless of what you do, would you choose to pick up barrels of trash, or would you sit on your couch and watch reruns on the professional fishing channel? A substantial percentage of people would choose to serve their tour of duty as a couch commando. This is especially true if you get the same house, food, and clothes as the person who sorts biotoxic waste at the asbestos factory. Socialism is very inefficient, if only because under such a system it is hard to motivate people to work and even harder to motivate them to seek efficiencies or to excel at their jobs. When the complete absence of competition means that a poorly run factory is treated the same as a well-run factory, how do you encourage workers to put in the extra effort it takes to run factories better? When there is no reward for finding a more efficient way to

---

[*]However, Marx would say that I have gotten this whole chapter totally wrong. Believing that each person's view of the world is shaped by the economic system under which he or she lives, he would argue that my view of human nature is shaped by the values—such as individualism, motivation, and competition—that are important for the continuation of the capitalist system. As such, Marx would say that I am guilty of "false consciousness," because I cannot properly judge human nature while viewing the world through my capitalist glasses. Marx was wrong. I'm a professor, so I'm always right. Deal with it.

do something, why look for it? When doctors are treated exactly the same as janitors, who would put in the extra years of training to become a doctor? Worse yet, if both good doctors and bad doctors get paid the same, what motivates people to become better doctors? Pride and integrity will provide some motivation, but is that enough? How many students in this class do you think would bust their asses to learn this material if there were no grading system and all the associated rewards and punishments for success and failure?

As you should easily be able to see, pure socialism and pure capitalism are both flawed. Neither could realistically function for any length of time in the real world. However, you must also realize that neither ever has been—or ever really could be—expected to exist in its pure form. As with many other concepts in politics, the ideal or perfect forms of these ideas are worth examining only for their dynamics. When it comes to the real world, the useful question is not whether to have a socialist or a capitalist economic system, but, instead, how to strike a balance between the two.

THE YIN AND YANG OF CAPITALISM AND SOCIALISM

In Chinese cosmology, the yin and yang are complementary forces, symbolized by the moon and the sun, which must remain in balance. Earth and heaven, cold and hot, female and male, vampires and werewolves—yin and yang represent the opposing forces of life. In many ways, this concept of complementary forces can be applied in the case of capitalism and socialism. When government regulates and polices the exploitation of the pool of labor by capitalists, it is, in essence, using principles of socialism to save capitalism. When it sets a minimum wage, limits working hours, creates safety rules, outlaws child labor, or in any other way limits the owner's management of the factory, the government takes some control of the means of production away from the capitalist and gives it to the society. All functioning capitalist systems in the world today are actually mixtures of capitalism and socialism, mixtures of private and societal control of the means of production. The real question is not capitalism versus socialism, but what balance between the two systems is best. As with most things in politics and government, there is no single answer to this question. Different cultures have struck different balances between these two ideals, and the balances are dynamic, always changing over time.

In Europe, particularly in Scandinavia, the balance is heavily tilted toward the socialist end of the scale. Society heavily regulates the workplace and provides extensive services and a high minimum level of wealth for all. In many developing countries, the political and economic systems are close to pure capitalism, featuring little regulation, few government services, and only the barest of minimum-wage and working-condition guarantees. Initially, it was a relatively pure and unregulated form of capitalism that replaced feudal and artisanal modes of production in Europe, North America, and elsewhere around the globe. However, the first century of capitalism witnessed the steady

JOHN STUART MILL

Team: **Capitalist Pigdogs**

Position: **Deep Mid Wicket**

Status: **Unfettered by the Mortal Coil**

It's an interesting question whether **John Stuart Mill** (1806–1873) should be enshrined in the economics chapter or the media chapter. In the end, economics makes the more compelling case, and not just because money talks. On Liberty[a] deserves a special place in the discussion of freedom of expression, which most people now think of as synonymous with press freedom, but it is a treatise about the liberty of the individual and isn't really about the press at all. And Mill's economics stuff is pretty damned impressive. He quite literally wrote the economics textbook.[b]

Building directly and explicitly from the work of Adam Smith, Mill introduced or developed the concepts of comparative advantage, opportunity costs, and economies of scale. All three of these concepts are central to today's politics and policy related to trade and economics.

Comparative advantage is perhaps the most important concept for many of the political and economic issues that today's nations confront. The basic idea of comparative advantage is that trade is not a zero-sum exchange. Both sides in a trade can come out of an exchange wealthier. It's as simple as apples and oranges.

If you live in upstate New York, it is possible for you to grow both apples and oranges. Apples are easy and cheap; the climate is perfect for them. Oranges are another matter. Even though there is an Orange County in New York, it's named after the Dutch royal colors, not a citrus spheroid that will turn into a green fuzzy lump if you leave it too long in the back of the fridge. The climate in New York is horrible for growing oranges. You could do it, though—you'd need a greenhouse and you'd have to pay to heat it through the winter and it would cost a fortune, but you could do it. Florida has, however, the opposite problem. The hot, humid weather wreaks havoc on apple trees, but orange trees grow like weeds there.

The result is that New York has a comparative advantage producing apples and Florida has a comparative advantage producing oranges. If they then exchange apples for oranges, the laws of supply and demand mean that they both end up with more total value in fruit than if they didn't trade. Producers in both states gain a higher price in the other market for what they can produce cheaply locally, and consumers get a lower price at home for something from far away that would be expensive to produce locally. New York apples sell for more in Florida than they would at home (benefiting New York farmers), but they are still cheaper than they would be if they were grown in Florida (benefiting Florida consumers), and the opposite as well.

This is the argument against protectionism and tariffs. In theory, a free trade zone such as that established by NAFTA expands the opportunities for pursuing these kinds of comparative advantages. The unfortunate difficulty with this idea in the real world is the problem of investments and sunk costs. If you were a New Yorker who invested heavily in the greenhouses needed to produce a modest quantity of very exotic and very expensive oranges, a free trade agreement with Florida and the flood of cheap oranges it would bring would drive you bankrupt. Wouldn't you fight like a screaming weasel to stop it?

How about the car factories in Detroit that are threatened by cheap labor in Mexico? Or the lumber mills in Oregon threatened by cheap Canadian timber? Or the Budweiser company, which is threatened by pretty much anything that might cause Americans to discover what a real beer tastes like?

[a]John Stuart Mill, *Principles of Political Economy with Some of their Applications to Social Philosophy* (London: Longman, Roberts, & Green, 1848).

[b]John Stuart Mill, *On Liberty* (London: Longman, Roberts, & Green, 1859).

introduction of societal controls, regulation, and policing of production, along with an increase in societal guarantees of a minimum level of wealth for all. Recently, most of the developed countries in the world have scaled back both regulation and societal guarantees of wealth, but the balance between degrees of capitalism and socialism is still the source of daily debate, particularly when the world's economy spirals down the toilet. Questions about issues such as what the minimum wage should be, how much health care should be provided to whom, what sorts of environmental regulations should be imposed, and whether the economy would be better stimulated by tax cuts or government spending are all part of finding the appropriate balance between capitalism and socialism.

Government and politics lie directly at the intersection of the society and the economy. When society wishes to exert more control over the means of production, it turns to government leaders. Capitalists use their wealth and power to influence those same leaders to reduce societal control over their factories, farms, and businesses. This regulation is just the basic, most fundamental role of government in the economy. Governments conduct countless activities—from the creation of money and the control of its supply to the building and maintenance of infrastructures, the sponsoring of research and development, and the education of future workers—to enhance and support the economic activity that transforms labor into wealth.

What is the perfect relationship between government and the economy? If I knew the answer to that question, I wouldn't be spending my time writing a political science textbook—I would be sipping beer on a beach in Aruba. In fact, as much as people act as if they know the answer, they do not. They think they know. In this sense, politics is very much about the battle among those who think they know what should be done. However, as I noted earlier, various countries have struck their own balances, just as Francie finds her personal balance between realism and idealism in *A Tree Grows in Brooklyn*. When countries identify the balance they want between capitalism and socialism, they not only pursue it through policy choices, but they also design their political structures in a manner that incorporates these choices into their governmental institutions. Therefore, it is the subject of structures and institutions that I will now beat into your head as best I can manage.

KEY TERMS

capitalism / 94
enlightened self-interest / 97
feudalism / 104
humanist / 103
laissez-faire capitalism / 106

Karl Marx / 101
means of production / 101
socialism / 94
the stag hunt / 97
tragedy of the commons / 95

CHAPTER SUMMARY

The relationship between government and the economy is more complex than most people realize. The need for government involvement in the economy is demonstrated clearly by the tragedy of the commons. This useful concept demonstrates that although people may know that overexploiting a common resource or abandoning a common effort is not in their long-term best interest, individual calculations may suggest that not cooperating is the more rational individual choice, because other people's actions must be taken into account as well. Although industrial capitalism had many advantages over the feudal system it replaced, it also had many flaws. Karl Marx exposed many of laissez-faire capitalism's imperfections, particularly its exploitation of workers and its inherent contradictions. While Marx recognized many of capitalism's problems, he did not foresee the defects in his own socialist prescriptions, which undervalued the role of human motivation. Students should learn two very important lessons from this chapter. First, there are no purely socialist or capitalist systems in the world today; most countries try to find a balance between these two economic ideals. Second, if you ever go stag hunting, make sure you really trust the people who go with you.

STUDY QUESTIONS AND EXERCISES

1. Think about some of the problems that the world confronts today—for example, the dwindling supply of petroleum, and arms proliferation. How does the tragedy of the commons help to explain why these problems are so difficult to solve?

2. How does the tragedy of the commons demonstrate the need for a basic and continuing economic role for government?

3. What is Marx's most pointed critique of industrial capitalism?

4. Do you think that Marx's communism could ever work? Why or why not?

5. What is the ideal balance between socialism and capitalism? Why?

WEB SITES TO EXPLORE

www.bunnygame.org/index.htm. Tragedy of the Bunnies is a site offering a game that illustrates the tragedy of the commons. Be sure to read the explanation of "the moral" of the game.

www.gametheory.net/dictionary/Games/StagHunt.html. GameTheory.net's version of the stag hunt offers a more mathematical approach to calculating the strategy of the hunt.

www.historyguide.org/intellect/marx.html. The History Guide's Lectures on Modern Intellectual History includes a biography of Karl Marx and some summaries of his major works.

www.marxists.org. The Marxists Internet Archive is a clearinghouse of information about and writings by Marx and Marxists composed by Marxists from around the world.

www.capmag.com. Capitalism Magazine is an opinion site that extols the virtues of laissez-faire capitalism.

Structures and Institutions

People like to watch other people building stuff. Pharaohs and pyramids, Chinese emperors and that fence or wall or whatever, William Randolph Hearst and that modest little cottage out in California—people have always liked watching other people build stuff. In fact, the official reason that cable and satellite TV were invented was so that we could have **enough channels for** the bazillion different programs about people building stuff. You can blame Bob Vila. I do. In the early days of cable, way back when there were only seventy channels, it was almost impossible to turn the TV on without finding him standing in the ruins of someone's home, talking about putting it back together. There were spin-offs and rip-offs, including a sitcom version, *Home Improvement*,[1] and today TV is well into what would have to be called the third generation of shows about other people building stuff. Most of the shows about other people building houses have gotten a bit boring,* except for maybe *Grand Designs. Grand Designs* is all about people who are at least a hop or a skip beyond the bounds of sane going totally freaky in the whole building or remodeling a house thing.[2] They buy old lighthouses, coast guard stations on big pilings out over the sea, medieval this, that, or the other things and then try to turn them into homes. Some of the resulting houses are awesome, but one of the coolest parts of the series is that sometimes the owners do a complete face-plant and fail to pull off their grand design. Sometimes the show ends with a visit six months later and we see the bankrupt, no-longer-quite-sane couple living illegally in a mess of plywood, exposed wiring, and despair. I'm just waiting for the spin-off series, *Grand Divorces*.

---

*Actually, I find a lot of these hip, new, and radical home improvement shows disturbing. Take *Extreme Makeover: Home Edition* as an example. Ty and his minions pounce on a desperate family, chase them out of town, tear down their house, build a monstrosity in its place, and then force the family to come back and live in it. Horrifying, yes, but that is not the most disturbing part. Consider that this act of vandalism is supposed to be a "makeover." If this concept of making over had been applied to the original *Extreme Makeover*, instead of giving people nose jobs, pretty new teeth, and exercise programs, the show's staff would have just sent them to the factory that makes Soylent Green and replaced them with robotic versions of Yul Brynner.

Unfortunately, if you're not careful, watching people build stuff can also be educational. If you watch enough *American Chopper,* Paul Teutul Sr. will teach you that you can replace any part of the English language, including punctuation, with an expletive. In fact, this learning effect is so powerful that if you let a ten-year-old watch enough of *Megastructures, Extreme Engineering,* and *American Guns,* he or she will inevitably build a full-scale battle-ship with a special deck just for ponies and unicorns.

Government **structures** are, conceptually at least, similar to that ten-year-old's building the capability to project extremes of military hubris to the far corners of the globe. They are the basic functions that governments need to perform. Wait, no, that isn't quite right. There is an analogy here, honest. Give me a second. Or maybe it's supposed to be a metaphor. Now a metaphor is like an analogy, which is like a simile but is actually a statement of logical . . . arrgh. Where's a copy editor when you actually need one? Seriously, hound me over commas and cut out all my favorite semicolons, but when I really need her . . .

Okay, forget all that.

Government structures are the interdependent essential elements of governing that deter-mine, enable, and limit the form and function of a government. In that way, they are like the essential elements of a house, such as plumbing or wiring and that is a simile, which is a type of metaphor . . . so there. This and the next few chapters focus on some of the big and obvious structures of government. Just as the foundation is a necessary part of every house, these governmental functions are a necessary part of just about any modern government. For example, all governments must establish the rules of acceptable behavior within their state boundaries. Consequently, every government must have a legislative structure for creating laws. That legislative structure might be a magic goat that whispers new laws to the king's favorite mistress, or it can be a bunch of rich old men arguing and voting, but no matter what form it takes, it has to be there. Because laws and decisions must be implemented, every government must have an executive or a political structure that acts on behalf of the state. There is also the duty of handling the mundane day-to-day tasks citizens expect of govern-ment. A bureaucracy handles these administrative functions in most modern states. Also, since the laws governing behavior must be enforced, every government needs some kind of policing and judicial structure. These are the metaphorical foundation, plumbing, roof, and electrical system of government when it's analogized to a house.

There are several other political structures I could include, and there are other ways I could categorize political structures, but most who teach politics will probably agree that these four are the basic structures critical for understanding how things work in modern government. The goal of the chapters in this all-important middle section of the book is to give you the back-ground and tools to understand how political **institutions** carry out governmental functions. During the course of this investigation,[*] I focus on the tension between ideal visions of how

---

[*]You have the right to remain silent, which is just as well, since I cannot hear you anyway.

government should operate and the imperfections of a hopelessly complex real world that refuses to quit changing long enough to get all this political stuff perfected.

We need to start by asking some very basic questions: What are government structures and institutions? Where do they come from? What forces shape them? Why are they so screwed up? And, of course, why do driver's license photos make everyone look like deranged lunatics? The chapters that follow look at specific structures in greater detail.

STRUCTURES OR INSTITUTIONS?

The house analogy—which might or might not be a metaphor but probably is an analogy, now that I think about it some more—gets the basic idea of a structure across quite well, and it also provides an opportunity to clarify the distinction between political structures and political institutions. Like structures, institutions are critical and relatively permanent parts of a government. However, structures are generic whereas institutions are specific. I can illustrate what this means by using our house analogy that might be a metaphor. A foundation is one of the key structures that you are going to find under any house, and all foundations have to share a few key characteristics, such as being under the house* and kind of sturdy, but the specifics of foundations can vary tremendously from house to house. In most places, a foundation can just be a big old slab of concrete, but it doesn't have to be. In places like New Orleans, where there isn't really any solid ground to be had, that slab of concrete has to be poured over the tops of pilings that are driven down deep enough to get to ground that is nonsquishy enough to hold the house up. In places like the North Pole, which is spelled Canada for some reason, foundations are usually concrete walls that go down far enough to get below the deepest the ground will freeze, so that the freezing and thawing won't shift the house about. An episode of *Grand Designs* featured the conversion of an old lifeboat station into a house in Tenby, Wales; the building needs a maze of steel girders to hold it above the raging surf. Other foundation choices are driven by construction costs, energy conservation, or architectural lunacy that is mistaken for design. Foundation materials can range from Styrofoam to stone, concrete, timber, steel, bales of cotton,† and papier-mâché.‡

To analogize with reckless metaphorical abandon, if the foundation is the structure, then any specific way someone decides to build a particular foundation would be an institution. In politics, the specific way that a critical political structure is implemented is an institution. A legislature is a political structure. The British House of Commons is an institution. A judicial system is a political structure. The U.S. Supreme Court is a political institution. This distinction is important because when I move from the discussion of basic functions to specific examples, I am also moving from the discussion of structures to the discussion of institutions.

---

*They work quite poorly on top of houses.

†Actually, this is a myth perpetrated by New Orleans tour guides. The Customs House and other old city buildings are only metaphorically built on cotton bales. They are actually built on foundations of cypress timbers that were purportedly purchased with the barter of bales of cotton.

‡The people on HGTV swear you can make anything out of the stuff.

When students hear the term *institution,* many think they would rather be locked up in one than have to study them. Your beloved textbook author thinks teaching about them is not that much fun either, even though he is certifiably insane[*] and quite likes the institution he calls home. But political institutions are a big—I'm talking extinct furry elephant-size big—part of how governments work. Political institutions are the organizational structures through which political power is exercised. They persist over time and provide a foundation of process, knowledge, and precedent for making decisions and performing actions. Getting at the underlying dynamics of institutions, however, is a bit of a challenge.

For instructors, it is hard to resist the temptation to catalog, categorize, and explain the various structures and institutions around us. Thus, political institutions are often presented in a straightforward descriptive fashion, usually in coma-inducing detail. Professors often emphasize things such as "there are two houses in the British Parliament," "there are 435 members of the U.S. House of Representatives," "the Israeli prime minister can call elections at any time," and, of course, "1600 Pennsylvania Avenue is not the address of Wrigley Field." Zzzzzzzz . . . Don't get me wrong, these details are important. I have often had to find incompetent but cheap lawyers for students who took one of my lame jokes seriously, packed up a few bratwursts, and downed a case of beer before trying to find the bleachers at 1600 Pennsylvania Avenue.[†]

If I never discussed specific institutions and what they do, it would be pretty tough for you to learn how they work. It would also be pretty tough to have an intelligent conversation about government. However, simply describing political institutions doesn't tell you everything there is to know about those institutions, nor does it help you build a dynamic understanding of the basic political structures that nations utilize. For students, understanding political institutions can be a challenge, if only because of the familiarity we already have with them. After all, most people who have been paroled from high school can probably name several political institutions. The presidency, the Congress, and the courts are among the most important institutions in the United States. Likewise, parliaments, monarchs, political parties, and the military are common political structures throughout the world. You see them, you occasionally interact with them,[*] and you talk about them all the time. However, it is this very familiarity that is part of the problem with studying and teaching about political institutions. As with the other aspects of government that you see or have experienced, it can be hard to find the fundamentals underneath the avalanche of details and nuances that you already know. It can also be difficult to remain objective about familiar institutions and remain open to alternative institutions that are used in other countries.

---

[*]There is an actual certificate involved. He framed it and it now hangs on the wall next to his diplomas.

[†]If you do decide to do the same, please remember that those guys dressed in cheap black suits are not umpires and they have had their senses of humor surgically removed. And you probably want to avoid saying anything about their mothers.

[*]Which reminds me, your mother asked me to remind you to renew your driver's license.

JAMES MADISON

Team: **Federalist United**

Position: **Cover Point**

Status: **Almost Completely Dead**

James Madison (1751–1836) was short and less than charming. He was also the fourth president of the United States and is often called the father of the U.S. Constitution. While he was quick to point out that he was but one of many who contributed to that document, his intellectual contribution to the design of the new government the Constitution produced is made quite clear in the *Federalist Papers*[a] that are attributed to him. Most notably are the papers that present the logic underlying the republican form of government (Papers No. 37–51), and the attribution of most of these essays to Madison is probably why he is given so much credit for the creation of the U.S. Constitution.

Many of ideas offered in this portion of the *Federalist Papers,* such as the separation of powers, are now such common and fundamental parts of most democratic governments that it can be a bit difficult to imagine a time before they were articulated as they are in the *Federalist Papers,* and it can be even harder to imagine bringing together all the hints and insights from British, Roman, and Greek history to assemble them into a coherent logic for a government that would balance the need to limit government from the excesses of kings and emperors, make it responsive to the needs of the people, avoid the tyranny of the majority, and still be dynamic enough to govern effectively and respond to the needs of the country. Madison himself discusses this challenge in *Federalist Paper* No. 37.

In terms of this chapter's focus on structures and institutions *Federalist Papers* No. 47–49 are, simply put, astounding. In these three essays, Madison describes the logic of a government structured around checks and balances, and about turning the danger of a jealousy for power into something that will prevent the transformation of a republic into a dictatorship. This simple explanation of the separation of powers, written for a general audience so they could be published in a newspaper, provide the logic that now defines the basic structure of almost every modern democracy.

[a]www.foundingfathers.info/federalistpapers/fedindex.htm.

HUMAN NATURE AND POLITICAL INSTITUTIONS

A society's basic view of human nature is a reasonable place to start working on a general understanding of political institutions. As James Madison put it, "But what is government itself, but the greatest of all reflections on human nature?"[3] Does the society view people as generally cooperative or selfish, rebellious or submissive, active or passive? This is critical because a political institution that is perfect for cooperative people, such as the Amish, would be a disastrous failure at dealing with selfish, performance-drug-abusing Major League Baseball players.

We can see this reflected in the work of Madison himself, because not only did James Madison occasionally comment on government and human nature, but he is also generally thought of as the father of the American Constitution.* His view of human nature was quite

---

*Notably, Dolley Madison is not considered the mother of the Constitution, and no one is talking about who is. I have no evidence, but some unusual family connections to the snack-cake industry lead me to suspect a woman who is known only as "Little Debbie."

pessimistic, and that perspective is abundantly clear in the basic construction of U.S. political institutions. Madison argued: "If men were angels, no government would be necessary. If angels were to govern men, neither external nor internal controls on government would be necessary."[4] Clearly, Madison was not anticipating a time when governors and citizens would come together, hold hands, and hum Disney songs while sitting around a campfire. In designing the American Constitution, Madison and his fellow architects built a system based on a basic mistrust of human nature. They drew the blueprints for a complex set of interlocking institutions with overlapping responsibilities that would pit separate portions of the government against one another. Each section jealously guards its power and the power of those that support it, and it is this pursuit of selfish interests that keeps the other sections honest.

The U.S. system, because of its separation of powers, is specifically designed to make it difficult for a less-than-angelic government to infringe on the rights of its citizens. The system also makes it difficult for any one portion of society to enact policies that infringe upon the interests of another. This kind of government has its good side in that it prevents many bad things from happening, but it also makes it hard to get much done at all—including passing very popular laws and laws aimed at ending discrimination or remedying its effects. Other governments based in a stronger belief in the natural goodness of humankind are more likely to have simpler governmental systems that make it far easier to enact policy. We see this, for example, in European democracies, where the winning party has a much freer hand in making changes. However, this ability to enact policy easily comes at the cost of stability over time. After all, the French change their government as often as they change their . . . their . . . well, let's just say they change their government a lot. These less restrained forms of governments also create an increased risk of putting one portion of society or government at the mercy of another as they swiftly pass laws and make sudden changes to the rules that define society.

The presumed nature of human beings—good or bad—is key to understanding the creation and evolution of political institutions. This is a great deal like saying that the intended use of a motorcycle—drag racing, motocross, or impressing girls with tattoos—shapes the way its basic structures are built. The exposed plumbing and pretty much every other aspect of the basic structure of a house built out of a nuclear missile silo are perfect for impressing girls with tattoos, but all wrong for many other contexts. No amount of altering and tinkering could change an underground lair into something that a flatulent claustrophobe could call home. Similarly, it is in the details of the local social context of a country—the worldview of its people, its geographic situation, and its economic realities—that political institutions are created and later evolve. Remember this as you seek to understand the underlying political structures that are expressed through the wide variety of institutions around the world.[*]

---

[*] That's an order.

ALEXANDER HAMILTON

Team: Federalist United

Position: Leg Slip

Status: Shot Totally Dead

Alexander Hamilton (1755–1804) liked guns. He enlisted in the militia during the U.S. war of secession (pronounced "Revolutionary War" in American), earned a commission in the continental army, did a bit of shooting during the battle of Yorktown, and ended up getting shot to death, presumably by Aaron Burr, who was the guy who didn't die in the duel. Of the Founders that participated in the writing of the U.S. Constitution, Hamilton was known as an advocate of strong government, and in the *Federalist Papers*[a] that are attributed to him we can see that he probably played a significant role in transforming the logic of the U.S. federal government structure into the specific institutions of the U.S. government.

In addition to the essays making the argument for a strong government that could dominate the states just enough to hold the country together, (No. 6–13), Al is given credit for most of the essays in the latter half of the *Federalist Papers,* which discuss the details of the government being formed by the constitution (No. 52–83). Everything from why there needed to be two legislative houses, to why the powers needed to be divided across the branches, to the role of the president as the executive, to the details of how the judicial branch would be its own, distinct branch of government separate from the others, it is all covered in explicit detail in the latter half of the *Federalist Papers.*

As a result, if you're looking for a theorist to put in a chapter on political structures and institutions, Al's your institutions go-to guy. In fact, he may not be the only one, but he is one of the few humanoids who ever wrote about the ideas behind institutions that were actually being created to transform the general structures of government into an approximation of the ideals of a government formed from something close to a blank slate.

[a]www.foundingfathers.info/federalistpapers/fedindex.htm.

THE REALITY OF POLITICAL INSTITUTIONS

Given the opportunity to craft ideal governmental institutions from scratch, we would all choose the types of institutions that we believe would support the values and traditions most important to us. Values such as democracy, individual rights, religious footwear, nationalism, strict regulation of the wearing of spandex at Walmarts, and so forth can all be bolstered and protected or weakened and repressed by the types of institutions a nation uses. Similarly, the personal wealth, power, and security of the leader are other values that can be bolstered or impeded by particular types of institutions. Connect this back to the personal nature of utopias and the variety of the people found in every governed society, and you will realize that the push for compromise quickly takes us away from anyone's ideal institutions.

Context, Evolution, and the Unbearable Weight of History

Of course, even if we could agree on every detail of the perfect political institution, in the real world, nations rarely have an opportunity to install their ideal institutions from scratch. First, most government institutions are not designed or even intentionally created. Instead, they evolve out of humble and sometimes downright unusual beginnings. For example,

Great Britain's Parliament, which serves as the model for most populist democracies around the world, evolved from a decidedly elitist source. Parliament was born out of the struggles between the wealthy nobility and the monarch. It was initially a means for the king to enlist the nobility in controlling, taxing, and ruling the peasants and exploiting the products of the land in an organized and efficient manner. Influence flowed from the royalty at the top to those who slaved away and paid taxes at the bottom. Over the decades and centuries, Parliament changed. It adjusted to economic shifts, demographic trends, and technological advances, until it ultimately developed into a democratic institution that aggregates the interests, desires, and demands from the ruled and sends that input from the bottom to the top. Today's British Parliament would likely horrify the elitist aristocrats who fought and killed to create it.

Even when institutions are rationally and intentionally designed, nations seldom, if ever, have anything close to a blank page when they create a government. Almost every government's institutions carry the legacy of generations. The U.S. political system represents a rare situation in which a government was actually designed. It was forged through careful consideration and impassioned debate, yet the vast bulk of the institutions in the fledgling U.S. government were inherited almost unchanged from the colonial government of the British. Everything—from the basic code of laws to the postal service, to the names of locations, the boundaries of the colonies, and even the local governing bodies within the thirteen colonies—came almost directly from the very same British colonial oppressors whom George Washington crossed the Delaware River to shoot.[*]

It is no different today. Revolutionaries still need the trains to run—and who better to run those trains than the experienced conductors and managers from the previous regime. The same goes for city governments, police officers fighting street crime, tax collectors, you name it. The very top of the political pyramid might be replaced by loyal revolutionary comrades in arms, but even with the most dramatic changes in government, the institutions beneath them seldom change much, if at all. In fact, if you turn this around, it is argued to be one of the big problems with the way the United States tried to rule Iraq after occupying that nation during the Second Gulf War. The United States excluded anyone from Saddam Hussein's Ba'ath Party from the new government. This removed a huge number of very experienced people from the government, so that simply conducting the basic business of running the country became difficult, and it also put those people out of work and left them little option but to oppose the U.S.-imposed government. Allowing the lower-level Ba'ath Party government bureaucrats to keep their jobs would have increased the immediate functionality of government, reduced the opposition, and probably reduced the cost and duration of the U.S. rebuilding effort.

At the extreme, a nation may not be able to implement its ideal institutions because its basic structures have been imposed upon it by another source. Newly independent colonies start

---

[*]When George crossed the Delaware River, he actually shot at German mercenaries in New Jersey, but let's not get picky.

with political institutions created by their former colonial masters, often with little or no consideration of the local cultures or realities of political power. At the close of World War II, the United States designed, and all but imposed, a new government for Japan. Various nations, including the United States, that were at one time colonies of European powers have governmental structures that mirror their former mother countries. In the words of The Who, "Meet the new boss, same as the old boss."

Even if you can suspend disbelief enough to argue that a nation can come up with and consciously go about trying to create ideal institutions, it is not necessarily true that what is planned will come to pass in the end. Like George Bailey in *It's A Wonderful Life,*[5] we find that our plans don't always work out in the way that we assume they will. Real life gets in the way. For George Bailey that means salvaging the family business, the Building and Loan, when he would have rather traveled around the world. In the real world the government structures that we erect, the plans we make as architects, do not always work out in the end. This happens with all kinds of structures. In the construction trade, so many adjustments always have to be made during the construction of a large building that *after* the project is finished, architects have to draw up a final set of building plans. These plans, called the "as-built drawings," show exactly how the planned building actually ended up being constructed. They are drawn up so that the designers of future renovations, or even those demolishing the building, will know exactly what is hidden inside the walls. The carefully designed U.S. government institutions had to be amended ten times before all the original states agreed to ratify them.

The imperfections of governmental structures go one step further. Even after accounting for all of these factors, we still must consider the effects of time and history as sources of many substantial deviations from the ideals we might dream up for our political institutions.

Take a plantation house built in the mid-1800s as an example of how history shapes the current expression of structures as institutions. In 1857, houses had foundations, walls, doors, and windows, but many other things we think of as basic to the structures of houses, such as electrical systems, did not exist or were vastly different. In a large expensive home of 1857, the kitchen was often not part of the house proper. The kitchen and its wood-burning stove was relegated to a separate building behind the main house, so the heat from the stove did not broil the occupants of the house during the summer, so the smells from unrefrigerated foods were kept out of the house, and, most important, so all the best parts of the house were protected from the dangers of kitchen fires.

As the years pass, the basic structural expectations for a house change; think of how such changes would eventually alter an 1857 plantation home. Central plumbing becomes a standard part of new houses, and eventually the women in the older home get tired of going outside to use the facilities, and they put their feet down and demand central plumbing.[*] From the point in time when central plumbing becomes standard, it is incorporated into the design of new

---

[*] I would humbly posit that the female members of a family are usually the more assertive proponents of indoor plumbing and other modern conveniences, given that men are generally willing to pee anywhere, but I'm open-minded on the topic.

houses. Once this happens, the other structural elements of new houses—walls, rooms, and such—are designed from the get-go to accommodate this new structure: fancy city plumbing. In new houses, the pipes are run inside the walls and the bathroom is included in the basic layout. In the old plantation house, the addition of plumbing has to be adapted to the existing structures. Pipes are run through the basement, and the coat closet under the stairs is converted to accommodate a toilet and sink.

Later, gas for lighting and cooking and then electricity are added to the plantation house. Eventually, the kitchen has to be moved into or added onto the basic structure of the house. With the development of central heating, an oil- or coal-fired boiler is shoved into the basement. This involves installing radiators and all the pipes needed to connect them to the boiler. Those new pipes have to be fitted in and around what already exists, so in an old house it's not unusual to see radiators blocking doors, exposed steam pipes in otherwise formal rooms, and all kinds of other makeshift fixes. More time passes. Showers, Jacuzzi tubs, air-conditioning, telephones, cable TV, a surround-sound media room, doggy doors, a library, a billiard room, Miss Scarlet in the conservatory with the revolver— everything that we now expect in a home has to be adapted to the basic form of that 1857 farmhouse. No one designing a new house would run pipes around on the outsides of the walls or turn a hall closet into a shower, but you see that sort of thing all the time in old houses. It's imperfect, but it's usually far too expensive to tear the house down and start again, so you must work with what you already have.

In short, the institutions you will find in today's governments are, in many ways, similar to an old house. Government institutions may not necessarily smell musty or make odd noises on a stormy night,* but they're the imperfect adaptations of structures. Their forms are shaped by history, culture, necessity, and circumstance. They're always imperfect.

Failed Institutions

Unfortunately, the imperfections that occur when ideal institutions are adapted to an imperfect world don't stop there. Political institutions sometimes just go wrong, and some do so quite badly. George Orwell's *Animal Farm*[6] clearly is meant to focus on the failed promise of communist revolutions. If we flippantly toss aside the whole communism and Cold War heart and soul of the book,[†] however, we see that the story can also demonstrate my point that attempts to shape ideal institutions can fail as individuals take advantage of the structures and context. The novel's plot describes a revolution in which the farm animals revolt and take over the farm. Motivated by the slogan that "all animals are equal," the animals are slowly co-opted by the pigs, who then alter the motto to indicate that some animals are more equal than others. Noble attempts to mold institutions can be pirated by those with less-than-noble purposes.

---

*Many do, however.

†I'm good a flippant. Probably because I learned to swim at a young age.

Further, regardless of intentions, statements, constitutions, or the detailed dictates handed down by the aliens who built the pyramids, political institutions are not always what they appear to be, and they may serve purposes that are not at first apparent. In *A Hitchhiker's Guide to the Galaxy,*[7] Douglas Adams's satirical jab at government is spun into a roundhouse left hook when the two main characters, Arthur Dent and Ford Prefect, run into Zaphod Beeblebrox, a two-headed being who happens to be president of the Imperial Galactic Government. As it turns out, the president has no power. The real job of the president of the Imperial Galactic Government is to do outrageous things that will distract attention from those who are truly in control. In fact, there is not even a galactic empire any longer. The only thing that remains is the name, which is kept alive solely for the purpose of allowing people to feel better about the government.

In Adams's skewering of all things official and proper, the institution of the presidency is used only as a distraction, but you do not have to travel along the fuzzy edge of literary insanity to find political institutions used as distractions, window dressing, or outright charades. Elections and parliaments in the real world can be prime examples. In 2002, Saddam Hussein was reelected as the president of Iraq. He was the only candidate, armed soldiers escorted people to the polling places, and voters had to sign their names to the ballots they cast, but no specific law said that everyone *had* to vote for a dictator known to slaughter entire villages. In Iraq there was also a parliament that debated issues. In reality, this parliament truly did make a few laws, but only as directed or allowed by Hussein. The Iraqi parliament's debates were as much a sideshow as Zaphod's presidency.

Too Legit to Quit: Legitimacy, Information, and Human Nature

Despite the variety of imperfections, complications, and difficulties that political institutions present, it's critical that you develop an understanding of these institutions. Even if a specific institution is a seemingly farcical sideshow or a pointless relic from a former age, it can still serve a purpose. For example, even without practical functions, institutions can build legitimacy for a government. The simplicity of my limited definition of legitimacy as the voluntary acceptance of the government or leaders should not detract from the fact that legitimacy is a key concept in political science. As an example of how institutions can enhance the voluntary acceptance of decisions, policies, choices, or even the leadership as a whole, remember why Zaphod was president even though the galactic empire had ceased to exist.

Even if an institution cannot affect the outcome of the policymaking process, keeping parts of history or tradition in the process can help convince people to accept the government's laws, processes, or policies. For example, when the U.S. Supreme Court declares that a law passed by Congress and signed by the president is constitutional, it convinces the public to accept the law. By affirming the law, it does not change or shape the law—indeed, often it will say that it is a bad law—but by declaring it constitutional the Court is saying to the public that the law has been examined and found to be within the bounds of

SOLVING ALL THE WORLD'S PROBLEMS, ONE TOPIC AT A TIME

As if I weren't already awesome enough, writing this textbook and all, I have also totally solved the problem of bad fiction, once and for all. I've spent a fair number of years as part of the slush reading team for *Andromeda Spaceways Inflight Magazine.* What's a magazine, you ask? Well, that's kind of an odd question, so I'm going to go right on as if you asked, What in the world is a slush reader? A slush reader is a poor sod who has to read through the stories that are submitted to a magazine and try to find the one or two out of a hundred that are worth passing on to the editor to consider. That's right, one or two out of a hundred. The sheer number of atrocious stories prompted me to start compiling a list of just what makes a story so horrible it could cause brain damage. Perhaps unsurprisingly, since I plopped this into a chapter on political structures, the most common reason a story is doomed to die in the slush pile lies in part of the structure of the story, the point where the author chooses to throw the reader in. Now, if just a few more of the authors out there would actually take a look at the list and at least try to avoid the obvious problems . . .

Douglas A. Van Belle, "A Comprehensive and Totally Universal Listing of Every Problem a Story Has Ever Had," *Andromeda Spaceways Inflight Magazine* online (2008), www.andromedaspaceways.com/EveryProblem.htm. Reprinted in *The New York Review of Science Fiction,* no. 248 (April 2009): 17–19. Sir Julius Vogel Award 2009— Finalist for Best Professional Publication.

the legally acceptable. This reassures the public and, in so doing, increases the public's willingness to accept the law. Across the pond, the queen of England opens meetings of Parliament by announcing what "Her Majesty's Government" will do during the upcoming session. This ritual increases the people's respect for the Parliament, draws their attention to it, and informs them of what is happening. The institution of the monarchy serves a purpose in this and other ways, even though the queen has virtually no true political power.

The example of the queen's role in opening Parliament is also important because of her role in informing the public. Governmental institutions can teach the public and shape the demands of the people as much as they react to the public's wishes or enact policy. Parliamentary and congressional hearings are conducted as much for the information they provide as they are for investigating what is needed to make good laws. The same can be said of legislative debates. The information that is provided to the public through a debate is often more important than the outcome, especially when legislation fails. From the debate, interested people will know the reasons particular legislation failed, and those who were in favor of the legislation can adjust their future demands to increase the chance of success. Debate can alert uninformed or unaware parties to the substance of the issue and provide the opportunity to generate input or feedback that will alter or even prevent the legislation. Think about an uncertain dictator who is facing domestic unrest and is worried about the reaction to a policy change. By staging a debate on the policy in his puppet

legislature, he can provoke a public reaction and get a hint of feedback without actually taking the risk of changing the policy and sparking a revolution.

It's also true that the institutions we utilize can go so far as to shape basic behavior in our day-to-day lives. Governments that demand citizen participation also demand that citizens be at least somewhat aware of public policy. Those governments that act in a paternalistic manner are likely to breed citizens who are dependent on strong leadership. Institutions that hunt down and punish dissent generate fear, isolation, and atomization. Nothing new with that idea: Aristotle, Rousseau, and many later theorists understood that human beings are the products of the societies they create. Furthermore, the institutions a nation utilizes reveal something about that society's overall view of human nature, and that connects to the earlier point that presumptions about human nature shape the ideals of a nation's political institutions.

SIMGOVERNMENT

The process of becoming a political science professor is much like a medieval apprentice-ship in which you sell your soul to an established professor and trade years of slave labor to learn the field and become a professor yourself. Then you get to torture your own students. Grad school feels a lot like signing up to become a troll in the hopes that you might one day become a swan. Part of this cycle of abuse is that political science graduate students spend enormous amounts of time reading books that no human would want to open, and they spend uncountable hours staring at computer screens full of mathematical hieroglyphics and other such gibberish.* Since the true revenge of the indentured servant is to avoid actually being helpful or productive, these political science trolls seek creative ways to look like they're working when in fact they're not. This is why computer games were invented, honest.

Computer solitaire has its limits. In fact, one student I knew got so bored with solitaire that he wasted nearly a month writing a program that played it automatically so he wouldn't have to waste his time wasting his time with solitaire. When I was in graduate school, one of the more popular computer games that helped students avoid doing any real work was Civilization. It wasn't quite Halo, but it was popular enough that it is still around. It's a great game in which you get to conquer the world, but aside from the fact that it is fun to build the pyramids in Cleveland and fight against Aztecs with cruise missiles, it does not work very well for the point I want to make. So I'm going to talk about SimCity instead.

For those of you who have never played SimCity or any of its progeny, the point is to start with a splat of land on a map and gradually build a functioning city complete with roads, airports, housing, businesses, Glorious Leader's Bountiful Carcass Pucks of Eternal Wonderfulness franchises, and so forth. You must accomplish all this while maintaining a balanced budget, a low crime rate, and general citizen satisfaction. It is an interesting, oddly noncompetitive, but highly addictive game that could consume an indescribable

---

*Am I selling you on it yet? I need a couple new trolls every year just to keep up with the boredom-induced fatalities.

amount of a graduate student's time. Even though some obvious problems have prevented me from finding a venture capitalist interested in creating a SimGovernment computer game, it strikes me that no one can stop me from torturing you with the idea. It also works pretty well as a framework for outlining some of the basic variations, decisions, and choices related to ideal and real political and governmental institutions.

Step 1: Choose a Terrain

The first step in SimCity is to select a terrain on which to start the city. If you were trying to build ideal government institutions out of thin air, you would pick a terrain that would be suitable for the type of government you want. That is, if you ultimately want to install a democracy, you would choose to construct a government in a place where the populace values participation, independence, and self-reliance. If you want to install a structure that emphasizes efficiency, you would build the government on a social foundation of people who like working obsessively and following orders. If you want fairness and equality, you would select a group that values community above all else. In short, the structures that you choose will be influenced by the basic **political culture**—the political aspect of the human nature of the local populace.

Political scientist Sidney Verba defines a nation's political culture as "the system of empirical beliefs, expressive symbols, and values, which defines the situation in which political action takes place."[8] This political culture can involve religious values, expectations, morals, ethics, and traditions. If you have taken a sociology class, you are probably very familiar with the notions of mores and traditions. Citizens do not often think about their political culture because they take it for granted. It is as fundamental and as absolutely natural as the basic personal hygiene skills you can reasonably assume your blind date will not possess. However, you notice immediately when you encounter someone who does not share your political culture, or for that matter the blind date who does not meet your expectations regarding an occasional encounter with soap.

Chinese political culture is radically different from the political culture in the Mountain West region of the United States, and no one who stopped to think about it would expect that we would be able to transfer Wyoming's political institutions to Beijing and have those institutions work effectively or at all in the Forbidden City. The basic expectations built into the two political cultures are different. How do you think the fiercely independent ranchers of Wyoming would react to the authoritative and dictatorial bureaucracies that are prevalent within Chinese political institutions?

The collapse of governments in many of the nations that had been colonized by Europeans shows the difficulties in installing representative democratic institutions in countries that have had no or very little experience with these types of institutions or among people who have no faith in democracy. If we took the political institutions of Denmark and simply transported them exactly as they are to Iran, would they succeed? Before you answer, consider the violent reaction a few Danish editorial cartoons managed

to spark across the Islamic world in September 2005. Cartoons that were perfectly acceptable forms of speech in Denmark sparked riots, murder threats, and efforts by Muslim countries to enact U.N. resolutions against Denmark. Clearly the Danes and the Iranians have different political cultures, especially in regard to freedoms of expression. Many of the countries of the former Soviet Union continue to struggle with their democratic institutions precisely because their dominant political cultures do not encourage participation, acceptance of the will of the majority, or a fundamental commitment to debate and voting as means of decision making. For that matter, although *democracy* is a Greek word, even Aristotle did not believe in democracy as we think of it now.

Thus, when designing your ideal government, you need to build your institutions in a place with the political culture appropriate to the type of government you want to build—or you will have to adjust your government to fit the political culture. When you design your simulated government institutions, you want to make sure that you do so in ways that maximize the degree to which they are wanted and voluntarily accepted. You need to maximize their potential for gaining and sustaining legitimacy.

Step 2: Choose a Basic Form

What is the basic form of government you would like to use? The form you choose will have a tremendous impact on how well different institutions serve their structural functions. For example, in the course of his examination of different constitutions, Aristotle identified six basic types. Of course, he recognized that many variations are possible, and that it is possible to mix the many types, but Aristotle was big on categories of ideal types, so he stuck with six. Among his six types of governments, he identified three *good* forms and three *perverted* forms (see my totally wonderful table 5.1). What differentiated the good from the perverted was for whom the government worked. If the government worked for the benefit of all of its citizens, Aristotle called it good. If it benefited only the ruling class, Aristotle labeled it a perverted type. The other major distinction Aristotle drew among the governments was the size of the group in charge.[9]

Table 5.1 Aristotle's Six Basic Government Types

Ruled by	Works for the benefit of all (good)	Works for the benefit of the ruling class (bad)
One	*monarchy*	*dictatorship*
Few	*aristocracy*	*oligarchy*
Many	*polity*	*democracy*

A nation that was led by one person could be either a **monarchy** (a good form) or a **dictatorship** (a perverted form). A government ruled by a few could be either an **aristocracy** (a good form) or an **oligarchy** (a perverted form). Finally, a government led by the many could be either a **polity** (a good form) or a **democracy** (a perverted form). One should not be too surprised that Aristotle labeled democracy a bad form. After all, in his day, democracy was synonymous with mob rule—that is, everyone acting in her or his own best interest with little or no regard for the community.

I will assume for this example that you do not want to use one of the perverted forms.* So, who will rule in your simulated government? Which institutions will you create? Will you choose to have a monarch? Before you jump to conclusions and say no to a monarchy, you should realize that I would make a pretty good king, and co-dictator of the universe is perhaps the one job that I would prefer over my current tenured position.

Also, there are benefits to having a monarchy. *Monarchy* literally means a single authority, and there are all kinds of situations in which having a textbook-writing professor as emperor would be a good thing. During a war, when decisions must be made quickly and decisively, or when a tough and unpopular choice must be made for the long-term best interest of the country, having a single decision maker can avoid the paralysis of committees and groups trying to make decisions. If you wish to have the most efficient form of government, why not just have one person make all of the decisions for you? Think of all the wasted time that can be eliminated by simply having a king decide—no long debates in Congress, no concerns about whether people really like an idea. Despite his faults, Mussolini was pretty much the only Italian leader ever to get the trains to run on time.† The pyramids were built by pharaohs, the Great Wall by Chinese emperors, Genghis Khan created the largest empire in the history of humankind, and you should have seen how I ordered around some of my graduate students to get this book done. There does tend to be a downside to most dictatorships—for example, death, war, slavery, the dead fish my downtrodden graduate students put in the bottom drawers of my desk at the start of every semester break; and do I have to mention Hitler?—but if you could only find a way to ensure that your dictator, or whatever else you want to call your monarch, would always be benevolent and would always avoid perverting government, you would be in business. However, even if you found the perfect person to take the job, how would you ever replace her when you eventually need to?‡ Make one of her kids the next king? What if her offspring are a pack of buffoons? From what I can gather from a study North Korean YouTube clips, the selection process for monarchs (and dictatorships) tends to be a bit irrational.

---

*What you choose to do in the private recesses of your own brain is your business, but please, not in my textbook.

†As noted in Chapter 3, I have been told that Italy has found a way to get its trains to run on time without resorting to fascism. However, I have never actually seen the trains run in Italy, and I would never let the facts get in the way of a good example.

‡I've actually come to the conclusion that a good dictator probably would have to be a woman. It's pretty obvious that all the men who have tried have failed.

In *Monty Python and the Holy Grail,*[10] the official and authoritative BBC documentary chronicling the rise of the monarchy in England, when King Arthur asks for directions from a peasant, the peasant asks how he became king and Arthur relates the story of the sword and the stone:

ARTHUR: The Lady of the Lake, [angels start singing] her arm clad in the purest shimmering samite, held aloft Excalibur from the bosom of the water signifying by Divine Providence that I, Arthur, was to carry Excalibur. [singing stops] That is why I am your king!

DENNIS: Listen, strange women lying in ponds distributing swords is no basis for a system of government. Supreme executive power derives from a mandate from the masses, not from some farcical aquatic ceremony.

ARTHUR: Be quiet!

DENNIS: Well you can't expect to wield supreme executive power just because some watery tart threw a sword at you!

ARTHUR: Shut up!

DENNIS: I mean, if I went around saying I was an emperor just because some moistened bink had lobbed a scimitar at me they'd put me away!

Clearly, the official process of selecting kings is less than perfect, even in a place that has gone through so many kings that kids have to use a song to remember them all, so you may want to consider limiting your monarch's power. But even if you do not actually give your monarch any real power, the central focus he or she can give to politics and government can be valuable for the group. Have you ever wondered why it is that Great Britain continues to have a queen? As institutions, modern monarchies serve as symbols for their nations. They bind the populace together and allow for a sense of national unity. In nations where monarchs coexist with parliaments, the monarchs often add legitimacy to these other governmental institutions by acknowledging their decisions as legitimate. Consequently, simply because you have a monarchy does not mean that you cannot still also have democratic institutions such as a parliament.

Still not convinced? Neither am I. Monarchs tend to soak up lots of their nations' money for no identifiable good reason, and with the exception of Yul Brynner's king of Siam, they tend not to be much fun at parties, so you may wish to choose some other form. If you choose not to have a monarch, your government is, according to one very basic definition, a **republic.** That does not mean you have a democracy; it just means that you do not have a single authoritative leader.

For example, if you value the promotion of a religion or an ideology, or you are a professional wrestling fan, you might prefer to hand power over to a few elites who could be

trusted to carry on the faith. Thus, an aristocracy might be for you. There is nothing quite like a group of religious leaders to watch over everything to make sure that the faith is being appropriately applied, supplied, and respected. In cases in which a secular ideology is the thing, there is often a ruling committee that makes sure the ideology is at the center of all decisions. Aristocracy would also be preferable if you could get the best people to rule the society. Of course, there are likely to be some knock-down, drag-out fights about what it means to be the best, and who qualifies. Even if you assume that the best leaders will be those who will make wise decisions for the good of the entire country, defining the good of the entire country is less than simple and certainly not obvious. Seems like a disaster waiting to happen, but before you get too down on aristocracy, you should bear in mind that many people argue that most of the countries that are considered representative democracies actually are ruled by small groups of elites. Further, many think this is a good idea. Winston Churchill purportedly once said, "The best argument against democracy is a five-minute conversation with the average voter." Elites tend to be well educated and well informed, and they often have the wealth needed to allow them to dedicate most of their efforts to governing rather than putting in overtime to buy a new snowmobile.

In fact, some form of aristocracy is actually a common feature of democratic governments. Many of the countries that you think of as democracies have constitutional courts similar to the U.S. Supreme Court—for example, Germany's Federal Constitutional Court (Das Bundesverfassungsgericht),* the Constitutional Court of Korea, and the Supreme Court of Canada. When the judges who sit on these courts make decisions, when they decide that certain laws violate their countries' constitutions and so they smite those laws to ashes,† are they acting democratically? These judges make up an aristocracy of legal and political elites who can, and often do, wipe out the results of massive democratic processes with the stroke of a pen.

Come to think of it, why would one choose to have a democracy? If you don't have an answer for that, you might want to hurry and think of something before you get to the democracy chapter. For now, however, you need to be aware that democracy is not the only alternative to monarchy and aristocracy. You should also be aware that perhaps those countries that you commonly think of as democracies contain some very undemocratic elements.

Step 3: Connect Your Government

Once you choose the form of government that you would like to have, it is important to decide how you would like to connect it and keep it together. Countries tend to be fairly big places, so big that they can strain the ability even to communicate from one end to the other. Hawaii is a full continent and half an ocean away from Washington, D.C. Russia covers eight time zones. And it takes hours to walk the length of Liechtenstein. Will all of the

---

*I didn't make that name up, honest.

†They are the Supreme Court, so they can do this even in a designated "no smiting" zone.

decisions in your government be made at one place, such as a very nice pub in the nation's capital? Or will some decisions be made at a more local level? If you do decide to divvy things up, where will those decisions be made and which level of government will have the ultimate authority to rule, in case there are conflicts or disputes between different local levels of government?*

There are essentially three systems through which the relationships among governmental levels can be ordered. Most often these are referred to as the **unitary system,** the **federal system,** and the **confederal system.** As I explained earlier, most nations don't *choose* to have one or the other. Rather, the makeup of the nation, its history, its culture, and its geography tend to determine the type of structure that will be used.

A unitary system is one in which sovereignty rests quite clearly on the shoulders of the national government. In other words, the national parliament, dictator, dancing llama, or whoever makes all the decisions for the entire nation. The laws apply to everyone regardless of where they live in the country, everyone shares all governmental benefits equally, there is no redundancy in services, and the whole plan is rather simple. This does not necessarily mean that there is no local-level government. It only means that the final word is always at the national level. The central national government can choose to allow some local governing boards to have a say in the decision making that will affect local communities; however, the ability to make these decisions is at the mercy of the national government, and that national authority could also choose to revoke this power from the local boards or to override any decisions the boards make. In France all of these decisions are made in Paris, in Syria they are made in Damascus, in Liberia in Monrovia, and I should not have to name many more before you get the idea. Seriously, pay attention, that was a pretty simple point.

Systems in which the final authority for at least some aspects of government is left to the local or subnational level are called federal systems. In a federal system sovereignty is, at least theoretically, shared between the national and the local government units. In the United States the national government shares its power with states, in Canada the sharing is done with provinces, in Germany there is sharing with *Länder.* The most obvious point of local political sovereignty in all three of these governments is education. Each state, province, or *Land* sets some or all of its own educational policy. Requirements for teacher preparation, funding schemes, curricula, even the number of school days in a year might be set at this or even more local levels.[†] Federal systems work well in diverse countries,

---

*In political science, the term used to describe the ultimate authority to rule is *sovereignty.* It is something akin to the unchallengeable right of all parents to end an argument with "Because I said so." Sovereignty is such an important concept in the discussion of international relations that I'll wait until that chapter before I talk too much about it. For the purposes of this discussion, sovereignty can be thought of as the ultimate power to decide, or who is the last person who can say "Because I said so" in the division of power among levels within your country. No matter how you set things up, it's important to decide where the final authority rests.

[†]Many, if not most, students in the United States assume that local control of education is the norm around the world. National education policy is actually far more common, especially in Europe, where education officials are often frustrated when they try to locate a U.S. national education ministry in the hope of exchanging information.

where variations in local conditions, economies, and cultures make it impractical or inefficient to try to impose a single system or make it difficult to enforce policy decisions from a central location. Think of why education policy is decentralized in the United States. It is unlikely that the forestry management class taught by my eight-fingered football coach in the small logging town outside of Seattle where I grew up would be of much value to the students of any of the high schools in the Bronx.

The Federation in *Star Trek* provides a perfect example. When Captain Kirk, and later his grandson or nephew or whatever Jean-Luc Picard was, puttered around the final frontier in the glorified intergalactic motor home they called the *Enterprise,* they talked a lot about the United Federation of Planets. Now, the temporal Prime Directive prohibits the transfer of knowledge from the future to the past,[†] so I can't give you much detail about the institutional arrangement that constituted this federation, but I can suggest that you presume that it was a federal system involving several planets. Further, if you stay sober through any of the episodes featuring negotiations for the entry of new members into the Federation, you'll find that consistent assurances of local sovereignty were made. From that you can conclude that within the bounds of the charter of the Federation, the individual planets ruled themselves.

While it is generally understood that in federal systems the governmental units share sovereignty, there are those who argue that shared sovereignty is not truly possible. These people believe that ultimate political power can never be shared and that one level must finally have supreme power. To the degree that this argument is true, you can assume that the national level would be the most powerful. However, perhaps the reality of where power resides makes it easier to see why it is so important for the people in a federal system to believe that the authority-sharing relationship is legitimate and robust. Without this belief, why would people invest effort in making local governments work?

Students in the United States often mistakenly equate federal systems with democratic systems. Most likely this is because they equate democracy with the structure that they know. A democracy, however, can use either a federal or a unitary system. The reality is that the unitary system is the more common form among democracies.

The least commonly used form is the confederal system. In a confederal system, it is the local government units that have the real power. They are the ones that have sovereignty. The key to the confederal system is that the individual units within it can defy the national or galactic level of government. They can even leave the system at any time they wish. The national government must maintain the continued willingness of all local units to stay in the confederation. This effectively gives every single local unit the power to veto any national-level policy by refusing to honor it or by leaving the system. As a result, it is usually the case that in confederations, the national or central government has very limited responsibilities.

[†] I know, I am a serious geek. I sincerely hope that by Chapter 5 you've gotten used to it. My kids have lived with it their whole lives.

The confederal type of government has been tried several times, but it has been about as successful as sitcoms about Ebola. It simply is too difficult to get things accomplished when you have so many parts of the system that can threaten to leave whenever they do not like something the central government is doing. The two closest things to a confederation that exist today are the United Nations and the European Union, and the European Union is a bit more like a halfway federation than a true confederation. Think about the difficulty that the United Nations has in getting anything accomplished, all the resolutions that are ignored by the relevant parties, and you will start to see the difficulty with confederacies. The European Union, which joins many of the nations in Europe to a common currency, joint trade policies, and a free trade zone, is a slightly more successful venture, but again, note how limited its authority is and the ongoing agony of the constant negotiations over Greece, Spain, Germany, and the fate of the Euro. There are huge economic and trade disincentives for leaving the EU, but that same system has no real way to enforce the national taxation and budgeting responsibility that is necessary for states to function within a system where they cannot fudge currency values to compensate. Everything, including the enforcement of financial agreements, is a point of constant negotiation, and it always seems to devolve into Germany acting like a parent who does not believe in punishment trying to bribe and cajole unruly kids into not throwing a tantrum in the grocery store. And thus, in one deft act of politically incorrect crassness, I have explained the ongoing crisis over the Euro and the ineffectiveness of the confederal system that supports that shared currency.

In reality, therefore, nations have only two real options: a federal system or a unitary system. Each has its benefits and its drawbacks. First, federal systems are more appropriate in large countries and in countries that have geographically diverse populations. Federalism allows for differences among the local government units that reflect differing cultures or traditions. Federalism can also be particularly appropriate for large countries that want democratic systems, since it is more likely people will have a noticeable influence on their representatives in smaller units. In large nations, such as the United States, a national representative can represent several hundred thousand people. Local government units allow the institutions that have the greatest direct effects on people's daily lives to be created on a smaller, more tractable scale that gives individual citizens more influence on the formation of policy.

Federal systems also allow for the local governments to act as what U.S. Supreme Court justice Louis Brandeis called "laboratories for social experimentation."[11] That is, these local governments can dream up and try out on a small scale several solutions to social problems. Those that work can then be copied or adapted by the rest of the nation, including other local governments that may have tried different solutions that failed. In this way, policy mistakes are confined to small areas, while policy successes can be shared with other states or perhaps the whole nation.

The refurbishment of areas known as brownfields—abandoned industrial sites, garbage dumps, and other locations where the land has been contaminated or seriously screwed up in one way or another—provides a perfect example. These eyesores exist all across the United States and drive down property values, attract crime, and encourage further degradation of the surrounding properties. Around the country a variety of efforts have been made to revitalize these properties; they have been used as locations for low-income housing, schools, new industrial parks, and almost every other kind of development you might imagine. It turns out that the best solution found so far is to put golf courses on them. Golf courses are green and open spaces that have two important characteristics. First, they look very pretty and enhance surrounding property values. Second, the people who use them are primarily adults who are on them for only a few hours at a time.

Since most of these brownfields have contaminant problems, building housing and businesses on them tends to create long-term exposure; even slight levels of pollutants can have detrimental effects on people who live on such properties or work long hours there. Think of young kids in low-income housing. They sleep there, eat there, and play in the dirt in the yard, all at a stage in their development at which they can be severely affected by even the lowest level of contamination. Levels of toxic pollutants that might be devastating for a toddler living every minute of every day in a revitalized brownfield are harmless to grandpa when he is there only for a few hours at a time as he putters around in a golf cart. The key is that the golf course solution came not from national decision making or from research at the national level, but from a local experiment dreamed up by someone who had to do something with an old garbage dump. Its success was then copied, improved upon, and adapted all across the nation.

One last benefit of federal systems is that they offer citizens more choices about the governmental institutions that fit them best. Like a shopper in a grocery store, a citizen can theoretically choose the kind of local government he or she would like to live under and then move to a place that has such a government. Have a high income? Move to a state with little or no income tax. Have lots of kids? Move to a community with good public schools. Approve of the death penalty? Move to Texas. Starting a business? Move to Delaware, where the business laws are quite liberal. Believe in limited government? Try Wyoming or Alaska. Want an activist government? Try California. This presumes you have the money and ability to move, but the general point is clear—variety gives you options.

Unitary systems also have their benefits. In a unitary system the governmental structure is easy to understand. Citizens do not have to worry about who has the responsibility to carry out policy. Furthermore, they do not have to worry about elections for multiple offices. As previously noted, in a unitary system every citizen in the country is entitled to the same rights and benefits. Some citizens do not have more money spent on their education, health care, welfare, and the like than others do simply because they live in one

state as opposed to another. Prisoners do not spend more time locked up in one state than they do in another for the exact same crime. Consequently, in comparison with federal systems, unitary systems make it easier to maintain a sense of national identity. Unitary systems tend to run more smoothly because they make the implementation of policy easier, and less effort is spent sorting out who should do what. Regulatory consistency across a larger entity also has economic benefits, since one product can be sold across the whole nation and the makers of products can more easily capitalize on efficiencies of scale.

On the other hand, some would argue that federal systems fit in well in countries with capitalist economic systems. Why is this? In federal systems, because both people and businesses have the capacity to move, local governments must compete to keep people and jobs within their borders. Local governments need businesses to pay taxes or to provide jobs to those who will pay taxes. Competition forces these local governments to optimize the business environments of their jurisdictions in one way or another. This might mean maximizing the education system or minimizing regulations. It could mean keeping taxes as low as possible by being very stingy in the benefits given to citizens—that is, spending little on welfare, education, or health care. Some local governments might seek an advantage by spending on infrastructure such as railways or anything else that makes for a very healthy business environment. This variety of ways of competing for wealthy private and corporate citizens can create niches for many different kinds of business, creating a diverse and healthy economy across the nation. Thus, you see again how the institutions you choose can affect the types of policies that your government will be able to enact, and I declare you duly educated according to all laws and regulations governing such activities.[12]

Step 4: Build Your Institutions

At last you are ready to build your institutions. Having put the basics in place—environment, form, and connections—you can design the specific mechanisms that you will use to accomplish the things that you need or want from government. How are you going to police your country, create your laws, or enact policy? In the following chapters you will be cruelly forced to examine the most important of the different structures and the different types of institutions more closely. However, before I begin this somewhat evil project, I want to clarify that I am talking about functions, not names or labels. All governments must perform different governmental functions. The legislative function is the making of law, the executive function is the enacting of law, and the judicial function is the interpreting and enforcement of law. However, simply because there is a legislative function, it does not necessarily follow that a legislature must perform that function. In fact, a person given the title of czar, king, shah, general, Glorious Leader, or El Presidente for Life can perform the legislative function—and such persons have done so throughout history.

After all, somebody has to make laws. Those laws can come from one person, several people, or lots of people. In reality, even where there are parliaments, other institutions still often perform legislative functions. For example, when bureaucracies issue regulations, they are making laws. It is also often the case that legislatures give executives the opportunity to make policy on their own. In these cases also the executive legislates.

Further, it is not necessarily the case that because a legislature performs the legislative function, the country is democratic. There is no such requirement. A dictator can appoint legislators who make the law. After all, being a dictator is a tough job. You have to be constantly worrying about those who have guns* and want your power. So, as a dictator, you may choose to turn over your legislative authority to a handpicked legislature that is responsible for making the laws for the country. After all, what dictator wants to create all of the parking regulations? As I noted near the beginning of this chapter, the British Parliament and many other such bodies actually originated not as democratic institutions but as bargains between kings and wealthy elites. The kings used the lords to raise cash, and, in exchange, the lords used their leverage to have some control over law. Later these bargains evolved into democratic legislatures.

It is equally true that other institutions can perform functions that are not necessarily part of the names of the institutions. Legislatures can and do perform judicial and executive functions. As we will see more clearly later, a major element of the American doctrine of separation of powers is just that, the blending of functions and institutions.

As you continue to build your imaginary government structures, I want you to make sure that your government will be successful. Over the long term, legitimacy tends to be an important factor in the success of political institutions, so as you dream up your perfect institution for making laws you may want to keep that in mind. The voluntary acceptance of these mechanisms serves as the glue that keeps a government together and functioning. In the idealized game of SimCity, you must keep your people happy to win—the same holds true for governments in the real world. Yeah, a dorky conclusion, I know.

KEY TERMS

---

*The ones with guns *and* bullets are particularly dangerous.

CHAPTER SUMMARY

Government structures are the basic things that governments need to do to govern; they are the basic functions that appear in every modern government. Political institutions are the particular mechanisms that a government uses to carry out essential government functions. For example, every government must have a mechanism to create laws—a government structure—but not every country has a Congress—a political institution. Institutions often reflect a society's view of human nature and its hopes; however, a society rarely has an opportunity to create institutions from scratch. In addition to the basic functions that institutions serve, they also can allow governments to build legitimacy for their policies. There are many different types of government, and Aristotle came up with one of the most commonly used typologies, which divides government types according to the number of people who rule and for whom the government works. Most countries utilize a federal or unitary system to structure their relations between the national government and its local entities. Students should learn two very important lessons from this chapter. First, there is more to studying government institutions than merely identifying the names of institutions in particular countries. Political institutions are reflections of a nation's culture, its aspirations, and its history, and these institutions also play a role in shaping a government's policies. Second, while SimGovernment might be a good way of thinking about structures and institutions, the author is not expecting any phone calls from software developers or venture capitalists.

STUDY QUESTIONS AND EXERCISES

1. What is the difference between government institutions and government structures? How many examples of structures and institutions can you identify?

2. Consider the impact of political culture on government structures and institutions and how the political culture affects what is possible in a given nation. How might this concept help to explain some of the difficulties that the United States has had with Iraq and other countries around the world?

3. Explain the differences among unitary, federal, and confederal systems. Under what circumstances might one system be preferred over another?

4. How did Aristotle differentiate among the types of government, and what basic types did he identify? What factors are likely to stand in the way of a nation that tries to create ideal institutions?

www.cia.gov/cia/publications/factbook. The World Factbook, the U.S. Central Intelligence Agency's profile of countries around the world, contains a wealth of historical, political, and geographic information.

www.foundingfathers.info/federalistpapers. This site offers the complete collection of the *Federalist Papers.*

http://lcweb2.loc.gov/frd/cs. The Library of Congress's Country Studies site contains information about the social, economic, political, and national security systems of countries around the world.

http://news.bbc.co.uk/1/hi/country_profiles/default.stm. The BBC's Country Profiles site contains historical, political, and economic information about countries around the world.

www.nytimes.com/pages/cartoons. The *New York Times* political cartoons section showcases a collection of current political cartoons by syndicated cartoonists.

www.parliament.uk/about/livingheritage.cfm. This site presents a good history of the British Parliament.

El Grande Loco Casa Blanca

The Executive (in Bad Spanish)

Sasquatch . . . For President. Given the nontraditionalities I've hurled at you in the first five chapters, you probably aren't going to blink when I start this chapter by telling you that Sasquatch would make a pretty good presidential candidate. He is tall, and taller presidential candidates consistently win more votes. He has a full head of hair, again something commonly associated with winning elections. He is elusive, which should serve him well at press conference time. His independent outdoor lifestyle gives him the right background to capture the rural vote, and he has great name recognition. Pair him with a hawkish, charismatic vice presidential running mate, maybe someone with a distinguished military record, perhaps someone like Captain James T. Kirk, and good old Bigfoot could easily stand for the Republican Party in 2020. I'd suggest that he wait until 2020 because I'm not too sure that the rather vocal pack of right-wing screaming weasels is yet ready to accept a candidate who doesn't shave, but if you would mention the idea to Sasquatch next time you see him and tell him to give me a ring about managing his campaign, I'd appreciate it.

The problem with Sasquatch, in addition to the shedding and the fleas, not to mention the way the absence of a Mrs. Sasquatch will inevitably stir questions and insinuations concerning his romantic preferences, is that even after a university professor surprises the world by leading his campaign to victory, he probably won't be anything close to the ideal president. He's more than a bit too camera shy for all the photo ops, he doesn't have a lot of experience with public speaking, and you have to worry about the leadership abilities of a mythical creature who's been hiding out by himself in the woods forever.

Perhaps a Kirk–Sasquatch ticket would be better. That way you could get the contribution of Sasquatch's appeal to the bomb-shelter-in-the-woods portion of the electorate, but then also get a

real leader in the White House. We all know that Captain Kirk has some kick-ass leadership abilities. Seriously, how many times has he rallied his crew against impossible odds and saved the girl, starship, planet, or galaxy? He's got the charisma and that indefinable personal presence that Americans expect in their presidents. And who better than a legendary starship captain to serve as commander in chief of the U.S. armed forces? But then again, Kirk's a hotheaded, impatient cowboy with a flagrant disregard for procedure, process, and propriety. He's been demoted or disciplined more often than they changed the oil on the *Enterprise.* And just like Bigfoot, he isn't married. Americans expect their presidents, even the ones who are "dating" their interns, to be properly spousified. And when Kirk actually gets into office, things will probably get a bit rough. As a starship captain he's used to unquestioning loyalty and immediate responses to his every command, and that's not the way the whole checks-and-balances, separation-of-powers structure of a modern democratic government works. Kirk really isn't the kind of person who is going to work well with Congress, and when he gets frustrated with the bureaucracy, he's likely to set his phaser to liquefy and blast away, which really, really isn't ideal. Besides, he's a fictional character. If there's even the slightest chance that Bigfoot exists, that's still more than a fictional character that everyone knows for certain is completely and totally made up.

Even though Kirk would make a lousy president, the U.S. presidency still provides a perfect example of the contrast between the reality and the ideal of the executive structure of government. Through fiction and the idolization of many past presidents, we have built up an ideal and impossible image of the presidency as a political institution. In truth, there are no superhero politicians who can step into the White House and get what they want accomplished while simultaneously staying above the fray of politics and occasionally leaping tall buildings in a single bound.* Instead, there are genuine human beings who operate within real and very imperfect political systems. Since the New Deal and World War II, the nation has expected a great deal out of its presidents, far more than is realistically possible, given the limitations of the office. Still, Americans want their presidents to have it all: the effectiveness of Franklin D. Roosevelt, but far more attractive; the toughness of Harry S. Truman, but without the abrasive eruptions of colorful and crass vocabulary; the bravery and honor of Dwight D. Eisenhower, but combined with the ability to speak in coherent sentences; the vitality and magnetism of John F. Kennedy, but without that whole starting the Vietnam War thing; the adroit deal making of Lyndon B. Johnson, but without that escalating the Vietnam War thing; the political skillfulness of Richard M. Nixon, but without the paranoid criminal antics; the honesty and intelligence of Jimmy Carter, but combined with the ability to master the insanity of Washington politics; the charm and

---

*Arnold Schwarzenegger does not count. First, he is not human; he is an android sent back from a heavily accented future. Second, all that bulletproof super-robot stuff was actually performed by a bulletproof stunt robot named Larry. And, as California politics have repeatedly demonstrated, not even "the Governator" can stay above the political fray.

media presence of Ronald Reagan, but without Nancy or the Alzheimer's; the foreign policy experience of George H. W. Bush, but with a better understanding of the economics of domestic policy; the education of Bill Clinton, but without all that Hillary and Monica stuff; and the ideological commitment of George W. Bush, but with the ability to pronounce *nuclear* correctly.[†] That's a tall order. Until some mad scientist perfects the genetic splicing and associated cloning technologies needed to create such a hybrid creature, that ideal president will never exist.[‡] Nevertheless, while the actual officeholders are bound to disappoint, the presidency as an executive institution remains, and we can discuss the ideal president as a way of understanding the U.S. executive and then contrast that with other executive institutions and structures.

Actually, I'm going to turn that plan topsy-turvy and discuss ancient executive institutions, then authoritarian executive institutions, and then finally the U.S. presidency in the context of democratic executive institutions, but you should keep in mind that I planned to work from the presidency, and then it all came out backward.

It's also important to keep in mind the distinctions among the president, the presidency as an American political institution, the presidency as a democratic political structure, and the executive as a universal political structure. Regardless of the opinions expressed about present and past presidents, Americans have tremendous respect for the office of the presidency, and consequently presidents begin their terms with a great deal of public support. Even though George W. Bush lost the popular vote in 2000, he entered office with an approval rating well over 50 percent. And even as individual presidents fail or embarrass, Americans remain faithful to the institution of the **presidency.** It is an institution, after all, that a number of men have used to great effectiveness at various points in American history. That brings up an important point: institutions become institutions, in part, by lasting over time. Further, institutions are larger than the people who occupy particular offices at any given time. The institution of the presidency, like all governmental institutions, includes all formal and informal powers, the offices, the staffs, and the historical precedents that define the institution. The United States has had many presidents. They arrive with parades and fanfare, and they leave by the side door with hastily packed suitcases full of stolen White House towels and little bottles of shampoo. Many of them even win elections. But the institution of the presidency exists and persists beyond those who sit behind the desk in the Oval Office.

Okay, back to the way I didn't plan to do this chapter.

[†] I am not ignoring the comments I could offer about Barack Obama; I just have a policy of not putting presidents on this list until they leave office and no longer control the CIA.

[‡] Also, the plots of countless B movies make it absolutely clear that even if you could genetically engineer such a president you would end up with a combination president and half-crazed, radioactive giant cockroach that would attack Tokyo and cause people to talk out of sync with the movement of their mouths.

OH CAPTAIN, MY CAPTAIN

Even though a Kirk presidency would be more disastrous than most, it is important to take a step back and realize that the U.S. presidency is just one of countless different executive institutions that exist or have existed in the world. It is just one of many presidential institutions, and you should remember that when you consider Kirk as a chief executive. There have been many military dictatorships, warrior fiefdoms, and reality television shows in which Kirk would have been the ideal executive.

At the most abstract and ideal level, the executive branch or executive office of a government would be something like a starship captain commanding the ship of state. Actually, more accurately, the executive would be the actual starship itself. We often think of the executive as the captain of the starship, the king, emperor, president, prime minister, or dictator, but the executive branch of a government includes far more than that. The executive is the implementer; it is the part of government that acts. It includes not just Caesar but also Caesar's armies, spies, and other operatives, and that probably includes people, offices, and agencies that you wouldn't think of as being part of the executive. I've given the bureaucracy its own separate chapter, but that's just because I've got a bitchin' bureaucracy story that needed a chapter so I could mention it. Most modern bureaucracies would fit under my "that which acts on behalf of the state" definition of the executive. So, technically speaking, you should include bureaucrats right up next to the generals, spies, and diplomats. Anyway, the point is that the term *executive* can be used to refer to the entire branch of government that performs actions on behalf of the state or to the office or position that an individual might hold. And just to make things even clearer, the individual holding the office of the executive may be referred to as the executive, though he or she usually has a title specific to the institution.

A second point that is probably worth noting, since this is a textbook and all, is that there is a difference between a **head of state** and a **head of government.** Generally speaking, when I refer to the executive as an individual or as an office that an individual might be chased out of by a torch-wielding mob, I am talking about the head of government. In contrast, the head of state is the person who symbolically embodies or represents the state. The head of government negotiates treaties; the head of state holds dinner parties. This distinction can be a bit difficult for American students to get used to, because the U.S. president is both head of state and head of government, but if you think about England, it helps. The British prime minister is head of government. When the prime minister sends troops marching, it's a war. The queen is head of state. When the queen sends the boys marching, it's a parade.

Several forms of executive, such as seventeenth-century kings, are both head of state and head of government, but when it comes to democratic executives, there are some points of discussion that make the distinction between these two roles interesting.

THE SCORPION KING ON GRANDPA'S FARM

I am neither an anthropologist nor an ancient historian. I am kind of ancient, but I'm not a historian, so discussing the early and primitive forms of executive institutions is a bit of a challenge for me.* I compensate for my lack of official expertise with questionable details and even more questionable jargon employed with unwarranted and irresponsible confidence.

The absolute and unquestionable truth of the matter is that the role of the executive was invented by a guy named Larry, on a Thursday. In the course of philosophizing about the hermeneutical nature of authority, Larry epiphanized a fundamental resonance that associopathed the cranial phalangial concussors with the evolutionized familial communicative infrastructurals, asserting the primal reproductive unit's subserventitude. Or, in layman's terms, Larry smacked his kid upside the head and yelled, "Because I said so!" and thus, the executive office of government was first established.

There are two points students should cull from that steaming pile of gobbledygook. First, even though your parents probably don't smack you upside the head all that often, they want to, often, very, very often. It's nothing personal. It's just a parent/teenager thing. I'm even less of a psychologist than I am an anthropologist, but I suspect that the instinct to smack teenage offspring arises from the very reasonable parental belief that if we could just rattle that stuff around in your head, you'd get smarter. Mathematically speaking, a random assortment of brain mush has to be smarter than whatever it is that you've been growing inside that skull. Second, family relations and the origins of the basic structures of government probably sort of go together. I should probably have started with that, since it's the relevant part.

I want to emphasize the role of the family straightaway because I think I need to correct what I believe is a common misperception regarding the earliest forms of the executive. If asked about the early executive, many students refer to some kind of warrior king and describe something similar to the dynamics of the baboon troop they saw on whatever Animal Planet show is the latest choice for irresponsible student drinking games. Fair enough. The baboon troop idea fits with what most of us have seen or think we know about early executives. Before Dwayne "The Rock" Johnson was abducted by Disney and tortured into family-friendly submission, he played the title role in *The Scorpion King,*[1] in which he basically out-babooned all the bad guys to become the king. Something like this can also be seen in *Alexander*[2] and *Braveheart,*[3] and even *The Lion King.*[4]

Further, if you were to take a Hobbesian view of the state of nature and combine that with the argument that security is the primary reason for government, the apparent prevalence of warrior kings and the quasi-military structures of executive institutions in a wide variety of governments, combined with the idea of personal combat or some other

---

*I had to go read some actual books and everything.

measure of personal military prowess as a method of executive selection, all seem to fit. After all, for the Hobbesians in the group of farmers that is not a tribe, it's a world full of rabid baboons, and the survival of your little colloquium would be best served if it was led by your biggest, baddest, and rabidest baboon. Making this scenario even easier to believe, the idea of a warrior king is not only common in fiction, but history is also littered with examples, such as Genghis Khan and Margaret Thatcher.

However, even with the numerous historical examples available, there are a couple of problems with thinking of the warrior king as the predominant form of the early executive. First, even if a leader won the executive role through some form of combat, there doesn't seem to be a lot of incentive for an incumbent executive, especially as he or she grows older, slower, and creakier, to do anything to encourage the institutionalization of personal combat as a means of executive selection. In fact, as my earlier discussion of the value of the leadership position and revolution suggests, it would seem that the incumbent executive has absolutely every incentive to discourage others from attempting to take the executive position through combat, assassination, or any other kind of potentially lethal personal confrontation. Instead, you would expect the warrior king to attempt to establish some kind of hereditary or other form of succession that doesn't involve the current leader ending up dead of anything but old age and maybe a bad case of exhausted-by-harem. In fact, if you look at the most famous historical examples of warrior kings, this indeed is something that you see. The conquerors usually work like the dickens[*] to put their children on the throne.

A second problem with thinking that the warrior king might be the predominant form of the primitive executive is that even though we see warrior kings so often in fiction and history, they were still probably quite rare. Just as wars are rare but grossly overrepresented in history books and in the study of international relations, it is reasonable to argue that the dramatic nature of the warrior sagas causes the warrior kings to be overrepresented and exaggerated in legend, history, and fiction. After all, do you really want to listen to the story of the village chieftain who inherited the office from his father, managed squabbles over wayward goats, made annual decisions on how many sheep would stay on the communal field over the winter, then died of ancientness and left the office to his nephew? For the vast majority of the vast, vast number of chiefdoms, tribes, independent village kingdoms, and city-states in the ancient world, the vast majority of the executives probably inherited or earned their positions, copied much of what their predecessors did, served as quiet managers of undramatic days, and passed it all on to the next heirs. We generally have reasonably good historical records only for the big empires of the ancient past, and since empires tend to be conquest oriented, you would expect their leaders to be more war oriented than the leaders of fishing villages and mountain towns where most primitive executives were to

---

[*]This one's for the nontraditional students in the class. You're welcome.

be found, but even if you look at the records of ancient Egypt, Greece, China, or just about any of the other big kingdoms or empires from anywhere in the ancient world, nonviolent succession seemed to be the norm, and most leaders seemed to spend most of their lives managing the mundane. Even the leaders who engaged in wars usually did so only for brief periods and spent more time at peace than they did killing their neighbors.

A second, and perhaps better, way of thinking about the earliest form of the executive is to think of it as a gradual institutionalization of **patriarchy** or **matriarchy** in a family or extended family group. The inheritance of the family business provides a good analogy. Each of the ships featured on *Deadliest Catch*[5] has to have a captain, which is quite fortuitously analogous to the executive of the ship of state, and most of those fishing ships are family ships. The captaincy of most of the ships has been inherited from earlier generations or is shared or transferred within the family, and each family has its own way of managing it. Sig took over the chair of the *Northwestern* from his father, and he doesn't give that chair up for anyone. The Hillstrand brothers take turns in the captain's chair of the *Time Bandit,* and Keith Colburn gave the chair of the *Wizard* to Monty for one of the opilio crab seasons. Sons, cousins, and younger brothers work as deckhands, training their way to either take over a family ship or otherwise take on captain's role when the captain needs to catch a couple hours of sleep, when he wants to spend a few months away from the ship, or when he wants to retire altogether.* Eventually, if these boats survive through enough generations, the precedents set by earlier generations become institutionalized and the transfer of the captain's chair becomes law-like. Further, certain characteristics about how the executive for each family captains the boat become institutionalized. If you watch *Deadliest Catch,* you can see that each ship has different ways of doing things, different ways of making decisions about where to fish and how to fish, and much of that process has been handed down from previous generations.

I would argue that the institutionalization of many, if not most, primitive executive institutions was probably similar. Essentially the executive role grows out of familial, business-like efforts to exploit resources, occasionally defend against other groups, and manage the cooperation needed to protect the group from lions, tigers, and bears. Eventually, both the methods of executive inheritance and some of the specifics of executive action become institutionalized. The postapocalyptic classic *Earth Abides*[6] provides a fictional example of this institutionalization process. A small number of plague survivors form a group akin to an extended family, and over the years, many of their unofficial leader's methods of doing things and even his habits become ritualized, and then institutionalized. Toward the end of the book, as the leader grows old and frail, the men who temporarily

---

*While it can be difficult to think of an example, particularly a pop-culture example, that is not heavily biased toward the testosterone-sodden half of society, do not take that to preclude the institutionalization of a feminine or gender-neutral executive in primitive societies. There are several historical examples, particularly from precolonial Africa.

step into that executive role for the tribe find that the tribe responds best when they use the same methods as the aging leader to do something, such as selecting a hunting ground. The last chapter of the book provides an interesting commentary on what has become institutionalized within the leadership position.

This is not to deny the Hobbesian view of the world, or to deny that we have plenty of examples of warrior kings. Instead, what I want to say is that if you were to put all the leaders of the millions of ancient tribes, chiefdoms, and kingdoms on a scale from the Scorpion King to the wisest grandpa shepherd, that scale would probably be tilted heavily toward the latter.

KINGS AND PRESIDENTS

The prevalence of **hereditary monarchies** throughout history and across cultures provides additional reason to argue that the nature of the primitive executive was skewed away from the warrior king and toward something like the family business analogy. Hereditary monarchies also provide a reasonable context for starting the discussion of the modern executive as a political institution. For this discussion—which really isn't much of a discussion, since I can't hear what you're screaming back at me and I probably wouldn't listen anyway—I am going to categorize modern executives as either authoritarian or democratic, and then further divide those two categories into two subcategories. Categorizing things is good. Very, very good.

Sticking to my strengths, I'm going to oversimplify and ignore everything I don't feel like talking about. Thus, I am going to skip right over a whole bunch of history and define things in modern terms. Thus, the authoritarian executive is a leadership institution that is mostly unconstrained by other branches of government. Authoritarian executives can be divided into monarchies and oligarchies. Democratic executives are executives that are significantly and intentionally constrained in the independence of their actions, usually by the threat of future elections, and they come in two flavors, presidential nut fudge and parliamentary berry swirl.

There is some method to my madness. More madness than method, obviously, but jumping past most of the Middle Ages avoids the worst of the plague years and also takes us to the point at which the ideals and the realities of leadership and government reemerged as topics of discussion, debate, and, in some cases, practice. Basically, I'm fast-forwarding to the good part.

Because GOD™ Said So

Nobody has actually trademarked GOD™, although you could argue that many a king and TV preacher have tried. In fact, it used to be relatively common for kings to claim that they were themselves divine. The Egyptian pharaohs, for example, were thought to be gods, and they were far from the only secondhand deities mucking about with us mere mortals

THINKER IN BOXES

AURELIUS AUGUSTINUS HIPPONENSIS

Team: *Algerian Old Boys*

Position: *Leg Gully*

Status: *Retired to Florida*

Better known as **Saint Augustine** (354–430), Aurelius Augustinus Hipponensis was a key contributor to the philosophical and theological foundations of early Christianity. He spent most of his life in small cities in North Africa. He also made a notable move to southern Europe, where he was so profoundly disappointed by his students that he gave up trying to teach and moved back to the North African boondocks. Apparently some problems are timeless in academia.

Philosophers get all twittery over his discussions of the soul, evil, free will, and predestination, but for the study of politics his distinction between the world of God and the world of men has to be considered a crucial text in the development of western political thought. *De Civitate Dei (On the City of God)* (circa 413–427) provides some key arguments that helped reconcile the divine mandate of kings with the less than divine nature of many, if not most, who inherited high royal office. The book itself might best be interpreted as a reaction to the sacking of Rome. It can be read as an argument for why God didn't protect Rome from the Visigoths and why Christianity was not to blame. Fundamental to this argument and much of Augustine's thought was the contrast between the earthly and the heavenly, which he defined largely as a dichotomy between the material and spiritual. Essentially, Augustine blamed the material, hedonistic excesses of the Romans for its downfall and prescribed a heavy dose of ascetic Christian spirituality, decongestants, and plenty of clear liquids.

It is not possible to catalogue all of the different ways that the tremendous volume of Augustine's writings, much of which survives to this day, influenced the development of western thought, particularly in philosophical and theological studies. However, the argument for the separation of the spiritual and material realms became one of the key elements of the theory of the divine right of kings.

and squabbling over who got to rule what bits of the planet. That changed as Europe stumbled its way through the Middle Ages. It's not exactly clear when, but one Thursday the conceptual foundation of the monarchy changed from "I am a God" to "Because God said I'm in charge."

It's impossible to identify the exact Thursday when this change occurred, but it's not that difficult to see the mix of historical, social, and political factors that coalesced into the concept that became known as the **divine right of kings.** It was largely a legacy of Roman rule and Christianity. The short and sweet version of the story is that the king as god thing doesn't fit too horribly well with the monotheistic nature of Christianity, and as Rome marched its way to the edge of Scotland something had to give, and it wasn't going to be the Romans.[*] Intellectually, most of the medieval European concepts of monarchy owe a great debt to Saint Augustine of Hippo's (354–430) *On the City of God,* which combined

---

[*]Obviously, Romans and Christianity didn't always go together, but for most of the centuries they ruled and dominated Europe, they did.

Greek, Roman, and Christian philosophical traditions to argue that there are two kingdoms of God—the heavenly, which God rules himself, and the earthly, which God appoints men to rule on his behalf. That separation allowed for the imperfection of governments and rulers on earth and was the direct antecedent of the concept of the divine right of kings. This and the other aspects of the debate about the divinity of the ruler were part of the Roman culture that the Roman legions carried into the rest of Europe with them.

While Roman conquests and the subsequent spread of Roman culture had profound effects on Europe, even on parts of Europe outside the Roman Empire, it is a mistake to think of the Roman Empire in terms of modern countries or kingdoms. The Roman Empire imposed some aspects of Roman government and culture over the areas it conquered, but it wasn't a big homogenizing beast. Most of the little European chiefdoms, towns, and villages that the Romans pulled into their empire retained a great deal of autonomy. Hereditary chiefs and princes, and whatever else they might call the executive ruling over a collection of filthy little huts along a muddy street, still reigned over their little patches of land, usually just switching their subservience—and related extortion/tax payments—from the latest barbarian king to a Roman governor. These little chiefdoms persisted, but any notion of royal divinity they might have held stood little chance of surviving against the combination of Christianity and secular Roman emperors and governors. Somewhere in there, the ideal of a divine prince had to be reconciled with the reality of Roman rule, and the idea of divine rulers was replaced by the idea of divine right.* The princess may not be a goddess—in fact, in the Middle Ages she probably didn't even have all of her teeth—but she was chosen by God to rule over the little swamp that her great-granddaddy conquered.

Within the bounds of the empires in which they were embedded—and usually the only bound that mattered to the emperor was getting the taxes paid on time—these little princes, dukes, and kings of Europe did whatever they wanted with their little realms. They even fought and conquered one another, and this is a reasonable example of the authoritarian breed. Authoritarian executives are mostly unconstrained leadership institutions, and even though I emphasize the unconstrained as a contrast to a democratic executive institution, the "mostly" qualification is important. Even divine or divinely selected monarchs face at least some constraints on their ability to rule. In the European example, the royal monarchs were constrained by the dictates and demands of both the empire and the church. The empire, or overarching kingdom, constraint was obvious: there were plenty of examples of emperors sending armies in to rearrange things in the principalities of any misbehaving nobles. But the church was also a very real, if more subtle, constraint. The blessing of the church was a necessary part of crowning a king or even naming an heir, and at the

---

*As with all the other simplified stories I offer, this medieval European example of the rise of the divine right of kings is far from perfect. The idea of divinely selected monarchs, as opposed to monarchs who themselves are divine, is as old as the notion of the monarchy itself, and its history is particularly strong around the Mediterranean basin. What makes the Roman/European example particularly relevant is the very large number of small principalities where the idea of divine right simultaneously arose and its resultant impact on later forms of government and modern philosophies of governing.

extreme, the church could excommunicate a ruler, essentially taking away the ruler's claim to being divinely selected to rule. In practice, something as extreme as excommunicating a prince rarely if ever happened, but through the Middle Ages the church had become increasingly organized, wealthy, and influential, well beyond the bounds of just holding the reigns of religious authority.

Nowhere was the influence of the church more evident than in the Thirty Years' War. In the 1600s the squabbling of the thousands upon thousands of little semi-independent fiefdoms in the middle of Europe escalated into the longest and, proportionately speaking, deadliest war ever fought.[†] Even though it's called the Thirty Years' War, the hostilities actually lasted closer to a century. Both the duration and the brutality of the war arose out of the witch's brew of nearly unconstrained kings exercising their divine right to rule as they wished and the church trying to use both its moral/religious influence and its wealth to maintain its authority over the rulers. There are plenty of reasonably historically accurate fictional works that give important glimpses of the politics from this period. *The Three Musketeers*[7] offers a fairly on-target depiction of Cardinal Richelieu acting as the effective leader of France and using that role to fight wars by proxy. However, if you can get past the rather absurd premise of a West Virginia coal-mining town being transported back in time and space to land in the middle of seventeenth-century Germany, Eric Flint's Grantville novels[8] provide an entertaining and perhaps even more impactful[*] contrast of modern and medieval ideas about the executive's role in government.

Perhaps it was the challenges and imperfections that reality imposed on the kings and princes of medieval Europe, particularly in the century preceding the Thirty Years' War and during the war itself, that generated the many discussions and essays from this period on the ideals of authoritarian monarchy. Though often called the first realist, Machiavelli described the ideal prince that was needed to unite his beloved Italy. In *The Prince* he addressed in some detail both the qualities an ideal executive needs to possess and how that ideal executive needs to act in order to rule properly. Later, I discuss Hugo Grotius (1583–1645) more in terms of his influence on modern discussions of law, but here I want to note that the natural law discussion he initiated was a huge and impactful part of the idealistic and theoretical discussions of the divine right to rule and the nature of monarchy. Jacques-Benigne Bossuet (1627–1704) built directly from Saint Augustine and medieval notions of kingship and wrote specifically about the divine right of kings and how kings were chosen by God directly and therefore accountable only to God. Bossuet specifically argued that because the king was accountable only to God, no one had the right to challenge that authority, including parliaments and protesters. Perhaps the most interesting of

---

[†]My copy editor has been nagging me since the first edition to put a footnote in here referencing the Catholic versus Protestant aspects of the Thirty Years' War. I did promise that I would, but I didn't say when. Maybe in the fourth edition.

[*]This is not a legal word, but I like it, and with the idea of publishing it so that it might someday become a legal word, I thought it was worth bribing my copy editor to look the other way.

JACQUES-BENIGNE BOSSUET

Team: French Monarchists

Position: Long Leg

Status: Died of the Stones

Jacques-Benigne Bossuet (1627–1704) is considered to be one of the best orators of all time. I'm not exactly certain what an orator is, but I'm pretty sure it has nothing to do with rowing a boat. He tutored the French dauphin (which is not an aquatic mammal) for King Louis XIV, was a favorite of the French aristocracy, and did some other things as well. He is perhaps most famous for his arguments regarding divine right and how that translated into the absolute authority of a monarch. The logic of absolutism was quite simple. Kings were divinely appointed. Therefore, they and their governments received their mandate from God and were answerable only to God. As a result, no man or collection of men had the right to question a king's authority.

Largely as a result of his involvement in the court of Louis XIV, Bossuet was intensely engaged in the grand politics of one of the most tumultuous eras in European history, and it would be fair to say that he was caught between a rock, a hard place, and another hard place in the form of the king of France, the Church in Rome, and the Protestant churches. First, Bossuet was placed in a less than comfortable position in a violent dispute between Louis XIV and the Church in Rome. Second, his commitment to reuniting the Protestant and Catholic churches by bringing the Protestants back into the Catholic Church endeared him to neither side and put him squarely in the middle of that conflict. The Protestants wanted nothing to do with someone trying to bring them back under the authority of Rome, and the hard-line Catholics railed at the moderate tone of his writings and their appeal to Protestant tastes. In both of these political/religious controversies, Bossuet argued for and pursued moderation and compromise, and that is a curious contrast to the immoderate and uncompromising logic and tenor of his argument for the divine and unquestionable authority of kings.

Finally, in one of the more unusual epitaphs of the dead theorists mentioned in this book, his death is attributed to "the stones." I was about to blame Mick Jagger, but then I noticed that *stones* wasn't capitalized and did some actual looking into things. If you can trust historians and all their history, the stones appears to be chronic kidney stones that caused a rapid decline in his health and his eventual death.

the period's discussions of monarchy and its concepts and ideals is *On the Divine Right of Kings* (1609), which was written by King James I of England (1566–1625) as a tutorial for his son and heir. It provides an interesting mix of idealism, religious piety, and the reality of ruling a kingdom, and it is notable for its assertion of the idea that the king embodied the state, an idea that was later taken to its extreme when Louis XIV of France said, quite simply, "I am the State." That notion of the monarch as the embodiment of the state lives on today with the constitutional monarchy, in which the king continues to embody the state in a symbolic role as head of state.

Another way that the authoritarian monarch lives on today is in the dictatorships that rise and fall around the world. While most modern dictators do not claim to have been appointed by God, they still rule largely as individuals who embody the state, and even though they often have constitutional, parliamentary, or other structures within their

governments, dictators are largely unconstrained by them or they dominate them nearly completely, and in many ways they behave like the princes of old.

Authoritarian Oligarchy

Authoritarianism, or mostly unconstrained rule by an executive, does not necessarily have to take the form of an individual as king or dictator. Oligarchic forms of authoritarian rule have been a significant element in recent history, particularly in single-party states such as China, Cuba, and Utah. In these states the executive is controlled through the cooperation of a small number of elites. These oligarchies can be carefully and extensively structured, as is the Chinese Communist Party, or they can be the largely informal products of dominant cultural, economic, or religious power bases, such as in Iran or Utah.

Most authoritarian oligarchies can be thought of as the descendants of revolutionary dictators. The Soviet Union, China, Vietnam, Cuba, and Iran all provide modern examples of revolutions that brought personalized, monarchical, or near-monarchical executives to power. Then, either through the necessities of ruling over a modern nation-state or through a conscious effort to build institutions that could persist past the death of the glorious leader, each of these countries established a small cadre of ruling elites that took over much of the executive and legislative functions in the government. The various communist politburos around the world are or were perfect examples of the authoritarian oligarchic executive. These small cadres of executive elites control recruitment of officials into the party and, through the party, into various institutions of government. Through a process of service and promotion in the party structure officials institutionalize their own eventual replacement. The single party in the state, though it is usually independent of the legislative institutions, also dominates the legislative function of government, at the very least, by vetting or otherwise selecting all of the candidates for legislative office. This effectively prevents the legislative branch of government from impeding or limiting the executive.

The degree to which the recruitment and replacement processes of these oligarchies are transparent or open to a broad section of society varies. The Chinese Communist Party is huge and heavily bureaucratized, and, at least officially, it appears to be mostly open, but the pattern of who is and who is not promoted to the highest ranks suggests that the higher up the structure one travels, the more politics and family outweigh merit in the promotion process. The upper echelons of Vietnam's Communist Party appears to be tightly tied to a small number of families, and Cuba's party elite is still focused on the Castro family.

While it is tempting to think of modern authoritarian oligarchies as dictatorship by committee, there is different dynamic apparent in **oligarchy.** The Soviet Union and China changed into completely different beasts after the deaths of Stalin and Mao, respectively. Whether that was a result of the group dynamics that came to the fore when a dominating leader had been removed or a result of the horse-trading, bullying, and bargaining that the persons and factions in the oligarchy had to employ in the process of selecting the leader

of leaders who would serve as the nominal executive is not clear. However, the ways these states behaved after the deaths of their first dictators were clearly different. And as the oligarchy persists beyond the lives of the key cadre of its founders that formed the first oligarchy, as in China, the oligarchy itself appears to become more and more bureaucratic, more and more impersonal, and more and more consistent over time. China is the best example of this process. This may not be something that generally happens, but it would seem to fit with the idea of how institutions evolve.

Another reason to avoid thinking of authoritarian oligarchies as dictatorships by committee is that I was only somewhat kidding when I mentioned Utah. Utah is perhaps the reddest of the red states in the United States, and in Utah conservative Republicans are such a predominant, wealthy, and powerful portion of the population that, for all intents and purposes, even though there is an election, it is the Republican nominee who is going to take the office. To the degree that the hierarchy of the Utah Republican Party influences or indirectly controls nominations, it acts as a single-party oligarchy within the democratic structure of the United States. Fortunately, the primaries in Utah are quite competitive, and that commitment to democratic competition within the Utah Republican Party keeps things from shifting too far toward oligarchy, but in other countries we do see elected authoritarian oligarchies.

Mexico provides what might be a controversial but still informative example. Prior to 2000, even though electoral competition was open, politics and government in Mexico had long been dominated by a single party. Because Mexico holds open elections, even if they are not really contested, it is controversial to talk about Mexico as an authoritarian oligarchy, but when the Partido Revolucionario Institucional (PRI) candidate was the only candidate who could win the presidency, it was the nomination process that mattered, and prior to the 2000 election the PRI did not hold any primary elections. Instead, the sitting president chose the nominee to succeed him, and the result was an authoritarian oligarchy within a democratic set of institutions. It is only since the turn of the century that this has begun to change. Japan has had a similarly dominant party. Though the oligarchic nature of its rule and its control over the executive have been less overt than in Mexico, Japan still lacks the kind of robust inter-party competition that is the hallmark of what most would consider to be democratic.

I'm going to call that a segue. I didn't actually mean to end the authoritarian executive section by talking about the claim that many oligarchic executives hide in democratic clothing, but I'm here and I'm tired of writing this part, so now I'm going to talk about democratic executives.

THE DEMOCRATIC EXECUTIVE

People, and a few very smart hamsters, usually think of democratic institutions in terms of the election of officeholders. However, the institutionalized constraint of the executive as a servant of a significant portion of the public is probably a better way to think about the most

KING JAMES VI AND I

Team: **Edinburgh Midges**

Position: **Forward Short Leg**

Status: **Not Buried in Grant's Tomb**

I don't claim to be an expert on kings or anything, and many of my students debate my claim to any expertise at all, but I have yet to hear a good explanation for how good old **King James VI** (1566–1625) could also be **King James I**. I suspect that time travel is involved. You see, he started out as King James VI, then he became King James I, but in both Roman numerals and the alphabet, I comes well before VI, so he must have traveled back in time or something to go from VI to I. Also, if he was both James I and James VI, that would make him his own great-great-grandfather, but that's what you get when amateurs mess with time travel. Putting aside James's failure to practice proper paradox prevention prophylaxis procedures, King James VI and I deserves a notable place in my executive chapter as a king who reflected upon and wrote about the role of the monarch.

The True Lawe of Free Monarchies[a] and *Basilikon Doron*[b] provide two very interesting insights into monarchy and the role of the executive. In terms of political theory, *The True Lawe of Free Monarchies,* also known as *The Reciprock and mutuall duetie betwixt a free King and his naturall Subiects,* is a key text on the subject of the executive role in government. It is notable in that it sets out the roles of the king and the subject as reciprocal and mutual responsibilities, while the argument itself is clearly a treatise asserting the divine right of the English king.

Basilikon Doron, also called *His Majesties Instrvctions To His Dearest Sonne, Henry the Prince,* was intended as, quite literally, a handbook for his heir. James I was not known as a great king of England, and his spelling seems suspect to me, but he did have a reputation as a studious man and a moderately accomplished writer. Never intended for the public—in fact, even when it was published, only seven copies were made—*Basilikon Doron* is notable for the frankness of the discussion, particularly when it comes to the king's role as both monarch and head of the Church of England.

The truly interesting thing about the writings of King James is that the combination of these two books provides insights into both a philosophical understanding of the executive and the practical concerns of a ruling monarch.

[a]King James I, *The True Lawe of Free Monarchies* (Edinburgh, 1598).

[b]King James I, *Basilikon Doron* (Edinburgh, 1599).

fundamental difference between democratic executives and authoritarian executives. After all, George Washington didn't actually win a presidential election. He was selected by sixty-nine electors, and those electors had been appointed as representatives by ten of the original thirteen states. And any George W. Bush fans should also remember that he actually lost the 2000 election but won the presidency based on the Electoral College system that evolved out of the original electors system that selected George Washington. Add to that the fact that Washington essentially ran unopposed, and even if you limit your idea of democratic elections to ones that are open and competitive, the election's distinction as the defining element of the democratic executive gets a bit squishy.

That election distinction for the democratic executive becomes further muddled when the elections are less than competitive. This is most obvious in the numerous elections that are structurally or procedurally noncompetitive or downright fraudulent. Oligarchic executives are often elected directly from limited or otherwise controlled sets of candidates, as in Mexico prior to 2000, or they are indirectly elected by being confirmed by bodies that have been elected from ballots for which the oligarchs determine all the "acceptable" candidates, as in the elections that were held in the Soviet Union. And the fraudulent elections, such as the 2008 election that Robert Mugabe "won" in Zimbabwe or the 2009 "victory" of Mahmoud Ahmadinejad in Iran, are even more obviously nondemocratic, despite all the voting that goes on. While the Soviet Union and Iran provide obvious examples of elections that weren't really democratic, it's not so easy to define what makes an election a good election. Most of the criteria that might be offered to define what makes an election democratic have difficulties in application when it comes to officially democratic but functionally oligarchic elections. Still, that's not really the problem. Defining what does not count as a democratic election is challenging, given that various points may be disputed, but it is not an insurmountable problem. The problem is that it isn't the election that matters. After all, Hitler was elected, fair and square, in a competitive democratic election. What matters is the way that all of the social and governmental structures of the country then translate that competitive election into constraints on the executive.

This is not to say that elections are not important. Ideally, the most fundamental of constraints on a democratic executive is the prospect of being held accountable by the electorate, either directly, as in a presidential system, or indirectly, as in a parliamentary system. However, it is the constraint part, rather than elections as a specific means of constraining, that is interesting for the democratic executive. In theory, if a means other than an election could systematically constrain an executive's behavior in a way that would keep it consistent with the needs, wants, and desires of a broad portion of the society being governed, then the country would be democratic even without an election. This is more than a philosophical point, since some argue that press freedom or freedom of expression can serve this function in the absence of democratic elections,[9] and there is some evidence to back that claim.

Still, elections are the tried and tested democratic constraining mechanism of choice, and the flavor of a country's democratic executive is largely determined by the mechanisms that connect the leader to the constraint created by future elections. Essentially, the choice is between a **presidential system** and a **parliamentary system,** and to use another of my famously questionable metaphors that might be analogies, this choice is tantamount to a waiter asking if you want your eggs sunny-side up or scrambled. To whom the executive is directly responsible is the fundamental difference between the two systems. In a presidential system, there is a separation of legislative and executive

SELF-REFERENCE THAT IS ACTUALLY QUITE NEARLY RELEVANT

I kind of make light of bribing my copy editor to let me slip in all these self-references just before the book goes to press, but the truth is, when this book actually comes out, I'm gonna have "a lot of 'splaining to do." And if you know who Ricky Ricardo is . . . what are you doing reading this textbook? Anyway, I figure if I slip enough references in that are actually in some way relevant, then I might be able to claim the irrelevant ones were accidents or something. I doubt if it will work, and I'm changing my phone numbers and e-mail address just to be safe, but I still gotta try.

So I now present you with a quite nearly relevant reference to *Press Freedom and Global Politics.* It's not really about executives at all, and I probably should have put it in the media chapter, where it really fits, but if I wait that long to put in a second reasonably relevant reference, nobody will buy it. *Press Freedom and Global Politics* provides some interesting evidence from the study of war that shows that press freedom just might constrain the executive in a very democratic way. Offering an explanation for the democratic peace, a phenomenon in which modern democracies do not seem to go to war against one another, it posits that the way people in free-press countries trust the information from other free-press countries makes it impossible for leaders of those countries to convince their populations that they need to break out the tanks and kill each other. Perhaps the most interesting part of the study is that press freedom shows this pattern better than do measures of democratic political structures. All of the contradictions to the rule of the democratic peace are countries that had democratic structures but not press freedom.

Douglas A. Van Belle, *Press Freedom and Global Politics* (Westport, CT: Praeger, 2000).

institutions (the yolk is separated from the whites), while in a parliamentary system there is a fusion of legislative and executive (the yolks and whites are scrambled together).

In a presidential system, the executive is separately elected and does not have to answer to the legislature. *El presidente mucho grande* has an independent base of democratic support that can be won or lost directly. In a parliamentary system, the executive is actually part of the parliament. The prime minister, as she or he is usually called, gets the position by first winning election to a seat in the legislature and then being elected to the post by fellow members of parliament (MPs). In a presidential system, the executive is elected through a system that is independent of the selection of the legislature and leaves office only after having served a fixed term or through a special removal process called impeachment. In a parliamentary system, the prime minister serves until the next elections are scheduled or until a simple majority of MPs votes him or her out. Under this system the prime minister remains responsible to the legislature and, through the next legislative election, responsible to the voting public, while in the presidential system the executive remains separate and primarily responsible to the electorate directly.

Both of these types of democratic executives have strengths and weaknesses, and both, interestingly enough, were created as reactions to the excesses or failings of the authoritarian monarchies that dominated Europe.

Sí, El Presidente

The modern democratic presidency originated with the U.S. Constitution, and it is probably fair to say that when it came to designing the executive, the Framers of the Constitution were profoundly worried about creating an institution that would simply replace a hereditary monarch with an elected one. They addressed this in part by separating the legislative and judicial institutions from the executive, but the Framers had good reason to fear an American monarchy.

During the two centuries before the U.S. Constitution was written, Europe was mired in war. The 1600s were a century of nearly constant warfare that included the Thirty Years' War, a war so long and so brutal that it killed half the population of the Holy Roman Empire and knocked huge swaths of Europe back to, quite literally, a stone-age level of subsistence. Many argue that the Thirty Years' War was actually a solid century of war that began when the Holy Roman Emperor Ferdinand of Styria began "liquidating" central European heretics in 1598, continued through the three Anglo-Dutch wars, the Wars of Louis XIV, the Wars of the League of Ausburg, and the Great Northern War, and it didn't really end until the end of the Spanish War of Succession, roughly around 1710.[*] Although even that date is contestable, since the Great Northern War continued until 1721, and the Austro-Ottoman War of 1716–1718 as well the War of the Quadruple Alliance (1717–1719) should probably be included as part of that nearly constant century of war. Nearly a decade passed before the War of Polish Succession (1733–1735) started everything up again, and from then until the American Constitutional Convention in 1787, scarcely a year would pass when at least two fairly large wars were not being fought in Europe, not to mention the wars the European kings were fighting in exotic overseas locals, such as Canada and New Jersey. And even though there would have been no way to predict the rise of Napoleon, at the time of the Constitutional Convention there were indications of the political and economic instabilities that would send Europe into yet another war of such massive proportions that you would almost have to call it a world war. The Napoleonic Wars involved armies larger than any ever seen before, ravaging and scavenging their way across all of Europe.

The men writing the U.S. Constitution, and the pixies who helped them with the spelling, blamed the kings and princes of Europe for all this unceasing warfare and the indescribable suffering imposed on the common people, who were bled dry with taxes and bullets, and

---

[*]The actual treaty wasn't signed until 1713, but the last of the serious fighting occurred in 1709.

that blame was well deserved. There is nothing simple about the causes of war, and one should not dismiss the economic and political dynamics arising out of untenable empires and fragile kingdoms that had evolved into impossible tangles of aristocracy and poverty, but the triggers of almost all of the wars seemed to involve royal succession, petty aristocratic squabbles, or aristocratic attempts to either quash or exploit peasant revolts in other people's kingdoms. The last thing the Framers wanted to do was to create a president who could, or would, recklessly throw American blood and money at war like a European king. That was why the power to declare war was given to the U.S. Senate and not the president.

The influence of kings and war on the presidency as the democratic executive did not end there, however. The Founders faced the very real fact that the United States would have to fight wars, almost certainly against those same kings they feared accidentally replicating, and to fight wars a country needed a powerful chief executive. Wars would require decisive action, deft diplomacy, and strategic maneuvering that no congress or senate could manage. Thus, the president was explicitly given the role of commander in chief of the U.S. armed forces and was empowered as both the head of state and the head of government. The president could not declare war, but he or she had the necessary authority to fight a war properly.

From the specifics of the U.S. presidency, a more generalized ideal of a presidential democratic executive has evolved. In terms of executive actions, presidential systems generally create a great deal of independence for the executive in relation to the legislature. Again, this helps the person in that role effectively lead a country in war, but in a more general sense, the stability of presidential executive systems is probably a more important point.

Presidents are generally elected separately from the legislature, and it is difficult for the legislature to remove a president from office. As a result, presidents typically serve their full terms and can usually ride out periods of domestic political instability. This avoids the kind of rapid turnover in leadership that can actually aggravate domestic political unrest in parliamentary systems. The stability of presidential systems also extends to the laws of the land. A modern presidency's official mechanisms for influencing legislation are generally limited to a mechanism for preventing legislation from becoming law, such as the veto, and/or a mechanism for refusing to execute a law. The result of this combination of a president with little influence over legislation and some sort of executive check on the legislature is that both the legislature and the executive generally have to agree to create and implement law. This again keeps the president from acting like a king, but it also makes it quite difficult for anyone to make changes to laws in a presidential system. This is stabilizing in that the law tends to remain constant over time, but that ability isn't always a good thing. The problem with institutionalized checks and balances is well-known to observers of the U.S. system: when one or more political parties decide to be aggressively obstinate,

it can be infuriatingly hard to get anything done, particularly if doing so means challenging entrenched interests. Because the checks are built into the system, there are so many ways to obstruct things that even a small minority can usually find someone with the ability to prevent changes to the status quo.

Again, however, presidential systems come back to the U.S. Founders' fear of kings. Preventing the rise of an elected king was the primary purpose behind the design of the American presidential system. Not only did the Founders distance the president from any positive role in the legislative function of government through the **separation of powers,** they employed **checks and balances**. Basically, everybody is always minding everybody else's business and always second-guessing what the other branches of government are doing, and every branch has the ability to stall or even stop the activity of the others. In a presidential system, not only does the president have the power to impede the legislative process through the veto or something similar, but also the legislature can impede the president's executive actions, particularly those outside of fighting wars. The legislature plays a role in presidential executive affairs through its powers to confirm appointments, ratify treaties, and approve budgets. These checks and balances of the presidential executive can be extended to the judiciary, as they are in the United States, but even without that, the isolation of the presidential executive from the legislative branch and the ease with which one branch can impede the actions of the other makes it almost impossible to meld legislative and executive power into something that can behave imperially. The downside of checks and balances, which I address more fully in Chapter 7, is that they can make it hard to get anything done in a presidential system. That actually creates another form of stability, since it means that laws are very slow to change and seldom change more than incrementally, but the difficulty in accomplishing things can be a very big problem in presidential systems.

Yes, Minister

The ease of obstructing governmental activity in the presidential system points to one of the strengths of the **prime minister** as the executive of a parliamentary system. The prime minister is the leader of the party or coalition that controls a majority in the parliamentary system. As a result, he or she has an easier time than does a president in shepherding legislation through the system—the legislation needed to pursue the course that the prime minister, as captain, has set for government. In fact, things happen quite swiftly and with little bickering in most parliamentary systems. The whole system is set up so that members of parliamentary political parties are far more likely to vote cohesively. Parties have a great deal of control—sometimes total control—over who gets seated after an election, therefore bucking the party in a vote is risky to the point of stupidity. Whenever the next opportunity to fill seats arises, why would the party waste a hard-won seat on someone who cannot be trusted to vote the party line? And if an MP breaks from the party line, that opportunity to

shuffle him/her/it out of a seat is likely to arise very quickly. In some parliamentary systems *any* failure of a piece of legislation automatically dissolves the government. This is not only embarrassing to the ruling party, but it also means that new elections must be held, which is not something a party wants after it has just been embarrassed by the defection of one of its own.

Because these institutional mechanisms reinforce party loyalty, an efficient parliamentary system holds the promise of a quicker and more certain ability to define and enact policy than is possible under a presidential system. The votes of party members in presidential systems are far less predictable and far more difficult to control. American presidents cannot necessarily count on all the members of their political party for support, and, in fact, many a presidential proposal has been defeated by a margin afforded by the defection of members of the president's party.

Interestingly enough, like the presidential system, the parliamentary system is in many ways a reaction to the kings of Europe and their warmongering predilections. The evolution of the parliamentary system is more relevant to the legislative aspects of that democratic structure, so I save it for the legislative chapter, which just happens to come next, but I want to note here that the modern prime minister is the end result of a centuries-long effort by the aristocratic legislature to pry the executive function out of the hands of the king. And it is in that light that I finish by returning to the distinction between the head of state and the head of government.

Democratic Executives as Heads of State

The role of head of state involves serving as the national symbol—the personification of the country and its people. This includes overseeing national celebrations, presiding over parades, christening ships, entertaining foreign dignitaries, and all of the other ceremonial aspects of the job. While this probably seems like a good gig, you should be aware of three very important facts concerning heads of state. First, heads of state can take different forms in different countries. The head of state can be a monarch, an elected president, or the guy with the most troops and biggest guns. In some countries the head of state is a king or queen, or even the king or queen of another country altogether. This figurehead role comes with little or no political power, but it also sometimes comes with a very big expense account and a nice house called a palace.* In other places, the head of state may be a king with a great deal of real political power; for example, the king of Jordan is more than just a head of state. In other countries the head of state is simply the dictator or el presidente for life.† The last avenue is to be elected to the job. Parliamentary systems that lack monarchs or dictators du jour usually have elected presidents. These presidents can be elected

---

*A palace seems to be a lot like the stuffy old-person version of a Barbie Dream House.

†Now that is not a bad gig, except of course for the fact that people tend to want to assassinate you, and your retirement home is a small pine box buried at least six feet in the ground.

directly by the people, or they might be chosen by the parliament. France, for instance, elects a president who serves as head of state but does not perform any of the executive functions of a U.S. president. It's kind of like voting for a queen.

The second thing you should know is that the whole head of state job is actually pretty important. The head of state can add legitimacy to a government.[‡] In other words, if the symbol of the country—say, a monarch—gives her blessing to a government, that blessing can strengthen the government's standing within the country. With the queen's blessing, the people may feel that the government ought to be given a chance to prove itself. In this way, many heads of state play important roles. In a parliamentary system, the head of state can be the one who formally authorizes the winning political party after an election to try to form a government. Some heads of state also have the authority to call for parliamentary elections. Heads of state generally do not have any influence over specific legislation or actions of government, but they can play a role in the overall direction of a country or government in the way they help or hinder diplomacy or the efforts of the government or challengers to gain or sustain broad-based public support.

The third thing you should know is that not all heads of state are created equal. A dictator du jour is going to have some extraordinary powers and will often also be the head of government. If there is a parliament in that situation, it is likely to have very little real power. The same thing is true of those countries with strong monarchies. There may very well be a parliament in Kuwait, but trust me, you would rather be the emir than the head of the parliament. Or perhaps you would rather be the king of Nepal, who in 2002 simply decided to dissolve the parliament he disagreed with.[*] Other monarchs are less powerful. These kings and queens, like most in Western Europe, are mere figureheads working within systems labeled as constitutional monarchies, where the parliaments have all of the real political power. Among presidents in parliamentary systems, however, there is a great deal of variety. For example, the French president is much more politically powerful than the Israeli president. The French president has more specific political responsibilities, particularly in diplomatic matters.

The point of skipping through the varieties of modern heads of state is to give me an excuse to say that it doesn't really matter. The head of state matters, but in terms of democracy, it doesn't really matter whether the head of state is a king, or a magic goat, or an elected official. When we are talking about the executive structure of government, we are almost always talking about a head of government, not a head of state. All the checks and balances, all the discussion of democracy as a constrained executive—it's really all about the executive as head of government, the one who sends the troops marching off to war, not marching in a parade.

[‡]In case you didn't catch on in Chapter 4, this whole legitimacy thing is pretty important for governments to have.

[*]Events that occurred in 2006—when protests forced the king of Nepal to reinstate the parliament—suggest that although he may have been able to dissolve the legislature, whether that was a good or effective political maneuver remains open to debate.

Democratic Executives as Heads of Government

If the head of state is the public face we see in the advertisements, the head of government is the manager who actually handles all the day-to-day "stuff."[†] As noted, the U.S. president plays both roles, but in parliamentary democracies the head of government is usually the prime minister. The prime minister is responsible for getting bills passed through the parliament, overseeing the running of the bureaucracy, dealing with disasters, commanding the military, and so forth. One becomes the prime minister by being the head of the party that wins a majority of seats in a parliamentary election. If no party wins a clear majority in an election, the head of state usually asks the head of the party that has won the most seats to try to form a government by forming a coalition with one or more of the other parties that won seats. The prime minister can stay prime minister only as long as he or she maintains the support of a majority of seats in the parliament. This means that the potential prime minister must try to broker some deals to bring a coalition together that includes more than half the members of parliament.

It is also technically true that the prime minister is nothing more than the first minister. Parliamentary governments are actually made up of many ministers that form the cabinet. Other ministers may include the foreign minister, treasury minister, defense minister, the minister of silly walks,[*] and so on. In an effort to form a government, a potential minister may offer another party a chance to have one of its members serve in the government as a minister in exchange for the party's joining and supporting the overall coalition. Once a majority coalition is constructed, however, the new prime minister also has a governing coalition, which is expected to pass laws.

Coming back to kings and war again, in most democracies, the head of government is the civilian head of the military. That means that he or she is responsible for sending troops abroad, defending the nation from foreign threat, and putting down domestic insurrections. At the same time, the executive is responsible for foreign relations; he or she must negotiate with the leaders of foreign nations, engage in diplomacy, and work out military and economic alliances. A president who "really performs poorly"[†] at the former will find it hard to excel at the latter.

While the chief executive must focus a great deal of attention abroad, he or she must also watch over the home front. The chief executive is responsible for overseeing much of the government's bureaucracy and making sure that government services are provided and

---

[†]I use quotes here because *stuff* or any other "acceptable" word just does not convey the very unglamorous and often unpleasant nature of this necessary function of government. The queen of England does nothing and gets palaces (note the use of the plural), while the prime minister of Britain does all the real work and lives in a sublet flat on Downing Street. That, dear readers, is a load of "stuff."

[*]Made famous in *Monty Python's Flying Circus*.

[†]I wanted to use a very crass phrase here, involving a colloquial term for a pet dog, but my copy editor insisted that I use "nice" language.

that laws are implemented and enforced. Also, in most modern democracies, the people expect the chief executive to manage the nation's economy effectively. Of course, democratic chief executives also have a purely political role that their authoritarian counterparts do not. Prime ministers are the heads of their parties, and thus they have a responsibility to campaign for their parties and make sure they help local candidates in every way they can. Presidents, too, are the heads of their parties. However, while prime ministers, as the leaders of their parties, decide who gets to run as their parties' candidates, the U.S. president does not have that luxury. Anybody can run for office as a Democrat or a Republican, provided he or she meets the requirements to get onto the ballot. Potential candidates do not need permission from the head of the party. Still, in addition to all of their other work, presidents are expected to raise enormous amounts of campaign funds for their parties and also to do what they can to get their parties' local candidates elected.

Given all of these roles, plus the unique roles of chief executives in various countries, it is no wonder that a fictional president would seem so appealing. Perhaps only a team of television writers could fix a plot so that a president could perform all of these roles with style and a flair for the dramatic.

KEY TERMS

checks and balances / 165
divine right of kings / 154
head of government / 149
head of state / 149
hereditary monarchies / 153
matriarchy / 152
oligarchy / 158

parliamentary system / 161
patriarchy / 152
presidency / 148
presidential system / 161
prime minister / 165
separation of powers / 165

CHAPTER SUMMARY

The executive is the government institution or the collection of government institutions that acts on behalf of the state. While the variety of executive institutions is boundless, most fit into one of four general categories. Authoritarian monarchies are single dominant leaders who are mostly unconstrained. Authoritarian oligarchies are executive leadership groups that are mostly unconstrained by other institutions of government. Democratic presidents are executives elected separately from their nations' democratic legislatures, whereas parliamentary prime ministers are executives who come directly from the democratic legislatures and are dependent on the legislatures for support to remain in office. The historical development of the executive has generally featured the slow separation of other functions of government from the executive.

Students should learn two very important lessons from this chapter. First, being a king just ain't what it used to be. Second, history has had a profound impact on the

development of the modern executive institutions. The U.S. presidency is an excellent example, in that many of the elements built into the American system were explicitly included to prevent the United States from suffering the excesses the Founders observed among the kings and princes of Europe.

STUDY QUESTIONS AND EXERCISES

1. What is the difference between an authoritarian executive and a democratic executive?

2. Why might authoritarian oligarchies be more stable over generations than authoritarian monarchies?

3. What is the difference between the head of government and the head of state, and what are the benefits of having the U.S. president perform both functions?

4. Why would we expect the institutionalization of executive selection by combat to be an unlikely thing?

5. Why might it be valuable to have the executive also be the head of the legislative function, as in a parliamentary system?

WEBSITES TO EXPLORE

www.whitehouse.gov. This is the totally official White House website.

www.thepresidency.org. The Center for the Study of the Presidency and Congress maintains this site.

www.thamesweb.co.uk/windsor/windsorhistory/kings_queens.html. This site explores the history of the kings of England.

The Confederacy of Dunces
The Legislative Function (Not in Bad Spanish)

So, what do I write in this chapter? Chapter 7 is sort of like the Wednesday of a textbook. The foolish enthusiasm that sent me hurtling headlong into Chapter 1 is long gone. It's so far behind me that I can't even remember what it felt like. And from here in the middle, the end of the book looks so far away that no matter how much I write, the back cover doesn't seem to get any closer. I don't even feel like trying to slip a slightly scandalous word or crude turn of phrase past the army of editors and the other evil mercenaries that my publisher has hired to thwart me.* And to make it even tougher, the Wednesday chapter is the legislative chapter. The legislative function of government is the lawmaking function. How much fun can that be? When was the last time you read a good book about a parliamentary debate? I named this chapter after John Kennedy Toole's novel, but *A Confederacy of Dunces* doesn't have anything to do with legislatures. The book is funny, in a creepy and uncomfortable chuckle kind of way, but it has nothing to do with legislatures. And there's no chance of finding a decent film on legislative politics. *The Phantom Menace* is about the intrigue and strategy involved in the maneuverings among members of a galactic legislature, and movies don't get much worse than *Phantom Menace*.[1] The best legislature movie I could come up with is *Mr. Smith Goes to Washington*. At first, when I heard that it was a Jimmy Stewart movie I was kind of excited, but then I discovered that *Jackie* Stewart is the race-car driver. *Jimmy* Stewart was just some crazy banker who hallucinated about giant rabbits and spied on his neighbors with binoculars. There isn't a single car chase in the whole Jimmy Stewart film. Still, even without

---

*It's not really even that much of a challenge anymore. The secret to getting all the naughty bits through is caffeine. I've bribed the manager of the Starbucks nearest the CQ Press headquarters so that on the days that I send in a completed chapter, my copy editor's hourly Kenya Bold grande with skim is replaced with decaf, my development editor's decaf mocha lattes are all made with triple shots of that same Kenya Bold, and everyone else gets herbal tea with black food coloring. By lunchtime they can hardly read, and by midafternoon none of them can find a footnote to save their lives.

car chases, explosions, gunfire, or anything else to keep students (or me) interested, I'm going to have to put together a serious chapter on legislative institutions. Senatorial debates may not make for good cinema, but in many ways the legislature is the heart and soul of modern government, so I have to write a chapter on it. And if I have to write a chapter on it, you have to read it. I recommend high doses of caffeine. I promise not to mess with your dealer.

It's tempting to jump straight into parliamentary versus presidential legislative systems, but since I did some of the historical stuff in the executive branch chapter, I feel kind of obligated to admit there is some history involved with the legislature, and, to be honest, some of it is actually important . . . to some people. Not to me. I also need to talk a little bit about the legislative function in nondemocratic governments. I'll save that for last. If I forget, remind me.

BORING HISTORY STUFF

The least boring part of the history of the legislative function of government is the way political struggles have gradually disentangled and distanced the legislative from the executive function of government. More often than not, the kings, chiefs, and fairy princesses who performed the executive function in ancient governments also performed the legislative and judicial functions. For the most part, a king's word was law, and that was that. Debate over the creation, execution, or adjudication of the law generally came down to "Because I said so," and people who wished to keep all of their favorite body parts attached to all the right places generally accepted that bellowing royal snarl as a compelling argument. Where this gets as interesting as a boring subject is going to get is when the legislative and executive functions of government begin to diverge. I am going to discuss three processes, or perhaps they are better conceptualized as social forces, that gradually created some separation between executive and legislative functions. These forces sometimes worked singularly and sometimes in concert, and the forms they took were as varied as the people and societies of the world. Certainly, forces and processes other than the three I'm highlighting were also involved, but for the purposes of gross oversimplification, I can talk about these three and only these three, and I can force you to think exclusively about these three and only these three because these three and only these three are what could be on the test.

The Tedium of Repetitive Redundancy

One way that a look at history explains the separation of the executive from an unfettered ability to make laws is through the importance of history itself. Tradition and precedent were incredibly powerful forces in early government, and once some law-like constraint on behavior became ritualized or otherwise entrenched, a king all but lost the ability to change it, or even circumvent it. This was particularly true for laws or law-like traditions with long-term economic or social consequences, such as those concerning marriage and inheritance.

Inheritance laws and land tenure laws provide a particularly useful example. Some societies essentially forced parents to split their estates equally among all their descendants. In fact, a form of this law still applies in Louisiana. This seems fair, in a socialist dictatorship kind of way, and it prevents a favorite child from getting all the good stuff, but in agriculture-intensive societies it had devastating consequences. Within only a few generations, most of the arable land ended up being divided into plots that were too small for a family to subsist on. Some societies avoided this problem by practicing primogeniture, in which the entire estate was inherited by the eldest son, or ultimogeniture, in which the entire estate was inherited by the youngest son. Both of these systems kept estates intact and avoided the problem of dividing the land into such small parcels that no one could survive on what they owned or what they had the right to farm. The problem these inheritance systems created was that each generation produced a whole gaggle of landless children, and there is no more powerful revolutionary force than a mass of landless starving people.

Regardless of the relative merits of any inheritance law, whichever one was practiced became so entrenched in tradition and practice that it was nearly impossible for a king to change it. History bound the king, at least partly, because so many economic interests were so firmly enmeshed in the existing law. Families literally lived their entire economic lives around whatever land inheritance traditions were practiced. In societies with laws calling for equal inheritance, parents with land would often try to purchase additional tracts to provide each adult son and his family with a plot big enough so that they could not only survive but also produce enough surplus to be able gradually to purchase additional land for their sons, and so forth. In places where estates were passed intact to an oldest or youngest son, parents often worked to provide for those who would not inherit, supporting their entry into artisan trades, funding their emigration, or helping them purchase land of their own. Changing the inheritance laws would upset all of that activity, destroying everything a mother and father had worked for over their entire lifetime. No matter what problems a set of inheritance laws might cause, if a king tried to change the laws, he would almost certainly face a revolt. Thus, history and tradition constrained the king's lawmaking ability.

Another way that history could pull some of the lawmaking function away from a traditional monarch was in the establishment of some kind of official veneration of the elderly. A wide variety of societies have or had something like a tribal elder or council of elders as lawgiver; this person or group literally embodied the delivery of tradition and law from one generation to the next. While the fact that one of my grandfathers was known for using $@^^& #*%/€ as a pronoun and another was evangelical about the use of diesel oil and a match as a way to weed the garden makes me a little reluctant to argue that age necessarily equals wisdom, still, in most contexts in which there is a council of elders or something similar, it would be most unwise for a chief, prince, or king to try to defy the law that

the elders carry down or interpret from legend and history. I have to emphasize that the interpreting of historical law to fit current circumstances is more than just remembering the good old days.* It is a form of legislation. It creates laws. New law was created through the adaptation of old laws, or simply through the application of the shared wisdom of the elders to decide what the law should be.

The Monotony of Religion

Religion was a second way that lawmaking power was pulled away from the executive. Even when the king was considered to be divine, there was almost always some kind of separate priesthood, with its own power structure and substantial influence over definitions of acceptable behavior. You can see this with the shamans of primitive tribes and in the Stone Temple Pilots* of established empires. In Egypt, for example, the priesthood was extremely powerful, and by defining pious behavior priests also defined much of the law of the land, including religious laws that would be difficult for the pharaoh to disobey without raising questions about his divinity. The Roman Catholic Church, particularly in the late Roman period and the Middle Ages, held considerable legislative or quasi-legislative power across thousands of independent or semi-independent kingdoms and principalities. Pious behavior, or at least some degree of deference to the idea of piety, was one of the corollaries of sustaining the claim of being divinely selected to rule, and the church controlled the definition and specifics of such behavior. Again, this is something you can see embodied in the struggle between kings and the priesthood. England's King Henry VIII had to form a new and totally official English church, and behead a wife or two, just because the Church in Rome would not let him make divorce legal. And then, after Henry went to all that trouble, that darn† new church started distancing itself from the Crown and refused to be completely controlled, making new law-like proclamations about how people, including the king, had to behave.

Religion is still a significant consideration today. For example, the body of Islamic religious law known as sharia constitutes a large, and in some cases predominant, portion of the law practiced in many regions and many countries, often in defiance of the officially legislated laws of civil governments.

As Exciting as Accountancy 101

While some might mistakenly believe that there is something interesting or—heaven forbid—exciting in the power struggles between church and king over lawmaking and legislative authority, even those foolish souls will have to admit that the third way that some

---

*I mean this quite literally, court order and all.

*Stone Temple Pilots was the name of a band that you've probably never heard of.

†I used a nice word here, since I'm talking about a church and all, you know.

The Confederacy of Dunces

legislative power was pried away from monarchs and other traditional supreme executives is tedious to the point of excruciation. It's all about the bankers. Don't worry, I'm not going to bring Jimmy Stewart and a rabbit named Harvey into this. I could, but I won't.

Kings, princes, and other forms of what I have been calling traditional monarchs all must confront one of the more fundamental dilemmas of power. It is, in fact, a dilemma that all governments face, but it was particularly troubling for monarchs trying to maximize their power by controlling both the executive and the legislative functions of government. Controlling the kingdom was one thing. That was critical to a king's power, but just as important, if not more important, was the power of the kingdom, and wealth was one of the primary determinants of a kingdom's power. Spain rose to global prominence largely because of the sheer volume of gold and silver it was able to extract from the Americas. The Dutch and the English dominated the world with the wealth they earned through trade. Half the stories from the Thirty Years' War are about the princes and kings who bankrupted themselves hiring mercenaries to attack their rivals and the princes and kings who bankrupted themselves hiring mercenaries to attack the princes and kings who had bankrupted themselves, and so on.

The difficulty that kings and queens faced was that even though the power of their kingdoms depended on wealth, monarchs had little if any ability to create wealth, and that presented them with a dilemma. In many ways the dilemma was a classic macroeconomic puzzle: How does the government balance levels of taxation and controls of society against incentives that encourage subjects to create wealth to maximize total tax receipts? As you would expect, boundless combinations of incentives and tax strategies were employed across the world over the centuries, but a general trend in European history is that monarchs gradually relinquished legislative authority in return for the acceptance of taxation by those being taxed, or they surrendered some degree of legislative authority to nobles and merchants with the expectation that those groups would use that freedom to create a greater taxable base of wealth. The Dutch Republic, which was formed in 1588, is frequently cited as an example of legislative power devolving to those with the economic power. In the United Provinces it was the wealthy merchants who controlled and dominated the government through the States-General. The States-General was a forum through which the largely independent provinces were represented in what was essentially a confederal government with a heavily constrained hereditary monarch. The problem with the Dutch example is that it was more anachronistic than typical. The States-General was largely a mechanism to create something coherent out of the fiercely independent Dutch provinces. Rather than wresting power from a monarch, that collection of provincial governors actually had to go out and find a monarch to serve as their executive.

The English Parliament is a better and more typical example. The English Parliament evolved out of a variety of traditional gatherings of advisers to the king that existed in medieval England. Through a combination of political maneuvering, revolt, war, and other

historical kinds of things, these occasional and often haphazard congregations of advisers, nobles, and city representatives grew into something of a representative body. In the thirteenth century, under Edward I, the English monarchy first accepted that taxation required the consent of those who would be most affected, and the council of nobles that eventually became the English Parliament was institutionalized as a way of obtaining that consent. The financial demands of the frequent wars that Edward I and his son fought transformed the need to gain the consent of the taxed into a tremendously powerful political lever, and the political history of thirteenth- and fourteenth-century England is largely a tale of Parliament using that lever to pry more and more legislative authority away from the king. Every royal tax demand was met with a reciprocal demand from Parliament for greater authority and legislative responsibility, and by 1327 Parliament had grown strong enough to remove Ed Jr. from the throne. The evolution of the English Parliament, which became the British Parliament, was a bit swift and a bit extreme compared to the norm, but it is reasonably representative of the economic dynamic that split legislative function from executive authority in the kingdoms of Europe.

The evolution of the English Parliament also segues into democratic legislative institutions. Ooooooh, fancy.

A DREARY DISCUSSION OF DEMOCRATIC LEGISLATURES

When it comes to legislative institutions, I want to spend most of this horribly boring chapter talking about demonic[*] legislatures. This is largely because the way that legislative institutions are integrated into democratic governments is marginally less mind-numbing than what you see in autocratic political systems. After all, if the English Parliament could uncrown a king, that's a pretty good hint that something other than soul-crushing monotony can happen with legislatures once in a while. Recently, there's also been a bit of less-than-mind-numbing debate about the value of democratic legislatures. Not too long ago, many scholars were declaring that legislatures had reached an era of decline, but that argument is falling by the wayside. In fact, writing in the 1990s, political scientists Gary W. Copeland and Samuel C. Patterson speculated that we might instead be in an age of parliaments.[2] It is probably true that legislatures were never quite as bad off as some political scientists claimed, and it is also likely that legislatures today are not as powerful as other political scientists believe them to be. Still, perhaps what is most impressive about legislatures as institutions is that even though they are so old they creak and groan with every movement, they remain viable. At the risk of sounding too conservative, it would seem that there must be some benefit to institutions that have lasted for hundreds of years.

After droning on and on, and on, about the endless bleak centuries that primal legislative institutions spent wresting legislative authority away from the authoritarian executives, I'm

---

[*]If this doesn't get corrected, it's a pretty good guess that this chapter has already bored my copy editor to death. CQ Press will probably forward letters of condolence if you can be bothered to send them.

going to turn around and go right back to the executive and categorize democratic legislatures in terms of their connection with executive institutions. If you're still conscious enough to remember Chapter 6, or at least remember that there was a Chapter 6, you might recall that I talked about the distinction between presidents and prime ministers as democratic executives. The key difference between the two is that a president has an independent electoral base but is distanced from the legislative process, while a prime minister is the leader of the party or coalition that controls the legislature and is closely connected to the legislative process. This difference has a huge impact on the nature and effectiveness of the legislature, not just as a lawmaking institution but also in its other political roles.

And just in case you missed that inelegant cue I tacked onto the end of the preceding paragraph, the topic of democratic legislatures also gives me the chance to expand the discussion beyond lawmaking. Lawmaking is probably the most fundamental role that legislative institutions play, but as the English example suggests, there is more to such institutions than just writing and revising laws. When you are pondering the idealism inherent in legislatures, it is best to think of fluffy kitties or something else that might reignite your will to live, but you might also want to consider the functions that you would like legislatures to perform. While there are many such possible functions, I arbitrarily identify the five I believe are the least unimportant. They are lawmaking, representing, checking, legitimating, and educating.[3]

The Humdrum Function of Lawmaking

The root of the word *legislature,* is, of course, *legislate,* which breaks down into the phrase "leg is late," which is meaningless and completely irrelevant. At the heart of the matter, however, is that you expect your parliaments or congresses, first and foremost, to make laws. Indeed, legislatures make laws, but often not in the way that one would expect. The making of laws doesn't entail a stately debate over nuance and detail. It often doesn't involve even an unstately debate. On the surface it looks like there's a lot of arguing, but, in fact, there isn't. The mistake is fair enough. At one time or another, everyone in the United States has flicked through the cable channels slowly enough to accidentally catch an instant of C-SPAN. C-SPAN is dedicated to covering the U.S. House of Representatives,[*] while C-SPAN2 covers the U.S. Senate. The thing about this legislative TV network is that it always seems to be showing someone in the well of the U.S. House of Representatives just yabbering away about something. Tune in at 3:00 A.M., and it looks like the debate is still going strong.

However, if you have a high tolerance for soul-crushing monotony and can watch C-SPAN closely, you will see that while the person at the podium is yelling[†] whatever it is that his or her speechwriter wrote, there is nobody in the chamber listening. It turns out

---

[*] The U.S. Surgeon General has determined that, despite rumors to the contrary, watching C-SPAN does not cause brain hemorrhaging. It is the beating of your forehead against the TV screen that causes the brain damage.

[†] Yelling in legislatures seems to be compulsory.

that even during debate few members are there to listen. Now, that might lead you to posit the philosophical conundrum, "If a congressman shouts in the House and no one is there to hear him, does he still make a sound?"* More to the point, if there isn't anyone there listening or shouting back, what exactly is the esteemed representative from Iowa doing? It can't be a debate. Instead, most of the speechifying on the House floor isn't about creating law. It's about one of the other things legislatures do, like educating.

In most democratic legislatures the actual process of making laws is largely completed by the time it comes to votes and debates. Bills can come from the minds of legislators, but they also may be suggested, or even written up in detail, by constituents, interest groups, the executive branch, or the political leadership of the congress or parliament. Furthermore, in most legislatures, much of the real lawmaking work goes on in committees rather than in the actual legislative chambers. Committees, and sometimes subcommittees, conduct research, hold hearings, debate, write bills, and amend them. Control of a committee can effectively give a representative or a party control of all the relevant legislation. Committees are generally there to whittle down the number of bills that get introduced in the legislature during any given session, to write the laws using the necessary precise, legally effective wording, and to allow members to specialize in specific areas of policy.

The actual process for the passage of bills differs from legislature to legislature. In *Mr. Smith Goes to Washington,* Saunders offers a pretty accurate description of how difficult it is to get a bill passed into law in the U.S. Congress. Some parliamentary systems make it easy for popular bills to pass, while others make it more difficult. My point here is that all the arguing and speechifying usually is serving one of the other functions of a legislature. Most of the lawmaking goes on behind the scenes in a largely bureaucratic and procedural machine that is so bland that it isn't even interesting enough for this beige-on-beige chapter.

The Lackluster Function of Legislative Representation

Another fundamental job of legislators is to represent their constituents. That is, legislatures play a key role in making people feel as if somebody is speaking up for their interests. Different democratic institutions provide different methods of accomplishing representation, and a great many of those institutional arrangements are driven by questions over representation priorities.

Mr. Smith Goes to Washington takes place in the Senate, and even though I haven't yet given in to the temptation to bore you with a lot about the movie, I'm still going to use it as an excuse to refer to the fact that the Senate is one of the two houses that make up the U.S. Congress, the country's legislature. The other house is the House of Representatives. Technically, a legislature with two houses is called a **bicameral legislature,** one with a single house is referred to as a **unicameral legislature,** and one with twelve houses is referred to as a dodecacameral legislature.

---

*The answer is no, but if a tree fell on him, he would make a sound . . . kind of a squawking, squishy, crunching sound.

GENERAL HENRY MARTYN ROBERT

Team: Ducks All in a Row

Position: Gully

Status: Unchanging

Many scholars argue that **General Henry Martyn Robert** (1837–1923) is the third-most boring person to have ever lived. It seems obvious to me that he's the second-most boring person in recorded history, but I don't really care enough to bother arguing about it, especially since General Robert was all about taking all the fun out of a good old argument. Actually, it's probably not fair to say that a man who almost fought a war over a pig is nearly the most boring person ever. The Pig War, which almost occurred on San Juan Island in the state of Washington, started out as a dispute between British and American settlers over a pig that got into a garden. The Brits brought in some warships, and General Robert gallantly responded to the provocation by digging a big hole in the ground, and somehow that action convinced the Brits not to blow anyone up. All in all, as the defining moment in the general's military career, it was a rather humdrum affair.

What truly cements Robert's place as an icon of the mundane is a little book he wrote, *Robert's Rules of Order*. Someday, in the not-too-distant future, when your very essence is being whittled away by the monotony of yet another pointless meeting about nothing, you will realize that *Robert's Rules of Order* is the cheese grater of the soul. General Roberts had an unnatural interest in parliamentary procedure and an obsession with efficient and orderly meetings. He combined these two mental defects and created a book that outlined, in excruciating detail, how to run an orderly meeting. For cooperative associations, legislative institutions (particularly town councils), county commissions, Luxembourg, and other tiny governments around the world, this book makes Robert a god. Every little council and commission in the world runs its meetings according to the holy word of Robert, and it is guaranteed that some uptight person on every committee will have every detail of *Robert's Rules of Order* memorized and will end up constantly shouting out the rules like a plastic-haired TV preacher quoting scripture.

Now, if you think about it, writing the rules that govern the vast majority of legislative debates in the world, that's a pretty big thing. It's not as interesting as almost fighting a war over a pig, but it is still a big thing.

Why choose the bicameral form over the unicameral? The more appropriate question is how you can justify splitting the legislative function into two units that are largely redundant in what they do. Except for some minor differences in specific responsibilities, both the Senate and the House of Representatives perform all of the same legislative functions. So why have both? On one level, this choice goes to a very realist theory of government. If one thinks that having a government is the next best thing to asking a thief steal all of your stuff, then it makes sense to create government institutions that will deter the kleptomaniac you elected. Adding a second house to a legislature makes it that one step harder to do things, because the two houses tend to check each other (something I talk about below as an important function of legislatures). But if you are more of an idealist and you want to accomplish important things with a government, slowing your progress down with a second legislative house, or with an additional eleven, does not seem like a good idea at all.

Another reason for choosing a bicameral legislature is to guarantee representation for different segments of society. This is true for the federal system in the United States. In the

House of Representatives, the congressional districts that the members represent have roughly the same numbers of people in them, therefore every person is represented equally in a national legislative assembly. In contrast, the Senate has two representatives from every state and the states are all equally represented regardless of their size, their proximity to Canada, or their populations. Wyoming and California have the same power in the Senate but vastly unequal representation in the House. This difference in representation allows the Senate to impede any legislation that would allow the densely populated parts of the country to impose their will on the lonely places. Where there is a need for the legislature to represent distinctly different segments of society, it becomes imperative to have two houses. This is not always a geographic distinction. Sometimes the origins of the legislature can be seen in the different segments of society that are being represented. This is the case with the British Parliament. The House of Lords in the British Parliament originally represented the interests of the nobility, while the House of Commons represented the filthy, stinking peasants.* The continuation of a bicameral legislature in Britain is now mainly an observance of tradition, although there have been pushes to do away with the Lords.

Subsection for Tiresome Details about Representation Strategies

When it comes to representation strategies, one of the most important decisions a nation makes about its legislature is how the seats, or the votes, in the legislature should be divided to represent the country. There are two basic plans for this, and each offers its own advantages. One method is to divide the legislature up according to geography. That is, if you have a legislature with one hundred seats, you divide the nation up into one hundred districts, all with roughly equal numbers of people. This provides **geographic representation**; that is, people are represented in reference to the areas in which they live. The assumption is that people living in a defined area are likely to share the same interests and concerns. When they go to the voting booth, voters choose the specific person they want to represent them as residents of Bobsville. They then know who to call, visit, or write to when they want someone to voice their opinions to. Each representative must also maintain contact with the voters who will decide whether he or she returns to the legislature. Furthermore, because only the candidate who garners a plurality can win in the most frequently used **first-past-the-post system,** the system favors moderate political parties that can create coalitions to gain sizable amounts of voters. The result is usually a **two-party system,** which tends to provide stability to a government.

The other common option is **proportional representation.** Under this system, there is little concern for geography.† When citizens enter the voting booth they do not vote for a

---

*This is a commentary on medieval hygiene, not the social status of the peasantry.

†Surprisingly, Americans have a far lower average knowledge of geography than do Europeans, but the United States uses a geographic district electoral system and most European democracies use proportional systems that require no understanding of geography whatsoever. So much for rational politics.

The Confederacy of Dunces

person, they vote for the political party with the platform that most closely agrees with their views. Each political party submits a list of candidate names prior to the election. In the example of the parliament with one hundred seats, the parties will submit up to one hundred names, the most they could possibly win if they get all of the votes. Roughly speaking, under this system, if a party gets 53 percent of the vote, it gets the same proportion of seats in parliament.[†] The primary concern of those who choose this system is **ideological representation,** which means that they want people's beliefs represented. In a piece he wrote for the *Los Angeles Times,* Andrew Reding reflected on his comparative voting options as an American with dual citizenship in Belgium, a country that uses proportional representation. He noted that in contrast to the district system in the United States, with its choice between the two major political parties, "the Belgian ballot offered a choice of 29 parties, covering almost as many flavors of policy alternatives as Baskin-Robbins offers in ice cream. Researching the party sites on the Internet, I found just the right flavor and color."[4] Proportional representation tends to produce **multiparty systems.** Somewhere in this textbook I might remember to explain why, but for now just trust me that there's a reason it works that way.

Some countries try to combine the benefits of both systems. For example, they might have multimember districts where more than one person represents a geographic area. Proportional representation is then used to divide up the seats within each of the districts. Other countries opt to choose part of their parliaments based on proportional representation and part based on districts. In the next boring section I might get around to talking about some of the positives and negatives attached to each of the systems. For now it is enough for you to recognize that each system emphasizes a different type of representation. Where regional interests are considered crucial, district representation is more likely to be accepted. Where people's political perspectives are of the utmost importance, proportional representation is likely to be selected.

A Monochromatic Subsection on Types of Representatives

While the district versus proportional question has to do with structure of representation, there is a second important choice to be made. The question is whether a legislator should be a **delegate** or a **trustee.** Essentially, this choice comes down to individual representatives and their views of their relationships with their constituents. A delegate is a representative who attempts to do exactly what his or her constituents want. In essence, representatives of the delegate variety wet their fingers and stick them in the air to see which way the wind is blowing. Delegates believe that it is their job to vote the way their constituents want them to on every piece of legislation. Is this possible? On one hand, you can ask whether it is physically possible for a legislator to know what constituents want on all issues. Is it

---

[†]For those of you who choose to work the swing shift so you can get home just in time to watch the 1:00 A.M. reruns of *Beavis and Butthead,* 53 percent would equal fifty-three seats in this fictional one hundred–seat parliament.

possible for a legislator to poll all constituents on these issues? Do the constituents know enough about all the issues to have clear opinions? On the other hand, you probably should ask whether you would actually want a representative's constituency to have a say on all issues. Do you trust your fellow citizens to have that direct an impact on public policy?[*] If so, why have representatives at all? With today's technology, it would, after all, be possible to have some sort of direct electronic voting that would take the place of representatives. That kind of direct democracy won't work, and somewhere in this textbook I should probably explain why, but if you need to know right now, just focus on the subliminal message about how sleepy you're getting. Very, very sleepy. You feel all warm and fuzzy, like a rotten orange sitting on a tropical beach. Your eyes are closing, and when you wake up you'll want to buy dozens of copies of all my books and you won't really care about the problems with direct democracy until I tell that you desperately need to wonder about it.

Other representatives believe that they should be trustees. Trustees believe that they have been selected by their constituents as political experts and everybody just needs to calm down and trust their experience and expertise rather than the whims of the public. Trustees argue that people who knew their general beliefs elected them to office, and those voters trust them to make the right decisions based on their background, education, and awesome intelligence. In the end, if people do not like what their legislators have done, they can vote against them during the next election.

In reality, most legislators are **politicos.** Depending on the situation, they sometimes act like delegates and sometimes act like trustees. When an issue is very important to their constituency and there seems to be a strong consensus, they will vote the way their constituents want. After all, they want to get reelected. However, when there is no clear consensus, or in the many, many instances in which the constituency is uninformed, the legislators vote the way they think is best.

Featureless Subsection on the Function of Checking

Another role that legislatures play is checking. When we refer to checking in this context, it does not involve bank accounts and little slips of paper that you can trade for money, nor does it involve hockey players trying to forcibly remove each other's teeth.[†] For governmental institutions, the checking function involves the responsibility of the institutions or officials to watch over other government institutions or officials to make sure they are performing correctly. In some instances this function is also called oversight. Parliaments perform this function through a variety of means. One particularly popular way is through the use of investigative hearings. Legislatures can scrutinize the work of the executive

---

[*]Before you answer, take a good look at the person next to you, but don't stare—they arrest people for that.

[†]For hockey fans, it is very important to note the spelling of this term. This is kind of like a check, as in physically impeding the progress of an opposing player, but it is clearly not *Czech,* as in a player from that country, nor is it a *cheque,* as in the slip of paper that lures all the good players away from Canada and into places where they have no business playing hockey at all. Seriously, hockey in Florida? They have to import ice from, like, Greenland.

branch and even force government witnesses to appear to explain policy or to testify during investigations of wrongdoing. In some parliaments, tribunals can investigate possible areas of corruption within the executive branch.

Another common type of governmental oversight or checking is performed in parliamentary systems by the **shadow government.**[*] The shadow government is made up of those members of the minority party who would take office were that party ever to capture a majority. Those in the shadow government keep a careful eye on their counterparts in an attempt to expose flaws in policies and possible wrongdoing. The specifics of how this works vary from country to country. However, by far the most entertaining form of this kind of oversight is the British Question Hour. During Question Hour, the prime minister must face questions from Parliament about the government's actions. Some of the questions are softballs thrown underhand by the MPs in the prime minister's party. These scripted questions allow the prime minister to get in sound bites for the evening news, but the opposition or shadow ministers often throw hardball[†] questions meant to attack and embarrass the government.

The British Question Hour is notorious for its raucous atmosphere and poignant humor. In one of the most famous Question Hour exchanges, a female MP once attacked Winston Churchill with the comment, "Sir, if I was your wife I'd poison your tea." Winston immediately shot back, "Madam, if you were my wife, I'd drink it."[*] When New Zealand prime minister Sir Robert Muldoon was asked during a question hour to comment on what he thought of the high levels of migration from New Zealand to Australia, he said that it was great because it served to increase the intelligence of both countries.

The legislative banter of the British Question Hour is not always that sharp and witty, but it is always lively. The Question Hour is regularly rebroadcast on C-SPAN on Sunday evenings, and it is certainly worth your time to try to catch it once or twice. Despite the fun, the Question Hour can be very serious, as the prime minister's remarks are watched by the entire nation. Of course a question hour is possible only in a parliamentary system in which the prime minister is responsible to the parliament. In a presidential system, there is no way to compel the executive to appear before the legislature. In fact, even during the impeachment proceedings against Bill Clinton for his poor taste in adulterous coconspirators, Congress had no way to compel the president to appear.

The Wearisome Legislative Function of Legitimating

In the context of the legislative structure in government, legitimating has nothing to do with determining which impossibly pretty person fathered the half-alien child on a soap opera.

---

[*]And, of course, if the shadow government is corrupt and secretly run by the CIA, it would be a shadow puppet government. Yes, unfortunately, that pun was intended.

[†]Actually, more of a slider or split-finger fastball, something that's got both some velocity and some bend in it.

[*]Unfortunately, someone went and checked the "factuality" of this example. Apparently this legendary exchange was between Winnie and someone called Lady Astor and it occurred at a weekend house party at Blenheim Palace in the early 1930s, not in the Question Hour, and the actual quote is: "Winston, if I were married to you I'd put poison in your coffee." . . . "Nancy, if I were married to you I'd drink it." But why let facts get in the way of a good example?

Instead, legitimating is a matter of establishing the law as something that should be accepted. A lot of the legitimating function of the legislature comes simply from the fact that when an issue is decided in the legislature, people feel that there has been some consideration of their views. As a result of the process and debate, even if that debate took place in front of an empty room, people tend to be more accepting of laws that stumble their way out of a legislature. Even if they do not agree with the ultimate decision, they can still believe that the policy was put into place after their perspectives were taken into account. People are more apt to believe that they should voluntarily follow the law—that the law is legitimate—if the legislature supports it.

A good example of the legitimating function can be seen with the second Bush administration's policy toward Iraq. Early on, President George W. Bush was advised by his attorneys that he did not need congressional authorization to invade Iraq. Despite this advice, he nevertheless sought a resolution from the Congress. Constitutional and other pragmatic arguments aside, Bush probably calculated that a positive vote by Congress would add legitimacy to his government's actions. Without that legitimacy, public support could have been even harder to secure, and his efforts might have generated an even more contentious reaction.

How Hard Would It Be to Convince You That the Educating Function Is Dull?

The last of the five most totally important functions of democratic legislatures and their members is to educate the general citizenry, a process often facilitated by the media. Through committee hearings, open debates, and television appearances by legislators the public learns about important issues and perspectives. Members with geographic constituencies keep their districts informed of important events and important pieces of legislation. Legislatures can also initiate important discussions. In the wake of the hearing surrounding Clarence Thomas's appointment to the Supreme Court, the issue of sexual harassment gained national prominence. The Iran-Contra hearings informed millions about the inner workings of the government.

Education is a lot of what the audienceless speeches on C-SPAN and Parliament TV are for. Even though no one may be listening, those empty-room speeches are going into the official record and are providing fodder for news coverage back home, both of which are ways in which legislatures lay out the details of how, why, and what for. They also lay out the implications for constituents and localize national laws.

It seemed unnecessarily[*] cruel to force you to read a whole legislative chapter straight through, so before I throw you into an uninspiring section contrasting ideals and imperfections, please endure a brief intermission.

---

[*]In this context, unnecessary means unamusing. Amusing cruelty is never unnecessary.

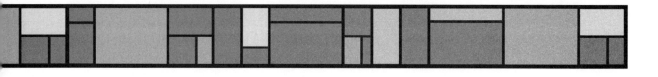

INTERMISSION

This intermission is sponsored by people I know who write things. They promised to pay me scads and scads of money, but they haven't yet. Maybe after the book comes out.

For sentimental, late-night TV junkies, *Mr. Smith Goes to Washington*[5] is a classic film that demonstrates the conflict between ideals and reality and how an institution continues to exist beyond the people attached to it. For the rest of us, it is a black-and-white movie written by a guy with a monument fetish and starring Jimmy Stewart, who was not a race-car driver.

The movie is about how a naive leader of the Boy Rangers, Jefferson Smith, gets selected to serve in the U.S. Senate. Along the way, he learns about corruption and graft, and he ultimately stands up to the political bosses by manipulating the rules of the institution to win. Jefferson Smith is clearly an idealist. He is appointed by the governor to fill a vacancy precisely because of his naïveté. The political bosses believe that he will not cause them any trouble. When he arrives in Washington, he demonstrates his idealized view of government by his blind admiration for his state's senior senator, Joseph Harrison Paine.

After touring the monuments around the capital, Mr. Smith slowly starts to feel like he is nothing more than the window dressing the state party bosses hoped he would be. Ultimately, with Senator Paine's approval, he introduces a bill to create a camp for boys that would be paid for with small donations from boys around the country. At first the bosses and Senator Paine are happy that Smith is busy with his Boy Ranger camp project. However, they eventually discover that he plans to build his camp in the same place reserved for a graft-related project contained in a public works bill. That graft is intended to line the pockets of the state's political boss, Jim Taylor, who could get any political official in the state to do his bidding.

At last, Senator Smith learns the truth from his secretary, Clarissa Saunders, who was originally hired by the bosses to babysit him but is now clearly rooting for him. Unlike Smith, Saunders is anything but naive. As she explains to her friend, "Look, when I came here, my eyes were big blue question marks. Now they're big green dollar marks." When Mr. Smith confronts Senator Paine, Paine tells him that he could not possibly understand all that is going on and that he should abandon the project. When Smith confronts Jim Taylor, he gets a real political education as Taylor offers him a job or the opportunity to continue serving in the Senate if he is willing to follow orders like Senator Paine.

Having none of it, Smith gets up to challenge the project on the floor of the Senate. He's quickly interrupted by Paine, who charges Smith with suggesting the boys' camp to make a profit for himself. Framed by false evidence, a seemingly defeated Smith disappears. Eventually, Saunders finds him visiting the Lincoln Memorial, this time with a more cynical eye. When he tells her that he plans to leave Washington, she uses the memorial to inspire him. Saunders then infuses Smith's idealism with some realistic political strategy. Smith returns to the floor of the Senate, and when he is recognized, he engages in a one-man **filibuster** of the graft-laden public works legislation. The filibuster—a tactic in which a senator or group of senators talk indefinitely about a bill—is intended to frustrate the proponents of the bill. Those employing the filibuster hope to keep the Senate from conducting any business at all, thus encouraging the other senators to stop considering the bill.

Jefferson Smith hopes to filibuster long enough to make the public aware of the graft contained in the bill.

Smith's ultimate victory puts a slightly different twist on the idealist/realist dichotomy I have thus far presented. It is incorrect to say that Smith has become a realist at the end of the movie; he clearly has not. If anything, his idealism wins out over realism. He defeats Taylor, he converts Saunders, and we are left to believe that the boys' camp will be built. What Smith does lose is his naïveté. He realizes that to accomplish his goals he must adjust his ideals so that he can deal with the way things are. Idealists need not be naive about politics and political methods. In fact, successful idealists learn to deploy tactics ideally suited to their political environments. Gandhi and Martin Luther King Jr. were certainly idealists who used practical political methods—boycotts, civil disobedience, and interest group pressure—designed to work and produce results in the real world.

During his filibuster, Smith lectures his fellow senators on how they have to rise to their jobs:

> Just get up off the ground. That's all I ask. Get up there with that lady that's up on top of this Capitol Dome. That lady that stands for Liberty. Take a look at this country through her eyes if you really want to see somethin'. And you won't just see scenery. You'll see the whole parade of what man's carved out for himself after centuries of fighting. And fighting for something better than just jungle law. Fighting so as he can stand on his own two feet free and decent, like he was created no matter what his race, color, or creed. That's what you'd see. There's no place out there for graft or greed or lies! Or compromise with human liberties!

Smith's ultimate victory is not just a victory over corruption and greed; it is a victory for the institution of the United States Senate. The goodness of the institution transcends those individuals who currently serve there. Even as reality constantly gets in the way, governmental institutions are meant to serve society. They are intended, at least, to do good things.

A REDUNDANT REPETITION OF THE THEME: CONTRASTING LEGISLATURES IN PARLIAMENTARY AND PRESIDENTIAL SYSTEMS

Belief in the idea that democratic legislatures actually perform the five functions I've discussed requires a fairly idealistic streak. It requires you to assume or presume that the institutions actually perform as desired and that the people in and around them aren't subverting or perverting their purpose. I know that's not the way the real world works, so I now need you to wade your way through the imperfections of democratic legislatures.

In Chapter 6, I contrasted the benefits of the ideal presidential system with those of the ideal planetary* system. The presidential system creates a strong and independent executive, while the parliamentary system offers an executive who is also a member of

---

*Again, just checking to see if the copy editor is in the house.

parliament and can work very effectively with the legislative branch. Whereas the presidential system maintains strong institutions through independence, the parliamentary system offers expediency and efficiency through the integration of the two primary political institutions. Strength and independence are positive virtues, as are expediency and efficiency. However, it is possible to have too much of a good thing. That strong president may, in fact, become too strong. The person serving as both head of government and head of state can effectively use modern technology to communicate with the people. This can allow presidents to go over the heads of the legislative branch to speak directly to the people. In the novel *All the King's Men,* Governor Willie Stark, who is facing impeachment by the legislature, appeals directly to the people to garner support to fight the impeachment.[6] This tactic, along with buying off key legislators, insulates him from the impeachment threat.

Presidents can also accumulate increased power at the expense of the legislative branch, ultimately making the president too strong for checks and balances to work properly. Remember that legislators always have reelection in the backs of their minds. This is particularly true when we are talking about a district-based electoral system. There is, therefore, an incentive for members of the legislature to avoid controversial political decisions so that they can stay in their constituents' good graces. This can lead to their delegating authority and power to the president on certain issues, and the president can take advantage of the situation. Delegations to the president are particularly common during international crises. At one such point, after presidents Lyndon Johnson and Richard Nixon accumulated tremendous power in the presidency, historian Arthur Schlesinger Jr., wrote *The Imperial Presidency,*[7] in which he examined the increasing power of the president. Ultimately, Congress did curtail the executive's increasing power, the **imperial presidency,** when the institution of the presidency was damaged by the Vietnam War and the Watergate scandal.

This potential for an overwhelming concentration of power is always a fear in presidential systems. The legislature and any other branches of government that are able to reign in the executive must always be vigilant and fight to ensure that their check on the executive remains effective. The imperial presidency can happen only if the legislature fails to check its rise. However, the danger of the imperial presidency is more of a monster under the bed than a bug in the day-to-day machinery of the presidential system. A more important difficulty is almost the exact opposite of the imperial presidency, and that is where the legislating part of it gets all mucked up.

The Monotony of Gridlock in Presidential Systems

While it is a bit of a fear that an imperial president will pull a full-on Godzilla* on the legislature, a far more commonplace problem is a situation often referred to as gridlock.

Full-on Godzilla is a technical term often skillfully deployed by extremely intelligent political science professors who watch too much late-night cable TV. In relation to politics, it refers to an individual politician gaining enough power to overwhelm any and all opposition. Contrary to the common mythology, radioactive waste plays no part in this process. It should also be remembered that the use of the term in political science is distinctly different from its use in professional wrestling.

The Confederacy of Dunces

Gridlock arises when the checks and balances within the presidential system work too well, and they not only prevent one institution from overwhelming the others but also prevent anyone from doing much of anything. Basically, it all just sits there like fuzzy green citrus. In the United States gridlock is often associated with **divided government,** when one political party controls the presidency and another party controls either one or both houses of Congress. Because the president can use the veto to check legislative initiatives and because the legislature can refuse to provide the funding for unpopular or controversial presidential policy efforts, it becomes very difficult for either the executive or the legislature to cooperate on anything outside what is likely to be a very narrow range of agreement between the two major U.S. parties. This is not the only time things grind to a halt inside the Beltway, however. Gridlock can occur anytime the Congress and the president end up stuck in a situation in which neither will allow the other to do anything, such as when a president's approval ratings crash and legislative members think that working with the president might hurt them in the next election.

This paralyzing division of government has been the norm in recent American history, and the term *gridlock* itself has worked its way into the speeches of politicians. Bill Clinton faced divided government for all but two years of his administration, and George W. Bush faced divided government for part of his first term. This may also be a source of many features of the modern U.S. presidency. Since a gridlocked president often finds it necessary to bypass the Congress and speak directly to the American people in order to try to get things done, we now see the direct appeal to the public as a significant, if not defining, part of the U.S. presidency. Gridlock can also lead to confusion over responsibility for policy, because when the president appeals to the public as a way to influence the legislature, the distinction between the institutions is blurred. When the news media report that the U.S. president has lost a legislative battle, they overlook the fact that the president cannot introduce legislation; the president cannot even vote in the Congress. This kind of commentary makes it even harder for the public to identify which branch of government is the one using its check to stop things from getting done, and because there is no identifiable villain, it is that much harder to escape gridlock.

One of the most significant negative effects of gridlock is the difficulty in passing any kind of broad or comprehensive policy changes, and the only way anything gets done is with what I call "the Bob solution."* In *What about Bob?*[8] Bill Murray plays a psychiatric patient who is paralyzed by his fear of everything. His new psychiatrist encourages Murray's character to take "baby steps," which is also the title of the psychiatrist's

---

*I call this the Bob solution only so that I can make a completely gratuitous reference to this movie. There is absolutely no reason to mention this movie, and I offer no justification whatsoever. *What about Bob?* has some funny bits, but the only real question is whether *Caddyshack* or *Stripes* is the best Bill Murray movie. As may be obvious, however, that argument is, in itself, little more than a shameless opportunity to provide two more completely unnecessary references to films I like just so that my blatantly self-indulgent references to my own work looks a little less crass.

self-help book. So Bill Murray literally starts to take baby steps and shuffles his way around. Because of the nature of the separation of powers and gridlock, in the United States policy is often reduced to baby steps. For example, Bill Clinton came into office promising major changes in policy, particularly the implementation of a national health care policy, but ultimately he managed only to make the smallest of changes in health care policy, such as portability of health insurance. The guarantee that you can take your old health insurance plan with you to a new job falls far short of a comprehensive national health care policy. But faced with the impossibility of fully implementing whatever grand dream a president may have, the Bob solution may be the only way to move forward.

In contrast, parliamentary systems are not subject to gridlock. Remember that the prime minister is actually a member of parliament and, by definition, always commands the majority of votes in the legislature. A politician becomes prime minister by garnering the support of a majority of the parliament. When one party manages to win a majority— 50 percent plus one—of the seats in the parliament, this is a quick and simple thing. The head of state asks the leader of the winning party to form a government, and the leader of the party becomes the prime minister. At most, sometimes a ceremonial vote is held during which the majority party elects one of its own as the prime minister. In other systems, coalitions between parties are formed after an election to get a majority of parliamentary votes. In either situation, the prime minister pretty much always has a majority in parliament to provide the legislation needed to back policy initiatives, and the majority in parliament can almost always count on the executive to support the legislation that is passed. No gridlock.

The Banality of Parliamentary Instability

There are two features of a parliamentary system, though, that might be considered bugs in the system, and both are related to stability. The first is pretty simple—**policy stability.** In a presidential system, in which big changes are difficult to enact, the social and economic environments within the country tend to be very consistent over time. This has a tremendous value to businesses and others who need to be able to plan over the long term. In a parliamentary system, sweeping change is far easier, and too much change can sometimes be a problem. A new party or new coalition coming into power can change just about anything and everything. Radical changes in tax laws can nullify a lifetime investment strategy in a second. Big changes in foreign policy can weaken or even shatter alliances. The effects are particularly obvious in business and other economic matters, in which stability of policy has a big influence on the investment of current wealth, the building of infrastructure, and research or production for future gains. Consistent policy is also valuable for educational systems, law enforcement, and any other long-term endeavors for which infrastructure, such as educational curriculum, needs to be developed for the

The Confederacy of Dunces

repeated performance of given functions. Any societal institutions that look to the future usually do better in a stable political and policy environment.

A second way that stability can be a problem in a parliamentary system is in the tenure of the government itself. In most parliamentary systems the government can be dissolved at any moment by a simple majority vote in the parliament. At any time, a party can call for a **vote of no confidence,** and if the prime minister loses that vote, the government is dissolved, and forming a new government begins immediately. In some systems there might be a window of a few days or weeks to negotiate a new coalition or a deal to win a new vote of support before an election is necessary; other systems require that new elections be scheduled immediately after a vote of no confidence. Essentially, this means that any scandal or policy failure that causes legislative support to waver can lead to an immediate change of government. In such a system, Ronald Reagan might well have served only two years. His unpopular policy of stationing U.S. Marines in Beirut, Lebanon, ended catastrophically in 1983 when the Marine barracks were bombed. Bill Clinton might have had an even shorter stay in office after the humanitarian intervention in Somalia—a policy he inherited from his predecessor—collapsed in disgrace and caused a serious backlash in Congress. In both of these cases, these presidents were able to carry on and recover sufficiently to win reelection a few years later. A prime minister would be unlikely to have such luxury.

France provides an excellent example of the difficulty governments in parliamentary systems can have in sustaining their tenure in office. Just during the period 1990–2004, there were twelve different French governments. While not all changes in French government require elections or bring a new prime minister into office, such constant turmoil takes up time and energy. Additionally, the uncertainty over who will be the prime minister next month means that everyone must always work with the knowledge that policy could change, quite literally, at a moment's notice. This instability problem with parliamentary systems is in many ways the opposite and equal to the gridlock problem with presidential systems. Each flaw is balanced by benefits. There is, however, a flaw that both systems share, and it is much more troubling for the ideals of democracy. Even if the whole process of voting is perfectly fair, neither a parliamentary nor a presidential system can ensure that every voter is represented equally and fairly by the government that is formed through voting.

The Unbearably Predictable Section Telling You That Representation Is Also Messed Up Because Both Single-District and Proportional Systems Can't Quite Manage to Function Ideally . . . Surprise, Surprise

As I've mentioned briefly before, votes are transformed into representation within government in two basic ways. The United States and several parliamentary democracies, such as Great Britain, use a single-member district system, in which voting is based on geographic districts and each geographic district elects a representative. An alternative that

many think is fairer is a proportional system, in which seats in a government body such as a parliament are assigned to parties based on the proportion of the votes they receive.

Both systems have advantages. A district system elects an individual who is clearly responsible for representing the interests of a specific community, and the specter of future elections tends to make that individual quite responsive to local needs. This helps preserve local and regional qualities in a geographically diverse country such as the United States. A proportional system allows a much wider variety of political perspectives to gain representation in the elected bodies of government, and it ensures that just about everyone's vote is translated to legislative representation. In a district system, if you vote for any candidate who cannot win a majority, you have wasted your vote and your preference will not be represented. In a proportional system, the party you vote for only has to exceed the qualifying threshold, sometimes as low as 1 percent of the vote, in order to win a seat and represent your opinion.

However, both systems are flawed as means of democratic representation. Proponents of proportional representation will immediately bristle at the suggestion that it is a flawed political institution. Proportional representation is frequently offered as the cure for the ills of district-based elections, and it does do most of the things its advocates claim. It increases the number of parties and the variety of policy perspectives officially represented in elected bodies, and it ensures that almost every vote is reflected in the final representation. However, that does not mean it is perfect. In the end, someone still has to govern, and it is in the steps between the votes and the final arrangement of who governs that the flaws in the proportional system become apparent. Specifically, minor parties, representing small percentages of the population, will often have a disproportional influence on the formation of a government.

One of the most obvious effects of proportional representation is the proliferation of political parties. Essentially, a party can form around any policy position that attracts enough votes to get the party past the qualifying threshold. Thus, there is usually a party representing the roughly 5 to 15 percent of the population that places their highest political priority on environmental issues, a party that caters to the roughly 10 percent of the population that votes on their socially conservative agenda, and so on. Multiparty systems are an important part of a proportional representation system, and when there are many parties in the legislature, it is usually very difficult for any one party to achieve the majority necessary to form a government on its own. Since a prime minister must always have the support of a majority of the parliament, this usually leads to coalitions between parties. Think of the alliances formed on one of the many incarnations of *Survivor*[9] or its reality TV progeny and rip-offs. Except for the fact that politicians seldom eat bugs, the alliances that are formed on *Survivor* are not very different from the coalitions that are formed in parliaments. They are ad hoc* agreements formed to win the executive—or the immunity

---

Ad hoc is not a reference to alcohol-induced regurgitation, nor does it refer to the sound a cat makes when hacking up a fur ball. It refers to an improvised or one-time-only action.

torch—but they are always uneasy alliances because all of the parties have their own political agendas.

Coalitions become a problem with democratic representation when a minor party finds itself in the key position to swing the vote for or against a prime minister. Minor parties in this situation are often called relevant parties, because, even though they do not have a chance of winning on their own, they can affect the outcome of the election and that gives them policy leverage far out of proportion to the votes they received. For example, consider a country that has proportional representation and three parties that attract votes: the right-leaning (conservative) Party A wins 43 percent of the seats in parliament, the more left-leaning (liberal) counterpart Party B wins 49 percent, and a religious Party C manages to get the remaining 8 percent. What happens then?

In order to govern, one party must put together a majority of support from the MPs. Usually, the head of state will ask the leader of the party with the most votes to try to form a government. Thus, Party B will talk to Party C. But clearly Party C has tremendous leverage here. No matter what either party offers in terms of policy concessions or ministerial positions in the cabinet, Party C can always go to the other big party and ask for more.

By supporting the conservative Party A, the religious Party C will be able to work out a deal to guarantee all kinds of conservative-friendly legislation. Furthermore, since the conservative party needs the religious party's support to stay in power, it is unlikely that Party A will enact any policies that would alienate Party C, because if the religious party were to leave the coalition, the government would fall. And in my little scenario, the religious party can play hardball in forming the coalition. Party C can coerce the liberal party with the threat of putting the smaller Party A in power and giving the conservatives control of policy and government for several years. However, even though there is a more natural policy affinity between the religious Party C and the conservative Party A, the conservatives still face a big risk if they do not make significant concessions. If neither Party A nor Party B is willing to give the religious party what it wants, Party C can refuse to join either of them, and thus force new elections. That would be extremely dangerous for the conservative party, because if the liberal party were to gain just 1 percent more of the vote in the new elections, it would have a majority and could rule unfettered by a coalition that dilutes its policy preferences. Thus, there is a flaw in the system: those small parties that are in a position that makes them necessary to form a government can gain influence that far outweighs the extent of their electoral support.

Given our three-party scenario, the negotiations are relatively simple. The religious party and the conservative party probably have enough in common that it would be in both of their interests to cooperate, and the liberal party is unlikely to be willing to offer enough to overcome that natural affinity. So, the conservative party should be able to form a coalition that completely shuts the party with the most votes out of government and gives substantial concessions to the party that won the fewest. That is far from perfectly representing the wishes of the public, and, to make matters worse, it is seldom that neat and tidy. Typically,

there is a proliferation of minor parties in a proportional system, and the interests of the minor parties seldom coincide enough to make for the easy formation of nice, rational coalitions.

A TIRED ATTEMPT TO MAKE COALITION POLITICS INTERESTING WITH A LAME EXAMPLE

Far from a match made in heaven, most coalition governments are put together like a TV reality matchmaking show in which a gender-nonspecific Pat, who has traveled all the way here from Chapter 1, is going to pick a future ex-spouse—from a cadre of far-from-perfect participants who were willing to sign the network's legal release form. It might go something like this:

"So, Chris, what does your party bring to the coalition table?"

"We're a radically conservative party that believes in restoring the nation to its former glory by kicking out all of the immigrants from countries other than the ones that kicked out our ancestors. Some of our leaders have made some disparaging comments about the minorities that voted for your party, but we've got 6 percent of the seats in parliament and we have a very active and growing membership."

"Terry, please tell me you have something better to offer?"

"Dude, we're a radical freedom suburban radical party for freedom.* We believe that the government should stick to providing only the bare minimum of necessary services—those that no private industry could provide—and it should stay completely out of all moral and social decisions made by consenting adults in the privacy of their own home, front yard, or driveway. We'll join your coalition, but the first thing that has to go is the repressive and hypocritical application of drug laws to hemp and hemp by-products. We think we might have something like 3 percent of the vote, or maybe it was 8 percent. Dude, does that look like an 8 percent? Or maybe a 6 percent? That is a percent thingy, right? Seriously, I know we got more than eight votes, man."

"Jamie, what have you got?"

"I am so very glad you asked, Pat, because we have got exactly what you want. We are a brand-new party, with new and completely unspecified ideas. We have a charismatic young and fiery leader who used to be an inspirational speaker and hamster therapist. Because our leader is so gosh-darned charismatic, we are going to have to demand that you give us a prominent place in your government from which we can threaten your party's authority with flashy

---

*The RFSRPF is a proud sponsor of the American Dodgeball Association of America.

The Confederacy of Dunces

and glib catchphrases that have little or no foundation in a coherent policy or the realities of government. We have 3.67 percent of the vote."

"Butch, what can you offer the coalition?"

"We're an ultrareligious party, Pat. We'd like to see the government take some long overdue action to restore the moral foundation of this country, starting with the elimination of all this tolerance for ambiguously gendered names. We are absolutely committed to universal adoption of the Ten Commandments, and we demand the immediate invasion of any country that objects. This country must stop its association with the morally corrupt nations of the world and France. We've got 5 percent of the seats in parliament and God's secret e-mail address."

Of course, the reality is that Pat does not really like any of these choices, and the coalition options for any political party are always imperfect choices. On top of the difficulties Pat will have in selecting coalition partners that fit with Pat's own party are the relationships between potential coalition partners that also have to be considered. Several combinations of the minor parties in the above example simply cannot coexist in a coalition, and this fact will give further policy leverage to some of these minor parties.

Therefore, while parliamentary systems do not suffer from gridlock, they can suffer from **immobilism** caused by the fragility of the ruling coalition. The more complex and more fragile the ruling coalition, the more difficult it is for the coalition to enact any kind of coherent policies, because any new policy that was not agreed upon by all parties at the formation of the coalition may cause a party to break away and force the government to collapse. This means that any party that can cause the coalition to fall apart has veto power over any legislation. Thus, multiparty systems can cause governments to teeter constantly on the brink of falling apart—a serious difficulty. Italy is perhaps the best example of this situation, as it has had fifty-nine governments since World War II, and, as a result, far from running on time, the Italian train system is so messed up that the company that prints the schedules is at risk of being sued for fraud.[*]

In rare instances, it is even possible for a country with a parliamentary system to have a **minority government.** In that case, the majority party does not share power with any other party, but it relies on an agreement in which another party will provide support or will abstain from voting if there is ever a no-confidence vote. For example, in 2005 Canadian prime minister Paul Martin's government was one vote shy of a majority and simply needed a party with two or more seats to agree to abstain from a vote of no confidence. This can work if there are several small parties that are willing to guarantee abstaining in return for modest policy concessions.

---

[*]I know, I know. Everyone says that Italy's trains now run on something reasonably close to a schedule, but when I was in Italy, a rail workers' strike prevented me from seeing any trains actually run, and until I see some evidence, I'm going to keep kicking this equine carcass.

Yet another variation is a **unity government.** With a unity government, the two major parties, though in opposition, work together to achieve a higher national purpose. For example, in Israel, Prime Minister Ariel Sharon's Likud Party worked with Shimon Peres's Labor Party for a time in order to show a united front during a recent period in the ongoing Middle East conflict. As one might imagine, such arrangements are difficult to maintain and are usually short-lived.

France has its own problems (aside from being French, that is). France's institutions are a little different from most. While the country has a parliamentary system, it also has a president with significant political power. That president is elected separately and at different times from the parliament. Nevertheless, the prime minister serves at the president's pleasure. Consequently, it is possible for the French president to be from one political party while a different political party controls the legislature.* This situation first occurred in 1986, when President François Mitterrand's Socialist Party lost parliamentary elections. The French refer to this as **cohabitation,** and I will leave it to you to employ a French stereotype to discover the obvious joke.

The Facile Cataloging of Representation Flaws in District Elections

If you are thinking that district elections are superior because of the imperfections of proportional representation, you need to look more carefully at districts—and I mean, quite literally, look at the districts. In nations that use district elections, legislators are elected to represent particular geographic territories, and the big problem with district elections is that someone must draw the district lines. In other words, if you want to have a legislature with one hundred seats, you have to divide up the country into one hundred districts. Who will do this? Politicians, of course. What could possibly go wrong with that? This is tantamount to allowing the richest team in baseball to dictate the rules for acquiring players.†

That analogy actually falls a bit short of the mark, because it is the politicians who already control the legislature who get to draw the lines. In the United States, the Senate's districts are, of course, the states. However, for the House of Representatives the responsibility for drawing district lines within individual states—or redistricting—lies with the state legislatures. Thus, whichever party controls a state's legislature gets to draw the lines for the seats within the state, and, of course, in doing so it puts the party's interests first.

Imagine the following extremely complex scenario in a very rectangular state, depicted in Figure 7.1, that has to be divided into three different districts with roughly the same number of people in each. The letter *L* stands for a pocket of about ten thousand people that is dominated by the Liberal Party. The *C* stands for a pocket of about ten thousand

---

*It is important to remember the distinction between head of state, someone like the queen of England, who serves as the symbolic embodiment of the country, and the head of government, who does all the real work of governing, like the prime minister of Great Britain. The U.S. president does both, but the French president is sort of like an elected queen.

†Oh, wait, that is what the Yankees do.

people that is dominated by members of the Conservative Party. If you are going to try to be the fairest you can be, you could divide the state horizontally into three districts—two with three majority-Liberal pockets and one with three majority-Conservative pockets. The final outcome would leave you with two districts where the Liberals are likely to win and one district where the Conservatives are likely to win. This is the fair way of doing it, since the number of districts each party would likely win is in proportion to the party's overall percentage of the total population. However, the concern is not with being fair, but with winning. What if you represent the Liberal Party and you are responsible for drawing these districts? Then you've got a different situation. Instead of drawing these districts horizontally, you'll draw them vertically and the Liberals will win three seats to the Conservatives' zero.

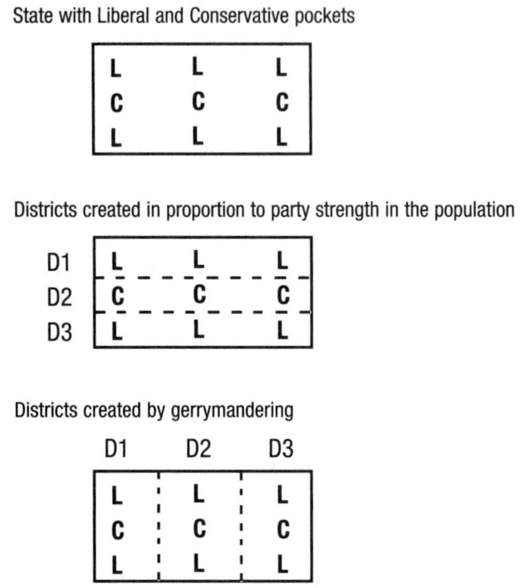

This process of intentionally drawing districts to gain a partisan advantage is called **gerrymandering.** In this scenario, the Liberal Party gerrymandered the districts to get an extra seat. Of course, in real life, at least in life outside the classroom, people are not arranged in neat little rows, but that does not keep those from drawing the lines from being creative. In fact, the word *gerrymander* comes from the name of an early practitioner of such redistricting. Elbridge Gerry, a signer of the Declaration of Independence, used his position as Massachusetts governor to manipulate the drawing of electoral districts in order to keep his political party in power. One of those districts looked like a salamander, and some clever political commentator, knowing that I would one day need a term in my textbook to denote this concept, noticed that *Gerry* plus *salamander* equals *gerrymander.*

In the state of Pennsylvania, roughly half of all registered voters are Democrats. Still, Republican redistricting has left the Republicans in control of twelve of the state's nineteen congressional districts. Don't feel too bad for the Democrats, though. As I've noted, there is a rich history of gerrymandering in the United States. The Democrats have done the same to the Republicans, and, given the opportunity in the future, you can be certain that they will do so again. Still, one has to wonder about how democratic such a system is.

Figure 7.1 Dividing a State into Districts

Certainly, with proportional representation the legislature will more accurately reflect the nation's partisan makeup even if a coalition arrangement distorts the policy impact of some parties at the expense of others. Gerrymandering is particularly common in the United States. Other countries that use district elections, such as Great Britain, Canada, and New Zealand, have independent commissions that attempt to create fair election districts in a nonpolitical manner.

Another problem with using electoral districts is that they can split the loyalty of the elected representatives. Voters ask their representatives to play two different, and often contradictory, roles.[10] On one hand, they ask their representatives to be part of the national lawmaking assembly. In this sense, the representatives are expected to enact legislation that is in the nation's best interest. Most people would see no problem with this. On the other hand, voters expect their representatives to be ambassadors from the districts and the geographic locations they represent. In other words, the representatives' constituents, the people they represent in their districts, want them to do what is in the best interest for the districts, and what is in the best interest of an individual state or legislative district is not always the same as what is in the best interest of the nation as a whole.

Sometimes local interests are the same as national interests, but there are many instances in which they are not. Take, for example, recent efforts to shut down military installations around the United States. With advances in transportation and with the end of World War II drastically reducing the likelihood that the Japanese will invade Oregon, it no longer makes economic sense to have thousands of small military bases scattered across the country. Consolidation of the military into a few large complexes makes economic sense, but what if you are a congressman with a naval base in your district? The district certainly benefits from the base; it brings jobs as sailors shop and eat at local establishments and keep the local independent contractors working in the oldest profession gainfully employed. Even though it is in the national interest to shut down many of these small bases, the local interests served by keeping the bases open will tend to drive U.S. senators and members of Congress to fight to protect them, even as they agree that many of the bases need to be closed.

Furthermore, this split can drive a wedge between national and local interests and weaken political parties. Because each individual representative owes his or her electoral success to a constituency and not to a political party, representatives may feel free to act in ways that are contrary to their parties' interests. Such attitudes on the part of representatives can make it very difficult for party leaders to maintain party discipline. The split loyalty can also encourage legislators to engage in **pork-barrel politics,** in which they use their political offices to bring federal money to their districts through projects and jobs. The first priority of these legislators is not whether the programs and jobs are necessary, it is whether they can bring home the bacon for their constituents, who will then return the

The Confederacy of Dunces

legislators to office. The more successful a legislator is at satisfying what constituents want, the better his or her chances for reelection. Again, it is difficult to reconcile some pork-barrel projects with the national interest, yet the funds for these projects come out of the national budget.

Furthermore, because local constituents are the ones who keep representatives in office, representatives feel obliged to provide as much service to their constituents as possible. Contrary to the image that most people have of their representatives engaging in important debates, much of the job of a legislator is constituent service. In fact, legislators often find themselves playing the undesirable role of ombudsmen, in which they and their aides help their constituents cut through the red tape of government to secure housing and other benefits. Sometimes representatives just act like bartenders and listen as their constituents tell them their problems, some of which have no solutions.[*]

A DREARY BLEAKNESS IN THE AUTHORITARIAN GLOOM: THEY ENDURE LEGISLATIVE INSTITUTIONS, TOO

I need to hurry up and finish this chapter before I run out of synonyms for boring and boredom, so I won't dwell too horribly long on authoritarian legislative institutions, but I am kind of obliged to discuss them, at least a little. As should be logically obvious from my discussion of legislative authority being slowly pried away from kings and queens, the authoritarian systems that have monarchs as executives must also, often, have some form of legislative institutions. After all, if there were no legislative institutions in authoritarian systems, there would be nothing there to enable all that prying and separating.

Since I mentioned the prying of legislative functions out of the hands of the authoritarian monarch, I probably have to mention the early forms of the English Parliament as an example. It may be uninteresting, but the fact that Parliament evolved out of a gathering of advisers and quickly became a means of representing the interests of the taxed to the monarch indicates two functions right there. For those of you who have slipped just a little too far into the coma to comprehend the sentence you just read, those two functions are advising and representing.

The advisory function is particularly noticeable in authoritarian oligarchies. It may be the politburo or another small committee of elites that actually determines most or all of the law, but the debates and discussions in the legislative institutions provide a great deal of advice and feedback on local conditions, local impacts, and the local needs of those represented.

---

[*]As the faculty supervisor of many legislative interns, I have heard some hard-to-believe tales of the strange requests that legislators receive from their adoring constituents. These can range from people wanting to get relatives into or out of the army to my personal favorite: the lady who called because she wanted her representative to do something about the roving band of stray cats infiltrating her neighborhood and stealing the pies out of her window. I think that one is better than the more routine calls about aliens, don't you?

Legislative institutions in authoritarian governments are also used to legitimate laws and decisions. In the days preceding the 2003 Iraq War, Saddam Hussein announced that he would let the Iraqi parliament decide whether the country should be opened to weapons inspectors. Shockingly, the parliament voted no. Iraqi officials argued that this demonstrated clear support for the Iraqi leader. Other countries might have taken this mandate a little more seriously if it had not been quite so obvious that the MPs would have surrendered several vital organs that they had grown fond of had they voted in a manner not to Saddam's liking. Still, what Saddam attempted to do was to have his parliament legitimate his policy. Generally speaking, the more a nation's people believe that their parliament answers to them, the more they believe that the parliament is truly representative, the more easily the parliament can perform a legitimating function.

Finally, authoritarian legislatures also perform an educating function that is remarkably similar to the educating function of their democratic counterparts. The debates, speeches, and discussions in these forums are often about the reasons and meanings of laws or executive actions rather than about actually implementing, preventing, or defining the laws.

KEY TERMS

bicameral legislature / 178

cohabitation / 196

delegate / 181

divided government / 189

filibuster / 186

first-past-the-post system / 180

geographic representation / 180

gerrymandering / 197

gridlock / 189

ideological representation / 181

immobilism / 195

imperial presidency / 188

minority government / 195

multiparty system / 181

policy stability / 190

politicos / 182

pork-barrel politics / 198

proportional representation / 180

shadow government / 183

trustee / 181

two-party system / 180

unicameral legislature / 178

unity government / 196

vote of no confidence / 191

CHAPTER SUMMARY

Legislative is an adjective, but if you put *the* in front of it, people will think it's a noun. In its narrowest sense, when used all proper and adjectivally, it links nouns to the lawmaking function of government. Thus, you have the legislative structure of government, legislative institutions, legislative branch, legislative process, and so on. Historically, the history of the legislative structure of government has been a gradual history of separating the legislative and executive functions of government, throughout the history of history. Legislatures serve five basic functions: lawmaking, legitimating, representing, educating, and one other one. While all of these functions, including the fifth one, are fairly obvious parts of democratic

legislatures, they can often be seen in authoritarian governments as well. Speaking of Ronald Reagan and Margaret Thatcher, democratic legislatures generally take one of two basic forms: proportional representation systems and single-member district systems. However, New Zealand mixes both together, and has yet to offer a good reason for doing so.

STUDY QUESTIONS AND EXERCISES

1. Identify and explain the different functions that legislatures perform.

2. This chapter makes the case that not all legislatures are democratic. Explain why this is the case. What are some aspects of the U.S. Congress that are not democratic?

3. Is C-SPAN or C-SPAN2 the most boring channel on cable?

4. What are the strengths and weaknesses of a single-member district process of selecting representatives for a democratic legislature?

5. Surprise . . . What are the strengths and weaknesses of a proportional representation process of selecting representatives for a democratic legislature?

6. Why would a dictator have a legislature?

WEBSITES TO EXPLORE

www.capsteps.com. The Capitol Steps are a group of former Senate staffers who satirize national politics through song.

www.c-span.org/international/links.asp. C-SPAN's Legislatures around the World page links to parliaments all over the globe and indicates whether their proceedings are televised.

www.parl.gc.ca/Content/LOP/researchpublications/bp334-e.htm. The Canadian Library of Parliament site reprints "Electoral Systems," Brian O'Neal's short 1993 paper on the different types of electoral systems and their importance.

http://www.nebraskalegislature.gov/about/history_unicameral.php. The Nebraska Legislature's site provides a history of Nebraska's decision to establish a one-house legislature.

Brazilian Bureaucracy
Do I Even Need to Bother with the Jokes?

Deep in the dark and constipated bowels of a well-worn bureaucratic agency, an insect falls into a printer and becomes, quite literally, a bug in the machinery of government. Terry Gilliam constructs the plot of an entire movie out of the resulting typo. Brazil is perhaps the darkest of dark comedies.[1] It ruthlessly spins our frustrations with administrative government into an Orwellian nightmare with just enough absurdity to take the edge off. A renegade plumber is killed and consumed by a swarm of the official paperwork that he refused to file. A man works in a nice secure government job, spending boring day after boring day torturing people to death at the office, and when it is his best friend in the chair, it is nothing personal. It is just his job; rules are rules, and all that.

Brazil expresses our collective frustration with bureaucracies. However, for the immediate purposes of this discussion, the film depicts the threat of what can happen to any institution. No matter how many experts are consulted, no matter how carefully plans are drawn, no matter how skillfully history is read, no matter how vast the understanding of politics, in real life no institution runs perfectly. There will always be unintended consequences, and something is bound to not go according to plan. A fly will land in the printer or someone will wiggle into an unanticipated situation that will have to be dealt with.

This is particularly problematic for bureaucracies, because inflexibility is actually part of the ideal of administrative government. Yes, Virginia, there is an idealist perspective on bureaucracy. In fact, the ideals of bureaucracy are some of the most clearly articulated and logically coherent ideals that have ever been offered for any structure found in modern governments.

CHAPTER 8

BUREAUCRACY, IT GOES TO ELEVEN*

If I had to offer a theme for the depiction of bureaucracies in film and literature, "ridiculous to the point of sublime" would be the first thing that probably comes to mind. *The Hitchhiker's Guide to the Galaxy*[2] opens with Arthur Dent lying in the mud in front of a bull-dozer. Arthur is neither intoxicated nor injured; he is simply trying to keep a wrecking crew from demolishing his house. It seems that the local bureaucracy has decided to put a highway bypass through his breakfast nook. Arthur's argument with the crew foreman is interrupted by Arthur's friend Ford Prefect. Ford not only reveals that he is actually an alien but also tells Arthur that the Earth is about to be destroyed so a hyperspatial express route can be constructed. When objections are raised, those in charge of both demolitions argue that notice had been given and Arthur had plenty of opportunity to respond and object. Of course, the paperwork for the demolition of Dent's house was posted in the unlit basement of a government building, and the Earth's notice was posted quite clearly on a notice board that just happened to be on another planet. Apparently the applicable rules said nothing about where the notice had to be posted.

Even if you have never faced the agency-mandated destruction of your house or home planet, bureaucracies are the one aspect of government that we all eventually end up wrestling with, and there is probably little need to convince you that they are flawed. Consider the film I opened the chapter with, *Brazil,* and the error committed by the infallible machinery of government. Or visit pretty much any department of motor vehicles office and time how long it takes before you hear every single one of George Carlin's "Seven Words You Can Never Say on Television" uttered by people trying to get something done. I could send you to Mercer Island in the state of Washington to get a permit to cut a tree out of your backyard. As ridiculous as that might sound, I am not making that one up. You need a permit to cut down a tree, even if a windstorm has already tipped it onto the roof of your home. Or how about a lawn-watering permit in Melbourne, which, despite the extraneous vowels, is in Australia, not France.

Actually, many of our frustrations with bureaucracies have less to do with their flaws and more to do with their ideals of strict adherence to rule-based actions. This is good, but the actual flaws of bureaucratic institutions are far more worrisome. In fact, the bulk of the academic literature on bureaucracies reflects a fundamental acceptance of the Frankensteinian image that most people in the general public hold. Bureaucracies are con-sidered to be unresponsive behemoths that not only frighten the average villager but also cannot be effectively controlled by the mad scientists who were elected to create them. Worse yet, once a bureaucracy has been set loose on the world, chasing it around with

---

*I take it for granted that you have all seen *This Is Spinal Tap.*

THE REAL REASON
I WROTE THIS CHAPTER

When this book actually comes out, I expect to get a lot of flack from my editor for including "inappropriate" and "irrelevant" references to my own stories and my own research in every chapter. So I decided to fix that by writing a chapter on bureaucracy so that I'd have plenty of totally appropriate and relevant stuff to reference. You see, I've actually done some research on the way foreign aid bureaucracies are influenced by the news media, so I could totally talk about that, and I might, later, if I feel like it. But right now, it's all about zombies.

"Zombies from Mars" is a most excellent satirical skewering of bureaucracy and all those aggravating little rules that attempt to politically correctivize everyone. Surprise, I don't like political correctness—bet you would never have guessed that. Anyway, stuck on a spaceship full of zombies, Gus, our hero, is bureaucratically thwarted at every turn. His desperate call for help is shunted over to an official in charge of personnel undisharmonization, who must chastise Gus for infringing on the empowerment of his crewmates by calling them "brain-eating zombies," and it goes downhill from there. In addition to poking fun at the bureaucratic instinct to throw a meeting or a form at everything, "Zombies from Mars" highlights the fact that bureaucracies simply are not designed to deal with anything out of the ordinary. Every action taken by the bureaucracy is in one way or another an attempt to force a zombie attack to fit into one of the categories of things that the bureaucracy has procedures for managing. There is actually, honestly, a relevant point here. Bureaucracies handle the routine stuff, and as I point out in this chapter, they actually do this quite well, but they are hopeless for things outside the bounds of their rules, regulations, and processes.

Douglas A. Van Belle, "Zombies from Mars," *Andromeda Spaceways Inflight Magazine,* no. 40 (2009).

torches and pitchforks does absolutely no good whatsoever. Academic research explicitly describes bureaucracies in terms of controlling them, taming them, overseeing them, influencing them, or capturing them—themes straight out of a monster movie—and it is safe to say that the struggle to cage bureaucracies has been the predominant theme in the researchers' studies.

In fact, the presumed impotence of political efforts to control bureaucracies drives an ongoing debate over the fundamental compatibility of bureaucratic and democratic government. Yet we must have bureaucracy. So many of the functions we demand of modern governments are routine, administrative tasks that repeatedly apply simple rules to regulate, distribute, gather, record, or otherwise interact with the mundane aspects of daily life that it would be impossible to manage them without the noble efforts of professional bureaucrats. Now can I have that permit to cut the stupid tree? I want to build a bridge out of it.[*]

---

[*] This is an obscure and oblique *Monty Python* reference. All real university students will have watched enough *Monty Python* to know exactly to what I am referring. For the rest of you, shame on you for having a life away from the telly, and it is the witch-trial scene from *The Holy Grail.*

Ideally, bureaucracies should be able to adapt to or respond to changes in or challenges from the world around them, but that flexibility conflicts with the ideal of a strict adherence to rule-based decision making.

SO, WHAT IS A BUREAUCRACY?

The word **bureaucracy** is derived from the French word for desk, which explains all the extraneous vowels in the middle. Its adoption as a political term reflects the idea that it is the position within the administrative political structure—the desk, not the person behind it—that defines the role or function to be performed. In other words, the role is separate from the person performing it. Once the role is defined, the person with the qualifications to fit that role can be hired or trained. If that person is fired, quits, runs off to Cuba with a mistress,[*] or retires, another with the necessary qualifications can replace the first with little or no disruption. This makes it possible to create professional administrative institutions that remain relatively consistent in their governmental functions and activities regardless of the turnover in personnel. Rules, procedures, and processes define the actions of these officials, and it is this *adherence* to the rules that both makes the desired consistency possible and creates the comedy of the mindless functionary who is unable to deal with anything that does not fit within the bounds of the rules he or she is supposed to follow.

After the Egyptians invented beer, but well before the Italians dreamed up pizza, the Chinese had some serious bureaucracies running a big chunk of the government in their very serious empire. The modern and Western take on bureaucracies arose when the medieval kingdoms and principalities of Europe grew beyond the effective scope of a personalized system of governing. As the demands for governance exceeded what a king and his personal advisers could manage, kingdoms began institutionalizing the more mundane functions and processes, such as accounting and record keeping. The scope of government's role in society, and, as a result, the scope of bureaucratic functions, has been growing ever since. Today's bureaucracies are huge, and they do all kinds of things. They regulate, license, procure, distribute, observe, preserve, encourage, police, study, and manage. In the United States, the Postal Service (USPS) delivers the mail, the Internal Revenue Service (IRS) gathers taxes, the National Science Foundation (NSF) funds research, the Citizenship and Immigration Services (USCIS) polices the borders, the Library of Congress preserves knowledge, and the Centers for Disease Control and Prevention (CDC) watches and protects us from the next killer plague, or, in the case of swine flu, helpfully tells us that we have it. The simple truth is that the vast majority of the "stuff"[†] that governments do is done by bureaucracies. Furthermore, this is true regardless of the form government takes—democracy, theocracy, monarchy, or whatever.

---

[*] If the person were a woman, would she run off with a misteress?

[†] I am not allowed to use the proper word to refer to anything that you might find in a steaming pile in your front yard.

Do We Really Want Bureaucracies?

No, of course not—dealing with a bureaucracy is seldom pleasant and usually infuriating—but bureaucracies are also indispensable. Think of the role that bureaucracy plays for government as analogous to the role of a thermostat in controlling the furnace in a house.* The thermostat performs a simple task, turning on the furnace when the temperature drops below a certain point and turning it off when the temperature exceeds a certain level. You might not think that's such a big deal, but realize that without a thermostat, you would have to perform that function yourself. When it got cold, you would have to get up out of your Couch Commando Barcalounger and flip the switch to turn the heater on. Then, sometime before the temperature rose to the point at which the paint blisters off the wall, you would have to put down the potato chips and get up again to turn it off. It seems simple, but then so is changing the channel on the TV, and how many of you crawl off the couch to do that when you can't find the remote control? Think of a cold winter night, one of those nights when the temperature plummets all of the way down to where even Canadians say, "It's cold." The furnace might come on for ten minutes once every half hour or so. Imagine trying to get a good night's sleep when you have to get up, turn on the furnace, get up ten minutes later to turn it off, then get up twenty minutes after that to turn it on again. Presumably—and I realize this may be a stretch—you have something better to do with your time and attention than turn the furnace on and off.

In the same way that the thermostat performs a simple task that frees you to do more important things, bureaucracies take on functions that would waste the time and effort of elected leaders or even barbarian kings. Every major U.S. city except Houston uses zoning laws and building codes to instill some coherence to urban growth, and even a small city issues hundreds of building permits a week.† As with the vast bulk of cases processed through the average bureaucracy, it is a fairly simple procedure for someone to make sure that all of the rules have been followed and to issue a building permit. But if not for the bureaucracy in charge of building permits, these tasks would have to be performed by other officials. Is this really what you want the mayor to be doing? If the mayor is reviewing hundreds of building permit applications a week, when is she going to find the time to schedule street cleaning, hire the new janitor for city hall, choose the flowers to be planted around the fountain at the park, issue dog licenses, inspect schools for fire safety, paint over the graffiti on the buses, or do any of the thousands of other things we ask a city government to do for us? We elect a mayor to make the big decisions for the city, not to implement or oversee every little detail in day-to-day management. That is what bureaucracies do. When you stop to ponder it, it quickly becomes clear that bureaucracies do pretty much everything that actually gets done by government.

---

*This one definitely is an analogy. I asked my brother and he's a poet.

†If you ever visit the Poconos, please bear in mind that it only appears that the region has no zoning laws and no building codes, and no tape measures. There are actually some zoning laws on the books. It's just that no one has ever taken up the task of enforcing them.

The Ideals of Bureaucratic Governance

There are few instances of fiction dedicated to the ideal bureaucracy, although one might argue that the bureaucracy in the movie *Logan's Run* functions with ideal perfection in its zeal to eliminate the world of those who are thirty years of age or older. The bureaucratic apparatus at work in *Nineteen Eighty-Four* is equally chilling in meeting its mission. Still, there are few if any instances in fiction in which bureaucracy is portrayed in a positive light. However, there have been academics who have approached the study of bureaucracies from an idealistic perspective that focuses on the effectiveness of administrative institutions. To his credit, the German sociologist Max Weber[*] (1864–1920) recognized that modern nation-states need professional bureaucracies. Furthermore, he argued that the ideal bureaucracy is both efficient and rational. It should function like a machine, with each of its parts playing a well-defined role. These parts should mesh perfectly with the roles and actions of the other parts to perform the administrative functions of modern society. Weber argued that a few elements are critical for achieving this ideal:[3]

Clear assignment of roles: To fit together and function in unison, each of the parts in the bureaucratic machine must know what it is supposed to do and how it fits within the larger organization. What are the responsibilities of a division or an individual? What are the expected outputs, and where should the bureaucrat look for input? When should something be handed to someone else, and what should be handed to that person? When is it someone else's problem? The whole idea of clear organization is to avoid overlap and duplication of effort, as well as gaps or failures in the process. Gaps and overlaps are wasteful and inefficient.

Rules, rules, rules, and more rules: For both efficiency and fairness, decisions and choices made by bureaucrats need to be impersonal and consistent. This is accomplished through careful adherence to rule-based decision making. To avoid favoring or discriminating against anyone, always follow the rules. To make certain you get the same output with every case—the output that the other parts expect—always follow the rules. If a situation cannot be resolved within the rules and roles defined for an individual bureaucrat or a division within the bureaucracy, see the next point.

Hierarchy: Bureaucracies are strictly hierarchical, with a clear chain of command from the king all the way down to the lowest peasant. Each person should have only one immediate supervisor and each supervisor should have only a limited number of subordinates. The result is a pyramid with the trolls slaving away at the direction of assistant troll managers, senior troll managers directing the assistant troll managers, super-important managers commanding the managers of troll managers, and so on. This is important not only for effective control of the bureaucracy but also for handling challenges to the

---

[*]Pronounced "Vayburr" not "Webber," and, no, he did not invent the barbecue.

rule-based decision making. In this idealistic version, deviant cases get passed up the food chain until they reach the level at which someone has the rule or authority necessary for resolving the issue.

Professionals: Finally, and most important, the selection of persons to fill roles within the bureaucracy, whether through promotion or recruitment, must be done on the basis of merit. For the engine of government to work at peak efficiency, the right parts—or people—need to be in their optimum positions. Someone without the necessary training or ability, who was hired or promoted on the basis of friendship, political or familial relationships, or the stunning good looks that will surely lead a soon-to-be disgraced senior troll manager directly into a sexual harassment lawsuit, will not be able to perform the functions expected of the role. Because of the integration and interconnections within bureaucracies, those without proper training and ability will cause difficulties for others as well. The call for professional merit-based bureaucracies was specifically meant to put an end to the spoils system, during which a new administration would fire everyone in the previous government and replace them with political supporters. And think about the harm that could be done by incompetent and unqualified bureaucrats. Would you want to climb into a rocket if the leading managers of NASA were not the best scientists but instead the best campaign fund-raisers?

If you do not think strict adherence to rules is an ideal, think about what it is like to be on the wrong end of bending the rules. Consider the small-town sheriff who doesn't like the way you look and decides to fix it with his nightstick. He can twist the rules of official behavior as much as he likes, because he knows that his brother the judge will ignore the rules and dismiss your complaints about missing teeth. Ponder the stereotypical B-movie plot in which the corrupt cop throws you in jail so the local drug lord can force your girlfriend/boyfriend/love-monkey to carry a shipment across the border. Reflect awhile on the bribed official who orders the demolition of your fire station to make way for a big developer, which somehow forces you to race a sentient VW Bug named Herbie against an evil race-car driver. The ideal of rule-based decision making is to protect the less powerful and the less influential from those with power and influence. The ideal is to make sure that everyone is treated exactly the same.

Policymaking versus Administration

However, even Weber's view of bureaucracy made many people a little nervous, particularly in democracies. As these organizations grew in size and number, so did the concern that bureaucracies might start to assume roles meant for the elected portions of the government. In other words, there was increased concern that bureaucracies would move from implementing laws to actually making the laws themselves. This possibility was particularly disturbing given that these organizations were not designed to be responsive to the people.

FRANK J. GOODNOW

Team: **Brooklyn Take Out**

Position: **Sweeper**

Status: **In Thirty Minutes or Less**

You probably didn't expect to see **Frank J. Goodnow** (1859–1939) highlighted as a theorist. This is mostly because you are students in an intro course, and if you knew enough to know who should be highlighted as a theorist of bureaucracy, then you wouldn't need to take an intro course and then you wouldn't be reading this book. However, Goodnow is also kind of a dark-horse candidate when it comes to the theorists I might have chosen. Your instructor probably expected Max Weber, but I decided to feature him in a different chapter, and unless your beloved teacher's primary field of interest is public administration, Goodnow probably isn't a familiar name.

Goodnow was a lawyer who studied administrative law. At the end of the nineteenth century and the beginning of the twentieth, he wrote book after book about public administrative law and administrative practice, covering topics ranging from city government to how to rule China. He was also the first president of the American Political Science Association and, as such, was something of a founding father for the modern study of politics. Conceptually, it is fair to say that the legalistic and procedural emphasis in the modern study of public administration comes from his work. I suspect he also invented the pen chained to a desk thing, but the CIA is hiding the evidence, for obvious reasons.

Of further concern in the late nineteenth century was the use of the bureaucracy for patronage purposes—that is, giving jobs as political favors.

In response to these concerns, Woodrow Wilson wrote an essay in which he declared that there should be a strict dichotomy between politics and administration.[4] Frank Goodnow picked up this theme and argued that there should be a clear and impenetrable distinction between the political branches making the laws and the bureaucracy implementing them.[5] However, the reality is that completely severing politics and administration would be a disaster for the whole concept of democracy. Nevertheless, Weber, Wilson, and Goodnow all viewed the often-infuriating inflexibility of bureaucracy as better than the alternative.

Bureaucratic Roles

Some of the more prominent things that bureaucratic agencies provide are services. In the list of bureaucratic functions above, I left out the big one. If you are at a public college, the whole enterprise is a vast bureaucracy, and therefore the education that you are receiving is a service that your state is providing. Even if you are not at a public university, you may eat the daily offering of the extruded meat-like product courtesy of the cafeteria. That, too, is an administrative service, and it often tastes like bureaucracy. Governments manage hospitals, carry out welfare programs, run public schools, operate parks, and so on. These are all service functions.

Administrative agencies also regulate. The FBI regulates personal behavior, the Food and Drug Administration regulates how much rat hair can end up in your hot dog,[*] the Securities and Exchange Commission (SEC) often tries to somewhat regulate Wall Street. Bureaucratic agencies watch over particular segments of the economy to make sure that they follow the law. Agencies are also primarily responsible for the implementation of legislation—making sure that the laws that legislatures pass get put into place. So, when the U.S. Congress decides that there should be a new immigration law, the U.S. Citizenship and Immigration Services puts it into place and figures out an exact set of rules for deciding which people getting off the international flight will get the genial wave-through and which will get the deluxe full-body search and the opportunity to discover the reason that large woman is wearing those special-color rubber gloves. When the Congress passes a new prescription drug program, the Department of Health and Human Services supplies all of the details to put it into place.

THERE BE FLAWS IN YONDER BUREAUCRACY, OBVIOUSLY

While it is important to establish that there are bureaucratic ideals, recognition of those ideals should not detract from a discussion of the very real flaws in bureaucratic government. Instead, it should serve as a foundation for understanding how these governmental behemoths actually function in the real world. Without understanding that inflexibility in the application of rules is an ideal, it is very difficult to come to grips with what is really involved in the problem of adaptation. In adapting, the commitment to consistency and equal treatment matters not just in terms of the variety of people needing services but also in terms of consistency of service across time; after all, it is very important that the person choosing between the house built in 2013 and the one built in 2012 can be confident that both were inspected and approved in the same ways and both meet the same minimum standards of quality. The concern is then all about the problem of balancing that consistency against dealing with and integrating new building materials, new building methods, and new products.

The real issue, however, is more fundamental than fitting the structural qualities of new building materials into existing building codes. Democracy itself is the real concern. Functionally speaking, a democracy is supposed to be a government that has institutionalized a set of procedures and mechanisms to force officeholders to be responsive to the needs, wants, and demands of the public. Once bureaucracies, which are designed to be consistent, not responsive, take on a significant role in government, does that limit or even prevent government responsiveness to the wants and needs of society? Does the growth of bureaucracy also replace democracy with bureaucratic authoritarianism?

---

[*]Seriously, there is an actual rule the FDA enforces regarding the amount of rat hair allowed in processed meat products.

WOODROW WILSON

Team: League of Nations

Position: Long Stop

Status: 6 over Par

In political science courses, **Woodrow Wilson** (1856–1924) is most often discussed in terms of idealism and international politics. He was personally involved in the Treaty of Versailles, which ended World War I, and most political scientists consider him to be the central player in the creation of the League of Nations. The problem with that designation is, however, that the League didn't work. It all failed quite miserably, actually. The Treaty of Versailles turned out to be one of the most catastrophic peace treaties ever imposed on the losers of a war. It saddled Germany with tremendous reparations commitments, which were an economic drain that prevented any real recovery after the war, and in doing so it all but guaranteed the economic collapse of that country. Probably not fair to blame Woody, but if he's going to take credit on his website, it's his own fault if I call him on the blame side as well, and the treaty really was one of the primary causes of World War II. The economic despair that the reparations caused, along with some of the more humiliating terms of the peace treaty, proved fertile ground for the rise of extremism in Germany. Hitler used the excuse of the Versailles "diktat" to seize power, and the downhill tumble into World War II inevitably followed. It can even be argued that Woody's famed League of Nations only made matters worse. Wilson was unable even to get his own country to ratify the treaty, and the absence of the United States turned the League into a weak, almost pointless institution that could do nothing except delay confrontation with Nazi Germany by providing a forum for idealists intent on avoiding war. The League seemed like a good idea and all, but like my investment in that chicken sushi chain, it was one of those good ideas that just didn't take off.

A less celebrated, but perhaps more positive, contribution of Wilson was his work on bureaucracy. "The Study of Administration"[a] laid much of the conceptual foundation for the rapid development of American bureaucratic government that followed shortly thereafter. In many ways, it was an argument against personalized government. Personalized government left too much discretion to individuals in positions of authority and was fertile ground for corruption. Personalized government was also a problem because the scope and complexity of many of the demands made on governments had grown far beyond what individuals could accomplish in an ad hoc fashion. Professionalism, organization, and structure were needed, and Wilson went about creating them. See, you can blame him for income tax and World War II.

[a]Woodrow Wilson, "The Study of Administration," *Political Science Quarterly* 2 (1887): 197–222.

Overhead Democracy and Authority Leakage

The most obvious way to integrate bureaucracies into a democratic system is to create what is called a system of overhead democracy in which elected officials—who are periodically held accountable to the desires of the voting public—are put at the top of the bureaucratic hierarchy or are otherwise entrusted with mechanisms that allow them to effectively control the unelected portions of the government. In this way, the public's influence on the bureaucracy is indirect, by operating through representatives, but it is still clearly democratic. However, from the moment the concept of overhead democracy

was first labeled and proposed as a means of conceptually integrating bureaucracies into the ideals of democratic government, the debate over the ability of leaders to exert control, even if they have the political impetus to make the effort, has cast serious doubts on a top-down model of a democratic bureaucracy. Anthony Downs described the concept of authority leakage as one problem. Given the emphasis Weber* places on hierarchy within bureaucracies, it is clear that if democratic responsiveness is needed it will come from the top down, but, as with everything else in the study of politics, it is never that simple.

Downs's concept of **authority leakage** questions if it is even possible for the pantheon of bureaucratic fairy princesses at the top of the hierarchy to effectively direct the actions of the trolls slaving away at the bottom.[6] Even if you assume good-faith efforts on the part of subordinates, the effort that top officials direct at controlling the output of a bureaucracy gets distorted as each successive layer of the bureaucracy interprets any ambiguities in an order and adjusts the order to fit its abilities to implement. Even if each of these individual alterations is minor, they multiply and accumulate and magnify one another as the order passes down through the levels within the bureaucracy. As a result, even assuming that the trolls are competent and dedicated to carrying out orders from their fairy-princess overlords, it becomes almost impossible for the top of the hierarchy to consistently and effectively direct the outputs at the bottom. Think of the distortion in terms of the kids' party game "Telephone," in which one child whispers a message to the next, who passes it along to the next. By the time the message reaches the last child in the chain it seldom bears any resemblance whatsoever to the original.

Memorandums go a long way toward getting commands from the top to the bottom with a minimum of distortion, but when the assumption that bureaucrats and bureaucracies are making good-faith efforts to serve the public interest is relaxed or abandoned, or when the very serious limits on the abilities or motivations of political leaders to invest the effort needed to oversee bureaucracies are recognized, the possibility that bureaucratic responsiveness and adaptation arise from the control exerted by leaders at the top of the hierarchy appears to be quite limited. This is particularly troubling for modern democracies, for which responsiveness is the most critical of ideals and in which leaders are elected with the expectation, or hope, that they will make government—including the unelected bureaucratic structures—respond to the needs, wants, and demands of the public. However, in applied research, authority leakage has been found to be less of a concern for democratic bureaucracies than the dynamics of representative democracy itself, and the failure of overhead democracy as a means of subjugating bureaucracies to the interests of either the public or the properly elected fairy princesses is most obvious in the concept of the iron triangle.

---

*The proper pronunciation of Weber was discussed earlier. Do try to keep up.

The Iron Triangle

The biggest problem with overhead democracy is that the same electoral dynamics that are expected to encourage the elected leaders to be responsive to the public create an imbalance of interests in the activities of the bureaucracies. This leads to agencies being "captured" by small interest groups, which are often those the bureaucracies are directed to regulate, manage, or otherwise control. The executive and legislature typically have little interest in bureaucratic oversight. The bureaucracies are performing repetitive and mundane governmental functions—nothing flashy that will get on the news. Democratic leaders are more concerned with electoral politics, and the oversight of bureaucracies is a high-cost endeavor with little promise of enhancing politicians' standing or providing salient services to the people who vote. It takes a great deal of effort to gather all the information about what a bureaucracy is doing, how well it is doing it, and alternative ways it could be doing things. In addition, the mechanisms that modern democracies give to their leaders to correct the courses of wayward bureaucracies are generally cumbersome and difficult to engage. As a result, elected leaders tend to have little interest in exerting the effort necessary to monitor and control bureaucracies.

In contrast, the interest groups directly affected by bureaucracies have a great deal of interest in those bureaucracies and in controlling or influencing their outputs. Farmers care a great deal about the Department of Agriculture. The airline industry has a great deal of interest in the Federal Aviation Administration. Given the effect that a bureaucracy can have on the welfare of a group it is supposed to regulate or assist, it is often worthwhile for those most directly affected to make the effort and spend the money to influence the bureaucracy. This creates a situation in which a bureaucracy can be captured and redirected so that it focuses on the needs of an interest group rather than the public interest or even its original mandate. The result is an **iron triangle** formed by the bureaucracy, interest groups, and elected officials, and it is all but impenetrable by outside actors (see Figure 8.1). Lobbying by interest groups encourages elected officials to craft legislation that reflects the preferences of those interest groups. In return, the interest groups then provide resources, such as cash or mobilized voters, to support the reelection efforts of cooperative elected officials. The bureaucratic agency that responds as the interest groups desire then receives rewards from elected officials such as preferences in budgeting. This gives the bureaucracy a motive to listen to the interest groups.

The fact is, however, that bureaucracies do function in democracies and democracies function quite well despite the necessary evil of delegating a substantial amount of executive responsibility to bureaucracies. There are clear and even disturbing examples of agencies, particularly regulatory agencies, being effectively captured by well-financed interest groups. In some cases the influence even extends to the point at which the government agencies actively work against elected officials and the broader public interest. Do these examples necessarily mean that bureaucracies are incompatible with the ideals of democracy?

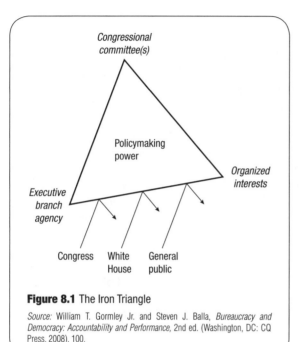

Figure 8.1 The Iron Triangle

Source: William T. Gormley Jr. and Steven J. Balla, *Bureaucracy and Democracy: Accountability and Performance,* 2nd ed. (Washington, DC: CQ Press, 2008), 100.

There are a huge, tremendous, and stupendous number of bureaucracies functioning in any modern government, and the vast majority of these agencies perform their assigned tasks quite effectively in the democratic context. They even adapt to changing needs or demands of society. I may poke fun at—or mercilessly taunt—the bureaucracy that is the U.S. Postal Service, for example, but it actually provides an incredibly difficult service with remarkable efficiency. You can send a letter, postcard, or a well-flattened fish head to a specific location on the opposite side of the continent for far less than the cost of a candy bar.

This creates a conundrum, which is basically just a plain old puzzle, but using a word that's hard to spell makes me sound a lot smarter. Most democratic bureaucracies work quite well and adapt to changing times, at least to some degree, even though they are not really democratic institutions. How can that be?

Exhibit no trepidation; I wouldn't posit the enigma unless I could conjure the appearance of extreme intelligence through its resolution.

Agency Theory and the Responsive Bureaucracy

From its introduction in the 1950s, the iron triangle or capture theory of bureaucracy was the central conceptual theme in the study of bureaucracies. The assumption that bureaucracies were fundamentally flawed to the point of threatening the very existence of democracy was the starting point for every analysis, critique, and call for reform. However, this began to change in the 1980s. Political scientists borrowed—as they often do[*]—from the study of economics and business the concept of **agency theory** and adapted it to the somewhat different context of government. With the results produced by some seriously fancy statistical analyses, scholars became more positive about the potential for bureaucratic responsiveness to the demands and desires of the broader public. New research seemed to show an interactive relationship between

---

[*]It was never returned, but it still wasn't stealing. There was a footnote involved.

bureaucracies and political forces in the democratic context. Bureaucracies appeared to adapt to their political environment, responding to both hierarchical (top-down) and pluralistic (bottom-up) domestic influences by incrementally changing their processes, their areas of focus, and even their levels of activity.

Agency theory, also referred to as the **principal-agent model,** is structured around the basic premise that bureaucracies are agents that act on behalf of the legislature in a relationship similar to a business contract. Bureaucracies are essentially hired by the legislature to perform specified sets of functions. The relationship is clearly hierarchical, with the bureaucracies treating elected officials as agents would treat customers or clients. However, unlike the conceptual foundations of earlier studies, which included an implicit assumption that bureaucracies are controlled or influenced only when their democratically elected masters are actively watching over their every action, the principal-agent model requires little if any direct monitoring by elected officials. The basic dynamic may be conceptualized as a contract made in a context other than the legislative-bureaucratic relationship.

This dynamic can be shown with a simple example. In the same way that a hypothetical suburban dentist with two kids and a blue Land Rover that he always parks right at the very edge of his neighbor's driveway, making it hard for the neighbor to get in and out of that driveway, does not sit and closely watch every action of the perpetually hungover landscaper he has hired to tend his yard, the legislature does not need to constantly supervise every action of a bureaucracy. Instead of the costly effort of constant supervision of the landscaper's activity, the totally fictional dentist, who really shouldn't let his dog bark all night, chooses the low-cost option of keeping an eye open for unsatisfactory results. Should a hedge be poorly trimmed or some flowers die, the dentist, who doesn't bother to scoop when he walks that annoying beast of a dog, can complain to the landscaper. If the problems go uncorrected, the dentist can withhold payment or hire a new landscaper.

Similarly, you can think of elected officials as the dentist. Not because you would expect elected officials to display such casual disregard for the simple acts of neighborly etiquette, but because elected officials are acting like someone who hired a landscaper to look after the yard—the principal—and they are hiring bureaucracies as the landscaper—the agents. If unsatisfactory output from a bureaucracy is brought to the attention of its elected overseers, they can complain or hold hearings, and if the problems go uncorrected they can pull out "the big stick behind the door" and threaten the budget of the bureaucracy, the tenure of upper-level officials, or even the continued existence of the bureaucracy as an entity. The elected officials do not have to watch the bureaucracy every minute, they just have to monitor the results and keep an eye out for something to go wrong. Bureaucracies do not want to get tagged as problems, and they generally try to do the best possible job so that elected officials will never see a need to intervene.

An alert student who has learned far more from this book than anyone really should have expected will notice how this occasional observation and punishment mechanism is

similar to the panopticon. For the rest of you, I'm pointing that bit out now so you don't look unprepared when it comes up. You're welcome.

The research conducted from the theoretical foundation of the principal-agent model has provided more than just the conceptual impetus for breaking away from the idea that constant monitoring was necessary for the control of bureaucracies. It has also led to a substantial foundation of evidence demonstrating the responsiveness of bureaucracies. Despite the fact that very few upper-level bureaucrats are political appointees and the ability of elected officials to monitor and direct the actions of their subordinates is limited, bureaucracies clearly do adjust, incrementally at least, to the will of U.S. presidents, becoming more conservative or liberal in response to the perspective of the president. They also shift their procedures and activities to address issues of particular interest to elected leaders. A trip to the department of motor vehicles may still be worthy of its own separate level in Dante's inferno, but bureaucracies, including notoriously indifferent state agencies, do respond to a wide variety of public and popular influences, including local politics, business groups, patronage institutions, and even large or loud expressions of public opinion. A summary of the most recent work from the agency perspective on bureaucracy might reasonably emphasize just how many different influences have now been shown to spur bureaucratic adaptations and adjustments. Scholars and critics still express concerns about control and responsiveness, but the idea that the uncontrolled growth of bureaucratic government could destroy democracy seems to be far less of a concern today than it was even just a few years ago.[7]

The Cockroach Theory of Bureaucracy

Caddyshack is an awesome movie. In addition to providing the best golfing advice ever, it gives you a hint at how I want you to rethink the whole bureaucracy and democracy thing. The pleasantly deranged and hygienically challenged groundskeeper in *Caddyshack*[8] seizes upon the task of eliminating a pesky gopher. In taking on such a dangerous mission, he knows that to survive he must immerse himself in the mind of the enemy. He must think like the gopher. He must act like the gopher. He must become one with the gopher. While most people would never have realized that gophers are so fond of plastic explosives, and that's a cool thing to know, the point about thinking like the gopher is inspiring.

To understand a bureaucracy, perhaps we need to think like the bureaucracy. One notable consistency in most of the studies and analyses of bureaucracies is that they all seem to come from perspectives outside the bureaucracies themselves. Though the imperatives that drive the bureaucracy are obviously central to the principal-agent model, the predominant questions addressed by principal-agent theory reflect the long-standing concern regarding the ability of the principal—the elected officials—to control or direct the agent—the bureaucracy. How do elected officials control bureaucracies? How do interest groups capture them? How can broader democratic forces influence them? Instead, perhaps we should think like the gopher. What motivates bureaucracies to act? What will motivate them to adapt or change? If agency theory is correct and bureaucracies consciously strive to avoid the

potential punishments that could rain down on them like anvils falling on a coyote, how does that actually work from the bureaucracies' side of things?

Bureaucracies must constantly struggle against other demands for limited funds within the government budget. Bureaucracies and bureaucrats realize that if they fail to provide a public good proportional to the government resources they consume, they face the prospect of being substantially sanctioned. At the extreme, entire bureaucracies could be eliminated by the public officials responsible for budgeting and oversight. A more realistic outcome for bureaucracies that fail to meet their public service mandate and that draw critical attention in the domestic political arena is that they will suffer a degradation of their position in the competition for resources. One of the first threats leveled at a wayward bureaucracy is the dreaded budget cut. Additionally, threats might be directed at the tenure of the bureaucracy's executives. An embattled bureaucracy might have its director or directors replaced, and/or the directors of the bureaucracy might try to fend off such replacement by "cleaning house" and shuffling lower levels of management within the agency. Both of these potential punishments motivate bureaucracies and bureaucrats to adjust to the demands and dynamics of domestic politics.

When considered from the perspective of the bureaucracy, however, the real question is, What happens when the infamous big stick that elected officials could use to beat them senseless stays behind the door?[*] The scramble to respond to threatened budget cuts is obvious, but how often is the full extent of possible sanctions against a bureaucracy even mentioned or considered in political discourse? We know that bureaucracies constantly make incremental changes that are not necessarily tied to any specific threats from elected officials. How do they know what changes to make? How do they monitor their political environment? What cues do they use to shape their choices to avoid even being threatened?

It seems logical to propose that bureaucracies would try to avoid the harsh negative sanctions that could be turned against them by adjusting their actions in accordance with the same cues they expect their potential punishers—elected officials—are using. In modern democracies, the news media provide the most prominent sources of political cues and offer an easy, inexpensive way for elected officials and bureaucrats to monitor the domestic political environment. High levels of coverage of an issue indicate that it is important or will be important, depending on whether you believe the media drive or follow the attention of the democratic political machine. Preemptively matching bureaucratic outputs with the indicators of public demand provided by the news media is an easy way for bureaucracies and bureaucrats to try to get their jobs right and avoid negative attention and critical scrutiny of their operations.

While most bureaucrats have neither six legs nor an exoskeleton, this idea of working to avoid negative attention allows me to compare them to cockroaches—and since I can,

---

[*]This is basically a counterfactual argument (what would happen if something didn't happen). It's the academic equivalent of jumping in front of a speeding bus and shouting "Stop!" and it should be attempted only by an overeducated jackass who has tenure and a flagrant disregard for lots of stuff.

MWAA HAA HAAA

It probably wouldn't surprise even a Kardashian to discover that I was the one who came up with the cockroach theory of bureaucracy. However, what might surprise even a Kardashian is that this is an actual, honest to god, serious theory, with research and everything. On top of that, it is totally relevant to the topic discussed in this part of the chapter. I know, I know, I wrote this whole chapter to give me someplace to reference something of mine that's relevant, but still, what were the odds I'd actually pull it off?

Media, Bureaucracies, and Foreign Aid: A Comparative Analysis of the United States, the United Kingdom, Canada, France, and Japan is a book that explores the cockroach theory of bureaucracy. I had to bring in a couple friends to help me, and most of my contribution was getting the incriminating photos that we used to coerce an editor to publish it, but still, that's the most critical part of any academic research project. The evidence that Jean-Sébastien and David found, that I totally take credit for, shows that aid bureaucracies around the world use the media as a means of keeping their aid responses in step with what they believe is or will be the public demand. There is a rough balance between media coverage and the weight that bureaucrats place on significant indicators of need and strategic importance. Further, when we talked to some aid bureaucrats, who will remain as nameless as they are faceless, they actually said that they kept track of media coverage but never really looked at it. They all thought that their own sources of information were far more reliable, but they wanted to know how much people cared about these places or about responding to specific catastrophes. That's pretty much saying that they were trying to be responsive to the public. Totally democratic.

Douglas A. Van Belle, Jean-Sébastien Rioux, and David M. Potter, *Media, Bureaucracies, and Foreign Aid: A Comparative Analysis of the United States, the United Kingdom, Canada, France, and Japan* (New York: Palgrave/Macmillan, 2004).

I will. Like the beloved patron insect of restaurant kitchens, the bureaucracy that finds itself caught out in the light is the one that is going to be stomped on. Thus, an effective strategy that both bureaucracies and roaches can use to thrive and survive is to avoid attention—to actively avoid the light. The **cockroach theory of bureaucracy** focuses on the glaring spotlight of the media, which are driven by business imperatives to seek out government failures that can be depicted as scandals and sources of political conflict. Thus, bureaucracies serve the public as best as they can and hope to stay hidden and well fed in the darker recesses of an anonymous bureaucratic government.

These failures, however, and the political grief they lead to for bureaucrats and bureaucracies, are also a necessary part of the system. Remember the panopticon? Remember the way that a few police officers can enforce the traffic laws on millions of miles of roads and highways? This is the same basic dynamic applied to bureaucracies: significant, salient, public punishments serve to remind bureaucracies of the consequences of their falling out of step with public demand. That is part of what motivates bureaucracies to self-police and actively adapt.

Tadah!

Conclusionoscopy

While I have not covered everything there is to cover about bureaucracy, I have managed to hit the key political elements, and the political is almost as important as they way I worked my stuff in. Bureaucracies and their internal functional dynamics, their procedural issues, and their role in creating and implementing policy all form a significant part of the public policy subfield of political science. While public policy is often a part of university political science or government departments, it generally focuses on applied issues. As a result, from a public policy perspective the politics and underlying theoretical issues concerning the reconciliation of bureaucratic and democratic ideals are secondary to the hows and what-fors of learning how to manage bureaucracies, or pursuing the efficient delivery of services, or maximizing the functionality of city service providers. The theories applied are more likely to be from University of Chicago business school management types than from philosophical Europeans. Since I am trying to force all that stuff about underlying theoretical dynamics into your head by contrasting the ideal with the real, I will leave the applied aspects of bureaucracy to public policy professors and skiptydoodle on to the courts and the law.

KEY TERMS

agency theory / 214

authority leakage / 212

bureaucracy / 205

cockroach theory of bureaucracy / 218

iron triangle / 213

principal-agent model / 215

CHAPTER SUMMARY

Bureaucracies are important. They do stuff. We want them to follow the rules so that we all know pretty much what they are going to do. Yes, they can be infuriating. Learn to live with it. The alternative is worse. People have fretted about how to enforce democratic control over bureaucracies. Overhead democracy didn't seem to fit with what was happening. Agency theory, in which bureaucracies are treated like subcontractors, seems to explain more. Comparing bureaucracies to cockroaches has three benefits: it is philosophically appealing, it lets me totally justify talking about myself so much, and it explains how bureaucracies monitor their environments and adapt to public demands.

STUDY QUESTIONS AND EXERCISES

1. Consider your personal experience with some bureaucracy—be it at the department of motor vehicles or in the financial-aid office of a public university. Do the characteristics of bureaucracy ring true given your experience?

2. What kinds of governmental functions do bureaucracies commonly serve?

3. Why are there extra vowels in *bureaucracy*?

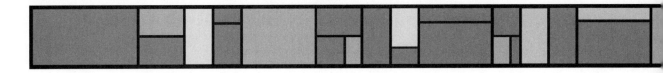

4. Why is strict adherence to rule-based decision making an ideal of bureaucratic government?

5. How does an iron triangle form?

6. Why isn't overhead democracy an effective means of subjecting bureaucracies to democratic control?

WEBSITES TO EXPLORE

www.dbh.govt.nz. This is the site for New Zealand's building codes. Try to find the section on the regulations regarding the installation of central heating, Go on, I dare you.

www.irs.gov. The site for the U.S. Internal Revenue Service (IRS) is all one thing: forms, forms, forms.

www.fema.gov. The site for the U.S. Federal Emergency Management Agency (FEMA) raises one simple question: Who you gonna call?

www.worldbank.org. This is the site for the World Bank, one of the best data-gathering bureaucracies around.

http://republic.cqpress.com/chap9/explore.asp. This site offers a collection of bureaucracy links from an American politics textbook.

Courts and Law

Politics behind the Gavel, Obviously, but What's under the Gown?

Imagine a golden age of idealism. Actually, the age was more greenish-mauve than golden, but it was still an idyllic time of joy and beauty. Video game graphics looked like they came from an electrocuted typewriter, but everyone still thought they were amazing. All the rock stars looked a bit electrocuted, too, with their hair either impossibly big explosions of frizz or sculpted to look like plastic laminated by a lightning bolt, but that was cool, too. It was the magical time when somebody came up with the idea of adding video to music to create video discography. VD turned out to be a poor choice of acronym, however, since no one wanted to admit to staying up late to catch the new VD from Madonna. But when some marketing genius started calling the combination of music and video "music videos," they became so popular that Thomas A. Edison had to invent cable television so everyone could watch them over and over around the clock.

In that idealistic, greenish-mauve age, if a professor stood in front of a class and stated that the law is political, many students in the class would have slapped their hands against their plastic-looking sculpted hair and loudly protested. From under their massive explosions of frizzy hair, other students would have argued that politics is about individuals maximizing their own advantage, about deal making, maneuvering, and scheming to get more. Law cannot possibly be political. Law is about justice, fairness, reason, principles, making a lot of money by suing HMOs, and doing what is right. Today, students are much brighter,* or at least a lot more cynical and critical, and it is difficult to find students who are the least bit surprised when their professors say that the law is political.

---

*This compliment is wholly unnecessary and should be ignored completely because I am actually referring to the reflectivity of your clothing. The always-ready-for-a-funeral look was big back then.

I blame TV.

Seriously. In every single one of *Law and Order*'s[1] forty-seven spin-offs, rip-offs, and competitors, every third episode has a plot about someone with wealth or political power thwarting, warping, or driving the personally motivated application of the law. *The Practice,*[2] *Boston Legal,*[3] and all the other law-firm shows are even worse, with story lines about twisting the law to the point of breaking it in the sometimes pathological pursuit of victory in court.* This was not always the case. In the old days, the law was the law, and television shows featured Joe Friday and Bill Gannon[4] methodically uncovering "just the facts, ma'am," or Perry Mason[5] finding the truth and winning the case at the very last second. Even when *L.A. Law*[6] added a bit of soap opera scandal to the 1980s law drama, the less than ideal parts centered on whom Arnie was sleeping with or fights within the firm. The law itself was always this ideal, abstract, absolute virtue, and it was always about the truth and righteous justice.

In the past couple of decades, not only did television fiction about the law change, but TV also thrust a number of troubling public events into our living rooms that eroded people's idealism about the relationship between law and politics:

- *Rodney King video and trial (1991–1992):* L.A. police officers were caught on videotape savagely beating Rodney King, an African American man, with their nightsticks, but they were acquitted by a jury after the state court trial was moved out of Los Angeles to a suburban venue. The officers were later found guilty of the filmed beating when a federal trial was conducted in an urban location.

- *O. J. Simpson (1995):* Despite a mountain of evidence against him, his dream team of defense lawyers was so successful that O. J. was acquitted of the murder of his ex-wife Nicole Brown Simpson and her friend Ronald Goldman after only a few hours of deliberation by the jury. O. J. was later found responsible for their deaths in civil court and ordered to pay massive damages, but, thanks to the deft use of bankruptcy laws, he paid little or nothing to the families of the victims, and until he suffered a serious bout of the stupids and robbed a guy at gunpoint, he lived an opulent lifestyle in Florida.

- *Robert Bork's Supreme Court confirmation hearings (1987):* Interest groups combined to defeat Ronald Reagan's well-qualified Supreme Court nominee Robert Bork because of his conservative political beliefs, especially concerning the use of the original intent of the Framers as a strict standard of constitutional interpretation.

- *Anita Hill's testimony regarding the Clarence Thomas Supreme Court nomination (1991):* On the Senate floor, George H. W. Bush's Supreme Court nominee

---

*With the end of *Boston Legal,* the world officially entered a legal-drama drought. Don't worry, though, legal dramas will be back. Nobody recycles like Hollywood screenwriters. In fact . . . *Fairly Legal, Franklin & Bash, Suits* . . . I see a storm a'comin'.

Clarence Thomas faced charges of sexual harassment from Anita Hill, who had worked under Thomas at the Equal Employment Opportunities Commission. This incident upset just about everyone—Thomas supporters believed the charges were politically motivated and unjust, while his opponents believed that he would not have been confirmed if the charges had been taken seriously.

- *Investigations of Bill Clinton (1998):* The president, a lawyer, testified under oath that the truth of an earlier statement—that he was not involved in a sexual relationship with Monica Lewinsky—he had given as part of a deposition in the Paula Jones sexual harassment lawsuit against Clinton all depended on what the meaning of the word *is* is. These verbal gymnastics confirmed some people's worst beliefs about the law and lawyers.

- *The 2000 presidential election (2000):* Florida state courts and the U.S. Supreme Court played significant roles in resolving the contested election results from Florida in the 2000 presidential election, and many believe that justices on both benches were eager to act in a highly partisan manner instead of distancing themselves and restricting their involvement to the detached interpretation of the law.

- *Hiring and firing in the justice system (2006):* How about Alberto Gonzales and the politically motivated hiring of Department of Justice lawyers? Or Dick Cheney, Karl Rove, and the firing of nine assistant United States attorneys (AUSAs) in 2006?

Scandals are nothing new, and fictional accounts of the politicization of the law predate the death of the eight-track tape. But the fiction and drama of the past few decades are indeed distinctly different in their intense focus on the political aspects of law as the driving forces behind plots and episodic story arcs. Still, even with the barrage of real and fictional events that have shown the political side of the law, the current willingness of increasing numbers of people to view the law and the courts in the context of politics is somewhat surprising. Even people who should know better have long been reluctant to surrender their ideals about the law. It took a long time for political scientists to study courts and law in the same way that they studied other political institutions. In fact, colleges still frequently offer courses, such as constitutional law, in which lecturers treat law as if it were drafted by the gods and delivered through the oracle at Delphi* rather than tainted by politics. For some strange reason, these idealistic courses remain very popular with those planning to go to law school, and even some of the less venomous and less reptilian creatures inhabiting universities find something naggingly appealing about the idea that the institutions of the law and the courts inhabit some kind of germ-free buffer zone protected from the noxious diseases affecting other political institutions.

---

*This is an ancient Greek thing and has nothing to do with satellite radios or the *Matrix* movies. Well, it might have something to do with the *Matrix* movies, but that is only because they stole the idea of the oracle as a source of ultimate truth. The Greeks did it first.

The current willingness of the public to accept the political nature of law appears even more confusing if you probe deeper. It turns out that most people still cling to the idea that the law is, in fact, different from other political institutions. Something about the law leads people to think about it first and foremost in terms of justice, fairness, and the protection of rights. If you are unconvinced, think of how much more disturbing it is to discover that a judge is corrupt than it is to see a politician claiming that a free weekend at a mobster's *Star Trek*–themed brothel was nothing more than an ordinary "campaign contribution."

LAW AND POLITICS

I am reasonably certain that somewhere earlier in this book I said that politics consists of the individual or combined actions of individuals, governments, and groups with public consequences aimed at accomplishing desired goals. If I take that definition seriously, it is difficult to argue that the law and the courts are anything but political. Whether it is the politics involved in writing laws, appointing judges to the bench, police selectively enforcing laws, prosecutors deciding to bring some types of cases and defendants to trial and not others, sentencing Bernie Madoff to a minimum-discomfort detention facility with cell-decorating contests instead of sending him to a real prison, or limiting the access of some plaintiffs to the courts, the law and the courts are clearly political institutions.

This tension between the real and the ideal, the tug between the political nature of the law and our feelings of ideal justice, emerges clearly in Harper Lee's *To Kill a Mockingbird,*[7] which I've chosen as an example because it's old and a classic, so no one is going to expect me to go updating this section or changing it with every edition. The story is narrated by Scout, who recalls growing up in Maycomb County in southern Alabama during the Great Depression. Her lawyer father, Atticus Finch, in one of the book's main story lines, is defending an African American man, Tom Robinson, who is being tried for rape. It is abundantly clear that Tom is being framed, and it is painfully obvious that even though everyone should be able to see this, he will still be found guilty, but Atticus is still compelled to defend Tom because, "If I didn't, I couldn't hold up my head in town, I couldn't represent this county in the legislature, I couldn't even tell you or Jem not to do something again."[8] Atticus Finch is a true believer. He believes in justice, he believes in the rule of law, and he believes that the system should work. He believes that it must be made to work.

However, despite his unwavering faith in the law, Atticus cannot totally ignore the obvious. The racist and segregationist political system of the day is thoroughly embedded in the courts, which cannot be counted on to provide the impartial justice in which Atticus believes. At trial, Atticus demonstrates that the disabled Tom could not have committed the crime, that his accuser is not trustworthy, and that the raped girl's father, Bob Ewell, is the likely culprit. Atticus appears to be making headway with the jury, and his closing argument is impassioned as it captures Americans' presumptions of justice:

I'm no idealist to believe firmly in the integrity of our courts and in the jury system—that is no ideal to me, it is a living, working reality. Gentlemen, a court is no better than each man of you sitting before me on this jury. A court is only as sound as its jury, and a jury is only as sound as the men who make it up. I am confident that you gentlemen will review without passion the evidence you have heard, come to a decision, and restore this defendant to his family. In the name of God, do your duty.[9]

Atticus does not win. The jury finds Tom Robinson guilty as the politics of the time win out over justice, but it is still a great speech that captures the coexistence of the ideal and the real. Real life and politics are contrasted with the ideal of law throughout the novel. At the end, Tom Robinson dies while trying to escape from prison. When Bob Ewell's attack on the Finch children ends abruptly with the pointy end of a knife stuck in Ewell's chest, Atticus, true to his faith in the law, insists that Ewell's death not be covered up even though he thinks his son, Jem, is to blame. The sheriff, however, claims that the attacker fell on his knife. This is obviously impossible, but the sheriff argues that even though this outcome may be outside the law, it fits the ideal of justice that is supposed to be embodied in the law. In the end, Atticus is convinced to abandon the law and the courts and accept this roundabout route to the justice that those institutions were supposed to have provided. Atticus decides to live with the political and social reality of the day.

To Kill a Mockingbird most clearly demonstrates how the politics of the day can permeate the legal system. While the racism of the 1930s is an extreme example, you should expect that today's politics also permeate the law and the courts. Law and courts are political institutions, and the legal system is but a subsystem of the larger political system. You should thus expect that political parties will make use of the courts to seek policy goals, that individuals will use the legal system to make their political careers, that those with resources will fare better in the legal system than those without resources, and that many of the same rules that apply to other political institutions will also apply to the courts.

Law on the Books versus Law in Action

Atticus's decision to go along with the sheriff's version of events also demonstrates one other important facet of studying the law. There is a fundamental difference—as the legal scholar Roscoe Pound (1870–1964) recognized—between **law in books** and **law in action**.[10] The law in books (or the law on the books) is the laws as they are written, while law in action (or the law in practice) relates to how laws are enforced in the real world. The law in books is the world of appellate courts, while law in action involves the way trial courts and other legal actors implement law in the real world. If he strictly followed the law on the books, the sheriff would have arrested Boo Radley, the man he knew delivered the pointy-ended knife blow that killed Ewell. The law on the books dictates that this must be done, regardless of how that action would affect Boo's life or the lives of the Finch children.

We all are aware of the difference between the law on the books and the law in action from our own interactions with the legal system.

When you drive through the Poconos on Interstate 80, the signs clearly say "Speed Limit 55 MPH." That is the law on the books. However, most people seem to believe that Interstate 80 means you have to drive 80 mph,[*] and anyone who drives at the legal limit is likely to get a sore neck watching people gesture rudely as they speed past. The law on the books says 55 mph, but even if you're not pretending it's the Poconos 500, you're probably driving 60 mph because you know that the law in practice is that no police officer is likely to pull you over until you hit 61 or more on the radar.

The U.S. Constitution requires that criminal defendants be read their *Miranda* rights before they are interrogated, but does that always happen? The law makes no distinctions based on race or wealth, but we all know these things do matter in reality. Even a constitutional right, James Madison once observed, is nothing more than a "parchment barrier."[11] A constitutional right is dependent on the people for protection. The reality is that laws depend on political actors for enforcement, and if we're relying on political actors, we should expect that laws will be political. We should also expect that if we really want to understand the way that the laws operate and if we really want to know how courts act, we must study the law as it is really enforced and how judicial officers actually behave. Thus, political scientists are interested not only in what the laws say but also in how they are put into practice. In other words, political scientists treat legal actors like other political actors.

Symbols

Even this far into the chapter, after I have been arguing the whole way that the law is political, a significant number of students will still have a lingering feeling that the law is somehow different from other institutions. Why? In part, it is because the courts use a variety of symbols and other tools to increase their authority and to encourage people to believe that something different is going on. Courtrooms are packed with symbols of authority: the judge's robes, the gavel, the raised platform, the Bible, the flags, the ornate seal that declares the jurisdiction, whether Hoboken or the State of West Virginia. The Supreme Court building in Washington, D.C., is quite literally a marble palace to house the law of the nation.

These symbols are more than mere ornamentation; the political actors in the judicial arena utilize symbols because people react to them. These symbols help create and sustain the perception that judges are different from politicians. People's beliefs that the courts are different, facilitated by the use of symbols, allow political participants in the law and the courts to operate with a legitimacy and a solemnity that is not found in other political

---

[*]Though this is incorrect, this belief seems to explain a great deal. It explains the way people drive in Daytona, Florida, which is on Interstate 95, and it also explains why Los Angeles has such traffic problems as Interstate 5 and Interstate 10 intersect in the middle of the city.

arenas. However, if we strip away these symbols, it becomes clearer that the law really is like other political institutions. Imagine a court case being held in a hotel meeting room with an ordinary person in charge. Envisage the Supreme Court justices in ratty jeans and sitting on folding chairs. Ponder what it might be like to have lawyers actually speak normal English.[*] When we strip away the symbols, courts do not seem quite so majestic.[†]

Words are symbols—perhaps the most powerful of symbols—and even the words used in the courts, the language of the law, reinforce the idea, belief, impression, conjecture, notion, postulation, and presupposition that something different is occurring in the courtroom. Of course this special language also allows lawyers to preserve their role as the translator for the courts, a role that serves them well both professionally and financially.[‡]

THE FUNCTIONS OF COURTS

Courts obviously play an important role in nations—clearly, every country has them—but what exactly do courts do that makes them so essential? In one sense, courts enforce the norms of society. Regardless of the type of government that exists or the amount of freedom citizens possess, it is nevertheless true that the courts are going to enforce the country's basic rules. If the nation is a dictatorship, the courts' treatment of protesters will send a message to those who may question the authority of the regime. In *To Kill a Mockingbird,* although everyone knows that Tom Robinson is innocent, the court's ruling sends a chilling message to Maycomb's African American population, and it reinforces the racial power relationships of Maycomb society. When an Islamic religious court in Nigeria sentenced a woman to death by stoning for the crime of conceiving a child outside of marriage in 2002, that court was also enforcing the norms of that nation.[§]

The courts also play more functional roles. According to judicial scholars Walter F. Murphy, C. Herman Pritchett, Lee Epstein, and Jack Knight,[12] courts play three principal roles in society. First, courts engage in **dispute resolution.** They peacefully settle disputes and keep order in society. Second, like other political institutions, courts make policy. Courts are involved not only in applying the law but also in shaping the law. Third, courts play an important role in monitoring governmental action, making sure that government entities act within their responsibilities and meting out punishments to government officials who run afoul of the law.

---

[*]Contemplate how many synonyms there are for thinking about things.

[†]The robes are one symbol we probably don't want to strip away. This is partly because we really don't want to know what Clarence Thomas is wearing underneath, but it is also because the robes are indicative of how much more symbol-laden the courts are in comparison to most other branches of government. Parliaments—other than the New Zealand Parliament, which is housed in something that looks like the internal workings of an electric razor—may have fancy buildings, but few have dress codes. Legislators can usually wear any old $2,000 Italian suits they have lying around.

[‡]Insert your own lawyer joke here. Do be kind and try your best to be witty, as someone in your classroom is likely to be studying for the LSATs and will sue you if it is not funny.

[§]A higher appeals court eventually overturned the penalty, but not before significant international pressure was brought to bear, and it is unclear if this result would have happened in the absence of outside intervention.

Dispute Resolution

Court cases are so much a part of the landscape that it is easy to take them for granted. But what would happen to a society if it had no courts? It might have the justice of the Wild West, vigilante justice, or just plain chaos. *To Kill a Mockingbird* shows what can happen when people try to take the law into their own hands as Atticus confronts an angry mob that is determined to lynch Tom Robinson. Perhaps the most important role of the courts is that of dispute resolution. Courts settle disputes peaceably through formal proceedings. The state brings charges against those accused of crimes. One company sues another for failing to meet the terms of a contract. Someone brings a malpractice suit charging a doctor with incompetence. By performing this function, the courts provide an avenue for citizens to settle their disputes in an orderly, organized, and authoritatively controlled fashion.

You are probably most familiar with the formal ways in which courts settle disputes, but courts often settle disputes in informal ways as well. For example, in sentencing those convicted of crimes, judges also help to set what might be called the "**going rate**" for punishment. In other words, judges set the context for plea bargaining, in which defense attorneys and prosecutors negotiate the appropriate penalties for plaintiffs who plead guilty to agreed-upon offenses. This is also true for civil lawsuits. Courts and juries are involved in deciding whether or not individuals and companies are liable for wrongdoing. Past decisions by the courts set the context for future relations between plaintiffs (those doing the suing) and defendants (those being sued). The litigants (those involved in a lawsuit) may choose to bargain in the hopes of reaching an out-of-court settlement instead of incurring the risks and costs involved in a jury trial. Once courts reach decisions, those decisions shape the advice given to potential future litigants. In other words, individuals, corporations, interest groups, and other parties decide whether or not to initiate lawsuits based on past court decisions and even alter their behavior because of the outcomes of previous cases.

Policymaking

Perhaps courts act the most like other political institutions when they make policy. Officially, courts are not supposed to engage in making policy—they are only supposed to resolve the disputes that others have over policy. Officially, the justices of the U.S. Supreme Court, for example, are supposed to use the official U.S. Constitution to find the appropriate resolutions to high-stakes disputes between policymaking branches of government, such as the official Congress and the official U.S. president. However, whether the official issue is the death penalty, abortion, sexual harassment, or any of the hundreds of other topics in which courts become involved, it is clear that in hearing those cases and making those decisions, the courts make policy.

In the most obvious way, judges set local criminal policy through sentencing decisions, bail decisions, their willingness to accept plea bargains, and their propensity to issue

warrants based on one type of evidence or another. Consider the mainstay of modern detective drama, the use of DNA for identification of suspects. In addition to the fact that it actually takes a fair bit of time to create a DNA profile, all of the rules about how DNA evidence can be used and what it means in a criminal court—in other words, the policy regarding the legal aspects of using DNA—have been set by judges who have listened to the testimony of experts and made decisions that stand as the precedents others will follow in the future.

Policymaking also occurs when courts are involved in **statutory interpretation.** That is, even if one were to accept the proposition that courts merely apply the law, by defining how those laws can and cannot be interpreted, courts set policy. Legislatures often pass laws that are vaguely written and thus open to a wide range of interpretations. Courts are then confronted with the question of whether these laws are meant to apply to specific situations and/or specific litigants. The application of laws requires specificity, so courts must interpret what particular statutes mean precisely—that is, they engage in statutory interpretation, and as soon as the courts start interpreting laws, they are, in effect, making policy.

Even well-written laws can be open to this kind of judicial policymaking. Because a nondiscrimination law meant to ensure that African Americans have the right to live in any neighborhood in a city says all persons must be treated equally, that law can be interpreted to mean that homosexuals must be allowed to march in the city's St. Patrick's Day Parade. A law intended to keep T-shirts with obscene slogans out of public school classrooms can be interpreted as giving school boards the power to require uniforms, or forbid lipstick, or ban unnatural hair colors such as red* as part of setting a minimum standard of dress and appearance. Going the other way on the school dress code issue, courts could rule that it is an infringement on freedom of speech for a school to allow some shirts but not others. That same court could turn around and rule that it is not an abridgment of the right of free speech when a local government restricts the posting of signs in a town. It is clear that the courts make policy through interpretation, and the courts' understanding of a law will stay in place unless the legislature chooses to pass a specific law that changes that interpretation.

Even if a legislative body passes a specific and clearly worded law, the courts can still become involved in policy through their interpretation of that law. Consider the question of the education curriculum in the U.S. public school classroom. In the United States, every state gets to set its own policy regarding what should be taught in its classrooms, and many states leave a great many of the details of school curricula to individual school districts. The lines of responsibility for this aspect of educational policy are clearly defined,

---

*Yes, this actually happened. The school official in question meant punk-rock totally red red as opposed to auburn and the other not-red colors that humans call *red* when referring to hair, and that official was actually quite clear about the distinction, but the ban on red hair still caused quite a stir and a bunch of shouting about racism against the Irish and that kind of hullaballoo.

and nowhere in any of the laws, bylaws, debates, or other documentation is any policy role reserved for the courts, yet through their decisions, the courts still set education policy.

Since 1925, when the so-called Scopes Monkey Trial brought the question of teaching evolution in the schools to the attention of everyone in the United States, the fight over the claim that your neighbor evolved from pond scum has been a contentious issue despite the obviousness of the family resemblance. Courts have become involved in this policy matter because of the constitutional requirement of a separation between church and state. Because public schools are government institutions, they are constitutionally prohibited from advocating religious doctrine or belief. Thus, they are not allowed to include the Hebrew/Christian biblical account of creation as part of their biology curriculum no matter how much a local community or local school board may wish to do so. As recently as December 2005, courts were still ruling on this policy issue, with a federal judge offering a sweeping and sharply worded decision against the school board in Dover, Pennsylvania, which had required statements regarding intelligent design in the biology curriculum. After an extensive trial this judge declared—and set the policy—that the argument that life is so complex that it had to have an intelligence behind its design was a representation of the biblical account of creation and, therefore, could not be part of the public school curriculum.

Conservatives generally find this kind of judicial policymaking to be anathema[*] to democracy and un-American and all that, but trust anyone over the age of thirty, you'd much rather listen to them bitch, whine, and scream over evolution than listen to them go on and on about abortion. With abortion they actually have something of a point about democracy and all that because U.S. abortion policy is almost entirely a result of court decisions. Also, environmental policy grew mostly out of court actions. So you could argue they've been on the wrong end of that judicial policymaking stick often enough to have reason to dislike it. However, if you give them that, then you have to decide if their court challenges to the Affordable Care Act ("Obamacare") and their evisceration of campaign finance regulations through suing in the courts to endow personhood on corporations are ironic or hypocritical. And if you go back further, the courts actually used to be the favorite tool of conservatives, who used them to block Roosevelt's New Deal legislation. It wasn't until the civil rights movement really got going that liberals started winning more than losing in the U.S. courts.

So, basically, if you really try, you can annoy anyone by talking about courts and policymaking.

Monitoring Government

The courts' setting of policy by preventing school boards from forcing intelligent design into the classroom reflects the final functional role of the courts, that of monitoring government.

---

[*]Cool word. Double points if you can sing the National Anathema.

This is essentially the check on the executive and legislative branches that the U.S. system gives the courts. The courts have the task of monitoring the actions of the government and governmental officials to make sure they follow prescribed rules and procedures, including the ones that check the behavior of the others. To fulfill this role, the courts generally have at their disposal the important tool of **injunctive power.** Courts have the power to stop the actions of government by issuing injunctions. Temporary or interim injunctions put policies or activities on hold until they can be examined at trial, and if in the course of such legal proceedings judges find that the governmental actions clearly violate established principles, they may decide to enjoin, or halt, the actions permanently.

Courts also monitor government action through prosecutions of corrupt or otherwise criminal government officials. By trying government officials according to the same rules and procedures as those used in trying everyday citizens, the courts send out the message that nobody is above the law. This monitoring function can have profound effects on the legitimacy of the government. Trials involving corrupt officials can become political spectacles, and the formality of the courtroom can reduce the possibility of violence that might occur if people did not believe that government officials were being held accountable to the laws of the land. In the United States, even President Bill Clinton was required to testify in court while he was a sitting president.

In some nations, the courts exercise a power called **judicial review,** which enables them to examine laws and government acts to determine whether those laws and acts are in violation of the nation's constitution or in some other way illegal under the structure of the country. Judicial review operates to allow courts to monitor governmental action directly. Both the Scopes Monkey Trial and the Dover intelligent design trial were instances of judicial review. In federal systems, which have multiple levels of government, such as the state and national governments in the United States, the courts also settle disputes between different levels of government. Questions often arise as to whether the national or local government has the proper authority to enact specific laws or to take specific actions or whether federal or local law should preside. For example, in *To Kill a Mockingbird,* the court in which Tom Robinson is tried is clearly a state court. As the nation moved away from the New Deal era and into the civil rights era, the federal courts began to assert their power over state courts to play a greater role in protecting the rights of African Americans. Had the novel been set in a later period, Atticus might have opted to try to have Tom released by a federal court.

Courts also determine whether government officials are acting within their prescribed authority. For example, members of Congress have gone to court to try to stop the president from acting in a manner that they believed exceeded his constitutional authority—for instance, exercising war powers without any official declaration of war or spending government money on something other than what it was budgeted for. On the state and local levels, too, courts are often called upon to determine whether officials, council members,

or mayors are acting within their spheres of power. This also frequently occurs with regulatory bureaucracies. Industries and businesses may use the courts to challenge particular agencies' authority to regulate them.

Judicial review is also at work when the courts strike down laws because they violate the constitutional rights of groups or individuals. Courts are frequently called upon to judge whether laws violate religious, political, and other human rights. When a court says that the nation may not prohibit the burning of the flag because such a ban violates freedom of speech, when a judge holds that Congress may not restrict access to Internet content, or when a court rules that the police have not properly read a defendant her rights, the court is, in fact, monitoring government action. In the United States, the courts receive a lot of respect for protecting citizens' rights. However, even this aspect of the courts is subject to the distinction between the law on the books and the law in action. Simply because a court declares that someone or some group is entitled to a right, that does not automatically change everything. In 1954, the U.S. Supreme Court declared, in *Brown v. Board of Education of Topeka,*[13] that the rule of "separate but equal" had no place when it came to education. Thus, segregated schools were no longer constitutionally permissible. Yet, ten years after the Court's momentous ruling, the schools in the Deep South were still largely segregated. It took the civil rights movement and congressional and presidential action to really begin the process of desegregation, and even today schools in many areas of the United States are still racially segregated because of the geographic distribution of populations and the ways officials have drawn school attendance boundaries.

TRIAL AND APPELLATE COURTS

Watching one of the marginally heroic lawyers rip up witnesses and give dazzling opening and closing arguments on the television show *Law and Order* or one of its kin can be something of a guilty pleasure for people who like to fight to win when they argue. Of course, the courts in *Law and Order* and pretty much all of the courts in the other police and lawyer shows are trial courts. Trial courts are the courts that exercise what is called **original jurisdiction,** which means that they are the first courts to hear a case (see Figure 9.1). They are like the tellers at the bank, at least at banks that still have human tellers. Like the customer-tolerant, "technically" pleasant people whom you go to first when you want your bank to do something for you, the trial courts are the first line of action and where the vast majority of judicial activity occurs. Criminals are tried, lawsuits are fought, and injunctions and search warrants are issued in trial courts. Trial courts are responsible for keeping records of their proceedings and for establishing the facts in the cases heard in the courts. The "finder of fact" in the trial court is either the judge or the jury, which means that it is up to the judge or the jury to weigh the veracity of the witnesses, assess the facts presented, and determine a winner.

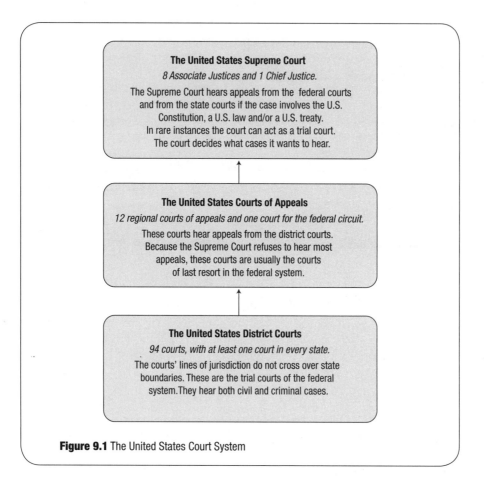

The United States Supreme Court

8 Associate Justices and 1 Chief Justice.

The Supreme Court hears appeals from the federal courts and from the state courts if the case involves the U.S. Constitution, a U.S. law and/or a U.S. treaty. In rare instances the court can act as a trial court. The court decides what cases it wants to hear.

The United States Courts of Appeals

12 regional courts of appeals and one court for the federal circuit.

These courts hear appeals from the district courts. Because the Supreme Court refuses to hear most appeals, these courts are usually the courts of last resort in the federal system.

The United States District Courts

94 courts, with at least one court in every state.

The courts' lines of jurisdiction do not cross over state boundaries. These are the trial courts of the federal system. They hear both civil and criminal cases.

Figure 9.1 The United States Court System

Appellate courts are like the bank manager in our bank analogy. You go to the manager if you do not get the service you requested from the teller or if you think the teller is not doing his or her job correctly. Appellate courts exercise **appellate jurisdiction,** which means that they review the records from trial courts. However, appellate judges cannot simply say they disagree with the factual conclusions in the cases they review. Rather, they are limited to decisions on matters of law and process only. Virtually every time a lawyer stands up in court and says, "I object," the lawyer is raising a point of law on which the trial judge must rule. Trial judges also rule on numerous pretrial motions concerning the admissibility of evidence. They provide instructions to the jury about what constitutes a crime

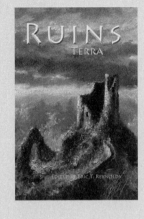

and on what the correct standards of evidence are. In addition, constitutional provisions regulate how the police conduct interrogations and searches and seizures. Appellate courts can rule on all of these procedural matters, but they cannot rule on or revisit the facts in the cases they review. Some countries provide for appeals of appellate court rulings, too. In the United States this occurs at the level of the Supreme Court.

LEGAL SYSTEMS

When appellate courts review the actions of lower courts, or when the judicial system reviews the constitutionality of laws that have been passed, those actions are not performed in a vacuum.* All judicial functions that take place in a given country or jurisdiction are shaped by the legal system of that country or jurisdiction. In other words, the law is not just the law, it is a social construction built upon a basic conceptualization of how the law is created and how it functions. In the modern world, three kinds of legal systems are most commonly used. The first of these is the civil law or code law system. This is the most widely used type of legal system in the world. The second major type is the common law system, which is used primarily in Great Britain and in countries that were either former colonies or members of the British Commonwealth. The last major type of legal system is religious; this kind of system is currently most commonly found in Islamic nations.

_____

*This is fortunate, as most scientists agree that a Supreme Court justice would survive for less than a minute in a vacuum. Ba-dum tshish. Thank you, folks, you've been great! Seriously.

The Civil Law System

The civil law system begins with the proposition that law is a codified, constructed entity that a legislature or some other lawmaking political body has constructed. Consequently, the process of compiling and writing down the law is a major component of the civil law system. The history of civil law really begins in the sixth century, when the Byzantine emperor Justinian codified what had been the law of Rome, hence the civil law system is sometimes referred to as the Roman law system. Justinian's work was completed in 534 A.D. and resulted in the Justinian Code, or the *Corpus Juris Civilis*. The second great codification came with the Emperor Napoleon. The Napoleonic Code was written by legal scholars and was made up of 2,281 codes built on many different sources of law. As Napoleon began his conquests, the Napoleonic Code accompanied his Grande Armée. The last major codification occurred with the German codification of 1900. Civil law is predominant in continental Europe, former French colonies, Quebec, and even in the U.S. state of Louisiana. Because the civil law system relies on written law, it tends to be more specific than common law, more readily understandable, and easier to apply to particular cases. However, the judge still has the ability to interpret the law.

Civil law systems utilize an **inquisitorial system,** which entails a rather prolonged pretrial investigative process. The goal of this process is to try to protect the innocent. Unlike the American system, in which prosecutors and the police play major roles in marshaling evidence against a suspect, in civil law systems all the courtroom participants participate in the investigation process. Information is also freely shared among all of the actors.

Common Law

The common law system began in 1066, when William the Conqueror began his rule as king of England. He set up a new legal system comprising the King's Court and judges who traveled the countryside to enforce the king's law and dispense justice among the various tribes that populated medieval England. Unlike under a civil law system, the judges had no written law to put to use. Instead, they based their decisions on custom and precedent (past judicial decisions). This explains why the doctrine of *stare decisis*—Latin for "let the decision stand"—is such an important part of common law systems, and why judges are reluctant to contradict earlier court rulings. The law that developed was, in essence, judge-made law. As time passed, English judges became more devoted to the body of law they had created than to the king's will. Furthermore, other types of law, such as equity and statutory law, supplemented the judges' common law. Nevertheless, the common law system is characterized by the strong role of the judge in cases and the importance of precedent.

One of the main components of the common law system is the adversarial process. Unlike the civil law system, which is marked by cooperation among the participants, in a common law system the legal actors battle it out. The judge is not an active participant in the dispute, but instead is more like a referee at a boxing match. Meanwhile, both the

HAMMURABI

Team: Babylonia Gardeners

Position: Third Man

Status: Immortalized, but still quite dead.

Hammurabi (long, long ago) lived from the late nineteenth century B.C. to roughly the middle of the eighteenth century B.C., and he may have been the first person who was so cool that he only needed one name. He is also the Babylonian king credited as the first to establish a code of laws. It's pretty clear that Hammurabi didn't create most of the laws in his famous codex. Instead, his codex is clarifying and organizing a very large body of existent law and tradition, but that is, in and of itself, a remarkable milestone in the history of law and society.

By organizing and publishing a code of laws, Hammurabi created a system in which all men could know exactly what was required of them and all men knew the punishment they would face if they failed to meet those standards of behavior or social responsibility. Babylon was the first real metropolis, and this organizational step was probably a necessary part of the city's development. As the city's population grew into the tens of thousands, the king could not take the time to personally deal with every petty criminal and every grievance, but the law still needed to be the King's Law. With the codex, judgment of crimes and other transgressions became a matter of interpreting facts or events in terms of the prescriptions of the written law. That made it possible for the king to delegate a great deal of judicial authority to others. It also laid out a standard for judges to be held accountable for their professional performance and prescribed severe punishment for judicial corruption or other misbehavior.

Thus, written law allowed delegation of adjudication of the law and that was the first step in creating a separate judicial branch of the government. This codification of law became essential to all kingdoms as they grew beyond the bounds of what an individual king could personally adjudicate.

---

prosecutor and the defense attorney do their best to try to win. Most students are very familiar with this adversarial process from the movies and television shows that feature dramatic questioning of witnesses, nail-biting cross-examinations, and dazzling closing arguments. It is important, however, to realize that what you see on TV is *fiction.* Very few real-life lawyers have the theatrical skills demonstrated on *Law and Order* or *The Practice.* Interesting cases are the rare exception rather than the norm, and even the best of lawyers consider themselves lucky if they ever get a case that might in some way set precedent on an issue. In fact, even the in-court maneuvering and all that hot trial action you see on TV are rarities in real courtrooms. Other than dealing with their own speeding tickets and divorces, the vast majority of lawyers never see the inside of a courtroom. Most lawyers spend their entire careers making a few hundred dollars at a time performing services such as drawing up contracts for house purchases. And even the criminal lawyers who do specialize in courtroom litigation spend most of their time researching facts, documenting testimony, and preparing for cases.[*]

---

[*]By admitting all of this I risk being served with an official cease-and-desist order from the Global Association of Political Science Departments. Prelaw students make up a significant proportion of the political science majors around the world, and it seems that the association doesn't want me saying anything that might discourage the next generation of lawyers from starting out as political science majors.

While I draw distinctions between the common law and civil law systems, it should be apparent that this division is simplistic. In fact, the United States uses a mix of common law and civil law, as Congress and state legislatures pass laws that are codified and the courts still have room for interpretation and precedent.

Religious Law

The third major type of legal system, religious law, is very different from the first two types discussed. While religious law is present in many countries, it is most common in Islamic countries, where it is based on **sharia,** or Islamic law. Unlike law in civil and common law systems, sharia in religious law systems is comprehensive, in that it governs every aspect of religious and secular life. Sharia is based primarily on rules laid out in the Koran as well as other legal sources, and the understanding and development of sharia, or *fiqh,* has been the work of religious jurists. Customarily, it is the *qadi*'s responsibility to resolve disputes by finding the law. The *qadi* may be helped by a mufti, an expert in Islamic law able to issue legal opinions called fatwas. This can sometimes lead to conflict, as different muftis can potentially offer contradictory fatwas.[14]

Many Muslims with intense religious convictions believe that it is obligatory to follow sharia even if this system of law is not acknowledged by the state. While some nations' justice systems are based entirely on sharia, such as those of Iran and Saudi Arabia,[*] in most countries where sharia is important it is mixed with either civil law (as in Egypt, Kuwait, Morocco, and Syria) or common law (as in Bahrain, Pakistan, Qatar, Singapore, and Sudan). In many, but not all, of the nations that utilize mixed religious and civil law systems, sharia is the basis for the underlying civil law. In Saudi Arabia, the monarch's ability to make law is limited because he may not make any law that contradicts sharia. Interestingly, the Canadian province of Ontario considered allowing Muslims to utilize sharia to settle family disputes if all of the parties agreed. This led to a good deal of controversy, as many Canadians were concerned, among other things, about how women are treated under sharia. Ultimately, the move was rejected.[15]

JURISPRUDENCE

While legal systems define how the law is created and how it functions, a more basic question concerns the underlying moral and philosophical basis for the law. The answer to this question depends largely on jurisprudence. Simply put, **jurisprudence** is a philosophy of law, and as one might imagine, there is a wide array of types of jurisprudence out there. There is a Marxist school, a critical legal theory school, a feminist school, and many more. In fact, within the feminist school, there is a Marxist school, a liberal school, a difference school, and so on. However, according to judicial scholar Harry Stumpf, three main schools of jurisprudence have vied for dominance in the United States—**natural law,**

---

[*]Sharia is very different, however, in these two countries.

HUGO GROTIUS

Team: Orange Crush

Position: Mid Wicket

Status: Escaped

Hugo Grotius (1583–1645) was kind of like the action hero of theorists. He survived shipwrecks, escaped from a prison, and is very popular in Berkeley. He is one of the more prominently cited authors in many arguments about natural law, and much of his writing engages the ideals of natural law and how it applies to the realities of the world. Natural law is generally considered in terms of laws that are innate to either the nature of the world or the nature of humankind and are thus universally applicable. This is the source of ideas such as human rights, and it is the legal foundation of the U.S. Declaration of Independence, which holds certain truths to be self-evident. The idea of natural law is also seen in much of the U.S. Constitution and rugby. Or maybe rugby is natural selection.

Self-evident laws of human nature, society, and morality also provide an interesting foundation for arguments for an international law. Since there is no overarching global authority to legislate or enforce international laws, much of what we use for international law must then be natural law, or laws that become self-evident extensions of the condition of humankind. It is through this adaptation or application of natural law that Grotius became one of the first scholars of international law. His argument that all nations have the right to sail the high seas, a subject near and dear to the hearts of the Dutch trading empire that employed him, eventually became accepted as the principle of freedom of the seas. His argument that nations have the right to control coastal waters up to the distance they can effectively defend those waters with cannons eventually created a distinction between territorial and international waters. This was first embodied in the principle of a three-mile limit, which was later extended to twelve miles, and is now embodied in exclusive economic zones.

Prelaw majors should familiarize themselves with all four ways his name might be spelled.

positivist jurisprudence, and **sociological-realist jurisprudence.**[16] I focus on these, but realize that these are not the only options, nor are these basic ideas expressed in the same ways in different cultures and legal traditions around the world. For example, a Chinese articulation of the concept of a natural law of humankind is likely to focus on society first and obligations rather than on the individual and his or her rights.

Natural Law

Thomas Jefferson's statement in the Declaration of Independence that "men . . . are endowed by their Creator with certain inalienable rights" captures the essence of the natural law tradition. Natural law presumes that there is some higher law that originates with God or nature, and that this higher law is discoverable through the use of reason. It presumes that there is a certain justice that everyone should simply know. For example, murder is wrong, you should not take other people's stuff, and you must urge your friends to buy this textbook and all the other stuff I've been pimping in it even if they are not taking this course.

Some people will immediately recognize that the concept of natural law plays a part in their belief systems, while others may not think it does. If you don't think you share these beliefs, think back to *To Kill a Mockingbird*. Was it wrong for Tom Robinson to be tried in the manner he was? Why? Was it unjust? Why was it unjust? If the laws of the state do not allow African Americans to sit on juries, why is that wrong? As it turns out, some of those who do not subscribe to the natural law tradition can answer these questions without resorting to explanations that invoke the idea of an underlying law applicable to all humanity, but for most people, the answers come down to the belief that there are just some things that are fundamentally right—that is, they believe in some notion of a higher law. As evidenced in Jefferson's words, the natural law tradition has always played an important role in the United States. Americans' fundamental belief in rights is rooted in a natural law sense of justice. In fact, Supreme Court justice Felix Frankfurter once wrote that the test the Supreme Court should use when determining if a state's action violated the principle of due process in a criminal case should be whether the action "shocks the conscience."[17]

While it is true that the natural law tradition has played and continues to play an important role in the United States, it is equally true that from an empirical perspective, natural law raises a lot of concerns. People do act rationally, but often people—and my very generous definition of people includes inebriated college students—can be found doing some very irrational things. Furthermore, what seems rational at one time may seem perfectly ridiculous at another. At one time Prohibition, the outlawing of alcohol, was considered to be such a good idea that it was written into the U.S. Constitution. Now, most people scoff at the idea.* Two seemingly rational people-like creatures can reach very different conclusions on a host of things. People in different cultures reach various conclusions on the basic question of the difference between right and wrong. And then there is the whole problem of proving it. How do you prove that something is a part of natural law? Take something as personal as your control over your own fertility. Now that is a totally safe topic for discussion in the current political climate in the United States, isn't it?

So, if you don't know why my editor scrambled to find her bottle of maximum-strength antianxiety medication when she realized I'd brought this up, then you'd better see a doctor about that coma you're in or find a new place to live that's not under a rock. I do have to admit that no matter how appropriate it is to the topic of natural rights, I'm a little leery of bringing up the recent screamfest on birth control. Not because I really care about upsetting people—it's more a matter of it being really hard to find something funny about it. The satirical "Republicans, Get in My Vagina!" Funny or Die video, with Kate Beckinsale, Judy Greer, and Andrea Savage, is pretty funny. And if my editor weren't popping antianxiety pills

---

*However, they might not be so quick to dismiss Prohibition if they saw some of those irrational things that college students do after consuming significant quantities of alcohol. I call particular attention to the practice of painting one's backside with school colors and running naked across football fields at halftime, in the snow.

like Pez already, dropping the V word *and* mentioning something that only liberals would find funny would have certainly got her going. More to the point, the whole Birth Control Brouhaha of 2012 can be reduced to a question of natural law and used as an example of just how far natural law is from an ideal form and how problematic natural law arguments can be. For religious conservatives, the issue at hand is the application of natural law to the unborn. Often quoting Planned Parenthood on how contraceptives such as IUDs and birth control pills function, they apply natural law to the fertilized embryo and label the prevention of uterine implantation of that embryo as a form of killing. For social liberals, the issue at hand is the application of natural law to women. They point to the right of a woman to control her own body, particularly in terms of fertility and reproduction.

You're probably going to object, fairly strenuously, to one of these two positions. Few people are indifferent on this topic. However, recognize that as a matter of natural law, they are both reasonably valid stances to take in the United States.

Just to be a jackass, I'm going to end this section by pointing out that since the U.S. Supreme Court has decided that corporations are people, that means that forcing a company into bankruptcy is murder.

Positivist Jurisprudence

The positivist school of jurisprudence begins with John Austin (1790–1859), who believed that the law had to be demystified. According to Austin, law is simply the command of the recognized sovereign authority of the state. In other words, though law is not void of morality, it is not the same as morality, and neither is it part of social and historical forces. Rather, those in the positivist tradition believe that law can be studied as a body of principles that originated with the state but then took on its own logic and rationality. Thus, law can be studied using formal logic. Under this theory of law, the job of the judge is to apply the law of the state to the particular facts of a case by using logic. In other words, judges merely discover the law as it has been documented by the legislature or through precedent. Consequently, it is very important for judges to be well versed in the case law and in applicable precedents so that they can reach the logically correct decisions.

What is interesting is that the seemingly strange combination of the natural law tradition and the positivist tradition took hold quickly in the United States. The influence of this odd blend can be seen in the popularity of Blackstone's *Commentaries,*[18] a legal text that covers all of the common laws of Great Britain, which early Americans studied to learn the law. This text had a profound and lasting influence on the American colonists and many of those who framed the Constitution. The view of the law and the role of the judge contained in Blackstone's work continued to shape the way that courts viewed their job as discoverers of the law. You can still hear the echoes of Blackstone today as politicians pledge to appoint only those judges who will apply the law, as opposed to judges who want to take away the legislature's responsibility to make the law. Atticus Finch's appeal to law in *To Kill*

a Mockingbird is firmly rooted within this combination of the natural law and positivist traditions. Atticus believes that there are principles of right and wrong that should be followed, and that there is only one right decision that can be reached in the case. Further, the key to reaching the right answer is strict adherence to the procedures and processes of the courts.

Realist Jurisprudence

Legal realism actually begins with a sociological critique of the law. According to that critique, the law is made up of a set of rules intended to meet the needs of society. Rejecting the natural law and positivist traditions, those in the sociological school argue that the law entails a lot of discretion on the part of the judge, and that discretion is best exercised with an understanding of the needs of society that could be met with the help of the social sciences.

In the early and middle twentieth century, legal realists went beyond this sociological critique to argue for legal reform. They also were distinguished from their sociological forerunners by their readiness to view the law in terms of the behavior of legal actors rather than as a body of legal rules. Some legal realists even argue that precedents are myths, that judges make their own decisions and only afterward justify them through legal precedent. In studying the law, then, legal realists focus heavily on the behavior of police, judges, juries, prosecutors, and other attorneys rather than on the content of law. For legal realists, the key to understanding the judicial system is to understand the tremendous amount of discretion that is available to legal actors. Police exercise discretion and can turn people's lives upside down by their decisions about whether to arrest or not. Judges exercise tremendous discretion in making rulings from the bench and sentencing. Prosecutors exercise enormous discretion in deciding what charges to seek against defendants, what plea bargains to accept, and what sentencing recommendations they will make.

The discipline of political science has always had a special relationship with the law. Political science departments traditionally offer classes, in subject areas such as constitutional law or civil liberties, that approach the study of law, at least partially, from a natural law/positivist perspective. However, political scientists have increasingly moved closer to the realist school, and, thus, since the middle of the twentieth century have started to treat the legal system as part of the larger overall political system. This has meant that there has been an increased focus on judicial behavior; on the relationships among judge, prosecutor, and defense attorney in criminal cases; and on the relationships among political actors inside and outside the legal system. Someone who adheres to the realist perspective would not be at all surprised by the result reached in *To Kill a Mockingbird*. For the realist, the focus would not be on the formal aspects of doctrine that guarantee people a right to a jury trial or on some abstract notion of due process. Instead, the realist would look at who is actually making the decisions in the case. Who is the judge? Who is on the jury? Who is the prosecutor? What are their motives and what kinds of logics are they likely to use in making their choices? These are the questions that legal realists believe are crucial.

TYPES OF LAW

One of the more daunting aspects of studying the law can be coping with the many distinctions that are made among types of law. I review some of the major distinctions below, but you should bear in mind that there are many others. I could have easily discussed contract law, tort law, family law, commercial law, patent law, intellectual property law, or Murphy's law.

Private Law versus Public Law

One of the most common distinctions made in the law is between private law and public law. On its face, the distinction is not all that complicated. **Private law** is concerned with the relations among private individuals and private organizations. In other words, government is not involved except in setting the rules and context of interaction. Thus, private law encompasses most contracts. Assume that the company Spacely Sprockets promised to purchase two hundred widgets from the Cogswell Cogs company for $2,000. Cogswell Cogs provides the widgets, but Spacely Sprockets does not pay. In other words, Spacely Sprockets and Cogswell Cogs had a contract that Spacely Sprockets apparently breached. This is an example of a relationship between private companies with which private law is concerned. Other examples of private law are marriages and divorces, wills and estates, landlord-tenant relations, malpractice, and other suits brought by individuals or private companies and directed toward individuals or private companies.

In contrast, **public law** concerns relationships involving the government and individuals or organizations. Criminal law very clearly is public law, as the government polices private behavior. Laws that enable bureaucratic agencies to regulate industries are also a form of public law, as are constitutional laws, taxing policies, and environmental regulations. The distinction between private and public law, while recognized in both the common law and civil law systems, is most important for nations utilizing the latter, which sometimes maintain separate courts to deal with public law.

When one thinks it through, it may seem that the distinction between private law and public law is problematic. If the basis for the distinction is the involvement of the government, how can any law that involves the courts be purely private? After all, the courts are part of the government. This distinction became particularly salient in the Supreme Court case of *Shelley v. Kraemer* (1948).[19] At issue in this case was whether someone could challenge a racially restrictive covenant, that is, a signed agreement by people in a neighborhood that they would not sell their houses to members of certain minority groups. The problem was that since this case involved relations among private individuals, it was a matter of private law. A constitutional challenge—a matter of public law—to a matter of private law seemed to be inappropriate. However, the Court ruled that the racially restrictive covenant was unenforceable. Since the courts were a part of government, they could

not enforce constitutionally prohibited discrimination. The *Shelley* case demonstrates how artificial the distinction between private and public law can be.

Furthermore, it is equally clear that private law can have very public consequences. Theoretically, malpractice suits are matters of private law. Yet they become matters of public consequence if, as some people argue, jury awards in malpractice cases contribute to the rising cost of health care. At one time, if someone was injured at work, it was considered a private matter; the injured party had the option of suing the employer if the injury occurred because of the employer's negligence. Eventually, this seemed like a draconian and inefficient way to look after those who could no longer work because of workplace injuries, so the government created a comprehensive system of worker's compensation, thus transforming a matter of private law into a matter of public law.

Criminal Law versus Civil Law

Criminal law is that body of law that defines specific crimes and details the punishments for offenses. Criminal cases are matters of public law in that they directly involve the government. The parties in a criminal dispute are always the level of government at which the crime has been defined and the defendant. Thus, cases may be listed as *United States v. Patrick Star* or *Commonwealth of Virginia v. Carrot Top.* While the victims of crimes have recently been recognized as having an interest in criminal cases, that interest is usually recognized by allowing victims to testify at the sentencing phase of a trial. Victims are not parties to the suits in which defendants are found guilty or not guilty. Consequently, the government may proceed with a criminal case with or without the victim's consent, though doing so without consent may prove difficult if the victim refuses to cooperate.

Serious offenses such as murder, rape, kidnapping, starring in a reality TV show, and arson are felonies, which usually carry a punishment of at least one year in prison. Less serious crimes, including traffic violations, public drunkenness, and simple assault and battery, are misdemeanors, which are usually punishable by less than one year in prison and a very serious frown from a judge. In a criminal case in the United States, the defendant is considered innocent until proven guilty, and to achieve a conviction, the prosecution must prove that the defendant is guilty beyond a reasonable doubt. In a criminal case, the judge or jury finds the defendant to be guilty or not guilty. Many in the media like to report that a defendant has been found "innocent," but courts do not actually do that.[*] Whether or not a defendant is truly innocent is between that person and his or her creator; no matter how many times someone is found not guilty, that does not prove he or she is innocent. As for courts, they only determine whether someone can be found legally guilty of a crime. You may be guilty as sin, but if the government can't prove it, you'll go free.

---

[*]The courts in some countries use the term *unproven* rather than *not guilty.*

Sometimes it seems as if there is someone out there getting paid to come up with terms designed to confuse people.[†] Take, for example, the term *civil law*. This does not refer to the civil law system, but instead refers to a particular body of laws. **Civil law,** in this context, is the law that governs relations between private parties. Sometimes, however, the government can be a party in a civil suit. For example, the government may sue on behalf of someone who has claimed a violation of his or her civil rights, it may be a party to a contract dispute, or it may bring a civil action against a corporation for violations of agency rules. More typically, however, civil law deals with relations among private individuals and groups. Someone who charges a physician with malpractice, sues the seller of a damaged automobile, or takes a relative to court for failure to repay a loan is bringing a civil suit. Think of civil law in terms of the kinds of cases you see on *Judge Judy, The People's Court,* or *Judge Joe Brown*. In a civil suit, the plaintiff will prevail if he or she can demonstrate that the defendant is liable by a preponderance of the evidence—an easier hurdle than the "beyond a reasonable doubt" required in a criminal case. Thus, O. J. Simpson was found not guilty of murder in the criminal case against him, but he was found liable for the deaths in a civil case.

Federal Law versus State Law

In the United States an important distinction exists between federal law, which is the law of the national government, and state law, which is the law of the states and their localities. In fact, there is a dual system of courts, with both the federal court system and a state court system in every state. Federal law comprises the law in the Constitution, treaties made under the Constitution, and congressional statutes passed under the authority of the Constitution. All other law is a matter of state law. Thus, states are responsible for the vast amount of law that regulates people's health, safety, and morality. Consequently, most law in the United States is state law, and the vast majority of legal cases are adjudicated in state courts. This includes the overwhelming amount of criminal law. Contrary to what many people think, it is also true that one cannot bring just any case to the U.S. Supreme Court. Like any other federal court, the Supreme Court can hear only cases that involve some aspect of federal law or a federal question.

However, it is true that a case may begin as a state court case and find its way to the Supreme Court. This usually occurs in one of two ways. First, while a case may be primarily concerned with state law, it may raise federal questions. Although a criminal prosecution is a matter of state law, several federal constitutional provisions may be relevant in a criminal case, such as the guarantee of due process or the bar against requiring a defendant to testify at his or her own trial. The second way that a case may wind up in the Supreme Court is if the matter has raised an issue of federal law from the beginning. State

---

[†]Technically, these people are called professors.

courts have concurrent jurisdiction over most federal law. However, remember the rule that the case must raise a matter of federal law to be heard by the Supreme Court. So if you do something stupid, like kick a hole in some guy's wall because he drank the last cold beer and didn't reload the fridge, and the guy says he is going to sue you all the way to the Supreme Court, you can reply with pride that his statement is inaccurate, because damage to property is a matter of state, not federal, law. I just hope you can get all the words out before he rearranges your face.

This discussion of the state/federal distinction has focused on American law, but in any country with a federal system, there will always be this distinction. For example, in Canada there is provincial law and national law. Even in countries with unitary systems there can still be municipal ordinances that are passed by local governments. However, these would be subject to the approval of the national government.

International Law

International law does not exist. I know, there are textbooks on international law and classes on it and all that, but there really is not an international law in the same sense that there is law within a country. International law, as you will find it in the textbooks, concerns conventions and agreements that govern behavior between nations, such as laws of the sea, but in reality, international law exists only to the point that there is a country or a coalition of countries with the power and the will to enforce a rule or norm of behavior. This is one of the fundamental principles of international politics, and it is the reason that there is no effective world government with the power to create and enforce a law globally.[*]

CONSTITUTIONAL REVIEW

Earlier I noted that one of the functions of courts is to monitor government action. One of the ways that courts do this is through the exercise of judicial review. Interestingly, the concept of judicial review originated with the United States, although the U.S. Constitution says nothing about the subject. In the very interesting case of *Marbury v. Madison* (1803), which will cause brain damage if you look at all that Latin too closely, Chief Justice John Marshall, writing for a majority of the Court, made the argument that since any law that is contrary to the Constitution is void, and since judges take an oath to obey the Constitution, they can hold that a law violating the Constitution is void. Today, it seems as if most Americans take the Supreme Court's power of judicial review for granted, although there is considerable debate about the conclusions reached by the justices. While there are many arguments surrounding the Court's use of judicial review, the principal one concerns what materials the justices should use when interpreting the Constitution.

---

[*]This could be connected to the concept of sovereignty, which can be roughly defined as the final political or social authority. If you had a true international law, including the enforcement mechanisms to make countries obey it, then leaders of countries would, in effect, be giving up that ultimate authority to the international courts. Few if any leaders are willing to do this.

Some legal scholars, judges, and political commentators argue for the idea of original intent—that the Constitution means only what its Framers and the authors of its amendments meant when they authored its provisions. To give meaning to the Constitution, the proponents of the concept of original intent would argue that the justices should be principally concerned with the text of the Constitution, the debates surrounding its drafting, and its authors' contemporaneous writings. The benefit of this proposition is that establishing a fixed meaning can provide certainty to the law, and the meaning of the Constitution would not be dependent on which justices are serving at any particular time. Those who argue for original intent quite obviously do so from a natural law/positivist perspective.

Those who oppose this position argue that it is not easy to determine the meaning of obscure phrases in the Constitution such as "due process" and "privileges and immunities," and that it is not always the case that all of the Framers agreed on one set meaning. More fundamentally, those who oppose limiting judicial review to original intent maintain that it is more appropriate to view the Constitution as a living document, a constitution of ideas that must be interpreted to reflect modern values and conditions. They argue that the Framers could never have dreamed of modern technology, the expansion of the nation and the government, or the fact that African Americans would somehow magically find the missing two-fifths of their personhood. Consequently, proponents of a living constitution would, for example, define "cruel and unusual punishment" from a twenty-first-century perspective rather than from an eighteenth-century view. It is clear that those who favor original intent would not condone the Court's reading the right to privacy or the right to obtain an abortion into the Constitution. Those who favor a living constitution do so from the perspective of the legal realist school of jurisprudence.

Regardless of the controversy that surrounds particular issues with regard to judicial review, it is clear that constitutional review serves important purposes for the nation. As stated earlier, judicial review can ensure that the government works properly and according to the rules prescribed in the Constitution. The Court ensures that government officials do not usurp the responsibilities of others and that the state and federal governments work properly within their spheres. Judicial review also allows for the protection of minority rights within a democracy. Constitutional provisions call for equal protections under the law for all, allow for the free exercise of religion, protect everyone's right to free speech, and guarantee that those accused of crimes receive due process. However, because the Court can spark great controversy when it declares laws and governmental actions to be unconstitutional, it is possible to miss the most important function of all. That occurs when the Court upholds law. By subjecting the nation's laws to constitutional scrutiny and upholding them, the Court confers legitimacy on the government's actions. Think of the Court's actions in the 2000 presidential election. Regardless of one's opinion about how the case was decided, it is nonetheless true that all parties accepted the Court's opinion.

Other countries have recognized the value of constitutional courts. Austrian, Irish, Japanese, and Indian courts exercise the power of judicial review. Even countries that use the civil law system have found the benefit of constitutional courts. Germany, Italy, Belgium, Portugal, and Spain, for example, all have constitutional courts, although these courts function differently than the U.S. Supreme Court. These civil law constitutional courts do not hear entire cases. Instead, if a lower court finds that a case raises a constitutional question, that question is sent to the constitutional court for review. The constitutional court then issues an opinion on the narrow issue, and the original court uses that opinion in deciding the case.

While many countries have adopted constitutional courts, the British have chosen not to have one. This decision does make sense because in England there is legislative supremacy. That is, the Parliament is viewed as representing the supreme will of the people, and for this to be true, there can be no higher authority on the law than the Parliament. However, Great Britain has been forced to accept a form of judicial review by its membership in the European Union. All EU member nations are under the jurisdiction of the European Court of Justice, which has the authority to review the laws of those nations to make sure they comport with the laws of the European Community.

At this point, the fact that governments derive benefit from judicial review should come as no real surprise. As I stated at the beginning of this chapter, we should view law and the courts in the context of the larger political system.

KEY TERMS

appellate jurisdiction / 233	law in books / 225
civil law / 244	natural law / 237
criminal law / 243	original jurisdiction / 232
dispute resolution / 227	positivist jurisprudence / 238
going rate / 228	private law / 242
injunctive power / 231	public law / 242
inquisitorial system / 235	sharia / 237
judicial review / 231	sociological-realist jurisprudence / 238
jurisprudence / 237	statutory interpretation / 229
law in action / 225	

CHAPTER SUMMARY

Despite recent events that have shown otherwise, there is still something about courts and the law that makes us feel as if they are separate from politics. Part of this feeling derives from the symbols and language that courts employ, the fact that people expect justice from the legal system, and the important functions that courts perform. However, the law and courts are political in that they fit in with the definition of politics used in this book. The

political aspects of the law become clearer when one ponders the difference between law in books and law in action. The political nature of law and the courts becomes further apparent when you realize that people have varying theories about the law and that different nations use different types of legal systems. When you learn about the many different types of law that exist and how these types of law apply in the real world, some of the mystery that surrounds the courts and the law is stripped away. Students should learn two important lessons from this chapter. First, a nation's legal institutions, like its other political institutions, perform important functions for its society. Second, there have been an amazing number of television shows dealing with the law, and it looks like we're in for another wave of them. Obviously, there are riches in store for the person who can come up with any original idea in this popular genre.

STUDY QUESTIONS AND EXERCISES

1. Almost every day it seems there is a news story that demonstrates the difference between "law on the books" and "law in action." Can you think of recent examples from the news that demonstrate this distinction?

2. Identify and explain the three major functions of courts.

3. How do trial courts differ from appellate courts?

4. What are the key elements of a common law system? A civil law system?

5. Of the types of jurisprudence identified in this chapter, with which do you most agree? Why?

6. What are the major types of law? Can you think of examples of each?

WEBSITES TO EXPLORE

http://jurist.law.pitt.edu/index.php. This site features jurist, law, and legal news from the University of Pittsburgh's School of Law.

http://curia.europa.eu/jcms/jcms/j_6. The site for the European Court of Justice contains information, case law, and news about the Court.

www.ncsconline.org. The National Center for State Courts offers a resource for research, publications, and educational material about the courts in the U.S. states.

www.stus.com. Stu's Views is a compilation of cartoons about the law and lawyers.

www.uscourts.gov. The Administrative Office of the U.S. Courts provides all types of information about U.S. federal courts.

www.venice.coe.int/site/dynamics/N_court_links_ef.asp?L=E. This site, maintained by the Council of Europe's Venice Commission, provides links to sites for the world's constitutional courts and equivalent bodies.

www.worldlii.org. The World Legal Information Institute presents an international directory of legal resources.

Not Quite Right, but Still Good
The Democratic Ideal in Modern Politics

Chances are, no matter who you are, the 2008 U.S. presidential election and its aftermath left you with a somewhat jaundiced view of democracy—the extreme partisanship and vicious electoral tactics, both of which have grown increasingly irrational since the early 1980s; the extremes of disrespect shown to the winners; the constant attacks to try to poison the waters for the incumbents for the next election cycle; the refusal to compromise in a system built upon an ideal of institutionalizing the need to compromise. However, in reality, you should be laughing so hard it hurts. In 1999 Al Franken wrote *Why Not Me?,*[1] a fictional account of his candidacy, victory, and eventual disgrace in the 2000 U.S. presidential election. In the book he runs on the platform that ATM fees are too high. He funds his campaign with the proceeds from a phone sex line. He smacks other candidates in the face with boards. All that, combined with some timely idiocy and stupidity, ultimately propels Franken to the presidency, after which he is promptly impeached for all the illegal things he did during the campaign. Franken is a comedian, a veteran of *Saturday Night Live,* and now, believe it or not, the junior senator from North Dakota or Minnesota, or one of those other really cold states in the middle of the United States. If you lean toward the red-state end of the political spectrum, you probably don't see anything at all funny about Al Franken as a senator. After all, he also wrote *Rush Limbaugh Is a Big Fat Idiot*[2] and *Lies and the Lying Liars Who Tell Them: A Fair and Balanced Look at the Right,*[3] and he admits to being a fuzzy-headed liberal. He even flaunts his liberalness in public. Still, regardless of whether you consider liberalism to be a lifestyle choice or a mental illness, you have to admit, Al Franken in the Senate is a nearly perfect example for a discussion of the issues inherent in applying the democratic ideal to an imperfect world.

Even if Al Franken had not won the Wisconsin Senate election in 2008, *Why Not Me?* would still have served as the perfect example to kick off this chapter—after all, I used it for the first edition,

which I wrote before he even ran for the Senate. Al's book is humorous precisely because the insanity it depicts comes so close to the absurdities of the real elections that take place around the world. The 2000 U.S. presidential election provides more than enough compelling examples of the sometimes-ridiculous imperfections of modern electoral democracies. Al Gore received the most votes overall, but he lost the election when George W. Bush won Florida, thus winning the most electoral votes and, consequently, taking the presidency. In the critical swing state of Florida—where *swing* usually refers to the big-band music your great-grandmother thought was risqué—thousands of elderly, lifelong Democratic voters "accidentally" voted for ultraconservative Pat Buchanan (running as a candidate on the Reform Party ticket) when they were confused by the poorly laid out ballots.*

Had Buchanan not benefited from the ballot confusion, Gore would have moved into the White House. Had it stopped there, that would have been noteworthy enough. But there was also Ralph Nader, the quite liberal Green Party candidate with the ongoing pledge to "protect everyone from everything everywhere by getting government out of everything except protecting people from everything everywhere." Had Nader not been in the race, or if even a modest proportion of the Floridian Naderites had voted strategically and picked Gore, the candidate closest to their political position who had a chance to win, Gore would have won the part of the election that actually counted. While some undoubtedly shudder that such a tiny vote difference was all that kept the critical selection of White House dinnerware out of the hands of Tipper Gore, the practical differences for most of us are even more profound. Putting Big Al in the White House would have changed the entire course of late-night TV, political cartoons, and other forms of satire for eight years. Satirizing a guy named Gore is funny, but could it have ever really surpassed the truckloads of jokes that have been made about George Bush the Younger?

And for those of you who shudder at the thought of Al Franken in the Senate, consider the very reasonable argument that if Al Gore had become president, then Al Franken could never have won his Senate seat. Franken won by just the thinnest of margins, and most pundits agree—and Al himself would probably agree—that many of the people who voted for him were voting against the Bush legacy and against the conservative establishment it represented.

Somehow, through all of the 2000 election nonsense and after a 2012 election that will almost certainly go down as the ugliest presidential election in history, most Americans still consider their country a democracy. Clearly, democracy—at least as mere mortals currently practice it—is not perfect. The imperfections of democracy make the absurdity in Franken's book—which I believe deserved a Pulitzer Prize, or at least a People's Choice Award—seem just a little too realistic.

---

*There are several good jokes I could have put in this paragraph, from some kind of self-exposure or flasher jokes about Al Franken writing an exposé about himself to Buchanan's claim that those elderly Democratic voters did really, deep down, want to vote for a loud and aggressive person who was too right-wing to run as a Republican, but sometimes one must pause to simply reflect on the rich humor inherent in life itself. Take thirty-seven Zen-like seconds to contemplate the nature of irony.

KENNETH ARROW

Team: **New York City All Rounders**

Position: **Silly Point**

Status: **Alive! Can you believe it? Alive, I say!**

Kenneth Arrow (1921–) is famous for more than being the only one of the dead white male theorists who isn't actually dead. He is an economist with an amazing knack for distilling the complexities of the world into simple and compelling logical discussions. Arrow's theorem, which explains exactly why it is impossible for voting to be a certain means of selecting the most preferred outcome when there are more than two choices, is the most obvious example. However, almost all of the larger body of social choice theory, which is concerned with the logic underlying how groups of people make and implement decisions, owes its existence, or at least a great big hug, to Arrow.

Arrow was awarded the Nobel Prize in Economics in 1972, and what may be more remarkable than that, he has seen several of his students win Nobel Prizes. And as remarkable as that all is, you would think I'd have a lot more to say about him, but then again, that is the kind of accomplishment that speaks for itself.

ARROW'S THEOREM

Alas, American democracy is no less imperfect[†] than that found in the world's other democracies. As it turns out, all democracies are fraught with problems. In fact, I just happen to have mathematical, scientific, absolute, geological proof that elections everywhere are imperfect. Using some serious math, an economist called Kenneth Arrow[*] demonstrated that the use of elections does not ensure that the majority's preference will be selected.[‡] How can this be? You would think that if everybody gets to vote, if all the votes are equal, and if all the votes are counted fairly, then you would clearly get the outcome preferred by the majority. After all, that is the whole democracy thing you learned in grade school, and now that you are all quite nearly grown up, you put a great deal of faith in election results, right? Unfortunately for those who are easily thrown into a crisis of faith, it turns out that whenever there are more than two choices in an election—even if you assume that every vote is counted and all votes are equal—the method used to add up the votes has a tremendous impact on who wins.

What? Addition is addition, right? It totally does not matter if you add the three to the four or the four to the three, it still comes out a seven, and that means you have "crapped out." The casino will now take your money; please pass the dice to the next person at the table.

[†]My computer's grammar checker wants to change "less imperfect" into "fewer imperfects." Thank you, Bill Gates and all you hard workers at Microsoft.

[*]Most people seem to call him Kenneth Arrow because that is his name.

[‡]This is true even in places other than Florida.

Well, not quite. Count on a professor‡ to figure out that when it comes to elections, addition is not that simple. Arrow found that different methods of counting votes lead to very different election outcomes. Moreover, he demonstrated that we can never be certain that any one method of counting votes will lead to the majority's single preferred option. Thus, even elections that most of us would consider perfectly fair may be imperfect because we cannot ever be certain the outcome is truly the one desired by the majority of the voting population.

Fortunately, I can demonstrate the idea behind Arrow's argument without resorting to anything beyond street-level math—Sesame Street–level math. Imagine you are all going to elect the king of the ice cream social. You have five candidates, cleverly named A, B, C, D, and Bruce, the singing wallaby,* who are artfully depicted in Figure 10.1. The most conservative candidate is on the right, advocating the imposition of vanilla for all and all for vanilla, and the extreme liberal is on the left, demanding that you must sample each of the twenty-nine flavors between Fiona Apple Crunch Nonpatriarchal Ice Cream and Rage against the Praline Socialist Ice Cream.[4] In the middle are the moderates, who generally think that something in addition to just vanilla would be nice, but these three candidates are deeply divided over the chocolate, strawberry, or rocky road issue. The figure also shows the percentage of the voters who prefer each candidate.

Now, if you go with a typical method of counting votes—each voter gets one vote and the candidate with the most votes wins—Bruce, the Australian conservative, wins the election with a mere 27 percent of the votes. This is a fair and simple way to count the votes

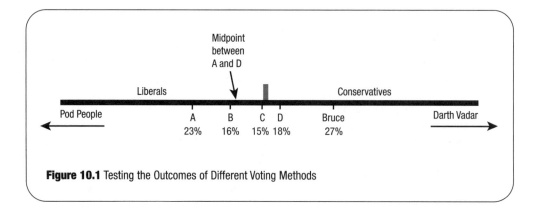

Figure 10.1 Testing the Outcomes of Different Voting Methods

‡Or, better yet, an economist.

*I'm not sure if it is a law or something, but it seems that all Australians are named either Bruce or Sheila. It also seems to be the case that sharks only eat Australians. I'm not sure why.

and it is the method you are probably most accustomed to. However, if you were actually to ask the voters, it turns out that the vast majority would rather have anyone other than that squawking marsupial as their duly elected monarch of frozen dairy. Despite the fact that every vote was counted and all votes were equal, does such an outcome actually represent the will of the majority? How can that be if the majority of the people are unsatisfied with the outcome? In Robert Penn Warren's novel *All the King's Men,* Willie Stark—whose later career is remarkably similar to that of the real-life Louisiana governor and U.S. senator Huey Long—as a relatively young and naive politician is supported in a bid for governor.[5] Stark's real-world political education begins as he realizes that his support is coming mainly from another candidate in the campaign who is just using Stark to divide his opponent's vote.

It may not shock you to learn that this sort of electoral result, in which someone with far less than half the votes wins, has actually happened several times in the United States. This was how Al Franken won the senate seat in Michigan or whichever cold midwestern state it was. It might even have been a Canadian province—Manitoba, maybe. Whatever. In the Saskatchewan Senate election, a third-party conservative candidate stole a good chunk of votes from Al Franken's Republican opponent, and Al won with only about 42 percent of the votes. One of the more interesting U.S. examples is Evan Mecham's election in 1986 as governor of Arizona. Mecham won the election with far less than a majority of the votes, and the result can only be called a political disaster. Not only did Mecham openly and quite seriously discuss alien landing sites in Arizona, which we all know are actually in Wyoming, he used an executive order to eliminate the Martin Luther King Jr. holiday in the state, and the politically correct backlash drove the Super Bowl and all of the money associated with it to California.

Mecham was quickly kicked out of office, but because of the chaos, insanity, dissatisfaction, and controversy that followed his ascent to the governorship, Arizona, like a few other states, adopted an alternative method of adding up the votes in an election with a large number of candidates to ensure that the voters will not end up with the election of someone with a very small percentage of the overall vote. For example, Louisiana and Arizona both now require a candidate to receive the majority of all votes cast before he or she can be declared the winner of an election. If there are more than two candidates in a race and no candidate wins more than half the votes, the two candidates with the highest pluralities—the most votes—must face each other in a winner-take-all runoff election.

If this system had been in place in my fictional—but still highly believable—election of the king of the ice cream social,* the outcome would have been much different. Bruce the conservative marsupial and the fuzzy-headed liberal candidate who thinks she is so cool

---

*Some may question the use of an ice cream social as an example. They may even say it trivializes the deeply held democratic ideal of elections. Obviously, these people haven't read the first nine chapters of this book if they are worried about that kind of thing at this point. They also don't realize that the real tragedy is the way I cavalierly mixed democratic and hereditary monarchical metaphors involved in electing a king. My copy editor really should have queried that.

she can simply go by the letter A, received the most votes in the first round, with 27 percent of the votes for Bruce and 23 percent for A. Then the two of them would have to face each other in a second round. If you look at the people who voted for the three eliminated candidates, most of them are closer to A on the ideological spectrum in my little figure than to that extremist honky-tonk Aussie, so the vast majority of them would probably prefer Candidate A over Bruce. Thus, in the second round of this different—but still fair—method of holding an election, candidate A would add B's 16 percent, C's 15 percent, and maybe even a few of D's supporters to the 23 percent she already had, pulling in about 55 percent of the vote to beat Bruce. However, does this method ensure that the election selects the candidate actually preferred by the majority of the population?

It might be tempting to say yes, this method of counting the vote gets you the will of the majority because it eliminates the undesirable outcome of electing a candidate that most of the voters dislike, but you should also realize that the single-vote system that elected Bruce and the runoff system that elected Candidate A are both fair ways to add up the votes to determine the winner of an election. Further, there are other fair ways of adding up votes that can produce outcomes different from either of these two methods. For example, what would happen if you go for reality TV democracy and start voting candidates off the island? Instead of voting *for* the candidate you prefer the most, you vote *against* the candidate you hate the most.[*] You do this round after round until just one candidate is left. With this method of counting the vote, in each round you vote against the candidate who is farthest from you on the ideological spectrum in Figure 10.1. Unsurprisingly, since so many people dislike him, the winner of the simple vote count this example first started with—Bruce—is the first one voted off the island. If you find the halfway point between the two most extreme candidates, it will be the point that marks the dividing line between the voters farthest from the candidate on the right and those farthest from the candidate on the left. If you are right of that line, A has to be the farthest away, and if you are on the left, Bruce has to be the farthest away. It can't be any of the candidates in the middle. No matter where you are on the line, either A or Bruce has to be the most-distant candidate. You don't have to believe me, you can check it out for yourself. No, seriously, go get the little pink plastic ruler out of your Hello Kitty pencil case, find the halfway point, pick some spots on the line, and start measuring the distances from those points to each of the candidates and see who is the farthest away. Go ahead, I'll wait.

Convinced yet? Not quite? Take a couple more minutes. I am very patient.

Look, just measure a few spots on the line.

Seriously, all the other readers are ready to move on, and it is hard enough keeping their attention as it is.

---

[*]Many people already do this, voting for a candidate not because they like or support him or her, but because they think it would be worse if his or her opponent won. In the first edition I predicted that this sort of voting against George W. Bush and his legacy would define the 2008 U.S. presidential election and, tadah, hello President Barack Obama.

Fine, but when the rest of us get back from the espresso stand, we are moving on with or without you.

Now that everyone is happily caffeinated, take a look at the halfway point between the two most extreme candidates A and Bruce, marked by the thick gray vertical line, and look at how many people fall on each side of that point. All of A's, B's, and C's supporters, and roughly half of people who should be D's supporters, will probably vote against Bruce. That's about 63 percent against the caterwauling Australian, and Bruce is off the island before he can win immunity in one of those silly games. However, once Bruce is off the island—safely shipped back to the outback, where he is using every last millisecond of his fifteen minutes of fame to cut an album and crank out a video—who is the next to get voted out? Assuming that voters will then turn against the remaining candidate who is most distant from them on my fancy graphic, you can again mark the midpoint between the most extreme candidates—this time they are A and D. In order to avoid any more unfortunate delays, I measured it myself and marked it on the figure for you. Even for those who made it to college but still for some reason cannot manage to operate a ruler, it should be obvious that Candidate A is the next one voted off the island. Bruce's supporters (27 percent), D's supporters (18 percent), C's (15 percent), and probably half of B's supporters (8 percent) all turn against the hapless Candidate A, and she is sent packing for her two-week publicity tour on every cable TV talk show with low enough standards to want her as a guest. Clearly, if Bruce and Candidate A are the first two kicked off the island, the winner of this election will not be same as the winner of either of the previous two elections. In fact, assuming that people keep voting against the candidate that is farthest from them on the figure, the last candidate standing is probably going to be Candidate C, the tall kind of gawky girl standing right in the middle.

In another variation, let's see what happens if you keep the reality TV style round-by-round voting system, but you do it *New Zealand Idol* style.[*] You vote *for* the candidate you like most, and the candidate with the fewest votes in each round gets kicked off the island. In that case the first one off the island is Candidate C, who was the winner of our third method of counting the votes. If you then split C's supporters evenly between B and D, B moves up to 23.5 percent and D gets 25.5 percent. Thus, A's measly 23 percent gets her kicked off. In the third round all of A's supporters go to their next-closest candidate, giving B 46.5 percent and leaving D's 25.5 percent to lose to Bruce's 27 percent. In the final round at least half of D's supporters jump to B rather than Bruce, and you have your fourth different winner—Candidate B—in this fourth way of counting the votes.

What if you were to use ranked votes? That is, what if you use the method the sportswriters use to give the wrong U.S. college football team the national championship?

---

[*]*New Zealand Idol* is just like *American Idol* or *Australian Idol,* but it is just far, far more painful to watch. Even if you turn the sound all the way down it makes the dog bark and whine.

Which candidate wins then? What if you have party-based primaries followed by a runoff election? Then A, B, and C have one election among just Democrats and D and Bruce have one among just Republicans, and those primaries are followed by the main event. What if you have party primaries, but allow everybody to vote in both primaries? Then you have the possibility of strategic voting, in which somebody can cast a vote in the other party's primary with the intention of selecting a candidate from the other party that her party can beat in the finals. Just try figuring that one out. All this, and I haven't even gone into all of the strategies about nominations and all of the other stuff that goes on before the vote itself.

At the very least, I've given you four different but fair sets of rules for tallying the votes, and each of those four accounting procedures produces a different outcome. How can you know which outcome is the will of the majority? It is true that I set up this distribution of candidates and votes to make it easy to come up with different winners when I used different methods of counting.[†] However, it is also true that I assumed that the process of conducting the election was perfect. Hanging chads, misprinted ballots, absentee votes from people who were never born, the mysterious voting habits of dead people, voting-machine failures, Kenyans born in "Hawaii," and all of the other things that might make the outcome of a real vote even more uncertain were not included in my example. Is the person who really "won" the 2000 U.S. presidential election the one who moved into the White House? Both the yes and no arguments have merit.

What **Arrow's theorem**[6] shows us is that elections cannot be the perfect means of making decisions because part of the process—the way the votes are tallied—can significantly alter the outcome, even when it is done perfectly and fairly. Since you have no way of being certain that any one of the various fair methods of counting is the correct one, you also have no way to guarantee that the outcome reflects the true will of the majority. Rather than sending you screaming in panic, the imperfect reality of using an election to achieve the ideal of democracy should serve as a reminder of my distinction between the ideal and the real and how that distinction affects politics.

I opened this chapter by spending a little quality time beating on your faith in democracy because it is important to get you to think about the distinction between the ideal of democracy and the reality. You have probably never been asked to make this distinction. You have probably never even thought about it enough to realize there is much of a distinction, but doing so—delving into the good, the bad, and the ugly aspects of democracy—is necessary to understand the critical role that elections and other democratic structures play in modern politics.

[†]I can do that. I'm the author and I might just be a little bit evil.

BARKING DEATH SQUIRRELS

Barking Death Squirrels has nothing whatsoever to do with democracy. There isn't a single election or vote in the whole thing. Not even a show of hands in a meeting. Honestly, what did you expect? It's a book about an alien invasion—who's gonna vote on that? Motion to run from giant man-eating squids. Second? Do I hear a second of the motion? AhhhahH! Chomp, chomp, gulp. And by this point in the textbook I really kind of expected you to have figured out I've just been mailing in the whole relevance thing. Truth is, all the bribing of copy editors and adding references to my stuff and pretending to care about having a reason to mention my stuff was all just so I could pimp this one.

First off, despite the kitschy title, there aren't any actual squirrels in the book, not one. It's a metaphor for the place of humans in a far future galaxy that's dominated by monstrous alien predators. At least I'm pretty sure it's a metaphor. Whatever. Point is, it's got kind of a classic science fiction storytelling vibe to it and I worked some literary kinds of things into it, and lots of politics—I am a professor—but for the most part, it is first and foremost a science fiction novel written by an author who really knows his science fiction.

Douglas A. Van Belle, *Barking Death Squirrels* (Wellington, New Zealand: Random Static, 2010). Sir Julius Vogel Award 2011—Finalist for Best Novel.

DEMOCRACY AND THE LIBERAL IDEAL

So far in this chapter I have not really spoken about the concept of democracy at all. Instead, I have been talking about elections, which is what most people probably think of first when they hear the word *democracy*. Given a more extended opportunity to speak about the concept, people might also mention presidents, prime ministers, legislatures, parliaments, and other aspects of modern democratic governments. However, in the modern world, pure democracy is not actually a viable form of government. Instead, democracy is an ideal, dreamed up by long-dead, slaveholding, wine-guzzling Greek men with lead-poisoning-induced sanity problems. And like all of the other ideals I have discussed, democracy is probably unattainable in practice. The various forms of modern democratic governments are merely efforts to approximate that ideal—and an emphasis should be placed on *approximate*.

Democracy quite literally means "rule by the people," at least it does in Greek, or Latin, or Egyptian or something old like that, and it reflects the ideal of people governing themselves, which may have been close to feasible in the ancient Greek city-state of Athens. Because ancient Athens was relatively small, all Athenian citizens could gather together to share perspectives, debate, and actually vote on policies in what we would now call

direct democracy. In reality, of course, Athenian citizens had time and space enough to engage in politics personally because they had slaves to do much of their work for them. Only "true Athenians" could be citizens, and that distinction did not include a lot of people—women, slaves, and the poor, for example. Other than that, everything was rosy. Still, the notion of people actually ruling themselves has a certain element of quirky charm to it. The idea was that democracy was more than a means of reaching a fair decision. Democracy also was seen as a means of improving the society. By sharing perspectives, empathizing with each other, and working out compromises, people created communities that worked to improve both the people themselves and their city-states.

All of this seems quite admirable—that is, at least until you ponder the trial of the great philosopher Socrates. The voters in that Athenian democracy gave Socrates a hemlock cocktail for challenging the Athenian democracy's accepted truths and for purportedly corrupting its youth.[*] The jury at the trial of Socrates comprised the citizens of Athens seated as one group, and it was they who voted to put him to death. That brings up a big problem associated with direct democracy. While it may create lots and lots of opportunity for the participation of those recognized as citizens, it also creates a situation in which there is often no tolerance for difference and dissent. A democracy in this sense is often associated with the **tyranny of the majority,** in which an unrestrained majority bands together to rule a society with a ferocity and cruelty that can be every bit as arbitrary and dictatorial as *Nineteen Eighty-Four*'s Big Brother.

Remember that Plato was not a fan of democracy, and Aristotle listed it among the bad forms of government. Quite possibly motivated by the death of Socrates, Plato believed that simply because a majority of people have an opinion, that does not make them or their opinion correct. Aristotle believed that democracies amount to mob rule in which self-interested factions fight for those things that suit them with no regard for the good of the larger collective. In fact, the Framers of the U.S. Constitution[†] shared this Aristotelian negative view of democracy. In fact, they would never have used the term *democracy* to describe the American government they created; they preferred to call it a **republic,**[‡] a government in which decisions are made by representatives of the citizens rather than the citizens themselves. One need only think of the many undemocratic features of the Constitution to get the point, such as the Supreme Court, with its members appointed for life terms; a Senate that would be chosen by the state legislatures; two votes for every state in the Senate regardless of state size; the Electoral College. Remember that while we

---

[*]Hemlock is a seriously deadly poison, and that is probably the reason the famous last words of Socrates were, "I just drank what . . . ?" Also, I stole this joke from Val Kilmer's best movie ever, *Real Genius.*

[†]Long, long ago in a chapter far, far away—Chapter 2—this material was covered. I should also note that the Framers were the guys who wrote it, not the ones who put it in that Plexiglas box in the National Archives. Not that there is anything wrong with the Plexiglas box. Seriously, it's a nice box, all clear and bulletproof and everything.

[‡]No, you are not hallucinating—at least I don't think so. In Chapter 6 I told you that according to one definition, a republic is a country without a single authoritative leader. However, this definition is the more common one.

ultimately wind up rooting for Jefferson Smith in *Mr. Smith Goes to Washington,* the filibuster he uses to win thwarts the will of the majority and is hardly democratic.

Yet, with all of its faults, democracy seems to have unending appeal. The idea that ordinary citizens should control their own destinies is a tremendously attractive one. The idea that democracy can promote moral values remains with us. Furthermore, it fits in well with the liberal ideal of limited government. In democracies the people ultimately rule, and government by the people should minimize the ability of a few powerful elites to extend government into the details of people's lives. Thus, democracy remains a powerful idea and an even more powerful ideal.

Direct Democracy

Exactly how a country would go about approximating the liberal democratic ideal of a government by the people is, in itself, an interesting question. If democracy had problems in ancient Athens, it is riddled with even more problems when it comes to modern nation-states. To distinguish the dead-Greek-men version from modern forms of democracy, people often refer to the Athenian model as direct democracy. As I have noted, direct democracy can devolve into little more than a polite mob that votes on whom they will lynch—or, in the case of Socrates, poison. Further, because in a true direct democracy everyone votes on every question of government, you should immediately be able to think of several problems that will inevitably arise. How can more than a few people all get together in one place? How will there be time for everyone to deal with every issue? How do you guarantee everyone an opportunity to participate? How will people find the time to participate? Except for perhaps the smallest of groups in the simplest of contexts, true direct democracy, as a system of government, cannot function efficiently or effectively.

Elements of direct democracy, however, can be valuable parts of modern democracies. The closest we probably get to direct democracy in the modern world is the *referendum* or *initiative* process employed by many, but not all, of the U.S. state governments. **Referenda*** are questions that legislatures put on the ballot for the people to vote on, while **initiatives** are questions that are put on the ballot by citizens, usually after some kind of qualification process, such as the collection of a significant number of signatures on a petition. These processes provide mechanisms that allow citizens to circumvent legislatures and other representative governing bodies and vote directly on policies, laws, and other actions that would normally be taken up by legislatures. Recent examples provide indications of both the difficulties and the values of this limited form of direct democracy.

Initiatives have been a particularly salient part of recent politics in Washington, that highly caffeinated state right next to Idaho that is not Montana. In 1999, Tim Eyman took

---

*Referendum is singular, *referenda* is plural. Also, the kiwi fruit is actually neither a native New Zealand plant nor what most would call a fruit. It is a berry, the Chinese gooseberry to be exact.

some time away from the unlicensed, possibly illegal mail-order business he ran out of his home—a lucrative career selling customized novelty watches to fraternities and sororities—and started an initiative campaign against car licensing fees. At the time, the fees for license tabs[†] in the state of Washington were based on a simple formula derived from the initial sticker price of the vehicle, the alignment of the planets during its most recent oil change, and the fractal derivative of the pattern of stains on its floor mats. The annual trauma of forking over several hundred dollars to keep mom's new SUV legal made the January 13, 1999, *Seattle Times* headline "New Initiative Would Set $30 Fee for All Vehicle Licenses"[7] an instant hit and an easy sell at the ballot box.

Anyone reminded of Al Franken and his fictional campaign theme of high ATM fees?

Mr. Eyman was remarkably successful at tapping into an issue of widespread public discontent. Nobody wants to pay taxes. That has always been an absolute and unshakable truth. Mr. Eyman's greatest talent, politically, at least,[*] was his ability to connect that discontent to a simple alternative that was extremely appealing to the average voter. Mr. Eyman seemed to understand how to connect with people whose political interest, involvement, and attention span tended to be severely limited. Drunk on the heady popularity of the car tab initiative and feeling pretty chuffed[†] about his new sombrero, Mr. Eyman offered initiative after initiative: to reduce property taxes, to limit property tax increases to 1 percent annually, to repeal a tax to build mass transit in Seattle, to use 90 percent of transportation funds for building and maintaining roads, to eliminate Seattle's light rail project, to open carpool lanes to all traffic during off-peak hours, to repeal the 5-cent-per-gallon tax increase on fuel that the state legislature passed to fund transportation projects in the wake of the massive revenue losses from the $30 vehicle licensing initiative that started it all. In 2006 Timmy pushed an initiative focused on overturning the state's gay rights legislation. In 2008 he put an elaborate, if not byzantine, traffic initiative on the ballot, and even though that initiative was defeated in a most resounding way, he was back at it in 2009 with an initiative that he said was about property taxes.[‡] In 2010 he started filing initiatives to fix his previous initiatives, and in 2011 he filed an initiative on bridge tolls. In 2012 he filed five, including an initiative to make the initiative process easier for him to get future initiatives on the ballot.

[†]And you thought you found a spelling error. I don't mean tags as in the pet license tags you put on your dog's collar, nor do I mean license plates. *Tabs* are what the good people of Washington—as well as the naughty ones—call the little stickers that people have to put on their license plates to show that they have paid their vehicle licensing taxes for the year.

[*]That thing he does at parties, with the sombrero, that's pretty hard to beat.

[†]Chuffed is the spiritual plane that teenage boys reach when they manage to avoid killing themselves when showing off for disinterested teenage girls. The word is derived from the term *chuffing,* which is what the males of certain kinds of game fowl do when they are strutting their stuff for the ladies of the species. It's a New Zealand colloquialism.

[‡]This raises another point about this type of direct democracy: Given that the author of the ballot question can make such a difference, is it democratic for only one person to set the agenda for an entire state?

Eyman's omnipresent initiative strategy enrages some and strains sociability. Ordinary political discourse has become impossible in Washington. The referendum and initiative processes are meant to be a safety mechanism. Structurally, the state government is not designed to function under such a constant barrage of initiatives. Eyman, however, has made a career out them, and his activities are, to say the least, controversial. So many people have become frustrated with the political dysfunction he is causing that they have begun attacking him personally. And they have turned to initiatives to make their point. State initiative I-831 asked voters to officially designate Eyman "a horse's ass." Some judge forced a revision in the official language of the horse's ass initiative, changing "a horse's ass" to "a vernacular term to denote the back end of a horse."[8] The courts later threw out the horse's ass initiative on technical grounds. Beyond giving us a few laughs, and giving me the chance to use "horse's ass" twelve times in a single paragraph, the horse's ass initiative does highlight the intensity of the debate. Browsing through the *Seattle Times* coverage of the Eyman initiatives that led to the horse's ass initiative is like reading a saga of old, with venomous editorials, personal attacks, harsh debates, court challenges, and a whole lot of old-fashioned arguing. And yes, "horse's ass" really is used twelve times in this paragraph, not including the way the judge revised "horse's ass" to something politically correct. Look again and see if you can find those two very clever ways I snuck a "horse's ass" into this paragraph.

Many of Eyman's initiatives have passed, but their success at election time has not been matched in subsequent legal fights. To this day, it still does not appear that any single one of Eyman's initiatives has actually become law in the state of Washington. The Washington State Supreme Court has eviscerated them all. In fact, the consistent failures of the initiatives in the face of legal challenges have even prompted some critics to argue that Eyman purposely writes illegally worded initiatives. The logic of why he would do that is a little shaky, and his critics have never managed to provide a good reason we should believe this interesting conspiracy theory to be correct, but it is clear that despite the failures and all of the side drama, Mr. Eyman's foray into direct democracy has changed the nature of taxation in the state of Washington.

The recent changes in taxation in the state of Washington highlight what Eyman and his supporters might argue is the true value of direct democracy. Even though Eyman has failed to actually get any of his initiatives enacted as law, his use of the initiative process has had tremendous effects. The cost of licensing a car for a year may not be exactly $30, as Eyman's initiative was declared legally invalid, the Washington State Legislature did initiate a flat licensing fee with limited local additions. At most, the fee is now about $50 — far below the several hundred dollars it could run before Eyman's first initiative. The initiatives injected the idea of a tax revolt into every political discussion and every action of the Washington State Legislature. You could also argue that the awareness of the threat of these kinds of initiatives, even when they are not used, has made every legislator in the

state of Washington more sensitive to what the public wants and how the public will respond to taxation and spending on transportation.

You could also argue, as many critics do, that these initiatives represent exactly what is wrong with direct democracy. The public's knowledge of the intricacies of politics, particularly in terms of taxes and economics, is limited, and the decisions made by the fleeting involvement of the public tend not to be of the highest quality. People are more interested in the daily challenges of dating, home life, career, dating, and figuring out how to TiVo the latest show that exploits pretty people in the name of reality television. Limiting car licenses to $30 sounds simple and appealing. In reality, however, what seems like a tax break for many is really a tax break that is limited to the owners of very expensive cars. With the change in licensing fees in the state of Washington, the owner of a Hummer received an annual tax break of more than $700, while the vast majority of car owners—particularly the professor who is still driving the rusted-out 1973 Dodge Dart that his parents tried to abandon by the side of the freeway—received absolutely no reduction in their annual licensing costs. And if you are a college student in the state of Washington, this is where union rules require your instructor to insert a screaming tirade about what the tax revolt has done to the funding of the state's universities.

Direct democracy can seem quite appealing to anyone who has struggled with, or just whined about, the inefficiencies, idiocies, and improprieties of a government that pays $200 for a toilet seat and gives subsidies to tobacco farmers while simultaneously suing the tobacco industry and making it illegal to smoke anywhere except the median of an interstate highway. However, the reality is that direct democracy usually does not work in the way that it might have sort of worked as a system of governing for the ancient Greeks. There are several reasons, but two simple and obvious ones stand out.

First, most people have neither the expertise nor the time to evaluate and consider all of the details of running a town, county, state, or country. Thirty dollars for an annual license: Does that include the fee for safety and emissions inspections? Does it apply to cement trucks, buses, pickups, motor homes, motorcycles, ATVs, snowmobiles, and parade floats? If you cut the licensing fee, where does the money for roads come from? Should the fee increase with inflation? What about those license plates with people's initials, cute seven-letter sayings, and tigers saying, "Save the rain forest"? All those used to cost extra every year. Are they all now $30? All of those questions and countless other details must be dealt with by those who govern. In a true direct democracy the public would have to deal with all of those details as they met together for discussion and debate. We often do not have the expertise and most of us do not have the time to go beyond the most basic aspect of $30 car tabs. Given the massive complexity of governing, it would be impossible for everyone to participate in every decision.

Second, most of the population does not want to. One thing that politicians, philosophers, and political scientists often forget is that many people would be perfectly thrilled if

they could just ignore politics and still get a reasonably tolerable government. Most people believe they have better things to do. For many students this involves the frantic quest to locate significant others of the desired gender with sufficiently low standards to consider dating said students—but that is far from the only thing that most students believe is more important than engaging in political debate. In fact, in terms of the things the average student has decided are worth panicking about, there are exactly 1,384 priorities above the politics of residential zoning laws. In other words, there is no better way to quiet a classroom than to ask a question like, "So, what do you think of the debate over the prime minister's new ministerial appointments?"

For the vast majority of us, putting food on the table, having a breakfast nook to put the table in, and all the little things it takes to someday buy, and hire a NASA scientist to assemble, the IKEA chairs for the three-legged table we found abandoned by the side of the road are the things that consume most of our lives. Politics and governing ourselves have to fit into what little time and energy we have left over, and then they have to compete with all the other things we would like to do, such as recovering from hangovers, learning how to program the clock on the stove, keeping that special person of the preferred gender happy enough, setting the world record for continuous viewing of the Home Shopping Network, finding enough money in the couch cushions to get one of those fancy foamed-up coffees, clipping toenails, and, of course, writing a best-selling novel about a goat, a robot, and the clone of Simón Bolívar getting stranded on the third moon of Saturn. Most of us do not want to govern ourselves because we have better things to do, and as long as the government does not get too far out of line or interfere too much with those other priorities, most of us are willing to leave most of the mundane governing tasks to others.

Still doubting? Well, stop to think about how close we actually are to being capable of instituting a system of electronic participation that could closely approximate a direct democracy. Assuming that we can get over some serious problems with computer security, we should soon be able to give everyone a password and ID that will allow him or her to vote on the Internet. But why stop there? Why not allow everyone to vote on every issue of concern? Every Saturday night can be voting night. Forget dating and finding the aforementioned significant other of the preferred gender, from now on, from 5:00 to 7:00 P.M. (Eastern Standard Time, of course), we can all discuss and debate the issues in one big national chat room. At 9:00 P.M. the vote can take place. Bone up on your knowledge of banking laws. Break out the books on issues of national security. Get ready to parse the specifics of energy policy. When you start really thinking about it, that pain you are feeling in your colloquial term to denote the buttocks of a human is the point. Most people just do not want the responsibility. Even those who still may be tempted are often dissuaded by the fact that their voice of reason may not win the debate. Consider those neighbors with the swastika tattoos, the families with small-scale hemp farms, the person with three hundred cats and nary a litter box in sight, or the former figure skating champion with a violent

streak and a collection of irreparable cars that she uses for lawn ornaments. Each of them would have the same ability as you to vote on issues of national importance.

There is a relatively simple solution. Pay someone else to do it. Find a specialist who knows what he or she is doing and hire that person to handle all that political and policy stuff. Whether it is governing society or fixing a toilet, when you have something that needs to be done and you lack the ability, the know-how, or the gumption to do it yourself, you hire someone who can and will do it for you. This has several advantages, the most obvious of which is efficiency. Hiring a specialist allows you focus on what you do best—say, the farming of a perfectly legal hydroponically grown crop—rather than on fixing the toilet. This allows you to become the best farmer you can be, and it allows those who fix the toilets, or govern, to become experts on fecal relocation. As any good capitalist will tell you, by specializing we are all more efficient, and that efficiency principle applies to governing as well as it does to any other task.

On the other hand, we do not want to surrender the role of governing to others completely. Think of Hitler, Stalin, Genghis Khan, George Steinbrenner, and James Cameron—history makes it clear that surrendering absolute power to others is not a good thing. It gives you movies like *Avatar.* So if we do not want to govern ourselves, and we know better than to trust others completely to do it for us, what do we do?

Representative Democracy

It is debatable whether or not the U.S. government was the very first modern democracy. The Swiss and a few others can make reasonable claims on that distinction. However, it is clear that many of the structures and processes that Ben Franklin and the other white-wig boys created to approximate government by the people have served as models for governments in an increasingly democratic world. Even the North Vietnamese communist government of Ho Chi Minh modeled significant parts of its constitution on the U.S. document. Whether or not the United States was the first modern democracy is less important than the fact that the Framers of the U.S. constitution[*] consciously and rationally designed it from nearly a blank slate. Without too many historical constraints or ongoing commitments, the Framers were able to invent and adapt structures, processes, and methods to create a government that could approximate the ideal of government by the people and still function in the real world.

Four factors are critical to the effectiveness and the remarkable endurance of the U.S. system. First, its designers used representatives as a way to create a democratic government of specialists. While the Framers did not create the idea of representative government, they understood those representatives to be servants of the districts they represented, and they intentionally apportioned the districts so that the representatives

---

[*]Again, not the guys who put it in the Plexiglas box.

could stay close to the people they represented. The second factor is the institutionalization of revolt, in the form of frequent elections, to select those representatives. Frequent elections—two years for members of the House of Representatives—are intended to keep those political experts focused on the demands, wishes, and desires of the people they represent. Third, the Framers of the U.S. Constitution recognized the potential downside of democracy. They limited the power of government in order to prevent people from voting to lynch others and otherwise imposing a tyranny of the majority. They did this in Article I, section 8 of the Constitution, which lays out Congress's powers, and then they added a whole bunch more with the Bill of Rights, particularly the Tenth Amendment, which specifically reserves all other power to the states and to the people. Further, through the use of "separation of powers" and "checks and balances," the Framers deliberately made it very difficult for the government to do much of anything at all. Fourth, as noted earlier, the Framers further recognized the limits of democracy by specifically adding a few, carefully chosen, undemocratic features. The most notable of these undemocratic features can be seen in the way that minorities and losers[†] are given specific guarantees of protection by the Bill of Rights. These protect dissent[*] and difference, and prevent the majority from exploiting minorities or killing a Socrates, even if they vote to do so. Thus, the U.S. Constitution really encapsulates the battle of the real versus the ideal when it comes to democracy. The Framers were able to promote government by the people by creating institutions that specifically limit the actual role that the people play.

For legal reasons, I am required to inform the readers of this textbook that this is the point when an argument broke out among the author, the fourth editor of this edition (the one who mysteriously vanished during a Dungeons and Dragons tournament), and a student named Larry. My now-missing editor suggested that I use this as an opportunity to connect the discussion to the theories of politics I introduced way back near the beginning of the book and the theorists that I have been spotlighting throughout the chapters. I used a very naughty word when I asked the seventh-level, half-elf magic user of an editor if he was referring to the Plato steaming pile of "stuff" on good and bad forms of government. Then Larry stuck his nose in. Larry—one of "those" kinds of honor students—was standing in the hall and promptly reminded this occasionally politically incorrect professor that the good and bad forms of government discussion was Aristotle's steaming pile of "stuff." A clerical "error" quickly followed, and after Larry discovered that his summer internship had somehow shifted from Boston to Botswana, the author and the editor debated the issue. There are, indeed, many ways that a discussion of the creation of the U.S. Constitution

---

[†]The Framers meant losers in the political forum, but this idea can be applied to losers more generally.

[*]Not to pick on George W. Bush and the conservative establishment that brought him to power, but this part of the Constitution suggests that calling people un-American for criticizing leaders and their policies is very un-American. Also, using the media to criticize the media is right up there near the top of the old irony scale.

could be connected back to some of my earlier discussions of political theory. Aristotle's good versus bad forms of government does fit here, but also how about Hobbes and the Constitution as an explicit articulation of a social contract? How about Locke's idea of limited government and civil society, and how that relates to the Bill of Rights? How about Machiavelli's discussion of power and the implementation of checks and balances as a means of using the lust for power to limit the power of leaders? How about Rousseau's argument about "forcing people to be free" and the social responsibilities that go with the rights being articulated in the first ten amendments? There are plenty of opportunities here, but with the "mysterious" and "unfortunate" disappearance of my fourth editor,[†] there was suddenly no one all that interested in pressing the issue, so I just decided to finish up the discussion of direct democracy.

Basically, your participation in democracy in the U.S. system is limited to choosing who will represent your interests in government, and your personal involvement in politics is usually limited to deciding whom you want to vote for. Not an ideal solution, but this imperfect compromise does attempt to address the most significant difficulty with direct democracy—at least much of the time. Of course, it doesn't take a rocket scientist to recognize that the U.S. system has, at critical times, failed to protect dissenters and minorities. Examples are abundant—slavery, Jim Crow laws, the long-lasting failure to give women suffrage, the internment of the Japanese during World War II, the squelching of dissent through the Alien and Sedition Acts, the stifling of protests during major wars, laws aimed at Jehovah's Witnesses, the detention center at Guantánamo Bay, the legality of double-extra-large bright-orange Speedos, and so on. The point is not that the United States is ideal; it is not. Rather, the point is that the U.S. system is an attempt—especially as it has been amended—to find a compromise between the real and the ideal when it comes to democracy.

AN ECONOMIC THEORY OF DEMOCRACY

The surgeon general of the United States has asked me to warn you that the next section of the text will discuss spatial distributions of voter preferences and the mechanisms through which the contours of opinion dispersal place practical constraints on the electoral system's political party structures through its effect on the electability of candidates of given ideological ontologisms.[*] There are two reasons, however, that you should not panic. First, this methodology is mostly harmless.[†] Side effects are mild and mostly self-inflicted, but are known to include acute disorientation, sobbing, and the loss of control of certain bodily functions that you thought you had mastered when your mother started buying you

---

[†]I did hire a nonplayer character to search for him.

[*]Gotcha! Don't let the constant asinine prattle that I throw about fool you. I really can talk and write like a professor when I want. I don't do it often, but every once in a while it does pay to keep students honest.

[†]Thank you, Douglas Adams.

big boy/girl underpants. Second—surprise—I used this methodology above in the discussion of the election for king of the ice cream social, and most of you survived, probably because I left out the big scary words.

When I discussed how the different methods of counting the votes in the election for king of the ice cream social altered the outcome, I put the conservative candidates on the right and the liberals on the left, and I said repeatedly that people would vote for the candidate who was closest to them on the spectrum shown in the figure or that they would vote against the candidate that was farthest away. This is the spatial distribution of voter preferences, and it is essentially what Anthony Downs did in *An Economic Theory of Democracy.*[9] This method of thinking about voters, voting, and elections is so effective that even after a half century, Downs's theory remains the best way to discuss much of the *why* behind what you see in modern representative democracies. In fact, it may be the most elegant work of political theory produced by a scholar other than the author of this text.

Figure 10.2 is roughly the same as Figure 10.1, with the same candidates competing for the same office. The one difference is that I have also graphed the concentration of voters along the line stretching from the liberals on the left to the conservatives on the right. The height of the curve indicates the number of voters holding a particular ideological preference. Notice that the curve is lowest at the ends and highest in the center. This represents the fact that most voters are concentrated near the middle of the political spectrum; they are moderate. While it often seems the opposite in the real world, public opinion polls, particularly in the United States but also in most of Europe and other developed countries, suggest that most people are in the middle. We all tend to notice extremists more because they have the motive to be more vocal and visible than the average person. And they often behave like a vernacular term to denote the back end of a horse. Furthermore, extremists tend to be less satisfied with the current state of affairs, so they scream about it more than the average person. However, extremists are few in number, and there are far more average people than there are goose-stepping militaristic fascists on the right or communal, free-love tofu sculptors on the left.

I am recklessly assuming two things that may seem obvious: (1) people will vote for the candidate who is as ideologically similar to themselves as possible, and (2) candidates wish to get enough votes to win the election. With these assumptions, I can use the spatial approach to make some interesting arguments regarding the likely ideological positions of successful candidates, the most effective ideological positions of political parties, and even the number of parties a democratic structure is likely to host depending on how its rules are structured.

Winner-Take-All Systems

Downs used graphs similar to this one to explain why the United States has, and will probably always have, a two-party system. He was also able to argue that those two parties will

Not Quite Right, but Still Good

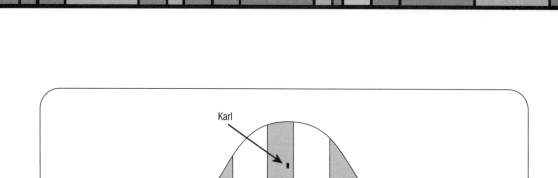

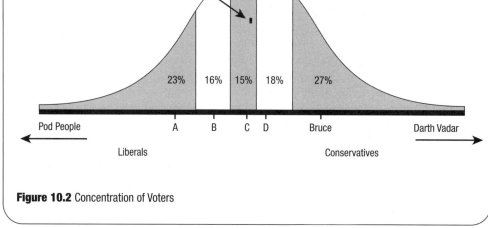

Karl

23% 16% 15% 18% 27%

Pod People   A   B   C   D   Bruce   Darth Vadar

Liberals   Conservatives

Figure 10.2 Concentration of Voters

always remain close to the nation's ideological center. The United States uses a **winner-take-all** (no proportional representation), **first-past-the-post** (no runoff elections), single-member district system.* In other words, each election has one winner, that winner is the sole representative of a given location, and winning is a simple matter of receiving the plurality (most) of the votes cast in the election.[10]

To get at these ideas, I'm going to send you tramping all the way back to the musical marsupial Bruce and the other characters in the beloved king of the ice cream social election example. Including the spatial depiction of voters in the discussion explains why some of the things happened. Specifically, in Figure 10.2 you can see how an extremist, representing the ideological preferences of only a small portion of a society, can manage to win an election when a large number of candidates are running. Most of the voters are in the middle of the political spectrum, but there are three candidates competing over this slice of the electoral pie. By dividing up the votes of the majority in the middle, it is possible for a representative of a more extreme position to win. Fewer voters overall are near Bruce, but he does not have to share those votes with any other candidate.

To identify the percentage of voters casting a ballot for each candidate, you draw a vertical line halfway between the candidate and the opponent nearest him or her on the ideological spectrum. I have put these lines in Figure 10.2, and the line between any two

---

*There are now a few exceptions to the first-past-the-post aspect, as noted earlier.

candidates represents the point at which voters go from being closer to one candidate to another. Thus, those on the left side of the line between A and B are closer to A, and they will vote for A. Those on the right of that line are closer to B, and they will vote for B. The number of people voting for each candidate is represented by all of the voters who are closer to that candidate than they are to any other. Thus, the number of votes for B includes everyone between the first voter to the right of the halfway line between A and B, all the way over to the last voter on the left of the line between B and C. Because the height of the curve represents the concentration of voters along the political spectrum, the area under the curve that is bounded by these two lines represents the total number of votes a candidate receives. Thus, the candidates in the middle get a narrower slice of the political spectrum, but that slice is taller, and the candidates at the extreme get a wider but shorter slice of the vote.

In most elections, the middle is where candidates want to be. Notice that in any scenario in which one or more of the middle-of-the-road candidates is removed, the extremists lose. In fact, pick any two of the five candidates and run them against each other, and the one closest to the center will always win. In a two-candidate election, the midpoint of this curve is critical. The area under either the left or the right half of the curve is the same.[*] Thus, if one candidate can push the dividing line between him- or herself and the other candidate just one voter onto the other side of the center, that candidate will have 50 percent + 1 votes. That one vote in the exact center is called the **median voter.** His name is Karl; he likes muscle cars, football, and *Sports Illustrated* swimsuit calendars; he works in an office; he talks about fishing but seldom does; he's lousy at golf; and his vote gives the winning candidate the majority needed to win. This fight over the median voter is why Downs argued that the United States has, and will always have, two political parties that are both very close to the political center.

The more generic version of the diagram offered in Figure 10.3 makes it easier to explain Downs's point. Consider a two-party system with one party on the right and the other on the left. To win the general election, which involves the final vote among the whole voting population for who will hold the office, a party must run a candidate who can capture the median voter of the overall population. So, the obvious strategy to win the general election is to try to get a candidate as close to the ideological middle as possible. The party that runs the candidate that is closest to the center—position 5 in Figure 10.3—will win. However, because the parties represent different sides of the political spectrum, the parties cannot rush all the way to the center. Within the context of a two-party system, with each party staking out one side or the other of the political spectrum, the candidate exactly in the center of the overall population is on the very edge of the political spectrum represented

---

[*]This is not exactly an accurate description of most developed countries. There tend to be slightly higher numbers of liberals in most countries, but that is roughly balanced by the fact that a higher percentage of conservatives vote.

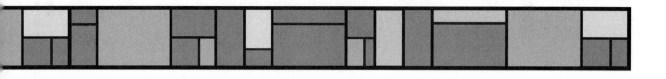

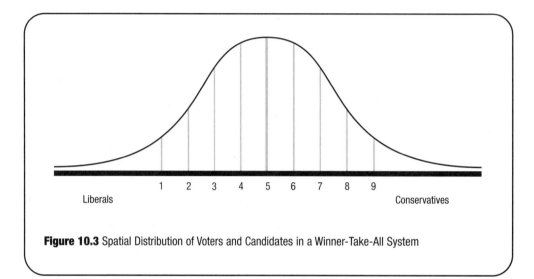

Figure 10.3 Spatial Distribution of Voters and Candidates in a Winner-Take-All System

by either of the two parties. This explains, in part, why people can complain, with some justification, that presidential candidates often tend to sound the same. To win the general election, presidential candidates must try to move toward the center, and this usually means the candidates are fairly similar.

However, the candidates cannot be exactly the same. There has to be some difference between the candidates of the two parties, because within the context of either party, the candidate who is exactly in the middle of the overall population is very much an extremist within the party and is some distance from the center of the party's ideological spectrum. With regard to the primary election, the election within the party to select the party's candidate for the general election, the candidate who wins the primary will have to capture the median voter within the political spectrum represented by the party. This requires candidates to always be on the party's side of the overall center. Thus, in a primary election, the candidates usually seem more ideological; Democrats tend to sound more liberal and Republicans tend to sound more conservative.

The result is a balance between these two electoral demands. The need to win the overall election drives the parties to run candidates near the median voter at the overall center. The need to win the primary drives candidates away from the overall center and toward the median voter of the party. Thus, you tend to get parties that claim ideological ground just to the right and the left of center, roughly locations 4 and 6 in Figure 10.3.

An Economic Theory of Democracy

Once these two parties are established, it is all but impossible to add a third party. The most obvious motivation to create a new party is to serve a portion of the population that is dissatisfied with the candidates offered by the existing parties. Because the bulk of the overall population is scrunched toward the overall ideological center, the median voter within the existing two parties will be skewed toward the overall center. This means that the most dissatisfied voters will be out at the extremes. They have the greatest motivation to try to start a new party and to run candidates that address their interests better than do the existing parties. The problem is that doing so is irrational. That kind of new party candidate will be further from the center than the candidates of the existing two parties, and rather than helping the dissatisfied voters get a representative that is closer to them ideologically, the new party will actually do the opposite.

If you start with candidates at positions 4 and 6 and add a candidate representing the more extreme ideological position of a new conservative party, say, at position 8, then you end up guaranteeing the election of the middle-of-the-road candidate that is farthest from your ideology. By running a candidate at position 8, the new conservative party steals the most conservative voters from the moderately conservative candidate at position 6, and by doing so guarantees that the more liberal candidate at position 4 will win the overall election. Thus, instead of a reasonable chance of getting a representative on their own side of the median voter, the members of the new party have made the outcome of the election worse for themselves by running a candidate that more closely represents their ideals. This is not just conjecture. Something like this scenario has happened several times in the history of U.S. presidential elections. Whenever an independent or third-party candidate has captured a significant share of the vote, the candidate from the established party that was ideologically closest to the added candidate lost the election. Many argue that Ross Perot cost George H. W. Bush a second term as president. While it would be a bit dangerous to assume that this is true, the real world being so untidy and unpredictable, it is a fact that if you were to add the votes for Perot to those of Bush the Elder, Bush wins a second term in a landslide and Bill Clinton is never elected president.

As long as you have a winner-take-all, single-member district system as in the United States, this will always be the case. Only the candidates that can win the overall vote in any election get the opportunity to actually participate in government. If you lose by even one vote, your party is shut out. Think about how frustrating this could be for a political party that is challenging the status quo. There are 435 seats in the U.S. House of Representatives. Imagine that the new political party wins 15 percent of the vote across the country, a remarkable start for a new political party. Yet it is almost certain that this new political party will actually gain *zero* seats in the House of Representatives. Remember, to win an election in a winner-take-all, single-member district system, a candidate must be able to achieve a plurality. Running candidates for political office is a costly, time-consuming, and exhausting task. It is little wonder that parties that can never get themselves up to a

Not Quite Right, but Still Good

majority in a significant number of locations quickly tire of trying. To add insult to injury, to the degree that a new party has ideas that may appeal to the center, the centrist parties will quickly absorb those ideas. Thus, the only viable parties are those that can win a majority reasonably often, and since the median voter is the key to winning, only the most centrist of parties will succeed and survive.

A big reason that Ross Perot's effort to build a new U.S. political party collapsed was that the party failed to win more than a tiny number of political offices, but possibly more problematic was that it also helped Democrats take offices from Republicans. The Republicans were closer to the conservative political base to which Perot was trying to appeal, thus his party tended to take votes that would have otherwise gone to the Republicans. Meanwhile, both the Democrats and the Republicans began to absorb Perot's deficit reduction message because it appealed to centrist voters. It is also true that the upstart Green Party in the United States did not endorse Ralph Nader in the 2004 presidential elections despite the fact that Nader is right there with them on the majority of issues. The Greens recognized that Nader would be siphoning votes away from John Kerry, so they would not support him because they wanted to be sure that those votes went to the Democrats. The Democrats were closer to the progressive liberal base to which the Greens were trying to appeal than were the Republicans, so the Democrats would have suffered the most if the Greens had supported a Nader candidacy.

Fine, but if this is true, how can there be so many democratic countries with more than two political parties? The simple answer is that not all democratic systems have rules like those used in the United States.

Winners-Take-Their-Share Systems

Modern democracies, unlike ice cream, come in two basic flavors:

1. The single-member district systems used in the United States, where one winner represents one location.

2. The proportional representation systems that are common in many parliamentary democracies around the world.

The differences between these two basic methods of selecting representatives have effects that permeate the political system all of the way down to the stability of the government.

One of the most significant ways in which modern democracies can differ is in how they translate the votes of the public into the people selected to actually govern in the name of the voters. The United States provides what may be the clearest example of a winner-take-all, single-member district system, but most democracies use a completely different system for using votes to select leaders.

The most common alternative to a winner-take-all system is a proportional representation (PR) system. PR systems are focused on political parties instead of on candidates. At election time, voters across the entire country cast their ballots not for specific candidates but for political parties. There are candidates—the parties offer long lists of candidates—but the transition from candidate to governing representative does not come from achieving a plurality of the vote. The seats in the parliament, Knesset, Diet, Babooska of the Holy Goat, or whatever else the legislative body might be called are divided among the parties based on the votes they receive. All of the parties that pass the qualifying threshold and get more than a certain minimum percentage of the vote (for example, at least 5 percent) win seats in the elected body. Once a party qualifies, the number of people taken from the party's list of candidates is based on the proportion of the vote the party has received; thus it is a proportional system.

Returning to the astoundingly wonderful figure I have been using throughout this most excellent chapter, I can use the spatial depiction of voters in Figure 10.4 to explain why political parties in proportional systems tend to proliferate like rabbits.

For the sake of the discussion, let's start out with two parties, A and B, fighting over the large number of voters near the center of the political spectrum. I could have started with a billion parties, or thirty-seven parties, and still have ended up in roughly the same place. However, starting with two makes it easier to make comparisons to the two I ended up with

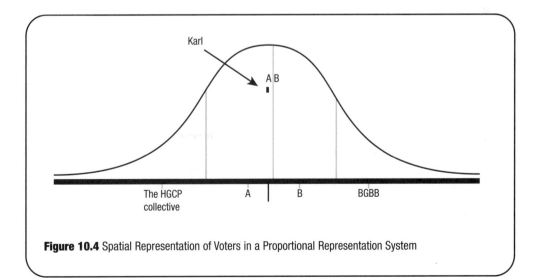

Figure 10.4 Spatial Representation of Voters in a Proportional Representation System

Not Quite Right, but Still Good

when I talked about the dynamics of a winner-take-all, single-member district system like that of the United States.

If you start out with two parties, each striving to dominate the political system by winning the most votes, both parties have the motivation to move toward the ideological center. People will vote for the party that is closest to them on the great horizontal line of ideology that defines all political beings. That means that the moderately liberal Party A will get the votes from the vertical line of political division separating it from the moderately conservative Party B along with all the votes out to the extreme left-hand edge of the spectrum. Since Party A is slightly closer to the center than B, the dividing line between them is on the right-hand side of the middle, and Party A will capture the greatest percentage of the votes. It is also true that since the seats in the parliament are divvied up to match that percentage, Party A will win the greatest number of seats in parliament and will have the majority it needs to win all the important parliamentary votes. Specifically, this means that Parliamentary Bill 56448 will pass, and all the members of Party B will have to sit on the wobbly old folding chairs at lunch.[*]

The problem with the strategy of capturing the middle is that it moves moderately liberal Party A away from the people out on the extreme left. Those people are quite dissatisfied with the arrangement, and they want representatives that better reflect their preference for beanbag chairs sewn out of the hemp cloth that they are finally willing to admit is too scratchy to use for underwear. Any rational political entrepreneur will quickly capitalize on the opportunity presented by this dissatisfaction by forming a party specifically to address the interests of this disenfranchised community. Thus, the Hemp Grower's Cooperative People's Collective (HGCPC) is born. The HGCPC assimilates the votes all the way in to the midpoint between it and Party A, thus capturing all the votes from the extreme left. In the example for the winner-take-all system, this leads to disastrous results for the interests of those supporting the new party. In each of the single-member local districts the extremely liberal HGCPC steals votes from the party closest to it, the moderately liberal Party A, and so the HGCPC actually helps moderately conservative Party B's candidates. Thus, it is irrational to form the new party, because in the election it will help the party furthest from it ideologically to win a majority of votes in districts where Party A might have had a slight edge.

In a PR system, however, the result is notably different. Voting is national, not local, and the key to success is the overall percentage of votes that the new party can get over the whole nation. If the HGCPC can capture more than the minimum percentage of votes, the qualifying percentage, it wins seats and wins the right to vote in the legislature. In fact, if the HGCPC can win just enough seats to prevent either Party A or Party B from holding

---

[*] Yes, lunchroom chairs are another dumb-ass example, and yes, I'm going to push it far beyond the bounds of prudence. Live with it.

more than 50 percent of the seats in the legislature, then it suddenly holds a power far beyond the number of voters it actually represents. In a PR system the new party suffers none of the frustration it would in a winner-take-all system, as it can immediately become an essential actor. It is essential because it controls the votes that either of the two big parties will need to get any bill passed in the parliament. Therefore, the HGCPC must be included if either party wants to get anything done. In any conflict or dispute between Party A and Party B, the support of the new party is necessary to win. Thus, both of the other parties have to cater to the needs of the HGCPC, and scratchy hemp beanbag chairs fill the lunchroom. Resistance is futile.

The dramatic gains in influence by the HGCPC do not go unnoticed, and nobody in their right mind wants to try to eat a tofu chili dog while sitting in a beanbag chair.[†] Thus, a new party springs up on the right, the Beer Guzzling Bambi Butchers (BGBB), whose members stagger in from their hunting lodges to offer a new alternative to this horrible state of affairs. Beyond an affection for bazookas, the new party hopes to capture enough seats to become an essential actor and redecorate the lunchroom with Barcaloungers and antlers. The proliferation of parties has begun. Any dissatisfied group, regardless of what kind of chair they have an unnatural obsession for, can offer up their own party. The only limiting factors are the percentage of votes needed to pass the qualifying threshold and gain at least one seat, and the strategic need to capture enough seats either to dominate or to be big enough that one or more of the other parties will need the new party to win the majority of votes in the parliament. Typically, this results in one or two large parties near the middle of the political spectrum and a large number of smaller parties vying to become just big enough to tip the scales for one of the larger parties. The lower the qualifying threshold, the easier it is to get a seat, and the greater the number of smaller parties there tend to be.

Israel provides what may be the best example of the proliferation of parties in a proportional representation system. With a qualifying threshold set at only 2 percent of the vote, Israel's 2006 election saw the seats in its Knesset split among ten parties as it took only 62,000 votes for a party to pass the 2 percent qualifying threshold and win a place in the Israeli government. This number of qualifying parties was down from 2003, when the threshold was only 1.5 percent, or 47,000 votes, and thirteen parties won seats. This is probably the extreme example of both a low qualifying threshold and the number of parties with seats.

The type of elections used to create a modern democracy is not an either-or proposition. Mixed forms are abundant. France has a PR system to select its legislature but also a popularly elected president selected in a winner-take-all national election. New Zealand elects some of its parliamentarians in a national proportional representation election and others as winner-take-all representatives of geographic districts. Neither method of electing

---

[†] If this stereotype upsets you, feel some sympathy for the conservatives who get it in the next sentence.

representatives is inherently superior to the other, nor has any particular mixture shown itself to be the magic combination to produce a perfect representational democracy.

New Zealand Elections—I'm Not Making This Up, Honest

On September 17, 2005, during the breaks between that weekend's National Provincial Championship rugby matches, New Zealanders voted. Other than the way political careers in the Southern Hemisphere swirl in the other direction when election results send them down the drain, the election seemed quite typical, except perhaps that a heck of a lot of people voted twice—and it was legal. When New Zealanders vote, they cast a vote for both their party preference, as you would in a proportional system, and a vote for a local representative, as you would in a single-member district system. It seems that when it came to the question of using proportional representation versus single-member districts, Kiwis formed a committee that took the sensible route of choosing neither and both. We know a committee made this choice because the resulting system is something that only a committee or an insane mathematician could have created. Or perhaps it was a committee of insane mathematicians.

There are many sane and simple ways that such a dual system could function. You could have two legislative houses, one filled through the proportional party vote and one filled through the election of the district representatives. Or you could have a single house with some proportion of the members selected through the party vote and the rest chosen to represent specific districts. Of course, if you are a committee, you will choose neither of these reasonable options. Instead, the Kiwi system is a little more complex and provides plenty of jobs for mathematicians. That is why I suspect the original committee was populated by insane mathematicians who were looking for a little extra weekend work on the side.

In New Zealand, a party that gets at least 5 percent of the party vote *or* has a candidate win an electoral district qualifies for parliament. Thus, in 2005, eight parties qualified. The Labour and National Parties won large percentages of the party vote and several electoral seats; New Zealand First and the Green Party won no electoral districts, but each received just over 5 percent of the vote; and four parties won an electoral district each but far less than 5 percent of the party vote.

Now follow carefully, this is where it gets a bit bumpy.

Once a party qualifies, its percentage of the party vote is used to determine the number of places it gets in the 120-seat parliament. The important detail that makes it insane is that the proportional distribution of seats according to party vote is applied to the entirety of the 120 seats in parliament. Kiwis do not allocate 69 electoral seats to the winners of the 69 electoral districts and then allocate the rest proportionally. Instead, they allocate all 120 seats according to the percentages of the party vote won, *and* the candidates who won electoral districts both count against a party's total number of seats won with the party vote

and they must be seated first. Thus, in 2005, the 31 Labour Party candidates who won electoral districts were seated in parliament, and they were subtracted from the 50 seats that the Labour Party won with its percentage of the party vote. This left 19 seats to be filled from the Labour Party candidate list.

At first, this system seems to nullify much of the motive for campaigning to win individual electoral districts (called electorates in New Zealand). However, if you go back to the "or" in the definition of the qualifying threshold, it is possible to see how—unlike the United States, where single-member electoral districts serve to exclude smaller parties—in New Zealand these electorates provide a mechanism for the smallest parties to establish or sustain a foothold in parliament. Any MP with solid support in his or her electoral district can keep a party alive as long as he or she can win that district and qualify the party. Once the party is qualified, it takes only a tiny percentage of the overall party vote to bring another party member into parliament to join the winner of the district. Thus, in 2005, when a policy shift by the large National Party subsumed many of the issues championed by the ACT Party and threatened the political survival of the ACT Party, party leader Rodney Hide focused all of his efforts on winning his electorate, and he was able to keep the party alive by winning it. Even though ACT New Zealand won only 1.5 percent of the party vote, it qualified by winning an electorate, and it had just enough of the percentage of the party vote to get a second seat to add the first person on the party's candidate list. It was still desperate times for ACT, and Mr. Hide lost his district in the 2008 election, casting doubt over the future of the party, but it stayed alive in 2005 because winning a single-member district kept it qualified.

This is in sharp contrast to the Green Party in 2005. The Green Party won more than three times as many party votes as ACT, but none of its candidates won individual electorates. With just 5.07 percent of the party vote that was counted on election night, Green Party members were biting their nails as every last absentee ballot was counted to determine whether the party qualified in the 2005 election. It came down to a matter of a couple thousand votes to determine if the Green Party would get six seats in parliament or none, and this uncertainty drastically reduced the party's leverage as a potential coalition partner in the new government. ACT, on the other hand, knew for certain it qualified, and even with just two seats it had far more leverage.

This is still not the most interesting aspect of the New Zealand system. What happens when a party wins more electoral districts than the number of seats the vote percentage entitles the party to fill? In 2005, the Maori Party won four electorates but only enough party votes to earn two seats in parliament. How does that fit into the scheme in which the electorate seats count against a party's total in the proportional system?

For a committee of insane mathematicians the answer is simple: you bring in a couple of folding chairs and seat 122 MPs in a 120-member parliament.

FRANÇOIS-MARIE AROUET

Team: **French Exiles**

Position: **Deep Point**

Status: **Free Agent**

You've probably never heard of **François-Marie Arouet** (1694–1778), but then you've also probably never heard of his more famous pen name Voltaire either. I considered grousing about that and inserting a snipe or two about the shortcomings of an educational system that could leave you so ignorant and so on, but it seemed like such an obvious thing to do that I thought I'd just change things up a bit and say how wonderful it is that you don't know anything at all about Voltaire. My logic is simple. If you don't know anything about Voltaire, then I have to teach you about him, and that means job security. So, hooray for a failing public school system.

Voltaire was French, but he was kicked out of France by the king, so he couldn't have been all bad. He was also a central figure in the development of modern liberalism. He was a playwright and poet who also write histories of questionable accuracy, and, most important, he wrote philosophical treatises. He wrote vigorous arguments supporting freedoms of speech and religion and the right to a fair trial, ideas that would later become central elements of most democratic systems in the world.

He did not write specifically about democracy, and his less-than-kind opinion of the masses probably would have made him cringe at the idea of universal suffrage, but the liberalism he espoused is critical to modern democracy. It may even be the necessary element of democracy. A vote means nothing without the freedom to debate, the freedom to disagree, and the freedom to try to convince others to join you to express that disagreement in the vote. Thus, it's to Voltaire that we owe a significant debt for those and other elements of freedom and fairness that define a functioning democracy.

THE REAL VERSUS THE IDEAL, AGAIN

Democracy in its ideal form holds great promise. The idea of the will of the people is one that has great symbolic and emotional appeal. It is so powerful that the rationale the United States used for entering into World War I was to "make the world safe for democracy." However, in the real world democracy is fraught with problems. Thus, to meet the conditions of the real world the common definition of the term *democracy* has undergone some changes. When we speak of democracy, we are no longer necessarily referring to **majoritarianism,** rule by the majority. In reality we have infused democracy with elements that are actually quite undemocratic. After all, freedom of speech, protection of minorities, freedom of the press, and freedom of religion are not democratic in any sense of promoting the majority's will. They are, in fact, limitations on what the majority can do to often unpopular minorities and ideas.

The modern definition of democracy has really been stripped down to its bare essentials. In his work *Capitalism, Socialism, and Democracy,* Joseph Schumpeter strips the term of all values. Instead, he sees it merely as a method of reaching decisions: "The democratic method is that institutional arrangement for arriving at political decisions in which individuals acquire the power to decide by means of a competitive struggle for the people's vote."[11] Gone is any attempt to infuse democracy with a notion of improving people's lives. This definition also is broad enough to encompass the many different ways of counting votes. We are left with a method of governance that is clearly not perfect but has still managed to inspire people to great acts of courage. It is the reality of democracy that led Winston Churchill to assert: "Many forms of government have been tried, and will be tried in this world of sin and woe. No one pretends that democracy is perfect or all-wise. Indeed, it has been said that democracy is the worst form of government except all those other forms that have been tried from time to time."

KEY TERMS

Arrow's theorem / 257

direct democracy / 260

first-past-the-post system / 269

initiatives / 260

majoritarianism / 279

median voter / 270

referenda / 260

republic / 259

tyranny of the majority / 259

winner-take-all system / 269

CHAPTER SUMMARY

While most people would argue that democracy is an ideal to which all nations should aspire, in reality, democracy has its problems. As the 2000 presidential election in the United States demonstrates, even long-established democracies have sometimes had problems in figuring out which candidate has actually won an election. In fact, in any election in which there are more than two candidates, the way votes are tallied will affect the outcome. Thus, every democratic system is flawed. Most people today think of democracy as the use of elections for the selection of governmental representatives; however, democracy actually means *rule by the people.* Giving all people the opportunity to rule can create problems, because the majority can overrun the minority, and people have come to expect that democratic countries will protect minority rights. While some democracies make use of the direct-democracy mechanisms of referenda and initiatives, most democratic countries are republics. Republics also have problems; for example, the type of elections that a nation employs will affect which candidates are elected. A winner-take-all system is likely to produce moderate candidates in a two-party system. Students should learn two very important lessons from this chapter. First, no nation can claim to represent its people perfectly; all systems, even democratic ones, are inherently flawed. Second, if you've ever thought someone was "a vernacular term to denote the back end of a horse" and wanted

to mobilize the electorate to do something about it, the state of Washington just might be the place for you.

STUDY QUESTIONS AND EXERCISES

1. Imagine that it is possible to have "electronic democracy"—that it is possible to have everyone vote via computer each night on the most important issues in the news. Further imagine that we have managed to get rid of any security concerns with electronic voting. Would you want this type of democracy? Why or why not?

2. What is the connection between the type of electoral system a country has and the number of parties it has?

3. Explain Arrow's theorem and how it is possible that different electoral systems can reach different results.

4. In most modern democracies, sizable proportions of the people who are eligible to vote do not actually turn out on election day. How might variance in voter turnout among different parts of the population affect the predictions of democratic theory? Can you think of any other pesky real-world factors that might affect the predictions of the idealized theories of democracy discussed in this chapter?

5. What four factors are critical to the effectiveness and the remarkable endurance of the U.S. political system?

6. Do you believe that the use of referenda and initiatives is a good idea? Why or why not? If you were going to propose an initiative or a referendum, what would it be?

7. Which state does Al Franken represent?

WEBSITES TO EXPLORE

http://cepa.newschool.edu/het/profiles/arrow.htm. The New School's Kenneth J. Arrow page, part of the History of Economic Thought website, provides a biography of and links to information about Kenneth Arrow.

http://edibleballot.tao.ca. The Edible Ballot Society, which criticizes elections, promotes people protesting by eating their ballots; recipes are included.

www.ciconline.org/elections. This site contains eLECTIONS, a very basic simulation of presidential elections that also has information about the U.S. electoral system.

www.fairvote.org. FairVote, the Center for Voting and Democracy, is an organization dedicated to electoral reform. This site provides news and information about elections.

www.iandrinstitute.org. The Initiative and Referendum Institute at the University of Southern California reports about initiatives and referenda and their uses.

www.vote-smart.org/index.htm. Project Vote Smart offers information about candidates and issues across the United States.

Media, Politics, and Government
Talking Heads Are Better than None

Many people mistakenly believe that plague, pestilence, war, and Will Ferrell hoisting his Oscar are the four signs of the apocalypse. It might be prudent to stockpile some Cheesy Poofs and other survival necessities before Will strips down to his tighty whities during his acceptance speech. However, as any hybrid-driving, eco-certified Brit will tell you, the real harbingers of doom, the true riders of the storm that will end all time, the legendary four horsemen of the apocalypse, are named Jeremy, James, Richard, and The Stig. They seem harmless enough, kind of goofy actually, and if you didn't know any better you might think they were just a few old guys who somehow ended up with a TV show that gave them an excuse to act like teenage hoons, but the greenies know better. There is little doubt that they will destroy the earth, and possibly the better neighborhoods on the moon as well. Even if you don't want to take the word of Jonathon Porritt, the Supreme Coequal of the Organic People's Infantry, you can just look at the evidence of evil that surrounds them. The Stig, once described as more machine than man, drove a rocket-propelled car off the end of an aircraft carrier and crashed into the ocean, but apparently to no ill effect. He was back the next season, a little paler and a little shorter, but otherwise none the worse for wear. When the undead begin driving cars very, very fast, clearly evil is afoot.

Actually, to quote another Brit, the *Top Gear* guys do seem to be "mostly harmless."[1] They test drive the kinds of cars that require bank-shattering mortgages to purchase, which in its own way is kind of funny, since the kind of people who could afford to buy that kind of car would never watch a show about three guys and an Imperial Stormtrooper acting like jackasses. They also compete in their own stupid little challenges, like turning cars into boats or riding $500 motorcycles from one end of Vietnam to the other or playing darts by using a pneumatic cannon to launch used cars at a

travel trailer.* Still, even if you consider the fact that Jeremy pretty much always cheats, or that they once accidentally set fire to an automated carwash, nothing they do seems all that apocalyptic. That's because what they do isn't the problem. The problem is that they do what they do on television.

It's not the CO_2 emissions The Stig generates by racing around in cars that get four miles to the gallon, or the environmental impact of destroying a Chevy Corvette with a helicopter-mounted Gatling gun. What worries environmentalists is the fact that *Top Gear* is one of the most popular shows on the BBC. Greenies worry themselves sick over the way that *Top Gear*'s millions of viewers in hundreds of countries might imitate or react to the amusingly stupid and crass things that Jeremy, James, Richard, and The Stig do. Officials of all types worry that people will hurt themselves or others trying to imitate the foolishness they see on the show. Petrol[†] station attendants worry that fans of the show will try to turn their minivans into homemade convertibles and end up destroying automatic carwashes everywhere.

Actually, to be fair, environmentalists do have reason to worry. Even if only a very small percentage of *Top Gear* viewers are convinced to spend that little extra for the higher-performance model next time they buy a car, that would mean tens of thousands of people could be purchasing cars with the bigger, hungrier engines that the show features, and the cumulative effect would be tremendous. Perhaps even more worrying for environmentally concerned elites and organizations is the way that the show frequently undermines the seriousness of the green message. When *Top Gear* does give in to the political pressure to highlight environmental issues and concerns, the boys inevitably twist it around into a joke. A segment on the future of mass transit consisted of testing the qualities of different kinds of buses by racing them on a rally-cross course. For entertainment value, there is nothing quite like watching a double-decker and a bendy bus banging doors as they race around a winding gravel track, but what kind of message does it send about using mass transit to reduce congestion and pollution? When testing a hybrid car, they raced it against a BMW with a massive engine and showed that when the BMW kept pace with a hybrid that was being pushed as fast as it would go, the BMW was actually more fuel efficient. The *Top Gear* guys claimed the point of that stunt was that mileage is more about how you drive than it is about what you drive, but for environmentalists, that reasonable point was a distant second to the damage they believed their campaign suffered by having such an important part of their message twisted into an embarrassment. After all, what was not part of that segment was any effort by the *Top Gear* guys to show how much fuel a high-mileage vehicle could save when driven properly.

Actually, to be fair, the *Top Gear* guys do produce some truly informative segments on minimizing fuel usage, such as comparing diesels to hybrids or showing how to stretch

---

*Pronounced "caravan" in British.

[†]Pronounced "gas" in American.

mileage so much that you can drive from London to the tip of Scotland and back on a single tank of fuel, or a variety of other challenges for which the point of the contest is getting from one place to another economically.

Actually, to be fair, there are so many ways to interpret the sniping between the *Top Gear* guys and Britain's ecowarrior bots that I could start another hundred paragraphs with "Actually, to be fair." Welcome to the power of the mass media.

Actually, to be fair, this is only a small part of how the media affect politics.

REALITY AND BEYOND

If the question of media's role in politics concerned just the multiplicative effect of mass communication, this would be a simple and short chapter. I could use a few communication theories to talk about factors related to the effectiveness of message transmission, such as signal-to-noise ratios, and I might talk a little about what makes a persuasive political argument, and that would be that. However, the effect of media goes far deeper than that, all the way to the nature of reality kind of deep.

Questions about the very nature of reality seem to be common in fiction of all sorts. In the *Matrix* movie trilogy, the whole story centers on the idea that what we call reality is actually a virtual reality designed to keep our minds content as our bodies are harvested for energy. The trilogy begs the question of why those responsible for the virtual reality we live in don't make the weather better, which would really make us happy in our slimy little energy pods, but the way *The Matrix*[2] and its sequels take on the questionable reality of reality is not all that new. In Ursula K. Le Guin's classic novel *The Lathe of Heaven,*[3] the main character changes reality and changes history through his dreams. In Marge Piercy's *Woman on the Edge of Time,*[4] the possibly insane main character skirts along an indistinct border between fantasy, insanity, and what might be time travel, constantly testing and questioning the definition of reality. *Alice in Wonderland*[5] has been connected with everything from quantum mechanics to the advocacy of recreational pharmaceuticals, but the way the story questions the nature of reality is perhaps its most interesting inquiry.

I do not even have to resort to bizarre fantasies in which impossibilities are tossed around like a poodle in the dryer. Magic, ghosts, vampires, imagined futures, possible pasts, that perfect family on the sitcom, a sexy spy who never quite dies while thwarting the latest attempt to conquer the world, the movie cowboy who saves the town that never actually existed, time travel in any form—fiction of all kinds is all about immersing the reader or viewer in an alternative reality for the duration of the story. This act constantly challenges assumptions about the nature of reality, if only by saying this could be or that could have been.

As a more believable fictional bending of the reality of politics some might point to *Wag the Dog,*[6] in which a U.S. president, facing a sexual scandal remarkably similar to the one President Clinton bumbled his way through, decides to create an imaginary war to distract

the public. For the politicians and the public, this imaginary war is as real as any other. Some might point to that movie to illustrate this point, but I will not. A better movie is *Capricorn One*.[7] Well, it may not actually be a better film. In fact, it is bad to the point of atrociousness,* but it is a far more obscure movie—one that you have probably never heard of—which makes me sound smart for knowing about it. It also fits better with some of the specific conceptual points I want to make in a chapter about the news media and politics.

The basic plot of *Capricorn One* is that one of the biggest moments in history was a complete fiction. The United States never actually landed on Mars and may not have landed on the moon. Instead, the whole NASA program was faked on a soundstage. In addition to the really nifty 1970s haircuts, the movie raises the question of whether or not the moon landings could have been faked. Is all that stuff in the textbooks and at Cape Canaveral just part of an elaborate hoax? The sane person's answer is no. The *MythBusters* team did a special episode in which they busted every single one of the myths underlying the moon landing conspiracy arguments, but there are plenty of websites out there that argue for the hoax and conspiracy.

What is the reality? Or, more important, how do you know what the reality is? *You* did not personally land on the moon. But you probably believe it happened. You also have beliefs about the reality of politics, but, like landing on the moon, most of the things you accept as part of the political reality are things that you have not directly experienced. Political reality is a **mediated reality.** That is, it comes to us through channels of information flow, primarily through the news media. In order to develop a critical understanding of politics and government, we need to understand first how information is selected, sorted, and presented to us through the news media to create what we believe to be reality.

THE WHOLE CHINA CHARADE

Many people believe that China exists. Don't feel bad if you are one of the many who have been duped. The global order of restaurateurs has concocted an impressive conspiracy of deception to sustain the illusion of that "country's" existence. The depth and extent of their effort is extraordinary, including creating a whole language complete with a system of writing that does not even use an alphabet. Then there's all of the work that went into faking all those maps in all those books. They even got supposedly "Chinese" athletes into the Olympics. How many bribes to the Olympic officials did that take? Still, anyone who is willing to do a little Internet research knows that "Chinese" food was actually invented in Manhattan's Upper West Side by Rachel Wise's great-granduncle Eli, who ran a delivery service but had nothing to sell that people wanted him to deliver.

---

*It is so bad that the only way I would ever give it two thumbs up is if I had a hundred hands. Two on a scale of a hundred still sounds a bit generous for this one, but hey, I'm a nice guy.

More seriously, how do you know China exists? If you haven't been to China, if you have not wandered down a Shanghai alley to a restaurant where you ate a bowl of soup that had a fishy, almost licorice taste that made you truly afraid to ask what the chewy bits were, how can you be sure that China exists? The answer that usually is offered is that there is just too much evidence that there really is a China for all of it to be faked. Even if you funded the China scam with every bit of the profits from the $6.83 billion that New Yorkers spend each year on Chinese takeout, a charade that monumental is just too much to pull off. It is too complex. Language, history, maps, Jackie Chan movies, the diplomats at the United Nations—why, the language thing alone would take way more work than it took to make up Klingon.[*]

If China is real—and I am not admitting anything by using that hypothetical—then what else is real? Are you sure? How many other things are there that you have not experienced directly that are actually real? The simple answer is that most things you believe to be real are things that you have never experienced directly, and the distinction between the realities you have personally experienced, or **experiential reality,** and the other things you take to be real, **agreement reality,** can be useful for understanding media and politics.

If you think about it, you'll realize that most of the things you believe to be true, most of your reality, consists of things that are outside your direct experience. From men on the moon to wars in places you never knew existed, to the money that changes hands in an eBay auction, to a date that does not end with a restraining order—how many things, processes, or other aspects of the world do you believe to be part of reality even though you have never personally seen them or experienced them?

This is particularly true in the study of politics. There is almost nothing about government or politics that you experience directly.[†] It is almost all agreement reality. At most, a few hundred people witness the workings of Congress on any given day. When was the last time you had a heart-to-heart talk with the prime minister of Tonga? Does Tonga have a prime minister, or a king, or is it the little island in the middle of the Pacific ruled by a magic goat? All of the decisions, all of the wars, all of the votes, all of the meetings—how much of the politics that affects your life do you actually witness or directly participate in? Most of the reality of politics is agreement reality. You come to believe that one political thing or another is true by putting together bits and pieces of information, much like the way many of you have been bamboozled into believing China exists. Moreover, how those bits and pieces of information are brought to you and how you use them to create your view of politics are critical to your understanding of politics.

---

[*]For my readers who spent the better part of their teens perfecting their fluency in Klingon instead of getting decent grades in their science courses, I'm really sorry to be the one to have to tell you this, but Klingon isn't a real language. It was made up by the Romulan Tal Shiar for some kind of temporal special-ops mission that was supposed to keep humans from developing warp technology. Speaking of the Romulans, I also have some bad news about the Easter Bunny.

[†]With the exceptions of, among some other things, sales taxes, right-to-work taxes, income taxes, property taxes, Social Security taxes, speeding tickets, parking tickets, and endless waits at the Department of Motor Vehicles. It's just shocking that people don't adore government.

YOUR NEW BRAIN AND THE CREATION OF REALITY

While it is, or should be, obvious how the things you experience directly become part of your understanding of reality, the creation of agreement reality is a bit more interesting. Take science, for example. In a widely used textbook on social science research methods, Earl Babbie argues that science is not really about lab coats, test tubes, pocket protectors, and all those other must-have fashion accessories that you just cannot buy at the mall.[8] Instead, science can be thought of as a set of rules developed to help us decide when to accept something as agreement reality. By conducting an experiment according to certain rules, a scientist convinces others to accept the resulting fantastic discovery as part of reality. Babbie wants students to learn the rules of science so they can create new bits of reality by conducting research. Thus, science is an intergalactic effort to create agreement reality.

Science is not the only intentional way that people try to convince each other to accept something as reality. Think of education. The professor, instructor, or homeless guy your university hired from the bus station to lecture for your class is intentionally trying to build a specific reality for you to accept. Beyond the detailed outline of the course and this fabulous textbook, the bus-station guy is also using the authority bestowed upon him by the structure of the university. Even the structure of the classroom is part of it. Do not underestimate the effects of small details like the shabby suit coat with the patches on the elbows and that little lectern at the front of the class. After all, if the bus-station guy were still standing next to his stolen shopping cart full of returnable aluminum cans, would you sit there for fifty minutes and listen to him babble? Would you read what he told you to read? Would you try to learn what he was teaching?

There are other ways you add things that you have not directly experienced to your understanding of reality. Naive science is really fun. As little as an afternoon spent in the company of a toddler is enough to make just about anyone willing to believe that it is part of human nature to consider the world around us in terms of patterns of stimulus and response, causes and effects. Academics have formalized this approach to understanding the world in the various methodologies we call science, but science is still all about the basics of pudgy little fingers repeatedly poking at bugs in the garden and looking for patterns of action and reaction. The problem is that without the rules that scientists have created for scientific inquiry, this natural instinct can lead us astray. People try so hard to put things together and generally we want so badly to find causes for things that we often fool ourselves. Superstitions such as the doom brought about by black cats crossing your path, bad luck from breaking a mirror, good fortune from rabbits' feet, the lucky jockstrap, all of those things that we all believe or sort of believe arise from the natural human instinct to find causes for all the effects we see around us. This instinct is a big part of what allows humans to make globe-transforming inventions such as belly-button piercing, the beer keg, and the iPod, but it also makes people prone to fooling themselves about reality, and it

9.8 METERS PER SECOND PER SECOND

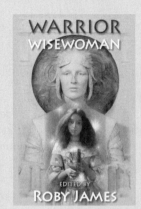

WARRIOR
WISEWOMAN

EDITED BY
ROBY JAMES

"Ungraceful Cliff Dwellers" is another almost-but-not-quite award winner, so it's probably fair to say it's a pretty good story. It's a little thin on violence and explosions, but it starts with a naughty bit, so that kind of makes up for it. "Ungraceful Cliff Dwellers" is a story specifically about how human societies use science and what happens when the cost of making new discoveries grows beyond the potential value of those discoveries. What happens when there is no real hope of

learning something new? For those of you who are already sick and tired of this class, and who probably have to smoke an antinausea "medication" just to get the nerve up to open this book, the idea of finally having discovered everything may not sound like much of an issue. However, even if you're not keen on the philosophical issues, gods, and the human drive to explore and discover and all that, consider the money. The economies of modern developed societies are built around growth through discovery and technological advance, so what happens when that goes away?

Douglas A. Van Belle, "Ungraceful Cliff Dwellers," in *Warrior Wisewoman,* edited by Roby James (Winnetka, CA: Norilana Books, 2008).

makes us susceptible to having our understanding of reality manipulated by people who want us to believe something.

For example, does a full moon really make people behave like insane wombats? This probably should come second to the question of whether there is any real difference between a sane and an insane wombat, but if you would just put that aside for a moment and let me finish what I was saying, we could get on with things. For a significant number of students, the insanity that is supposedly caused by a full moon is an unshakable, unquestionable part of their reality. How else can you explain waking up in the chemistry lab wearing someone else's clothes? However, even a quick search of the Internet[*] reveals that scientific efforts to find some actual evidence of this phenomenon consistently demonstrate that there is no such relationship. No matter what concrete thing you might use to measure the effect of a full moon, there is simply no evidence to support the claim that full moons cause insanity. Mental hospital admissions, arrests, injuries, emergency-room visits, accidents, overdoses, and alien abductions—none of these kinds of events are more common on nights with a full moon than on other nights. Yet many of you will continue to insist that lunacy is obvious; you have seen it.

The difficulty lies in the way that we humans perceive the world around us. We constantly see, hear, and smell far more than our brains perceive. The last time you walked into a classroom, your eyes saw every person sitting in there, but an instant after one of them

---

[*]Try a search with the keywords "full moon insanity research."

points out that you have arrived to take the midterm in your underwear, you would find it impossible to describe everything your eyes saw. At most, a couple of bits and pieces of that reality might stick in your head, for example, the sweaty rugby player who exceeds the legal weight limit for orange spandex bicycle shorts, the person(s) you find attractive, the uniform of the police officer waiting to talk to you about the events related to your over-nighter in the chem lab, or the vendor who is selling peanuts to the crowd of students waiting to see if you will—yet again—show up for a test wearing nothing but your worst set of underwear. Your mind uses a set of instinctual and learned filters, **cognitive frameworks,** for sorting the mass of incoming information and selecting which bits it will recognize and pass on to the thinking parts of your brain. Every person has several unique sets of mental filters, and you use different ones in different situations: being chased across a football field, driving a car, dating, going to school, hanging out with friends, or doing all of those things simultaneously. The diversity of frameworks that people use to filter informa-tion and make sense of the world is amazing, but there are a few predispositions that are common across all approximately sane people, and these are particularly relevant for this discussion.

When you are looking for something, you notice things that fit your existing beliefs and often fail to notice things that do not. When you search for something, you look where you expect to see it. If what you are looking for is not in a place you think it might be or should be, you will often fail to find it, even if it is sitting out in the open. More generally, when something fits with what you believe or expect, you are prone to notice or remember it in terms of the cognitive framework or understanding that was at the front of your mental queue at the time. Thus, if you believe in the whole moon and insanity connection, you are very likely to notice that there is a full moon out when you see someone knitting an invisible sweater and arguing with Millard Fillmore's ghost. You connect the moon and the insane behavior you just witnessed and chalk it up as further proof that your belief is valid. In contrast, you are far less likely to recognize or remember things that do not fit in with your belief. You are particularly prone to missing the absence of one of the two things connected by your belief. Seeing that same insane person in the afternoon, you are unlikely to notice that the invisible sweater is being knitted when there is no moon to be found in the sky. Similarly, when a night with a full moon is downright boring, you are unlikely to realize that this runs counter to your belief, and you are unlikely to think of it in terms of disproving the moon and insanity link.

In essence, you are prone to fooling yourself. Once you think the moon-insanity linkage or any other aspect of reality is true, you notice the things that fit that belief, and when you do, they reinforce the belief. However, you tend to miss contrary information. I've known this all along; it's the reason I gave you that whole bit at the very beginning of the book about using fiction to understand politics. I want you to use fiction to get around the beliefs you already have and the things you already know. I am trying to get you to step outside

the cognitive frameworks you have already created and consider other perspectives on politics and society.

Beyond the possibility of fooling yourself about things, the way you perceive things can create situations in which others, intentionally or accidentally, can manipulate your reality. By using a speech to provide a cognitive framework for understanding an issue, policy, or candidate, a politician can predispose people to interpret myriad facts and snippets in one way rather than another. By carefully choosing and building that framework, the politician can lead the public toward a desired conclusion. Some people call this **spin,** and others call it **framing.** Is global warming the absolute most totally dire threat the world faces? Is it all just liberal media hype? Is it a Canadian conspiracy? Should you blame the oil companies or vegan zombie vampires? While everyone has seen roughly the same information in the news, the reality created from the information depends largely on the particular framework you initially chose and how you have filtered information through that framework in deciding what to pay attention to. That framework provides organization to the overwhelming mass of information, and it shapes your reality.

NEWS MEDIA AND POLITICS

A vast proportion of the political information in your head comes to you through the news. In fact, modern politics is often discussed as mediated politics. I could even depict the very nature of politics as a process of strategic communication and social coordination that occurs through the content of the news media.

The news media provide an accessible, inexpensive, communal, and reliable source of information to form agreement reality about politics and government. As a result, the way the news media filter and select the information they print or broadcast, the way they present the news as stories, can favor certain cognitive frameworks over others. The processes and imperatives that operate in the news media can have a tremendous influence on how you understand the reality of politics.

Notice that I have carefully avoided saying or implying that the news media present an accurate reflection of political reality. You might think that, ideally, news media would provide us with a perfect reflection of political reality. Ideally, the media would be full of reliable and accurate information upon which we could base judgments and decisions. As with so much else about politics, however, the real is far from the ideal. And in this case, those imagined ideals are not actually the ideal media coverage. Ideals of media coverage reflect which of its many roles is invoked as its purpose, and these ideals never demand an accurate depiction of reality. They all involve selective distortions.

The image of politics presented to us by the media is distorted—drastically distorted—but not in the ways you might think. The conservatives may whine about a liberal bias in the news, paranoid people may make claims that various kinds of conspiracies are in the works, and liberals may agonize about evil corporations brainwashing us with the news,

THOMAS JEFFERSON

Team: American Eagles

Position: Spin Bowler

Status: Buried

It would be negligent to the point of criminal to write a chapter on the press and politics without highlighting the contribution of Stephen Colbert. **Thomas Jefferson** (1694–1778) was also kind of important.

Thomas Jefferson was so passionate about the essential nature of a free press in a democratic society that he said, "Were it left to me to decide whether we should have a government without newspapers or newspapers without a government, I should not hesitate a moment to prefer the latter."[a] His logic was quite simple: "The force of public opinion cannot be resisted when permitted freely to be expressed."[b] His passionate support for freedom of the press and freedom of expression is evident in the sheer volume of quotes attributed to him on the subject, but he also believed that these freedoms should be limited to the expression of truth. He made several statements that clearly show his opinion that libel, slander, and other damaging falsehoods should not be protected as free speech.

Also, if you look through the larger pattern of his statements on the subject, it becomes clear that Jefferson viewed the freedom of the press as more functional than ideological. The unhindered press is meant to serve certain social and political functions, such as exposing truths that selfish politicians might wish to keep secret, informing citizens, allowing discontent to be expressed, and enabling political debate. Someone searching for a more philosophical or artistic idea of the freedom of expression, as it might apply to fiction, literature, and free Internet pornography for all, won't find much from Jefferson on the subject.

[a]Letter from Thomas Jefferson to Edward Carrington, 1787.

[b]Letter from Thomas Jefferson to Lafayette, 1823.

but these and similar complaints almost never stand up to any kind of systematic scrutiny. They are a lot like the full moon connection with insanity. If you believe that certain things are happening, you see examples everywhere, but you also fail to notice the evidence that does not fit with your expectations. Still, the news media do not present perfect representations of reality, and you must examine the ways in which the news distorts, overemphasizes, or ignores information to fully appreciate how the media might best be utilized to understand politics. Once you know what the distortions are, you will be better prepared to deal with them in understanding politics or even acting politically.

The Business of the News

While movies and TV shows about newsrooms are less common than they used to be, there are still enough out there that you have probably seen at least a few here and there. Reruns of *WKRP in Cincinnati,*[9] *Murphy Brown,*[10] *NewsRadio,*[11] and even *The Mary Tyler*

Moore Show[12] can be found in the wee hours of the morning on many cable networks. Many movies, such as *State of Play*,[13] *Broadcast News*,[14] *Network*,[15] *The Paper*,[16] and *Fletch*[17]—I especially recommend *Fletch*—have some elements of the business of the news as part of their plots. The newspaper editor or TV news producer is always screaming about deadlines and trying to cut costs at every turn. The harried reporter is always trying to survive the pressure and fighting the constant demand to produce news. Everybody wants to grab the huge story that will beat the competition and blow everyone away. There is always some larger force, such as a corporation or a politician, trying to use power or money to stop a story or to get the dogged reporter off the case.

News is a business, a big business. No surprise there, and the truth about the business of the news is that the demands and limitations that arise from the drive to make money have tremendous, predictable, and consistent effects on the content of the news. These effects are not usually as dramatic or blatant as the movies would have us believe, but they are there. In fact, the subtle ways in which the demands of the business side of the news shape its content may be more important than the dramatic bits in stories about the news business.

First, a trick question: If the news is a business, it must sell a product. What is the product being sold by news outlets? The obvious answer is the news—the stories and pictures we see in newspapers and magazines and on TV.

Since this is a trick question, however, the obvious answer is not going to be the correct one. Of course, if I wanted to make it a really tricky trick question, I could have told you it is a trick question, then made it a question for which the obvious answer is the correct answer. Sort of a trick, trick question.

The answer to this relatively mundane and normal trick question is that the news outlets are not selling the news, they are selling *you,* or, more accurately, your attention.

Newspapers and magazines can be kind of tough to steal, so you might hand over a dollar or two here and there for that particularly important news package you have been eyeballing, and recently there has been a bunch of ballyhoo over getting people to pay for the news online and such. However, what you pay for the news is a pittance compared to the cost of producing something like a newspaper. Often, most or even all of what you pay for a hard copy of a newspaper goes to the person who delivers the paper to the puddle in your front garden or to the person who sells it to you from the newsstand. Even if every cent of the $1.50 or so you might spend on the paper were to go to the publisher, it would not begin to cover the cost of producing the paper. A daily paper for even a modest-size city has more text in it than a novel, and the Sunday edition of the *New York Times* is longer than all three volumes of the *Lord of the Rings* together, plus one of those bodice-ripping romances with a cover that features a girl passing out from the body odor of the hunky guy. In the United States, a paperback novel costs five or six times what a news-paper costs, and outside the United States it is more like ten to twenty times. In

New Zealand, a paperback book sells for twenty-five dollars and a daily paper costs just one little New Zealand dollar, about forty pence, three quarters of a euro, eighty U.S. cents, a hundred yen. There is no way a dollar or two, even multiplied by many subscribers, is going to cover the cost of the work put in by the hundreds, sometimes thousands of people who create the paper that you read while you eat your Cap'n Crunch cereal.

Not convinced yet? Think about this one: TV news is *free.*

What the news sells is your attention. Advertisers, with all the things they want to sell to you, pay good money for even a brief moment in front of your eyes, and the more eyes looking at a news product, the more the news outlet can charge for the space or time advertisers want. The audience is the primary product being sold by a news outlet; the actual news is only the means by which that audience is created. Everything about the business side of the news is focused on the audience as a product, and the cost of creating the audience must be balanced against the size and value of that audience. Thus, news outlets are constantly trying to find the story that will keep your eyes glued to the screen, but they want to do so as cheaply as possible.* Much of the politics of the news media builds from the tension between these two business imperatives.

The news itself may not be the product the news media are selling, but it is still the key to the commercial news industry. Everything about the news, down to the very structure of a news story, is focused on attracting an audience that can be sold to advertisers. The simple fact that we apply the word *story* to the presentation of the news is telling. All stories are structured based on the conflict-driven interaction of protagonists, antagonists, heroes, villains, and alien ninja robots. The conflict in a news story always has an introduction, a climax, and a resolution. News stories also have theme music. This is obvious on TV, where you can actually hear the theme music at the beginning of the stories, but even newspaper stories have theme music. It's just that most people don't realize they are supposed to hum the theme music for the news they read in the paper. Hum the intro music from *Raiders of the Lost Ark*[18] for a story about whatever country the United States happens to be invading, the theme from *Phineas and Ferb* for all those stories about kids falling in wells, and, of course, the chicken dance music for stories about the British Parliament. A full listing of news story musical themes, along with the sheet music, might be available on BarkingDeathSquirrels.com.[†]

The Political Soap Opera

One of the most important things to understand about the presentation of the news is that reporters write news items using the dramatic structure of stories, whether or not the news actually fits that structure. Thus, the complex and often interactive dance of a debate on a bill in the Israeli Knesset is discussed in terms of a simple conflict, a fight between its

---

*This explains all the stories about those newborn zoo animals. Aren't they just adorable?

†Yes, I own this domain name and check its usage stats regularly to see how many of you actually go there.

supporters and detractors, the struggle to pass or defeat the legislation. Even when a news event stretches out over days or weeks, every individual report still must be a story, and the conflict in each story must conclude with one side winning and the other losing some small battle within the larger war. A news story can be an episode within a larger story arc, but just as in a television series, every episode must contain within it a whole story that carries the larger plot forward. Thus, the coverage of a war, a large piece of legislation, an electoral campaign, a scandal, or a debate takes on the basic form of a television soap opera, with continuing episodes and a large cast of characters. Television soap operas are much better than politics at getting attractive people to play all the important parts. Seriously, Al Franken is funny, but certainly not pretty. Still, politics and soap operas are both presented in much the same way.

Actually, soap operas provide some reasonably good examples to help make sense of what makes one thing a better news story than another. The same things that are ridiculously overdone in the hyperdramatic afternoon shows that most people do not admit they watch are essentially the same elements that guide the selection of news stories and get overemphasized by reporters in their efforts to fit news into the dramatic story structure.

Conflict Makes the World Go 'Round

The first intergalactic law of the soap opera is that everybody is always fighting over pretty much everything. Wealth, power, love, sex, good, evil, the secret decoder ring at the bottom of the Cap'n Crunch cereal box, it doesn't really matter what the entire make-believe town is fighting over, it is always on the verge of Microsoft World War 3.7 beta. The wealthy bad guy, the nasty and aggressive woman, the confused young girl, the noble young man, the crazy lady who walks around with a puppet that comes to life when no one is looking, the aerobics-addicted housewife, the twenty-two-year-old brain surgeon, mix and match, there is always a web of conflict and it is a constant war in which everyone eventually ends up fighting with everyone else at one time or another. The conflicts in soap operas, like everything else in the soaps, are ridiculously overdone, but they are only an exaggeration of the most basic element of the dramatic story structure.

The very premise of the dramatic story structure is action and change driven by conflict. Antagonist and protagonist are locked in a death struggle that must be resolved. Thus, war is a better news story than peace, conflict on the campaign trail is sexier than candidates' explanations of where they stand on the issues, a trade dispute is more newsworthy than the trouble-free trading of billions of items between one place and another. This emphasis on conflict even extends to the norms of fairness and objectivity that journalists swear by. These norms exaggerate the emphasis on conflict even further. To be "objective," reporters will often provide equal coverage of the arguments of opposing sides in a story even if one side represents a near consensus. This exaggerates the conflict by making it look as though the disputants are locked in a debate, even if it is just one crackpot shouting about how real China is. This phenomenon shapes much of the coverage of global warming, for

example. There is a near consensus among scientists in every relevant discipline that human-driven global climate change is real; the only question is the magnitude of the problem and what should or should not be done about it. However, the minority of scientists who disagree get a disproportionate amount of attention and coverage because reporters are constantly trying to provide both sides of the lopsided debate with equal and fair coverage in their stories. This is an important point, remind me to get back to it later, but for now, it is important to note that the emphasis is on conflict in a literary sense, not violence. The struggle of man against man, man against nature, man against his nature, us versus them—these are the things that capture a reader's attention.

There is tremendous emphasis on conflict in the news media, but it is not just a fight that makes something newsworthy. More generally, newsworthiness has to do with presumptions about what will entertain the audience enough to keep them tuned in or turning the pages long enough to see the ads. What characteristics of an event or issue contribute to its ability to capture the attention of an audience?

Sex and the City

The second universal law of the soap opera is that sex sells. In every soap opera around the world just about every cast member is beautiful. It is hard to miss. In fact, just to make sure that the viewers realize that the actors are beautiful, all the women and about half the men in Mexican soap operas are forced to wear spandex pants and halter tops all the time. It is the law. The lone exception to this universal rule is New Zealand's biggest soap opera, *Shortland Street*,[19] which is filled with some very bad actors whose limited acting ability actually shines in comparison to their personal appearance. Further, promiscuity is so rampant in these imaginary little soap opera worlds that any character might be pregnant at any time and the paternity—sometimes even the maternity—of every baby is a mystery worthy of dramatic music at the end of each episode.

Sex gets people's attention, and this obvious fact is not lost on the editors, reporters, and producers responsible for creating news products to capture audiences for advertisers. While not all papers go so far as *The Sun* (London), which is famous for putting a full-page picture of a topless woman on page 3 in every issue, you can still see the evidence everywhere. Look at any magazine rack in any store in any country. At least half of the magazine covers will feature impossibly beautiful women: women made up, dressed up, lighted up, photographed, touched up, and Photoshopped to unattainable perfection. It doesn't even matter what type of news or information is under the cover. Fashion, personal advice, housekeeping tips, sports, photography, knitting, architecture, boating, motorcycles, cars—it does not seem to matter what the subject is or who the desired audience is, impossibly pretty women are the norm for magazine covers.

This imperative has ramifications beyond the fact that it effectively prevents the author of this text from ever looking out at you from the cover of a magazine. It also influences the

content of newspaper and television news by shaping the very idea of what stories should be covered. A sexual element adds to the presumed newsworthiness of a story, sometimes to the point that the media obsess over stories that are about little or nothing. In the 1990s, President Clinton's affair with Monica Lewinsky had almost no substance, and it took a valiant effort on the part of his political opponents to even come close to connecting it to his ability to lead the country. In the end it was not the actual affair that had political repercussions, but the fact that Clinton lied about having an affair.

While the president's choice to have a relationship with an intern might be slightly newsworthy, the real story was about little more than infidelity in the White House; yet it was all over the news for just less than three centuries. Sex, especially when it comes with a bunch of scandalous little details, such as an infamous stain on Monica's blue Gap dress, gets people's attention. Thus, it is newsworthy. More generally, think about all the news about the private lives of celebrities. Divorces, affairs, dates, and marriages of movie stars and athletes—why is any of that news? Where is Kardashia and why do we need a documentary on its "special" people? They are probably in the news because it is the adventure of the soap opera. The masses want to experience the sexual lives of impossibly pretty people vicariously.

Honey, the Dingo Stole Another Baby

The third interstellar law of the soap opera is that there is no such thing as a normal day. When is the last time a character on a soap opera got a cold? Ebola, leprosy, amnesia, spinal gingivitis, hysterical blindness, Bolivian brain fever, rabies—those are ailments you will see on the afternoon shows, but never a common cold. You can't just have a baby of indeterminate parentage, that baby has to be stolen by a dingo. Wild dogs carrying off children are surprisingly common occurrences on Australian soaps. You would think that after losing the first dozen or so infants, the impossibly beautiful residents of the fictional neighborhoods and outback outposts would put up fences or at least make a point of keeping their babies up and out of the dingoes' reach, but they don't. Pick any long-running U.S. soap and ask how many of the people have been kidnapped in that little town or been jailed for bizarre crimes they did not commit. The unusual is dramatic. Would you watch a show about a guy who rides the bus to work, shuffles papers for eight hours, rides the bus home, treats his hemorrhoids, orders a pizza, and watches TV until he falls asleep, and then gets up the next day to start it all over again? Unless something unusual or dramatic happens to that little bureaucratic troll, why would you want to watch?

Newsworthiness is related to unusualness, or the degree to which an event deviates from the norm. No one wants to read about the routine functions of government or the commonplace occurrences we all expect to happen. This is summed up with a classic and quite snappy snippet—the headline "Dog Bites Man" is not newsworthy; "Man Bites Dog," now that is something to write about. The more common something is, the less newsworthy

it is. Even if it is important, if it is commonplace it is not news. In Washington, D.C., murders are unfortunately common, sometimes numbering in the hundreds a year. Despite the other things that might make murders newsworthy, most of those murders do not make the front page of the paper or the TV news outside the Washington metro area, and some do not even make it into the local news. They are just too common. In New Zealand, where violent crime is rare, any murder is a national story even if it occurs more than a thousand miles from Auckland. Can you imagine New York newspapers covering every murder in Chicago? In North Dakota, an average blizzard seldom makes the news beyond the weather report. It takes a monstrous snowstorm before anyone other than the weather girl mentions it. In Florida, the threat of frost is a lead story and can cause panic buying of antifreeze, bottled water, canned goods, and electric blankets.

The Tragically Hip

The final hyperspatial law of the soap opera is that all of the sexy, unusual conflict is nothing unless it somehow is or could be tragic. The evil plot in Bay City is kind of boring unless it could destroy someone's life. The rare disease is no big deal unless it will spread to the whole town or kill the psychic half-alien baby that the dingo stole from the unknown father. The affair matters only if it will break up Bo and Hope. It just is not drama unless it has an impact on "real" people. If a tree falls in the woods and no one pretty is there to get crushed, who cares?

Human impact is one more aspect of newsworthiness. A small fire that destroys the home of a family is far more newsworthy than a huge fire out in the woods. Even when a wildfire hits the news, it is usually because it has begun to have a human impact, burning through another Sydney suburb, killing firefighters, or blanketing a city in smoke.

As a result, when we turn to the news, we see a world of war, death, and disaster. We see the rare and unusual events that have tremendous impacts on people. War is always newsworthy, peace seldom so. When we read the paper it seems like the whole world is at war all the time, but peaceful interaction between countries is the norm; war is the exception. The **dramatic imperative** of commercial news outlets distorts the news. Since we build much of our understanding of the reality of politics from this distorted image, awareness of this imperative is critical to our understanding of politics. It surprises most people to discover that cooperation runs rampant among the gladiators we elect to rampage around the political capitals of the world. Outside the United States—and, to be honest, even in the United States—politicians often agree on things and a great deal of stuff gets done, but these accomplishments are lost behind the bickering we see on TV and in the newspapers.

Will He Bring Balance to the Force?

As noted earlier, journalistic norms of objectivity and fairness actually make the distortions caused by the dramatic imperative, particularly the overemphasis on conflict, even more

problematic. How can the effort to be fair and objective possibly distort things even further? Glad you asked. If you are trying to be fair, it would not be objective to take a side in a conflict. The best way to cover a conflict objectively, even if it is a conflict that the reporter had to search hard to find among all that cooperation, is to present both sides of the issue on an equal and fair basis. The problem is that not all conflicts are made up of two reasonably equal sides. This can cause tremendous distortion when a journalist tries to be objective by presenting the views of a small but vocal minority on the same terms as those of a much larger majority. In the news, it almost always appears that two roughly equal sides are engaged in a battle to the death, but that is often not the case.

Nowhere is this more apparent, and more misleading, than in the coverage of policies and politics related to science education in the United States. Take, for example, the issue of teaching evolution in classrooms. It is a simple debate. In the blue corner, wearing a white lab coat and horn-rimmed glasses, is the "We evolved from pond scum" team, offering explanations for less evolved creatures such as politicians and lawyers. In the white corner, wearing fancy robes and tall mitred hats, is the "God did it in a week" team, offering explanations for the completely illogical animals that could not possibly have evolved, such as egg-laying venomous mammals like the platypus and all those Kardashians over there in Kardashia.

If you were to follow the debate over evolution in the general news, the clear conclusion you would reach is that Darwin versus God is a point of controversy and uncertainty. For every quote from a guy in a lab coat there is almost always an equal and opposite quote from the universe-in-a-week team. Stories about evolution are often presented as two sides in dispute over the validity of a theory, and both sides are presented fairly, which on the news means equally. This creates the image of scientific division over this subject, and you would be forgiven for concluding that Darwin's theory of evolution is a hotly disputed topic among scientists. You would be wrong, but still forgiven. While the assertion offends those who would rather not see evolution taught in the classroom, scientists of all stripes overwhelmingly agree—and I mean overwhelmingly agree—that the general framework of ideas that Darwin offered about the evolutionary process is the best conceptual framework for explaining critical aspects of the natural world. It is a tiny minority of scientists—most of them at small religious universities—who disagree. It is literally a dozen or so people disputing the scientific consensus supported by tens of thousands of scientists, but because of the news media's emphasis on conflict and fairness, whenever that tiny minority of scientists screams and shouts, it is covered on nearly equal terms as the overwhelming consensus.

Similarly, global warming is real, deal with it. I was going to say chill, but that was too much of a dorky pun, even for me. Point is that the scientific debate on climate change is so lopsided that the media have resorted to quoting former tobacco industry advocates such Steve Milloy as if he knew something about science in order to present climate

change as something that is scientifically contentious. It is a political conflict, and the rather hysterical efforts of deniers have built a significant number of believers of the denialist position, but this is not by any means a scientific debate.

Speaking of conflict, how many of you are sputtering and fuming right now? If you are growling as you try to find that fiddled-with bit of temperature graph that shows temperatures actually fell since 2008, don't bother e-mailing it to me. First, if you actually believe that a graph covering four years from one source of data disproves global warming, go back to the sixth grade and get a refresher on drawing graphs. Second, I seldom read more than a fraction of the e-mails that I'm contractually obligated to pretend I care about, so even if your very very importantly urgent e-mail gets past the spam filters that I have set to block exactly that kind of e-mail, I'm unlikely to read it or care about it. Third, ecofascists can't climb out from under that cloud of purple smoke long enough to agree on whether to worship or protest wind turbines. Do you really think they could run a conspiracy encompassing tens of thousands of scientists? Finally, quit hyperventilating long enough to go back up a couple paragraphs and take a look at what I said *is* a point of contention in both evolution and climate change: the politics.

The *politics* of climate change are a point of reasonably balanced conflict, and by this point in the book you should be starting to get a feel for what aspects of a political debate are amenable to influence. Assuming you aren't on the ecofacist side,* denying the science is a losing battle, or maybe a delaying tactic. If you seriously want to engage that issue and keep them from outlawing V-8s, better to jump in on the policy aspects of the debate. Personally, I prefer my corporate overlords to be techie and geeky, but if you want to go with Detroit, big oil, and coal, fair enough. Old school can be cool when it's done right, and by done right I mean the whole V-8 thing. Nothing quite like a supercharged V-8 interceptor racing through the outback to take on a motorcycle gang. And since we're talking about science I do have an issue with Mad Max's supercharger. I've never seen one you can turn on and off like that, and I don't think it's technically possible. And, uhmm . . . what was I ranting about? Probably doesn't matter. The whole section here had something to do with the media and balancing two sides or something. Whatever. I forget where exactly I meant to go with it so I'll just jump ahead to . . .

The political and religious aspects of the debate over evolution may be more reasonably depicted on equivalent terms. There is a clear division in the United States, and the political conflict is significant, with substantial numbers on both sides. Judging by public opinion polls, presenting the *political* debate over teaching evolution or climate change as two roughly equal sides does not distort reality too much, if at all. However, this is simply not true for the coverage of the science of evolution or climate change. The scientists agree, but the scientific consensus is ignored. Actually it is more distorted than that. The fact that

---

*If you are an ecofacist, whoa man, cool, go buy a Snickers bar and chill because for once I'm not making fun of you, honest.

there is an overwhelming consensus among scientists is almost completely buried by the media's business emphasis on conflict and the journalistic ideal of impartiality and fairness.

Elite Dominance of the Sources of News

Beyond the exaggeration of conflict and an obsession with odd or unusual things that have impacts on people, another way the journalistic presumptions of newsworthiness influence the content of coverage, particularly the coverage of politics, is by supporting a preponderance of elite voices in the news media. Elites, whether they rose to social prominence through politics, business, religion, athletics, entertainment, inheriting the fortune daddy made with his hotel chain, creating paintings of soup cans, or some other means, dominate the news. The latest matrimonial disaster of the aging rock star is all over the news, while your neighbor's divorce, despite the thrown dishes and juicy details about a dental hygienist named Trixie, is not. The opinion of the pope is news, but not the opinion of the local minister/waiter at Bob's Temple of Heavenly Pancakes. The president's musings on just about anything are global news, yours are not. George H. W. Bush (George Senior) made news all over the world for saying he hates broccoli. You have been saying that since the third week of second grade, when you finally learned to talk, and no one cares, least of all the news media. Even the all-star athlete who cannot spell *environment* is likely to get his expert opinion on that "globe warmin' thang" reported, while nobody quotes the environmental studies major who has spent her entire junior year obsessing about it from beneath a cloud of purple smoke.

The presumption among journalists is that elites, because they are already prominent focal points for society, are newsworthy. The actions or words of the president, the pope, an aging rock star, or a steroid-using athlete are going to capture or hold people's attention; they are going to contribute to drawing an audience that can be sold to advertisers. Elites are, by definition, unusual, and through their status they can often have tremendous effects on people's lives. Elites who fight with one another are even more newsworthy. Thus, when the aging rock star's divorce devolves into a fight over custody of the naughty home videos, the news media coverage is relentless.

A VAST CONSPIRACY?

Elites also have the motivation and the resources to actively try to gain beneficial news coverage. Actors might complain about the invasive paparazzi, but being the object of the public's attention is a big part of why producers pay $20 million for the star who can bring people in to see a wretched movie. Talent is often a secondary concern. How else can you explain Madonna starring in movies or the careers of any of the Baldwins other than Adam? Name recognition is perhaps the biggest factor in democratic elections, and it often does not matter where that recognition came from. Ronald Reagan, Jessie Ventura, Arnold Schwarzenegger, Steve Largent, Fred Grandy (Gopher from the *Love Boat* for the

JOHN MILTON

Team: **Dead Poets Society**

Position: **Short Fine Leg**

Status: **Free of Spirit**

When it comes to thinking of press freedom in philosophical terms, **John Milton** (1608–1674) is your go-to guy. Areopagitica: A speech of Mr. John Milton for the liberty of unlicensed printing to the Parliament of England,[a] was delivered in 1644, and it is the first, and perhaps the most magnificent, grand polemic ever to argue for freedom of the press.

In the speech, Milton quite literally referred to the freedom of the press. He was talking specifically about the right to publish books without prior censorship, and not the more general concept of freedom of expression and the right to voice dissent that we now think of as freedom of the press, but he was making that freedom of the press argument in philosophical terms. Milton drew support for his position through reference to classical history and theology, not the political or social-functional logic that would later dominate the American debate on the topic. In doing so, Milton planted the seeds of a more general notion of freedom of expression that would eventually find a great deal of support in philosophical and theological argumentation, and from those origins, the idea of more general artistic freedom arose.

Despite Milton's use of philosophical arguments and evidence, the speech itself was transparently political. Milton was unabashedly and quite obviously trying to flatter the English parliamentarians by comparing them and their country to the pinnacles of Greek and Roman civilization. He also blatantly pandered to the predominant religious factions in England with more than a little Catholic bashing. Still, despite such obvious political savvy, Milton failed. At first Parliament simply ignored him. He eventually had the last word, but by then he was too dead to care.

[a]The text is available online through several sources, one of which is www.dartmouth.edu/~milton/reading_room/areopagitica.

rerun-deficient), Al Franken—none of them won their first elections because the voters recognized their lifelong commitment to political service. A big part of why they won is that the voters recognized who they were. In democratic nations, the ability to gain coverage in the news media is tremendously valuable. It gets people into the theater, into the voting booth, or even out marching in the street. That attention can be used to create wealth or influence politics. Continued attention is usually necessary for someone to remain an elite public figure, and news media coverage can help sustain that attention.

Given a reasonable motivation to seek coverage, it should be no surprise that members of the elite actively do things to encourage the news media to cover them. Think of the red carpet at a movie premiere. What is that but a big event orchestrated for the purpose of getting the stars' pictures taken and, by association, creating public exposure for the movie? Or consider statements by publicity secretaries—elites often have employees they have hired just to get the media's attention. Or how about ridiculous stunts? Do you think

Britney Spears and her first, twenty-four-hour "accidental" marriage might have anything to do with a shortage of musical talent? Or how about Billy Connolly? As the waning of his comedic career became painfully obvious, he bungee jumped naked to get some news media attention for his tour of New Zealand. That's a lot of work to get the attention of a country with fewer people, but more sheep, than the state of Alabama.

For political elites, news coverage is even more of a consideration. In addition to being the focus of a great deal of public interest, political elites make decisions and take actions that have tremendous impacts on people's lives. Except for an occasional stalker or celebrity impersonator, the aging rock star does not have such a regular or substantial impact on people's lives. Votes in parliament and the decisions of a president can quite literally have life-and-death consequences when the bombs start falling. And for politicians, the ability to keep their jobs, the ability to get reelected, is often dependent on their attaining and sustaining favorable images in the news that most people rely on for their understanding of the reality of politics.

Elites want to get coverage and the media want to cover elites; it sounds like a conspiracy. In fact, the way that the news media feature political elites so prominently, combined with the value political elites place on generating favorable media coverage, makes the conspiracy obvious. Clearly, newspaper reporters are just zombified stooges of the rich and politically powerful. Every day, an e-mail arrives from The Man's office and outlines exactly what the day's news will look like. Reporters are not completely controlled, however. They get to choose every third adjective.

There is no conspiracy!

The prominence of conspiracies in discussions of the news, and the degree to which people truly believe that there is a conspiracy that defines the news, is hard to describe and even harder to explain. There are far too many people involved in the news media for any kind of conspiracy to ever be possible. It takes only one person—the weakest link—to blow the cover off of a conspiracy, and there are hundreds of thousands of very weak links in the chain between politics and the newspaper that gets thrown into your rose garden every morning. If there were a conspiracy, it would have to encompass thousands of people. Think about how hard it is to get your buddy to shut up about the moderately illegal string of events that led to your overnighter wearing someone else's ball gown in the chem lab, and then ask how hard it would be to keep up a conspiracy among thousands. As I have mentioned a time or two already, in any decent-size college classroom it is almost certain that there will be at least one person ready to enlighten the class with the juicy details about how liberal reporters and editors conspire to attack and defame any politician who dares represent the red-blooded American conservative majority while hiding the indiscretions of their liberal political brethren. In that same classroom will be a student— probably not the same student—arguing that the wealthy and conservative business elites who own media outlets conspire with editors and reporters and use their money to kill any

story or report that might bring the "truth" to the public about cars that run on switchgrass or other things that could save the environment or end poverty.

There is no conspiracy. Conspiracies have to be limited to three people, two of whom must be dead. People just will not keep their mouths shut.

The conservatives wailing and gnashing their teeth about the liberal news media have a hard time explaining the media's obsession with Bill Clinton and Monica Lewinsky or any of the other times the media have feasted on the carcass of a liberal politician. The liberals who are horrified that conservative big-business owners of the media are controlling everything we read have a hard time explaining the coverage of Watergate, Martha Stewart going to jail, Rupert Murdoch's recent troubles, or any other media evisceration of a conservative politician or wealthy media figure. It is that whole moon and insanity thing again. You notice and remember what you already believe to be true.

There is no conspiracy!

The Mutual Exploitation Model

The reality—if I dare refer to reality in a chapter on mediated politics—is that there is a tremendous coincidence of interests between the news media and elites. The result of this shared interest is not a conspiracy, but what is commonly referred to as a **mutual exploitation model** of the news-elite relationship. The news media exploit elites by using them for cheap sources of news that they know will interest the public. At the same time, the elites exploit the news media by using them to communicate with the public and present public images that will help their political, economic, and social ambitions. The reason there is no conspiracy is that there is no need for a conspiracy. For the most part, economic forces and self-interest drive the media and elites to choose to cater to each other's needs. You do not need mysterious men in trench coats causing "accidents" to befall those who stray. Reporters and editors will choose to cover elites, and they will tend to cater to the images those entertainers and politicians wish to present because they want to preserve future access to those newsworthy individuals. Elites will cater to the reporters' and editors' business needs and will give them the resources to produce inexpensive newsworthy copy whenever possible so that they can exploit the reporters in order to get images, ideas, and words to the public. Why in the world would you try to organize a conspiracy to do something that everyone is already doing?

Still, the biggest reason I feel comfortable arguing that there is no conspiracy is that, if given sufficient incentive, either side will turn on the other. Elites who use the media for their own political and personal ends will turn against the media and attack individuals or the entire system if there is enough benefit or if they are sufficiently angered. Richard Nixon used the news media's interest in him as a political elite to save his career. In the famous/infamous "Checkers Speech,"[20] Nixon used his pet dog to create the image of a real human being behind his political ambition and showed that he knew how, and was willing,

to use the media. Yet later, as president, Nixon viciously attacked the media. He threatened reporters and news outlets, trying to intimidate editors with threats of FBI and IRS investigations and generally being more unpleasant than a rabid walrus at a dinner party. A decade after Nixon used the media to salvage his career, he turned against it because he could gain politically by doing so. By arguing that the liberal media were creating a distorted image of his policies and the Vietnam War, Nixon managed to convince much of the public that the war looked worse than it actually was and the media, not the president or his policies, were responsible for how bad it appeared. Have you ever thought that it's ironic that Rush Limbaugh and other vocal conservatives attack the liberal media establishment from the platform of syndicated radio shows, radio shows that are broadcast on the stations of that same liberal media establishment? They attack the media because it gives them a salable point that a conservative audience wants to hear.

The way that politicians turn against the media, however, is nothing compared to the way the media will turn against a member of the elite if the story is sufficiently newsworthy, as the coverage of the Watergate scandal shows.

The Watergate Is a Hotel, No?

There is no better example of the political power of the press than Watergate. Not the Watergate Hotel, the Watergate scandal. It is a perfectly nice hotel and all, with curvy hallways, mints on the pillows, and freshly vacuumed carpets, but it is the political scandal associated with the hotel that every professor will point to when introducing the political role of the free press in a democratic society.

Even after several movies and books on the subject, some of the facts are still a little unclear, but roughly what happened was that Robert Redford and Dustin Hoffman were doing something in a parking garage and Hal Holbrook told them something naughty and the *Washington Post* fired President Nixon. Okay, that is not really even close to what happened, but you can always just go and watch one of the Watergate movies yourself.

What really happened is that during the 1972 U.S. presidential election campaign, the Democratic Party's election headquarters, which were housed just off one of those curvy halls in an office suite in the Watergate Hotel, were burglarized. Nothing much was stolen, and it never would have been much of an issue, except for the fact that two reporters, Bob Woodward and Carl Bernstein,[*] investigated and exposed a connection back to President Nixon. Once the sordid details of Nixon's illegal and unethical campaign tactics were reported by the *Washington Post,* it became impossible for the Nixon administration to bury, hide, or ignore the news story, and it eventually led to Nixon's resignation.

The real key to the Watergate scandal was the role that the press played throughout. The official law enforcement mechanisms of the U.S. government failed to expose the

---

[*]No relation to the bears.

burglary's connection to President Nixon—the reporters did. The official mechanisms of government also did not remove Nixon from office. They may have, if given enough time, but it was the public pressure created by the relentless press coverage that forced Nixon to resign from office. You can go further and argue that it was the public nature of the scandal that forced many of the official government agencies and processes to engage the scandal, and that engagement was critical to exposing the full extent of the criminal activities and keeping the scandal at the forefront of the public's agenda.

Even though Deep Throat is an awesome code name for a secret informant, some have vilified the man who tipped off Woodward and Bernstein, and others will argue that the news media should not have the political power that they demonstrated during the scandal. Still, what is made absolutely clear by Watergate is that the media play a huge role in modern democratic politics, and knowing something about the details of the Watergate scandal is an absolute necessity for anyone interested in the role of media in politics. Fortunately, it has been fictionalized for your protection. There is a book about the actual events, Bob Woodward's *All the President's Men,* but it is also the center of several films, so you do not even have to learn to read. It is in *All the President's Men* (1976), *Secret Honor* (1984), *Nixon* (1995), and *Dick* (1999), and you can find hints of it all over the place, from *Forrest Gump* to reruns of the *X-Files.*

The Watergate scandal may be the most obvious example of how the media will turn against even the most powerful of elites if the story is good enough. The relentless coverage of the issue was the prominent story across the news media for months and the subject of significant coverage for years. Watergate also shows that this kind of coverage has tremendous costs for elites who are at the center of a storm. Entertainment elites, political elites, any kind of elites always face the reality that any scandal or conflict they might get caught up in will be newsworthy and will get reported by news media obsessed with drama, regardless of the impact that coverage has on the elite individual.

Watergate also gives us a bit of insight in the democratic role of the press. Journalism not only exposed the illegal activities that cost Richard Nixon the U.S. presidency; the simple fact that every bit of that political catastrophe was so heavily and thoroughly covered was a significant factor in making it impossible for Nixon to remain in office. Media coverage was key to the end of Nixon's presidential career.[*]

Watergate is not the only example of a political career flushed down the toilet by a flood of news coverage. Because of media coverage, many democratic leaders have lost their offices or their standing as the result of far less substantial scandals. In fact, the effect of scandal goes beyond just demonstrating that the media will turn on the elites they are so fond of covering. The fear that a career-ending scandal creates in politicians may be the biggest part of how the news media keep democratic leaders from doing things for which

---

[*]Years after leaving office, however, Nixon enjoyed a resurgence as a domestic and international political elder statesman and analyst.

the public will punish them. It only takes an occasional Gary Hart or Gary Condit to convince other politicians that they should not change their name to Gary and to remind them that getting on the wrong side of a media scandal can cost them their entire careers. Gary Hart had a fair chance of becoming the Democratic presidential nominee until a picture of him wearing a blonde woman on his lap was sold to the tabloids. In a fit of unbelievable stupidity that transcends Bill Clinton waving his finger and saying that he did not have sexual relations with that woman, Hart had actually dared the media to follow him when rumors of an affair emerged. A few days later, he was caught sitting under a young blonde, on a yacht named *Monkey Business* of all things. Gary Condit's political demise is even more telling. After the disappearance of an intern who was both young and female, suggestions that he might have at one time or another smiled at her in the office spun into rumors of an affair, which led to stories about a murder conspiracy. There was no evidence or anything of that sort, but the relentless media coverage drove Condit from office. While many people will recall that part of the saga, few know about the evidence that later indicated that it was almost certainly a random attack in a Washington, D.C., park that led to the disappearance of the intern. That a politician might possibly, maybe, perhaps be involved was newsworthy. More than a year later, the fact that Condit was almost certainly not involved was not all that newsworthy. Or how about a South Carolina governor shacking up with an Argentinean woman on the side? Or a New York governor with a well-stamped customer loyalty card from a prostitution ring?

Of Cockroaches and Politicians

These media-induced political vivisections are significant not just in the way they remove misbehaving or unfortunate politicians from office, but also in how they influence the activities of other political actors or politics in general. The greatest fear of any modern democratic politician is to get caught in the middle of a media feeding frenzy over a scandal or disastrous policy. In fact, I can argue that the way the media can turn on a politician is the most important role the media play in democratic politics. Call it the **cockroach theory of politics**.[*] Like the beloved insects, politicians do not want to be spotted anyplace where they can be stomped on. When the media rip the liver out of a politician caught in a scandal, this tells all the other politicians they had better not do the same stupid thing, and you often see evidence of a scramble among other politicians or officials to avoid getting noticed for similar indiscretions.

As an anecdotal example, consider the case of the parking enforcement division of the police in an unnamed city that used to be in the middle of the swamps at the very end of the Mississippi River an hour's drive south of Baton Rouge. The parking police were well-known for their extremely aggressive enforcement of the city's bewildering codex of

---

[*] Yes, this is pretty much the same thing as the cockroach theory of bureaucracy I talked about in Chapter 8. Recycling is good, ask an environmentalist.

parking regulations. Some even carried rulers with them to measure the exact distance of tires from curbs, writing citations for cars that had one wheel as little as one-quarter inch over the maximum distance from the curb. Further complicating things, decades of poor maintenance practices meant that most of the city's streets no longer had anything that might be called curbs, in which case this exact and precise measurement was made in relation to the imaginary place where a curb might go.

Surprisingly enough, these valiant defenders of automotive order refused to confront the egregious activities of the most blatant and persistent parking renegades in the unnamed city that was hit by Hurricane Katrina. A facility that provided services to senior citizens was experiencing tremendous difficulties with people parking in a passenger-loading zone. The facility was located on Canal Street, a six-lane parkway that serves as a major thoroughfare into the city, and the curb in front of the facility was designated as a passenger-loading zone. At stake was the safety of the hundreds of senior citizens who were brought in daily from around the city for services ranging from physical therapy to small social events. This loading zone, however, was always full of cars that didn't just exceed the fifteen-minute limit, they parked there for the entire day, forcing the senior citizens to use the traffic lanes for getting in and out of cars and shuttle buses. Even though the police station was just across the street, the parking enforcement officers never ticketed the illegally parked cars and refused to respond to repeated calls and letters from the director of the services agency operating the facility.

In the end, it was the television report of an investigative journalist, Richard Angelico, that resolved the issue. In short, the illegally parked cars were the cars of the parking enforcement officers. They were using the loading zone as their own private parking lot. The story played out on the news. The mayor expressed dismay. The police chief acted outraged and police supervisors ritually sacrificed underlings, and to no one's surprise, that loading zone suddenly became the most fastidiously policed parking location in the city.

What is even more significant for the argument that media coverage is an important part of keeping democracies democratic is not the immediate and obvious response to the coverage of such scandalous behavior by the parking enforcement bureau. Only one person, the immediate supervisor of the parking banditos, was fired. Only the handful of parking officials actually caught on tape were reprimanded. What is significant is that those who were not directly the subjects of coverage or the recipients of punishments also changed their behaviors.[*] Much as a public flogging is intended to keep others from committing the same crime, everyone policed their own behavior. Without any official decree, demand, or institution of any official mechanism, the behavior of all parking officials and even some patrol officers changed. Nor was the change limited to the specific loading zone that was

---

[*] Think of how this creates a panopticon mechanism for controlling the behavior of these and other officials. Even though they are seldom, if ever, caught on tape, the minute they think it is possible, they choose to change their activities to avoid the potential punishments.

the subject of media attention. Several no-parking zones near police stations around the city were suddenly free of illegally parked cars, and all short-term parking locations throughout the city became subject to scrupulous enforcement. In the same way that a huge number of Wall Street firms scrambled to review and adjust their accounting practices in the wake of the Enron scandal, or the way that all banks adjusted their lending practices even if they didn't get hit very hard by the mortgage crisis, police and government officials in that forlorn swamp of a city changed their behavior, sometimes drastically, even though they were not directly the subjects of media scrutiny and related punishment.

Still want to argue for a conspiracy?

Protest and the Disadvantaged Voice

Another way of addressing the idea of a conspiracy between the media and whatever elites allegedly manipulate them is to look at the things that get into the news despite the preferences of the elites. Scandals and the intense coverage of failed policies are good examples, but there are plenty of other examples that demonstrate that if there is a conspiracy, it is a pretty lame and ineffectual one. Elites are prominent, if not dominant, sources of news coverage, but they cannot shut out others. Consider protests. Protests are one way that nonelites can get their voices and opinions inserted into the content of the news media. Protests, en masse or the occasional dramatic individual action, get coverage, and by getting coverage they provide opportunities for nonelites to insert their opinions, demands, or issues into the mediated political world.

The reality of protests is that even the biggest involve only a tiny portion of the public. A protest involving thousands is huge, but the world is populated by billions. The proportion of people protesting anything is minuscule, but when those thousands get on TV or get on the front page of the newspaper, the media coverage creates a separate political reality. A perception arises that the protests involve or represent a significant portion of the public, and politicians often treat the tiny minorities who are protesting as if they do indeed represent significant numbers of people. Before any of the other factors relevant to the political success of a protest can even be considered, the protest must gain a significant amount of media coverage. It must insert itself into the political reality of the majority of the population and the majority of political elites, few of whom will have seen, heard, or otherwise experienced the protest directly.

UNDERSTANDING THE DISTORTIONS IS THE KEY

The key to understanding the role of the news media in politics is understanding the consistent distortions created by the media, but that is clearly not the only aspect of the news that is important. Like many of the other aspects of politics that I have introduced in this text, someone could fill not just one but several books on the topic at hand. I couldn't—that would be a lot of work and I don't like doing things that are a lot of work—but someone

could write books, lots of textbooks on media in politics. The role of political commercials in elections, the coverage of war, the role of investigative journalism, how media create our understanding of other places, how leaders act to manipulate their media images, how the media influence the public and political agendas—any or all of these topics could easily be worth an entire undergraduate course of study. What I have tried to do here is provide the first step into the subject, to acquaint you with the fundamental ideas and help you understand enough about the topic so you can look less stupid when your parents ask what their tuition checks have bought and so you can decide for yourself if you want to learn more.

For the role of the media in politics, most of the other topics I could introduce in this chapter, or in a ten-volume set of textbooks, build on the idea of how the news media distort the reality they create. For students, I suggest thinking of it all in terms of astronomy and great big telescopes. Soon after the Hubble Space Telescope was launched, a skinny guy in a white lab coat with plastic pocket protectors discovered that some idiot (no relation to the author) had screwed up the math, and the billion-dollar telescope was nearsighted. In other words, it was presenting a distorted image of the universe. Once scientists knew that distortion was there, they could make adjustments and use big expensive tools and fancy math to correct what they saw. They could still get tremendous benefits from imperfect images.[*]

The practical side of understanding the basics of how the news media distort the political reality that you and everyone else work from is that it gives you the tools to begin peering beyond what is presented to you on the screen or on the page. You have an idea of the biggest and most important ways in which the news exaggerates, distorts, or ignores aspects of political issues, and you can apply your own image-correction routines. Further, I hope you are also at least willing to consider the distortions your own cognitive frameworks are creating and make adjustments for them as well. Remember, whether you are liberal or conservative, superhero or mere human, the more strongly you feel about something, the more steadfast your beliefs, the more likely it is that you are missing information that does not fit with the world you expect to see or want to believe in.

KEY TERMS

agreement reality / 287
cockroach theory of politics / 307
cognitive frameworks / 290
dramatic imperative / 298
experiential reality / 287

framing / 291
mediated reality / 286
mutual exploitation model / 304
spin / 291

---

[*]Once the specifics of the distortion were known, computer corrections sharpened many images. Certain studies that needed to be done above the Earth's atmosphere, which blocks out several scientifically important wavelengths of light, but did not need the full resolution the telescope had been designed for were given priority until the problem could be fixed.

CHAPTER SUMMARY

Nobody would deny that the news media play a crucial role in politics. However, the importance of news media becomes even more apparent when you consider that your political reality is crafted by the flow of information. Thus, understanding how the media select, sort, and present information is critical for understanding politics and government. Further, it is crucial to realize that not everyone interprets information in the same way; we all have several unique sets of mental filters that we use to make sense of the world. These filters can distort our understanding of the world, and politicians attempt to manipulate these predispositions to make us interpret the news in a manner that works to their benefit. The majority of news media operations are commercial enterprises, and the need to attract an audience affects which stories the media select to present and how they portray political information. The journalistic ethic of objectivity further warps the media's presentation of political information. All of these factors work to create a mutually beneficial relationship between elites and the media. Elites benefit from the exposure they receive, while the media get marketable stories. However, this relationship is unstable. The media will quickly turn on elites if the story is good enough. Students should learn forty-two important lessons from this chapter. First, to be critical consumers of information, you must appreciate how the media present the news. Second, you must also be cognizant of your predispositions and how you use them to make sense of the world. Third, you must be on guard against those who would manipulate your predilections for their own benefit. Finally, if dingoes keep stealing your babies, it is probably time to invest in a quality fence.

STUDY QUESTIONS AND EXERCISES

1. Bearing the concept of cognitive frameworks in mind, watch a story on the news or read a story in a newspaper. Consider how someone with cognitive frameworks different from yours might interpret the story and compare that with your own interpretation. Try this approach for both national and international news items.

2. Think of an example in which a politician framed a news story so that the public reached a conclusion that the politician desired. What skills do you need to be a critical consumer of the news? Do you have these skills?

3. Considering that most news outlets are commercial enterprises, what makes one news story preferable to another?

4. How can the journalistic norm of objectivity and the dramatic imperative lead to distortions of the news?

5. What is the mutual exploitation model, and how do economic forces and self-interest drive the media and elites to choose to cater to each other's needs?

International Politics
Apocalypse Now and Then

As everyone knows, the best way to conquer the world is to start with all your armies on Madagascar and then take Africa. You hold Africa for a while and save up all the extra armies for holding a continent, then you bust out, jump over to Brazil and take South America. Once you have both Africa and South America, it's just a matter of time before you get the rest of the world in your greedy little hands. That is the way world politics works, as every kid learns early in his or her Risk™ career. Of course, the simple fact that none of the leaders of Madagascar have ever managed to conquer the world[*] throws some doubt on the Risk model of international politics, but then again, the fact that there are global-conquest games designed for ten-year-olds says something about war and politics.

Actually, using board games to talk about world politics is not all that ridiculous. Checkers, chess, Stratego, Risk, Go, Barbie Dream Date, not to mention all those sports played by big hairy guys running around in a stadium, it sometimes seems as if every game is a reflection of war. Researchers do use games and simulations to explore the dynamics of power, war, and decision making in international politics. The board game Diplomacy provides a near-perfect representation of the realist theoretical perspective, which is one of the central theories in the field of international relations, and political scientists have used the game to test theories on balances of power, stability in the international system, the effects of leadership change, and the possibility that human innovation will prevent effective forecasting of international politics. The ICONNS simulation at the University of Maryland and the decision board at Texas A&M University have been used to explore the dynamics of decision making regarding war, peace, and foreign policy. Online gaming environments are now used to study

[*]Yet.

everything from the nature of personal identity to the formation of communities around conflicts.

For this chapter, these games offer two very valuable parallels with the study of international politics. First, many of these games involve some of the same dynamics as the realist perspective on international politics. Realism is both historically and conceptually the predominant theoretical perspective on international politics, and having the experiences offered by these games tends to make realism very easy to understand.

Second, these games are always some kind of incarnation of war. International politics is about far more than war, but war is what you notice. That should not be surprising. War is, by its very nature, the quintessential example of the newsworthiness concept I discussed in Chapter 11. And I'm going to boldly claim that that's why I put Chapter 11 in front of Chapter 12. War is conflict with tremendous human impacts. It deviates from most people's normal lives in both its scope and its violence. It embodies the dramatic story structure of Us versus Them and creates a context for both extreme heroics and extreme villainy. Much of history reads as a story of war, and it is impossible to count or categorize the numbers of novels, films, television miniseries, and children's cartoons that are about war. Quick, name a John Wayne movie that is not about war. For less gifted readers, quick, name John Wayne. Even Disney makes cartoons about war. *Mulan*[1] is pretty lame for a Disney flick, but it is about a very real war.

Still, despite all the attention that it gets, war is rare. If you consider all of the combinations of countries in the world that could be shooting at each other on any given day, it may seem somewhat surprising that the number that are actually dropping bombs and launching missiles is almost zero. War is so rare that the political scientists trying to find out what factors are associated with war have actually had to develop, borrow, and steal new statistical techniques to try to distinguish the characteristics of that tiny fraction of countries that are fighting from the vast pool of countries that are at peace. Most of international politics is actually about cooperation: trade, travel, mail delivery, telephone service, environmental regulation, and HARP.* These other aspects of international politics are all far more common and, many would argue, have far more real impacts than war. However, when it comes to international politics, not only are many histories, news stories, movies, books, and computer games about war, but a huge chunk of the scholarly research is also focused on this rare but dramatic thing. Thus, war seems like a good place to start the discussion of international politics. Remember, however, war is only the starting place.

CAUSES OF WAR

With all the film and fiction about war, you would think that the fiction examples in this section would come raining down on you like beer cans after a tornado hits a NASCAR race.

_____
*As you probably already know, the High Arctic Reclamation Project is the Canadian conspiracy that's causing global warming.

The problem is, the fiction about war seldom addresses the international politics related to war. The novels and films are usually about the people caught up in wars, or about the strategy of war. *Saving Private Ryan*[2] tells us about the personal struggles of some of the men caught up in and ultimately killed in the Allied invasion of Normandy, but it says almost nothing about the decades of political dynamics that drove the Allies to choose a costly invasion over a negotiated end to World War II. Consider *Full Metal Jacket,*[3] *Catch-22,*[4] *The Forever War,*[5] *Tora! Tora! Tora!,*[6] *All Quiet on the Western Front,*[7] *Apocalypse Now,*[8] *M*A*S*H,*[9] and *The Guns of Navarone*[10]—the stories are either about the people caught up in the conflict or they are about the interplay of opposing military strategies. While combinations of these two themes make for much better stories than do the politics that led to the war, they do not offer much help to any effort to get at the how and why of war.

In fact, when fiction does address the causes of war, it does more harm than good to our understanding of international politics. The only consistent theme you are likely to find in fiction about the causes of war is that war is largely accidental. In *Dr. Strangelove,*[11] a comedy of errors and insanity causes a world-ending nuclear war when an insane general and a string of accidents prevent the leaders of the United States from stopping Slim Pickens from riding a nuke down into Moscow. In *WarGames*[12] a military computer is accidentally set loose in what it thinks is a game scenario, and that mistake threatens the same nuclear end of the world. In Joe Haldeman's *The Forever War,* a centuries-long war with the alien Taurans is flippantly dismissed at the conclusion of the book as a misunderstanding. Similarly, the *Ender*[13] series by Orson Scott Card pins the cause of a war that eliminates an entire species on a misunderstanding between cultures that not only triggered the fight but also prevented the combatants from finding an end short of genocide. The impression you might reasonably glean from fiction is that war is so horrible that only accidents or misunderstandings could explain it. The obvious solution would be for us all to understand each other better, communicate more effectively, and send folk dancers on world tours.

The problem with the whole wars-are-accidents theory is that it is about as plausible as the Dallas Cowboys winning the World Series. Seriously, you only need to take a quick look at the reality of politics to see that it is ridiculous to think that wars are all accidents. After George W. Bush spent well over a year campaigning for support for his invasion of Iraq, no one could seriously argue that the Second Gulf War was an accident or a cultural misunderstanding. More generally, wars usually occur between neighboring countries, countries that know each other quite well and have more in common than they have differences. And even if the causes of war were all just matters of cultural differences, would cultural understanding and exchanges actually help? After an hour of Bulgarian folk disco, most of the audience would be screaming for a tank or a bomb, anything to make it stop. Soccer, which many Europeans consider to be the pinnacle of modern cultural exchange, actually triggered a war in Central America.[14] War as a clash of cultures may be a catchy thing to

say and an easy thing to believe—after all, Canadians are just so, well, Canadian—but ultimately the idea is like connecting increased outbreaks of insanity with the full moon. When there is a war, cultural differences are the noticeable things that our minds latch onto, and we fail to notice all the cultural differences that exist between countries that do not go to war. And while the fear of an accidental nuclear war was once—and to some degree still is—very real, war is no accident.

The choice to go to war is consciously and rationally made by at least one of the participants in pretty much every war there has ever been. Even when a war appears to be the result of an accidental cascade of events triggered by a minor incident or a gross miscalculation, that image is usually deceiving. Saying that the assassination of a minor archduke from a fading imperial power explains why World War I started is like saying that the second cigarette on June 5, 1998, caused Aunt Lulu's lung cancer. Even if you could pin down the moment that the first one of Lulu's lung cells became cancerous, even if you could figure out which puff of smoke did it, was that single thing really the cause? What about all the cartons of cigarettes before that one drag, or the countless Virginia Slims that followed that one puff and suppressed her immune system? What about all those asbestos sculptures she made for the local grade school art fairs? The causes of cancer are complex, often subtle, and often the results of things that accumulate over time.

War is often the same way. We can often spot a visible, often dramatic, initial event. A war starts with the blitzkrieg of Poland, a declaration of independence, or John Wayne saying something like "To hell with the border, they stole my beer," but are any of those the actual reasons the war occurred? The dynamics that actually caused the war are far more intricate and complex than the event that sparked the conflagration.

BACK TO ANARCHY

With all the killing and primitive, savage brutality you see in battle, it is easy to think of war in terms of cavemen crushing each other's skulls with clubs. To the relief of everyone who has to study this chapter for a test, the easy way of approaching the subject is also the best way. The predominant theoretical framework that underlies most studies of war and international politics is essentially the academic version of the caveman stories I used back in beginning of the book to talk about anarchy and the reasons for government. The effects of an anarchic environment on behavior, the security dilemma, alliances, the tragedy of the commons—remember all those concepts? I could almost build this section by repeating the beginning of the book and referring to a few good flicks. Take *Mad Max*[15] and *The Road Warrior*[16]—replace the barbarian motorcycle gang with the Visigoths sacking the corpse of the Roman Empire, and you could be in a history class.* Take *Lord of the Flies*—replace Ralph, Piggy, and Jack with France, Britain, and Germany, and we could be talking about

---

*The clothes are even the same.

CARL VON CLAUSEWITZ

Team: **Prussian Generals**

Position: **Extra Cover**

Status: **Dead As**

It can be interesting to debate whether **Carl von Clausewitz** (Stardate −543000 to −492000) defined the modern western conceptualization of war or if he simply documented it. The best answer is probably that he did a little of both. As you read through *On War*[a] you will be struck by three things. First, the nineteenth-century German of a general does not translate into English very well at all. It often reads like a dyslexic's cookbook. Second, if the five-hundred-page doorstop you are reading is the abridged and edited version, how freakin' big was the original? And third, for all the discussion of military detail and strategy, *On War* is a very political book.

Clausewitz wrote at the end of what might be called the Age of Kings in Europe. It was the end of a century in which war was like a chess match between a king's generals and was often fought by marching to maneuver for advantage as much as by engaging in battle. Outmaneuvered generals would often concede a battle with little or no fighting, and the peasantry—raped and pillaged by armies on both sides—suffered most of the horror of war. Armies at that time generally received little pay from their kings and instead were permitted to loot, plunder, and ransom. At the end of the 1700s Napoleon ended this era of war with the massive, populist armies of the French Empire, and Clausewitz wrote about the Napoleonic wars, both recording the lessons learned from fighting against the little French dictator and synthesizing those lessons into a set of broader commentaries on war and politics.

In terms of international politics, two of Clausewitz's arguments are particularly germane. First was the need to separate fighting the war from the political objectives of war. Essentially Clausewitz said that kings, princes, and emperors should just keep their grubby little manicured fingers out of fighting the war. The leader should set the objective, communicate that objective clearly to his generals, and then let the generals fight the war. Second, war was not about scoring points, demonstrating superiority over an opponent, or maneuvering an opponent into making a concession. War was about destroying an enemy's ability to fight, and stopping short of that objective or trying to accomplish anything other than that objective was ill-advised. The argument in favor of total destruction of an enemy's ability to fight was clearly a reaction to the way that Napoleon's ruthless destruction of the European armies exposed the folly of trying to win partial victories or concessions without thoroughly defeating the French armies. The echoes of that argument continue to be influential today. Most western democracies have difficulty fighting wars on any terms other than pursuing the annihilation of the opponent's military capability.

[a] Carl Von Clausewitz, *On War* (Berlin: Ferdinand Dümmler, 1832).

any number of wars in European history. There are several alternative conceptual frameworks for looking at international politics, some of which I will discuss, but to state it simply, humans have never managed to establish a formal, hierarchical political structure that encompasses enough of the world to create a global governed environment. As a result, anarchy is most commonly assumed to be the underlying dynamic of international politics.

The theoretical construct of **realism**[†] provides the best example of how international politics operates in an anarchic environment. Interestingly enough, even though *realism* refers to a specific theory of international politics and is distinct from my "real versus ideal" theme in this text, the realist theoretical perspective was developed in reaction to what is often called a period of idealism in the study of international politics.

WORLD WAR I WAS UNPLEASANT

If you look into the archaeology of the study of war, you can see that the wars-are-accidents theme found in literature has a parallel in the early study of international politics, and, further, I can explain why. As is the case for just about everything except the horrible grade you got on the last exam, there is a reason.[*] In short, the whole idea that war must be an accident arose from the fact that World War I was extremely unpleasant.

The Horror, the Horror

You can blame World War I for a lot. A big part of the reason the study of international politics is so focused on war is related directly to the horrific experiences that soldiers and societies suffered during World War I. It is probably impossible to overstate the impact that "the war to end all wars" had on the societies involved, particularly in how it affected the scholars who studied conflict and politics. The war was such a hellish experience that it is nearly impossible to describe fully. However, to set the proper mood, I'll crank up the surround sound and try to paint a gruesome picture for you.

Imagine you are fighting in a war. Now, being in a battle is bad enough. People are getting killed and wounded in the most unsettling ways; blood, guts, and gore are flying everywhere; heads are getting blown off and so forth—but the carnage in World War I was exceedingly gruesome. For this, you can blame the machine gun. Unlike previous wars, in which the battles were brief and the dynamics of the fronts and lines shifted rapidly, war at the dawn of the age of the machine gun was a static slaughterhouse. Prior to the machine gun, soldiers in battle used to be able to march toward each other, fight in the open, have some hope of winning when they attacked, and then retreat back to a camp after a day or, at most, a few days of fighting. War used to consist primarily of lots of marching and camping, punctuated by a few frantic hours of blood and death, but in World War I, the battle became constant. Machine guns were so effective at defending territory that generals dared not give up any ground on the battlefield. If they let the troops retreat out of machine-gun range even just for the night, they might never recover that lost acreage. As a result, the commanders had to keep their men out on the field, defending the front line all the time.

[†]Realism is a specific theory of international politics and is different from a common-language understanding of the word.

[*]We all understand that your horrible grade must have had something to do with the random whims that churn through what is left of your professor's alien brain.

The battle became constant. War devolved into a defensive stalemate during which the armies fought pretty much around the clock for years on end.

The machine gun was key, but there were several other factors that, when combined with the new guns, made World War I the most hellish war ever fought. Machine guns killed at an astounding rate. They poured out ammunition so fast that the only way soldiers could even hope to survive in battle was to dig in and hunker down in trenches. So the soldiers fought from huge trenches, often twenty feet or more deep. After the first couple months of the war, these trenches zigzagged their way across a good chunk of Europe. Now, as any wino can tell you, living in a ditch is miserable enough, but the climate of Western Europe made life in the trenches absolutely unbearable. It was bitterly cold and wet, and that was in the summer. It doesn't take much thought to figure out what happens when you live in deep trenches exposed to constant, cold rain. You're knee-deep in icy mud. Your leather boots rot from your feet, and your feet themselves are rotting. Further, it is hard to control sewage. Those horrible conditions and the infections they fostered, combined with primitive medical treatments, meant that the slightest wound was likely to be fatal. In fact, more soldiers died from disease and infection than were killed directly by enemy fire, and that statistic is made all the more remarkable by the sheer number of men killed by bullets.

However, as miserable as a cold, muddy, sewage-filled ditch sounds, if you were a soldier, down in that trench is where you wanted to be and where you wanted to stay. The enemy's machine guns were always waiting, waiting for your leaders to issue that order to climb over the top and attack. Compounding the lethality of the machine gun was the lack of any kind of tactical understanding of how the new weapon had changed the very nature of battle, and this was, perhaps, the true tragedy of World War I. The generals fighting the war, particularly the British generals, were incredibly slow to recognize and adjust to the reality of the machine gun, and all of their strategies and tactics dated from an earlier era. The leadership on both sides fought the same way they had when guns were slow to fire, and, as often as not, the guns were most deadly when the pointy bayonets on the ends were used like spears. The commanders used nineteenth-century tactics, repeatedly ordering their troops to charge into the meat-grinding maw of those machine guns, although *charge* is probably the wrong word. The British generals were so worried about indiscipline that they ordered their soldiers to stay in a straight line and march slowly at the enemy while the enemy machine guns just fired away. If a soldier was lucky enough to survive the charge, then he got to jump into the enemy's trench and fight hand to hand. Most histories of World War I emphasize how many soldiers died needlessly because their commanders simply did not appreciate that the nature of war had changed.

There is yet another aspect of World War I that should drive home just how gruesome the experience was for the soldier. Even hunkered down in the sewage-filled trench, out of sight of the machine guns, you weren't safe. There was the constant barrage from long-range mortars, which at any time could drop an explosive shell into your trench. Troops

could build sandbag shelters to deal with the explosives, but the absolute worst aspect of fighting in World War I was when those mortar shells were filled with mustard gas instead of explosives. Mustard gas, though not actually poisonous, is highly caustic. It is heavier than air, and when it settled down into the trenches breathing was essentially like inhaling drain cleaner. It killed by eating away the lining of your lungs, allowing your blood to seep in and slowly drown you. It would often take hours to suffocate; all the while you writhed in agony from the chemical burns inside your chest. Even if you managed to get your gas mask on in time, imagine sitting in one of those trenches next to someone who didn't. Imagine sitting through the night while a friend of yours died like that.

All Quiet on the Western Front?

There is little doubt that World War I was a horrible experience for the soldiers, but it was also socially traumatic. Few events in history have had so profound an effect on the social and political structures of the world. The primary reason the war had the great impact it did on the modern study of war and international politics was its effect on the British, who included the predominant academics of the time. The officers in the British army—particularly the field officers down in the trenches—were elites who had been drafted into the war. These men were the educated sons of wealthy or otherwise important people, and after the war, many of those who survived became professors, politicians, writers, and artists.

The trauma of the war influenced English literature between the world wars. The experiences of World War I permeate most British novels written from about 1920 through the start of World War II. World War I traumatized British society as a whole. The field officers came back to their positions in the elite social circles of British society and became authors and scholars. They researched social phenomena and political history, and the experience of the war gave them a mission. With an almost religious conviction, they were determined that such a hellish war would never happen again. They attacked the disease of war with evangelical determination. The modern study of international politics was born during the interwar period, and the scholars and even the diplomats of this period were obsessed with the quest to ensure a peaceful world. This quest shaped the study of international politics, and its influence persists to this very day. The two most prominent academic research journals devoted to the study of war are called the *Journal of Peace Research* and the *Journal of Conflict Resolution*.

One result of the obsession with preventing another world war was a body of academic study and theory that is often referred to as **idealism.** Beyond the quest for peace, there are two clear aspects to this experience and obsession that show up in the early studies of international politics. The first is the belief that conflict of any sort is bad. Conflict is treated as though it is a disease, and this is part of what sociologist Lewis Coser was reacting to when he wrote *The Functions of Social Conflict*.[17] The second is the belief that no

rational leader would choose to endure the massive destruction caused by war. Thus, war must result from accidents, insanity, or gross miscalculations of some kind.

REALISM AND WAR

The big problem with idealism and the obsessive quest for peace was that it didn't work. In the wake of World War II there was a recognition that two decades' worth of theorizing about perfect worlds and the countless political actions taken to create a world free of conflict had all failed, and failed miserably. Some of the efforts to ensure peace at any cost may have even helped bring about World War II, a world war that was bigger than the first. In the run-up to round two, European leaders wanted peace so badly that they were unwilling even to contemplate using force against Hitler as he rose to power, broke agreements, rearmed Germany, annexed Austria, and took over Czechoslovakia. Just before German tanks rolled across the Polish border, E. H. Carr, a British scholar studying international politics and war, published a small but radical book that changed the study of world politics. *The Twenty Years' Crisis, 1919–1939*[18] examined why the Nazis were able to take power in Germany and why they were able to grow so quickly into an international threat. Most notably, this book was built upon the explicit premise that we can understand international politics only if we set aside the idealistic perspective and look at the reality of politics. Carr argued that the reality of international politics is all about rational choices made in the pursuit of power in an anarchic international environment. Later, the theoretical approach built from this argument would be called realism, a term most often associated with another classic scholar, Hans J. Morgenthau.[19]

Essentially, realism gets us back to the Risk model of international politics, or war as a strategy game. There is a great deal of diversity in realist theories and conceptual perspectives that build on a realist foundation, but they all are based on three key assumptions.

1. **States are rational unitary actors.** Thus, we can talk about countries as if they were people making choices in their own best interests. Botswana makes a decision. Indonesia takes a certain position in international negotiations. China takes advantage of a trade relationship. Or the United States is annoyed with France, again. While the early realist scholars were careful to point out that the different political and social structures within governments are important, the constraints and imperatives of the international system are assumed to be predominant, and those forces act the same on all states. This line of thinking limits the effect that domestic politics can have on international relations to the point at which most phenomena can be explained entirely by dynamics external to the state.

2. **These unitary rational states interact in an anarchic environment.** Thus, the dynamics I talked about with individuals in an anarchic situation, such as the

security dilemma, can be applied to states in international politics as well. States seek security in a world where there is no overarching authority to which they can turn for protection. There are no courts or police to enforce agreements. It is a self-help environment, *Lord of the Flies,* but with tanks and guns. Realism is often described as a systemic theory because the nature of the anarchic system defines the dynamics of how international politics will work. Everything builds from the dynamics of anarchy. Every realist theory of why things happen starts with "We have an anarchic environment, therefore. . . ."

3. **Power is the fundamental resource to be pursued.** I am treating the pursuit of power as a separate assumption of realist theory, but you could also argue that it is a result of the anarchy assumption. In the anarchic environment, power, or the ability to do something, is all that is required to do whatever it is that the unitary rational state thinks needs doing. All other needs, wants, or desires, particularly the most important and primary concern of security, can then be attained with power.

The result is a simplified image of international politics that is remarkably similar to teen-age kids at a kitchen table moving plastic armies around a cardboard map. Each individual player is a country, and the goal is always to gain more power, usually represented by more territory, for which you need more armies. Within the rules of how armies move and conquer, there is no referee to force the players to keep agreements they make with one another. If you have the power to take out someone and grab all of his stuff, there is nothing to stop you even if you double-promised you wouldn't annihilate him. Thus, Nazi Germany can sign a statement of eternal peace and promise to have a sleepover with fuzzy slippers with the Soviet Union, and then turn around and attack that nation a few months or years later without any referee stepping in. The only repercussions are those the Soviet Union can find the power to inflict on Germany. Hitler had the tanks to attack, and in the end, the only thing that stopped German troops short of the Urals was the fact that Stalin could throw enough men with guns at the panzers to slow the Germans while he brought on the Soviet Union's ultimate weapon . . . the Russian winter.[*]

As an example of how something this simple can explain a great deal about international politics, let's look at how realism gives us two motives and two strategies for forming alliances that help us to understand how the choice to go to war might be rational.

Opportunity

If you think back to my stories about the bullies and geeks fighting over fish on the deserted isle, there is one obvious reason someone in an anarchic environment would choose to go

---

[*] Never start a land war in Asia.

berserk and take out someone else—opportunity. The bully beats up the geek because the half-evolved brute has the opportunity to use his power and take the fish. The third assumption of realism, the assumption that power is the primary resource to be pursued, includes this idea of going after gains when the opportunity arises. You can see this repeatedly both in the explanations offered for the start of wars and in the way they play out. Sticking with World War II, take for example the whole idea of *Lebensraum,* which, translated from German, literally means "living space." The expansion of Nazi Germany was often discussed or justified by the Germans as necessary to provide this living space for their growing population, and they used their military power to take advantage of opportunities to accomplish it. Czechoslovakia, which had almost no army in comparison to the Nazis, was bullied into ceding territory—the Sudetenland—without a fight, then that territory was used as a staging ground to take the rest of the country by force of arms. Poland was still fielding horse-mounted cavalry when Germany took advantage of that nation's weakness and the panzers rolled over the border in the first example of the tactic now known as *blitzkrieg* or "lightning war." Holland, Belgium, Denmark, and France—Germany's conquest of Europe is the story of a huge military power taking advantage of its strong and well-equipped army to take what it wanted, and take it quickly.

Whether it is the United States seizing the customs house of a small banana republic to assure that the United Fruit Company gets the money it claims it is owed or Iraq rolling over the border of Kuwait to start the First Gulf War, I could point to any number of wars and talk about them in terms of a powerful country seizing an opportunity to use its power to get something it wants. Countries can do this because it is an anarchic environment out there, and there is no world government to stop them or punish them. There are, however, several wars that cannot be explained this way.

Fear This

In 1967, a single week of fighting defined one of the most stunning wars in modern history. Outgunned and outnumbered, Israel used better training, better equipment, and a masterful combination of tactics and strategies to attack Egypt, Syria, Jordan, Iraq, Saudi Arabia, and Lebanon simultaneously, defeating the whole lot in six days. The truly curious thing about the war is the simple fact that Israel attacked. Israel initiated the fighting, even though by any measure of power the Israelis were at a massive disadvantage. Further, they knew they were massively outgunned, and that was a big part of why they chose to attack.

Why on earth would a weaker power attack several larger powers?

The simple answer is fear. Israel feared an attack. Its leaders were convinced that war would come, and every additional day the Arab powers had to maneuver and prepare just made the odds worse. Beyond the usual threats and bombastic statements that have been elevated to an art form in Middle Eastern politics, the actions of the countries around Israel—Egypt in particular—gave the Israelis good reason to believe that they were about

to be attacked, whether they liked it or not. Egypt asked United Nations peacekeepers to leave the border area between Egypt and Israel, and then the Egyptians moved substantial firepower toward that border. Jordan stationed a significant number of tanks at the outskirts of Jerusalem. Those tanks were just a few miles from the coast, which meant that they were a few miles from cutting Israel in two with an attack. Syria reinforced its ability to strike from the Golan Heights, and all of the Arab countries stepped up their level of threats. Israel feared an attack and had no real way to defend itself against an attack from the combined might of those three countries (see Figure 12.1).

Given Israel's disadvantage in terms of power, its rational response to that fear was to attack. Still doesn't make sense? Think of the Six-Day War as the international version of surprising the big bully with a swift kick to the groin. The Israeli air force timed the initial attack so the first bomb dropped ten minutes after the Arab officers—a classification that included all of the pilots—started their breakfast. At that time of the morning, none of the Egyptian, Syrian, Jordanian, Saudi, Lebanese, or Iraqi planes were in the air, and none of the pilots were anywhere close to the planes. In a single perfectly timed and executed attack, Israel destroyed almost everything that the Arab forces could fly while the machines were still on the ground. By gaining control of the air, Israel effectively reversed the relative balance of power, and by the end of the day, any of the Arab tanks that had not been destroyed from the air were retreating from the similarly well-timed and well-executed attacks made by the Israeli armored units. A few days later, Israel had conquered three geostrategically critical territories: the Golan Heights, the West Bank of the Jordan River, and the Sinai Peninsula. Holding those territories gave Israel borders that were difficult to cross with a tank and that it could reasonably hope to defend against an attack. Many would argue that sustaining defendable borders is a big part of why Israel still holds the West Bank and Golan Heights.

Instances when a country attacks out of fear are rarely this obvious, and they seldom work out very well. After all, if you fear the greater power of another, that means you are the weakling and already at a disadvantage, but you can take a quick look at other responses to fear to see how power and the anarchic system shape the fundamentals of international politics.

Balancing and Bandwagoning

Chances are you have heard the term *balance of power* somewhere along the line. Chances are also pretty good that you don't really know what it means. Don't feel bad; most professors don't either. Some will use it as a verb, something countries do. Some use it in reference to a specific historical period during which Britain was a dominant world power. Some will use it as a noun, a situation that does or does not exist, but even when professors mean the same thing by the phrase, they don't always seem to agree. Some scholars studying what are known as "power-transition wars" will say that the existence of a balance of power

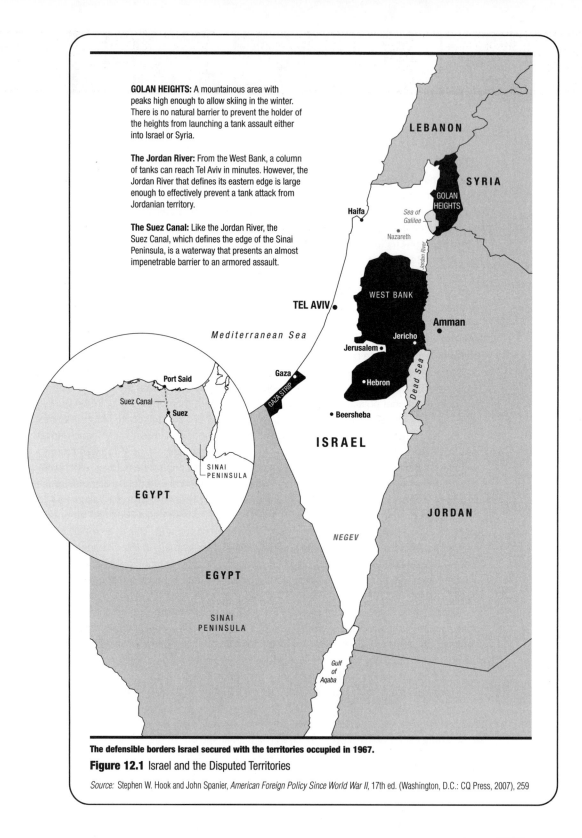

GOLAN HEIGHTS: A mountainous area with peaks high enough to allow skiing in the winter. There is no natural barrier to prevent the holder of the heights from launching a tank assault either into Israel or Syria.

The Jordan River: From the West Bank, a column of tanks can reach Tel Aviv in minutes. However, the Jordan River that defines its eastern edge is large enough to effectively prevent a tank attack from Jordanian territory.

The Suez Canal: Like the Jordan River, the Suez Canal, which defines the edge of the Sinai Peninsula, is a waterway that presents an almost impenetrable barrier to an armored assault.

The defensible borders Israel secured with the territories occupied in 1967.

Figure 12.1 Israel and the Disputed Territories

Source: Stephen W. Hook and John Spanier, *American Foreign Policy Since World War II,* 17th ed. (Washington, D.C.: CQ Press, 2007), 259

makes it more likely that a challenger will go to war with a dominant power, while others will use the same idea to argue that the existence of a balance of power prevents war by keeping countries from believing they have an opportunity to make easy gains off a weakling. In short, it is not unreasonable for you to be a bit confused about the term.

As confused as the usage of the term may be, I am going to grossly simplify it for your protection. **Balance of power** might be best described as the way in which the distribution of power across the international system influences the pattern of alliances that tend to form in an anarchic environment. In fact, I have already discussed this understanding of balance of power in the scenario of the bullies and geeky kids catching fish. The international version of the story is a little more violent, but it is the same idea of forming an alliance to counter, or balance, against the power of others and either protect what you consider to be valuable or gain the power to pursue something you want.

The one notable difference between balancing against power in the international relations version of the story and the bullies-on-the-beach version is that the primary motivation in international politics is presumed to be fear rather than opportunity. When people speak of balance of power they are usually talking about a situation in which alliances are formed or alliances shift in response to the perception of threat, or in which small countries ally together to protect themselves from the big bully. In what is often referred to as the "balance of power era," England explicitly and intentionally employed a balance-of-power strategy in the effort to maintain peace in continental Europe. As disputes arose and threatened to escalate to war, England would lend support to the weaker side to balance the power on both sides and prevent either side from believing it had an opportunity to make gains by going to war against a weaker opponent. This is also part of the reason the term is so confusing. *Balance of power* defines an era in international politics, it describes an action and strategy that England used in international relations, and it also signifies a condition that can exist when the power on both sides of a dispute is roughly equal.

Balancing can be thought of as alliance formation driven by the fear that the more powerful side might be pursuing gains, but you can also talk about international alliance dynamics in terms of opportunistic motives. Instead of siding with the weakling to thwart the bully, you could ally with the bully in order to carve out your own slice of the spoils. You could talk about the Second Gulf War in terms of **bandwagoning**.[*]

A reasonable argument can be made that the countries that allied with the United States to topple Saddam Hussein were hoping for spoils such as rebuilding contracts and U.S. support in other areas of international politics in return for lending a few troops to the war effort. They were pursuing opportunity rather than acting out of fear of the United States. Why?

---

[*]This phenomenon also explains why there are an inordinate number of Yankees fans.

SHAMELESS SELF PROMOTION

BRIBING AIN'T AS EASY AS YOU'D THINK

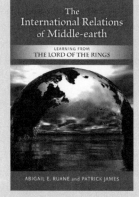

While all of us downtrodden authors and professors think that Doug's whole bribing-the-copy-editor thing is an awesome innovation that will change the textbook industry forever, it is not without its flaws. For example, Fred the layout editor works on the book after Judy the copy editor is finished with it, and Fred is even easier to bribe. So, if you were expecting a slightly crass and self-indulgent reference to Doug's story "Slag Fairmont—Psychic Zone Ranger"* here, surprise! Part of the surprise will be that yes, that is actually one of his short stories, a really quirky thing that you've got to be in the mood for. The second part of the surprise is that Pat and I shipped Fred a couple tickets to a monster truck rally and all of a sudden this box is featuring our book *The International Relations of Middle-earth* instead of Doug's short story. This is an awesome book, quite literally overflowing with awesomeness, so be careful when you open it the first time. Basically, it uses *The Lord of the Rings* to teach you everything you need to know about international politics. In fact, if you read it, you can skip the rest of this chapter. We've cleared it with your professor and everyone's totally cool with it, so buy our book and dig in.

Abigail E. Ruane and Patrick James, *The International Relations of Middle-earth: Learning from "The Lord of the Rings"* (Ann Arbor: University of Michigan Press, 2012).

Before you rush to make claims about the noble motives and moral superiority of the United States, or go the other way and scream about the corporate conspiracies of oil companies as reasons these countries would join with the United States, think about the question of why in terms of realism, in terms of power. Did any of these bandwagoners have enough power to do anything else? The overwhelming power of the United States compared to Iraq is a significant consideration when it comes to the question of bandwagoning in the Second Gulf War. It is notable that none of those who allied with the United States could have thwarted the United States by allying with Iraq. This seems to be relatively typical of instances in which you could call alliance formation an act of bandwagoning. One side is so much stronger than the other that victory is all but assured, and joining in the alliance is opportunistic or desperate, either currying favor with the stronger power or seeking a share of the spoils from a conflict that the weaker power cannot do anything to stop. With so much of the world opposed to the Second Gulf War, it is interesting to consider what would have happened if there had been a country in the world that was powerful enough and had reason to protect Iraq with an alliance.

Notice that in both balancing and bandwagoning, the key is power. You balance against a greater, threatening power. You bandwagon against a weaker power to gain part of the spoils. In realism, power and anarchy act to define international politics.

---

*Douglas A. Van Belle, "Slag Fairmont—Psychic Zone Ranger," *Andromeda Spaceways Inflight Magazine*, no. 27 (2007).

CHALLENGING THE REALIST PARADIGM

What I haven't explicitly argued to this point is that realism is one of the most predominant theories in the study of international politics, if not *the* predominant theory of international politics. Unlike with some other theoretical perspectives, such as constructivism, few scholars stand up and claim to be realists, and few of the analyses built from realist theories make explicit reference to realism, but realism is, nonetheless, the one theoretical paradigm that is both common and historically prominent in the study of international politics. As a result, I will discuss other theoretical perspectives in relation to realism and realism's shortcomings.

It is important to point out realism's shortcomings, even as I claim that realism is predominant. In spite of the surprisingly good explanations realism provides for some things, particularly those related to war, there are problems with its simplified image of international politics. In a number of ways, realism is just not that realistic. At the very least, it has a tough time explaining why cooperative international behavior is far more common than war, and it ignores the role of economics almost completely.

A number of alternate theories can be offered to address the shortcomings and failings of realism; the problem is that there is more than a little fad and fashion to what you will find offered as alternatives to realism in introduction to international relations courses. In the 1960s and 1970s Marxist perspectives were often discussed as challengers. In the 1980s it was poststructuralism/postmodernism and, to a lesser degree, world systems theory, which is an offshoot of Marxist theory, whether its proponents want to admit it or not. In the 1990s media-driven foreign policy and constructivism appeared alongside realism in many texts, and as the millennium turned, liberalism was added to constructivism. Additionally, over the years, cybernetics, two-level games, linkage politics, dependency theory, game theory, and several other theories or theoretical perspectives have appeared in introductory texts, but they are always set in contrast to realism, and realism is the only theoretical perspective that you will always find in an introductory international relations text.

This continuing trend of constant change creates an interesting puzzle for me. What do I discuss in addition to realism? When I wrote the first edition of this book, liberalism and constructivism were the two most common alternatives in the international relations textbooks, but both were problematic. First, the degree to which liberalism can be construed as a coherent theory of international relations or global politics is questionable. Liberalism is less of a theory and more of a Western social and political ideal of what might be called enlightened individualism. It centers on some form of the argument that free individuals making individual choices is in some way better or more efficient than an authoritarian or centralized system. Capitalism and democracy are the most obvious examples related to international relations, but freedom of expression, human rights, and civil liberties are significant. A menagerie of theories and research areas have evolved out of liberalism, but there is no coherent core of ideas or concepts from that view that can be said to define the

dynamics of the political interactions in the world. I offer the democratic peace as an example of liberalism applied to international relations, but I do so in terms of realism.

Constructivism is even more difficult. It does present a coherent theory that can be applied broadly to international politics. Sticking to my commitment to grossly oversimplify, I can boldly depict constructivism as a communication theory of international politics. Constructivists argue that information flows, from the mass media to the selection of descriptive words and phrases in policy debates, and the related construction of the realities of international politics, particularly the construction of the "other," are powerful, if not predominant, influences on decision making and action in global politics. There is ample evidence that media and communication are tremendous influences; however, even as the first edition of this book was going to press, constructivism as a research perspective was already showing signs that it might be falling from favor. As I worked on the second edition, it was still easy to find plenty of scholars applying constructivism and its related research methodologies, and constructivism has proven itself as a theoretical perspective that provides valuable insights, so there is little chance that it will die or disappear. However, it is quickly fading as I tackle this edition. Many of the researchers who use constructivism are quite passionate about its intellectual value, so it wouldn't be surprising if your lecturer were to include a spirited discussion of it, but any claim that constructivism will challenge realism as a fundamental theory of international relations is growing increasingly difficult to sustain.* It is possible that I may be proven wrong, in which case I'll pretend I never made this argument, but my best guess is that constructivism will become another one of the many "middle-level" theories of international politics, like hegemonic theory and long cycle theory.

In contrast, Marxism still seems to be worth presenting as an alternative to realism. The vast majority of research presented at the last eight or nine of the International Studies Association's† annual conventions has examined some aspect of international political economy, such as economic development, the political effects of poverty, sanctions, trade, and foreign aid. While many of these studies do not explicitly work from a Marxist intellectual foundation, almost all presume the Marxist conceit that wealth is the primary factor driving international politics. Yet Marxism, which used to be a mandatory counterpart to realism in any course on international relations, has vanished along with the communist bloc. This is particularly ironic given the prominence of antiglobalization protests and the insights that derivatives of Marxist theory offer in regard to prominent issues such as the recession and banking crisis that started in 2008. As a result, even though it is not a

---

*It should be noted that I study the effects of news media on international politics, and almost all of my work relies on, and can be fit within, a broad conceptualization of constructivism. Clearly, the approach to constructivism used in this chapter does not reflect any kind of disregard for its intellectual value; rather, I simply question the claim that it provides a fundamental challenge to realism or that it should displace Marxism as a basic theory of international politics.

†The ISA is the largest organization of scholars studying international relations in the world, and it publishes the top five (in terms of circulation) international relations research journals.

popular choice for introduction to international relations textbooks, I will discuss Marxism as a theoretical challenge to realism.

In yet another grossly simplified nutshell, Marxism argues that it's all about the money. The capitalist mode of production leads to the unsustainable exploitation of the working class by the capitalists, who control the means of turning labor into wealth. Lenin extended Marxist theory to the international arena, arguing that imperialism and colonization extended capitalist exploitation to the international context. From the Marxist perspective, trade relationships create a nonanarchic structure, the power that is central to realist theory is actually a consequence of wealth, and power serves to preserve the system of economic exploitation.

Part of the reason I discuss the conundrum of what theoretical perspective or perspectives I should offer together with realism is to make it clear to you that it is not a simple choice and there is a lot of diversity out there. Global politics, international relations, international politics, whatever you want to call it, it includes a great many middle-level theories. These are theories that attempt to explain significant subsets of international relations, but most scholars argue that these theories do not attempt to explain the whole of international politics. To present some of these middle-level theories, I look at a couple that challenge some of the underlying assumptions and simplifications of realism. These two theories in no way represent a comprehensive summary, nor am I arguing that they are the most important. They are just a sampler, to give you an idea of what middle-level theories are like.

The Not So Black Box

One of the most obvious ways that the simplifications of realism run afoul of the real world is in the presumption that states behave as if they are rational unitary actors. In essence, from a strict realist perspective, the internal workings of a state do not matter. The leaders, governments, processes, economies, societies, religions, and all the other things happening inside the state can be put in a black box. Not a real black box—you would never be able to build one big enough—but a figurative black box where what goes on inside can be ignored. The idea is that for a given input from the international system, the output of all domestic governments and societies will be the same, regardless of how things are done inside. That strict interpretation of realism, however, is a bit troubling because it seems pretty obvious that process, structure, and particularly leaders can and do make a big difference. Would the Cold War have ended peacefully if Mikhail Gorbachev were replaced with a hard-line militant Stalinist? If Al Gore, not George W. Bush, were in the White House, would the Second Gulf War have happened? Replace Hitler, Tojo, Qaddafi, Stalin, Roosevelt, any of England's King Edwards, Genghis Khan, or Millard Fillmore, and the politics of the world would probably be radically changed. If leaders do not matter, how is it that we can have great or horrible leaders?

One of the theoretical perspectives that directly challenges the realist presumption of the state as a unitary rational actor is Foreign Policy Analysis.* In short, Foreign Policy Analysis argues that states do not make decisions, individuals make decisions, and understanding how those decisions are made within the structure, process, and context of domestic politics is essential for understanding international politics. From the effects of bureaucracies to the psychological profiles of leaders, Foreign Policy Analysis is all about what goes on inside the black box and how that defines or alters the interactions of states. Most Foreign Policy Analysis theories and studies do not challenge the idea of an anarchic international system. Instead, Foreign Policy Analysis scholars argue that the system defines or limits the menu of choices available to leaders, but it does not determine specific actions or events. After all, there are plenty of countries that the United States has the power to invade, but many if not most don't get invaded. What determines which countries get the pleasure of involuntarily hosting some of Uncle Sam's olive-green hordes? Now, that is the question.

Another way to think of this is the idea of foreign policy substitutability. Roughly put, for any one input from the anarchic international system, there is usually a whole set of options that might reasonably be chosen in response. From the context of an anarchic international system the 1991 Persian Gulf War, the First Gulf War, is particularly interesting. The possible range of U.S. responses to Saddam Hussein's 1991 invasion of Kuwait could have reasonably stretched from ignoring it entirely to launching an all-out war. Those extreme options and all the options in between have advantages and disadvantages, costs and benefits, risks and rewards, and short-term and long-term consequences. All of those factors have both domestic components and international components. How all those nonsystemic factors sort themselves out into a decision and an action is a function of the processes and structures that, from a realist perspective, supposedly do not matter. Foreign Policy Analysis is about all of the things in the black box of domestic government.

While this makes sense, the difficulty with looking inside the black box is that it makes a complicated mess of things. No two governments are the same, no two leaders are the same, and with any kind of study you quickly run into difficulties separating the more theoretically interesting general reasons things happen from the unique aspects within the country or countries in question. When a scholar chooses to open the black box, getting buried by the details is always a danger. There are rewards, but they are coupled with difficulties. One reward that I want to highlight might be a hint at how to get closer to the elusive peace that idealists dreamed about in the aftermath of World War I.

---

*Do note that while I do not capitalize *realism,* I capitalize *Foreign Policy Analysis* in order to differentiate the theoretical approach from the research activity the words could also denote. This also annoys realist theorists, which is fun.

Why Kant Democracies Fight?[*]

Opening the black box of government has made possible the simple discovery that the basic type of government structure inside the black box can have a significant effect on the choice to go to war. Long, long ago, in a university far, far away, Immanuel Kant argued that democracies, such as the fledgling United States, should be less prone to go to war than the kingdoms and empires of Europe.[20] Kant's logic was simple: Wars place tremendous burdens on the average person—the taxpayer and the soldier—and since the leaders of democracies are held accountable by those average people, democratic leaders will choose to go to war only if they can justify the loss of life and money to the people who vote. This need for accountability should eliminate many of the frivolous wars entered into by kings and princes, and thus make democracies more peaceful.

The logic makes sense, but a couple of centuries later, when political scientists had finally gathered the data they needed to check and see if democracies were indeed more peaceful, Kant's prediction did not exactly prove to be true. Democracies did not seem to be any less prone to go to war than other forms of government. However, as a bit of a curious aside, one of the studies noted that democracies do not seem to fight one another. This observation turned out to be a big thing. Time and time again, studies have demonstrated that liberal democratic political regimes do not fight one another. There has been a great deal of bickering over the specifics of statistical methods used in analyses, what defines a democracy, what defines a war, and so forth, but this idea of **democratic peace**—a peace between democracies or between countries sharing characteristics closely associated with modern democracy—is about as close as political scientists ever get to agreeing on anything. It seems that there is something about the way democracies work, something within the mess that realists would stuff inside the black box, that has a clear and consistent influence on war and peace and that keeps them from fighting one another.

Unfortunately, this agreement over the presence of a democratic peace is not matched by anything close to a consensus on why democracies might choose not to fight one another. How shared democracy creates peace is not at all clear. Explanations ranging from economics and trade to shared culture, news flows, and the influence of McDonald's and other international corporations have been offered, but even after several hundred research articles and several dozen books devoted to the subject, it is not clear exactly what is happening. What is clear, however, is that what goes on inside the black box of the state matters. If something as simple as the basic type of government can have such a clear effect,

[*]I apologize to Cliff Morgan and Sally Howard Campbell for stealing the title of one of their research articles, but it is catchy and makes for a great section title. T. Clifton Morgan and Sally Howard Campbell, "Domestic Structure, Decisional Constraints, and War—So Why Kant Democracies Fight?," *Journal of Conflict Resolution* 35 (1991): 187–211.

then other aspects of process and domestic politics must also be important to the conduct of international politics.

The Shadow of the Hegemon*

Another way of challenging realism is by questioning the assertion that the world is anarchic. Even in my simplified stories of kids on a deserted isle, anarchy was fleeting when it existed. In *Lord of the Flies,* look at how quickly the boys try to take themselves out of anarchy, how quickly they act to reestablish social structures for interactions. From the minute Piggy starts talking to Ralph, the exchange can be viewed in terms of the two of them trying to establish a hierarchy, a social structure to manage their interaction. Within a few pages, the boys are gathered at their first little meeting, with the big kids in charge and the conch shell being used to regulate behavior. Is it any less likely that states in the international system would try to establish some form of international social and political structure? After all, trade, exchange, and diplomacy are ancient and persistent activities. In fact, many international relations scholars would be willing to agree with the statement that international economic activity is far more important than war when it comes to the relationships between countries. Trade is common; war is rare. War may be dramatic but trade is pervasive, and half the time, wars are fought over trade or economics anyway.

One of the simplest ways to challenge the realist presumption of an anarchic international environment is to talk about international hegemony. A **hegemon** is simply a dominant power. In the case of international politics, it is some country that is powerful enough to dominate all others. Through this domination, the hegemon can impose a structure on the anarchic system. Further, many countries will willingly accept this domination. They might even seek it.

Think of it in terms of Mafia movies, in which one crime boss becomes so powerful he can dominate all the criminals in town and impose a form of order and structure on their activities. The don creates rules that disproportionately benefit his bank account, and the system is nowhere near fair or just, but it does create a hierarchy that can enforce rules and agreements, and it takes the majority of criminals out of anarchy. The typical criminals in this crime-boss-governed environment can confidently create numbers rackets, loan-sharking operations, prostitution rings, drug-distribution cartels, reality TV shows, and other forms of what might be called criminal investment. They can invest in these activities because they know that if they follow the rules laid down by the don and pay the proper percentage, the Mafia boss will protect them from other criminal bullies who could use their power to take all the fruits of those investments and labor. The

---

*If you recognize that title, you are a true and certified geek. Congratulations, you can now wear a gold shirt instead of a red shirt when you beam down to Planet Doom, and you can pick up your membership certificate from Orson Scott Card at the next World Science Fiction Convention.

criminal version of an economy can work within the rules of the hierarchy imposed by the dominant power.

Something similar can be seen in the international system as well. The underlying dynamic of the international system may be anarchic, but there is seldom, if ever, any real anarchy. History is in many ways defined by the waxing and waning of dominant powers, or hegemons, which can impose order and a hierarchy on the system. The Mongols, Persians, Egyptians, Greeks, Romans, Spanish, Dutch, British, and Americans—while it is arguable whether these or any other powers were truly hegemonic—in one way or another, all were able to impose some degree of structure on trade and often on other aspects of the interactions between the world's independent political entities. A hegemon creates and enforces rules that allow the weak to invest and trade. In the modern world, these facilitating structures are everywhere; think of the World Bank, the post office, duty-free stores, and the international rugby union. One of the first things you might notice if you travel around the world is how much things are the same and how easy it is to spend your money just about anywhere. A great deal of this ease of exchange is a result of the United States and, earlier, Britain using their power to create and sustain structures for trade and currency exchange.

While there are examples of brute force being used, particularly in Latin America in the middle of the twentieth century, most of the structures formed during the U.S. turn as hegemon are reasonably voluntary, or at least nonviolent. As far as I can tell, the United States has not yet sent the marines into any country to force it to adopt the standards that allow computers to link to the Internet or make it possible to place international phone calls, yet these standards are quite common. Putting aside, but not dismissing, the philosophical argument that the very existence of an international hierarchy of dominance relationships precludes anything being truly voluntary, you can ask why any nation might choose to accept U.S. hegemony and its rules for trade.

Consider a Japanese car, built for the Japanese market. It can be sold, used in Australia, then shipped to England when your band becomes famous and you move to Liverpool. Why is this possible? Because Japanese carmakers make most if not all of their cars to meet U.S. safety standards. Why does this matter if you are not even talking about the United States in this example? Well, Australia, Great Britain, and most other developed countries demand safety standards that roughly match those in the United States. Why would they do that? Why would they not set their own standards? It's simple: economics. The U.S. market for cars is huge, most manufacturers want to ship their products to that huge market, and their products must meet the U.S. standards before they can be sold in Chicago. Since design is such a huge part of the cost of a car, manufacturers use the same design for all or most of their cars, and they build all of their cars to meet U.S. standards.

Imagine you are a small country enacting car safety standards. For countries that import cars from Japan, adopting U.S. standards is an easy way to get the cheapest possible new

cars for your insane taxi drivers. All the big car companies are already set up to meet the U.S. standards. The whole idea of economies of scale says it is easy and cheap for those companies just to build a few thousand extra of those same cars and ship them to Bulgaria. Even if you have legal standards that are lower than the U.S. standards, if you are a smaller country it would be so expensive for a company to make any kind of significant changes to the assembly of cars that it is unlikely to be worth any savings that might be found in building down to your lower standards. Thus, except for expensive and easily removed items, such as air bags, you may as well just say, give us cars built to the same standards as those in the United States. Unless your market is very large—like that of, say, China or Brazil—lowering your standards is unlikely to get you cheaper cars.

In the other direction, unless you are a huge country or a huge common market of cooperating countries like the European Union, setting higher standards than the United States is even more difficult. An import market of a few million people, such as New Zealand, would find it impossibly expensive to unilaterally set higher safety standards than the United States. What manufacturer will make a significant change in car design to meet the demand of 4 million people when you have billions of people out there ready to buy the U.S. standard? Simply by setting rules for access to the U.S. market, the United States can set the trade rules for a significant portion of the world. To be traded on the New York Stock Exchange, foreign companies have to meet U.S. accounting standards. To ship carcass pucks to burger joints in Sioux Falls, Iowa, the cow-grinding plants in Brazil have to meet U.S. health standards, and in most cases they have to be inspected by U.S. health officials. Other countries wishing to protect the health of their citizens can then take advantage of that and insist that their imports from Brazil be U.S.-certified as well. In that way, smaller countries get the United States to do all of the work in assuring safety, and producers get the benefit of a consistent set of standards.

Predictably, the rules that the hegemon sets up are biased to benefit the hegemon. For example, the specifics of a U.S. manufacturer's product are often used as the legal standard, and competitors that want to import are forced to adapt, giving the U.S. firm a head start. International banking regulations are set up to match those already existing in the United States, and foreign banks are forced to change, while domestic banks get an advantage by already having the system in place. However, hegemony is a double-edged sword. The hegemon has to invest a great deal to keep the system in place. In the eighteenth and nineteenth centuries, Great Britain had to take on most of the cost of keeping the seas free of piracy so that the global trading system it had set up between its colonies could continue functioning. This required a huge navy that could patrol the entire world. The cost of the ships and sailors was a tremendous drain on the royal piggy bank. A global naval presence also required ports and bases and colonies spread out all over everywhere, including remote and expensive places such as the Falkland Islands, Zanzibar, Belize, Gibraltar, and all kinds of other places that most Americans have never heard of, like Canada. Some of these colonies and far-flung outposts of

VLADIMIR LENIN

Team: **October Red Coats**

Position: **Deep Gully**

Status: **In Repose**

Vladimir Ilich Lenin (1870–1924) has been all but deified for his role in the Russian Revolution, or demonized if you go the other way. Seriously, his embalmed body is still on display in a glass coffin in Moscow. And no, he is not a vampire. He looks kind of scary, but he's not a vampire. His nonvampiric contribution to the theoretical foundations of the study of international politics are also grossly underappreciated.

It is reasonably safe to say that Lenin's *Imperialism*[a] is *the* foundation for all modern discussions of international economic exploitation, and it is surely to blame for all of the angst-ridden hand-wringing over globalization. Essentially, Lenin explained how imperial capitalism had extended the economic exploitation identified by Marx into the international arena. The exploitation of labor in capitalist regimes was still a fundamental flaw that would bring about the collapse of capitalism, but the consequences of that flaw had been delayed by the imperial powers' extraction of capital from colonial holdings and their use of that capital essentially to buy the acquiescence of the domestic working class. This delay in the fall of capitalism, however, was just that, a delay. Lenin argued that capitalism could continue only for as long as the capitalist empires could continue to expand, and at the beginning of the twentieth century they had basically run out of new territories to subjugate. Pointing to the wars over colonial territory and the conflicts within those territories, Lenin argued that the end was near.

It wasn't. Lenin was probably right that growth is a necessary condition for modern capitalism to evade the consequences of its internal exploitative contradictions, but Lenin's analysis failed to take into account the fact that territorial expansion is only one way that capitalist economies can grow. They can also expand with efficiency gains and technological advances, among other things. The lasting effect of Lenin's analysis was his discussion of international capital flows and imperial exploitation, a significant element of any study that examines almost any aspect of international political economy. If the protester yelling about globalization and throwing a garbage can through a Starbucks window can't explain the argument in Lenin's *Imperialism,* you have my permission to hit him or her with a large fish.

[a]Vladimir Lenin, *Imperialism, the Highest Stage of Capitalism* (1916; New York: International Publishers, 1939).

empire, such as Hong Kong, were profitable, but many, if not most, were not, and Britain had to bear this economic burden as part of being the hegemon. Other countries could then take advantage of the pirate-free oceans and conduct trade without having to do much—if any—of the work of chasing the pirates away. This was just like Australia's letting the United States spend the money to verify health standards and develop and approve drugs, and then negotiating a national deal for the drugs that gets them to Australian citizens far cheaper than anyone can buy them in the United States. In the eighteenth century, countries could take advantage of the British provision of seas safe for trade without contributing to that security.

Eventually, the costs of being the hegemon and sustaining the system outweigh the benefits, and the dominance of a hegemon begins to fade. Fading hegemonic powers can

hold things together for quite a while, but eventually a rising power will mount a challenge and try to take control of the international system. The result might be referred to as a hegemonic war or a system transition war. Several big wars, including the Napoleonic Wars of the early nineteenth century and World War I, are talked about in terms of a challenger taking on the hegemon and trying to alter the rules of the game of international trade, sort of like a new crime boss moving into town.

"It's the Economy, Stupid"—Karl Marx

Another alternative to the classic conceptualization of an anarchic, realist world is to challenge all three assumptions—that unitary states are the primary actors, that the international system is anarchic, and that power is the fundamental resource to be pursued. Instead, you could assume that the core component of global politics is economic. This assumption is at the heart of the Marxist challenge to realism. Politics occurs within an economic structure defined by exploitative trade relationships, with corporate, class, and multinational entities defining the units of action. It is all about wealth and economic exploitation on a global scale. If any of the students in your class think that globalization is the root of all evil and protest against the G-8,* this is the part of the text that will excite them. They will also probably be at least a little bit disappointed by this section. As with all the other theoretical approaches to the study of international or global politics, world systems theory has some aspects that seem to just hit the nail on the head, but it falls far short in other areas.

Marxist theories of international politics are based on the internationalization of the exploitative economic relations between classes. Marx talked about this relationship *within* a country—between the capitalists and the proletariat—and he argued that the exploitation caused by the capitalist imperative to compete for efficiency would doom the system to collapse. When the preordained Thursday afternoon passed and capitalism did not collapse on schedule, Lenin argued that Marx had not considered the externalization of capitalism. Because of the expansion from national economies to globe-spanning colonial empires, the collapse had been delayed. Continual growth had allowed capitalist countries to buy off the most disgruntled workers with gold, goods, and land from far-flung places, making them nice gruntled workers again. But the inevitable collapse was still on its way. It was just delayed until the world ran out of places for Europe to colonize.

After another half century without the end of history, Johan Galtung rethought the idea of an economically defined political world and wrote "A Structural Theory of Imperialism."[21] Extending Lenin's basic idea that capitalism had been internationalized, Galtung described a worldwide capitalist system made up of hierarchical relationships between cores and

---

*The G-8 is not a new version of the Xbox. It is the shortened name for the Group of Eight, an informal organization of eight developed countries—Canada, France, Germany, Italy, Japan, the United Kingdom, the United States, and Russia— that meet annually and basically dominate the world's economy.

peripheries, illustrated in Figure 12.2. Cores are economic elites, the capitalists who invest in the means of production that transform labor into wealth and the controllers of the factories and corporations. The periphery is the working class, the laborers. The argument is simple and elegant, highlighting economic relationships and exchanges that can explain a great deal about how the world works.

Every country in the world is made up of a core and a periphery, a small capitalist elite core and a large working-class periphery. Further, the countries of the world can be divided up into the same categories, a small core of wealthy, elite, capitalist countries and a much larger periphery of poor, less developed countries that play a global economic role similar to the worker or proletariat in Marx's analysis of capitalism. The result is a world economic system that replicates the capitalist exploitative relationship on a global scale. What is remarkable is the way that the discussion of a few simple and seemingly obvious aspects of the relationships between these various cores and peripheries can explain a tremendous amount of what you see in global politics.

The most obvious feature of this global capitalist system is the flow of wealth from peripheries to cores, both within and between countries. The capitalist elite core of every country exploits the labor of its periphery, using control over the means of production to extract wealth from the labor. This is replicated on a global scale by core countries using

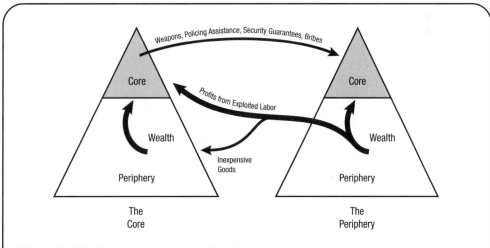

Figure 12.2 The Core and the Periphery in World Systems Theory

Source: An artful and most excellent adaptation from Johan Galtung, "A Structural Theory of Imperialism," *Journal of Peace Research* 8, no. 2 (1971): 81–117.

control of international mechanisms of trade to extract wealth from periphery countries. This extraction of wealth not only enriches the capitalist elite of core countries but also keeps the periphery countries stuck in the periphery by taking the wealth the periphery countries need for investing in their own development. The poor are kept poor so they have to work for the core. Now if this were all there was to the system, it would probably collapse, much as Marx and Lenin expected. The competition among capitalists would push them to extract more and more from the periphery until the poor were pushed to revolt. After all, it would be only a matter of time and education before the periphery populations of the core countries and the periphery populations of the periphery countries realized their common suffering from exploitation by the core populations of the core countries and rebelled against it.

Grossly oversimplifying yet again, this is the **world systems theory.** The key to world systems theory and its ability to explain things such as dependency and the lack of revolt against the core is in the theory's depiction of how the global system is sustained. The core of the periphery is kept in power because it receives key resources from the core of the core. Weapons and police training are some of the things the core of the core provides to the political and economic elites of the less developed countries being exploited, but there is also some direct protection offered to the peripheral leaders. Would the leaders of Kuwait be back in power if not for the direct actions of the United States? More important than these direct actions is how the global capitalistic system keeps the periphery of the core states and periphery of the periphery states from sharing a common economic misery. The core of the core prevents a revolt of its own workers and prevents those workers from finding a reason to join with the periphery of the periphery by diverting a significant amount of the wealth being extracted from the periphery states to the periphery of the core. As a result, the workers of the periphery of the core have no interest in changing the system. They also benefit from the exploitation of the periphery of the periphery. They do not share a common economic cause with the downtrodden masses in less developed countries. In short, the average person in the United States, Europe, or any other developed capitalist country gets paid off with wealth extracted from the less developed.

What's that, you say? You haven't gotten your world systems periphery exploitation check? Well, actually, you are wearing it. Inexpensive clothes are one particularly obvious way that the average person in a core country benefits from the economic exploitation of the periphery. Heard about all of that protesting of Nike's Malaysian sweatshops? Well, the use of cheap foreign labor leads to more than just corporate profits. It also leads to less expensive, much less expensive, shoes. Forget the superflashy basketball shoes that will never actually get anywhere close to sweaty feet on a court; go into a discount store and look at the price on an average pair of shoes that a normal human would use to play basketball. I can even be generous and tell you to avoid the really cheap stuff and look only at the ones that are marked, say, fifty dollars a pair. What would it cost to make those in the

United States or Europe? Well, find another store and see how much cash it takes to buy a pair of Italian designer shoes. Even at a discount store an average pair of Italian-made shoes will cost at least twice what you lay out for the sneakers. The biggest part of that difference is the cost of the labor. Shirts, pants, coats, even your underwear—they are all far cheaper because they are made by the periphery workers of the periphery states. Even if you do not find cash falling into your wallet, your dollar, yen, pound, or euro buys far more stuff because of the exploitation of the periphery. If you united with the periphery of the periphery and overthrew the global economic system, you would also be giving up all that cheap stuff.

You don't rebel because you like your cheap stuff.

So you are kept happy and nonrevolutionary with your cheap stuff, and that bit of insight is what separates Galtung and world systems theory from other Marxist or economics-first theories of politics. Galtung not only explains why the system keeps poor countries poor, but he also demonstrates how the system is sustained and why it doesn't collapse. This is also what all the noise regarding antiglobalization is about. The antiglobalization demonstrators who can think beyond the catchy slogans and actually understand why they are harassing the G-8 meetings and smashing the windows of Starbucks are protesting against the fundamental unfairness of this global economic capitalist system. For wealthy countries, the infrastructure of the global system for trade acts much as the ownership of factories did for the early industrial capitalists Marx wrote about. By controlling the World Bank, monetary exchange systems, and access to sources of investment capital, developed nations force less developed nations to play by unfair economic rules. Loans, development grants, foreign aid, and trade agreements are all self-serving actions by the developed countries. These actions build economic infrastructures not for local development but to facilitate the exploitation by the economies of core countries, and they tie developed countries to debts that extract capital at an alarming rate through interest payments.

An entrepreneur in the Republic of the Congo has no realistic hope of becoming the next Bill Gates. The infrastructure of the Congo will not provide him the education, nor will it allow him to develop the products needed to bring wealth to his country. As for computers or communications lines, even if you could get access to reliable electricity in the Congo, it is almost impossible to buy a lightbulb there. If Einstein's smarter brother were to be reincarnated in the Congo he would have to go to a developed country to succeed in business. He would have to leave to even be educated enough to understand what his less gifted, crazy-haired brother said. Developed countries not only keep the wealth flowing home, but they also keep the opportunities at home and extract everything that less developed countries would need to build economies that do anything more than service the dominant, wealthy parts of the world. The core even extracts people from the periphery. Most of the foreign students you see on campus are the brightest and best their countries

have to offer. They represent the best resources those countries might have for development, and most of those students will stay in the United States or Europe to work after they complete their educations. Except for money sent home to families, those students will contribute to their adopted developed economies instead of their less developed homelands; they will pay taxes, create businesses, and contribute to your standard of living instead of going home. In the Congo, there is very little work available for molecular biologists. Thus, the Congo and all the other developing countries have little hope of keeping their best and brightest at home to pull the countries up economically. The unfairness of all this is what the antiglobalization demonstrators are really protesting about.

Now I said that the antiglobalization crowd would be displeased with this section, and here is the part they really will not like: there are two big problems inherent in the politics and the reality behind all the antiglobalization protests and window smashing. Pointing these things out never fails to really irritate a few people, but if I were worried about upsetting people, it would be awfully hard to teach about politics.

The first problem is that not everything about globalization is bad and evil. That is not to deny that there are truly wretched things that we can blame on the effects of global capitalism, but if you look at all of the ways capitalism has changed the world over the past couple centuries, or even over the past half century, you'll likely agree that there are several good things. *Better* and *worse* are value judgments, and they depend greatly on what you, personally, value, but there is enough of a variety of good things that I can probably find something you think is good.

You're in college, so maybe you like education. I'm not going to make any presumptions on this topic, but if you do like education, it might interest you to know that there are more literate people in the world right now than at any other time in history, and more people than ever have access to basic, advanced, and technical education. Maybe you like being alive. Many people do. In that case, consider that basic health care and vaccinations have become more available in just about every country around the world than they were in *any* country before capitalism became a prominent economic phenomenon, and when the entire globe is considered, the likelihood of surviving childhood is now higher than it was for any previous generation. What about bananas? Do you like them? Many of the foods you enjoy are probably not native to the country you live in, but are available to you through international trade. How about something more esoteric, like human rights? While there are still some notable and ugly exceptions, basic rights for women—almost nonexistent prior to the capitalist economic revolution—now exist in some meaningful form for the vast majority of the better-smelling gender.* There are currently more democracies in the world and more people living in democracies than ever before in history. At the very least, before

---

*I included a weasel word here by saying *meaningful*. While many places, such as China and India, are difficult to consider equal to Western European standards, women in these and most other countries around the world have rights that almost no women anywhere had before the Industrial Revolution.

you smash that Starbucks window, you should look at both the good and the bad things that you might reasonably blame on capitalism. For the past half century, the United Nations has been gathering and publishing data on living conditions around the world. Even a cursory examination of these data on the U.N. website reveals many things that have improved. Some things are worse, some are better, but the balance between the good, the bad, and the ugly is a matter of judgment and personal values. That is a judgment you should make in an informed and considered manner.

The second thing that will displease an antiglobalization protester is a simple question: What do you think you want? "Stop globalization" may be what you spray-paint on the side of the cow you stole and tied to the front door of the McDonald's in a lame stab at irony, but is that possible? Globalization is a phenomenon created by advancing technology, increasing worldwide education, and the aggregate economic choices of billions of people around the world. It is not like the global release of *Indiana Jones and the Kingdom of the Crystal Skull,* which somebody could and very well should have stopped. Is there anyone, any country or any group of countries, that could actually stop or reverse globalization? What alternative is there to globalization? The technology is already out there; can we take it away? Certainly there must be things that leaders or countries could do to reduce the negatives and enhance the positives, but can the increasing economic integration of the world be stopped? Can it be reversed? If you were to cut a country off from all aspects of international trade and international communication, would it really be better off? North Korea suggests the answer might be no, but having an insane dictator might be part of the problem there. Even if you are a leader who wants to give the antiglobalization protesters what they want, what is it that you could give them?

Imperfection Is Cool, Honest

It is all but impossible to offer a coherent and comprehensive introduction to international politics in a single chapter. Not only is the study of international politics conceptually and theoretically diverse, but the size of this subfield of politics is also difficult to misunderestimate. The International Studies Association's Compendium of International Studies uses roughly 4,000,000 words of summary essays in its attempt to review the field. That's not a typo, 4,000,000 words, roughly the equivalent of thirty copies of this book, just to try to summarize the field. I've offered some commentary on the choices I've made as a way to alert you to the fact that I was making compromises and judgment calls, some of which your instructor or some future instructor of a global politics course might very well disagree with. Keep that in mind. That's an order.

As a way of concluding this most imperfect chapter, I want to mention two things. First, I want to raise the idea of a global tragedy of the commons. For those of you with a green tweak inside those heads of yours, particularly those who don't shake your heads in confusion at the mention of the Gaia hypothesis, this should be particularly relevant. Second,

even though I dissed constructivism a little earlier, I want to end with a mention of it and what it offers.

Dude, Think about the Fish

The tragedy of the commons represents another way the study of international politics can mirror the caveman stories from the beginning of the book and yet another way that international politics diverges from the simplistic model of realism. Collapsing fisheries, disappearing forests, transnational pollution, population pressures, and plagues are all issues the world has seen before. The Roman Empire had serious problems with airborne pollution from silver smelting. Historically, deforestation has repeatedly been a problem for naval powers from the Greeks to the British, often sending them to farthest reaches of their trade networks for the timber needed for shipbuilding. Ancient civilizations from Cambodia to Peru appear to have fallen victim to the cumulative effects of intensive agriculture, causing regional, and sometimes continental, economic and social collapses. Many of these transnational or regional catastrophes, however, occurred in the shadows. The overexploitation and collapse of communal resources left little or no impression in written histories and were usually discovered by archaeologists digging in the dirt rather than historians digging through archives.

Today, the struggle with the forces driving us into the tragedy of the commons has gone global, and every year the number of ways that the feeble humans of planet Earth face problems that threaten the global commons increases. From population pressures to collapsing ocean resources, to ozone depletion, to access to fresh water, to acid rain, to disease control, to reality TV,* a list of global tragedy-of-the-commons issues could grow very long. The length of this list might reasonably be attributed to the forces of globalization. With capitalist pressures becoming ever more universal, the numbers of ways those economic dynamics drive people to overexploit common resources increase and become all-inclusive. Further, the economic pressure driving overexploitation is now relatively consistent around the world, driving everyone everywhere toward the same tragedies and making it difficult for regional booms and busts to average themselves out.

Fisheries have often been overexploited to the point of collapse. The California anchovy fishery that collapsed right about the time Steinbeck was writing *Cannery Row*[22] is just one example. Previously, however, an event like that was isolated, and when the fish were gone, the world's consumers could go elsewhere for another tin of salty pizza toppings. The fishermen would abandon a commercially unworkable area and essentially leave it to recover while they destroyed someplace else. Now, it is all happening at once. The

---

*Obviously, this is a joke. There is nothing more horrific than reality TV, and it should clearly be first on the list of things that threaten the very existence of the human race.

Canadian Atlantic cod fishery has already collapsed, and the Icelandic, North Sea (European), Alaskan, Japanese, Peruvian, and Antarctic fisheries are all under intense commercial pressure. Globally, the levels of exploitation appear to be well beyond what might be sustainable, and if these fisheries are driven to collapse, there is nowhere else to fish for something to go with your chips. For a particularly grim take on this subject, try *Earth,*[23] by David Brin.

However, part of the increase in attention paid to the exploitation of the commons in international politics might be attributed to an increase in education and awareness. Almost unheard of a half century ago, environmental and shared-resource issues have become such an integral part of education that in 2002 the Europe-Wide Global Education Congress included international environmental cooperation next to literacy, history, and mathematics in the definition of a basic education. Recycling, energy conservation, deforestation, endangered species, acid rain, global warming, the global spread of disease, the French tolerance of body odor—we may not agree on what if anything should be done about these environmental issues, but they are issues on the international political table and they are all new. Fifty years ago none of them were any part of the mainstream political debate, and today they are global issues.

These global tragedy-of-the-commons issues are also well represented in fiction.[*] The most relevant for today's students might be the movies about global epidemics, such as *12 Monkeys.* In addition to making it uncomfortably clear that Brad Pitt is just a little too good at playing the part of a lunatic, *12 Monkeys*[24] shows just how hard it is to generate the collective actions needed to protect even the most precious of global commons. It would not take much to stop the release of the virus that is about to destroy life on Earth, but convincing anyone to act against an abstract and seemingly distant threat turns out to be an impossible challenge. If it is that hard to convince just a few people to act, how hard must it be to get the massive and coordinated action necessary to combat bird flu as a likely pandemic or swine flu as an actual pandemic?

This is, and likely will continue to be, a significant part of global politics, but there is no tidy theoretical perspective with a catchy name to attach to the study of the political dynamics of a global tragedy of the commons. Still, a few dynamics are becoming apparent. The first is that it is difficult to label this as international relations. Rather than being part of the politics *between* nations, it is more of an issue and a dynamic that extends *across* nations. It is a transnational issue involving nations, but it also includes groups and organizations that can't be put in that category. Subnational political units such as cities, political parties, states, and provinces are acting across and beyond national borders. Multinational entities such as the United Nations, NAFTA, the International Whaling

---

[*]David Brin's *Earth,* James P. Hogan's *Thrice upon a Time,* Kim Stanley Robinson's *Mars* Trilogy, *Soylent Green,* and *Omega Man* are all stories of environmental collapse. Larry Niven's Gil Hamilton stories, and many of his *Known Space* stories, are built on themes about population pressures and the limits of the biosphere.

SUN TZU

Team: Imperial Dragons

Position: Silly Mid On

Status: Unconfirmed

Sun Tzu (sometime in the Land that Time Forgot) may have never existed, or he may have been another philosophically inclined time traveler. Supposedly, he wrote *The Art of War*[a] around 500 B.C., but scholars argue that many of the details of warfare that Sun Tzu describes, such as the use of the crossbow, did not exist or did not appear in China until at least 50, and possibly as many as 250, years later. Others argue that certain historical details indicate that *The Art of War* had to have been written before 474 B.C., when the Wu kingdom was destroyed, and that makes the 500 B.C. date a pretty good approximation. Regardless of when *The Art of War* was actually written, it is notable that Sun Tzu was supposedly a great and distinguished general, but the histories of this period do not mention him—thus, the questions of whether he ever existed at all arose. Various scholars have suggested that Sun Tzu was actually a fictitious character invented for story-telling purposes, that he existed but a later disciple actually wrote the book, that he merely collected and edited together existing anecdotes and stories, or that he was actually a teenage girl pretending to be the son of a warrior, who with the assistance of a tiny talking dragon accidentally won a war and then hired Walt Disney to ghostwrite her memoirs in cartoon form.[b]

Nevertheless, the discussions of the philosophical and political foundations of war that are attributed to Sun Tzu have had an extensive and lasting effect on everything from business to international politics. Notable in *The Art of War* is the very clear argument that war is essentially a political activity, and as a result, the politics involved affect the way in which a war must be fought. One of the clear corollaries of this line of reasoning is the argument that destroying the enemy's ability to fight is not the only way to win a war. In fact, it may be one of the most inefficient and costly ways to win. Destroying an enemy's will to fight is often a better way to win a war, and better still is maneuvering your opponent into a position that convinces the opponent to concede without fighting.

This emphasis on winning the political side of the battle as the key to waging war has been argued to be a defining aspect of an Eastern, or perhaps Asian, philosophy of war, exemplified by the Vietnam War. The vastly outgunned North Vietnamese defeated the U.S. superpower not by winning battles but by constantly attacking the U.S. will to fight. The Tet Offensive is the best example of winning the politics. By any reasonable measure of military and tactical accomplishment, the offensive was a failure, but it dealt a devastating blow to U.S. morale, and its effect on the U.S. desire to continue fighting is often cited as the turning point in the war. Similarly, demoralizing the United States and forcing it into immediate negotiations over trade embargoes was one of the primary objectives of the Japanese attack on Pearl Harbor. The tactic backfired, but the Japanese strategy to damage the U.S. will to fight reflects the impact of Sun Tzu.

[a]Sun Tzu, *The Art of War,* translated by Samuel B. Griffith (New York: Oxford University Press, 1963).

[b]Except for the Disney part, discussions of these arguments about the authenticity of *The Art of War* and the identity of Sun Tzu are common features of published versions of the text, and the details of these and a variety of other aspects of the work can be found there. See, for example, the Griffith translation cited here.

Commission, and the World Bank are involved. Transnational organizations, entities that exist outside and across the geographic definition of states, are involved, such as Greenpeace, the Sierra Club, Doctors Without Borders, and international businesses. Additionally, economic dynamics, political dynamics, and issues of science and research all come into play. How all of these additional factors sort out into a simple model of how the world works is an interesting and complicated question.

Constructivism

Finally, it's important that I give constructivism a fair mention. There is a reason that it has been popular in introduction to international relations textbooks, and students do need to have some idea what it is and why it is valuable.

While it can be a challenge to get everyone to agree on a definition of **constructivism,** or even to agree on whether it qualifies as a theory of international relations, constructivism can reasonably be depicted in terms of its fundamental claim that human beings construct the reality around them—the reality upon which they base their decisions and choices—through language and communication. The conceptual framework used to describe something enables certain actions and prevents others. The analogy chosen for thinking about something defines the logic by which all current and future information on the subject is interpreted. What is communicated—or, more important, what is not communicated—drives politics, because what we do not hear about, we cannot address. From this perspective, international communication, both in terms of capabilities and in terms of filters on the content, becomes the critical consideration in the study of international relations. With all of the technological, social, and political interest in the recent and rapid advances in communication technology, it should not be surprising that constructivism has garnered a great deal of attention.

In the study of international politics, constructivism is certainly equal to or more significant than many of the perspectives, issues, and ideas highlighted in this chapter, and as an explicit challenge to the realist perspective, its claim is unquestionable. Arising out of postmodern critiques directly attacking, if not assaulting, realism as a theory,[25] it has an antirealism pedigree that not even Marxism can match. It would appear that all the factors have aligned for a big and flashy section on constructivism, parade and all. However, in addition to the technical challenge of including a parade in a textbook, there are several reasons for exercising caution in regard to constructivism. Four are particularly troublesome:

1. As a theory, constructivism is still new, very new. It has now been a little over a decade since it first began coalescing as any kind of coherent approach, and there simply has not been a lot of time for academic research to sort out its strengths and weaknesses thoroughly. In contrast, realism and Marxism have been around longer

than almost any of the professors currently studying them. There has been plenty of time to sort through their implications and the limits of how much they can explain in international relations.

2. The enthusiasm inherent in many of the earliest studies on constructivism may have distorted assessments of its scope and applicability. The "CNN effect" is the primary example. The moment it was suggested that the real-time global news media are driving leaders into actions they would rather avoid, the idea was touted as a revolution in the very nature of international politics even before any significant research had been conducted. Subsequent research has shown that the CNN effect is extremely limited, particularly in terms of how far it can push a leader against the flow of other influences. In fact, the CNN effect seems to be largely confined to an influence within the limits of policy action defined by either the economic constraints of the world system or the power constraints of a realist political environment.

3. Claims that constructivism represents a new way of understanding a new world are a bit questionable. It may be reasonable to say that constructivism is coalescing into a new way of understanding international politics, but the claim of a new world order is not holding up well in the face of most research. As far back as existing records make it possible to study, the news media have always had a modest but clear influence on international politics. One of the best explanations for choices the United States made in the Vietnam War involves media coverage and the use of analogies to conceptualize and debate the issues. Another example is the way in which President Truman's presumptions and beliefs about the Soviet Union prevented him from even considering cooperative options, and the way those cognitive frameworks appear to have been significant factors in the beginning of the Cold War. In short, many of the elements of a constructed reality of politics are not new phenomena that have arisen out of the latest revolution in communication technologies.

4. In 2012 there was a noticeable drop in the number of papers presented at key academic conference on international studies that were explicitly presented as constructivist theory approaches. Fluctuation in the research topics presented at such conferences is a normal thing to see, but the change in 2012 was significant enough to make me worry about having to totally rewrite this chapter for the fourth edition in order to replace constructivism with something else.

However, all of these cautions concern the place of constructivism as equal to Marxism as a challenger to realism, not its inherent value as a new and interesting theoretical construct. Research will eventually tell us exactly where constructivism fits; we just have to be patient. I've never been good at being patient.

Roaring Mice and Vacation Hot Spots

Like everything else in politics, international relations is probably best discussed not in terms of which theoretical approach is correct but instead in terms of how different ideas help us understand what is going on. To quit teasing you and actually conclude this chapter, I ask a simple question: Why does Barbados exist?

No, I am not talking about how the island was formed—by aliens setting off volcanoes— but the mere existence of Barbados as an independent country, which is a very interesting thing to consider. Barbados has absolutely no power in the traditional, international relations sense of the word—no army, no navy, no air force, no Girl Scouts brandishing pointy marsh- mallow roasting sticks. The United States could conquer the island without mustering any forces beyond the guys hanging around a typical Minnesota hunting lodge griping about Al Franken. If the world is anarchic and you can survive only if you have the power to protect yourself, how can Barbados exist? Is the answer economic? Is it a moral issue? Is conquer- ing Barbados just something the United States hasn't gotten around to doing? Watch *The Mouse That Roared*[26]—either the movie or the *Pinky and the Brain* cartoon version—and then ponder how it is that a powerless country like Barbados continues to exist as an independent entity. None of the theories of international politics in this text can offer a satisfactory answer.

KEY TERMS

balance of power / 326

bandwagoning / 326

constructivism / 346

democratic peace / 332

hegemon / 333

idealism / 320

realism / 318

world systems theory / 339

CHAPTER SUMMARY

When we think about international relations, we most often think about war. Given the hor- rors, tensions, and fears associated with war, this is understandable. However, given the number of countries that exist, war is rare. In fact, most of international politics concerns cooperation. Thus, a truly interesting question is, Why do wars happen? The tendency in fiction to explain wars as accidents flies in the face of reality. Wars are not accidents; they are the results of conscious, rational actions. Spurred by the horrors of World War I, schol- ars were motivated to focus on peace. World events ultimately put a damper on idealism, which led scholars to embrace realism as an explanation. Realism, with its presumptions that international relations can be explained in terms of strategy, rational action, and power in an anarchic environment, did not explain every war. Scholars taking the approach of Foreign Policy Analysis challenged liberalism's presumptions that the internal workings of governments do not matter. Political scientists have paid a lot of attention to the fact that democracies do not fight one another, although scholars do not agree about why this is. Other schools of thought have emerged to explain international relations. Among these,

one focuses on the dominance of a nation, another focuses on the global economy, and yet another focuses on the global influence of the news media. Students should learn two very important lessons from this chapter. First, there is no one simple theory that explains global interaction; international relations are complex and multifaceted. War, albeit attention grabbing, is only one part of this complex labyrinth. Second, from now on you will find it difficult to purchase a pair of sneakers without your mind wandering off to consider cores and peripheries.

STUDY QUESTIONS AND EXERCISES

1. This chapter discusses a number of theories that seek to explain international relations. Which of these theories do you believe best explains the current world situation? Why?

2. What are the three key assumptions that underlie the realist perspective on international relations?

3. What are the flaws in the realist perspective? What are the flaws in the other perspectives?

4. What prompted the development of idealism as an approach to international relations?

5. Find an article or editorial that discusses the issue of globalization. Do you agree with the perspective expressed in the piece you have selected? Why or why not?

6. What is a hegemon? What role does a hegemon play in international relations?

WEBSITES TO EXPLORE

http://europa.eu/index_en.htm. The Europa: Gateway to the European Union site includes news and information about the European Union.

www.du.edu/~bhughes/ifs.html. Barry B. Hughes's International Futures site links to a computer simulation of global systems for classroom and research use.

www.imf.org. The International Monetary Fund's site provides information on this organization of 184 countries that aims to foster global monetary cooperation, secure financial stability, facilitate international trade, promote high employment and sustainable economic growth, and reduce poverty.

www.library.gsu.edu/research/pages.asp?IdID=41&guideID=101&ID=560. Georgia State University Library's International Relations Resources Web page includes general resources, gateways, proprietary resources, and international law resources.

www.library.yale.edu/ia-resources/polecon.html. Yale University Library's Political Economy and Development Resources Web page provides links to relevant organizations, journals, data, and more.

www.library.yale.edu/ia-resources/resource.html. Yale University Library's International Affairs Resources Web page includes links to international organizations, news, and research institutes.

www.un.org. This site provides information about the United Nations, its member nations, its policies, and more.

www2.etown.edu/vl/research.html. The World Wide Web Virtual Library: International Affairs Resources page contains a list of research institutes focused on international relations.

Secret Government
Spies, Lies, and Freedom Fries

Somewhat naked goldfish ▮▮▮▮▮▮▮▮

▮▮▮▮▮▮▮▮▮▮▮▮▮▮▮▮

▮▮▮▮▮▮▮▮▮▮▮▮▮▮▮▮

▮▮▮▮▮▮▮▮▮▮▮▮▮▮▮▮

▮▮▮▮▮▮▮▮▮▮▮▮▮▮▮▮

▮▮▮▮▮▮▮▮▮▮▮▮▮▮▮▮

▮▮▮▮▮▮▮▮▮▮▮ second at Daytona ▮▮

▮▮▮▮▮▮▮▮▮▮▮▮▮▮▮▮

▮▮▮▮▮▮▮▮▮▮▮▮▮▮▮▮

▮ rabid pixies ▮▮▮▮▮▮▮▮▮▮

▮▮▮▮▮▮▮▮▮▮▮▮▮▮▮▮

▮▮▮▮▮▮▮▮▮▮ barking death squirrels ▮

▮▮▮▮▮▮▮▮▮▮▮▮▮

dyslexic coloring book

ungraceful cliffdwellers

clonehenge

burning epiphanies

nearly heroic

Political Culture

Sex and Agriculture, Getting Rucked Explains It All

Quick, what's the most commonly spoken language in New Zealand? If you've seen all the reruns of Flight of the Conchords, or if you think that New Zealand is one of those province things up in Canada, you will probably guess English. Technically, that is correct. The reality, however, is a bit more complicated. Consider the following:

When the gang from Morningside accidentally gives the first fifteen food poisoning, the little hoons get thrown into the scrum and they are all that stand between the St. Sylvester Savages and an inglorious rucking from the old boys. The consequences of this latest misadventure could be worse than when the class visited the *marae,* found themselves in the middle of a *tangihanga,* and Jeff the Maori was mistakenly asked to decide the fate of his *iwi.* It could be worse than all the girls left up the duff after the St. Sylvester ball. This disaster could even be worse than when Mack gets the Fa'afafine Brother Ken thrown in jail and everyone in Morningside spits the dummy. It could be worse than Mack breaking into the totally flash bach and all the tog jokes in the episode about Sione and the Brazilian. Yes, it could be the worst yet. However, in the tradition of all good comedies, it's not about whanu, it's not about the yakka, in the end we all learn the lesson that it doesn't matter how much of a zonk you are, you're in good nick as long as a zambuck hauls you off the domain.

While the lingo may not be exactly spot on and a fair bit of that Kiwi slang is dated—I am a crusty after all—it still should get the point across. It isn't exactly Walter Cronkite's standard mid-western American English. It isn't even the Queen's English. In fact, of all the English dialects around the world, New Zenglish is probably the second most colorful, after Jamaican. In addition to a healthy portion of slang from every corner of Britain, and a fair bit brought across the ditch by the dingoes, New Zenglish includes a great deal of Te Reo Maori, the language of the Polynesians

native to New Zealand, and is full of words from all across Polynesia. Even the words that are common English words are colored by Polynesian ideas and are often pronounced with shortened vowels and the Polynesian emphasis on the first syllable. New Zealand's version of English is also remarkably diverse within the country, ranging from a heavy Scottish influence and accent in the Deep South to a predominance of Polynesian accents and idioms in the Auckland region to the north, a distinctive Wellington accent, and a very interesting pocket of slang unique to the Gisborne* area.

What's important here is not just the slang and the colorful idioms, or the extra vowels in words like *labour* and *colour* or the extra syllable in *aluminium.* The slang is just a hint at the surprisingly big cultural differences between New Zealand and North America. Even the things that seem familiar tend to be quite different, and nowhere is that more obvious than in the humor (or humour).

Like any good cartoon, *bro'Town*[1] exploits the theme of the social value of violent injury. In the very first episode, Valea became a genius when he gets hit by a bus. However it is the raw ethnic humor in *bro'Town* that sets it apart from most other satiric cartoons. The show is littered with toilet humor and stuffed with sexual jokes, and it makes a point of skewering religion, even beginning one episode with God playing strip poker with Buddha. Still, it is *bro'Town*'s casual use of impolitic racial references and crass ethnic jokes that is most striking. "Jeff's Maori, he can break into anything." Pacific Islanders are referred to as "Taro Eaters." If you want to butcher an old racehorse, you take it to Tommy the Tongan Butcher because Tongans will kill anything for you. Abo is an Australian Aborigine running around in a loincloth and eating grubs. The "fat brown kid" is obviously a good flanker because "those pollywogs have it in their blood," and all the Chinese kids are masters of martial arts who are caught up in organized crime and eat stir-fried puppy-fetus rice. It is not as crude as *South Park,* but *bro'Town* is politically incorrect to its core.

As a student who is misspending the last and best part of your youth at a North American university, you are probably immersed in U.S. and, to a lesser degree, Canadian culture,[†] and that is why you cannot hope to understand even half of the references in *bro'Town* and you will never get any of the jokes. If you are on that side of the world, it probably means that you do not know that "Sex and Agriculture" actually refers to the best CD since the Bronze Age. You probably don't even know who the Exponents are or why four million people—and roughly sixty million sheep—will instantly associate the chorus from "Why Does Love Do This to Me?" with grown men crashing headlong into each other. If you happen to know what scrums, rucks, and mauls are, then you will know that getting rucked is nothing even remotely close to a sexual reference,[‡] and you just might know what

---

*Pronounced Giz-B'n.

†Yes, Canadians have culture.

‡*Rucking* is a rugby term for stomping on someone who is lying on the ground and obstructing the ball. However, there is a rule against rucking someone's head. Rugby players aren't savages, at least not completely.

a *haka* is, but how about a *hongi*? What kind of a beast is a Pakeha, and what should you do if one gets loose while you are at the zoo?

Jemaine, Bret, and Murray actually make it a bit worse. Flight of the Conchords is a New Zealand comedy act about a clueless folk duo, but the television show of the same name is an American production for an American audience, and half the jokes fall flat, or worse, in New Zealand. Most of you are probably realistic enough to realize that *Lord of the Rings* was a fantasy trilogy that was filmed in New Zealand, not a documentary on New Zealand history, but even that has served to create some interesting distortions of Kiwi culture. And that is, perhaps, the point. Culture is a tricky subject, and when you mix it with politics, it becomes even less straightforward.

POLITICAL CULTURE

It probably seems strange to you that one of the subjects I have barely mentioned in a textbook that uses pop culture to examine politics is political culture, but *bro'Town* is the reason. Well, not specifically *bro'Town,* but rather what it represents in terms of political culture. Put succinctly, culture is a somewhat problematic issue for the study of politics because by providing a seductively simple explanation for just about everything, it risks telling us nothing.

One of the most common ways to define **culture**—the set of values that a group shares—is in terms of implicit and explicit beliefs, practices, and expectations. In an ideal world, all peoples would share enough culture to be able to communicate clearly with one another, and everybody would agree on common terms for understanding the best solutions to key problems. And except for the toilets, when the 747 dumps a North American student at the Auckland airport, said student will find a lot about Kiwi culture to be quite familiar.* Prospects look good for communication and understanding. However, what the *bro'Town* example shows us is that in the real world, even when two societies share most key aspects of culture, the cultural gap between them can still be huge. Even when the two societies are both developed, Western, capitalist, democratic societies that are, for the most part, populated by people who share the same ethnic and religious background, even when they almost speak the same language,† culture can still impede communication and understanding. Even with the briefest of exposures, there is no mistaking the differences—sometimes subtle, sometimes huge—between North American and New Zealand cultures.

---

*Unlike the dainty little water-saving, environmentally friendly low-flow toilets that decorate the bathrooms of North America, New Zealand toilets are notable for generating a thundering rush of water that is powerful enough to flush a buffalo. This is all the more remarkable for the fact that there are neither buffalo nor bison in New Zealand.

†Just in case you haven't figured it out yet, New Zealand English and U.S. English are *not* the same language. Consider the words *bum* and *fanny.* In the United States, *bum* refers to a homeless alcoholic, whereas in New Zealand it refers to a portion of the anatomy used for sitting. In the United States, one way to refer to that part of the anatomy used for sitting is to call it a fanny, but that is definitely not what a fanny is in New Zealand. In New Zealand, a fanny is a part of the female anatomy that you cannot refer to on TV, not even New Zealand TV.

Humor is particularly good at exposing the width and depth of that gap because humor works by subtly twisting some bit of truth in an unexpected direction. Because of that need for subtlety, until you have spent a good year or more living in New Zealand and have picked up some of those subtle bits of Kiwi culture, you will miss half the jokes in *bro'Town*. Similarly, urban humor—particularly the variety of New York humor found in Woody Allen movies—is completely lost on the populace of New Zealand, a country with a capital city that is smaller than Toledo, Ohio.

Consequences of Culture

Beyond which jokes do and do not work, there appear to be some obvious political consequences of culture. Take the regulatory standard for broadcast TV as an example. In New Zealand, sex, religion, and ethnicity are fair targets for a comedy that airs at 7:30 P.M. on broadcast TV. Partial nudity is allowed after 9:30 P.M., so most nonviolent films with a U.S. "R" rating can be shown uncut late in the evening, but many "PG" films that would have to be edited for content to be broadcast at all in the United States can be shown at any time of day in New Zealand. For New Zealand broadcast TV, the rules regarding foul language are also far more liberal, even for TV commercials. In a government-funded public service spot aimed at discouraging drunk driving—shown during afternoon and weekend shows targeting an adolescent audience—one teenager calls his friend a "dick" and the friend retorts, "Well, at least I've got a dick." In the United States, because of that language, that commercial would never be broadcast. Similarly, in the United States, *bro'Town* would definitely be relegated to cable, if it were shown at all. Even if it were on cable, can you imagine the uproar over a cartoon that spends an entire episode making jokes about a kid getting an erection from watching Xena: Warrior Princess putting a condom on a banana? And *bro'Town* would not fare any better in the Great White North. The crassness of the ethnic humor, particularly with so much of it directed at native peoples, would probably keep *bro'Town* off Canadian TV altogether. All of this, however, is acceptable in New Zealand. Clearly, New Zealand's more liberal political culture has a profound influence on the nation's broadcast standards.

Or does culture have anything to do with it?

At first glance, it seems obvious that a few small but important cultural differences explain the divergence between what is shown on New Zealand and U.S. broadcast TV. Clearly, New Zealand must be a more liberal country. One only has to look at the arguments in the United States over birth control and teaching evolution to see that the political power of the religious right and social conservatives is far greater in U.S. culture than in New Zealand. In New Zealand, the conservative National Party was recently criticized by the ultraliberal Maori Party for giving women free access to government-funded birth control. Can you imagine the Republicans giving away free birth control? That cultural difference surely explains why you get some naughty words and an occasional glimpse of naughty bits on New Zealand broadcast TV but not on the U.S. networks.

However, that cultural argument cuts both ways. In comparing the two countries, it also becomes clear that Kiwis as a whole seem to be more sensitive to the value inherent in racial and ethnic diversity than Americans are. Kiwis engage racial and ethnic political issues, particularly those involving indigenous peoples, far more effectively than do Americans, or anyone else in the world for that matter. If anything, when it comes to race, Kiwis seem to be far more like Canadians than Americans,* and a cultural explanation for the differences in broadcast television content would lead to the expectation that in New Zealand, ethnic humor—especially when it targets the indigenous Maori—would be treated as ethnic humor is in Canada, discouraged to the point of being shunned. However, *bro'Town* makes it clear that that is not the case.

If Not Culture?

Instead of culture, perhaps one could use a simple market model to explain the differences between U.S. and New Zealand broadcast television standards. In the United States, cable TV has been around for more than a quarter century and has been available almost everywhere in the country for the past twenty years or so. This is significant because you have to pay for access to cable TV, and that means that the content of U.S. cable TV has always been governed by a different, and far more liberal, set of rules than broadcast TV. The argument that you have to shield those who do not wish to see a few naughty bits does not apply if they have to pay to watch. As a result of the availability of cable TV and its more liberal rules, in the United States shows that pushed the boundaries of social acceptability had an outlet other than broadcast TV. That alternate outlet may have eliminated, or at least severely reduced, most of the social pressure to liberalize broadcast rules, and the United States ended up with what, by a global measure, can only be called prudish standards for broadcast television.

In contrast, there was no alternative outlet for that boundary-challenging television content in New Zealand. With a population roughly equal to that of Connecticut, and most of that population rural and spread out over a mountainous country that would cover the entire West Coast of the United States, stretching from Los Angeles to Seattle, simple geography prevented New Zealand from experiencing the cable TV boom that hit the United States in the early 1980s. In New Zealand, it was just too expensive to hook everyone up, and until the quite recent expansion of satellite TV delivery, most New Zealanders had access to nothing but the two government-sponsored, nationally broadcast television channels. As a result, there were no alternate channels available and any demand for content that challenged the limits of social acceptability could be addressed only through adjustment of the broadcast standards governing the limited channels that were available.

---

*While Canadians live in the chilly part of North America—the part that justifies adding North to the continent name and that does make them, technically, Americans—I would rather not insult the Canadians by referring to them with the term most of the world uses as a disparaging reference to the United States.

As a result, political pressure was brought to bear that led to far more liberal broadcast standards in New Zealand.

But then again, maybe it was just culture. Kiwi conservatives are far, far less prudish about sexuality than American conservatives, and Kiwis in general don't dwell on sexuality in the same way Americans do. There are almost no thematic references to virginity and little social value placed on chastity in New Zealand literature and popular culture. Prostitution is legal in New Zealand, and brothels can be found in any phone book. On the other hand, Kiwis have trouble understanding the American tolerance of, if not affection for, graphic violence, and any imported U.S. films or shows that are edited are usually censored for violence.

Culture as Explanation

The problem with using culture to explain political phenomena is that culture—political or otherwise—offers a universal explanation. Everything political can be distilled down to some group's shared beliefs, or shared expectations, or shared linguistic referents. Why are the Nordic countries of Europe far closer to the socialist end of the economic spectrum than the rest of Western Europe? You could argue that it is simply a reflection of their culture. If you visit Norway, Denmark, Sweden, or Iceland you will discover that a sense of social responsibility seems to be a very big part of the culture. When you visit, it actually feels very socialist there. In the Nordic countries many clearly believe that society has a responsibility to take care of those who fail economically. In fact, saying that a person "fails" economically, or in any other way suggesting that an individual is responsible for his or her own poverty, is something that really would not fit well at all with Nordic cultural norms, but is that really an explanation for why they are the most socialist of the developed countries in the world? Is it enough to say that the economy is that way because the inhabitants share the belief that it should be that way? Does that really tell us anything? Isn't it possible that the economy was that way first and that after adjusting to it the people found they liked it?

Some would argue that this culture of social responsibility arose out of the extreme winters, where not looking out for a neighbor could be deadly, and the Nordic countries do seem to share a belief that something like that community responsibility should be extended and applied to society as a whole.

If culture is enough of an explanation, then how do we explain change? How do you get from raiding and pillaging Vikings literally slaughtering people to take their wealth to a Norway that is synonymous with the Nobel Peace Prize and abhors the very idea of people suffering for want of money? Perhaps culture could change that drastically over the course of a few centuries, but gradual change does not explain how culture could account for both China's embrace of communism and the ferociously competitive, almost predatory capitalism that has evolved there over the past few decades. Could Chinese culture, built upon a historical foundation stretching over several millennia, whipsaw back and forth that

quickly? If culture is enough of an explanation for national economic models, then how do we explain when vastly different things happen in similar cultures or when similar things occur in vastly different cultures?

There is no denying that culture is real and has a significant influence on politics. It is almost certain that the Swedish economic model would never work in Australia. It does not take much research to see that a heavily socialist economic model just does not fit with the rugged-individualist ideal of Australian culture. Crocodile Dundee and Steve Irwin may both be caricatures of Australian culture, but caricatures always have to reflect a fair bit of truth in order to work. However, that very same example also makes it clear that you must be very careful in what you attribute to culture. In addition to what Australians think might be culture,[*] an explanation of the current nature of the Australian economy would have to address all of the historical, political, geographic, demographic, economic, domestic, and international factors that have shaped all the choices and decisions that have led to the nation's current economic model. The lonely, uninhabitable stretches of desert that dominate most of the country, where the monstrous ranches dwarf those of even the United States, explain a lot about the Australian economic model. They also seem to explain a great deal of the country's culture, but then again how does that rugged, extremely rural explanation fit with the fact that Australia is one of the most urbanized countries in the world?[‡] Or the fact that Australia is an intensely regulated society, with lawn-watering permits and an almost stifling regime enforcing political correctness in the workplace? A common quip in Australia is "If you can't drink it or &%$# it, regulate it. In fact, we may as well regulate that too." Culture clearly does matter, since it effectively rules out certain possibilities and probably favors others, but it is also clearly not deterministic. The hard part is figuring out how much culture matters. When does culture matter and how does it matter relative to other forces shaping politics? And what influences culture? Clearly, if a comparison of the Romans and the Tifosi[†] is any indication, culture is not static—so something must influence it.

The short answer is that political scientists really do not have an answer for how to factor culture into the study of politics. Many political scientists ignore culture entirely. Many argue that culture is merely a universal term to cover what cannot be explained through other factors. Some political theorists argue that culture or some aspect of culture, such as language, and the choices of shared cognitive referents are the most important factors in politics and define all but a few details of events.

---

[*]As a resident of New Zealand, I am legally required to disparage Australia at any opportunity, but don't worry, Australians don't know what *disparage* means.

[†]Even with a whole continent at hand, the vast majority of Australia's nineteen million inmates live in cities, with 64 percent of the population living in the capital cities of its states and territories. Any measure of urbanization that takes into account the total space available puts Australia at the very top.

[‡]Tifosi are the rabid and radical fans of Ferrari's Formula 1 team. Even the non-Italian ones are very Italian.

KARL EMIL MAXIMILIAN WEBER

Team: **Prussian Aristocrats**

Position: **Mid On**

Status: **Medium Rare**

It is an interesting question where to highlight **Max Weber (1864–1920)** as a theorist in this book. My first instinct was to put him in the chapter on the bureaucracy (Chapter 8). The theories and ideas in Weber's *Economy and Society* are still central to the study of administrative government. With a rather significant portion of his work focused on capitalism and related politics, I could have also put Weber in the economics chapter (Chapter 4). Similarly, many of the arguments he puts forth in *Politics as a Vocation* address the central role of government, and Weber was the first to claim that the state has a monopoly on the legitimate use of violence. This idea is so central to the foundations of modern government that I could have highlighted him in the anarchy chapter (Chapter 2), or the structures and institutions chapter (Chapter 5), or even the international politics chapter (Chapter 12). Finally, I could also have put good old Max in the conclusion since many people consider him to be the first true social scientist and pretty much all of the subdisciplines of political science can trace their roots to his expositions on methodology and research.

Plenty of academics and other researchers have highlighted Weber's contributions to these areas, so I decided to highlight his work in a slightly different way. In terms of cultural politics, Max Weber deserves far more credit, and far more attention, than he tends to receive. *The Protestant Ethic and the Spirit of Capitalism*[a] was the first, and is perhaps still the best, research ever to posit that culture could be a central determining factor in politics, society, and related economics. Weber's detailed and extensive historical analysis is probably the best model for anyone considering the study of culture and politics. Most important is the fact that his explanation focused on functional mechanisms through which specific cultural elements of Western Europe influenced productivity, tolerance of disagreement, and populist political participation. There was nothing vague or all-inclusive about Weber's application of culture as an explanatory variable, and for anyone thinking of exploring political culture, that is the best lesson anyone could teach.

[a]Karl Emil Maximilian Weber, *The Protestant Ethic and the Spirit of Capitalism,* translated by T. Parsons (1904–5; London: Routledge, 1992).

This unresolved—perhaps irresolvable—issue is a big part of why I have put off addressing the question of political culture. Political culture is an excellent example of a seductively simple explanation that seems to cover everything, but in truth it is neither simple nor universal. Wealth, power distributions, geography, gender, cognition, rational choice, social psychology, family structure, religion, the evolution of the human brain, grand conspiracies, and alien interventions are some of the countless, often compelling, explanations that have been offered to explain it all, or at least to explain huge swaths of phenomena from the Mongols conquering Kardashia to the likelihood that a given country can embrace democratic values. The problem is that even though all such universal explanations are problematic, you cannot simply dismiss them. Most do offer some insights. It is hard to believe that war and the global obsession with nuclear missiles can be entirely

explained by insecure men compensating for small . . . um . . . for personal shortcomings that threaten their confidence in their masculinity, but it is also hard to deny the conceptual value in many of the more moderate feminist arguments regarding international politics. Wealth may not explain everything, but Marxist theories, such as world systems theory, provide valuable perspectives that show how wealth shapes the nature of the world. Aliens do not control everything, but it is pretty obvious that the Eiffel Tower is a thinly disguised Model Number 3FB transgalactic broadcast station.

In most cases, these grand explanations can be neither simply accepted nor rejected.[*] Instead, the best approach may be one of informed skepticism—dismissing the universal but assuming that there is some value in there and considering the hows and whys of the idea to try to find that value. The analytical skills that this book was designed to help you develop can be particularly valuable, enabling you to act as an "informed consumer" when it comes to explanations for political phenomena. To provide an exercise of those skills, I discuss below two aspects of New Zealand politics that might easily be explained or described in terms of political culture. In addition to highlighting some of the difficulties with the very concept of political culture, this will give you an opportunity to exercise those analytical skills.

APPLYING POLITICAL CULTURE

To start, I take a careful look at how people have defined culture and how it might be applied to politics. Culture has been defined as everything from language to a shared appreciation for a particular body shape.[†] One constant throughout those definitions is the idea that culture is shared by a group. It is something that helps individuals identify with the larger group and provides a context for action by and within that group. Thus, for this analysis I am going to define **political culture** as the shared social context from which people make political choices. Related to that is **political socialization,** the process by which the group teaches the shared context to the members of society. And related to that are **agents of political socialization**—or those from whom the group learns the political culture—which can include schools, parents, the media, politicians, friends, religious leaders, and so on. And related to that is the whole global obsession with boobs on TV. It's sort of a circle-of-life thing.

One can understand New Zealand political culture in terms of the things that make it a way better culture than Australia's, such as knowing that people shouldn't live on a continent full of poisonous critters. You could also add in there factors such as extreme geographic isolation, a largely agricultural economic base, historical and legal inheritances from British colonialism, and the fact that descendants of the precolonial inhabitants, the

------

[*]The exception, of course, being the role of aliens. Resistance is futile.

[†]Body shape is a surprisingly common referent in discussions of culture. From Renaissance art to advertising to African cultures that associate obesity with social and economic success, body shape is in there a lot.

Maori, make up enough of the population to have a successful political party. Within countries, you often find **subcultures,** which are smaller cultures within the main political culture. Within New Zealand, I could talk about regional political cultures, the most obvious being the noticeable differences between the North and South islands.

From that foundation I can apply the idea of culture as shared social context and look at the role of culture in two different ways that it might be related to politics. First, there are the influences culture could have on politics, specifically how a culture of isolation has shaped New Zealand's foreign policy. Second, there is the intentional use of culture as a means of attaining a political end, such as using culture to establish and enhance local and national identities within New Zealand. Finally, I conclude by asking a few questions about the politics of what might be called cultural ownership and cultural preservation.

A Thousand Miles to Nowhere: Isolation and Foreign Policy

From New Zealand, it is quite literally a thousand miles to nowhere. Even if you were to convince Kiwis that Australia is more than just a bunch of louts with surfboards stuck between all that poisonous stuff on the land and the sharks in the ocean, that nearest of New Zealand's neighbors is still a very long way away. A thousand miles in a plane leaves you with 334 miles of swimming before you can rescue Nemo from the dentist in Sydney, and the next-closest country of any significant size is on the other side of that quaint little continent full of toxic frogs, poisonous snakes, deadly spiders, and venomous egg-laying mammals.* Los Angeles, Tokyo, and Singapore are all about a thirteen-hour flight away, and for most other destinations you have to fly through one of those cities. The mostest totally directest flight to London, not including the three-hour stopover in Los Angeles, will take more than twenty-five hours. No matter how you measure it, New Zealand is, without question, the most isolated of all the developed countries, and except for perhaps a few very small Pacific island nations, it is the most isolated country in the world.

There are clear cultural effects that seem to follow from that geographic isolation. The "overseas experience," or OE, is encouraged both socially and officially. Even though the costs of travel from New Zealand are tremendous, a large percentage of Kiwis enhance their educations with extended stays somewhere else, often arranged with the help of schools. Similarly, a trip overseas is unquestionably accepted as a justification for an extended absence from school, and families are encouraged to take advantage of those types of travel opportunities no matter when they might arise during the year. This is a stark contrast to most states in the United States, where schools are required to fail students for extended absences from school, regardless of the justification. As a result, a far higher percentage of Kiwis have traveled overseas than Americans, even though it is far easier to travel from the United States.

---

*The male platypus has a barb on its hind legs that injects what some consider to be the most painful venom produced by any animal on the planet.

New Zealand's isolation also has a practical effect in terms of border-related politics, such as immigration, and that is associated with some cultural differences as well. New Zealand has extremely strict immigration laws, and with all that ocean for a border, it is probably the second-most effective country in the world at enforcing its immigration laws.[†]

As a result, all the U.S. and European political conflicts over immigration, particularly illegal immigration, usually lead to a confused shake of the head in New Zealand. In New Zealand there is no question that a country has the absolute right to regulate everything about immigration. There is broad acceptance of strict laws that are overtly crafted to ensure that people moving to New Zealand will contribute significantly to the local economy. To gain a work permit to move to New Zealand you have to pass medical exams to prove that you will not be a burden on the country's health care system, and you generally have to be under the age of fifty, to guarantee that you will work long enough to cover the burdens your retirement years will place on the society. These aren't just laws on the books, they are strictly enforced, and more than a few would-be immigrants have been turned away because they failed to measure up.

Not only are these laws accepted, but opinion polls suggest that the majority of Kiwis would like the immigration laws to be even stricter and more forcefully implemented. For all but the most liberal of Kiwis the idea of an obligation to accept or support impoverished or unskilled immigrants, particularly those who arrived illegally, seems bizarre. One of the most telling comments was offered by a student during a classroom discussion of U.S. immigration issues: "What part of 'illegal' makes those immigrants anything but criminals?"

The culture of isolation also affects attitudes toward material possessions. New Zealand is a very small market, far too small to support the manufacture of many things, except for equipment related to raising sheep, and it costs a lot to ship things to New Zealand. As a result, things such as cars and building materials are expensive. The average car in New Zealand is far older than the average car in most other places around the world. New cars are rare. In fact, the majority of cars that arrive in New Zealand have already had a full automotive lifetime of use in Japan or Britain. Building materials are so expensive in New Zealand that a prominent industry has been established by the building recyclers who buy and resell everything from windows to doorknobs. There is a building recycler in every town. This is related to a whole set of norms and shared beliefs regarding the nature of houses. In New Zealand there is more than a little admiration for a bach built out of whatever random bits and pieces might have fallen into someone's hands.[*] Even this has political ramifications. Currently, this cultural idealization of the bach is clashing with an effort to improve housing quality through the strict regulation of building practices and laws regarding the approval of building materials.

[†]North Korea probably gets the nod for number one.

[*]A bach is something like a cabin in the United States. The word comes from the ramshackle bachelor housing that used to be built for miners, loggers, whalers, and farmhands. Now bachs are generally used as beach and forest retreats. Most have no power or other services, and many are still accessible only by boat or horse.

However, of all the cultural aspects of New Zealand that might be attributed to its geographic isolation, the one with the most obvious political ramifications is a sense of political isolation from the rest of the world. In debates over foreign policy, it is clear that there is little evidence of any kind of geostrategic motive. There is no sense that anyone feels that it is necessary to engage directly most of the major issues that arise in world politics.*

What may be the most obvious reflection of the political effect of a culture of isolation is that moral, not geostrategic, reasoning is the primary benchmark for current New Zealand foreign policy. Foreign policy actions based on a moral obligation to act are common, and this was clear even in the decision to send troops to Afghanistan and Iraq after the U.S. invasions. New Zealand refused to participate in the invasions, and when it sent troops, its leaders bent over backward to make it absolutely clear that the Kiwis were in those countries to protect the innocent victims of the conflict and help them rebuild, not to support the U.S. occupation. In fact, some of the strongest reflections of this culture of isolation can be found in the arguments against committing troops to postinvasion Iraq and Afghanistan.

In New Zealand, there is a strong sentiment that the country has a moral obligation to defy the United States when the world's most powerful nation acts geostrategically at the expense of democratic and liberal ideals. As a result, far from any interest in trying to win favor from the United States, the arguments for acting in Afghanistan and Iraq had to *overcome* the fact that to do so would give the appearance that New Zealand supported the U.S. invasion. The presumption is that New Zealand will defy any U.S. demands unless a solid moral justification can be made for going along with the United States. You can see this in nuclear policy. Despite long-standing and intense pressure from Washington, New Zealand still refuses to allow nuclear-powered ships or any ship that might carry nuclear weapons to enter its territorial waters. In the recent elections, the mere suggestion that one of the parties wanted to capitulate to U.S. demands to drop the nuclear ban was considered to be an underhanded slur against the party's leader. New Zealand also defied the U.S. attempts to politically isolate Cuba and, later, Vietnam.

However, it could also be argued that culture has nothing to do with any of these aspects of New Zealand politics. Perhaps the physical distance that separates New Zealand from the rest of the world, in and of itself, explains New Zealand foreign policy. Not only does a thousand miles of ocean make New Zealand safe from any plausible direct threat to its physical security, it also makes it pretty much impossible for New Zealand to threaten anyone else militarily. This effectively takes issues of threat, force, and power out of both sides of the foreign policy equation and means that, culture or not, New Zealand foreign policy would have to focus on something else first.

---

*There is a clear indication of loyalty to the Crown, and with that a need to support the British Commonwealth, and that support does lead to some engagements with the world that would otherwise be hard to explain from a strictly isolationist cultural perspective.

IT ISN'T COMEDY WITHOUT A FART JOKE

Culture is a truly interesting beast when you start looking at things that most people who talk about culture would dismiss with a huff and an upturned nose. Fantasy tales are a prime example. A look at the fantasy novels on the shelves of your local Barnes & Noble will reveal a flood of European cultural imperialism. From Middle-earth to Hogwarts, it's all Euro-Anglocentric, usually a twist on myths and a bit of post-Roman/pre-Enlightenment European historical setting. *The Care and Feeding of Your Lunatic Mage* shakes this up a bit by asking what would happen if that magical Europe tried to colonize the South Pacific. By placing the European fantasy tropes in a South Pacific cultural context, the book makes the contrast between these cultures a point of political and comedic action.

Douglas A. Van Belle, *The Care and Feeding of Your Lunatic Mage* (Melbourne: Andromeda Spaceways, 2010). Sir Julius Vogel Award 2011—Finalist for Best Collected Work.

Arguably these actions reflect a culture of isolation because Kiwis feel distanced from the security imperatives that drive the foreign policies of most other nations. That ocean is very comforting. Despite being a tiny country, New Zealand can defy the United States because Kiwis neither feel threatened by U.S. military might nor feel a need to seek U.S. protection from the threats of others. Threats are far away and almost never invoke any sense of a need to act to protect the homeland. The dynamics of the foreign policy debates in New Zealand are remarkably similar to those of the United States from a century ago. When the Atlantic Ocean gave Americans a similar sense of isolation from the politics of Europe, there were intense political pressures on leaders to avoid foreign entanglements despite plenty of evidence of economic engagement.

Culture and Social Distance

Perhaps the most interesting aspect of the relationship between culture and isolation is not how isolation might lead to some aspects of culture, but how culture seems to shrink the reality of distance. Despite the fact that London is twice as far away from them as Los Angeles, Tokyo, Shanghai, or Singapore, New Zealanders are both far more culturally affiliated with England and far more politically engaged with London than they are with any of those other locations. When Kiwis talk about travel, trade, or political issues they tend to equate the distance to England with the distance to the United States even though they fly through the United States to get to England. Kiwis think of Japan as being much farther away than England even though Japan is actually half as far away.

More telling is the New Zealand relationship with the island nations of the Pacific. The Maori of Aotearoa* are Polynesians, related to Hawaiians, Samoans, Fijians, and other Pacific island communities. This cultural connection serves to shrink the extremely large distances that separate New Zealanders from these small island nations. These islands are thousands of miles away, yet Kiwis consider them to be neighbors. By any kind of global measure these island nations are economically insignificant, yet New Zealand puts a priority on economic relations with them, including sending almost all of New Zealand's foreign aid to them. By any global measure these nations have no military might or power, yet New Zealand is intensely concerned with their security, and theirs is the one region in the world where New Zealand will send troops in response to security threats. It is hard to find an explanation other than culture for New Zealand's interest in these island nations.

Culture as Politics

The political aspects of culture extend far beyond the possibility that culture influences politics and policy. Culture can also be applied to the pursuit of political and social goals. During the Cold War, the Russian Bolshoi Ballet frequently toured the world and served as a means of establishing some nonhostile interactions between countries that were otherwise engaged in the most protracted security crisis the world has ever known. Sporting events, particularly the Olympics, have similarly been used intentionally to bridge the rifts between countries.

Culture is constantly used to define or justify policy. For example, using the story of "The Rape of Kuwait" to explain the need to act in the First Gulf War resonated with an American culture obsessed with stories of selfless heroes riding in from afar to rescue virtuous damsels from the hands of evil and power-hungry villains. Not only did the invocation of this cultural framework shape policy by eliminating policy options that contradicted the story structure, it was intentionally used to generate overwhelming domestic support for the First Gulf War. The first Bush administration went so far as to orchestrate events that reinforced this cultural ideal, with the most blatant example being the congressional testimony of an "eyewitness" to the atrocities of the Iraqi occupation. This fifteen-year-old girl was later identified as the daughter of Kuwait's ambassador to the United States, and she had not witnessed what she had claimed.[2] However, what she said fit so strongly with what Americans wanted to believe that even after her true identity was exposed, the vast majority of Americans continued to believe her story. The shared knowledge created by U.S. sports was also used to great effect during the invasion, with military officials describing events to the public using football and baseball terms.

Aotearoa is the Maori word for New Zealand. Its literal meaning is the land of the long white cloud, signifying the way that clouds form along the ridge of mountains that defines most of the country.

From politicians slipping out of their Italian shoes for an afternoon to make a show of hunting or fishing to connect with a rural constituency to American television creating overseas demands for U.S. products by featuring them in sitcoms, the use of culture for political or other ends appears commonplace. However, one of the most interesting ways that culture can be used politically is to influence group identity. Not only do the Olympics provide an example of modern sporting culture being used to build bridges between estranged countries, but they—and sports in general—also provide an example of how cultural and sporting events can be used to enhance national or other group identities.[*]

The Soviets invested a great deal in sports such as gymnastics, partly as a demonstration of Russian power to the world, but also to use the Olympics to enhance a sense of national identity in a country that included hundreds of nationalities that had been forcibly incorporated into the Russian Empire and carried forward into the Soviet Union, or brought unwillingly directly into the Soviet Union. Schools, cities, and regions around the world use athletic teams as a means of generating community identities. The display of jerseys, caps, and posters identifies members of particular communities to one and all and remind the people who see them of those communities.

In Liverpool, the red jersey, scarf, or cap means you will never walk alone. In the United States, high school homecomings are annual events that create shared identity across generations of students and help bind small towns into communities. It is no accident that colleges and universities in the United States invest tremendous amounts of time, money, and effort not just into athletics but also into the logos, mascots, school colors, and all of the other signifiers of community associated with them. The sense of ongoing community that keeps wealthy alumni and their donations connected to the university makes that kind of investment perfectly rational. The broader sense of community created among locals who never attended the university but still root for its teams bolsters demand for government support of universities and, again, makes it rational to invest in the athletic programs and the sporting events that provide the means to create that community.

The Sound of Black

Sport as culture and its role in community building can be applied directly to New Zealand. It is unlikely that any other athletic team in the world is as intimately connected with a nation's identity as the All Blacks are connected to New Zealand. Kiwis find it easier to recognize the All Blacks' flag than they do their own national flag, which is unpleasantly similar to the Australian flag. In fact, over the past few years there has been a recurring debate over calls to adopt the All Blacks flag—or a close facsimile—as the national flag, and when New Zealand won the right to host the 2011 Rugby World Cup, someone climbed up on top of the parliament building and replaced the New Zealand flag with the All Blacks' flag. The stylized silver fern on

---

[*]I hope that the discussion of the political aspects of group identity and the sociology of groups is still floating around in your head somewhere.

a black background not only fluttered and flapped on parliament's rooftop all day, but no one complained. It really wasn't all that surprising. Kiwis are astoundingly passionate about their rugby. How else can you explain the fact that a country of just four million people can produce a team that far larger countries—some of which are fifteen times as large as Aotearoa—strive to match and often struggle even to compete with? The passion for the All Blacks is so all-encompassing that it is hard to find a young Kiwi-born bearer of a Y chromosome who does not spend every possible moment running around the schoolyard tackling anything too slow to get out of his way and dreaming of wearing the coveted black jersey.

New Zealanders' team loyalty, however, is not the best example to use. The All Blacks are an indispensable part of the heart of New Zealand,[*] but it is the All Blacks' *haka* that provides the more interesting example of culture being used to create a shared identity. Quite literally, *Ka Mate* is a part of a traditional culture being used to create a larger shared culture for a nation.[†]

A *haka* is a Maori call to battle, and the All Blacks' *haka, Ka Mate,* was created[‡] in the 1820s by Te Rauparaha, the high chief of the Ngati Toa *iwi.*[§] It has been a part of the All Blacks' history since the beginning, some one hundred years ago. As old footage shows, for most of that history the *haka* bore little resemblance to the modern version. Roughly twenty-five years ago, one of the Maori All Blacks decided that the *haka* needed to be done correctly, and he taught the others the traditional form and how to give it the passion of a warrior's challenge. Now it literally thunders through the stadium and you can see its effect on the opposing players.

A lot could be said about how the *haka* creates a team unity that transcends what can normally be created in a national all-star team, or the way it intimidates opponents, but the social effects of the way the *haka* resonates with all those Kiwi boys dreaming of a black jersey is more interesting. That piece of Maori culture and heritage that was shared through the All Blacks became accepted as not just Maori culture but New Zealand culture. Though there is obviously a mélange of cultural, economic, and political forces at play in New Zealand, the *haka* appears to be a significant part of the current and growing respect and acceptance of Maori culture as a significant, if not defining, facet of a New Zealand culture.

The relationship between Pakeha[¶] and Maori is certainly far from perfect, and it would be impossible to argue that any relationship between colonizers and indigenous

---

[*] The left ventricle, to be specific.

[†] There is a link to all kinds of information on the *haka,* including video clips and a history, on the All Black Web site: www.allblacks .com.

[‡] Some suggest it was adapted at this time rather than created.

[§] *Ka Mate* is of the *ngeri* style, which does not involve weapons. Also, an *iwi* is a social/political/spiritual Maori group. It shares many characteristics with a Native American tribe, particularly in its legal standing and the way it serves as a social and political entity, but in comparison with Native American tribes, there appears to be far less emphasis on language that is unique to an *iwi* and a greater emphasis on spiritual matters and local community activities.

[¶] Pakeha are New Zealanders of European heritage, and it is notable that these pale and sunburned Kiwis frequently use this Maori term to refer to themselves.

populations can ever be considered ideal. However, the rest of the world could learn valuable lessons from what New Zealand has accomplished in this area. There are still significant political, economic, and social conflicts, but the average Pakeha has a knowledge and understanding of Maori culture that is far beyond the understanding of native peoples by all but the most informed Americans, Canadians, or Australians. Maori language is taught in grade schools, including grade schools with few Maori students. How many Americans outside a reservation can offer a greeting in Navajo or Chinook? How many Canadians know any of the First Nations' creation myths? There is also a great deal of respect that accompanies that knowledge. *Kapa haka* groups, which perform competitively, are common at all school levels, for the most part irrespective of the ethnic mix in the schools. Many, if not most, of New Zealand's English place-names and geographic references have been replaced by the original Maori names. And while it might seem trivial to point out that *all* New Zealanders grumble when they see a foreigner sporting a *moko,* a Maori tattoo, the sense that these cultural referents are shared across ethnic lines goes a long way toward reducing the otherness separating Maori and Pakeha. Again, that is not to claim that the situation is perfect, but in comparison to the many nations where horrific relationships exist between colonizers and indigenous peoples, New Zealand is far less imperfect than most.

There is no need to accept my assertion regarding the respect for Maori culture in New Zealand. New Zealand filmmakers are better at making the case anyway. *Whale Rider,*[3] *River Queen,*[4] *Once Were Warriors*[5]—pick any New Zealand film you might get through Netflix, and if it is a recent film funded and produced by Kiwis, it will almost certainly place Maori culture and society front and center.

Of course, the *haka* might have nothing to do with it. It could all just be a practical reflection of a liberal political system and the fact that Maori make up enough of the New Zealand population to have some political and economic clout. It could be that in the Treaty of Waitangi the Maori managed to retain enough assets to make them, their culture, and their interests a significant factor in New Zealand's future. Perhaps the sharing of the *haka* explains nothing.

Regardless of what conclusions might be drawn from this or any other discussion of *Ka Mate* and New Zealand national identity, this *haka* is also significant in the way it relates to cultural ownership, the concluding topic for this chapter. Despite the role *Ka Mate* seems to play as a part of New Zealand national identity, it is not in the public domain. Its "ownership" is, in fact, legally protected.

Culture has value. In addition to all of the innate aspects of culture that make it something that is valued, if not treasured, the fact that culture can be used to accomplish things indicates that it has instrumental value and that connects directly to the issue of cultural ownership. When something has instrumental value—when it can be intentionally used as a means of accomplishing something—it is likely, if not inevitable, that someone will attempt to possess it to control its application in the pursuit of economic, political, or other ends.

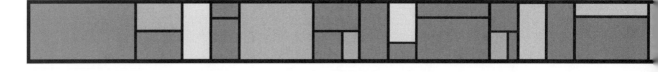

A member of the British and Irish Lions rugby team (R) performs the Hongi with a Maori Warrior during the team's visit to New Zealand. This ritualistic touching of noses and foreheads symbolizes the uniting of two breaths of life together. Like the distinctive but undefinable pattern of Ta Moko facial tattoo, it is another Maori cultural tradition that is widely considered to be a part of a larger New Zealand identity.

The *Haka* in Texas

Euless, Texas, might seem like the last place you would expect to see one of the best examples of how the *haka* creates a shared identity. The most distinguishing characteristic of Euless was the fact that it is close to the Dallas-Fort Worth airport, and Euless Trinity High School was known primarily for how kids came and went as airport jobs brought their parents into town and took them away again. However, largely because of the *Ka Mate haka,* all that changed in the fall of 2005.

As with all great stories, it started on a dark and stormy night. Actually it was a rained-out high school football practice, but that is pretty much the same thing. The coach had caught one of the players showing another the video of the *haka* from the All Blacks' website, and they were all talking about it. One of the many Tongan players on the team knew the *haka* well enough to start teaching the others, and by the end of that rained-out practice, something magical had started. *Ka Mate* united the team. The *haka* united the school. The *haka* brought alumni back to the stands for the games. It created something that all of the Euless Trinity Trojans shared, something they called their own, something that distinguished them as a group from all of the thousands of other high schools in Texas. In the fall of 2005 they adopted *Ka Mate,* and it carried their football team to the Texas State Championship.

There is a story here about the way this aspect of Maori culture created a sense of group identity for Euless, much as it has done for New Zealand, but there is also a story about cultural ownership here that has yet to play out. *Ka Mate* belongs to the Ngati Toa *iwi* and

is licensed to the All Blacks, which means that every time the Euless Trinity Trojans perform the *haka,* they are breaking the law. Ngati Toa has yet to act to protect its ownership right. In fact, at the time this edition of the textbook went to press it is not clear if the members of the *iwi* are even aware of what is happening in Texas, but in general the Maori of Aotearoa have been both aggressive and effective in using Western legal mechanisms to protect their culture, and the legal relationships between New Zealand and the United States probably gives the *iwi* exactly the mechanisms it would need to pursue this legally. Further, there are several aspects of how this high school is using *Ka Mate* that are unlikely to endear them to the *iwi,* such as raising money by selling "Got Haka?" T-shirts. The members of Ngati Toa probably have every legal right to gut the treasury of the school, the school district, and perhaps several of the individuals involved.

Will they?

Should they?

Can anyone really claim ownership of heritage and culture?

More interesting, why do the Euless Trinity Trojans use *Ka Mate*? Tonga has a culture very similar to that of the Maori, and Tongans have many of their own *haka.* Why did these Tongan students choose to adopt the *haka* used by the All Blacks?

Cultural Ownership

Navigating through this aspect of the relationship between politics and culture is more than difficult. Just referring to cultural ownership in a textbook is fraught with known and hidden hazards because the very idea that something that is part of a group's shared identity can also be owned is antithetical to the foundations of many cultures. However, many, if not all, of the cultures that disagree with the concept of **cultural ownership** must also contend with the reality of the global reach of the Western economic model that embraces and legally entrenches the ownership of pretty much anything and everything. Companies have claimed ownership of everything from a particular shade of purple to the genome of a traditional food plant.[*] At the very least, ownership of culture must be established in the legal system to prevent someone else from doing so. This leads to the problem of having to redefine culture into things—artifacts, patents, trademarks, and other legal entities that can be owned—even when the idea of owning the things that are treasured by the community is foreign to the culture of the group seeking those protections.

BACK TO THE QUESTION OF "WHAT IS CULTURE?"

When it comes to the politics of cultural ownership, there are really two interrelated questions that one has to consider. First is the question of how to define culture. That question has to come first because even if we all agreed that culture should be protected, it is pretty

---

[*]Cadbury holds a trademark for the shade of purple used for its candy wrappers, and the University of Hawaii raised a bit of a stink when it filed for patent protection for the genomes of certain varieties of taro.

tough to engage the second question—how to protect culture—until we know what we are including.

Consider some of the names of a few U.S. sports teams: Florida State Seminoles, Cleveland Indians, Atlanta Braves, Washington Redskins, Minnesota Vikings, Boston Celtics, Kansas City Chiefs, Golden State Warriors, Seattle Thunderbirds. At what point does the name or the icons associated with a team cross the line and become the exploitation of a group's culture? Is the war paint on the face of the fan in a Tallahassee stadium too much? How about the tomahawk chop in Atlanta? The profile of a Native American chief on a helmet in Washington, D.C.? If any of those cross the line, then the horned helmets and furry vests in Minnesota must also, right? Or what about the Harvard lacrosse team? Lacrosse is, after all, a Native American sport.

Where the line is drawn is a tough question. Is it a matter of who makes the money? Is the tiki god coffee mug—treasured because it holds twenty-two ounces of caffeinated sludge—acceptable because it was made in Hawaii by Hawaiians? Or is it simply a matter of asking permission? Applying that logic, the tomahawk chop cannot be protected because it is not clearly associated with any one tribe that might have the legal standing to claim ownership, but something specific, such as the hula, can be protected. What then of all the unlicensed non-Hawaiian dance teachers teaching the hula to little girls in their ballet classes?

The various incarnations of a Western legal system seem to have proven reasonably effective at protecting some things, such as dances, icons of cultural mythologies, and spiritual traditions, but what about language and linguistic referents to particular cultures? When it was discovered that a major tobacco company was selling a "Maori-blend" cigarette in Israel, New Zealanders were displeased, to say the least, and it did not take much of an expression of that displeasure to get the tobacco company to back down and pull that brand from the shelves. No one in New Zealand was happy that there had been a Maori-blend brand of cigarettes, but most seemed to agree that quickly pulling it from the shelves was a reasonable response to the situation. Similarly, when Major League Baseball arrived in Arizona, there was some suggestion that the team be called the Apaches. That was shot down, quickly, by critics who argued that no one but the Apache tribe had the right to use that name, but what does that say about the Yakima ski and sport racks that keep half the continent's Volvos securely centered under their mountain bikes? By the logic that got the Maori-blend cigarettes off the shelf and made the baseball team the Arizona Diamondbacks,[*] only the Yakima tribe should be able to use that name, or at least should get to decide who gets to use it and perhaps get a little cash in return. Tillamook cheese, Snoqualmie Vineyards, Motel Puyallup[†]—it can be a challenge to find a North American

---

[*]Do note that no one seemed to care about the cultural rights of the diamondback rattlesnake.

[†]"*Pyew*-al-up" not "Pu-*ya*-lupp."

Indian tribal name that is not used as part of a business name or trademark. How does that fit with the examples of the baseball team that never came to be called the Arizona Apaches and the Maori-blend cigarettes?

Beyond the fact that many tribal names are also used as place-names in the United States, this question of the use of words or names as cultural referents becomes particularly difficult to manage in the face of the argument that language is either the key aspect of culture or the one and only true representation of culture. When it comes to political efforts to address culture, such as the efforts to preserve indigenous cultures around the world, language always seems to be the first target on any list. Quite a bit of time and effort is put into recording languages and teaching them to kids in order to keep them alive as spoken languages. How does that concrete acknowledgment of language as the central core of culture fit with cultural ownership? If language is the heart and soul of a culture, it seems reasonable that it should be the first, and perhaps most important, thing a group should be able to protect from exploitation, but can you copyright a language? And if you could, how would you charge royalties for use of the language? Maybe you could use something like the swear jar that your mother made you constantly feed your allowance into when you used those certain words; then again, maybe not. And if people could charge for the use of language, would you have to pay the French for all those extra vowels that never get pronounced?

Ultimately, I could spend forever and a day discussing the French vowel fetish and other imponderable questions regarding culture—including what is part of culture and what should or can be protected against exploitation by others—but in the end, much of it boils down to political questions, political debates, and political attempts at resolution. Politics truly does seem to permeate everything.

KEY TERMS

agents of political socialization / 361

cultural ownership / 371

culture / 355

political culture / 361

political socialization / 361

subcultures / 362

CHAPTER SUMMARY

Political culture causes a great deal of difficulty for political scientists. While it is clear that societies share contexts from which they make political choices and that these contexts are learned, it is not clear how valuable political culture is as an explanation for political phenomena. Political culture does have some explanatory value; however, it cannot explain all differences among nations. In fact, political scientists disagree about whether and how to factor culture into the study of politics. Despite the disagreement about political culture as an explanatory variable, it is clear that it is related to politics in three ways. First, culture can affect a nation's approach to policy choices. For example, a country's shared context

can explain how it relates to other nations. Second, politicians can use a nation's culture as a powerful tool to achieve political ends and to establish group identities. Third, culture poses a particular problem as countries struggle over the question of how to deal with cultural ownership. Students should learn two important lessons from this chapter. First, while political culture can be an amorphous topic, it cannot be ignored. On top of the fact that culture resonates strongly with people, it is clear that it can have an effect on politics. However, it is important not to overly generalize the explanatory import of political culture when other factors may provide satisfactory answers. Second, quit asking about hobbits when you visit New Zealand. It was just a movie. Get over it.

STUDY QUESTIONS AND EXERCISES

1. Consider how political culture can influence policy preferences within a country. What regional political subcultures can you identify?

2. This chapter discusses how culture can be used to build group identity. What examples can you come up with to demonstrate how culture has been used in this way?

3. What is political socialization? Which agents of political socialization have had the greatest effects on your view of the world?

4. Think about the United States' war with Iraq. To what degree, if any, did culture play a role in the decision to go to war, the public's support of the war, and how public officials discussed the war?

5. Why should students be wary of those who explain politics solely in terms of political culture?

6. Explain the concept of cultural ownership. What factors make discussions about cultural ownership complex?

WEBSITES TO EXPLORE

www.brotown.co.nz. Check out the official site for *bro'Town,* New Zealand's first prime-time animated TV show.

www.civilsoc.org. Civil Society International assists organizations that work for democracy and civil society in hostile countries.

www.fowler.ucla.edu. UCLA's Fowler Museum of Cultural History explores past and present art and material culture to foster an understanding of cultural diversity.

www.haka.co.nz. This site is all about New Zealand rugby.

www.uiowa.edu/policult. The Center for Media Studies and Political Culture, Professor Bruce E. Gronbeck's site at the University of Iowa, seeks to examine how political processes and technologies intersect.

The Lastest and Bestest Chapter
The Study of Politics

In November 1987, the Godfathers played the Ballard Firehouse, a club in . . . Ballard, Washington, of all places. The Godfathers were known for grinding away at guitar riffs and angry, angst-ridden lyrics, and they were the perfect contrast to the giddy fascination with electronic everything that had defined the music of the 1980s. The band was also a total contrast to the kind of band you would expect to see playing a gig in a tiny bar in a Norwegian suburb of Seattle. In between booking the gig and rolling into town in their graffiti-covered double-decker tour bus, the band had gotten big—figuratively—and their sound system had gotten even bigger—literally—and that was why that cold November night would not be remembered for the music, or even for the odd theft from the nearby hardware store. That night would be remembered for the way the show abruptly ended.

First, the opening act refused to quit playing, and the management had to organize a posse from the audience to force the issue. It was a lame posse, but then again, it was a lame band with a lead singer who dressed like a Nazi boy scout, so there was balance to the Force. Once the lame posse had escorted the slightly lamer band off the stage, the Godfathers quickly pushed their way through the crowd, leapt onto the plywood-covered plastic milk crates being used for a stage, and launched into their first song even before the volunteers from the audience had finished hauling the opening act's drum set out of the way. The Godfathers were a big-time band playing a small club. They were anxious to get started and worried about having enough time to get through their set before Ballard's 1:00 A.M. curfew for live performances shut everything

down. And they were also trying very hard to look the part of angry boys singing angry songs.

Unfortunately, the Godfathers were too big of a band for that too-small club. Halfway through the first song, they blew out the electrical circuits powering their amps. Circuit breakers were flipped, but to no avail. Those big black banks of speakers just sucked too much power. Someone broke into the hardware store across the street, and dozens of orange extension cords suddenly appeared, running everywhere, over the bar, into the bathrooms, around and back into an office, connecting some of the amps to different circuits. That got the band through the first song, but ultimately the jury-rigged fix just made things worse. Halfway through the second song the band blew the main breaker for the whole building, taking out the lights and everything else.

At this point the lead singer was so incensed that he climbed up on top of a speaker and shouted, "Tear this $(%&* place apart!"

The response to that irresponsible, but in many ways predictable, incitement of an already riled-up crowd by a band who worked very hard to look like the angry boys their angry lyrics deserved, was swift and immediate. It was the stuff of legends.

No one did much of anything.

The club was in Ballard, after all. Ballard was known for the prevalence of "uff da" bumper stickers on cars driving five miles per hour. It was known for bakeries where old Norwegian men sat around making fun of old Swedish men. Ballard was not really a looting and rioting kind of place. Not even the pale skinny guys sporting brightly colored Mohawks[*] were interested in actually breaking anything, especially with all the cops across the street investigating the robbery at the hardware store.

The lead singer was a bit confused, but not that easily thwarted. He took charge, pointing and shouting at some truly ugly guys who were wearing torn-up leather jackets and penny loafers, "You ugly #$@@&%'s. Throw that %*&^# table through that %*&^# window."

The appearance-challenged group of gentlemen complied. They opened the glass doors before carefully tossing the small bar table out onto the patio.

It wasn't very riot-like at all, and the lead singer was furious. He was so furious that he almost looked angry enough to sing his angry songs. He stomped. He screamed some very complex, almost literary profanities, and the band left the stage, never to return. That was how the show ended. The crowd was a bit riled up, but those riles were quickly soothed by a cute bartender's bold and brilliant decision to open the taps and give away all the beer left in the kegs, and the crowd ended up voting against rioting. There actually was a formal motion made and a show of hands. Instead, the crowd elected a representative to negotiate a refund of the cover charge from the club owner. It all ended quite civilly. But then again, it was in Ballard, and no matter what unnatural color your hair might be, you just do not riot in Ballard.

---

[*]Unless someone uncovers photographic evidence, I am not going to admit anything at all about a purple Mohawk.

HERE'S WHERE THE STORY ENDS

Everything must end, even a textbook that students have grown to love more than beer itself, and I have spent a great deal of effort trying to create just the right ending.

I failed.

I tried lots of things:

- A section on religion and politics that showed the uncomfortably extensive parallels between the Crusades, Osama bin Laden's jihad, and recent Republican campaign rhetoric

- A short chapter on conspiracy theories and alien abductions

- A humorous rant about picture of a monkey trying to shove something that looked suspiciously poo-like into a ballot box

- A reprint of an article claiming *The Wizard of Oz*—the book, not the movie—was a political statement about abandoning the gold standard for U.S. currency

- A textual-historical analysis of one of those letters from Nigerian katrillionaires asking if you will help him stash his money in your bank account

- A short story about a robot, a priest, and a farmer, made up entirely out of quotes from the U.S. tax code

None of it worked, and I finally gave up. It was another one of those instances when the ideal crashes headlong into the real and you have to settle for something less than what you had hoped. The end of the Godfathers' show was close, but not quite it, and you will have to settle for a very mundane ending for this most excellent of all excellent textbooks.

THE STUDY OF POLITICS

The study of politics is usually divided into several subfields. There is nothing remarkable about that. Most academic disciplines have a variety of subfields. What is interesting about the study of politics is the degree to which most scholars agree on what the major subfields are. Except for the odd affection for the black shoes, brown corduroy pants, and dark-blue sport coat teaching ensemble, there really isn't that much that political scientists agree on. We like to debate and argue over just about everything, but in just about any political science department in the United States you will find the same four major subfields represented in about the same way. The big ones are American politics, international relations, comparative politics, and political theory. Depending on the organization of your university or college, the three more applied subfields of political science may be included with

INSANITY THAT IS NOT SO INSANE

"A Small Blue Planet for the Pleasantly Insane" is a flat-out comedy. It's one of my favorite stories, and if I hadn't already used up all my pimping energy on pushing *Barking Death Squirrels,* I'd be pimpin' up a storm here. However, despite serving no philosophical point other than trying to make people laugh, it does offer a point about the very real issue of competition between academics. When the alien arrives to study humans and gets pulled into a struggle between competing paleontologists, that prissy little fight strikes a chord with anyone who has ever worked as a researching and teaching academic. Academia actually is a pretty brutal and cutthroat world, filled with bright people who are determined to the point of obsession. This is then made all the worse by their being the constant targets of budget cuts. While it might seem silly to talk about wholly arbitrary distinctions between subfields or to separate applied from academic, these things have huge impacts on who gets jobs and on the kinds of resources that are available for conducting the research that will get a professor tenure. If a job teaching about bureaucratic government is in a public administration department, then some hands-on experience in government is all but required, but if that same job is listed as part of an American politics subfield, then practical experience in government would actually be something of a strike against you. With a hundred or more applicants for every entry-level academic position, those kinds of little things become very, very big things.

Douglas A. Van Belle, "A Small Blue Planet for the Pleasantly Insane," *Andromeda Spaceways Inflight Magazine,* no. 16 (2004–2005).

political science, or they may be housed in a separate department, usually called a public administration or public management department. The three more applied subfields are public administration, public policy, and public law.

American Politics

American politics is the largest of the political science subfields in the United States. Some suggest that this is due to a poor diet and lack of exercise. Its favorite color is beige and its favorite summer activity is counting things. Part of the reason that American politics is such a large subfield is that there is such high demand for people wearing mismatched shoes/trousers/sport coats to teach it. In Texas, every university student has to pass an introduction to American politics course to earn a degree. We call that lovely little law the Political Science Professor Employment Act. Texas is the only place where that is an actual law, but the American Political Science Association is lobbying intensely for the adoption of that law in all the other states that start with a *T.* I have high hopes, but even if the lobbyists are unsuccessful, the simple fact is that an introduction to American politics course is a mainstay of every political science department. Not only is it required for almost all political science majors, but it is also one of the more commonly chosen social science electives and is probably the most taught social science course in the country.

I often joke about American politics scholars and their number fetish, but like any good joke, this one has a bit of truth to it. Empirical studies dominate the published research, but that is largely a reflection of the nature of the subject of study. The governments in the U.S. federal system provide an incomparable wealth of reliable and accessible data on just about every aspect of their function. The results of every election in every district, town, city, county, and state are public record. The budgets of every state, county, city, town, planning commission, and rural health board are usually public record. Nearly all meetings of all governing assemblies in the country, including the votes of every member, are usually public record. Bureaucratic agencies have to provide almost any information that is formally requested, including historical records, and government and private agencies gather, catalog, and make available a great deal of information. The United States is one of the most consistently surveyed populations in the world, and the quality of U.S. census data is highly regarded throughout the world. With all those data right there to be statisticallymanipulatedforanalysis[*] it is no wonder that data-intensive empirical analyses dominate the subfield. Other forms of analysis are not excluded, but they are a distinct minority.

International Relations

Many say that the little boys who pretend that every stick is a gun all grow up to be international relations scholars. This is patently not true. The little girls who pretend that pinecones are hand grenades also grow up to be IR scholars. Okay, that's not true either. The truth is that the study of IR is largely driven by people who like short and catchy abbreviations, like IR for international relations. Okay, that's not true either, but it is true that war is a big part of the study of IR. Honest.

IR scholars study the interactions of nations and, to a lesser degree, those of subnational and supranational organizations. War is far from the only thing that IR scholars examine. In fact, war probably comes second to the study of the international political economy, but international conflict is such a big and attention-grabbing part of global politics that most people associate IR with the study of conflict and peace. In contrast to the study of American politics, the study of IR sports a broad, if not eclectic, mix of analytical approaches. A significant number of empirical, statistical data analyses are published, and they may be the majority, but only by a modest margin. Again, this largely reflects the nature of the subfield. Some areas of IR, such as trade, aid, and certain kinds of conflicts, naturally provide a significant amount of data or are important enough to merit the commitment of significant funds and time to gathering difficult-to-acquire data, but many areas and subjects are simply too difficult, or even impossible, to study through the statistical analysis of large numbers of cases.

---

[*]In the study of American politics, this is properly pronounced as a single word.

Empirical analyses require large numbers of events in order for the statistics to be an effective means of identifying patterns and commonalities, and it is relatively common for there to be too few of certain events, such as revolutions that evolve into international wars, to allow any kind of meaningful statistical analysis. Statistical analyses also require reliable, consistent, and unbiased data, and in many cases, standards of information collection and provision by different countries vary so much that the data simply cannot be used. The information we have about North Korea is, at best, estimated, and often it is outright fiction manufactured for propaganda purposes. Even countries that are relatively open and honest often simply do not record various kinds of information in the same ways as other countries. Additional, some of the phenomena studied in IR are simply too complex to distill down to a few key variables. Conflict in the Middle East is a perfect example. History, religion, ideology, external political interests, oil, poverty, water . . . the list of significant factors quickly grows beyond what can be reasonably measured and combined in a meaningful way. This is probably why case studies and qualitative analyses are far more common in IR than they are in the subfield of American politics.

Comparative Politics

No one ever calls comparative politics CP. I'm not sure why, probably because comparative politics scholars never pretended sticks were guns when they were kids. Or maybe it's because comparative politics scholars are just a little confused. That's fair enough. It can be a little difficult to figure out exactly what constitutes comparative politics. The simple definition of comparative politics is that it is the study of political systems other than the United States. Thus, if you have a professor who examines Lithuanian parliamentary procedure, and she has multiple personalities, she is a comparative politics scholar. This is relatively simple until you get to the comparative politics scholars who study regions, such as Latin America or East Asia. Once they begin studying the interactions among multiple nations, they are starting to slip into the study of IR, even if their work is largely limited to a geographically defined region. And where do you draw the line between comparatively studying a group of nations and the very large number of IR empirical studies that examine a few key characteristics or factors across all or most of the nations in the world?

The simple answer is that we often don't bother to make the distinction. Sort of like soap opera characters—who tend to be either mostly married or mostly notmarried, but never completely one or the other—the majority of comparative politics scholars also consider themselves to be at least partly IR scholars, and vice versa. The key difference in the way these scholars tend to view themselves is where they choose to direct their focus. Comparative scholars tend to focus their attention and efforts primarily on the elements that define a nation or region. They usually have detailed backgrounds in the histories and politics of their geographic areas of expertise, and they often have learned the local languages and have spent significant time living in the countries or regions they study. Thus,

scholars who study Latin America usually speak and read Spanish and often Portuguese. They often have spent the early part of their careers developing extensive networks of contacts and friends in the area they study, are familiar with local customs and cultures, and use that background to examine some aspect of politics. In short, comparative politics scholars emphasize what makes a country or region unique, while IR scholars try to minimize those differences in their analyses. One result of the emphasis on the uniqueness of countries or regions is that empirical statistical analyses are not very common in comparative politics. Deeply contextual and historically detailed descriptive analyses are more the norm.

Political Theory

It would be wrong to suggest that political theorists are all descended from the kids who practiced massnonconformity and wore their best goin'-to-a-funeral clothes all the time, but if I let right and wrong define what I put in this book, it would be a very short book indeed. The truth is, when you penetrate the swirling purple fog that obscures this subfield,[*] most of what falls under the label of political theory reflects or engages the philosophical foundations of the study of politics. This includes the following:

- **Classical theory,** which addresses the political aspects of enduring arguments regarding the nature of the human condition, the nature of knowledge, and the nature of reality.

- **Political philosophy,** which mixes cultural, historical, and philosophical perspectives to discuss the deeply contextual nature of politics. Political philosophy is often closely associated with classical and/or normative theory.

- **Normative theory,** which addresses questions regarding moral or social imperatives, and/or questions over what "should" be done.

- **Critical theory,** which questions the presumptions underlying the scientific approach to the study of politics and/or the social academic structure that defines, enables, and limits the pursuit of knowledge across the discipline.

- **Constructivist theory,** which examines the impact of language and the construction of meaning on our understanding of politics. The role that language plays in many critical theoretical analyses makes separating constructivist theory from critical theory a contestable point.

- **Philosophy of knowledge,** which examines the application of philosophy of science arguments to the process, means, and procedures of academic study in the

---

[*]Okay, now I'm just being mean. I admit it. I'm not going to stop it and I'm certainly not going to play fair, but I do admit it.

discipline. Including the philosophy of knowledge as a separate subset of political theory is a debatable choice, but one of the unique aspects of political science is the relatively extreme degree of attention that most of its scholars pay to questions of philosophy of science and philosophy of inquiry debates.

There is little or no empirical work that would be considered political theory. Most of the research in the subfield is published in the form of narrative arguments, although a notable minority of the work employs a form of mathematical and philosophical analysis called formal logic. A great deal of political theory appears as a small part of larger analytical studies, but generally speaking, most people exclude that aspect of theory from their conceptualization of political theory as a subfield.

Political theory is the smallest subfield in the discipline, and this is at least in part because there is so little demand for political theory courses. If you look at a typical course catalog, political theory courses tend to be rare in comparison to courses in the other subfields.

THE APPLIED SUBFIELDS

In some ways it is unfair to call public policy, public administration, and public law as applied subfields, but fair and unfair have little or no relevance to this book, so I'm just gonna hitch up the wagon and shout, "Westward Ho!"

The reason it might be a bit unfair to refer to any field as an applied subfield is that there is quite a bit of ivory-tower snobbery toward anything that is intentionally oriented toward developing insights into practical matters and has a significant teaching emphasis on skills that can be directly applied. To quote a colleague whose nationality shall go unmentioned[*] and who has a very big nose that is always raised well clear of the horizontal, "A university is about pursuing knowledge, not teaching a bunch of bloody fools how to drive a lorry." Political science is not the only discipline for which this is an issue; education programs actually get a far worse beating from the snobbery stick, but it does tend to be a bit divisive, often to the point of pushing public administration and public policy into a separate department.

Public Policy

The subfield of public policy can be thought of as the study of how "stuff" gets done. Largely this is focused on how government, policy stakeholders, and the public interact to set and implement policy. The dynamics of bureaucracy are a significant part of the subfield, but it is probably fair to say that most of the research in this area focuses on questions of what does and does not work in specific policy areas. The research methods applied are

---

[*] Is British actually a nationality, or should it be broken down to Welsh, English, and so on?

typically detailed descriptive analyses of procedure, process, intent, and outcome. They often explore the dynamics of policy implementation efforts or compare the relative effectiveness of similar policy initiatives in different times or places. The implicit, or sometimes explicit, goal of study is to understand how things get done to improve the government's ability to attain social or political goals.

Public Administration

A few universities call this subfield public management rather than public administration, and that management idea is probably the best way to think about public administration. Think of it as the MBA program for government. In fact, when public administration departments are separate from political science departments they are often associated with business schools. Research in public administration generally reflects this management idea, exploring the organizational dynamics within governments and quasi-governmental organizations. This involves more than just comparing how the inner workings of government are similar to and different from the management dynamics within business. The differences from traditional business programs are often seen in public administration studies, but several aspects of government are so fundamentally different from business that they must be studied in their own right. Notable is the absence of a profit incentive to provide a shared cognitive structure for those working in government. Unlike businesses, which usually have some sort of incentive system in place to encourage divisions and individuals to pursue lower costs and/or greater profits, governments must find other ways to pursue efficiency and thrift. Along these lines, research into the relative effectiveness of privatization versus public management in different areas has been significant lately.

Public Law

Although public law might better be called the politics of law, it isn't. Unlike public policy or public administration, public law usually isn't sent away to live with a business school. Every once in a while a university will be big enough, or it will be focused enough on proto-lawyers, for public law or prelaw to become a degree in and of itself, and then you sometimes see public law attached to a law school, but for the most part, public law is usually hiding in a dusty corner of the political science department. There are two major avenues of research that I have noticed in public law. There are probably more, but I don't really pay all that much attention.

One general avenue of research and teaching in public law is the study of the role of the judiciary in politics or as a branch of government. Often you will see this research couched in terms of the subfield of American politics, but it occasionally surfaces in comparative politics. Studies of judicial activism, judicial interpretation, and, in the United States, the process and dynamics of judicial review are common areas of research in this regard. Judicial-executive relations and dynamics have also been prominent recently, with

high-profile issues such as Clinton being naughty and Bush doing that whole Guantánamo Bay thing.

A second avenue of research is the impact of policing and the court system on the public or society. A lot of this might get siphoned off into the category of criminal justice and treated as a separate discipline all its own, but it clearly fits under the public law heading to which all of our proto-lawyers flock.

Methodological Divisions in the Study of Politics

I would be criminally negligent if we didn't provide a thorough discussion of the methodological debates in the discipline.

CONCLUSION

The conclusion for the discussion of the subfields of political science is fairly simple.

Don't take them too seriously.

There are no hard-and-fast divisions within political science, and pretty much every scholar is a little bit of one and a little bit of another. Is the study of American foreign policy part of American politics or IR? Does the study of congressional process fit in American politics or public policy? Should we put a study of Japanese foreign aid in the comparative politics column or is it IR? The answer to all of these questions is yes. The divisions and definitions of subfields are solely for convenience and reference. Ideas pass back and forth between subfields all the time, and few scholars fit in one and only one area. In fact, most graduate programs in the United States require their doctoral students to pass comprehensive examinations on at least two of the subfields.

The conclusion for the whole textbook is a little more difficult. There are a lot of ways I could conclude this, and the temptation is to go back to the monkey stuffing poop in the ballot box, but I've decided against that, reluctantly, and instead have chosen to end things by making a brief but important point.

There has been a method to all this madness.

The two biggest challenges your instructor faces are getting past what you already think you know and getting you to actually read and pay attention to the material. I've made it clear from the beginning that the use of fiction here is intended to help get you past your preconceptions and beliefs, and perhaps now I should make it clear that the sarcasm and foolishness are more than stylistic affectations.

Think of the journey through the text as a very long road trip. Turning each page is like a glance out the window. What you see each time you look out that window will always be a different bit of the journey, but if every time you look you see a paddock full of sheep, you will very quickly begin to miss the details, and you could be twenty miles into dairy farming country before you realize that those mooing things are not just very big sheep. However, when you are driving through varied terrain you never know what you will see in that glance

out the window, and even when one glance is largely the same as the last, when you start expecting difference instead of sameness, your mind has to take that extra moment to really look at what you are seeing. You have to consider whether the view is different, whether it might be something new . . . you have to think about it a moment before you can categorize it as the same as the last glance. The humor and other foolishness in this textbook has been very carefully designed and presented to make sure that you are never quite certain what you will find when you turn the page. Anything has been fair game. I've even mixed up the chapter structure in a few places.

Most of you will have found it quaintly sanitary,* and some of you will think the humor has been overdone, but even if it was a little much for your taste, the fact is that you never knew when or where I might drop a twisted phrase or a tongue-in-cheek snipe into the text, and that is the point. You knew that you couldn't be sure what to expect, and that kept the cognitive function of your gray squishy parts engaged as you read. Hopefully some of it was actually amusing, but I'll happily settle for annoying if that was what it took to keep you thinking as you read.

The risk I've taken in doing this is that you might have mistaken form for substance. If you get to this point and you don't think that there has been much "real" material in this book, might I strongly suggest that you reconsider that conclusion. One of the values of using examples from pop culture and fiction to teach politics is that they help us to get at the complex dynamics and ideas underlying politics. As a result, I can put far more of the why of politics into fifteen weeks of study than is usually possible. I can also get you to think more than you normally would in an intro course, and as far as I'm concerned, learning to think is what it's all about.

---

*Believe it or not, I am really pushing the bounds of the language I can get away with in a textbook, and my development editor is very nervous about the fact that I very nearly referred directly to *Cannabis sativa* in the text.

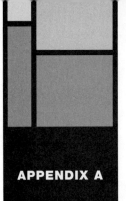

APPENDIX A

Fiction Appendix

 ### Alexander
Oliver Stone (Warner Bros., 2004)

A labored and surprisingly boring attempt at a sweeping epic film. The historical accounts of Alexander are actually far more interesting. While the film tries to spin some personal, mommy issues in, Alexander actually had daddy issues. He was the son of a rather unpleasant king after all. Key political point revolves around his failure to establish a line of succession and institutionalize the empire he conquered.

   The Executive (chapter 6); *Empire Building* (chapter 12)

Alice in Wonderland
Lewis Carroll (1865) [film adaptation: Clyde Geronimi and Wilfred Jackson, directors (1951); Tim Burton, 2010]

Sorry, kids, this is one of those where you have to read the book. The Disney version is cute and all, but it leaves out all the hints and teases at the odd stuff that was floating through Carroll's brain. The Tim Burton adaptation gets the weird, as you would expect, but really twists the story and fails miserably on the point of choosing to be a hero. Alice really didn't get much of a choice Tim. Anyway, in the book, there is some serious social commentary hidden in this journey through an imaginary and quite insane world.

   utopia (chapter 2); *mediated reality* (chapter 11)

All Quiet on the Western Front
Erich Maria Remarque (1929)

This novel is part of the social, political, academic, and artistic reaction to World War I I talk about in chapter 12. Even though it sounds like this guy might be French, he was actually a German who moved to the United States and married a very pretty movie star. Good job mate. The idea behind this story—finding humanity in the enemy—is often imitated, though never with the finesse or impact of the original.

   alliances (chapter 2); *security* (chapter 2)

All the King's Men
Robert Penn Warren (1946)

After Hurricane Katrina, picking on Louisiana has gone out of style, but this book will help students understand why the Bayou State has always been in the satiric crosshairs. If anything, the reality of the corruption and insanity is understated here, and students might wish to refer to *A Confederacy of Dunces* for a better insight into the raw comic material available in those swamps. Actually, *The Water Boy* isn't that far off either.

   realism (chapter 1); *institutions* (chapter 5); *presidency* (chapter 6); *Arrow's Theorem* (chapter 10)

All the President's Men
Alan Pakula, director (1976)

This is the film for understanding Watergate.

   government (chapter 2); *power* (chapter 2); cockroach theory of politics (chapter 11)

 ### American Chopper
Creator: Hank Capshaw, co-executive producer (2003-)

You don't know what American Chopper is? Get a life and start watching some TV.

   institutions (chapter 5)

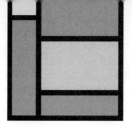

Animal Farm
George Orwell (1945)

Some animals are more equal than others. There is no line that better captures the way that institutions and ideologies can be twisted to serve the interests of leadership.

institutions (chapter 5)

 *Apocalypse Now*
Francis Ford Coppola, director (1979)

Speaking of New Orleans, flying into the city is eerily similar to the opening scene of this Vietnam War movie. When the 737 drops down low over the swamp on approach, the only thing that is missing is the "Flight of the Valkyries" blaring in the background. With all the refineries out by the airport, it even smells like napalm when you disembark.

alliances (chapter 2); *security* (chapter 2)

 *Avengers, The*
Joss Whedon (2012

Just gonna talk about the film here, don't want to scare anyone off with the serious geek it takes to delve in to the comics. Joss, take a bow. And if any of you don't know who Joss Whedon is, you may not be suited for this textbook.

idealism (chapter 1)

Barking Death Squirrels
Douglas A. Van Belle, Random Static, 2010

Mentioned in Chapter 10, for no good reason, Barking Death Squirrels actually addresses several salient political issues, such as the question, "Why don't the French have a word for Surrendermonkey?" Oh, and there is stuff on idealism in practice, the security dilemma, and alliances/conflict.

idealism (chapter 1); *security* (chapter 2); *alliances* (chapter 12)

Batman
Bob Kane and Bill Finger, character creators; William Dozier, series creator (1966–1968)

Production values? We don't need no stinking production values. That may not have been the motto of the 1960's TV version of *Batman,* but it probably should have been. It was such a horrible show that even a six-year-old could spot the continuity flaws, and the lines they wrote for Adam West were so cheesy that mice would rush the screen whenever he spoke. Still, it was probably the first real multimedia phenomena, going from comic book, to TV, to film, to Saturday morning cartoon, and the merchandising . . . there are a lot of old Batman lunchboxes out there.

idealism (chapter 1)

Boston Legal
David E. Kelley, creator (2004–2009)

Denny Crane is William Shatner's best character, best role, best performance ever, and I am one of those old geeks who loves the original *Star Trek.* Not to be overlooked is the way that Denny Crane uses his supposedly failing mind to evade the restrictions of social and political structures—insanity as a source of power.

power (chapter 2); *law in action* (chapter 9)

Braveheart
Mel Gibson, director (1995)

Think what you want of Mel Gibson and his recent issues with divorces, drunken anti-Semitic tirades and wife beating, the princess in this one was very pretty and that's what really matters. There is also a bunch of stuff about diplomacy and the executive as an institution as Mel runs around killing Englishmen. Film is also notable for including

every Scotsman who has ever appeared on screen except for Billy Connelly.

executive (chapter 6); *diplomacy* (chapter 12)

 Brave New World
Aldous Huxley (1932)

This is a must-read for any kind of examination of the modern take on utopian thought. Written during the hedonistic excesses of the economic boom that preceded the Great Depression, it makes some serious statements about the hollowness of the unrestrained pursuit of pleasure. Can also be read as a very precognizant anticipation of the 1960s and the social politics surrounding the hippies.

utopia (chapter 2)

 Brazil
Terry Gilliam, director (1985)

Warning: if you ever have the opportunity to see the four-hour director's cut of this film, pass. I am a devoted fan of Gilliam, but this is one of those instances where some interference in the creative process by the studio executives saved the film and actually made it great. I seriously wish that someone had done the same with Peter Jackson's take on *King Kong*. Seriously, Peter, cut thirty minutes, and you would have the best movie in years. What? Oh, the plot of Brazil . . . uhm . . . well, the infallible bureaucracy makes a mistake, and a guy gets caught up in the chaos, sort of. Seriously, you just gotta trust me and watch it.

bureaucracy (chapter 6)

 Broadcast News
James L. Brooks, director (1987)

This is a pretty good one for getting a feel for the dynamic of the newsroom and how that might influence what does and does not end up on the TV during dinner.

dramatic imperative (chapter 11); *mediated reality* (chapter 11); *mutual exploitation model* (chapter 11)

 Bro'Town
The Naked Samoans, creators (2004)

Good luck finding this in North America, and it really is too bad. It provides a great twist on the British-style, intellectual slapstick that made *Monty Python* such a hit, and it adds a touch of New Zealand's innocent, slightly naïve take on social responsibility to give it just that bit more than the laugh. One of its most interesting serious questions concerns the nature of satire in the relationship between minorities and dominant groups in a society. When a minority culture inserts itself into the mainstream through self-satire, does that help or hinder its acceptance as a meaningful part of the whole?

culture (chapter 14)

 A Bug's Life
James Lassiter, director (1998)

Call me naïve, but I suspect that if a kid ever actually encountered a bright blue ant that talked, hysteria would ensue. The grasshoppers are supposed to be bad, though the thought of Dennis Leary as a ladybug is actually the scary part. Kids are supposed to learn that they should team up with circus freaks to form a street gang.

alliances (chapter 2); *collective action* (chapter 2); *security* (chapter 2)

 Caddyshack
Harold Ramis, director (1980)

I have no real reason for including this movie in the textbook, other than it is the funniest

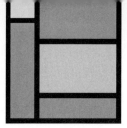

movie that students might have never seen. Best golf movie ever.

cockroach theory of bureaucracy (chapter 8)

 Cannery Row
John Steinbeck (1945)

This is one of those books that misses the target—not its target, my target. It is an excellent social and political commentary on life in hard times—a pretty good book even if it counts as literature—but it doesn't quite tell us enough about the collapse of the anchovy fishery to really drive the tragedy of the commons story home.

the tragedy of the commons (chapter 4)

 Capricorn One
Peter Hyams, director (1978)

This movie provides a classic example of what is meant by the term mediated reality. How do you really know what is and is not real if you haven't experienced it yourself?

mediated reality (chapter 11)

 Care and Feeding of Your Lunatic Mage, The
Douglas A. Van Belle (2010)

This is part of my self-promotional shtick for this edition of the textbook, but it has a surprising variety of points that are significant to the text. I'd highlight the political culture bit, as it takes the Eurocentric magic and wizardry bit and projects that forward into the attempted colonization of the Pacific. However, I could also go with power politics, the executive, imperial politics and political economy.

Awesomeness (Totally the whole book)

 Casino Royale
directed by Martin Campbell (Eon, 2006)

A James Bond flick that spends a boring half-hour setting up a cliché, there's always a better hand at the table, poker scene. Cut that half hour out and this is one awesome action flick. Key here is the set up of the economic foundations of politics as the bad guy is trying to manipulate the stock market in a very very naughty way. Not like Bernie Maddoff or anything.

political economy (chapter 4)

 Castle
Andrew W. Marlowe (ABC, 2009)

The only thing better than Nathan Fillion in a TV series, is Nathan Fillion in a Joss Whedon TV series. Seriously Fox TV executives, what kind of drugs were you on when you cancelled Firefly? But this show is pretty good. In addition to the detective and cop stuff, there is a nice bureaucratic politics undercurrent to this one as Rick Castle is the fly that the Mayor shoved into the police bureaucratic machine.

all kinds of law stuff (chapter 9), bureaucracy (chapter 8)

 Catch-22
Joseph Heller (1985)

This is one of those rare stories where either the book or the movie works. The story attempts to capture the irrationality of war, but also can be interpreted in terms of power and the structure of society.

security dilemma (chapter 2)

 A Christmas Carol
Charles Dickens (1843)

First, the Timmy in this story is not the Timmy from South Park. Second, maybe he should

have been. This tale really could have used a bit of Cartman's eloquence and grace. Enough already—rampant unchecked capitalism is miserable—we get it.

laissez-faire capitalism (chapter 4)

A Christmas Story
Bob Clark, director (1983)

The NRA was widely rumored to have bankrolled this seemingly charming tale of Christmas wishes. All Ralphie wants from the jolly fat man is a Red Ryder BB gun—but it seems everyone is saying no—and he has to deal with a bully who really needs shooting.

forceful control (chapter 3); preference falsification (chapter 3); safety valve (chapter 3)

A Clockwork Orange
Stanley Kubrick, director (1971)

This is one seriously disturbing movie. From the choreographed rape scene to the brutal murders, it is supposed to make us question where we draw the line between the needs of society and the rights of criminals, but the biggest questions it raises usually center around the exact formulation of the drugs Stanley must have been on when he made it.

personal nature of politics (Introduction)

Clonehenge
Douglas A. Van Belle (2007)

This is mostly a story about hypocrisy, so you can probably fit it in anywhere.

Cryptonomicon
Neal Stephenson (1999)

A story about secrecy, information, cryptology and politics it is referenced in chapter 3 right about in the whole panopticon thing, but

it is also clearly relevant to international politics, secret politics and media and politics. It follows to parallel stories, two generations apart, about cryptology in WWII and in the late 1990s.

Panopticon (chapter 3); conspiracies and secret politics (chapter 13); media and politics (chapter 11)

Dances With Squirrels
Douglas A. Van Belle (2013)

A story primarily about the differences in the way men and women conceptualize the world, the human half of this story is set against the alien story of a struggle to fulfill roles and excel as an individual when trapped inside a strict hierarchical political structure of ship's crew.

Hierarchy (chapter 2)

The Dark Knight
Christopher Nolan (2008)

Will the real Batman please stand up? The original comic-book Batman was a tortured soul who tread a narrow path between heroic and criminal and with *The Dark Knight,* the world finally got to see him on film.

Detritus of a Second-Hand Mind
Douglas A. Van Belle (2010)

Human cognition is a bitch of a topic to work into fiction, but I managed.

idealism (chapter 1)

Dick
Andrew Fleming, director (1999)

This satiric version of the Watergate story that puts forth the novel idea that the scandal was

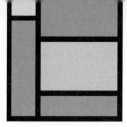

all caused by the bubble-headed blondes that Nixon hired to walk the presidential dog should not be taken seriously—unless of course, you are a die-hard Nixon supporter.

authority (chapter 2); *government* (chapter 2); *hierarchy* (chapter 2)

 ### The Dispossessed
Ursula K. Le Guin (1974)

This book might just be the best literary take on socialism ever. A must-read for anyone who thinks they might be either a socialist or a capitalist.

utopia (chapter 2); *capitalism* (chapter 4); *socialism* (chapter 4)

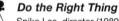 ### Do the Right Thing
Spike Lee, director (1989)

Who would have thought delivering pizza could be this troublesome? Sal's pizzeria is the central location in Spike Lee's graphic portrayal of racial tension in Brooklyn, New York.

safety valve (chapter 3)

 ### Dollhouse
Creator: Joss Whedon, creator (2009-)

Well . . . it survived for most of the first half of its first season. The idea was cool. Downloading personalities into pretty bodies for secret agenting all about and stuff is cool. And even if Eliza Dushku can't act to save her life, she does have a certain . . . uhm . . . screen presence. One of the few times that Joss Whedon has failed to spin enough of his magic to turn something into the kind of classic series he's famous for, like *Firefly* or *Buffy*.

experiential reality (chapter 1)

 ### Dr. Strangelove: Or How I Learned to Stop Worrying and Love the Bomb
Stanley Kubrick, director (1964)

Kubrick's twisted mind really works to perfection in this prototype of the "war as accident" story line, and it is unquestionably Peter Seller's best performance ever.

causes of war (chapter 12)

 ### Eagle Eye
D. J. Caruso, director (2008)

Some might say that this is yet another incarnation of Orwell's Big Brother from 1984; They're wrong. It is more of a Frankenstein's monster kind of story, where the creation escapes the control of its master. The plot is a little predictable, and it does choose action over nuance, but it is a nice twist on the surveillance theme.

panopticon (chapter 3)

 ### Earth
David Brin (1991)

The best population and ecological collapse novel ever written. David Brin manages to capture the meta struggle of humanity to survive on a worn out earth and still bring the individual drama to the fore. Crazy lady as bad guy isn't bad.

tragedy of the commons (Chapter 4)

Earth Abides
George R. Stewart (1949)

Interesting twist on the post apocalyptic story, where there are just a few survivors of a plague and they struggle to remodel themselves into a tribe. An excellent story on the

institutionalization of political actions and the beginning of political structures.

political structures (chapter 6)

 Enchanted
Kevin Lima (2007)

Satirical take on the ridiculous idealism and utopianism of Disney films, done by Disney.

Idealism and utopia (chapter 1)

 Ender's series
Orson Scott Card (1977)

Originally appearing as a short story in the August 1977 issue of *Analog,* I'll leave it to the true geeks in the class to debate if the expansion into first a novel and then a series of novels was brilliant or tragic. The end of childhood and exploitation of innocence themes of the short story were powerful, but they get lost in the novel's and the series's focus on the nature of humanity, construction of the other, essence of souls, religion, and the meaning of life.

causes of war (chapter 12); *culture* (chapter 14)

The FairlyOdd Parents
Butch Hartman, creator (1998)

Is there anyone better than Cosmo? We don't think so. This ranks right up there as one of the top cartoons of all time. Subversive, fun, twisted, but still innocent enough to let little kids watch—it is great.

utopia (chapter 2)

 Field of Dreams
Phil Alden Robinson, director (1989)

I say more than enough about this one in the text. Try reading chapter 2.

ideology (chapter 1); *utopia* (chapter 2)

 Fletch
Michael Ritchie, director (1985)

This is the best movie ever for one-liners. It seems that every line Chevy Chase has is a one-liner. I use its depiction of newsroom dynamics as an excuse for putting it in this textbook.

mediated reality (chapter 11)

The Flintstones
Joseph Barbera and William Hanna, creators (1960–1966)

The modern Stone Age Drama with the Flintstones and their neighbors the Rubble clan. Fred and Wilma, Barney and Betty—all you needed was a bridge night. I have always been kind of surprised that the kids didn't get their own series: "Pebbles and BamBam Got Married."

power (chapter 2)

The Forever War
Joe Haldeman (1974)

Classic, award-winning science fiction novel. I reference it as a wrong example of the causes of war, but as the characters skip forward through time, and we see not only the way society changes but also the way normalcy changes, it has a lot to offer for that dreaded term paper about politics in fiction.

causes of war (chapter 12)

 Forrest Gump
Robert Zemeckis, director (1994)

Stupid is as stupid does. This movie probably has the oddest spin-off of any feature film ever, the Bubba-Gump Shrimp Company restaurant. Today's students probably do not realize that one of the big talking points about

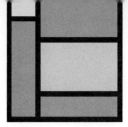

the film was the way the special effects people managed to insert Forrest into real archival footage. Everyone was wondering if we would ever again know what was real.

government (chapter 2); *the other* (chapter 2); *politics* (chapter 1)

 ### The Front
Martin Ritt, director (1976)

It is a question as to whether this or the original *Manchurian Candidate* is the best film about McCarthyism. Both tell us something extremely relevant in the post–9/11 era. Just replace communists with terrorists and the parallels are scary.

communism (chapter 1);

 ### Full Metal Jacket
Stanley Kubrick, director (1987)

This straight-up war flick really gives a solid kick to the "horribleness of being a soldier" story line.

alliances (chapter 2); *security dilemma* (chapter 2)

 ### Gilligan's Island
Sherwood Schwartz, creator (1964–1967)

In the original *Lost,* seven men and women, including the hapless Gilligan, are stranded on an island after their boat is lost in a tropical storm. The real question is: If the professor can build a satellite receiving station out of coconuts and a car out of bamboo, why can't he just build a boat?

alliances (chapter 2); *anarchy* (chapter 2)

 ### Game of Thrones
George RR Martin

If I need to point out the politics in Game of Thrones, then you really need to read the books and giver yourself a fighting chance of seeing something other than the nudity.

naughty bits (chapter 14)

 ### Gil Hamilton Series
Larry Niven, creator

In this collection of short stories, Gil Hamilton is a detective working in a far future of extreme resource scarcity and overpopulation. By looking at it from the angle of the crimes that arise in that context, Larry Niven provides a uniquely personal perspective on these increasingly salient global challenges.

tragedy of the commons (chapter 4)

 ### Girl Named Rabies
Douglas A. Van Belle (2010)

A man gets stuck waiting on standby, for 600 years, and wakes up in a bizarre bureaucratic utopia. A girl named Rabies and after mugging him becomes his guide to this wonky bit of the future.

utopia (chapter 1); *bureaucracy* (chapter 8)

 ### Gladiator
Ridley Scott, director (2000)

I'm not sure if this is a great film or a horrible one. I suspect the latter. I suspect that too much cinematic spectacle and not enough meat in the story line will make it one of those films that vanishes from the collective consciousness by the end of the decade. A must see if you have a leather and bondage fetish.

authority (chapter 2); *leadership* (chapter 3)

 ### Grantville Gazettes (1632)
Eric Flint (2000)

1632 and the series of novels that follow are perhaps the best, explicitly political novels

out there. I know, it's a bit tough to take the whole idea of a West Virginia town being transported back to the middle of the 30 years war. In fact, many of you probably find it difficult to take the whole idea of West Virginia, but push past that and just explore the politics. Flint did an awesome job researching these novels and gives a very accessible take on everything from democracy, to land tenure laws, to diplomacy, to capitalistic politics.

everything (whole book)

 Great Expectations
Charles Dickens (1861)

In the grand tradition of British comedy, Dickens has to be the humorist I understand the least. Boy growing up to fall in love with a cruel woman and then loses everything. I just don't get the joke. Dark humor still needs to be funny. Try *Shaun of the Dead* instead.

laissez-faire capitalism (chapter 4)

 The Green Hornet
Michel Gondry, director (2011)

Crap film. Comics have some geek appeal.

ideals versus reality (chapter 1)

 Green Lantern
Martin Campbell, director (2011)

See Green Hornet and double the crap part.

ideals versus reality (chapter 1)

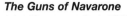 **The Guns of Navarone**
J. Lee Thompson, director (1961)

Great flick, but not much use in talking about the causes of war.

security (chapter 2)

 A Hitchhiker's Guide to the Galaxy
Douglas Adams (1979)

This is the first book in a four or five novel trilogy that ruthlessly skewers government and all things related to social propriety. Adams originally wrote this as a radio play, adapted it for television, and eventually packaged it into a book. It provides the perfect case study for the differences in story construction and the nature of comedy for these different mediums. Students should be aware that the movie sucked in comparison to the earlier versions, and I refuse to acknowledge its existence even though I think Zooey Deschanel is very pretty.

institutions (chapter 5)

 Home Improvement
Matt Williams, Carmen Finestra, and David MacFadzean, creators (1991–1999)

Incompetent to the extreme, Tim Taylor is the host of a cable TV tool show. The plot of half the episodes can be summed up by the fact that he has his own coffee mug at the emergency room. This is one of those sitcoms that is actually good. The writing is good. The characters are good. The performances are good. And it has something of a soul to it, with Wilson and the family angle and everything. The reruns of this will be floating around for a very long time.

structures (chapter 5)

The Hunt for Red October
John McTiernan, director (1990)

Another great flick, but I use it as an example of how socialism and communism are misrepresented in terms of the cold war, which really isn't what the film is about at all.

socialism (chapter 4)

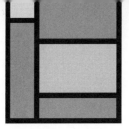

Iron Man
Jon Favreau, director (2008)

Believe it or not, I still haven't gotten around to watching Iron Man 2 yet. I have had the blue ray sitting on my shelf forever and I guess I really am just that lazy. Now, to be fair, the rugby world cup was on right when I got the disk, and then it was summer, and then the Super 15 Rugby season started up and when you're watching 7 rugby matches a weekend, there isn't that much time for watching movies, unless they have a lot of nudity in them. Speaking of Game of Thrones. . .

real versus ideal (chapter 1)

It's A Wonderful Life
Frank Capra, director (1946)

Yeah, it's a classic. Whatever.

institutions (chapter 5); *structures* (chapter 5)

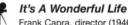 The Jackal's Waltz
Douglas A. Van Belle (2008)

Another of those surprisingly relevant bits of self-promotion, the ceremonial hunt at the center of Jackal's Waltz is a metaphor (that might be an analogy) for diplomacy in a predatory universe that is probably an analogy (but might be a metaphor) for anarchy.

anarchy (chapter 2); authority (chapter 2); diplomacy (chapter 12)

Jackass: The Movie
Jeff Tremaine, director (2002)

Take stupid people off the television and give them a movie deal. Whoever came up with this idea should really be shot—and as soon as we finish rounding up the reality TV people, Mr. Knoxville and company are our first priority.

politics (chapter 1)

Jerry Maguire
Cameron Crowe, director (1996)

Tom Cruise plays a sports agent who loses it all for being foolish enough to say something when he realizes that he actually believes in something. "You had me at, 'Hello'" is now officially the most over- satirized film line ever.

power (chapter 2)

The Jetsons
Joseph Barbera and Oscar Dufau, creators (1962–1988)

The theme music is supposed to be exactly the same as *The Flintstones,* but I'm not sure if I believe that.

power (chapter 2)

Judge Joe Brown
Peter Brennan, creator (1998)

A bad version of Judge Judy, if that is possible.

civil law (chapter 9)

Judge Judy
Peter Brennan, creator (1996)

Bad. Worse than reality TV.

civil law (chapter 9)

Julius Ceaser
That Shakespeare dude

Play, hard to understand, lots of stabbing in one part.

monarchy (Chapter 5)

 The King and I
Walter Lang (1956)

It's a musical, so I hate it. The king of Siam hits on his kid's teacher or nanny or something like

that, sort of like *The Sound of Music* with dancing instead of singing, and without the Nazis. There was actually a king of Siam, but Siam was bought out by a shaving cream manufacturer and renamed Burma. Now it's Myanmar; no one is really sure why.

monarchy (Chapter 5)

 L.A. Law
Steven Bochco and Terry Louise Fisher, creators (1986–1994)

This used to be the prime-time soap opera to watch. They never, ever let the lawyering part get in the way of the melodrama.

power (chapter 2); *dispute resolution* (chapter 9); *going rate* (chapter 9); *law in action* (chapter 9)

The Lathe of Heaven
Ursula K. Le Guin (1971) [TV adaptation: David Loxton and Fred Barzyk, creators (1980)]

Forget the TV show, read the book. It isn't that long, and it is pretty good. Ask yourself questions about the power of social structures when you do. Actually, even though I mention this in terms of mediated reality in the text, it is probably a better example of the subjectivity of utopias. Wait, I do mention it in the utopia chapter. Somebody should have caught that before I wrote this part. Why is there never an editor around when you need one?

utopia (chapter 2); *mediated reality* (chapter 11)

 Law and Order
Dick Wolf, creator (1990)

This must be the most ripped-off and spun-off TV series ever. It is also a fantasy. It is just not possible to have that long of a run of sexy female district attorneys and handsome male cops replacing the sexy and handsome ones who quit or die.

power (chapter 2); *common law* (chapter 9); *criminal law* (chapter 9); *going rate* (chapter 9); *original jurisdiction* (chapter 9)

 Lawnmower Man
Brett Leonard (1992)

Uhm, stupid guy gets an upgrade and is hooked to a computer or something. This thing makes Inception look downright straightforward. It's one of those all seeing menace kinds of things so I mention it with the panopticon stuff.

panopticon (chapter 3)

 **Lies and the Lying Liars Who Tell Them: A Fair and Balanced Look at the Right**
Al Franken (2003)

A satirical jab at Fox News.

News (chapter 11)

The Life of Brian
Terry Jones, director (1979)

Monty Python's second best film. It beats out *The Meaning of Life* by just a smidge. There actually is a fair bit of political story in here as the characters are caught up in a political struggle against the Roman Empire.

ideology (chapter 1)

Lion King
Roger Allers and Rob Minkoff (1994)

Disney's remake of Hamlet.

authority and hierarchy (chapter 3); *hereditary monarchy* (chapter 6)

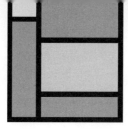

Logan's Run
Michael Anderson, director (1976)

This film is another one of those "be careful what you wish for" stories. Yes, everybody is young and beautiful, but that is because they are killed on their thirtieth birthday.

utopia (chapter 2); *bureaucracy* (chapter 8)

Lord of the Flies
William Golding (1963)

Your high school English teacher probably told you this story was about the fragility of civilized society or about the animal in people and the descent into savagery. We say it is about the dynamics of anarchy. Who are you going to believe? Remember, your grade depends on your answer.

anarchy (chapter 2); *group identity* (chapter 2); *security* (chapter 2)

Lost
Jeffrey Lieber, creator (2004–2010)

How far can you twist and spindle a plot before it falls apart? Tune in for season six and see for yourself.

anarchy (chapter 2); *authority* (chapter 2)

Lucifer's Hammer
Larry Niven and Jerry Pournell (1977)

The comet hitting the earth was just the beginning. The real story is about the struggle to survive in an anarchic environment.

anarchy (chapter 2); *group identity* (chapter 2); *security* (chapter 2)

Mad Max
George Miller, director (1979)

This is a classic Australian film, which tells you everything you need to know about Australia. The stunts are amazing, so amazing that you will actually be surprised to learn that none of the stuntmen died while making this film, but it is the violence that sets this apart as an iconic film. It isn't all that gory, but it feels very, very real and if you don't find yourself cringing and curling your toes, you might want to consider having yourself committed before you turn into a serial killer. All those directors of all those lame and bloody horror flicks could learn a thing or two from George Miller.

anarchy (chapter 2); *security* (chapter 2)

Mad Max 2: The Road Warrior
George Miller, director (1981)

Americans know this one as *The Road Warrior*, and most do not know it was a sequel. One of the best Aussie films ever made. I realize that isn't saying much, but it is a great flick, and the Aussie part should not be discounted too hastily. When Hollywood tried to make a *Mad Max 3*, they really stuffed it up. This is a seriously good story about anarchy and the search for security.

alliances (chapter 2); *anarchy* (chapter 2); *security* (chapter 2); *the tragedy of the commons* (chapter 4)

Mars Trilogy (Red Mars; Green Mars; Blue Mars)
Kim Stanley Robinson (1993; 1994;1996)

Ecopolitics writ large, very, very large. One big long story spans a bajillion pages of this trilogy as human kind terraforms Mars while the ecosystem of the Earth collapses. The *Red Mars, Green Mars, Blue Mars* series has a lot to offer for that paper you are being forced to write on the politics in a novel. Try environmentalism, socialism, self-determination, terrorism, the role of technology in society, or the changing conceptualization of humanity, for a few themes.

anarchy (chapter 2); *equality* (chapter 3); *tragedy of the commons* (chapter 4)

The Mary Tyler Moore Show
James L. Brooks and Allan Burns, creators (1970–1977)

This is another one of the newsroom television shows that have fallen out of favor—in fact it was the first one. It is also the one with the least to say about the dynamics of the newsroom and might be better used as an example of a feminist statement about the empowerment of women in a male-dominated society.

mediated reality (chapter 11)

 M*A*S*H
Robert Altman, creator (1972–1983)

This is possibly the best comedy/drama ever made. 'nuff said.

security (chapter 2)

 The Matrix series
Andy and Larry Wachowski, directors (1999)

The Matrix films provide the object lesson that no matter how successful the first film was, some directors should not be given free rein on the sequels. The first movie is the perfect mediated reality, "how do you know what is real" kind of flick. The second two wallow so self indulgently in Christian, Greek, and even Egyptian mythology that there is little worth watching.

Plato (chapter 1); *mediated reality* (chapter 11)

 Monty Python and the Holy Grail
Terry Gilliam and Terry Jones, directors (1975)

This is the funniest film ever made, bar none—the best work by the best comedy team ever.

institutions (chapter 5)

 Moon over Parador
Paul Mazursky, director (1988)

Little-known actor Jack Noah is working on location in the dictatorship of Parador at the time the dictator dies. He is made an offer he cannot refuse—run the country. One of those pretty good films that tends to get lost in the mix and overlooked when it comes to scheduling old flicks on cable.

legitimacy (chapter 3); *revolution* (chapter 3)

 The Mouse that Roared
Jack Arnold, director (1959)

A classic. Rent it and watch it.

world systems theory (chapter 12)

 Mr. Magoo's Christmas Carol
Abe Levitow (1962)

It's a cartoon version of *A Christmas Carol,* fully bastardized by UPA animation studio. Don't watch it unless you're seven years old.

experiential reality (chapter 1)

 Mr. Smith Goes to Washington
Frank Capra, director (1939)

This actually could be a film about unnatural fetishes and obsessions. Monuments, monuments, monuments—enough already.

idealism (chapter 1); *institutions* (chapter 5); *bicameral legislature* (chapter 7); *filibuster* (chapter 7)

Mulan
Tony Bancroft and Barry Cook, directors (1998)

This is supposed to be a "girls can be heroes, too" kind of story, but that benevolently feminist moralizing just does not work, and not

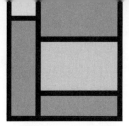

even Eddie Murphy can save this rather lame Disney film. If you want a Disney film with a strong female lead struggling successfully against a male-dominated society, try *Beauty and the Beast*.

the other (chapter 2)

 Murphy Brown
Diane English, creator (1988–1998)

A comedy series about the newsroom. The dynamics of the news as a business are hidden beneath the comedic insanity of the quirky collection of characters, but it is there and surfaces now and again.

mediated reality (chapter 11)

 National Treasure
Jon Turteltaub, director (2004)

I forget why I mentioned this and I'm too lazy to go back through the book and figure out what chapter it was in and why.

For some reason (somewhere probably)

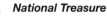 **National Treasure 2: Book of Secrets**
Jon Turteltaub, director (2007)

Even less sure about why this one is in here and even lazier now than I was a few minutes ago.

Maybe for some reason (somewhere probably)

 The Net
Irwin Winkler, director (1995)

One of the first real attempts to take a serious shot at the internet as Panopticon story. Not the best, but gets a mention for being the first.

panopticon (chapter 3)

 Network
Sidney Lumet, director (1976)

This is probably the best film about the newsroom.

mediated reality (chapter 11)

 Nineteen Eighty-Four (1984)
George Orwell (1949) [film adaptation: Michael Radford, director (1984)]

Takes a light-hearted romp through the cheery little nightmare of life under the unblinking gaze of Big Brother. Government is everywhere, watching everything and everyone, and it is a crime to think the wrong thoughts.

utopia (chapter 2); atomization (chapter 3); government control of individuals (chapter 3); panopticon (chapter 3); peer policing (chapter 3); preference falsification (chapter 3); self-policing (chapter 3); bureaucracy (chapter 8)

 Nixon
Oliver Stone, director (1995)

This film got a lot of attention when it came out, but *All the President's Men* is probably a better film and is certainly a more accurate one.

politics (chapter 1); *hierarchy* (chapter 2); *power* (chapter 2)

 Oliver Twist
Charles Dickens (1838)

Again, I don't get the joke. What is so funny about starving orphans and clouds of coal smoke so thick that they block the sun?

laissez-faire capitalism (chapter 4)

 Omega Man
Boris Sagal, director (1971)

Omega, the last letter of the Greek alphabet and as such it has been abused to the point

of despair as a symbol of the last or the end. Give it a rest people. Last healthy man on Earth is trying to find a cure for the plague that's turning everyone into Zombies. Gets an extra point or two for Zombies

tragedy of the commons (chapter 4)

 Once Were Warriors
Lee Tamahori, director (1994)

This movie depicts the struggle of trying to live when you are caught between a traditional society of warriors and the demands of a modern, Western European society. On the lighter side, the director was arrested, in drag, on a street corner.

cultural ownership (chapter 14); political culture (chapter 14)

 The Paper
Ron Howard, director (1994)

This movie is a seriously good depiction of the business imperatives and structural dynamics of the newsroom.

mediated reality (chapter 11)

 Peanuts
Charles M. Schulz, creator

Snoopy—widely regarded as the most famous dog in history—and his owner Charlie Brown first appeared in print in 1950. This cartoon continues to feature in print, television, and movies fifty-five years later.

security (chapter 2)

 The People's Court
Stu Billett, creator (1981)

How many synonyms for wretched are there in the thesaurus? Not enough.

civil law (chapter 9)

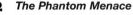 **The Phantom Menace**
Steven Spielberg is totally glad he didn't direct this (1999)

Legislative politics made even less interesting than it actually is.

legislatures (chapter 7)

 The Postman
David Brin (1985)

Yeah I know there was a film. Read the book. Pretty good depiction of the unpleasantness of anarchy but could also be shoehorned into the news chapter as a commentary on the communicative needs of society and the place given to the messenger.

anarchy (chapter 2)

 Popeye
E. C. Segar, director (1956–1963)

The original Popeye appeared in a 1933 cartoon, but made it onto television for a seven-year stint. The often graphically depicted brutal violence is argued to be one of the inspirations for the Itchy and Scratchy characters on *The Simpsons*.

security (chapter 2)

 The Practice
David E. Kelley, creator (1997–2004)

This show that came before *Boston Legal* offers probably the best peek at the unpleasant side of the law. Most of the drama was angst over the fact that these defence attorneys were far too committed to winning at all costs, and they were far better at it than they wanted to be. It lasted two years longer than it should have, but the Alan Shore character—who moved to *Boston Legal*—was brought in for part of the last

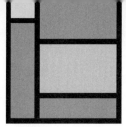

season and made the extra forty episodes worthwhile.

power (chapter 2); *common law* (chapter 9); *criminal law* (chapter 9)

 ### The Probability Broach
L. Neil Smith (1981)

Hidden gem, underappreciated—there are a lot of ways of describing this book. It uses that well-worn and often abused "parallel worlds" plot device, but it more than makes up for that by providing what may be the closest thing to a workable anarchic political environment that has yet been dreamt up. And for the record, Neil is an unabashed libertarian anarchist with a web site and everything.

utopia (chapter 2); *anarchy* (chapter 2); *hierarchy* (chapter 2)

 ### Quantum of Solace
Marc Forster, director (2008)

I needed a movie for the Q section of the appendix so I shoved this into the political economy chapter. It fits, because the bad guy is trying to set up a monopoly on a communal good, but still.

filler (appendix A)

 ### Raiders of the Lost Ark
Steven Spielberg, director (1981)

Raiders is the quintessential action film, combining good visual effects with a story line that is more than strong enough to carry them. With the Nazis and World War II elements in the story line, there is probably a lot that could be said about the politics of war, power, and such, but we don't ever get around to that in the text.

mediated reality (chapter 11)

 ### Rainbows End
Vernor Vinge (2006)

Vernor pronounces the e on the end of his last name and note that the lack of an apostrophe in the title is not a typo. This is a full on, frontal assault on the information politics thing. This is worth a relaxed, contemplative read, Vernor gets my vote for the best living science fiction author out there. After me of course.

panopticon (chapter 3)

 ### River Queen
Vincent Ward, director (2005)

Supposedly, this film was cursed. It did suffer from more than its share of production problems, but it is also a cinematic treat. *River Queen* won some awards, but none of the big ones. In addition to the cultural bit I use it for in chapter 14, it could also be used to discuss the politics of war, colonization, and race.

cultural ownership (chapter 14); political culture (chapter 14)

 ### Roger and Me
Michael Moore, director (1989)

This is the documentary that thrust Michael Moore—who has sometimes been called the attack dog on the liberal side of the fence—into the limelight. Unabashedly political, this film would be interesting to talk about in the text box on politically effective protest. Michael is clearly protesting.

politics (chapter 1)

Rush Limbaugh Is a Big Fat Idiot and Other Observations
Al Franken (1996)

This is Al's take on the attack, attack, attack, political strategies of the Republicans in the

1980s and early 1990s. Al is far funnier when he's satirizing himself than when he's hitting conservatives. Even though he does an excellent job of satirizing the beast that grew out of Newts electoral strategy, and the hypocrisy of Newt himself, there is just a little bit too much real feeling in this to get more than a chuckle as you read.

elections (chapter 10)

 Saw
James Wan, director (2004)

Saw is, perhaps, the perfect starting point for discussing how lazy the horror genre has become. The iconic moment, cutting off the leg to escape, was stolen from Mad Max 2, and there really isn't all that much more it has to offer. Horror used to be scary because of the struggle inherent in the drive to survive an inhuman threat, not because you cringe at the thought of having to cut your leg off, or rip your eyeball out. If you want to cringe at eyeballs getting ripped out, watch Against the Fall of Night instead. The fact that the woman VOLUNTEERS to be blinded by having crows peck out her eyes, really makes the religious power aspect, and its abuse, horrifying.

A writer's laziness (chapters 1-15, plus introduction and appendixes)

 Saving Private Ryan
Steven Spielberg, director (1998)

Private Ryan is another "horrors of war" flick. In fact, the extended opening scene is probably the best "horrors of war" example there is, and if my description of World War I did not faze you, imagine, it was worse than Normandy.

group identity (chapter 2)

 **Scorpion King**
Chuck Russell (2002)

Winning the throne through battle. Used as a counter example of the institutionalization of the executive.

kings (chapter 6)

 Secret Honor
Robert Altman, director (1984)

This film depicts a Nixon supporter's version of the Watergate scandal. The most telling point about it is that nobody remembers it, and it is almost impossible to find a copy of it. Did it really exist?

politics (chapter 1); *power* (chapter 2); *presidency* (chapter 6)

Sex and the City
Darren Star, creator (1998–2004)

I suppose there might be something to say about the shock value of the naughty bits on screen, and there is the novelty of seeing a group of reasonably pretty women who are a bit too old obsess about sex as much as men do, but this has got to go in the category of shows that got very tiring very fast.

cognitive frameworks (chapter 11)

Shortland Street
Created by Patricia Morrison (TVNZ, 1992)

A New Zealand soap opera which serves as a warning for what happens when you forget the pretty part of soap operas being all about pretty people who can't act.

newsworthiness (chapter 11)

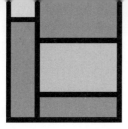

The Simpsons
Matt Groening, creator (1989)

The longest running cartoon ever, may- be the longest running series ever—*The Simpsons* covers it all. From ecology to racism, pick a political topic and you can probably find an episode with something relevant to say.

politics (chapter 1)

Small Blue Planet for the Pleasantly Insane
Douglas A. Van Belle (2004)

The politics of academic rivalry, with a stupid alien thrown in the mix.

academic debates (chapter 15)

Snow Crash
Neal Stephenson (1992)

Another Panopticon story, Snow Crash is also a utopia story. It depicts the increasing irrelevance of physical location and physical boundaries as information driven societies lead to topical groupings of people over the physical. Probably overplays that, as people have a countervailing interest in expanding the reach of their physical security, but that is what utopian fiction does, push those kinds of things to the extreme.

security (chapter 2); panopticon (chapter 3)

Soylent Green
Richard Fleischer, director (1973)

Tastes like chicken.

tragedy of the commons (chapter 4)

The SpongeBob SquarePants Movie
Stephen Hillenburg, director (2004)

You know, I really didn't want to refer to the movie. I was talking about the cartoon series when I mentioned SpongeBob. The movie really wasn't all that good. If you want to see the very best of SpongeBob, you have to see the imagination box episode.

power (chapter 2); laissez-faire capitalism (chapter 4)

Star Trek
Gene Roddenberry, creator (1966–1969)

Despite all my self-deprecating jokes about being a *Star Trek* geek and all, this really was one of the most influential shows of the twentieth century. You could pick just about any theme in this book and find that one of the original *Star Trek* episodes has something to offer. The first show to put a black woman in a position of responsibility and command, it tackled the social issues of its time and pulled no punches.

utopia (chapter 2); federal system (chapter 5)

Star Trek: Insurrection
Jonathan Frakes, director (1998)

While this may not be the best movie in the world, or even the best of the *Star Trek* movies, it does have an interesting take on the socialist commune as an idyllic utopia.

group identity (chapter 2); socialism (chapter 4)

Star Wars
George Lucas, director (1977)

This is the movie to end all movies. A lot of people got caught up with the spectacle created with the special effects, but we would argue that it was the heroic story line—the humble farm boy following his heroic instinct and rescuing the princess— that made this movie such a phenomenon. The parallels with Christian religious

beliefs were made obvious by the fact that Luke wears very Jesus-like clothes. The clash of the realist and the idealist hit all of the right chords with an American society that was in the depths of one of the worst economic and political times since the Great Depression.

idealism (chapter 1); *realism* (chapter 1)

 ### Star Wars, the other five episodes
George Lucas, director (1983–2005)

I can forgive George for not stopping with the first one, which was actually the fourth episode, and *Empire Strikes Back* and *Return of the Jedi* were both okay, except for the Ewoks. But those three prequels were wretched. I didn't even watch the third one until it came out on cable. Seriously, George, legislative intrigue is pretty seriously boring. What made you think you could make it exciting?

idealism (chapter 1); *realism* (chapter 1)

State of Play
Kevin Macdonald, director (2009)

It's a crime flick. Investigations, murder . . . yawn.

mediated reality (chapter 11) mutual exploitation model (chapter 11)

 ### Survivor
Charlie Parsons, creator (2000)

Surprisingly, these are not the people to blame for the reality TV pandemic. The Norwegians—or maybe it was the Swedes— came up with the idea. Just to be safe, we should just forbid anyone north of Munich from ever making a TV show ever again.

alliances (chapter 2); *group identity* (chapter 2); *Arrow's Theorem* (chapter 10)

 ### Team America: World Police
Trey Parker and Matt Stone, directors (2004)

This is a "love it or hate it" kind of movie. It either causes laughter that threatens bladder control or bores you to tears. I tend to like the more subversive and subtle parts of Trey and Matt's humor, like the way they turned the *South Park* movie into a satire of a Disney cartoon. This one was just too much crass "in your face" slapstick. The one funny part was the Film Actors Guild, but there just wasn't enough of that kind of fun in it.

socialism (chapter 4)

To Kill a Mockingbird
Harper Lee (1960)

This is another one of those "must-read-even-though-it-counts-as-literature" kinds of books. There's plenty of discussion of it in the text so back off.

politics (chapter 1); institutions (chapter 5); dispute resolution (chapter 9); law in action (chapter 9); law in books (chapter 9); natural law (chapter 9); positivist jurisprudence (chapter 9)

 ### This is Spinal Tap
Rob Reiner, director (1984)

This documentary on the world's loudest band is the unchallenged best example of the mockumentary. Some of the best one liners ever

not really relevant at all (whole book)

 ### Thrice Upon a Time
James P. Hogan (1980)

Geek factor 5 if you recognize this one. James P. Hogan wrote some really interesting stuff in the 1980s and commanded a big swath of the bookstore shelves during his time, but for all

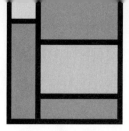

that success he just didn't manage the staying power that you would expect. He's still writing books, but they can be hard to find beyond the pages of Amazon.com. Thrice Upon a Time was his try at an ecological time travel thriller, seriously. It actually is pretty interesting and could be said to presage the current and growing problem with dead zones in the ocean from fertilizer pollution.

ecopolitics (chapter 4)

 Top Gear
Andy Wilman, producer (1977–2001)

Three blokes and a cyborg spend an hour every week screwing around with cars and behaving like jackasses. TV at its finest.

mediated reality (chapter 11)

 Tora! Tora! Tora!
Richard Fleischer and Kinji Fukasaku, directors (1970)

This story of Pearl Harbor is not much use here as it doesn't really tell us a great deal about the politics surrounding war, but it may be the best of the World War II movies.

conceptual frameworks (chapter 1); security (chapter 2)

A Tree Grows in Brooklyn
Betty Smith (1943) [film adaptation: Elia Kazan, director (1945)]

Ah, yes. Professors really like assigning this one, so beware and be warned. If you really like sucking up to the teacher, choose this book for your writing assignment. That said, for such a dreary story line filled with human misery, it is not that intolerable to read. The standard plot summary is that that the Nolans manage to enjoy life, despite . . . (insert unpleasantness of life here) . . . but something

touchy-feely about family might be better. Oh, and tell the professor that you cried while reading it. The professors who assign this one are always real big on that touchy feely empathy stuff.

idealism (chapter 1); *realism* (chapter 1); *laissez-faire capitalism* (chapter 4)

 12 Monkeys
Terry Gilliam, director (1995)

A disease has wiped mankind off the face of the earth, and only a handful of B-list actors are managing to survive in a soundstage that looks like a psychotic interior designer went nuts with chain-link fencing. Bruce Willis travels back in time to pull out his own teeth. Brad Pitt is all too convincing in the part of a raving lunatic, and the world still ends.

collective action (chapter 2); the tragedy of the commons (chapter 4)

 The Untouchables
Brian De Palma, director (1987)

A movie that uses the "Good cop versus bad mobster" theme. The gritty old realist teaches the idealist to cope with the reality of fighting crime in gangland Chicago.

idealism (chapter 1); *realism* (chapter 1)

Ungraceful Cliffdwellers
Douglas A. Van Belle (2008)

By the time you realize that I was hiding a philosophical story behind the opening sex scene, you'll be far enough into this one that you may as well finish it. Basic question revolves around the political economy of science and what happens when the diminishing returns on investment catch up to us.

discovery and science (chapter 15)

Utopia
Thomas More (1515)

The original *Utopia* turns out to be a horrible and miserable place. The book is worth a read if only to drive home the point that utopias are subjective.

utopia (chapter 2)

Wag the Dog
Barry Levinson, director (1997)

This movie is an unconvincing attempt to tell a horror story about the mediated reality of politics. There are a lot of ways this could have been done well, but there are just too many holes in the idea that a president could create an entirely imaginary war. In the end, the viewer feels beaten about the head by the heavy-handed moralizing in the story.

legitimacy (chapter 3); *framing* (chapter 11); *mediated reality* (chapter 11); *spin* (chapter 11)

War Games
John Badham, director (1983)

Computer goes nuts and takes over the U.S. nuclear launch system in a classic example of the "war as accident" story line with a teenage kid saving the day.

causes of war (chapter 12)

Watchmen
Zack Snyder, director (2009)

Give me my three hours back, damn you!

ideal versus the real (chapter 1)

The West Wing
Aaron Sorkin, creator (1999–2006)

One of those realistic political dramas, this series provided a reasonably not-outlandish depiction of what life in the White House might really be like. The drama is a bit overdone, and the sinisterness of the political confrontations is a bit over the top, but still, it's better than most.

politics (chapter 1); *institutions* (chapter 5); *presidency* (chapter 6)

Whale Rider
Niki Caro, director (2002)

One of the best examples of the cultural emphasis of the New Zealand film industry. There are numerous political themes that could be examined from the story, ranging from the clash of modern versus traditional cultures to the role of leadership. However, we recommend the *Bro'Town* satire of it where Jeff the Maori plays the Keisha Castle-Hughes part and has to save his Iwi from developers.

cultural ownership (chapter 14); political culture (chapter 14)

What About Bob?
Frank Oz, director (1991)

I had no good reason for including this in the book.

gridlock (chapter 7)

White Nights
Taylor Hackford, director (1985)

White Nights provides an excellent representation of the Soviets as the "Evil Empire" fictional depiction of socialism and communism. An emergency landing puts a former Russian Ballet star back in the hands of the big bad communists, and he has to dance or die. Okay, it's not quite that extreme, but they do hold him prisoner and just generally are not very nice to him, and it takes the sacrifice of

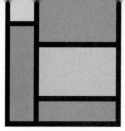

a friend to help him escape back to freedom. Just remember that socialism is an economic term that is conceptually distinct from evil dictatorships.

socialism (chapter 4)

 Why Not Me?
Al Franken (1999)

Franken pulls off this pseudo-autobiography perfectly, and by portraying himself as an idiot rather than attacking the real idiots playing politics out there, it takes the partisan edge off. That makes it, perhaps, the funniest political satire ever written.

Arrow's Theorem (chapter 10)

 WKRP in Cincinnati
Hugh Wilson, creator (1978–1982)

Another media as a business show with Les Nessman as the intrepid anchorman who pronounces Chihuahua—Chee-hooah-hooah.

mediated reality (chapter 11)

 Woman on the Edge of Time
Marge Piercy (1976)

This is another one of those books that professors really like assigning. The story is littered with lots of complex ways to discuss power relationships and structural violence and to question the nature of reality. Basically, you are never sure if the woman committed to the asylum is insane or gifted as she struggles against the constraints the structures of society place upon her.

mediated reality (chapter 11)

 X-Files
Chris Carter, creator (1993–2002)

Here is the ultimate alien conspiracy theory series. In addition to what it says about cognitive frameworks and the interpretation of incoming information, it could be used to discuss the role of secrecy in democratic governance, technology, and myth.

cognitive frameworks (chapter 11)

 **Zombies From Mars**
Douglas A. Van Belle (2009)

One of the best examples of zombies as bureaucracy that I have ever written about someone trapped on a space ship.

bureaucracy (chapter 8)

 Zoolander
Ben Stiller, director (2001)

Awesomeness. Satire in it's highest form.

Idealism (chapter 1)

A Strategic Approach to Writing for the Classroom

James G. Van Belle | Douglas A. Van Belle

Most students are more than capable of writing a most excellent essay. Even if they have difficulties with the more mechanical skills of writing—spelling, grammar, and punctuation—they are usually still quite capable of constructing sentences and stringing them together to make coherent paragraphs. However, undergraduates almost universally abhor this seemingly simple task. More often than not the mere mention of a paper or essay exam in a syllabus is enough to start a stampede to the registrar's office to beg for a different class. Even for the better students, a simple essay assignment may be a daunting, almost Herculean task. Why, if students are capable of writing these essays, does writing cause such a visceral reaction? And why do birds continue to fly south every fall when they could just land on the top of a southbound semi and ride I-95 to Florida?

Though there are probably several complex social and psychological processes that combine to cause both students and birds to behave irrationally, one of the biggest and most constant sources of the students' fear seems to stem from a more straightforward source, uncertainty over the content of an essay. There are several books and other types of guides that tell a student how to write an essay—formats, styles, citations, and such— but when it comes to what to put in those properly formatted sentences and paragraphs, the vast majority of students, even the studious and hard-working students, are clueless. A few have a natural knack for it, an intuitive feel for what a professor or a boss wants to see in there, but for most it is a shot in the dark and they all end up trying to hide it all behind the selection of a tasteful Book Antiqua font.

Combining the often-divergent insights derived from teaching introductory composition courses, teaching writing-intensive political science courses, and watching documentaries on bird migration, a lecture-style description of a strategic approach to writing is presented here. The primary objective is to provide students with something they can use to help focus and organize the content of a brief, report, or other type of essay. Obviously, every paper is going to be different, and it is impossible to tell a student what he or she should put in any specific essay. However, just as it is possible to teach a mechanic methods and techniques to more effectively use the tools of the trade to attain an end such as fixing a car, it is possible to outline a method students can use to more effectively construct an essay. By focusing on the effort to persuade the reader and adding a few other suggestions regarding the content of writing, students can make the whole process easier and more effective.

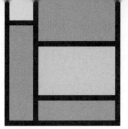

THE GOAL OF WRITING

Writing is a goal-oriented process, a means to an end, and it needs to be approached as such. In short, you are not just writing an essay, you are trying to accomplish something with your essay. Specifically, in writing an essay you are presenting an argument. You are trying to convince the reader of something. At the very least you should be trying to persuade a reasonable and open-minded reader that what you are arguing, what you are trying to say, the position you are trying to defend, the opinion you are trying to express, is reasonable. When you are writing for a boss, or judge, or banker, or client, you are not filling pages so you can get enough and stop typing, you are trying to convince them to sell this widget, to let your client go, to loan you this money, to follow this advice. When you are writing for a professor, you should also keep in mind that you are doing more than regurgitating the information that has been delivered to you throughout the course. We call that brain vomit. Professors don't like brain vomit any more than they like any other form of vomit. Professors want you to use that information in a novel way. They want you to take what you have been given and form it into an argument that will convince your professor that you understand the material and its application. You have to use that material to convince your professor of two things: you know the topic well enough to be writing an essay about it, and that he/she/it should take your argument seriously.

How does this focus on convincing the reader of something translate into a strategy for writing an essay? Perhaps the simplest starting point is to use this goal as a point of reference throughout the writing process. When you are faced with the task of writing, ask yourself, "What am I trying to convince my reader of?" Often this will help determine what material should go into an essay and how it should be organized.

For example, pretend you are sitting across the dinner table from your less-than-bright Uncle Larry. Everybody has that grudgingly tolerated relative who occasionally shows up for a holiday meal here or there. Everyone has that uncle who talks with his mouth full and is just a little slow on the uptake but who does not let either get in the way of a good debate.

"Why do you have to go off to college? You don't need to go to college. I did just fine working at the gas station," Uncle Larry's mashed potatoes say.

You sit there, and for some unknown reason you feel compelled to explain to Larry why you went off to college. It is that effort at explanation that captures the essence of what you should be trying to do every time you write.

What do you do? You probably start with something along the lines of, "Going to college was the best thing for me to do."

A statement like this is more or less the topic sentence that everyone talks about when they try to teach you to write. Whether it is called a thesis, hypothesis, proposition, or something else, a topic sentence for an essay is nothing more than a simple statement of what you are trying to convince the reader to believe; in this example you are trying to

convince Uncle Larry that going to college was a good thing. In a way, this statement or proposition is merely the simplest version of your argument you can make. You know, of course, that Larry is going to challenge your assertion, so you need more support and examples to work with.

A crucial aspect of making an argument is to explain why your reader should believe your thesis. Describe the basic logic, the reasons why the reader should consider your argument to be reasonable. What reasons do you give to Larry to make him believe that going to college was the best thing for you to do? This can be thought of as the "because" portion of the argument, and a simple set of statements starting with "because" can be an easy way to get yourself used to thinking in this way as you write.

- Because—People who attend college, on average, make more money than people who do not.

- Because—People who go to college are more likely to find a job that provides full benefits such as health care, vacations, and retirement plans.

- Because—People who go to college tend to do less physically demanding work and are more likely to be healthier in their old age.

- Because—Going to college is the only way that I can get the job I want.

You have just laid out several reasons why Uncle Larry should agree with your assertion that going to college was a good choice. You have also just outlined your essay. In fact, you have almost written the first paragraph.

When you approach an essay for an exam or a short paper, you should employ this same strategy. You start out by saying, as clearly and simply as you can manage, this is what I want to convince you of. For an essay exam this can be as simple as "this is the best answer to the essay question." Don't be afraid to simply answer the question being posed. For example, a sociology exam that asks the question, "Is the Internet good for society?" is begging for a straightforward answer. An effective response to this question could start by simply answering the question: The Internet is good for society. The writer then goes on to say that the reader should believe this answer because . . . and states what that reason is and adds a second reason, and a third reason, and possibly even a fourth reason.

That is your first paragraph. It clearly and blatantly states what you are arguing and why it should be accepted as reasonable. That first paragraph also outlines your essay. You can call it what you want, topic paragraph, introductory paragraph, or whatever, but that is all there is to it. Now, if you think about it, this is pretty much the same thing your high school English teacher taught you about an introduction to an essay, but what was probably missing in high school was the part about what actually goes in an introduction. What is the logic behind a topic sentence? What is it supposed to accomplish? How can you write a

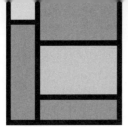

topic sentence if you don't know what it is supposed to accomplish? How can you write that first paragraph if you don't know what you are trying to use it for? The first sentence of the first paragraph unambiguously lays out what you are arguing, then the remainder clearly states the logic so that the reader knows exactly what to expect from the rest of the essay. If this is done properly, a professor should be able to grade the entire essay just by reading the first paragraph. This emphasis on directness and clarity is one very important way in which this strategic approach might differ from the way composition is often taught.

When you are using writing as a tool for making an argument, subtlety is bad. Outside of literature, subtlety just doesn't work; it can't work. Why? Well, there is a practical reason. First, think about your professor. He/she/it is probably going to have to sit down and read at least twenty of these essays, more likely twice that many, and sometimes hundreds. What are the chances that anyone, Cylon or human, could sit down in front of all those essays and be able to tease out subtle details or catch understated nuances? Similarly, your boss isn't going to want to take the time to eek out subtle allusions from a strategy document. And do you really want to take the risk that he or she misses them? Be clear, be direct, and by all means state your argument early.

There is also a very practical, psychological reason for presenting the logic of your argument clearly and unambiguously at the beginning of the essay. Human cognition works by sorting incoming information according to logical frameworks or logical constructs. If you provide a reader with YOUR logical framework at the beginning of that thing you are calling a term paper, then the reader is almost certain to use that framework or something quite close to it to sort through the narrative atrocity that follows. The reader will actually help you connect the information you provide to the argument you are making. If you don't provide that logical framework at the beginning, readers will pick or create their own, and who knows what kind of logic a clinically insane university instructor is going to use to try to make sense of a collection of grammatical errors so horrific that the result is almost poetic?

If a clear statement of the point being argued and a succinct outline of the logic constitutes your first paragraph, what comes in your next paragraph? Think of your next paragraph as your first "evidence" paragraph. What you do is you take this first reason, the first "because" statement, and give the reader the evidence. Give the details, and explain how this evidence demonstrates what you are trying to convince the reader of.

In your effort to convince Larry, the first reason you gave him to explain why people should go to college was that they make more money. In your second paragraph you should tell him how much more money college graduates make. How do you know this? How quickly will that extra income make up for the costs of college and cover the costs of not working for the seven and a half years it will take you to graduate with your certificate in TV and DVD repair? Anticipate Larry's questions and critiques. Tell the reader the answers to unasked questions. Convince them that you have thought it through, give the details, and, most important, explain why it supports your argument. Explain why that evidence should make the reader believe.

You do this convincing with about one or two paragraphs for each one of the points you made in your first paragraph. Each "because" you offered in the introduction paragraph should have at least a paragraph worth of evidence and explanation. If you cannot fill a paragraph, perhaps you should revise your "because" statement to be slightly broader, or perhaps you should add something to it. If you cannot fit all of the explanation for the "because" statement into a couple of paragraphs, perhaps you should try to split it up or narrow it to make it a little more exclusive. Overall, you should probably have at least three "because" statements and three evidentiary paragraphs to support your argument. If you fall short, you might want to consider revising your argument to be a little broader, or try searching for some other evidence and other reasons it should be believed. Similarly, you should probably try to avoid going beyond five or six reasons, or seven or eight long evidentiary paragraphs that support your argument. If you have more than that, you might want to think about splitting up the argument, narrowing the focus, or using some form of larger organizational scheme like the one discussed near the end of this essay.

It seems simple, but that is almost it. That is really all there is to writing an essay. If you put together a first paragraph that lays out your argument with some specific reasons for the reader to consider it reasonable, then write a handful of evidentiary paragraphs, you are just a concluding paragraph away from finishing an essay that is about the right length for a one-hour, in-class, essay exam.

That leaves just one thing left to talk about. What should you do with your last paragraph? If asked, most students who think a great deal of their intellectual abilities will quickly say, "Restate your hypothesis like your composition teacher told you in high school."

Wrong. Absolutely not.

Your hypothesis is your topic sentence, the statement of what you are trying to convince the reader to accept as reasonable. If the reader gets to the last paragraph, if your professor gets to this last paragraph, and does not already know what you are trying to argue, you have pretty much failed. Actually, if your reader gets to the end of that first paragraph and does not know exactly what you are arguing and the logic you are offering to support your point, if he/she/it does not finish the first paragraph knowing exactly what is coming, you have not done your job. The reader should know your argument from the very first paragraph, often the very first sentence. It should be absolutely clear and unmistakable.

Instead of restating something the reader should already be quite aware of, you should instead remind yourself that everything in an essay must contribute to the effort to convince the reader. Don't waste space and don't waste the reader's time.

Does restating a hypothesis add anything for your reader?

Instead, what you should do is use that last paragraph to accomplish something. But what?

Well, here is where you have some options, and what you choose to do will depend a great deal upon what you arguing and who you are trying to convince. The last paragraph

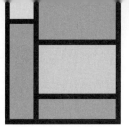

is where you can do some additional tailoring to fit the audience you are trying to convince. You could add little tidbits of evidence that don't require much if any explanation and don't fit in with your larger evidence paragraphs. This is particularly effective if you have something you know will strike a key with your reader or readers.

For example: "And Larry, there's a party every night at college."

Larry will buy that. You wouldn't use that to convince your mother, but for Uncle Larry, that might work.

Another thing that often works well is to use the last paragraph to demonstrate that you know both the strengths and the weaknesses of your argument, the scope and limitations.

For the going to college argument you also could acknowledge that college isn't for everyone. If we were making this argument to Uncle Larry we might use the example of a good friend from high school. He was more than capable of going to college, honor student, good SAT scores, and all that, but he was passionate about cars. Instead of going to college he decided to go to England for a couple years and work in a mechanic's shop. He came back and opened up a shop that repairs and restores British sports cars. For what he wanted to do, college wasn't the right choice. By showing Larry that you understand the limits of your argument, you demonstrate that you have thought through the entire argument, and your argument should be more convincing overall.

Keeping a constant and conscious focus on making an argument will almost certainly make your essays easier to write. Whenever you get blocked, whenever you have a question of what to put in, what to say, how to word something, just remind yourself to think of the argument, the effort to convince. In many cases just that focus can improve the quality of the essays. It will give you instant coherency because you are constantly organizing what you are writing around this goal of convincing the reader of something. This ties everything together because whenever you are not sure, whenever you have a question about how to handle something, you are constantly referring back to that goal of making an argument, convincing the reader of something.

LONGER ESSAYS

This strategy for developing the content of an essay, when combined with the structure outlined above, gives you an essay that is about five to ten paragraphs long, just about the right size for an in-class essay exam. What do you do if you need to write something bigger?

To write a longer essay you should still keep the focus on making an argument, keep the conviction that everything in the paper should be part of that effort to convince, and keep the basic strategy. All you really need to do differently is adjust the structure to something that can accommodate a lengthier, more complex argument. One of the best ways to do this is to nest several related, five- to ten-paragraph arguments within a similar structure that makes a larger argument.

Take a look at your evidence paragraphs; isn't each evidence paragraph really an argument? In each one you are making an argument that explains how this evidence supports

the overall point you are trying to make. Well, there is no reason that the arguments regarding the evidence cannot be made in the essay form outlined above. In other words, look at the outline for the essay, then replace each evidence paragraph with an essay-length argument that makes a point supporting the overall argument. Do that, and before you know it, you have a ten-page essay. Repeat that three times to create three essays that fit together to converge on a point you are trying to make, and you have a twenty-five-page paper, nest those within an even larger argument, and you are approaching a dissertation. You have built a pyramid crafted out of these small essay chunks.

Don't believe us? Fair enough, most people don't until it is too late, which is why we never did very well as crossing guards. Fortunately, in this case, there are no large trucks involved, and you don't have to believe us. Look at well-written research articles, and we will bet that some form of this structure is exactly what you find. You will discover something akin to the nested sets of essays described here. The research article is split up into small sections and each section makes an argument that it is trying to convey information to the reader. A research article starts with an introductory section that states the question being researched. This is immediately followed by an argument regarding why this subject or approach to this subject is important. Then there is a section that presents a nested set of arguments regarding what other research is relevant, how it is relevant, why it is relevant, and how it relates to the question at hand. The next section is an argument that states how the author(s) decided to research the question and that section also probably tries to convince you that the chosen approach is reasonable. The next section goes into what is discovered and why you should consider it reliable or useful. Finally, the article concludes with a section that includes arguments for how it all fits together, why the finding is important or what implications it has for the question being addressed.

This research article is simply the nesting of small arguments within the context of a broader question. Nesting arguments like this has the added advantage that you can take this monster essay you have to write, such as a senior thesis, and break it down into a bunch of small, manageable parts that you can tackle one by one.

CONCLUSION

Using a strategic approach to the content of an essay can help many, if not most, students tackle writing more effectively, with less effort and better results. Though focusing on making an argument and organizing your essay as suggested above is effective, it is not a cure-all. Writing, translating your thoughts and ideas first into language and then into written form, is such a complex process that the only real way to learn to write better is by writing. This strategy, or any other help that might be offered for writing, can only be effective if applied, repeatedly.

Just write, then write some more. Your first assignment is to explain why birds don't ride on the tops of semi-trucks.

NOTES

Introduction

1. *Two and a Half Men,* created by Chuck Lorre and Lee Aronsohn (Warner Bros. Television, 2003).
2. *A Clockwork Orange,* directed by Stanley Kubrick (Warner Bros., 1971).
3. *Phineas and Ferb,* created by Dan Povenmire and Jeff Marsh (Walt Disney Television Animation, 2007).

Chapter 1

1. *The Dark Knight,* directed by Christopher Nolan (Warner Bros., 2008).
2. *Star Wars,* directed by George Lucas (Lucasfilm, 1977).
3. *The Untouchables,* directed by Brian De Palma (Paramount Pictures, 1987).
4. William Shakespeare, *Julius Caesar* (New York: Folger Shakespeare Library Washington Square Press, 1992).
5. *West Side Story,* directed by Jerome Robbins and Robert Wise (MGM, 1961).
6. Stephenie Meyer, *Twilight* (New York: Little, Brown, 2005).
7. William Shakespeare, *Romeo and Juliet* (New York: Folger Shakespeare Library Washington Square Press, 2004).
8. *Indiana Jones and the Kingdom of the Crystal Skull,* directed by Steven Spielberg (Paramount Pictures and Lucasfilm, 2008).
9. *Watchmen,* directed by Zack Snyder (Warner Bros. and Paramount Pictures, 2009).
10. *Green Lantern,* directed by Martin Campbell (Warner Bros. and De Line Pictures, 2011).
11. *The Green Hornet,* directed by Michel Gondry (Columbia Pictures and Original Film, 2011).
12. *The Avengers,* directed by Joss Whedon (Marvel Studios and Paramount Pictures, 2012).
13. *Enchanted,* directed by Kevin Lima (Walt Disney Pictures, 2007).
14. *The Republic of Plato,* translated by Francis MacDonald Cornford (New York: Oxford University Press, 1981), 14–29.
15. *Dollhouse,* created by Joss Whedon (Fox Television, 2009).
16. George Orwell, *Nineteen Eighty-Four* (New York: Harcourt Brace, 1949).
17. William Golding, *Lord of the Flies* (1954; repr., New York: Capricorn Books, 1959).
18. Thomas More, *Utopia* (1516; Baltimore: Penguin Books, 1965).
19. Ursula K. Le Guin, *The Lathe of Heaven* (New York: Scribner, 1971).
20. *Logan's Run,* directed by Michael Anderson (MGM Studios, 1976).
21. Aldous Huxley, *Brave New World* (New York: HarperCollins, 1932).
22. L. Neil Smith, *The Probability Broach* (New York: Del Rey Books, 1980); *Star Trek,* created by Gene Roddenberry (NBC, 1969).
23. *The Front,* directed by Martin Ritt (Columbia Pictures, 1976).
24. Robert C. Tucker, ed., *The Marx-Engels Reader,* 2nd ed. (New York: Norton, 1978), see esp. pt. II, 203–465.
25. *Field of Dreams,* directed by Phil Alden Robinson (Gordon Company, 1989).
26. Karl Marx and Friedrich Engels, "Manifesto of the Communist Party," reprinted in Tucker, *Marx-Engels Reader,* 469–500.

27. Charles Dickens, *A Christmas Carol,* illustrated by Greg Hildebrandt (1843; New York: Messner, 1983).

28. *Mr. Magoo's Christmas Carol,* directed by Abe Levitow (NBC, 1962). In 1997, Disney released a live-action film of Mr. Magoo based on the 1962 cartoon.

29. Some, however, argue that the distinction between ideologies and theory is used to improperly denigrate ideologies. See Nancy S. Love, *Understanding Dogmas and Dreams: A Text,* 2nd ed. (Washington, DC: CQ Press, 2006), 9–11.

30. Adam Smith, *The Wealth of Nations,* edited by Edwin Cannan (1776; New York: Collier, 1902).

31. *Monty Python's Life of Brian,* directed by Terry Jones (HandMade Films and Python (Monty) Pictures, 1979).

32. Eduard Bernstein, *Evolutionary Socialism* (New York: Schocken Books, 1961).

33. *Jacobellis v. Ohio,* 378 U.S. 184, 197 (1964), Stewart, J., concurring.

34. Harold D. Lasswell, *Politics: Who Gets What, When, How* (New York: Peter Smith, 1950).

35. David Easton, *The Political System* (New York: Knopf, 1964), 129–134.

36. See Sandra Guy, "McDonald's Issues Report on Social Responsibility," *Chicago Sun-Times,* April 17, 2002, 67; and Roger Cowe, "Rules of Engagement: Ethical Investment: A New Approach Will Help to Balance Financial and Social Demands, Says Roger Cowe," *Financial Times* (London), April 4, 2002, 20.

37. *The Simpsons,* created by Matt Groening (Fox Broadcasting, 1989).

38. *Roger & Me,* directed by Michael Moore (Warner Bros., 1989).

39. *The Politics of Aristotle,* edited by Ernest Barker (New York: Oxford University Press, 1981).

40. Aristotle, *Nicomachean Ethics,* translated by Terrence Irwin (Indianapolis: Hackett, 1985).

41. This is the approach of W. Phillips Shively's "little book" *The Craft of Political Research,* 4th ed. (Upper Saddle River, NJ: Prentice Hall, 1998), which does a masterful job of introducing the basics of the political science research enterprise.

42. Earl Babbie, *The Practice of Social Research,* 10th ed. (Belmont, CA: Wadsworth, 2004).

Chapter 2

1. *Mad Max,* directed by George Miller (Kennedy Miller Productions, 1979).

2. *Saw,* directed by James Wan (Evolution Entertainment, 2004).

3. Thomas Hobbes, *Leviathan* (1651; New York: Penguin, 1985).

4. *The Road Warrior (Mad Max 2),* directed by George Miller (Kennedy Miller Productions, 1981).

5. David Brin, *The Postman* (New York: Bantam Books, 1985).

6. Larry Niven and Jerry Pournell, *Lucifer's Hammer* (New York: HarperCollins, 1977).

7. Brian L. Job, ed., *The Insecurity Dilemma: National Security of Third World States* (Boulder, CO: Lynne Rienner, 1992).

8. *The Office,* created by Greg Daniels, Ricky Gervais, and Stephen Merchant (NBC, 2005).

9. *The Jetsons,* created by Joseph Barbera and William Hanna (Hanna-Barbera, 1962).

10. *The Flintstones,* created by Joseph Barbera and William Hanna (Hanna-Barbera, 1960).

11. *SpongeBob SquarePants,* created by Stephen Hillenburg (Nickelodeon, 1999).

12. *Game of Thrones,* created by David Benioff and D. B. Weiss (HBO, 2011).

13. *Castle,* created by Andrew W. Marlowe (ABC, 2009).

14. *Kitchen Nightmares* (Fox Television, 2007).

15. William Golding, *Lord of the Flies* (1954; repr., New York: Capricorn Books, 1959).

16. *Survivor,* created by Charlie Parsons (CBS, 2000).

17. Lewis Coser, *The Functions of Social Conflict* (New York: Free Press, 1956).

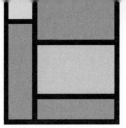

Chapter 3

1. *Eagle Eye,* directed by D. J. Caruso (DreamWorks Pictures, 2008).
2. *The Net,* directed by Irwin Winkler (Columbia Pictures, 1995); *The Lawnmower Man,* directed by Brett Leonard (Allied Vision, 1992); *1984,* directed by Michael Radford (Umbrella-Rosenblum Films, 1984); Vernor Vinge, *Rainbows End* (New York: Tor Books, 2006); Neal Stephenson, *Snow Crash* (London: Penguin, 1992); Neal Stephenson, *Crytonomicon* (New York: Avon Books, 1999).
3. *Jerry Maguire,* directed by Cameron Crowe (Columbia/TriStar Pictures, 1996).
4. Michel Foucault, *Discipline and Punish* (New York: Random House, 1975).
5. *V for Vendetta,* directed by James McTeigue (Warner Bros., 2005).
6. *A Christmas Story,* directed by Bob Clark (Paramount Pictures, 1983).
7. Georg Simmel, *Conflict and the Web of Group Affiliations* (1908; repr., Glencoe, IL: Free Press, 1964); Lewis Coser, *The Functions of Social Conflict* (Glencoe, IL: Free Press, 1956).
8. *Do the Right Thing,* directed by Spike Lee (Columbia Pictures, 1989).

Chapter 4

1. *National Treasure,* directed by Jon Turteltaub (Walt Disney Pictures, 2004); *National Treasure: Book of Secrets,* directed by Jon Turteltaub (Walt Disney Pictures, 2007).
2. *Zoolander,* directed by Ben Stiller (Village Roadshow Pictures, 2001).
3. *Iron Man,* directed by Jon Favreau (Marvel, 2008).
4. *Casino Royale,* directed by Martin Campbell (Eon, 2006).
5. *Quantum of Solace,* directed by Marc Forster (Eon, 2008).
6. *A Tree Grows in Brooklyn,* directed by Elia Kazan (20th Century Fox, 1945).
7. *Robin Hood,* directed by Allan Dwan (United Artists, 1922).
8. For a good collection of edited Marx works, see Robert C. Tucker, ed., *The Marx–Engels Reader,* 2nd ed. (New York: Norton, 1978).
9. Adam Smith, *The Wealth of Nations* (1776; New York: Everyman's Library, 1964),1:4–5.
10. Charles Dickens, *Great Expectations* (1861; New York: Dodd, 1942); Charles Dickens, *Oliver Twist* (1838; New York: Tom Doherty Associates, 1998).
11. Charles Dickens, *A Christmas Carol* (1843; New York: Weathervane Books, 1972), 12–14.
12. Vladimir Lenin, *Imperialism, the Highest Stage of Capitalism* (1916; New York: International Publishers, 1939).

Chapter 5

1. *Home Improvement,* created by Carmen Finestra, David McFadzean, and Matt Williams (ABC, 1991).
2. *Grand Designs* (Talkback Thames, 1999).
3. James Madison, *Federalist* No. 51, 322 (1788), in *The Federalist Papers,* edited by Clinton Rossiter (New York: New American Library of World Literature, 1961), 320–25.
4. Ibid.
5. *It's a Wonderful Life,* directed by Frank Capra (Liberty Films, 1946).
6. George Orwell, *Animal Farm* (1945; New York: New American Library, 1996).
7. Douglas Adams, *A Hitchhiker's Guide to the Galaxy* (New York: Ballantine, 1979).
8. Sidney Verba, "Comparative Political Culture," in *Political Culture and Political Development,* edited by Lucian W. Pye and Sidney Verba (Princeton, NJ: Princeton University Press, 1965), 513.

9. *The Politics of Aristotle,* edited by Ernest Barker (New York: Oxford University Press, 1981), bk. IV, 154–202.
10. *Monty Python and the Holy Grail,* directed by Terry Gilliam and Terry Jones (Twickenham Film Studios, 1975).
11. *New State Ice Co. v. Liebmann,* 285 U.S. 262, 311 (1932), Brandeis, J., dissenting.
12. For a good discussion of federalism, exit costs, and public choice, see James Eisenstein, Mark Kessler, Bruce A. Williams, and Jacqueline Vaughn Switzer, *The Play of Power: An Introduction to American Government* (New York: St. Martin's Press, 1996), 141–44.

Chapter 6

1. *The Scorpion King,* directed by Chuck Russell (Universal Pictures, 2002).
2. *Alexander,* directed by Oliver Stone (Warner Bros., 2004).
3. *Braveheart,* directed by Mel Gibson (Paramount Pictures, 1995).
4. *The Lion King,* directed by Roger Allers and Rob Minkoff (Walt Disney Pictures, 1994).
5. *Deadliest Catch,* created by Thom Beers (Discovery, 2005).
6. George R. Stewart, *Earth Abides* (New York: Random House, 1949).
7. Alexandre Dumas, *The Three Musketeers* (1844; New York: Oxford University Press, 1998).
8. Eric Flint, *The Grantville Gazettes* [The 1632 series] (Riverdale, NY: Baen Books, 2000).
9. John Mueller, "Democracy and Ralph's Pretty Good Grocery: Elections, Equality, and the Minimal Human Being," *American Journal of Political Science* 36 (1992): 983–1003.

Chapter 7

1. *The Phantom Menace,* directed by George Lucas (Lucasfilm, 1999).
2. Gary W. Copeland and Samuel C. Patterson, *Parliaments in the Modern World: Changing Institutions* (Ann Arbor: University of Michigan Press, 1994), 1.
3. For another look at legislative functions, see Gerhard Loewenberg and Samuel C. Patterson, *Comparing Legislatures* (Boston: Little, Brown, 1979).
4. Andrew Reding, "'Baskin-Robbins' Voting; European Systems, with '31 Flavors,' Offer Citizens Better Representation," *Los Angeles Times,* July 6, 2003, 5M.
5. *Mr. Smith Goes to Washington,* directed by Frank Capra (Columbia Pictures, 1939).
6. Robert Penn Warren, *All the King's Men* (1946; Orlando, FL: Harcourt, 2005).
7. Arthur M. Schlesinger Jr., *The Imperial Presidency* (Boston: Houghton Mifflin, 1973).
8. *What about Bob?,* directed by Frank Oz (Touchstone Pictures, 1991).
9. *Survivor,* created by Mark Burnett (CBS, 2000).
10. For discussion of the U.S. case, see Roger H. Davidson and Walter J. Oleszek, *Congress and Its Members,* 12th ed. (Washington, DC: CQ Press, 2009).

Chapter 8

1. *Brazil,* directed by Terry Gilliam (Universal Pictures, 1985).
2. Douglas Adams, *The Hitchhiker's Guide to the Galaxy* (New York: Pocket Books, 1985).
3. Max Weber, "On Bureaucracy," in *From Max Weber* (New York: Oxford University Press, 1946).
4. Woodrow Wilson, "The Study of Administration," *Political Science Quarterly* 2 (June 1887): 197–222.
5. Frank J. Goodnow, *Politics and Administration* (New York: Macmillan, 1900).

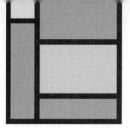

6. Anthony Downs, *Inside Bureaucracy* (Boston: Little, Brown, 1967).
7. Most of this research has examined bureaucracies in the United States, but the findings apply to bureaucracies in all representative democracies. See Douglas A. Van Belle, Jean-Sébastien Rioux, and David M. Potter, *Media, Bureaucracies, and Foreign Aid: A Comparative Analysis of the United States, the United Kingdom, Canada, France, and Japan* (New York: Palgrave/Macmillan, 2004).
8. *Caddyshack,* directed by Harold Ramis (Orion Pictures, 1980).

Chapter 9

1. *Law and Order,* created by Dick Wolf (NBC, 1990).
2. *The Practice,* created by David E. Kelley (ABC, 1997).
3. *Boston Legal,* created by David E. Kelley (ABC, 2004).
4. *Dragnet,* created by Jack Webb (NBC, 1967).
5. *Perry Mason,* executive produced by Gail Patrick Jackson (CBS, 1957).
6. *L.A. Law,* created by Steven Bochco and Terry Louise Fisher (NBC, 1986).
7. Harper Lee, *To Kill a Mockingbird* (1960; New York: Warner Books, 1982).
8. Ibid., 75.
9. Ibid., 205.
10. Roscoe Pound, "Law in Books and Law in Action," *American Law Review* 42 (1910).
11. James Madison, letter to Thomas Jefferson, October 17, 1788, "Madison-Jefferson Correspondence on a Bill of Rights," http://1stam.umn.edu/main/historic/Jefferson%20Madison%20correspondence.htm, accessed June 4, 2006.
12. Walter F. Murphy, C. Herman Pritchett, Lee Epstein, and Jack Knight, *Courts, Judges, and Politics: An Introduction to the Judicial Process,* 6th ed. (Boston: McGraw-Hill, 2006), 44–46.
13. Harry P. Stumpf, *American Judicial Politics,* 2nd ed. (Upper Saddle River, NJ: Prentice Hall, 1998), 5–17.
14. Islamic law is quite complex, and different Muslim nations and sects have different means of interpretation and mechanisms for interpretation of the law. See generally Sami Zubaida, *Law and Power in the Islamic World* (London: I. B. Tauris, 2005).
15. Prithi Yelaja and Robert Benzie, "McGuinty: No Sharia Law," *Toronto Star,* September 12, 2005, A1.
16. Stumpf, *American Judicial Politics.*
17. *Rochin v. California,* 342 U.S. 165, 169 (1952).
18. Sir William Blackstone, *Commentaries on the Laws of England,* available from the Avalon Project at the Yale Law School, http://avalon.law.yale.edu/subject_menus/blackstone.asp (accessed June 28, 2012).
19. *Shelley v. Kraemer,* 334 U.S. 1 (1948).

Chapter 10

1. Al Franken, *Why Not Me? The Inside Story of the Making and the Unmaking of the Franken Presidency* (New York: Delacorte Press, 1999).
2. Al Franken, *Rush Limbaugh Is a Big Fat Idiot and Other Observations* (New York: Delacorte Press, 1996).
3. Al Franken, *Lies and the Lying Liars Who Tell Them: A Fair and Balanced Look at the Right* (New York: Dutton Press, 2003).
4. With apologies to *Mad Magazine;* www.ariekaplan.com/benandjerrys.htm.

5. Robert Penn Warren, *All the King's Men* (1946; Orlando, FL: Harcourt, 2005).
6. Kenneth J. Arrow, *Social Choice and Individual Values* (New Haven, CT: Yale University Press, 1963).
7. Barbara A. Serrano, "New Initiative Would Set $30 Fee for All Vehicle Licenses—Voters Would Also Have to OK Every Tax Increase," *Seattle Times,* May 8, 1999, B2.
8. Erik Lacitis, "The Man Who Has Gone from Rhymin' to Eyman," *Seattle Times,* March 6, 2003, F1.
9. Anthony Downs, *An Economic Theory of Democracy* (New York: Harper, 1957).
10. In 1946, the French sociologist Maurice Duverger demonstrated that "(1) a majority vote on one ballot is conducive to a two-party system; (2) proportional representation is conducive to a multiparty system; (3) a majority vote on two ballots is conducive to a multiparty system, inclined toward forming coalitions." Duverger, *Party Politics and Pressure Groups* (New York: Thomas Y. Crowell, 1972), 23.
11. Joseph A. Schumpeter, *Capitalism, Socialism, and Democracy* (New York: Harper & Row, 1976), 250.

Chapter 11

1. *Top Gear* (BBC, 2002).
2. *The Matrix,* directed by Andy Wachowski and Larry Wachowski (Warner Bros., 1999).
3. Ursula K. Le Guin, *The Lathe of Heaven* (New York: Scribner, 1971).
4. Marge Piercy, *Woman on the Edge of Time* (New York: Knopf, 1976).
5. Lewis Carroll, *Alice in Wonderland* (New York: Norton, 1971).
6. *Wag the Dog,* directed by Barry Levinson (New Line Cinema, 1997).
7. *Capricorn One,* directed by Peter Hyams (Warner Bros., 1978).
8. Earl Babbie, *The Practice of Social Research,* 10th ed. (Belmont, CA: Wadsworth, 2004).
9. *WKRP in Cincinnati,* created by Hugh Wilson (CBS, 1978).
10. *Murphy Brown,* created by Diane English (CBS, 1988).
11. *NewsRadio,* created by Paul Simms (NBC, 1995).
12. *Mary Tyler Moore,* created by James L. Brooks and Allan Burns (CBS, 1970).
13. *State of Play,* directed by Kevin Macdonald (Universal Pictures, 2009).
14. *Broadcast News,* directed by James L. Brooks (20th Century Fox, 1987).
15. *Network,* directed by Sidney Lumet (Metro-Goldwyn-Mayer, 1976).
16. *The Paper,* directed by Ron Howard (Imagine Entertainment, 1994).
17. *Fletch,* directed by Michael Ritchie (Universal Pictures, 1985).
18. *Raiders of the Lost Ark,* directed by Steven Spielberg (Lucasfilm, 1981).
19. *Shortland Street,* created by Patricia Morrison (TVNZ, 1992).
20. Richard M. Nixon, "Checkers Speech," September 23, 1952. An audio portion and text of the speech are available at www.historyplace.com/speeches/nixon-checkers.htm (accessed July 3, 2012).

Chapter 12

1. *Mulan,* directed by Tony Bancroft and Barry Cook (Walt Disney Pictures, 1998).
2. *Saving Private Ryan,* directed by Steven Spielberg (Amblin Entertainment, 1998).
3. *Full Metal Jacket,* directed by Stanley Kubrick (Warner Bros., 1987).
4. Joseph Heller, *Catch-22* (1961; New York: Dell, 1985).

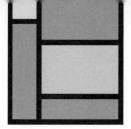

5. Joseph Haldeman, *The Forever War* (New York: St. Martin's Press, 1974).

6. *Tora! Tora! Tora!,* directed by Richard Fleischer and Kinji Fukasaku (20th Century Fox, 1970).

7. Erich Maria Remarque, *All Quiet on the Western Front* (Boston: Little, Brown, 1929).

8. *Apocalypse Now,* directed by Francis Ford Coppola (United Artists, 1979).

9. *M*A*S*H,* directed by Robert Altman (20th Century Fox, 1970).

10. *The Guns of Navarone,* directed by J. Lee Thompson (Columbia Pictures, 1961).

11. *Dr. Strangelove: Or How I Learned to Stop Worrying and Love the Bomb,* directed by Stanley Kubrick (Columbia Pictures, 1964).

12. *WarGames,* directed by John Badham (Metro-Goldwyn-Mayer, 1983).

13. For example, Orson Scott Card, *Ender's War* (Garden City, N.Y.: Doubleday, 1986).

14. Ryszard Kapuscinski, *The Soccer War,* translated by William Brand (New York: Knopf, 1991).

15. *Mad Max,* directed by George Miller (American International Pictures, 1979).

16. *The Road Warrior,* directed by George Miller (Warner Bros., 1981).

17. Lewis Coser, *The Functions of Social Conflict* (Glencoe, Ill.: Free Press, 1956).

18. Edward Hallett Carr, *The Twenty Years' Crisis, 1919–1939: An Introduction to the Study of International Relations* (1939; London: Macmillan, 1949).

19. Hans J. Morgenthau, *Politics among Nations: The Struggle for War and Peace,* 5th ed. rev. (New York: Knopf, 1973).

20. A copy of Kant's 1795 essay "Perpetual Peace: A Philosophical Sketch" can be found on Mount Holyoke College's International Relations Program's Web page at www.mtholyoke.edu/acad/intrel/kant/kant1.htm (accessed July 2, 2012).

21. Johan Galtung, "A Structural Theory of Imperialism," in *Transnational Corporations and World Order: Readings in International Political Economy,* edited by George Modelski (San Francisco: W. H. Freeman, 1979), 155–171.

22. John Steinbeck, *Cannery Row* (New York: Viking Press, 1945).

23. David Brin, *Earth* (New York: Bantam Books, 1991).

24. *12 Monkeys,* directed by Terry Gilliam (Universal Studios, 1995).

25. As an example, see Richard C. Ashley, "The Poverty of Neorealism," in *Neorealism and Its Critics,* ed. Robert O. Keohane (New York: Columbia University Press, 1986).

26. *The Mouse That Roared,* directed by Jack Arnold (Columbia Pictures, 1959).

Chapter 14

1. *Bro'Town,* created by the Naked Samoans (New Zealand: TV3, 2004).

2. Arthur E. Rowse, "Teary Testimony to Push America toward War," *San Francisco Chronicle,* October 18, 1992, 9.

3. *Whale Rider,* directed by Niki Caro (ApolloMedia, 2002).

4. *River Queen,* directed by Vincent Ward (Silverscreen Films, 2005).

5. *Once Were Warriors,* directed by Lee Tamahori (Avalon Studios, 1994).

GLOSSARY

agency theory: Also called the principal-agent model, the basic premise is that bureaucracies are agents that act on behalf of the legislature—the principal or "client"—in a relationship similar to a business contract.

agents of political socialization: The sources from which a group learns the political culture, which can include schools, parents, the media, politicians, friends, and religious leaders.

agreement reality: Things that we believe are real even though we have never directly experienced them through our five senses.

alliances: An agreement between groups or individuals to join resources and abilities for a purpose that individually benefits the members of the alliance.

anarchists: Radical ideologues who long for a lack of authority or hierarchy because they believe that human beings are capable of peacefully intermingling and ordering society without broad, formalized governmental structures.

anarchy: The absence of any kind of overarching authority or hierarchy.

appellate jurisdiction: A higher court's authority to review the record from a trial court.

Aristotle: An ancient Greek philosopher and political theorist who categorized types of government and believed that people should work toward building the best government possible for their situation.

Arrow's Theorem: The idea that elections cannot be the perfect means of making decisions because the method by which the votes are tallied can significantly alter the outcome.

atomization: The deliberate isolation of people from each other in society to keep them from forming a group that could threaten a leader's hold on power.

authority: Where knowledge, natural ability, or experience makes it rational for people to choose to place themselves in a subordinate position to another individual or group.

balance of power: The way in which the distribution of power across the inter-national system influences the pattern of alliances that tend to form in an anarchical environment.

bandwagoning: Opportunistic international alliances in which nations ally with the bully in order to carve out their own slices of the spoils.

bicameral legislature: A legislature with two houses.

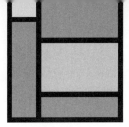

bureaucracy: The position within the political administrative structure—the desk, not the person—that defines the role or function to be performed.

capitalism: An economic system based on the free market and individual competition for profits.

checks and balances: A system whereby each branch of government can limit the powers of the other branches.

civil law: The branch of law that typically deals with relations among private individuals and groups.

classic conservatism: A political ideology that maintains that unrestrained individual human reason cannot take the place of long-standing, traditional institutions.

classic liberalism: A political ideology that emphasizes the belief that people should be generally free from governmental constraints or interference.

cockroach theory of bureaucracy: The idea that bureaucracies serve the public as best as they can and hope to stay hidden from the media and well fed in the darker recesses of an anonymous bureaucratic government.

cockroach theory of politics: The idea that politicians do not want to be spotted anywhere where they might be stomped on; thus, when they see others caught by the media in a scandal they try to avoid getting noticed for a similar indiscretion.

cognitive frameworks: The set of instinctual and learned filters the human mind uses for sorting the mass of incoming information and selecting which bits it will recognize and pass on to the thinking parts of the brain.

cohabitation: Under the French political system, when the president is from one political party while a different political party controls the legislature.

collective action: Coordinated group action that is designed to achieve a common goal that individuals acting on their own could not otherwise obtain.

communism: A political ideology that advocates, via revolution, a classless, socialist society in which justice and fairness for the whole prevail over the interests of individuals.

conceptual frameworks: The personal experiences, preferences, and expectations that we all use to make sense of the world.

confederal system: A system where the local governmental units have all the real power.

constructivism: A theoretical perspective in international relations that holds as its fundamental claim that human beings construct the reality around them— the reality upon which decisions and choices are made—through language and communication.

criminal law: The branch of law that concerns relationships involving the government and its relationship with individuals and organizations.

cross-cutting cleavages: When a group contains many different points of conflict, thus allowing people to find many points of agreement and conflict within the group.

cultural ownership: The idea that something that is part of a group's shared identity can also be owned.

culture: The set of values, conventions, or social practices associated with a particular field, activity, or societal characteristic.

delegates: Representatives who attempt to do exactly what their constituents want.

democracy: Rule by the people, usually through elected representatives, under a constitution that provides protection for basic rights and majority rule.

democratic peace: The observation that liberal democratic political regimes do not fight one another.

democratic socialism: A political ideology that advocates for a socialist state through democratic means.

dictatorship: Form of government in which power is centralized in a single person or possibly a small group of people.

direct democracy: A political system in which all citizens gather together to share perspectives, debate, and vote on policies.

dispute resolution: The role of courts to peacefully settle disputes and keep order in society.

divided government: When one political party controls the presidency and another party controls either all or part of the legislature.

divine right of kings: The principle that earthly rulers receive their authority from God.

dramatic imperative: The need for commercial news outlets to focus on rare and unusual events that have a tremendous impact on people in order to draw an audience.

enlightened self-interest: The idea that people will restrain their self-interest in recognition of the need to preserve a common resource.

experiential reality: Things that we directly experience through our five senses.

fascism: A political ideology that argues for the supremacy and purity of one group of people or nationality in a society.

federal system: Systems where the final authority for at least some aspects of government are left to the local or subnational level.

feudalism: An economic system under which peasants raise crops and livestock on small plots within the landlord's estate and are obligated to give a substantial percentage of their production to the landlord in exchange for protection.

filibuster: A delaying tactic used by a senator or a group of senators—who indefinitely talk about the bill—to frustrate the proponents of the bill and ensure defeat of the measure.

first-past-the-post system: An electoral system where the candidate with the most votes wins regardless of whether that person has a majority of the votes cast; there is no run-off election.

foreign policy analysis: A theoretical perspective in international relations that holds that understanding how those decisions are made within the structure, process, and context of domestic politics is essential for understanding international politics.

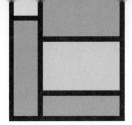

framing: The use of a speech to provide a cognitive framework for understanding an issue, policy, or candidate to predispose people to interpret a myriad of facts and snippets in one way rather than another.

geographic representation: A legislature divided according to geography, in which people are represented by the area they live in.

gerrymandering: The process of intentionally drawing districts to gain a partisan advantage.

going rate: When judges, through past sentencing, set the context for plea bargaining as defense attorneys and prosecutors negotiate about what the appropriate penalty should be for an offense for which a plaintiff pleads guilty.

government: The creation of institutions or structures to provide the security that people continually need; the result of a group's need to institutionalize, or make permanent, its power.

gridlock: When the checks and balances within the presidential system work too well so that they not only prevent one institution from overwhelming the others, but also prevent anyone from doing much of anything.

group identity: The degree to which members identify with a group, and conversely, identify who is not part of that group, a process that affects the group's strength, cohesiveness, and survival.

head of government: The political role of a country's president or ruler as the leader of a political party or group and chief arbiter of who gets what resources.

head of state: The apolitical, unifying role of a country's president or ruler as symbolic representative of the whole country.

hegemon: A dominant power, either an individual or, in the case of international politics, a country powerful enough to dominate all others.

hereditary monarchies: The most common form of monarcy; used by almost all of the world's existing monarchies. Under a hereditary monarchy, all rulers come from the same family, and the crown is passed along from one family member to another.

hierarchy: A societal structure that elevates someone or some group to a position of authority over others.

Hobbes, Thomas: An English political theorist who believed that without government, life would be chaos.

humanist: An idealist who is interested in and motivated by concern for the broader human condition and the quality of people's lives.

idealism: A way of looking at the world where the focus is on what we would like to do; what we would like the world to be. Also refers to a theoretical perspective in international relations that stresses the quest for peace.

idealist period: The two decades between the world wars that were marked by the effort to envision and attain a perfectly peaceful world.

ideological representation: Representation in which people's belief is the main concern of leadership.

ideology: A body of work aimed at organizing and directing goal-oriented action.

immobilism: When, because of the complexity and fragility of a ruling coalition, it becomes nearly impossible to enact any kind of coherent policies out of fear that a coalition party will break away and force the government to collapse.

imperialism: The extension of an empire's or nation's rule or authority over foreign countries, or the acquisition and holding of colonies and dependencies for the purpose of economic gain.

imperial presidency: The accumulation of tremendous power in the presidency at the expense of the other branches of government, especially the legislative branch.

individual security: Focus on the continued safety of the individual.

initiatives: Questions that are put on the ballot by citizens, usually after some type of qualification process, for example, the collection of a significant number of signatures on a petition.

injunctive power: The power of courts to stop governments, individuals, or groups from acting.

inquisitorial system: In a civil law system, a prolonged pretrial investigative process.

institutions: The organizational structures through which political power is exercised.

iron triangle: The situation where the bureaucracy is captured and redirected to focus on the needs of an interest group rather than on the public interest or even its original mandate.

judicial review: The power to declare laws and government acts to be in violation of the nation's constitution or in some other way illegal under the structure of the country.

jurisprudence: A philosophy of law.

laissez-faire capitalism: An economic system allowing very little, if any, government involvement, interference, or regulation.

law in action: How laws are applied and enforced in the real world.

law in books: The laws as they are written.

League of Nations: An international institution created after World War I that attempted to bring nations together to peaceably resolve conflict in a form of collective security.

legitimacy: People's voluntary acceptance of their government and its exercise of authority.

Locke, John: An English philosopher and political theorist who believed that people hand over only a limited number of their rights to the government in exchange for protection of their person and property.

Machiavelli, Niccolò: An Italian political theorist often referred to as the father of the modern theoretical tradition known as realism.

majoritarianism: Rule by the majority.

matriarchic: A form of social organization in which the mother is recognized as the head of the family or tribe, and descent and kinship are traced through the mother's side.

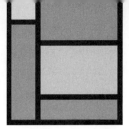

Marx, Karl: A German economist, theorist, sociologist, and philosopher most notable for his works criticizing capitalism and advocating communism, a classless, collective socialist society.

means of production: The mechanisms for transforming labor into wealth.

median voter: The one voter in the center of the ideological spectrum.

mediated reality: Reality that comes to us through channels of information flow, primarily through the news media, and our understanding of how information is selected, sorted, and presented to us through the news media.

minority government: When the majority party does not share power with any other party, but relies on an agreement where another party will provide support or will abstain from voting if there is ever a no-confidence vote.

monarchy: An authoritarian government with power vested in a king or queen.

multi-party systems: A system comprised of multiple, distinct, and officially recognized groups, otherwise known as political parties.

mutual exploitation model: The idea that the news media exploit elites by using them for cheap sources of news that they know will interest the public while, at the same time, the elites exploit the news media by using them to communicate with the public and present a public image that will help their political, economic, or social ambitions.

national security: Encompasses the requirement to maintain the survival of the nation-state through the use of economic, military, and political power and the exercise of diplomacy.

natural law: A type of jurisprudence that presumes that there is some higher law, which originates with God or nature, and that this higher law is discoverable by the use of reason.

oligarchy: Government by the few, especially for corrupt and selfish purposes.

original jurisdiction: A court's authority to be the first tribunal to hear a case.

"the other": Someone who is identified as an outsider and not part of the group, defined as a means of initiating conflict, and is therefore identified as the enemy.

panopticon: A social mechanism of control where people know that while they are not watched all the time, they may be watched at any time.

parliamentary system: A system in which there is a fusion of legislative and executive institutions.

patriarchic: A form of social organization in which the father is recognized as the head of the family or tribe, and descent and kinship are traced through the father's side.

peer policing: A system in which people police each other.

Plato: An ancient Greek philosopher and political theorist who believed that the best form of government was one where enlightened philosopher-kings should rule.

policy stability: When the social and economic environments within the country tend to be very consistent over time.

***polis*:** The ancient Greek notion of a state or country.

political capital: An individual's or institution's reserve of power that can be called upon to achieve political goals.

political culture: The shared social context from which people make political choices.

political science: Field of study characterized by a search for critical understanding of the good political life, significant empirical understanding, and wise political and policy judgments.

political socialization: The process by which the group teaches the shared context to members of society.

political theory: A body of work aimed at developing knowledge about politics and political systems.

politico: A person active in party politics.

politics: Individual or combined actions of individuals, governments, and/or groups aimed at getting what they want accomplished; when those actions have public consequences.

polity: Constitutional government that is a mixture of democracy and oligarchy.

pork-barrel politics: Where representatives use their political office to bring federal money to their districts through projects and jobs.

positivist jurisprudence: A type of jurisprudence that views law as simply the command or will of the recognized sovereign authority of the state.

power: The ability to get something done.

preference falsification: When people hide the way they truly feel while publicly expressing what those in power want them to communicate.

presidency: An executive institution that includes all formal and informal powers; the offices, the staffs, and the historical precedents that define it.

presidential system: A system in which there is a separation between legislative and executive institutions.

prime minister: A member of parliament, who, as the leader of the winning party in the parliament, exercises some of the functions of a chief executive.

principal-agent model: Also called agency theory, the basic premise that bureaucracies are agents that act on behalf of the legislature—the principal or "client"—in a relationship similar to a business contract.

private law: Law that is concerned with the relations among private individuals and private organizations.

proportional representation: A system in which there is representation of all parties in a legislature in proportion to their popular vote.

public law: Law that concerns relationships involving the government and its relationship with individuals and organizations.

realism: A way of looking at the world where the focus is on what we are able to do; what is possible for the world to be. Also refers to a theoretical perspective in international relations that views international politics as a strategy game.

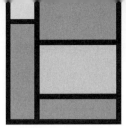

realist jurisprudence: A school of jurisprudence in which the key to understanding the judicial system is to understand the tremendous amount of discretion that is available to legal actors.

referenda: Questions that legislatures put on the ballot for people to vote on.

reform liberalism: A political ideology that argues that within a capitalist system, government should play a role in regulating the economy and removing major inequalities.

regime security: The leaders' ability to protect their hold on power.

republic: A government in which decisions are made by representatives of the citizens rather than by the citizens themselves. Also refers to a country without a monarch or an authoritarian leader.

revolutions: Mass uprisings focused on the goal of tearing down and replacing the current government.

Rousseau, Jean-Jacques: A French philosopher and political theorist who argued that society should be governed according to the general will rather than by a majority of people voting for their own interests.

safety valve: A mechanism that allows people to blow off steam in order to avoid larger conflict.

scientific method: A specific set of rules and processes for pursuing knowledge with observation, hypothesis-building, experimentation, and replication.

security: The ability to protect oneself and one's property.

self-policing: A social mechanism where only a few enforcers are needed to maintain control of the population because the fear of being punished keeps people in line.

separation of powers: A system designed so that no one branch of government can become too powerful over the others.

shadow government: A type of oversight or checking performed in a parliamentary system by those members of the minority party who would take the office if that party were to capture the majority.

shari'a: The system of Islamic law.

Smith, Adam: An English economist whose *Wealth of Nations* argued that individual rational choices in a free market are the ideal way to foster efficient economic activity.

socialism: An economic system in which society controls the means of production.

socially responsible investing: The purchasing of stock in corporations or the acquiring of proxy votes from willing corporate stockholders by groups seeking to change or influence the direction of corporate policies.

sophist: One who in ancient Greece taught promising young men practical skills, such as rhetoric, so that they could be successful in public life; they did not focus on metaphysics or ethics.

spin: The use of a speech to provide a cognitive framework for understanding an issue, policy, or candidate to predispose people to interpret a myriad of facts and snippets in one way rather than another.

stag hunt: A commonly used parable that demonstrates how the interdependence of actions and choices affects collective efforts to attain a goal.

state security: The ability at the governmental level to protect borders and governmental structures from outside threats.

statutory interpretation: When courts must interpret what a law precisely means to maintain specificity.

structures: Basic elements that governments need in order to govern, which determine, enable, and limit how the particulars of the government take shape.

subcultures: Smaller cultures within the main political culture.

Sun Tzu: A Chinese political theorist whose *Art of War* is the oldest secular text still in existence.

tragedy of the commons: A problem that demonstrates how the rational choices of individuals collide with the needs or interests of the larger community.

trustee: A country or government charged with the oversight of a trust territory.

two-party system: A system that favors moderate political parties that can create coalitions to gain sizeable amounts of voters.

tyranny of the majority: An unrestrained majority that bands together to rule a society with a ferocity and cruelty comparable to a dictator.

unicameral legislature: A legislature with one house.

unitary system: A system in which sovereignty and authority rest quite clearly with the national government.

unity government: When the two major parties, though in opposition, work together to achieve a higher national purpose.

utopia: An ideal world.

vote of no confidence: A parliamentary device by which the government can be dissolved by a simple majority vote of the legislature.

winner-take-all: An electoral system in which there is no proportional representation.

world systems theory: The idea that politics occurs within an economic structure defined by exploitative trade relationships, with corporate, class, and multinational entities defining the units of action.

INDEX

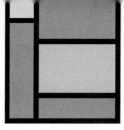

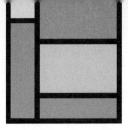

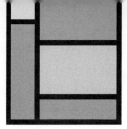

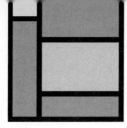

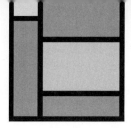

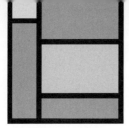

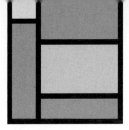

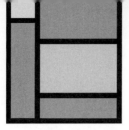

SAGE researchmethods

The essential online tool for researchers from the world's leading methods publisher

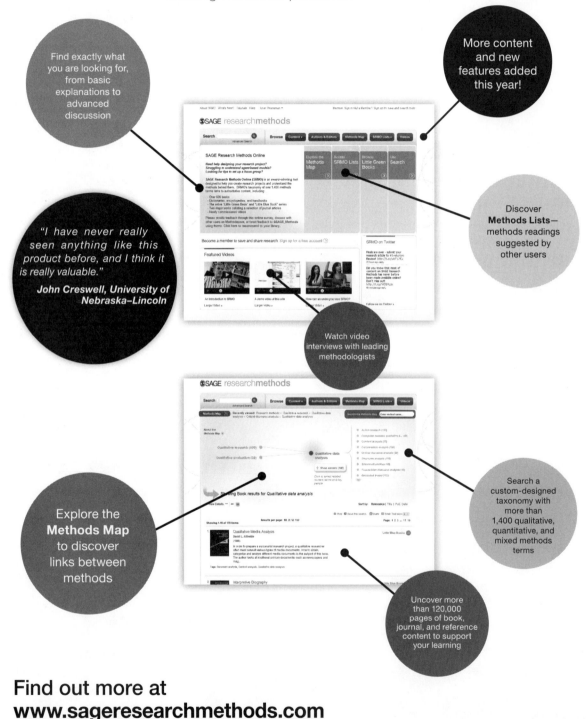

Find exactly what you are looking for, from basic explanations to advanced discussion

More content and new features added this year!

Discover **Methods Lists**— methods readings suggested by other users

"I have never really seen anything like this product before, and I think it is really valuable."

John Creswell, University of Nebraska–Lincoln

Watch video interviews with leading methodologists

Explore the **Methods Map** to discover links between methods

Search a custom-designed taxonomy with more than 1,400 qualitative, quantitative, and mixed methods terms

Uncover more than 120,000 pages of book, journal, and reference content to support your learning

Find out more at
www.sageresearchmethods.com